THE RADICAL RIGHT: A WORLD DIRECTORY

KEESING'S PUBLICATIONS

Other Keesing's Reference Publications (KRP) titles (all published by Longman Group UK Limited) include the following:–

Border and Territorial Disputes (2nd edition), edited by Alan J. Day (1987)

Revolutionary and Dissident Movements of the World, compiled by Henry W. Degenhardt (1987)

Trade Unions of the World, edited and compiled by F. John Harper (1987)

The World Financial System, compiled and written by Robert Fraser (1987)

Political Parties of the World (2nd edition), edited by Alan J. Day & Henry W. Degenhardt (1984)

State Economic Agencies of the World, Edited by Alan J. Day (1985)

Maritime Affairs: A World Handbook, compiled by Henry W. Degenhardt (1985)

Latin American Political Movements, compiled by Ciarán Ó Maoláin (1985)

Communist and Marxist Parties of the World, compiled by Charles Hobday (1986)

OPEC, Its Member States and the World Energy Market, compiled by John Evans (1987)

Treaties and Alliances of the World (4th edition), compiled by Henry W. Degenhardt (1987)

Peace Movements of the World: An International Directory, edited by Alan J. Day (1987)

The following titles are currently available in the Keesing's International Studies series (all published by Longman Group UK Limited):–

China and Soviet Union 1949–84, compiled by Peter Jones and Sian Kevill (1985)

Conflict in Central America, by Helen Schooley (1987)

From the Six to the Twelve, by Frances Nicholson and Roger East (1987)

Keesing's Record of World Events (formerly Keesing's Contemporary Archives), the monthly worldwide news reference service with an unrivalled reputation for accuracy and impartiality, has appeared continuously since 1931. Published by Longman Group UK Limited on annual subscription; back volumes are also available.

THE RADICAL RIGHT: A WORLD DIRECTORY

A KEESING'S REFERENCE PUBLICATION

Compiled by
CIARÁN Ó MAOLÁIN

Longman

THE RADICAL RIGHT: A WORLD DIRECTORY

Published by Longman Group UK Limited, Longman House,
Burnt Mill, Harlow, Essex CM20 2JE, United Kingdom

Distributed exclusively in the United States and Canada
by ABC-Clio, Inc., 2040 Alameda Padre Serra, PO Box 4397, Santa Barbara,
California, CA 93103-4397, USA

ISBN 0-582-90270-3
ISBN 0-87436-514-7 (ABC-Clio)

British Library Cataloguing in Publication Data
Ó Maoláin, Ciarán
   The Radical Right: A World Directory.
   1. Conservatism – Directories
   I. Title II. Series
   320'.025   JF2051

   ISBN 0-582-90270-3

Printed and bound in Great Britain by
Adlard & Son Ltd, The Garden City Press,
Letchworth, Herts

Contents

Introduction

This book is designed as a reference tool for political activists, academics, journalists, state agencies and others concerned with the activities of those organizations and individuals around the world who fall within a broad definition of the radical right wing. Few areas of political science, political practice or political journalism are as contentious as the definition of fascism and of the radical non-fascist right-wing – usually referred to collectively as the far-right, the ultra-right or the extreme right. In attempting to present an accurate and objective account of the organization and activities of radical right-wing organizations around the world, this directory casts its net rather wider than some stricter definitions would permit, in order to serve both the non-specialist reader and those specialists whose definitions do not coincide. The title of "The Radical Right" should not be taken in the sense used by Weber to distinguish between "conservative, reactionary and radical" right-wing movements.

(If this writer may suggest one usage which ought to become conventional, it is that the terms "nazi" and "fascist" ought not to be used randomly as pejoratives, but should be restricted to the pre-war nazi and fascist parties and to the post-war groups which readily acknowledge their ideological, and in some cases organizational, descent from such parties; "neo-nazi" or "neo-fascist" should be used only of modern groups which espouse ideologies very similar to the pre-war nazi and fascist parties, but which find it expedient to deny any sympathy with or descent from such groups. Thus, John Tyndall's National Socialist Movement in Britain in the 1960s was a nazi group, but the same man's 1970s National Front was neo-nazi. An effort has been made to use terms fairly consistently and in those senses in the present work.)

Rather than contributing to a terminological debate better conducted in academic or polemical works than in a reference volume, it may be helpful at this point to set out the tendencies, attitudes, attributes and ideologies which have been treated as pertaining to the radical right for the purposes of this book. The author regards the radical right as consisting of three broad and overlapping strands, within which there are numerous competing world-views, policies, strategies and priorities. For the sole purpose of clarity, and without discussing the merits of the terminology, we may follow popular practice in describing these strands as ultra-conservatism, anti-communism and right-wing extremism. The first term would encompass fringe groups of, say, the British Conservative Party (e.g. the Monday Club) or the US Republican Party (the Heritage Foundation), and other "new right", right-wing libertarian, militarist and moralist pressure groups. The second term covers both domestic and international groupings opposed to communism *per se* (the John Birch Society, the World Anti-Communist League, the TFP network), and émigré groupings mainly concerned with opposing the communist governments of their country of origin; it may also be applied to armed subversive groups in communist countries, and to the Moon cult and some anti-trade-union organizations. The third strand consists of movements which see themselves as presenting a revolutionary challenge to the existing social order, and it includes groups openly in sympathy with Hitlerian national socialism (the FANE in France, the US New Order), fascist terrorists (the Italian NAR), groups which are regarded as neo-nazi or neo-fascist (the South African AWB, the Italian MSI, the UK National Front), white supremacist movements (the Ku Klux Klan, the Aryan Brotherhood), anti-semitic conspiracy theorists (the New Christian Crusade Church, the British League of Rights), Latin American death squads and so on.

Within each of the three strands are many movements which have one or more of the following attitudes or attributes, which are commonly, but not exclusively, found among the radical right: (i) commitment to, or admiration of, violence as a political tactic; (ii) support for an authoritarian, centrally controlled structure for both party and state; (iii) nationalism, to the point of xenophobia; (iv) a belief in the inherent supremacy of the "white race" (the definition of which may differ from one movement to the next), coupled with opposition to the immigration of, or interbreeding with, other "races"; (v) a belief that the wrong side won the Second World War; (vi) a tendency to assert that the nazi holocaust of European Jewry either did not take place, or was not as extensive as generally thought; (vii) a belief that considerable power is held by a secret world-wide cabal of Jews, bankers, freemasons or other minorities; (viii) commitment to the patriarchal nuclear family and "traditional values", and opposition to feminism and "immorality"; (ix) rejection of class conflict in favour of national solidarity against a perceived external threat; (x) opposition to communism as an ideology, to communist governments, to trading or other relations with communist countries, and to domestic communist parties; (xi) admiration of individual heroism, strong leadership, sacrifice, discipline, courage and chivalry; (xii) opposition to free speech, particularly for left-wingers; (xiii) belief in the construction of a ruling élite, which may be regarded as genetically self-perpetuating; (xiv) perception of the existing social order as decadent and corrupt, and (xv) a belief that the nation must be rescued from a decline, possibly resulting from some great wrong done it by other nations or by misguided or evil leaders.

Although the 3,000-odd organizations mentioned herein fit within one or other of the author's three categories of radical rightism, it must be said that a large proportion of them would find many of the stated positions quite repugnant and that they would deeply, and rightly, resent any implication that they are in sympathy with, or even tolerant of, all other movements included. It cannot be stressed enough that the mention of any movement or individual in this book does not mean that that movement is fascist or that person is a dangerous extremist. A large proportion do not regard themselves, or do not wish to be regarded, as anything other than conservatives, and a larger proportion of self-acknowledged far-right groups would find themselves discomfited at being listed on the same pages as nazi parties and anti-semitic pressure groups. Inclusion in this book means only that the groups or individuals concerned have espoused or have been reported as espousing policies which, in the opinion of the author, conform with one or more of the list of fifteen characteristic attitudes presented above.

The book is arranged alphabetically in country chapters, covering each country in which there has been organized ultra-right activity in the post-war era. (There are no entries for countries with no such history.)

Within each country chapter there is, firstly, an introduction which sets out basic facts about the political system and recent history, followed by an outline of the origins and development of far-right activity there.

After the introduction there is an alphabetical listing of far-right groups thought to be active in 1985–87, the period during which most of the research was carried out. The nature and content of each entry is described below. This section is followed by a listing of the more important of the apparently defunct far-right groups, giving rather less information on each group; there follows a listing of less important and lesser-known right-wing groups, and finally, there is a listing of individual right-wing activists associated with that country but not, so far as has been ascertained, with any listed far-right group.

Each organization entry has a number of headings, designed for comparability and ease of use. First, the name of the organization is given, in the vernacular and in English if applicable. The address is then given if known, sometimes with a telephone number. The leadership of the group is then stated, with posts held (president, general secretary, etc.), so far as is known; in some cases the names given will be those of individuals quoted in press reports and may not be the actual leadership. There are frequent leadership changes in most small political groups and it is entirely possible that a high proportion of the names and positions recorded over the last three years will be out of date. A brief description of the political orientation of the group is given – nazi, anti-semitic, white supremacist, ultra-conservative or whatever. There follows an account of the history of the group, which in some cases is extensive but in many consists merely of an account of its most recent reported public activities. Other headings follow depending on the amount of information available in each case. These optional headings include Policies (a short account of the ideology, aims and priorities of the group); Membership (based on own claims or press or author's estimates); Publications (periodicals and other media); Associated Organizations (front groups, youth sections, allies and co-ordinating committees), and International Affiliations (membership of international bodies, corresponding organizations overseas and so on).

A single index provides page references for organizations (in English and in the vernacular), for periodicals and for personal names, and cross-references for acronyms and initials.

Given the extreme, even obsessive, secrecy of many far-right organizations, the short life of many such groups, with frequent splits and regroupings and reliance on press and other second-hand sources, including disaffected ex-members and political opponents, I have to acknowledge that this work will contain numerous errors and omissions, for which I accept full responsibility.

Conversely, the merits of this book are due in large measure to the work of others, and I must single out the courageous and tireless researchers, reporters and other staff of *Searchlight* magazine, a British monthly which provides an invaluable and unique reference resource for journalists, historians and anti-fascist activists. In researching this work I made extensive use of *Searchlight* and its resources, although the *Searchlight* staff were not directly involved apart from answering some specific queries and providing general advice. The late Maurice Ludmer, a former editor of *Searchlight*, is a model and inspiration for committed journalists everywhere. It is with proper humility that I dedicate this work to Maurice and to his American counterpart, Dixon Gayer, either of whom would have written it so much better.

Other anti-fascist organizations and individuals around the world have helped in the preparation of this book over the past ten years, and if I refrain from mentioning individuals it is because some of those who helped most may not be named because of the risk to their work and to their persons. There is an extensive international network of anti-fascist groups, some of which are exclusively concerned with the issues of fascism and racism while others are left-wing political parties or Jewish or black pressure groups with a greater or lesser interest in those issues. I have relied heavily on their archives and publications and on the advice of their experts.

In many cases information was supplied directly by the groups concerned, although an early attempt at questionnaire research demonstrated that many of the groups would not have co-operated had they known why the information was required. Thereafter I chose from time to time to conceal the purpose of my enquiries. I apologize to those who would have co-operated with a more overt approach.

I want to give special thanks for the help which I received from the staff of Longman's World Affairs and Politics department, and more particularly from Alan Day, now a freelance publishing consultant; from his successor as my editor, Roger East, and from my erstwhile colleagues in *Keesing's* (formerly *Keesing's Contemporary Archives*), the monthly record of world events, who were of considerable assistance in monitoring the international press for reports of ultra-right activity. I have aspired in the present work to the standards of impartiality and accuracy which have gained *Keesing's* its reputation. Finally, I have to thank my wife, Mary, for holding off editors and creditors during a hectic year.

Some of the material in this book has appeared in my *Latin American Political Movements*, published by Longman (and Facts on File) in 1986.

June 1987   *C.O.M.*

ix

Afghanistan

capital: Kabul   **population: 16,500,000**

Political system. Afghanistan has since 1978 been governed by the communist People's Democratic Party, the sole legal political party, through a Revolutionary Council. There are plans for the introduction of a new Constitution to be ratified by an elected assembly.

Recent history. Afghanistan was a monarchy until 1973, when a coup installed a military regime which was itself overthrown by the "Saur Revolution" of 1977. The communist government thus established has undergone three changes of leadership, including a coup in December 1979 which brought a pro-Soviet faction to power. The government has faced a widespread insurrection by Muslim fundamentalist tribesmen and has had to rely heavily on Soviet military and economic support, although there were indications in early 1987 that the Soviet Union was seeking to scale down and eventually terminate its direct military involvement.

The evolution of the far right. The deposed King of Afghanistan maintained for a time a right-wing government-in-exile, one of whose Ministers of Security was the late Mitch Werbell III, a leading mercenary associated with the "Soldier of Fortune" operation (see United States).

Today the right in Afghanistan, if it may be so described, consists of the tribal rebel movements, which are based in Pakistan and have received extensive assistance from the United States, Saudi Arabia and other Western countries, with funds, military supplies and diplomatic support. These groups are certainly not fascist, nor do they share many of the ideological positions of the European or North American right; most are fundamentalist Islamic organizations, which as such fall outside the scope of this work. However, the more right-wing of these groups are mentioned below because of their uncompromising anti-communism and their partial reliance on Western anti-communist and ultra-right groups. Some of these rebel groups, which are collectively known as the *mujaheddin* (holy warriors), belong to the anti-communist Democratic International (see United States), with Dastagir Ghulam Wardiah their main representative on that body. Funds are also channelled from private sources, such as the US Council for World Freedom, which maintains a permanent representative in Pakistan for that purpose.

Mujaheddin organizations

The Afghan rebel movements are many and ideologically various, with leaderships and the composition of alliances changing too frequently to permit a thorough analysis of their composition here; what they have in common is that virtually all are based in Pakistan, mostly in Peshawar, and virtually all are dependent to a greater or lesser degree on the support of the US Central Intelligence Agency, which supplies both US government funding—about US$700 million in 1980-86—and secret Saudi Arabian funding, which probably exceeded $100 million in the same period.

In 1986 the main rebel coalition was the National Alliance, based in Peshawar and comprising seven political-military groups. It was founded in 1980 as the Islamic Alliance for the Liberation of Afghanistan (IALA), by which name it is still sometimes known, and was led by Prof Ghulam Abdurrasul Sayaf. Four leaders of the Alliance, including Burhanuddin Rabbani (leader of *Jamaat-i-Islami Afghanistan*), met President Ronald Reagan of the United States in June 1986.

Other rebel groups reported as active between 1979 and 1987 included the following:

1

Afghan Islamic and Nationalist Revolutionary Council (AINRC): a defunct member of the IALA, succeeded by Surrah-e Melli Inkalab-i Islami.

Ekhwamis: the Muslim Brotherhood, one of the first guerrilla groups to emerge in the late 1970s.

Harekat Islami Afghanistan: Islamic Movement of Afghanistan, led by Sheikh Mohammed Assef Mohseni.

Harkat-i Inkalab-i Islami: Movement for the Islamic Revolution, a member of the IALA, of Islamic Unity and of *Teiman Atahad-Islami*; led by Mohammed Nabi Mohammedi.

Hedadia Mujaheddin Islami Afghanistan: Alliance of Afghan Islamic Fighters, founded in 1979, led by Wali Beg.

Hizb-i-Islami: Islamic Party; two factions, only one remaining in the IALA; leaders Gulbuddin Hikmatyar and Yunus Khalis.

Islamic Unity of the Mujaheddin of Afghanistan: an alliance founded in 1981.

Jamaat-i-Islami Afghanistan: Afghan Islamic Association, a member of the IALA and of *Teiman Atahad-Islami*; led by Burhanuddin Rabbani. Its offices in Peshawar were bombed on Feb. 19, 1987, killing at least 14 people.

Nejat-e Melli Afghanistan: Afghan National Liberation Front, founded in 1979 by Imam Sebghatullah Mujjaddedi, and a member of the IALA and of Islamic Unity.

Setem-i-Melli: Against Tyranny, a defunct group which killed the US ambassador to Kabul in 1979.

Surrah-e Melli Inkalab-i Islami: National Islamic Front of Afghanistan, successor to the AINRC; a member of Islamic Unity.

Supreme Revolutionary Council: founded in 1980 as a provisional government.

Teiman Atahad-Islami: Sworn Fighters for Islam, an alliance founded in 1979.

Other active organizations

Afghan Youth Council in America

Address. 214 Massachusetts Avenue NE, Washington, DC 20002, United States

Leadership. Omar Samad (leader)

Orientation. Anti-communist

History. The Council was established in 1982 with the support of the Heritage Foundation (United States).

Policies. The Council aims to unite Afghan exiles in the United States in support of the *mujaheddin* rebels and to publicize and oppose what it terms the Soviet occupation of Afghanistan.

Publications. Afghan Information, monthly.

Afghanistan Information Center (AIC)

Address. 20 West 40th Street, New York, NY 10018, United States

Leadership. Rosanne Klass (director)

Orientation. Anti-communist

History. The AIC was established in the early 1980s to provide a publicity and support service for the Afghan rebel movement.

Policies. The Center seeks to publicize alleged abuses of human rights by the Afghan government, to supply information on the situation in Afghanistan and to support those working for change in that country.

Associated organizations. The AIC is supported by Freedom House of USA, a lobbying organization which concentrates on denouncing human rights abuses under communist regimes.

American Afghan Education Fund

Address. 214 Massachusetts Avenue NE, Suite 510, Washington, DC 20002, United States

Telephone. (202) 547 0201

Leadership. Andrew Eiva (director)

Orientation. Anti-communist

History. This grouping, founded in 1983, is one of several North American anti-communist organizations which have provided propaganda, advisory and financial support to the cause of the *mujaheddin*. In 1986 it released news of the acquisition by the rebels of US-supplied Stinger anti-aircraft missiles, although both the US government and the rebels were denying at the time that any such transfers had taken place. It was revealed in early 1987, in the aftermath of the so-called "Irangate" scandal (concerning the Reagan administration's funding of Nicaraguan rebels by arms sales to Iran), that tens of millions of dollars of Saudi funding intended to buy Stingers had been diverted from a Swiss bank account, although only a small quantity had in fact reached the rebels.

Policies. The Fund lobbies for increased US support for the rebels and attempts to increase public awareness of and support for their cause.

Publications. *Afghan International Update*, quarterly.

Associated organizations. The Fund is closely associated with the Federation for American Afghan Action, and is supported by the Heritage Foundation, the leading US right-wing conservative lobby, whose address is used by both the Fund and the Federation.

American Aid for Afghans (AAFA)

Address. 6443 SW Beaverton Highway, Portland, Oregon 97221, United States

Telephone. (503) 297 4743

Leadership. Dr John Lorentz (executive director)

Orientation. Anti-communist

History. AAFA was formed in 1980 and has become one of the largest pro-*mujaheddin* lobbies in the United States.

Policies. The organization raises and distributes private-sector funds for "non-military" supplies for rebel groups, and lobbies the US government for increased and unrestricted aid to such groups.

Membership. 1,500 (1986).

Publications. Free Afghanistan Report, quarterly; pamphlets and mailings.

Federation for American Afghan Action (AAA)

Address. 214 Massachusetts Avenue NE, Suite 510, Washington, DC 20002, United States

Leadership. Andrew Eiva (director)

Orientation. Anti-communist

History. The Federation was formed in 1983 as the activist arm of the American Afghan Education Fund.

Policies. The Federation lobbies the US administration for increased governmental aid to the anti-communist rebel groups, and solicits private donations for forwarding to the Pakistan-based groups.

Associated organizations. American Afghan Education Fund; Heritage Foundation (United States).

Albania

capital: Tirana   **population: 3,000,000**

Political system. Albania is a People's Socialist Republic led by the Albanian Party of Labour. There are no other political parties. The national parliament is known as the People's Assembly; there are also local and regional People's Councils.

Recent history. The Marxist-Leninist ruling party came to power in 1944. It dissolved the monarchy in 1946 and has since taken a Stalinist line, rejecting the ideologies of both the USSR and China as deviations from the correct path. It has pursued an isolationist foreign policy, although there have been signs of a softening of its stance in recent years.

The evolution of the far right. Albania was invaded by Italy in 1939 and subsequently annexed. It was occupied by German forces in 1943 but was liberated in 1944. The communist regime then established has not faced any serious challenges from within Albania or from the substantial émigré community. There have been occasional allegations of attempted coups and assassination plots, but these are thought mainly to have arisen from personal or ideological clashes within the ruling party.

Active organizations

Free Albania Organization

Address. 409 South Broadway, South Boston, Massachusetts 02127, United States

Leadership. William Johns (president)

Orientation. Anti-communist

History. The Organization was formed by Albanian exiles in 1940.

Policies. It seeks the creation of a non-communist independent Albania, and works for the preservation of Albanian culture and traditions among the exile community.

Membership. 1,000 (1985 estimate).

Publications. Liria, weekly.

Defunct organizations

National Organization of the Legality Movement: a Paris-based opposition group with some support among the exile community. It was founded in the mid-1970s by Ydriz Basha i Novosejt.

Résistance Albanaise: this anti-communist organization, which claimed to have members in Australia, France, England and the United States, published a monthly journal until the late 1970s.

Individuals

Leka I: the exiled pretender to the Albanian throne, who has adopted the title and style of Leka I, is the son of ex-King Zog, who was deposed in 1939, reinstated in 1944 and deposed again in 1946. Leka I was reported to have formed a guerrilla group in the late 1970s. In September 1982, after the failure of a sea-launched rebel invasion of Albania, he said that he knew the rebels' leader but denied personal involvement in the venture.

Angola

capital: Luanda   **population: 8,700,000**

Political system. Angola is a People's Republic led by the People's Liberation Movement of Angola—Party of Labour (MPLA-PT or MPLA). There is a People's Assembly, elected indirectly every three years. An executive President, who is the President of the MPLA, heads a Council of Ministers.

Recent history. Angola gained independence from Portugal in November 1975, after a lengthy guerrilla war led by the MPLA, which agreed a ceasefire after the April 1974 coup in Portugal. Since 1975 the MPLA government has faced an insurrection by South African-backed rebels, but has held on to power with the assistance of a large number of Cuban troops.

The evolution of the far right. The principal far right organizations were founded, at least nominally, as pro-independence movements, but following the formation of the MPLA government they carried on fighting and proclaimed a provisional government. By 1986 only one of these groups—the UNITA—continued to pose a serious threat to the MPLA regime.

Active organizations

American Angolan Public Affairs Council

Base. Washington DC, United States

Orientation. Anti-communist

History. This lobbying organization was founded in September 1985.

Policies. The Council seeks to increase public awareness of the Angolan conflict and to win support for the UNITA from American legislators, officials, media and public.

Associated organizations. Other North American right-wing groups active in the pro-UNITA lobby are the American Republican Foundation, the American Security Council, and the College Republican National Committee. The last-named, a youth affiliate of the ruling Republican Party, called in 1985 for a consumer boycott of Gulf Corp., the US oil company (which in July 1985 merged into Chevron Corp.) on the grounds that its commercial activities and those of its Angolan subsidiary Cabinda Gulf Oil Co. supported the Angolan government. It also produced a film biography of Jonas Savimbi and other propaganda materials. In November 1985 the UNITA engaged a Virginia-based public relations company—Black, Manafort, Stone and Kally—to promote its image in the USA. The UNITA's more vocal supporters among the US establishment have included the late William Casey, a former head of the Central Intelligence Agency (CIA); Jeffrey Gayner of the Heritage Foundation; Congressmen Jack Kemp, Claude Pepper and Mark Sijlander, and Thomas Henriksen of the Hoover Foundation.

Frente de Libertação do Enclave de Cabinda (FLEC)
Cabinda Enclave Liberation Front

Orientation. Right-wing regionalist guerrilla movement

History. This group, founded under colonial rule in 1963, has since Angolan independence continued with an intermittent guerrilla campaign against the MPLA government with a view to securing the separate independence of the coastal district of Cabinda. It has suffered numerous factional disputes and is not very effective. In October 1985 it was reported to have entered into secret peace talks with the government.

Associated organizations. There have been other Cabinda regionalist movements, mainly splinter groups of the FLEC and including the Military Command for the Liberation of Cabinda, the *Movimento para a Libertação de Cabinda* (Molica—Cabinda Liberation Movement) and the *Movimento Popular de Libertação de Cabinda* (MPLC—Popular Liberation Movement of Cabinda). Little has been heard of these groups in recent years.

União Nacional para a Independência Total de Angola (UNITA)
National Union for the Total Independence of Angola

Leadership. Dr Jonas Savimbi (president); Miguel N'zau Puna (general secretary)

Orientation. Anti-communist guerrilla group

History. The UNITA was established in 1966 during the armed struggle against the Portuguese colonial regime, and was initially committed to the country's total independence. It subsequently accepted Portuguese support in return for fighting the main liberation movement, the MPLA, and since independence has continued to harrass government forces and disrupt economic activity with the support of South Africa and the United States. It was almost destroyed in the campaign of 1975-76, despite clandestine support from the US CIA, but it has staged several offensives since then, sometimes with overt South African assistance, and directed mainly against the transport infrastructure.

In 1985 there were persistent reports of tensions within pro- and anti-South African elements in the UNITA, culminating in the dismissal and disappearance of the then chief of staff, Demostenes Chilingutila. Covert US assistance to the movement restarted in 1985, in which year supplies and funds to a total of US$15,000,000 were sent. Despite a non-aggression pact signed in 1985 by Zaïre and Angola, it was reported that in 1986 a UNITA base at Kamina, in Zaïre, received three shipments of arms from the United States, through the CIA's "Santa Lucia Airways".

Policies. The UNITA demands the withdrawal of foreign (mainly Cuban) military personnel attached to the Angolan government forces as a precondition for peace talks with the government. The guerrilla forces of the UNITA engage in raids against civilian and military targets throughout southern Angola, and infrequently in other parts of the country.

Membership. The movement is thought to have up to 15,000 armed supporters, mainly in the south of the country.

Associated organizations. The UNITA joined forces with the now defunct FNLA guerrilla movement in 1975.

International affiliations. The UNITA has the financial and political support of numerous foreign anti-communist organizations, notably in the United States (see American Angolan Public Affairs Council). It also receives covert South African funding, in common with the Mozambican MNR with which it agreed in 1984 to share a South African-based radio transmitter partly funded by the USA. In late 1985 the US Defense Department and the CIA were said to be backing efforts to increase US funding for the UNITA from tens of millions of dollars to something approaching US$300 million.

Defunct organizations

Frente Nacional de Libertação de Angola (FNLA): the National Front for the Liberation of Angola was formed by Holden Roberto in 1962, took part in the pre-independence guerrilla war and became a junior partner in the transitional government set up in 1975. Within months it had resumed its guerrilla activities, this time directed against the MPLA, and had secured the financial, logistical and political support of several Western countries, including South Africa, the USA and Zaïre. By the end of the year it controlled two north-western provinces and was allied with the UNITA, which it joined in a "government of the People's Democratic Republic of Angola".

Over the following years it suffered numerous setbacks, including the loss of external funding, and in 1980 it collapsed in disarray, with Roberto forming a *Conselho Militar da Resistência Angolana* (Comira— Military Council of the Angolan Resistance). By 1985 this Council was more or less defunct. Roberto attended the 1985 Dallas conference of the World Anti-Communist League (see South Korea).

Argentina

capital: Buenos Aires   **population: 30,000,000**

Political system. Argentina has an indirectly elected executive President and a bicameral Congress consisting of a 254-seat Chamber of Deputies and a 46-seat Senate, elected respectively by direct popular vote and by the 23 provincial legislatures, to which substantial powers are devolved under the federal Constitution.

Recent history. There have been several periods of military rule in the present century, most recently in 1966-73 and 1976-83. The centrist civilian government installed in 1983, after the failure of the military to regain control of the Islas Malvinas/Falkland Islands from the UK, has carried out numerous reforms of the armed forces and has brought to trial a small number of those involved in the military regime's "dirty war" against the left, in which up to 30,000 people were killed.

The evolution of the far right. A right-wing military regime was in power from June 1943 until the end of the world war. There is considerable debate as to whether the unique form of authoritarian populism practised by Gen. Juan Perón, who ruled Argentina from 1946-55 and 1973-74, may be classified as fascist. It can at least be said that fascist elements were present in Peronism, and that ultra-right death squads, known as the AAA (Triple A—see below), flourished under the protection of the second Peronist government. Perón's exile, from 1955 to 1973, was spent in Franco's Spain. However, there is also a left-wing brand of Peronism which has even given rise to Marxist revolutionary guerrilla movements. Tensions between right and left resulted in a split in the core of the movement—the Justicialist Party—in 1984-85, with the far-right *oficialista* tendency (under Herminio Iglesias) appearing to win control. Between the Perón regimes there was at least one unsuccessful right-wing coup attempt (in 1962).

The military junta installed in 1976 under the leadership of Gen. Jorge Videla had a vehement and violent anti-communist philosophy. In the 1976-78 "dirty war", and to a lesser extent from 1978 to 1983, the police and armed forces carried out a ruthless assault on left-wing guerrilla movements and their supposed sympathisers. Torture, arbitrary arrest, murder and "disappearances" became common, and many thousands died at the hands of the armed forces or right-wing death squads operating under their protection. The junta was led from early 1981 by Gen. Roberto Viola, who started a process of liberalization, and from late 1981 by Gen. Leopoldo Galtieri. In 1982 the junta was replaced by a military presidency. Since the restoration of democracy there has been relatively little right-wing activity outside the mainstream conservative parties, although there were unsuccessful military rebellions in early 1987.

Active organizations

Círculo Europeo de Amigos de Europa—Sección Argentina (CEDADE-Argentina)
European Circle of Friends of Europe—Argentinian Section

Address. a/c Sr Alvaro F. Martín Frey, Poste Restante, Sucursal 26, Buenos Aires

Leadership. Alvaro Martín (contact)

Orientation. Nazi

History. CEDADE-Argentina is the local branch of a youth-oriented nazi grouping based in Barcelona and with groups or correspondents in most Spanish-speaking, and some other, countries. The Argentinian group was active from at least 1977, when it had branches in Buenos Aires and Misiones, but it failed to respond to a communication to the above address in 1986.

Policies. The group's policies, in line with those of the parent body, are based on a white supremacism which does not exclude those of Mediterranean origin; national socialist economic and political precepts; anti-semitism, and belief in a world-wide Jewish conspiracy; nationalism and authoritarianism.

International affiliations. See CEDADE (Spain, Ecuador, Uruguay, France and elsewhere).

Democracia Social
Social Democracy

Leadership. Adml. (retd) Emilio Massera (leader)

Orientation. Ultra-nationalist

History. This grouping was formed in 1981 by a right-wing former naval officer. In November 1982 Massera was arrested after praising Licio Gelli, leader of the clandestine right-wing Italian masonic lodge P-2, for his "valuable service to Argentina in the war against terrorism".

Policies. The party is not social democratic. It has described itself as "the sole force capable of bringing the national movement to a new phase". It supports authoritarian rule and military intervention in national politics.

Defunct organizations

Alianza Anticomunista Argentina (AAA or Triple A): this network of right-wing death squads was reportedly founded in 1973 by José López Rega, who was Gen. Perón's private secretary from 1968 until the latter's death in 1974. He served as Minister of Social Welfare (perhaps the most important post in the Peronist hierarchy) from 1973-76 and was also the author of a number of esoteric astrological texts, including one written in collaboration with the Archangel Gabriel. The alleged operational commander of the AAA was Aníbal Gordon, with Raúl Antonio Guglielminetti as his deputy. Between 1973 and 1976 about 2,000 killings and numerous kidnappings, shootings, bombings and beatings were attributed to AAA squads, most of whom were thought to be military or police intelligence agents.

The AAA's controllers were thought to have extorted millions of dollars from the families of their victims, who included academics, businessmen, journalists, parliamentarians, left-wing politicians and trade unionists. Several AAA activists continued their activities after the 1976 military coup and a small number remained in military posts even after the establishment democracy in 1983. Gordon was arrested in 1984 after the kidnapping of a right-wing nationalist leader, Patricio Kelly; Guglielminetti was extradited from Spain (with two colleagues) in 1985, but failed to answer bail, and López was extradited from the United States in 1986 after a long exile in the Bahamas and Switzerland.

Este y Oeste: this magazine (East and West), founded in 1963, was published at least until the late 1970s. It analysed world events from a right-wing nationalist and anti-communist standpoint.

Frente Nacional Socialista Argentino (FNSA): the Argentinian National Socialist Front bombed several synagogues in the mid-1970s. It issued a statement to the effect that Argentina was suffering from a conspiracy by a "Judaeo-Bolshevist plutocracy". In 1975, after protests at the Front's activities, the production and dissemination of anti-semitic literature was banned, halting the activities of the pro-nazi *Editorial Milicia* and *Editorial Odal* publishing houses which had been the country's leading sources of fascist material; however, Federico Rivanera Carlos, owner of both firms, had resumed his activities by 1978, trading as Ediciones "Mi Lucha" ("*Mein Kampf*" Publications).

Movimiento Nacionalista Argentino (MNA): the Argentinian Nationalist Movement was in contact with foreign fascist groups, including the Spanish CEDADE, in 1977-78. Its symbol was a spread eagle over two crossed swords. This group may be the same as the *Movimiento Argentino Nacional Organizado* (Mano), which was active around 1980.

Other organizations

Minor right-wing organizations which have been active in recent years, but are thought to be defunct, include the following: *Asociación Patriótica Argentina* (Argentine Patriotic Association); *Cabildo* (a nazi magazine edited in the late 1970s by Ricardo Curutchet); *Editorial Heumel*(a Buenos Aires publishing house specializing in the works of the Argentinian fascist Bruno Genta), and *Partido Nacionalista Integral*(Integral Nationalist Party).

There was an Argentinian section of the Christian Mission to the Communist World (see United Kingdom) in the late 1970s. There was also a local chapter of the World Anti-Communist League (see South Korea), which hosted the organization's 1980 conference in Buenos Aires at which Gen. Videla was guest of honour. A leading figure in the Argentinian WACL was Gen. Guillermo Suárez Mason, whose extradition was sought from the USA in early 1987 in connection with murders and kidnappings in 1976-83.

Individuals

Dr Walter Beveraggi Allende: the Argentinian correspondent of the anti-semitic US newpaper, *The Spotlight* (see Liberty Lobby, United States), was also listed in 1983 as an editorial advisor to the US Institute for Historical Review, which denies the facts of the nazi Holocaust. Beveraggi is a minor academic in the University of Buenos Aires.

The names of *Juan Carlos Monedero* (believed to be a publisher) and *Francisco D. Argiro*, both of Buenos Aires, appeared on anti-communist and fascist address lists circulating among foreign groups in the early 1980s. No further information was available on their activities or affiliations.

Australia

capital: Canberra   **population: 16,000,000**

Political system. Australia is a constitutional monarchy with a federal system of government. There is a bicameral Federal Parliament, elected by universal adult suffrage, and a Cabinet headed by a Prime Minister, with similar arrangements in most of the six states.

Recent history. Government has alternated in recent years between the social democratic Australian Labor Party and a right-wing coalition led by the Liberal Party. The current 1987 Labor government is led by Bob Hawke.

The evolution of the far right. Australia has traditionally received large numbers of UK and other white immigrants and until the late 1960s operated a racially discriminatory "White Australia Policy", supported by the main political parties, which sought to keep out Asians and other non-white immigrants. This policy has now been formally abandoned but racial discrimination remains and is advocated by a number of right-wing pressure groups. On the other hand, the left is taking an increasingly liberal stance on immigration and race issues, as evidenced by the campaign in mid-1984 against a Melbourne university professor, Geoffrey Blainey, who made controversial statements opposing Asian immigration.

Another focus of right-wing activity is anti-communism, particularly among the émigré communities from Yugoslavia, Hungary, Vietnam, the Ukraine, Lithuania and elsewhere. The most important such groups are the Hungarist Movement and the Croatian *Ustase* (see under countries of origin). The most significant local anti-communist group, not covered here because of the moderation of its stance over the years, is the Democratic Labor Party, a small group formed by right-wing defectors from the Labor Party in 1956.

On the right of mainstream conservatism, an interesting development in the past few years has been the arrival of American-style employer groupings engaging in sophisticated union-busting activities. To date these have been ad hoc coalitions to fund legal disputes but there are indications that something more permanent will emerge.

Out-and-out nazism has never been a significant force although there have been numerous attempts to organize nazi parties; these have failed because of what an Australian anti-fascist author, David Harcourt, has termed the "everyone wants to be Führer" syndrome. Thomas Messenger, the leader of a Melbourne neo-nazi group, was killed in a shootout with police in 1985. In the following year his group was suspected of involvement in the car-bombing of the Victoria state police headquarters.

Active organizations

Australian League of Rights (ALR)

Address. PO Box 1052J, GPO, Melbourne

Leadership. Eric D. Butler (national director)

Orientation. Anti-semitic, white supremacist

History. This organization, whose early history is detailed in Ken Gott's *Voices of Hate* (1965), was formed in 1946 by Butler, a social credit activist in the 1930s. Butler was the author of *The International Jew*, an anti-semitic tract published by his New Times press shortly after the war. In the 1970s the League spawned similarly named affiliates in Britain and elsewhere, with the help of Butler's Australian-born associate Don Martin.

In the early 1980s the ALR became involved in campaigns against Aboriginal land rights, alleging that there was a Marxist-inspired plan to found an Aboriginal republic. One of these campaigns, the Save Victoria Committee, was reported to have staged joint activities in 1984 with members of the Victoria branch of the Liberal Party. The League was also reported to have infiltrated the Australian National Party.

Policies. The League is active on a number of issues; it opposes the fluoridation of water, it supports the old White Australia policy and it supports links between

Australia and other white countries of the "Old Commonwealth". The League's founder is one of the leading anti-semitic propagandists of the post-war world, and advances the theory that communism is a Jewish conspiracy "inspired by Satan".

Publications. On Target, weekly; *Ladies' Line*, fortnightly

Associated organizations. The League operates partly through groups such as the Australian Heritage Society. A League sympathiser, John Bennett, ran the Victorian Council for Civil Liberties throughout the 1970s; in the early 1970s he was one of few advocates of unrestricted freedom of speech and assembly for the National Socialist Party of Australia (some of whose members were at that time also active in the League, despite the latter's stated opposition to nazism). Around 1980 Bennett became an editorial advisor to the Institute for Historical Review (United States), a Holocaust-denial group.

International affiliations. Through the Crown Commonwealth League of Rights (see United Kingdom) the League has links with sister organizations in Canada, New Zealand, the UK and the United States.

Australian People's Congress

Leadership. Robert Pash (leader)

Orientation. White supremacist

History. Pash, who is also the leader of the National Vanguard, visited Libya in December 1985 and returned to publish a pro-Gaddafi magazine.

Policies. Pash advocates the formation of an anti-Zionist, anti-capitalist "New Left" comprised of white nationalists. He also publicizes the teachings of Gaddafi's "Green Book" and organized a conference on that topic in 1986.

Publications. The Green March.

Associated organizations. See National Vanguard.

International affiliations. Pash claims to have the support of the Libyan government, but the Libyan representation in Australia denies any relationship with him.

Australian Populist Movement

Base. Perth, Western Australia

Leadership. Jack Van Tongeren (leader)

Orientation. Neo-fascist

History. This Movement was established by Van Tongeren, a Vietnam war veteran, reportedly as a front for his National Action group. Graffiti in support of the Movement was found on Communist Party offices attacked by arsonists in 1985.

Policies. The Movement describes itself as opposed to both communism and capitalism and in favour of a nationalist revolution.

Associated organizations. See National Action and National Vanguard.

National Action

Base. Sydney, New South Wales

Leadership. Jack Van Tongeren (president); Mark Ferguson (vice-president); Jim Saleam, Lina Reyes

Orientation. Neo-fascist

History. This group, formed in the late 1970s, has presented its leader as a candidate in local elections. In 1983 it organized a "Rock Against Reds" concert. There were reports in 1984 that it had engaged in paramilitary exercises, had carried out bombings and attacks on leftist bookshops and on a Trotskyist group in Sydney and was stockpiling weapons. Saleam, then the group's leader, and a member, Peter Coleman, were charged with burglary, receiving stolen goods, and insurance fraud later in 1984; Saleam was in early 1987 sentenced to two years' imprisonment, while Coleman was acquitted.

In 1985 the group was reported to be working partly through other organizations including National Vanguard and the Australian Populist Movement.

A National Action member faced explosives charges in 1986 after a series of attacks on anti-racist activists.

Policies. National Action has revolutionary nationalist policies and opposes "the rot which calls itself liberal democracy". It opposes capitalism and advances pseudo-socialist economic policies.

Publications. Audacity.

Associated organizations. National Action runs a small right-wing bookshop in Sydney.

International affiliations. The group has extensive links with foreign fascist parties, including the New Zealand Nationalist Workers' Party. In 1984 it was said to be in contact with the French PFN and the South African HNP.

National Vanguard

Leadership. Robert Pash (leader)

Orientation. White supremacist

History. This organization was active in the mid-1980s.

Policies. It seeks to build an alliance of left- and right-wing groups opposed to Zionism and capitalism and in favour of the construction of an international union of white states.

Associated organizations. Pash also leads the Australian People's Congress. In 1985 it was reported that National Vanguard was a front for the National Action movement, and that it was producing Ku Klux Klan propaganda.

International affiliations. There have been suggestions, encouraged by Pash but denied by the Libyans, that Pash has the support of the Libyan government.

Victorian Council for Civil Liberties: see Australian League of Rights.

Defunct organizations

A.R.C.: an ultra-right magazine of the 1970s which circulated particularly among youth and student movements.

Australasian Union Party: founded in 1956 by Graeme Royce (also known as Peter Huxtable), formerly of the Australian Party and later of the Australian Nationalist Workers' Party, this grouping opposed all existing political parties and called for the creation of a united white-ruled state in Australasia. It was dissolved in late 1957.

Australia-Rhodesia Association: this group was active in the late 1960s and the '70s in support of the white minority regime in Rhodesia prior to its attainment of recognized independence as Zimbabwe. Its treasurer was Robert Clark of the Immigration Control Association in Sydney, and active supporters included Johnny Macleay and nazis such as Jerry Hardy (see Church of God) and Ross May of the ANSP. Members of the NSPA and the Australian League of Rights were also involved in this group. The Association maintained contact with the Rhodesia Information Centre in Sydney, which published *Rhodesian Commentary* on behalf of the illegal Smith regime.

Australian Assembly of Captive Nations Organizations: this coalition of anti-communist émigré groups from non-Soviet Eastern European countries was active in the 1970s. Its address (PO Box 535, Parramatta, New South Wales 2150) was shared with an anti-communist newsletter called *News Digest International*.

Australian Catholic Association Against Decadence: this group, led by Yves Dupont, was active in the 1970s. It published a magazine, *World Trends*, which sought to expose a Jewish and masonic conspiracy against Christianity. Through Tenet Books it also published a number of Catholic traditionalist and anti-semitic books.

Australian National Front for Social Justice (ANFSJ): founded in 1967 by Graeme Royce, this neo-nazi party opposed both communism and unrestrained capitalism; it opposed Zionism (and was involved in the Free Palestine Committee), and was ultra-nationalist and white supremacist. Its journal, *Action*, had among its contributors the British nazi leader, John Tyndall (now of the British National Party). After a year the Front merged into the National Democratic Party.

Australian National Renascence Party (ANRP): this tiny organization was founded in 1963 by Robert Pope, and was based in Victoria. In 1964 it joined the Australian National Socialist Party, of which Pope became deputy leader.

Australian National Socialist Party: one of the more successful and longer-lived of the Australian fascist groupings, the ANSP was formed in Sydney in 1963 by Arthur Smith, late of the Australian Party and the ANWP, together with Don Lindsay and Edward Cawthron. From the beginning it favoured jackboots, uniforms and other paramilitary trappings, and with the native penchant for diminutives it gave the Australian language the word "stormie" (for stormtrooper).

The Party was raided by the police in 1964; Smith was jailed on arms and other charges, together with three followers, and was ousted as leader by his deputy, Robert Pope, who had recently joined the group along with members of his ANRP. The ANSP declined in Smith's absence but he reorganized it briefly in 1966 and again in 1967. It suffered a split in 1968, with most of its few dozen members joining Cawthron's National Socialist Party of Australia. It revived somewhat in 1970, with Frank H. Rosser as national secretary. The Party remained in existence during the 1970s but there have been no recent reports of its activities. Its publications have included *Brownshirt*, *National Socialist Newsletter* and *Australia Awake!*.

Australian Nationalist Workers' Party (ANWP): founded in 1957 by Arthur Smith after the collapse of the Australian Party, the ANWP attracted very little support for its neo-nazi policies before adopting more openly nazi policies in 1963 and becoming the Australian National Socialist Party. The ANWP secretary was Graeme Royce, formerly of the Australian Party and the Australasian Union Party. The ANWP sought the liberation of Australia from "Jewish financial domination", withdrawal from the "Jewish-controlled" United Nations and the strengthening of the White Australia Policy. It was based in Sydney and had overseas contacts including the National Socialist Movement (United Kingdom).

Australian Party: an ultra-nationalist party founded in 1955 by journalist Frank Browne, the Australian Party was disbanded in 1957, with several of its leading members (including its secretary, Arthur Smith, later a nazi leader) going on to form the Australian Nationalist Workers' Party. Browne's party had called for "freer finance and a more virulent nationalism", for the retention of the White Australia policy, for Australian control of the Pacific, and for the abandonment of both capitalism and communism. The deputy leader, John Webster, was formerly a leader of the pre-1945 British National Party and the English Legion; he ran an ultra-right bookshop, Essential Books, and joined Mosley's British Union after the war. He emigrated to Australia around 1950. In 1958 he changed his name to Muhammed and he remained active on the Australian right for many years, being associated for a time with the ANSP.

Baltic Council of Australia: a coalition of émigré groups representing the Latvian, Lithuanian and Estonian communities, the Council was active in the 1970s and was based in North Melbourne.

British Israel World Federation: this group was active around 1980 and may well continue in existence. It is debatable whether this organization, which claims that the British and white Commonwealth peoples are the chosen people of God, may be described as white supremacist and/or anti-Jewish; however its philosophy has certainly attracted racists and anti-semites. (See British Israel movement, United Kingdom.)

Captive Nations Committee: this anti-communist pressure group was formed in Sydney in the 1960s, mainly by members of Eastern European immigrant groups. Its president was Douglas Darby, a state assemblyman for the mainstream conservative Liberal Party. Its supporters included active nazis.

Church of God: this church, and the related Church of God of Prophecy, attracted a neo-nazi following in the 1960s, mainly because of an Irish pastor, Jerry Hardy, who denounced the "Jewish-Bolshevik conspiracy" from the pulpit and blessed Australian National Socialist Party banners. Hardy later opened a fruit shop and joined the Pentecostal Church and the National Democratic Party.

Conservative Immigration Movement (CIM): a Perth (Western Australia) group opposed to any coloured or Asian immigration into Australia, the CIM stood unsuccessfully in Senate elections in 1970. Its secretary was E.J. Langhorn. The CIM pursued anti-communist policies and was informally linked with other racist groups such as the New South Wales Immigration Control Association and the National Socialist Party of Australia.

Eagle Corps: the Elite Australian Guard for Law Enforcement, or Eagle Corps, was the paramilitary wing of the National Socialist Party of Australia. It was active in the early 1970s.

Fourth Reich Motorcycle Club: a gang of "bikies", or Hell's Angels, based in Woolongong in the early 1970s. The Club members wore nazi emblems and participated in right-wing demonstrations.

Free Palestine Committee: this nazi front group had a brief existence around the time of the Arab-Israeli war in 1967. Its leaders, Ted Cawthron, Frank Molner and Graeme Royce, were associated with the NSPA and the ANFSJ.

Immigration Control Association (ICA): led by Robert Clark, this New South Wales movement was active in the 1970s in opposition to "multi-racial" immigration. It favoured the abandoned White Australia policy and "desirable immigrants...

preferably, but not exclusively, Anglo-Saxon, Nordic or Teutonic". Its newsletter was *ICA Viewpoint*. Like the CIM, the ICA was a middle-class, non-fascist organization.

Ku Klux Klan: there have been a few attempts to organize Australian branches of US-based Klan groups, most of which nowadays profess a neo-nazi ideology. Graeme Royce, associated with the ANWP and other fascist groups in the 1950s and '60s, was one of those behind the invariably unsuccessful efforts.

National Australia Party: this grouping emerged in Sydney in 1964 under Ernest de Carleton and other ex-members of the ANSP, including ANSP secretary Trevor Evans (also known as Ralph Benson or Ralph Betsonby) who became secretary of the new party. It described itself as "violently anti-communist" and called for racial purity and white rule. It collapsed within a year.

National Civic Council: a non-fascist right-wing pressure group led in the 1960s and '70s by Bob A. Santamaria.

National Democratic Party (NDP): was formed in Sydney in 1968 by N.A. Harper, whose supporters included Jerry Hardy (see Church of God) and Graeme Royce (a former member of various fascist groupings). The Party opposed both communism and socialism but denied that it was a nazi group.

National Front: this offshoot of the UK party of the same name was led around 1980 by Terry Rowling. It has had addresses in Melbourne and Brisbane and has also been known as the Australian National Front. It is almost certainly extinct.

National Socialist Party of Australia (NSPA): this Canberra-based nazi group broke away from the Australian National Socialist Party in 1967 under the leadership of Edward R. (Ted) Cawthron, a long-standing rival of the ANSP's Arthur Smith. In 1970 Cawthron became the first parliamentary candidate to stand in any English-speaking country as a National Socialist since the war, winning 0.32 per cent of the vote. He suffered a severe bout of mental illness in 1971, and a pro-ANSP faction temporarily gained control of his group with the help of Cawthron's deputy and self-proclaimed successor, Frank Rosser. By 1972 control of the NSPA had passed to Cassius and Katrina Young, who withdrew from the alliance with Smith's ANSP. Party publications included the quarterly *Australian National Socialist Journal*, of which Cawthron remained editor after his 1971 retirement from the leadership; the monthly internal *National Socialist Bulletin*, and short-lived newsletters called *Action Report*, *National Socialist Newsletter* and *Stormtrooper*. Unlike the parent party, the more moderate NSPA preferred to present itself as a legitimate political party and its paramilitary activity was confined to its Eagle Corps section. The NSPA, despite the support of the fascist Hungarist Movement (see Hungary), faded away in the mid-1970s. It probably had fewer than 100 members in its heyday. It was affiliated to the World Union of National Socialists and was particularly close to the sponsors of the WUNS in the now-defunct National Socialist White People's Party (United States).

Nationalist Workers' Party: the ANWP occasionally used this name; it was also known as the Workers' Nationalist Party and as the National Workers' Party, and for a time maintained a front called the Australian National Unity Movement.

New Times Ltd: an anti-semitic publishing house run in Melbourne in the 1940s by Eric Butler (see Australian League of Rights); it published a journal, *New Times*, which became the organ of the League of Rights.

Odinist Faith and Culture Mission in Australia: this group, which reflected the nazi fascination with paganism and Nordic mythology, was formed around 1964 by Don Lindsay after his departure from the ANSP.

Rationalist Association: this grouping, about which little information has come to light, had at least some involvement with fascists in the 1950s.

Social Credit League: the social credit political philosophy, which is based on the monetary reform teachings of Maj. C. H. Douglas, is not strictly fascist but has been attractive to believers in a Jewish conspiracy theory of history; it has had some electoral success, notably in Australia, New Zealand and Canada. The League was the main Australian social credit party from the early 1930s—becoming the country's fifth-largest party by winning 133,000 votes (but no seats) in the 1934 elections—and in the 1970s it had a limited overlap of membership with the Australian National Socialist Party; for its part, the rival NSPA once described its own economic policies as virtually identical with those of social credit.

Truth and Liberty Mission: the Rev. William Carter, an anti-semitic propagandist, ran the Mission in the 1960s and '70s. Its journal, *Truth and Liberty*, opposed communism, immorality, Judaism and Catholicism, and supported the White Australia policy, the Vietnam war, apartheid, capital punishment and the replacement of democracy by theocracy. It serialized the Tsarist forgery, *The Protocols of the Elders of Zion* which became a standard source for 20th-century anti-semitism around the world.

Viking Youth: this white supremacist boy scout organization, most of whose members were in Western Europe, claimed around 1980 to have a small following in Australia.

White Australia Legion: organized in the mid-1960s by Harry Brus, a veteran racist who died in 1971, the Legion's main purpose was to unite ultra-rightists and right-wing conservatives in defence of the White Australia immigration policy. Brus was subsequently close to the NSPA.

Other organizations

Minor far-right organizations which have been active in recent years include the following: *The Black Rat* (a magazine); *Books for Freedom*(PO Box 35, Kilgoorlie, Western Australia 6430), distributing far-right propaganda; the *Call to Australia Party* (no information available); the *Commonweal Club* and the *National Alliance Party*. From the late 1970s the Christian Mission to the Communist World (see United Kingdom) has also been represented in Australia.

Individuals

Les Shaw: the Australian correspondent of the anti-semitic Liberty Lobby journal, *The Spotlight* (United States).

Austria

capital: Vienna

population: 7,550,000

Political system. Austria is a federal republic and a parliamentary democracy with a popularly elected non-executive President and a two-chamber legislature.

Recent history. Austria was assimilated into the Third Reich in 1938 and was liberated by allied forces in 1945. The resulting occupation administration lasted until a treaty in 1955 established Austria as an independent state. A long period of centrist coalition government gave way in 1966 to majority rule, under which power alternated between the conservative People's Party (ÖVP) and the social democratic Socialist Party (SPÖ), but in 1987 the two parties once again entered into coalition.

The evolution of the far right. Austria's pre-war nazi movement included the clerical-fascist *Heimwehr* group of Prince Starhemberg, whose *Heimatschutz* paramilitary wing staged an unsuccessful putsch in 1931. There was also an Austrian Nazi Party, which allied with the Pan-German Party and other groups in calling for the unification of the country with Germany. This was achieved with the German invasion and *Anschluss* of March 1938. The Nazi Party and other German fascist bodies were subsequently organized in Austria on the same basis as in Germany, and at the end of the war the NSDAP had about 700,000 Austrian members. The Third Reich era is amply documented elsewhere; we are concerned here solely with the post-1945 period.

Fascist parties have had little electoral or other success in post-war Austria, and in early 1986 the *Verfassungsgerichtshof* (constitutional court) ruled that the formation of nazi parties was forbidden under the 1945 Constitution. The 1955 State Treaty has also been used to suppress neo-nazi groups rejecting the established borders of the state. The largest existing far-right group is the National Democratic Party. In 1983, during the trial of nine neo-nazis for a series of bombings of Jewish targets in 1981-82 and for various other paramilitary offences, it was estimated that ultra-right parties had between 15,000 and 20,000 supporters in Austria.

Austria's nazi past has resulted in two major political controversies in recent years. In 1985 an Austrian war criminal, ex-SS major Walter Reder, was released from an Italian prison on health grounds and on his return to Austria was met by the Defence Minister, occasioning widespread protests and an unsuccessful vote of no confidence in the government. Reder was given a "badge of honour" by an SS veterans' group later in 1985.

The election in 1986 of former UN secretary-general (1972-82), Kurt Waldheim, as President of Austria caused international controversy in view of revelations about Waldheim's activities as an intelligence officer in the nazi armed forces in Yugoslavia and Greece and his alleged subsequent lies and omissions in his accounts of the war years. It was maintained by the World Jewish Congress and others that Waldheim must at least have known about atrocities committed in the areas of the Balkans where he had served, and there were claims that he had been directly associated with war crimes. Waldheim had joined the SA (Brownshirts) in 1938 and had also belonged to the Nazi *Studentenbund*.

The Liberal Party (*Freiheitliche Partei Österreichs*, FPÖ), which was the minority partner in coalition with the SPÖ after the 1983 election, came under severe internal strains in 1984 when a right-wing nationalist element fought the Carinthian *Landtag* (state assembly) elections on a platform of opposition to bilingual education for the region's Slovene minority. Agitation for and against Slovene rights had led to periodic violence since the early 1970s. The right wing won control of the FPÖ at national level, causing the SPÖ to withdraw from coalition and call an election in late 1986.

The FPÖ, though not yet regarded universally as a party of the radical right, is causing increasing concern to Austrian anti-fascists.

Active organizations

Aktion Neue Rechte (ANR)
New Right Action

Base. Vienna

Orientation. Neo-nazi

History. This ultra-right youth organization ran candidates in university elections in the mid-1980s.

Policies. The policies of the ANR are identical with those of the NPD; although organizationally autonomous, it functions as the NPD youth and student wing.

Arbeitkreis Internationale Zusammenarbeit
Action for International Co-operation

Base. Vienna

Orientation. Nazi front

History. This group was reported in 1984 to be a front for the US-based NSDAP-AO nazi party, and to have links with nazi activist Walter Ochenburger (see *Österreichischer Beobachter*).

International affiliations. See NSDAP-AO (United States).

Committee for Truth in History

Base. Vienna

Leadership. Dr Norbert Burger (president)

Orientation. Neo-nazi

History. The Committee was established by Burger after his replacement as leader of the neo-nazi NPD. Burger, a veteran right-winger, has been convicted in his absence in Italy for bombings carried out in the 1960s as part of a campaign for the return to Austria of the German-speaking South Tyrol, ceded in the aftermath of the First World War.
In 1984 the Committee invited a British revisionist historian, David Irving, to give a lecture tour of Austrian cities. Irving was expelled from Austria in June on suspicion of threatening public order by spreading nazi ideology.

Policies. The Committee is part of the international historical revisionist movement, which is primarily interested in rewriting 20th-century history in a way favourable to nazism.

Deutsch-Österreichisches Institut für Zeitgeschichte
German-Austrian Institute for Contemporary History

Base. Vienna

Orientation. Nazi front

History. In 1984 the Institute was reportedly a front for the US-based NSDAP-AO nazi group.

Policies. The Institute promotes a revisionist view of recent history.

Associated organizations. See *Österreichischer Beobachter.*

Institute for Historical Research

Orientation. Nazi front

History. The Institute was reportedly operating in 1984 as a front for the activities in West Germany and Austria of the NSDAP-AO nazi party.

International affiliations. See NSDAP-AO (United States).

Kärntner Heimatdienst (KHD)
Carinthian Homeland Order

Base. Carinthia

Leadership. Dr Josef Feldner (chairman)

Orientation. Anti-Slav

History. The KHD is the post-war successor to the Carinthian Homeland Union, a pro-nazi pressure group which sought to ensure the ascendancy of German-speaking Austrians over the Slovene minority in the province of Carinthia. The KHD has the support of the nominally-liberal FPÖ under the leadership of the party's current president, Jörg Heider, who took office in 1985 (and saw his party's vote rise to about 11 per cent nationally in the 1986 election).

Policies. The KHD campaigns against Slovene linguistic and cultural rights, notably the constitutional right to bilingual education for Slovene children. It appears to regard the minority as a "fifth column" preparing the way for a takeover by communist Yugoslavia.

Publications. Call of the Fatherland.

Kritische Studenten-Zeitung
Critical Student News

Address. Postfach 440, 1071 Vienna

Orientation. Ultra-right

History. This youth-oriented tabloid newspaper was in business in 1986.

Policies. The paper is ultra-nationalist and authoritarian.

International affiliations. Exchange advertising indicates informal links with a number of foreign ultra-right publications, including *Scorpion* (United Kingdom).

Nachrichten Austauschdienst
Information Exchange Service

Orientation. Nazi front

History. This group was active in 1984 as a front for the US-based NSDAP-AO of Gerhard Lauck. Walter Ochenburger of the *Österreichischer Beobachter* was also involved in the Service.

Policies. The Service exists to produce and distribute fascist propaganda.

Nationale Demokratische Partei (NPD)
National Democratic Party (NDP)

Address. Landstrassergürtel 19/3, 1030 Vienna

Leadership. Dr Norbert Burger, Franz Stourat

Orientation. Neo-fascist

History. The NPD was founded in 1966, and was regarded as a more moderate successor to the illegal nazi party established in the late 1950s by Karl Windisch. In the presidential election of May 1980, the then chairman of the Party, Burger (see Committee for Truth in History), came last of the three candidates, with 140,741 votes (3.2 per cent). In 1982 Burger was responsible for the arrest of a West German neo-nazi, Ekkehard Walter Weil, who had fled to Vienna after being charged with shooting a Soviet soldier in Berlin. Weil had allegedly conspired with a group of Austrian sympathisers to bomb Jewish targets and establish a nazi army; Burger regarded him as an agent provocateur.

Policies. The NPD has authoritarian, ultra-nationalist and anti-communist policies. It also seeks to vindicate the wartime nazi leadership and supports the reintegration of the South Tyrol into Austria.

Associated organizations. Aktion Neue Rechte functions as the NPD youth wing.

Der Nationalrevolutionär
The National Revolutionary

Address. Postfach 442, 1011 Vienna

Orientation. Nationalist

History. This journal was being produced six times per year in 1986.

Policies. Its position has been described as "national left with new right influences".

Österreichische Beobachter
Austrian Observer

Base. Vienna

Leadership. Walter Ochenburger (alleged publisher)

Orientation. Nazi

History. This unreconstructed national socialist newspaper was being published in Vienna in the early 1980s. Ochenburger, an Austrian nazi activist, was generally supposed to be its publisher.

Policies. The paper calls inter alia for an immediate Europe-wide pogrom, for the development of an Aryan master race and for the abolition of democracy.

Associated organizations. Ochenburger is also involved in what are believed to be front organizations for the NSDAP-AO, namely the *Nachrichten Austauschdienst,* the *Deutsch-Österreichisches Institut für Zeitgeschichte*and the *Arbeitkreis Internationale Zusammenarbeit.*

International affiliations. See NSDAP-AO (United States).

Stop the Foreigners

Base. Vienna

Orientation. Anti-immigration

History. The group secured 0.03 per cent of the vote in the 1983 general election.

Policies. The policies of this group are comprehensively stated in its name.

Defunct organizations

Nationale Front: a meeting which was to have launched this new nazi party was banned in November 1984 by the Interior Ministry, on the grounds that the party's manifesto supported the *Anschluss*, contrary to the 1955 State Treaty. No further reports of Front activity have come to light.

Other organizations

Minor right-wing organizations active during the last decade have included the following: the *Bund Volkischer Jugend* (BVJ—People's Youth Alliance); *Huttenbriefe* (Strauchergasse 23, 8020 Graz), a pan-German nationalist periodical; *Inter-Media News* (Hohenstaufengasse 2/8, 1010 Vienna); the *Kameradschaft Babenberg* (a veterans' group); the *National-Europäische Partei* (National-European Party); the *Nationalistischer* (or *Nationaler*) *Bund Nordland*; the *Österreichise Bürgerpartei* (Austrian Citizens' Party), *Österreichise Nationalpartei* (Austrian National Party) and *Österreichise Sozialbewegung* (Austrian Social Movement); the RFS; *Der Stosstrupp* magazine; the *Study Group Ottokring* and the *VDU*. There is also an Austrian affiliate of the *Christian Mission to the Communist World* (see United Kingdom).

Bahrain

capital: Manama   **population: 380,000**

Political system. The State of Bahrain is ruled by an Amir, who is assisted by an appointed Cabinet. A National Assembly was elected in 1973 but was dissolved in 1975, leaving absolute power with the Amir.

Recent history. Bahrain, formerly a British protectorate, became an independent state in 1971. Sheikh Isa bin Sulman al-Khalifa thereupon became Amir.

The evolution of the far right. Since political parties are banned, there are no native right-wing organizations. There is, however, a chapter of the World Anti-Communist League (see South Korea), which paid US$10,000 towards the WACL's 1985 conference expenses.

Belgium

capital: Brussels   **population: 9,850,000**

Political system. Belgium is a constitutional monarchy with a cabinet system of government. There is a 181-seat Senate and a 212-seat Chamber of Representatives, directly elected by universal suffrage for four-year terms, with the exception of 75 senators chosen by other means.

Recent history. Since the Second World War, in which Belgium was under German occupation, the country's political life has been dominated by the linguistic, cultural, ethnic and political differences between the north's Dutch-speaking Flemish community and the French-speaking Walloons of the south, forming about 55 per cent and 44 per cent respectively of the population. Recent governments have been centre-right coalitions mainly involving Flemish and Walloon Christian democrats with or without socialists.

The evolution of the far right. Pre-war fascist groups in Belgium were led by the Rexist movement. In May 1934 Belgium outlawed the use of political uniforms. The Pierlot government which took power in 1939 remained in office throughout the occupation, which began in 1940. The volunteer Westland SS regiment was recruited from 1940 from the majority Flemish community and in the occupied Netherlands, and fought on the Russian front.

In the post-war era most ultra-right activity has taken place in the Flemish community, and has supported demands for Flemish autonomy or independence; a typical group in the 1970s was the *Vlaamse Militanten Orde*(VMO), now banned, which formed links with many foreign fascist groups and participated with other Flemish nationalist groups in annual rallies at Diksmuide, held in July and known as the *Ijzerbedevaarten*. A feature of the *Ijzerbedevaart* is a commemoration of those who died fighting for the Nazis in the last war; this has led to frequent protests from Jewish groups and calls for the banning or restriction of the rallies. Some Flemish nationalist groups, and numerous cultural organizations, exist across the French border. In the Walloon community autonomist and pro-independence organizations have, for historical reasons, been identified with the centre and left rather than with the extreme right.

There have been violent clashes between Fleming and Walloon groups over linguistic and regional political issues. Anti-semitic violence has been reported from time to time, including the bombing of a bus in 1980 and of a synagogue in 1981, and the machine-gunning of worshippers in a synagogue in 1982; four died in these incidents. The most serious political violence in more recent years has, however, emanated from the extreme left.

Active organizations

Algemen Vlaams-Nationaal Jeugdverbond (AVNJ)
United Flemish National Youth League

Address. Ooststatierstraat 363, 2550 Kontich

Leadership. Marc van Reeth

Orientation. Flemish ultra-nationalist

History. Members of the AVNJ, a smaller and more radical Flemish youth organization than the better-known VNJ (from which it had split in the late 1970s) organized paramilitary training camps for Western European right-wing youth movements from 1980 onwards. It participated in the 1984 *Ijzerbedevaart*.

Policies. The group has called for greater autonomy for Flanders, for the preservation of the Flemish way of life and for the release of a jailed VMO leader.

Altair

Address. BP 1446, 1420 Braine L'Alleud

Leadership. Jean-Paul Hamblenne (publisher)

Orientation. White supremacist

History. This magazine started publishing around 1980.

Policies. Altair has been described as a "racial-nationalist" journal working for solidarity between the countries of Western, and more particularly Northern, Europe.

International affiliations. Exchange advertising has appeared in foreign ultra-right publications, but there is no evidence of formal links with any group.

L'Anneau
The Ring

Address. BP 436, Centre Monnaie, 1000 Brussels

Leadership. Ralf van den Haute (publisher)

Orientation. Pan-Europeanist

History. L'Anneau began publishing around 1984. It has dealt primarily with cultural and intellectual aspects of "national-revolutionary" thought.

Policies. This publication advocates nationalist revolution throughout Europe.

International affiliations. Contacts are maintained with similar publications abroad, including *Scorpion* (United Kingdom).

AVH-Video

Address. Postbus 10, 1510 Buizingen

Orientation. Historical revisionist

History. In 1984 this firm was advertising a German-language videotape, *Das Problem der Gaskammern*, which expounded the Holocaust-denial theses of Robert Faurisson, one of the leading French revisionist historians. Other titles were forthcoming.

Berkenkruis—see *Sint-Maartensfonds*.

Dietsland Europa—see *Were Di*.

Europese Partij/Parti Européen (EPE)
European Party

Address. 90a Avenue Milcamps, 1040 Brussels

Orientation. White supremacist

History. This organization was active in the early to mid-1980s. It does not appear to have a large following and there have been few recent reports of its activities. The party symbol is a broadsword pointing upwards on a black lozenge.

Policies. The main concern of the EPE is opposition to "third world" immigration into Belgium. It has participated in protests at the imprisonment of VMO leader Bert Eriksson.

Publications. *Vox Europae; Europe en Avant.*

Associated organizations. The Party engages in exchange advertising with other Belgian rightist groups including the *Instituut voor Europese Studies*. A Hitler birthday party which it organized in 1984 (the Führer being referred to obliquely in publicity material as "notre chef historique") was attended by members of the Instituut voor Europese Studies, the *Mouvement Social Nationaliste* and the *Odalgroep*. The EPE had in 1983 joined other right-wing groups, including the VMO, in an alliance known as the *Front nationaliste*.

International affiliations. The Party claims to have established branches in Switzerland and in the Flemish communities across the French border. It is in contact with several foreign ultra-right groups, several of which are openly nazi, including the French *Faisceaux Nationalistes Européens*.

Front national
National Front

Base. Brussels

Orientation. Ultra-right

History. This party was founded in 1983 as a sister party to the French group of the same name. It reportedly drew most of its membership from the banned VMO.

Policies. The Front opposes non-white immigration and calls for strong law-and-order policies.

Hulpkomitee voor nationalistische politieke gevangenen (HNG)
Aid Committee for Nationalist Political Prisoners

Address. p/a W. T'Jolijn, 13/5R St. Paulusstraat, 1000 Antwerpen

Telephone. (03) 233 7888

Leadership. Walter T'Jolijn (chairman)

Orientation. Flemish nationalist

History. The HNG was formed around 1983 following the imprisonment of VMO leaders Bert Eriksson, Ludo Haenen and others on arms and other charges.

Policies. The HNG seeks to publicize the cases of Flemish nationalist "political prisoners" and to create pressure for their release. It also encourages sympathisers to correspond with the convicts and with the Belgian authorities.

International affiliations. The Committee is modelled on the West German HNG, which has similar aims and objectives.

Instituut voor Europese Studies/Institut d'Études Européennes
Institute for European Studies

Address. Postbus 35, 9300 Aalst

Leadership. L. van den Bossche (publisher); G.L. Bosmans (editor)

Orientation. Fascist

History. This organization was established around 1982 by Bossche (of Molenstraat 31, Dendermonde) to provide a point of contact for Belgian and foreign nazi, fascist and racist groups, including Flemish nationalists.

Policies. The Institute appears to favour the maximum co-operation among ultra-right groups, particularly in Western Europe.

Publications. Euro-forum, cheaply-produced bulletin. The Institute also sells a range of books on the SS, Hitler, Hess and other Nazi leaders and groups.

Associated organizations. Among Belgian groups which have advertised or been featured in *Euro-forum* are *AVH-Video*, the EPE, the HNG, the *Odalgroep*, *Rex National* and the VMO.

International affiliations. Foreign advertisers or featured groups include the DNSU (Denmark), *DNZ Verlag* and *Unabhängige Nachrichten* (West Germany), *Consortium de Levensboom* (Netherlands), and *Euro-American Quarterly*, the Mountain Church and New Order (United States).

De Keikop

Address. Nauwstraat 109, 9180 Belsele

Orientation. Flemish nationalist

History. This group was active in the early 1980s.

Policies. The group describes itself as a nationalist union "for Flanders, the Netherlands and Europe"; it is not known whether it has a specifically right-wing ideology.

Mouvement contre l'insécurité et l'immigration abusive (MIIA)
Movement against Insecurity and Immigration Abuses

Leadership. Léon Delwart (leader)

Orientation. White supremacist

History. This group organized an anti-immigration demonstration in February 1984.

Policies. MIIA opposes non-European immigration into Belgium, principally on the supposed grounds that immigrants are more likely than native Belgians to become involved in crime.

Associated organizations. Other groups involved in the 1984 rally included *Organisation Delta* and the *Ligue Civile Belge.*

Mouvement Social Nationaliste (MSN)
Social Nationalist Movement

Orientation. Nazi

History. This group was formed around 1983 after its predecessor, the *Mouvement National Socialiste*, had been proscribed by the Belgian authorities. No further information has come to light.

Associated organizations. MSN members reportedly attended a Hitler birthday party held by the EPE in 1984.

Nation Europe/Natie Europa
European Nation

Address. rue de Montigny prol. 128, 6000 Charleroi

Orientation. Pan-Europeanist

Associated organizations. It has not been possible to confirm whether this group is identical with the Éditions Machiavel publishing company of the same address, or whether it is responsible for *Volonté européenne* magazine.

Nationalistisch Jong-studentenverbond (NJSV)
Nationalist Youth and Student League

Leadership. Lieven van Mele (contact)

Orientation. Ultra-right

History. The NJSV was active in the mid-1980s among Flemish secondary school students. It held a variety of events including camps, dances and meetings.

Policies. The NJSV describes itself as "conservative-revolutionary", right-wing, "solidarist" (opposed to class struggle), anti-communist, anti-immigration and nationalist. It opposes federalism and confederalism and works for an independent Dutch-speaking state including Flanders, the Netherlands and the French Flemings.

Publications. Verbondsberichten, internal bulletin; *Branding*, monthly.

Associated organizations. The NJSV is the under-18 affiliate of the NSV. It has collaborated with several other nationalist groups including the AVNJ and the *Alternatief Vredeskomitee* (Alternative Peace Committee, an anti-Soviet "peace through strength" pressure group).

Nieuwsbrief
Newsletter

Address. Lode van Berckelaan 125/5, 2600 Bechem

Leadership. Edwin Truyens (editor)

Orientation. Flemish fascist

History. This publication was produced from around 1979 by Truyens, who had been a leader of the paramilitary VMO at the time of its banning.

Policies. The bulletin reports the activities of the Flemish ultra-right and supports demands for Flemish autonomy.

Publications. Nieuwsbrief (officially, *Nieuwsbrief uit Zuid-Nederland*), Dutch and French-language versions.

Odalgroep
Odal Group

Address. Ballaerstraat 80, 2018 Antwerp

Leadership. Albert Eriksson-Godon

Orientation. Flemish fascist

History. The Group was established around 1983 as the *Werkgroep Alarm*, while Bert Eriksson, leader of the banned VMO, was serving a one-year prison sentence resulting from that group's racist and paramilitary activities. In a letter from prison Eriksson referred to the Group as "ex-VMO", implying that it was the direct successor to the latter organization. In 1984 three former VMO men linked to the *Odalgroep* were imprisoned for shooting into a café in a French-speaking part of Fourons during a long-running dispute in that area over linguistic matters; the *Odalgroep* became involved in a campaign for their release.

Policies. The policies expounded by the Group are identical with those of the VMO; it terms itself *volksnationalistisch* (for an ethnically-oriented nationalism), *solidaristisch* (opposed to class war), against monopoly capitalism and Marxist collectivism, for a right-wing revolution and for European solidarity against "Soviet imperialism and American power-politics".

Publications. Alarm!, monthly, formerly the organ of the VMO.

Associated organizations. The Group's address is that of a bar, the Lokaal Odal, which describes itself as the "meeting place for the International Right".

Rex National
National Rexist Movement

Address. c/o BP 754, 1000 Brussels; or rue du Page 99, 1050 Brussels

Leadership. Emil Robe

Orientation. Fascist

History. This group is the direct descendant of the Rexist movement which was the main pre-war fascist grouping. The Rexist Movement still follows the teachings of its founder, the wartime SS general Léon Degrelle, who fled to Spain in 1945. In 1986 he was cleared of causing distress to a Jewish woman by claiming in an interview that the Holocaust never happened.

The original Rexist movement, which took its name from the fascist newspaper *Rex*, was founded in 1935 and secured 271,000 votes and 21 of the 202 seats in its first parliamentary election in May 1936. Most of its votes appeared to come from the Catholic parties' traditional following; a pro-German nazi party formed in Belgium in 1934 had called for a boycott of the poll, with success in some border areas. In June 1936 the Rexists won 78 of the 696 provincial council seats. In 1936 the movement won eight of the 101 Senate seats and it retained its parliamentary representation until the war.

Policies. The group seeks to vindicate the Belgian fascist movement and its collaboration with the German occupation. It continues to advance fascist policies on contemporary issues.

Publications. L'Europe Réele; Bec en Ongles, monthly.

Scoutsverbond Delta
Delta Scouting League

Orientation. Pan-Dutch nationalist

History. This youth organization was active in Flemish districts in the mid-1980s.

Policies. The League promotes a pan-Dutch philosophy, seeking the creation of a Dutch-speaking state of all 17 Dutch, Belgian and French provinces where the Dutch languages, or variants thereof, are currently spoken. It is seeking to organize in all 17 provinces.

Septentrion
North

Address. Murissonstraat 160, 8530 Rekkem

Orientation. Flemish nationalist

History. This magazine, subtitled "a review of Dutch culture", was being published (in French) in the early 1980s.

International affiliations. It has been advertised in the French neo-nazi magazine, *Devenir européen.*

Sint-Maartensfonds (SMF)
St Martin Fund

Address. Postbus 408, 2000 Antwerp 1

Orientation. SS veterans' group

History. The *Fonds* was established after the war as a social and welfare organization for veterans of the Flemish volunteer SS battalions which fought on the Eastern front.

Policies. The *Fonds* organizes reunions and carries out welfare work with veterans and their families. It also seeks to provide moral support for veterans and to defend their rights and interests.

Publications. Berkenkruis, monthly.

Taal-Aktie-Komitee (TAK)
Taal Action Committee

Address. Edegemse Steenweg 2 (bus 5), 2550 Kontich

Leadership. Erwin Brentjens

Orientation. Flemish ultra-nationalist

History. Members of the TAK met the French ultra-right leader, J.-M. Le Pen, in Antwerp in 1984. The group also participated in the 1984 *Ijzerbedevaart*.

Policies. The group, which is non-party political, seeks to defend Flemish cultural and political rights and to work for a democratic Flemish republic in a "Europe of the peoples".

Publications. De Taktivist, every two months.

Associated organizations. The TAK has co-operated or maintained contact with a large number of Flemish cultural and political organizations, only a few of which are openly fascistic. These groups include: AVNJ and VNJ (youth groups); *Bormskomitee* (nationalist group); *Davidsfond* (Christian social and cultural group); *Gebroeders van Raemdonck kring* (social club); *De Keikop* (nationalist group); NJSV and NSV (youth and student right-wing groups); the pro-VMO *Odalgroep* (in 1983, when it functioned as the *Werkgroep Alarm*); *Sint-Maartensfonds* (SS veterans); *Verbond van Vlaamse Oud-Strijders* (nationalist group founded in 1919); *De Vlaamsche Vlagge* (ultra-nationalist youth group); *Volkskunstgroep Boerke Naas* (cultural group with South African links); *Wase Jonge Leeuwen* (non-party Flemish nationalist youth group).

Vlaams Blok
Flemish Bloc

Address. Pletinckxstraat 38, 1000 Brussels

Telephone. (02) 511-27-62

Leadership. Karel Dillen (president)

Orientation. Flemish nationalist

History. The Bloc was founded in May 1979 on the basis of an earlier (1978) alliance between Dillen's *Vlaams Nationale Partij*, founded in 1977, and the *Vlaamse Volkspartij*, founded in 1977 by Lode Claes, formerly a senator for the *Volksunie* (People's Union; one of the more moderate Flemish nationalist groups). In the November 1981 general election it won 66,422 votes (1.1 per cent) and retained the one seat (for Dillen) which it had held since 1978 in the Chamber of Representatives. In the October 1985 elections it increased its vote to 85,330 (1.4 per cent), with a slightly higher share in the simultaneous election to the Senate.

Policies. The Bloc works for increased autonomy for Flanders, and regards the current devolution process as insufficient. Although its policies are right-wing nationalist rather than fascist, it appears to command the electoral support of numerous followers of more extreme nationalist groups. It opposes the main Flemish parties including the *Volksunie* and the Flemish-speaking sections of the non-nationalist parties.

Publications. Vlaams Blok, monthly.

Associated organizations. The party has a youth organization known as the *Jongeren-Aktief* (Active Youth).

Vlaams-Nationaal Jeugdverbond (VNJ)
Flemish National Youth League

Address. Te Bolaerlei 156, 2200 Borgerhout-Antwerp

Orientation. Flemish ultra-nationalist

History. This uniformed group, which was founded in the early 1960s, is open to Flemish nationalists between the ages of six and 18. It is not directly linked with any senior groups but provides a recruiting ground for many of them.

Policies. The VNJ advocates Flemish autonomy and the eventual unification of Flanders with the Netherlands.

Vlaamse Militanten Orde (VMO)
Flemish Militant Order

Orientation. Flemish fascist

History. The VMO, one of the most successful Flemish supremacist groups, was established in 1950 and reorganized in 1968. It was led until the late 1970s by Xavier Buissert. He was succeeded around 1978 by Albert Eriksson of Antwerp, who was arrested in 1979 and imprisoned in 1983 after a number of violent incidents attributed to the group. Other prominent members were Roger Spinnewijn and Jimmy Bosman. The VMO was particularly active in the district of Fourons (or Voeren), whose status has long been disputed by the Walloons of Liège province and the Flemings of Limburg (to which province the district was assigned in 1962).

Sixty VMO members were arrested on arms charges in 1979, with 33 eventually having prison sentences confirmed on appeal, and the group itself was partially suppressed. It was banned by the Belgian authorities in 1982 as a private militia, but its members have regrouped under several similar names or acronyms, including *Vlaamse Nieuwe Orde* and *Vornming Mootschappelijke Outurkkeling*, as well as forming the *Odalgroep* (which remains under Eriksson's leadership) and the HNG prisoner support group. One of the VMO's last leaders, Edwin Truyens, now publishes *Nieuwsbrief;*Buissert, who left the group in late 1978, publishes Haro. The occasional reappearance of the VMO name or acronym at nationalist gatherings gives rise to doubts as to whether the ban has been enforced and the group actually dissolved.

Policies. The VMO is or was a "national-revolutionary" grouping which supported Flemish cultural and political autonomy while calling for a pan-European alliance of fascist groupings.

International affiliations. The extensive international links of the VMO arose mainly from its role in the annual *Ijzerbedevaart* gathering at Diksmuide. It was particularly close to UK fascist groups such as the League of St George, the British Movement and the National Front, although occasional conflicts, for example over the Irish question, have given rise to violent confrontations between and within British and other contingents at the Diksmuide rallies. Other groups attending the rallies as guests of the VMO have included the MSI and NAR (Italy), CEDADE (Spain), the National States' Rights Party (United States), and the FANE or FNE (France).

Vlaamse Nieuwe Orde (VNO)
New Flemish Order

Address. Brugsweg 229, 8921 Poolkapoelle

Orientation. Flemish fascist

History. This group was formed around 1982 and won the support of a number of prominent followers of the banned *Vlaamse Militanten Orde*. It is unclear whether the group was formed purely to circumvent the ban on the VMO or whether it was a genuinely-independent splinter group. It may be defunct.

Volksmacht
People's Power

Address. 121 Wetstraat, 1040 Brussels

Orientation. Flemish nationalist

History. This weekly magazine, which is one of the leading organs of the Flemish movement, has been published continuously since 1944.

Volonté européenne
European Will

Address. BP 1560, Centre Monnaie, 1000 Brussels

Orientation. Pan-Europeanist

History. This magazine was being published in 1986 as a successor to the similar journal, *Conscience européenne*. It deals mainly with intellectual and cultural matters.

Policies. The magazine espouses the pan-Europeanist new right ideas of Jean Thiriart, leader in the 1960s of the *Jeune Europe* group.

Associated organizations. The magazine is published by Éditions Machiavel of rue de Montigny prol. 128, 6000 Charleroi; this is also the address of the *Nation Europe* group, which may be connected with the magazine.

International affiliations. The reviews published by the French group, GRECE, are the nearest foreign equivalents to this publication.

Voorpost

Address. Postbus 45, 2100 Deurne

Orientation. Pan-Dutch nationalist

History. This group was formed in the late 1970s around a nationalist magazine. The group took part in the 1984 *Ijzerbedevaart*.

Policies. The organization terms itself a non-conformist all-Dutch nationalist action group, opposed to the Belgian state, opposed to communism and for a "Europe of the peoples" in which a combined Dutch and Flemish nation would have its place.

Publications. Revolte, quarterly.

International affiliations. In keeping with its pan-Dutch philosophy (regarding the Dutch and Flemish as one nation), there are *Voorpost* sections in the Netherlands (Postbus 109, 4730 Oudenbosch) and in French Flanders.

Vouloir
Will

Address. BP B41, 1970 Wezembek-Oppem

Leadership. Robert Steukers (editor)

Orientation. New right

History. This review was founded in the mid-1980s by Steukers, who had been involved in Jean Thiriart's *Jeune Europe* group in the 1970s before becoming an assistant to Alain de Benoist, leader of the French GRECE movement.

Policies. The review presents itself as an independent journal for right-wing thought, above party politics. It is generally pro-European.

Publications. Vouloir; periodicity, price and extent variable.

Were Di

Address. Victor Govaerslaan 19, bus 3, 2060 Merksem; magazine has been published from Jordaenskaai 3, 2000 Antwerp

Leadership. Bert van Boghout (editor); Frank Goovaerts (member of editorial board); Geert van Lommelen, Jos Vinks

Orientation. Flemish fascist

History. The editorial committee of this group's magazine met the French ultra-right leader, J.-M. Le Pen, during his visit to Antwerp in 1984.

Policies. The magazine promotes contact between new right groups throughout Europe, and provides a forum for their political theories. It also works for the rehabilitation of wartime collaborators.

Publications. Dietsland Europa, monthly.

International affiliations. Typical of the foreign groups with which Were Di has links is the French neo-nazi organization, *Devenir européen*.

World Anti-Communist League—see under Luxembourg.

Defunct organizations

Back to Liège Movement: a Walloon agitation, led in the 1970s by Jean Happart, to reverse the ruling which in 1962 transferred the district of Fourons (in Flemish, Voeren) from Liège to the Flemish province of Limburg, leading to frequent and sometimes violent clashes between nationalists of both communities.

Belgian National Socialist Party: founded in 1934, this group never achieved the popular following of Degrelle's Rexist party. In 1936, rather than field candidates, the party called for a boycott of the general election, with appreciable results in two or three provinces.

Dinasos: a Flemish paramilitary national socialist movement, it was dissolved by its leader, van Severen, in August 1934, after the passage in July of legislation prohibiting uniformed political groups. It was reported to have about 5,000 members at the time of its disbandment.

Front de la Jeunesse: this Waloon right-wing youth group was banned by a Brussels court in May 1981, when 14 of its associates received sentences in connection with the 1980 arson of a refugee centre.

Nouvel ordre belge: a grouping formed in 1972 by elements of several small right-wing movements, including *Jeune Europe*, the FGE and the CEN.

Pour une renaissance européenne: this magazine was published by a Belgian section of the Paris-based intellectual new right group, GRECE, until 1982.

SS de la Toison d'Or: a volunteer SS battalion recruited from the Belgian fascist movements in 1940-45.

Westland Neue Post: the WNP neo-nazi group was set up in 1980. The purpose of the group was to collect and disseminate information on "racial enemies". The group had an armed paramilitary wing, three of whose members - Michel Libert, Korel de Lombarde and Paul Latinus, all former military personnel—were arrested in 1983 on charges of stealing secret NATO documents. Latinus, a former environmental activist, killed himself during pa police investigation in 1984.

3a Diffusion: a Walloon nationalist publication and group which was in contact with foreign nazi groups in the early 1980s.

Other organizations

Minor right-wing and ultra-nationalist organizations which have been reported as active in the last few years have included the following: *Agence Nationaliste d'Information* (Nationalist News Agency); the neo-nazi journal *Alliance*, published since the 1970s; the *Blauwvoetjeugdtverbond*, a radical pan-Dutch youth group; the *Centre de Liaison et d'Action Nationaliste*; an affiliate of the Christian Mission to the Communist World (see United Kingdom); *Europawinkel*, a magazine; *Haro* magazine, published since 1978 by former VMO leader Xavier Buissert; the *Hertog Jan van Brabant*, an Eastern Front veterans' group; *La Lettre de Bruxelles*, an "intelligence" bulletin published since the mid-1970s (93 rue Souveraine, 1050 Brussels); the *Ligue Civile Belge* (Belgian Civic League, an anti-immigration group led by Omer Molle); the *Mouvement Occident* and *Occident* magazine (BP 65, Centre Albert, 6000 Charleroi); *La Nation Européenne*, a fascist journal founded in the late 1960s and linked with Palestinian groups; the *Nationalistische Studenten Vereninging*, a senior (high school and university) student group allied to the NJSV; the anti-immigration *Organisation Delta*; the *Rubenskelder* beer cellar (Cordolanstraat 1a, Bruges); *Taboe* magazine; the *Viking Jeugd Vlaanderen*, the small Flemish counterpart of the West German Viking Youth fascist scout group; *De Vrijbuiter* and *De Vrijburger* magazines.

Belize

capital: Belmopan   **population: 150,000**

Political system. Belize, formerly British Honduras, is an independent state with the UK monarch (represented by a Governor-General) as head of state. The National Assembly consists of a 29-seat directly elected House of Representatives and an eight-member appointed Senate. The Prime Minister, who leads the majority in the House, is assisted by a Cabinet.

Recent history. Since independence in 1981 Belize, which is claimed by Guatemala as an integral part of its territory, has been dominated by the mainly left-wing People's United Party (PUP), which controlled the local parliament from 1954 to 1984, and the right-wing United Democratic Party (UDP), which opposed independence and was involved in strikes and demonstrations in 1981.

The evolution of the far right. The UDP and other opponents of the PUP have on occasion adopted strongly anti-communist language, but the UDP itself is of the democratic right. There have only been two other right-wing movements of importance, both of which appeared to be dormant by 1987.

Defunct organizations

Anti-Communist Society (ACS): founded in 1980 by a former PUP Trade Minister, Santiago Perdomo, the ACS was accused of involvement in attacks in 1980 on left-wingers. It was thought to be influenced by Guatemalan anti-communist groups.

Belize Action Movement (BAM): the BAM, a right-wing anti-independence formation, emerged in 1980 as a pressure group within the UDP. It was involved in anti-independence demonstrations in 1981.

Bolivia

capital: La Paz   **population: 6,300,000**

Political system. The Republic of Bolivia has an executive President, a 27-seat Senate and a 130-seat Chamber of Deputies, all directly elected for four-year terms. The President has extensive powers, partly because of the unusual brevity of congressional sessions, and heads a Cabinet.

Recent history. Changes of government in Bolivia have generally been effected by military coup rather than by election. Most governments in recent decades have involved either right-wing (or occasionally left-wing) factions of the military, or the main political party, the National Revolutionary Movement (MNR), which has a number of factions and offshoots, most of which profess a social democratic ideology.

The evolution of the far right. Several of the recent military governments have been of the extreme right, including some which have been funded by the cocaine trade which has become the country's largest export industry. Right-wing military regimes were in power in 1951-52, 1964-66, 1969-70, 1971-78, again briefly in 1978, and in 1979, 1980-81 and 1982. Perhaps the most notorious of these regimes were those of Gen. Hugo Bánzer Suárez (1971-78), who was backed mainly by the *Falange Socialista Boliviana* (FSB), and Gen. Luis García Meza (1980-81), who was later put on trial for his involvement in a massive drugs operation involving German Nazi war criminal Klaus Barbie, known as "the butcher of Lyons". There have also been numerous failed right-wing coup plots, most recently in June 1984 (when the President was kidnapped), September and December of the same year and January 1985.

An ex-President, Juan José Torres, was assassinated in Argentina in 1976; in 1985 his family accused a US citizen, Michael Townley, of involvement. Townley had earlier been accused of the killings of two Chilean exiles in the USA and Argentina.

Active organizations

Alianza Democrática Nacionalista (ADN)
Democratic Nationalist Alliance

Base. La Paz

Leadership. Gen. (retd) Hugo Bánzer Suárez (leader)

Orientation. Ultra-right nationalist

History. The ADN was founded by Bánzer after his presidential term of 1971-78, during which he was supported mainly by the FSB. He came third as the ADN candidate in the 1979 presidential election, with 14.9 per cent of the vote. He increased his share by two points in the 1980 election, and initially supported the subsequent military coup, although he was deported in April 1981 for allegedly plotting a counter-coup.

The ADN called for democratization in 1982, and contested the 1985 presidential elections. Bánzer secured 28.6 per cent of the vote - the largest share, but not a majority - and the party simultaneously won 51 seats in the Chamber of Deputies. The presidency was given by Congress to a centrist candidate.

Policies. The ADN is anti-communist, populist and nationalist.

Centro Nacionalista (CEN)
Nationalist Centre

Address. Héroes del Acre 1746, Oficina La Voz del Pueblo, La Paz

Leadership. Dr Roberto Zapata de la Barra (leader)

Orientation. Ultra-right

History. The CEN was formed around 1978 and gave its support to the 1980 right-wing coup.

Policies. The party has stated its rejection of both "liberal democratic bourgeois capitalism" and Marxist scientific socialism, opting instead for a nationalist and autarkic policy.

Publications. La Voz del Pueblo.

Falange Socialista Boliviana (FSB)
Bolivian Socialist Phalanx

Base. La Paz

Leadership. David Añez Pedraza (president)

Orientation. Right-wing nationalist

History. The FSB, which was modelled on the Spanish *Falange* which provided the main support for the Franco regime, was founded in 1937 and gained its first congressional representation in 1946. In 1970 a left-wing element broke away from the party, and the rightist rump supported the Bánzer coup in the following year. A further split in 1974 left the right in control of a faction known as the FSB-Moreira, under the leadership of Gastón Moreira Ostria and Augusto Mendizabal.

In 1978 Moreira's FSB supported Bánzer's nominee, who lost the presidential election, and in 1979, in alliance with the ADN, it supported Bánzer himself, again unsuccessfully. In September 1984 a retired colonel, Rolando Saraíva, was charged with involvement in pro-FSB coup plot in June and early September; the President, Hernán Siles Zuazo, had been kidnapped in the course of the first unsuccessful attempt. The Moreira wing of the party remained in existence in the mid-'80s but its support had declined to little more than 1 per cent by the 1985 presidential election.

Policies. The FSB is populist, nationalist and anti-communist; it has favoured military intervention in politics and a mixed economy.

Defunct organizations

Legión Boliviana Nacional Socialista: the paramilitary Bolivian National Socialist Legion, which ceased to exist in the late 1970s, had published *Combate* magazine since the mid-'50s. Its leader was Guido Alarcón Zegada. The Legion supported the 1971 coup against the Torres government but opposed the resulting Bánzer dictatorship. During the 1970s it also functioned as the *Movimiento Paramilitar Anticomunista del Nuevo Orden Corporativo Católico,* and it sought to oppose "Yankee and communist imperialism and the Jewish-masonic controllers of both".

Los Novios de la Muerte: one of the more notorious of the countless drug trade death squads, the Fiancés of Death group was formed and led by Klaus Barbie, a German war criminal who settled in Bolivia in the 1950s (under the pseudonym Klaus Altmann), with the assistance of a German nazi fugitive, Joachim Fiebelkorn. Barbie had organized a substantial group of ultra-right supporters, including Italian and German neo-nazis, and was deeply involved with cocaine growers (principally Roberto Suárez) and right-wing military officers from the early 1970s until his arrest and extradition to France in 1983. His colleagues included fugitive Italian terrorists Stefano delle Chiaie and Pierluigi Pagliai, and Friedrich Schwend, another German Nazi settled in Peru. From their formation around 1974 until the early 1980s the *Novios* were involved in several major incidents, including the 1980 coup and the murder of socialist leader Marcelo Quiroga Cruz.

In 1984 it was reported that Barbie had sent a message from prison to ask a neo-nazi business associate in Bolivia, Alvaro de Castro, to organize right-wing paramilitary groups; de Castro and an Italian terrorist associate, Emilio Carbone, were arrested shortly afterwards, and details were disclosed of an alleged plan to kidnap French public figures to secure Barbie's release.

Barbie's capture resulted in the disclosure in 1983-86 of details of the use made by Allied intelligence services of Nazi war crime suspects in the immediate aftermath of the Second World War. Barbie, and many others, were permitted and in some cases assisted to escape by means of a "Rat Line" of secret routes to new lives in South America or elsewhere. About ten books have since appeared on the Barbie affair; more information emerged during his trial in France in mid-1987. Delle Chiae, who was wanted in connection with the Bologna massacre of 1980, the Borghese coup plot of 1970 and other fascist crimes in Italy, was extradited from Venezuela to Italy in early 1987.

Other organizations

Minor organizations reportedly active in recent years on the right wing of the Bolivian political spectrum have included the following: *Comité Unidad Nacional* (National Unity Committee); *Frente Nacional de la Juventud*(National Youth Front); *Movimiento Anticomunista Nacional Organizado* (Mano--Organized National Anti-Communist Movement), linked to similarly-named groupings in Argentina and Guatemala; *Partido Unidad Boliviana* (Bolivian Unity Party), and affiliates of the UK-based Christian Mission to the Communist World and the Spanish-based CEDADE nazi group.

Brazil

capital: Brasília   **population: 134,000,000**

Political system. Brazil is a federal republic with a bicameral National Congress consisting of a Chamber of Deputies and a Federal Senate, each with a variable number of members, most of whom are elected by universal adult suffrage. An executive President, elected by a college consisting of federal and state legislators, heads a Cabinet; each of the 23 states has its own government with extensive powers.

Recent history. There has often been direct or indirect military rule in Brazil, most recently in 1964-85. For much of the latter period there was fierce repression of opposition groups, involving torture, imprisonment without trial, censorship and death squad activities, but there was a period of liberalization prior to the return to civilian rule with the election as President of Tancredo Neves, whose term is now (1987) being served by José Sarney following Neves' death in 1985.

The evolution of the far right. Although Dr Getúlio Vargas, who seized power in a rebellion in 1930, established a corporate state on the Italian model and assumed dictatorial powers, he brought Brazil into the Second World War in 1942 on the Allied side. Opinions differ as to whether his first regime may be regarded, in whole or in part, as fascistic. His second period in office, from 1950 to 1954, ended with his suicide.

The 1964 coup was led by an anti-communist General, Humberto Castelo Branco, who became dictator in 1965 and outlawed all political parties; a pro-government party, the ARENA, was later created along with an artificial opposition. Other military presidents continued to use the ARENA as their political organ until its dissolution in 1979. Its successor, the Social Democratic Party, is not sufficiently right-wing to concern us here.

During the recent period of military rule there emerged a number of right-wing death squads, most of them apparently consisting of police officers and concerned with killing criminals and peasant activists as well as left-wingers. Church sources stated in 1979 that since 1964 there had been 179 known deaths and 53 disappearances in which security forces were thought to be involved. Landowner resistance to the agrarian reform programme introduced in May 1986 has also given rise to death squads, directed against clerical and lay proponents of the reform, and to the *União Democrática Ruralista* (UDR—Democratic Ruralist Union), a landowner pressure group which seems likely to become a major far right political party.

Legislation prohibits the advocacy by political parties of racialism.

Active organizations

Europinion

Address. Caixa Postal 10624, São Paulo CEP 01000

Orientation. Ultra-right

History. This magazine was advertised in European neo-nazi publications in the early 1980s. No further information has come to light.

Tradição, Família e Propriedade (TFP)
Tradition, Family and Property

Address. Rua Martim Francisco 669, 01226 São Paulo

Leadership. Dr Carlo Barbieri Filho (leader)

Orientation. Anti-communist

History. The TFP (formally the *Sociedade Brasileira de Defesa da Tradição, Família e Propriedade*) was founded by Barbieri in the 1960s.

Policies. The group and its foreign affiliates seek to alert the public to the communist threat by means of propaganda campaigns including full-page advertisements in leading newspapers.

International affiliations. There are national TFP groups in several countries, including the United States (where it is known as the American Society for the Defense of Tradition, Family and Property), Canada, Argentina, Bolivia, Chile, Ecuador, France, Portugal, Spain, Uruguay, Venezuela and the United Kingdom. The TFP is itself an affiliate of the World Anti-Communist League (see South Korea), and its Latin American affiliate, the Fedal (see Paraguay). Barbieri is vice-president of the Fedal, as he was of its predecessor, the fascist-controlled CAL.

União Democrática Ruralista (UDR)
Democratic Ruralist Union

Orientation. Ultra-right

History. This organization was formed by landowners in order to co-ordinate their campaign of resistance to the land reform programme planned by the Sarney government installed in 1985. The group was said to have links with far right politicians and with right-wingers in the intelligence service, the SNI. It sponsored several right-wing candidates in the November 1986 congressional elections.

Policies. The UDR was regarded in late 1986 as primarily an anti-land reform group, but was developing a wider-ranging right-wing political platform.

Membership. By July 1986 the group claimed to have 1,500 members in half the 23 states of Brazil.

Defunct organizations

Aliança Anticomunista Brasileira (AAB): the AAB carried out several bombings and beatings in the mid-1970s, directly mainly against progressive churchmen.

Aliança Renovadora Nacional (ARENA or Arena): the National Renewal Alliance was formed by the Castelo Branco dictatorship in 1965 and was one of only two parties permitted to function until the liberalization of 1979, when the party was dissolved and replaced by the less right-wing Social Democratic Party.

Esquadrão da Morte: this group or network of groups, whose name means Death Squad, was formed in 1964 by policemen seeking to avenge the death of a colleague. It carried out about 1,000 killings in its first six years, and in 1968 began to issue messages claiming responsibility for its acts. A crackdown in 1972-76 resulted in the conviction of several policemen, and the alleged leader died in an apparent accident in 1979, but the group continued its activities into the 1980s. About 250 deaths were attributed to it in 1980, but fewer in subsequent years.

Falange Pátria Nova (FPN): this right-wing terrorist group bombed a number of news-stands in Brasília and Río de Janeiro in 1980, killing at least one person, in order to discourage the sale of left-wing journals.

Frente Nacional: the National Front was an openly-nazi organization active around 1976. It opposed the Geisel regime as insufficiently radical, and sought to combat capitalism and race-mixing.

Sociedade de Estudos Políticos, Económicos e Sociais (SEPES): the Society for Political, Economic and Social Studies was active throughout the 1970s as the Brazilian branch of the World Anti-Communist League (see South Korea). It was then the largest and most organized right-wing grouping other than Arena. It had extensive foreign contacts.

Tenente Mendes: Leonel Brizola, a leading progressive politician, was the target of an unsuccessful assassination attempt claimed by this group in 1980. It also attacked several left-of-centre publications.

União Obreira e Camponesa Brasileira (UOCB): the Brazilian Workers' and Peasants' Union was a right-wing nationalist pressure group formed in the late 1960s. It followed fundamentalist Catholic ideology based on the teachings of Plínio Salgado, who as leader of the pre-1945 "integrist" movement was in contact with German and Italian fascist movements in Europe and among the immigrant communities in southern Brazil. The UOCB supported the military regime and the Arena party, and was particularly close to Gen. Geisel. From 1968 it published a newspaper, the *Diário de Divulgação Doutrinário e de Notícias*, which became *Renovação Nacional* in the early 1970s. The UOCB faded away in the late '70s.

Vanguarda do Comando de Caça aos Comunistas (CCC): in 1980 this group was collaborating with the better-known *Esquadrão da Morte* in killing about 100 people a month; the CCC concentrated on attacking political activists rather than alleged criminals. In 1980 it bombed a school in Río de Janeiro.

Other organizations

Minor right-wing groupings which have been active in recent years, and may or may not remain in existence, include the *Movimento Anticomunista*(MAC) and a local branch of the UK-based Christian Mission to the Communist World.

Bulgaria

capital: Sofia   **population: 9,000,000**

Political system. Bulgaria is a People's Republic with a 400-seat National Assembly elected by universal adult suffrage for a five-year term. The Assembly elects a 28-member State Council and a Council of Ministers. The only legal political parties are those of the communist-led Fatherland Front.

Recent history. Since the Fatherland Front seized power in 1944 the country has been ruled by the Bulgarian Communist Party. Todor Zhivkov, party leader from 1954, became President of the State Council (and de facto head of state) in 1971, when the present Constitution was adopted.

The evolution of the far right. Right-wing military coups took place in 1923, when the Agrarian Party Prime Minister was assassinated, and in May 1934, when the same conspirators overthrew the parliamentary system and installed a dictatorship under Col. Kimon Georgieff (with the approval of the King, Boris). A sizeable fascist movement developed, the main element in which was the National Legion. Bulgaria allied itself with the Axis powers in March 1941 and participated in the invasion and occupation of Yugoslavia.

The uprising of 1944 resulted in the dissolution of all native fascist movements and there has been no evidence of organized internal right-wing activity thereafter, although there was an attempted coup in 1964 and there have been isolated reports of sabotage. Normal, though illegal, dissident activities such as those of the ABD in 1978 fall outside the scope of this work, as do those of the émigré Social Democratic Party.

In 1982 a Turkish fascist, Mehmet Ali Agca, who had tried in May 1981 to kill Pope John Paul II, alleged that his action had been the result of a conspiracy involving the Bulgarian secret service. No evidence of the connection was produced and it is now generally accepted that he was working with non-Bulgarian fascists. There were allegations in the mid-1980s that the Bulgarian government was engaging in a forcible campaign to assimilate the ethnic-Turkish minority which was estimated to account for some 5 per cent of the population.

Active organizations

Bulgarian National Committee (BNC)

Address. 109 Amherst Street, Highland Park, New Jersey 08904, United States

Leadership. Dimitar Petkoff (president)

Orientation. Anti-communist

History. The BNC was founded in 1949 by anti-communist émigrés.

Policies. The Committee seeks to unite Bulgarian refugees and Bulgarian-Americans to ensure the wellbeing of refugees, to publicize the Bulgarian national question and to work for the downfall of the communist system and the creation of a free and independent Bulgaria. It provides employment advice, educational and social welfare services for refugees, and co-ordinates the work of local and foreign Bulgarian émigré groups.

Publications. Free and Independent Bulgaria, quarterly; bulletins and pamphlets.

International affiliations. Apart from 57 local groups in the United States the Committee has affiliates in Australia, Canada, France, New Zealand and other countries.

Bulgarian National Front (BNF)

Address. PO Box 46250, Chicago, Illinois 60646, United States

Leadership. Dr Ivan Docheff (president)

Orientation. Anti-communist

History. The BNF was founded in 1948.

Policies. The goals of the BNF are essentially the same as those of the BNC, although it is perhaps more explicitly anti-communist.

Membership. The Front has fewer than 4,000 members, most of whom are Bulgarians or of Bulgarian descent.

Publications. Borba, quarterly.

Defunct organizations

National Legion: a pre-war national socialist paramilitary movement, the Legion had about 30,000 members when it was ordered to disband in 1934. It was revived in July 1935, with the intention of forming part of the right-wing government's proposed State Party, but it was again dissolved in January 1936, when it claimed 40,000 members.

Rodna Zachtita: the Home Defence organization, modelled on the Austrian *Heimwehr*, was established around 1930. By 1934, when it was prohibited, it had about 7,000 members; it was revived briefly in the latter half of 1935.

Other organizations

Emigré organizations which profess to be concerned principally with human rights issues, but which have attracted the support of anti-communist activists in the emigré and host communities, include the Vienna-based *Civil Rights Group*, active in the late 1970s, and the Paris-based *Collectif de Soutien de la Lutte du Peuple Bulgare* (Support Collective for the Bulgarian People's Struggle). Both organizations have engaged mainly in publicizing allegations of the maltreatment of political prisoners in Bulgaria.

Canada

capital: Ottawa   **population: 25,500,000**

Political system. Canada is a parliamentary democracy with the UK constitutional monarch as its head of state and a federal system of government. There is a popularly elected 282-seat federal House of Commons and a 104-seat appointed Senate.

Recent history. The Liberal Party, which formed the government almost continuously since 1968, lost power to the Progressive Conservative Party in 1984. The main political issues in recent years have been federal-provincial relations and separatism, but there are now indications that French-speaking Quebec has largely accepted its position as one of the 10 provinces.

The evolution of the far right. Canada had a small pre-war fascist movement, which was suppressed in 1939-40. The country still has a substantial Social Credit Party, which controls the provincial government in British Columbia. The social credit philosophy, based on monetary reform and developed in the 1920s by Maj. C.H. Douglas, was taken up by the Social Credit League which formed the Alberta government from 1935; it has in other countries been adopted by quasi-fascist movements, but the current Canadian party is centrist (although it has some fascist members; see Jim Keegstra, below). Some United States fascist groups, such as the Aryan Nations and various Ku Klux Klan factions, have enrolled Canadian members, and there is also a native fascist movement typified by the Western Guard Party.

There are many Eastern-bloc émigrés in Canada, as well as very long-established Russian and Ukrainian communities, but there is not much evidence of anti-communist or fascist activity among them. There are numerous Lithuanian, Hungarian, Ukrainian, Russian and other émigré publications and societies. Some Ukrainians, however, came to Canada after serving in the Nazi forces during the Second World War, and they protested strongly during a public inquiry held in 1985 into war criminals living in Canada.

The legal position of fascist agitation in Canada is somewhat unclear. Legislation has been enacted against the promotion of racial hatred, but has been used only twice. On the other hand a Charter of Rights enacted in 1982 has been used by fascists to prevent the seizure of hate literature, most of which is imported from US groups. An unusual False News Act has been used against a revisionist history publisher (that is, one active in the movement which seeks to deny that nazi Germany had a deliberate policy of exterminating Jews).

Active organizations

Aryan Nations

Leadership. Terry Long (spokesman)

Orientation. White supremacist

History. This ultra-right organization (see main entry under United States) has a number of Canadian members, and came under police scrutiny in 1985 for advertising computerized data banks containing lists of "race traitors".

Policies. The group has advocated the extermination of homosexuals. Long, a prominent Canadian member, has been quoted as saying that all Jews should be hung for treason. The group has made a special effort to recruit Vietnam war veterans.

International affiliations. In 1986, when aged 73, John Ross Taylor was the "ambassador to Canada" of the US branch of the Aryan Nations movement.

Bureau Tradition, Famille, Propriété pour le Canada (TFP)
Tradition, Family and Property Canada Office (TFP)

Address. 244 rue Notre Dame, Sainte Suplice, Quebec

Orientation. Anti-communist

History. This pressure group originated in Brazil but now has branches in several Western countries.

Policies. The group seeks, mainly by means of full-page advertisements in the mainstream press, to warn of the dangers to individual freedom posed by communism and socialism.

International affiliations. See TFP (Brazil, United Kingdom); American Society for the Defense of Tradition, Family and Property (United States).

Canadian Knights of the Ku Klux Klan

Address. Box 2415, New Westminster, British Columbia

Leadership. James McQuirter (grand wizard); William Lau Richardson (intelligence director)

Orientation. White supremacist

History. The KKK was reportedly organized in Canada in 1980, although there have been reports of occasional Klan activity there since the 1960s at least. In April 1981 Mary Ann McGuire, a Canadian Klanswoman, was arrested in Dominica after the discovery of a plot to invade the island.

Policies. Like its many US counterparts, this Klan group is anti-black, anti-abortion, anti-semitic and authoritarian.

Associated organizations. The group has links with the NSWPP.

International affiliations. The Canadian Klan corresponds with several US Klan organizations, and took part in the 1982 gathering at Stone Mountain, Georgia, which attempted to co-ordinate the various Klans.

Canadian League of Rights (CLR)

Address. PO Box 130, Flesherton, Ontario N0C 1E0

Leadership. Ron Gostick (national director)

Orientation. Ultra-right, anti-semitic

History. This organization, founded around 1963 by Pat Walsh, was represented by Gostick at the 1985 Crown Commonwealth League of Rights (CCLR) conference in London, UK. In his address to the gathering Gostick defended the Canadian revisionist historians, Ernst Zündel and Jim Keegstra (see Individuals, below).

Policies. The League shares the anti-Jewish and white supremacist beliefs of its foreign sister organizations.

Associated organizations. The publishing arm of the CLR is Canadian Intelligence Publications, at the same address, which produces the quarterly *Canadian Intelligence Service* in English and French since 1963.

International affiliations. The League is linked, through the CCLR (see United Kingdom), with similar bodies in Australia, New Zealand, the UK and the United States. It has also been linked with the World Anti-Communist League (see South Korea) but was included in the WACL's early 1980s purge of anti-semitic groups.

John Birch Society—see United States.

National Socialist Alliance (NSA)

Address. 812 O'Connor Drive, Toronto, Ontario M4A 2B0

Orientation. Nazi

History. The Alliance emerged in the early 1980s, possibly as a splinter group of the NSWPP.

Policies. The Alliance follows classic nazi policies on racial, political and economic matters.

National Socialist White People's Party (NSWPP)

Leadership. George Graham (member)

Orientation. Nazi

History. Like the former US party of the same name, whose successor organization is known as the New Order, the NSWPP has attracted the support of most of the country's overt nazi sympathisers. Graham, a leading activist with a history of infiltrating and disrupting left-wing groups on behalf of US and Canadian official and private agencies, was allegedly assaulted together with a Klan activist at a 1984 anti-abortion demonstration.

Policies. The NSWPP openly admires and follows the ideas of Adolf Hitler. It believes in the unification at national and international levels of the white "race" under a hierarchical and authoritarian leadership, and it opposes black immigration and "race-mixing".

International affiliations. The party has links with several foreign nazi groups, mainly in the United States.

Nationalist Party of Canada

Address. 685 Danforth Avenue, Box 473, Station J, Toronto, Ontario

Orientation. White supremacist

History. The Nationalist Party has been active since 1982.

Policies. The Party has neo-nazi policies.

Publications. Nationalist Report

Associated organizations. There appear to be close links between the Party and a Klan-type organization called the White Knights of Columbia.

International affiliations. By the mid-1980s the Party had established contact with several foreign fascist groupings, including some affiliates of the World Union of National Socialists (see Denmark and United States).

Speak Up Publishing Co. Ltd

Address. Box 272, Station B, Toronto, Ontario M5T 2W2

Orientation. White supremacist, anti-semitic

History. This company was founded around 1977 and remained active in the early 1980s.

Policies. The magazine published by the company propounds a Jewish conspiracy theory.

Publications. Speak Up, monthly.

International affiliations. Speak Up is very similar in its content and thrust to *The Spotlight* and other publications of the Liberty Lobby (United States).

The Spokesman

Address. 2800 Keele Street, Box 610, Downsview, Ontario M3M 3A9

Orientation. Ultra-right

History. This publication was circulating among Canadian and foreign far-right groups in the early 1980s. It has not been possible to confirm that it is still produced.

Publications. The Spokesman, monthly.

Western Guard Party

Address. Box 193, Station J, Toronto, Ontario M4J 4Y1

Orientation. Neo-nazi

History. The Party was formed as the Edmund Burke Society by Canadian adherents of the US-based White Power movement in the early 1970s, and adopted its present name in 1972. It has contested local and provincial elections without success, although its then leader, Don Andrews, came second in the 1974 Toronto mayoral election.

Policies. The Party has white supremacist ideas and is anti-communist and anti-semitic.

Publications. Straight Talk, party organ, monthly.

International affiliations. There is a branch of the Western Guard Party in Buffalo, New York. The party corresponds with many foreign nazi parties, Klans and other groups, and has been particularly close to the National States' Rights Party (United States).

Western Unity Movement

Address. PO Box 156, Verdun 19, Quebec

Orientation. White supremacist

History. The Movement was founded around 1980.

Policies. The Movement's publications are concerned with the maintenance of the cultural, political and racial integrity of the white peoples.

White Christian Patriots Association (WCPA)

Address. Box 116, 20483 Fraser Highway, Langly, British Columbia U3A 4G3

Orientation. White supremacist

History. The WCPA was active in the mid-1980s.

Policies. The Association promotes belief in a Jewish conspiracy for world domination, and in the natural superiority of the white "race".

Young Americans for Freedom—see under United States.

Defunct organizations

Federation of Labour Clubs of Quebec: this association formed the basis of the Canadian Fascist party, formed in September 1933. The party, which claimed to have 25,000 members at the outset, adopted a nazi uniform and salute. It was suppressed during the war.

Falange d'Action Fasciste des Travailleurs: the Workers' Phalanx for Fascist Action was established around 1975 as a successor to the *Mouvement d'Assaut Révolutionnaire Socialfasciste* (MARS—Social-Fascist Revolutionary Assault Movement), which was itself a successor to the *Parti National-Socialiste Canadien* (Canadian National Socialist Party) formed in 1968 and banned in 1970. All of these tiny and openly nazi movements were led by M. von Reuters and were based in Quebec, publishing a journal called *L'Assaut* with a swastika symbol. The *Falange* established contact with several foreign groups, such as the Spanish CEDADE, before it dissolved in the late 1970s.

Friends of Rhodesia: a racist pressure group based in Oakville, Ontario, in the 1970s.

Michael Fighting League: a fiercely anti-semitic "integrist" grouping based in Rougemont, Quebec, it fought in the 1970s to expose alleged communist subversion of the Catholic Church.

National Front of Canada: formed in the 1970s by immigrant supporters of the British National Front, this grouping failed to take off and is thought to have disbanded around 1984. It was based in Sarnia, Ontario.

Other organizations

Other groups which have been reported as active on the right-wing fringe of Canadian politics within the past decade include the following: the *Association to Defend Property Rights* (PO Box 7456, Station E, Calgary, Alberta T3E 3M2), a libertarian "objectivist" group; the *British Commonwealth Alliance*; the *British Israel World Federation—Canada*, and the rival *Canadian British-Israel Association* and *Association of Covenant People* (see British Israel movement, United Kingdom); *Campus Alternative* (PO Box 332, Rexdale, Ontario M9W 5L3), for right-wing students; the *Canadian Freedom Foundation* (55 Cockburn Drive, West Hill, Ontario M1C 2T1), a libertarian grouping; *Canadians for Responsible Government* (PO Box 4111, Station E, Ottawa, Ontario K1S 5B1); a branch of the UK-based Christian Mission to the Communist World; *Countdown* quarterly (PO Box 278, Station K, Toronto, Ontario M4P 2GS), founded around 1974 by Paul Fromm as an offshoot of the racist Edmund Burke Society; *Editions Celtiques*, founded in the mid-1970s by the fascist New European Order (see Switzerland) to distribute the publications of its *Institut Supérieur des Sciences Psychosomatiques, Biologiques et Raciales* (also known as the *Akademie für Psychosomatik, Biologie und Rassenkunde* and as the *Academy for Psychosomatic, Biological and Racial Sciences*; the *Libertarian Party of Canada* (which, in common with most libertarian groups, denies that it is of the right, but has a philosophy attractive to the traditional following of right-wing groups), based at PO Box 190, Adelaide Street

Postal Station, Toronto, Ontario M5C 2J1; founded in 1973, and led by Victor Levis and Dennis Corrigan; the *Monarchist League of Canada*; the *National Association for the Advancement of White People* (a Ku Klux Klan front, modelled on the US group of the same name, it opened a Toronto office in 1980); the *National Citizens' Coalition* (74 Victoria Street, Suite 902, Toronto, Ontario M5C 2A5); the *National Party*; the nordicist and anti-semitic *Odinist Movement*, led by E. Christensen and publishing *The Sunwheel* and *The Odinist* quarterly; the *Parti de l'Unité Nationale—Parti National Social Chrétien* (National Unity Party - National Christian Social Party), an openly fascist grouping (banned during the war) which was founded in 1899 by Adrien Arcand as the PNSC, becoming the PUN in 1930; the *Party for the Commonwealth of Canada*; *Samisdat* bulletin (206 Carlton Street, Toronto, Ontario), which carries a broad range of national socialist and "national revolutionary" propaganda; an anti-communist Quebec regional party, *L'Union Nationale*, of 580 est, Grand-Allée, Bureau 20, Quebec, Quebec G1R 2J5, led by Jean-Marc Béliveau; the *United Empire Loyalists Association*, the Canadian affiliate of a precursor of the UK National Front; and the libertarian *Unparty* of Box 6069, Station A, Toronto, Ontario M5W 1P5.

Individuals

Jim Keegstra: an anti-semitic activist, former mayor and dismissed high school teacher from Eckville, Alberta, he was prosecuted in 1985 for wilfully promoting racial hatred by publicizing his belief in an international Jewish conspiracy and in the theory that the Holocaust never happened. He was fined $5,000 and had his collection of anti-semitic publications confiscated. The case, which went on for 67 days, received widespread publicity. Keegstra was one of few extremists in the Social Credit Party; he had become a vice-president of the party, was then expelled (when details emerged of the impending prosecution) but was subsequently reinstated and was an unsuccessful Social Credit parliamentary candidate in 1984.

Patrick Walsh: the former leader of the Canadian League of Rights, and Canadian correspondent of the anti-semitic Liberty Lobby's magazine, *The Spotlight* (United States).

Ernst Zündel: a German-born "revisionist" history publisher, and author of *The Hitler We Loved and Why*, he was convicted in February 1985 of "publishing false news" and was sentenced to 15 months imprisonment after claiming that the nazi Holocaust was a fiction invented by the Jews. His lawyer was Doug Christie, who also defended Keegstra. In evidence Zündel stated that he supplied nazi literature in 18 languages to 45 countries. In early 1987 the Ontario Court of Appeal overturned the conviction on procedural grounds, but in May 1987 the Attorney-General was appealing to the Supreme Court to restore the conviction.

Chile

Political system. The Republic of Chile is governed at present (1987) by a military dictatorship, installed by a coup in 1973 which purported to establish an "authoritarian democracy" by means of various "constitutional acts" and a "fundamental law" proclaimed in 1976 and 1981. The head of the military regime has assumed the title of President of the Republic.

Recent history. In the present century the *Partido Nacional* (PN—National Party, representing the landed oligarchy) has competed for power with the centrist Christian Democratic movement and the Socialist and Communist parties. The left-wing coalition government installed in the elections of 1970 was overthrown in a US-backed military coup in 1973; President Salvador Allende, the Socialist leader, died in the fighting. Gen. Augusto Pinochet Ugarte headed the four-man military junta which seized power, and in 1974 he had himself proclaimed President. He remained in power in early 1987. Civil liberties and political rights have been suspended in much of Chile for most of Pinochet's rule.

The evolution of the far right. Apart from the PN, which is really a right-wing conservative grouping with a more radical rightist fringe, there were few successful ultra-right movements in pre-1973 Chile. There was a small nazi movement before the war, and after 1944 several war criminals (the most notorious of whom was Walter Rauff, inventor of the mobile gas chamber), settled in Santiago and northern Chile. Rauff died in 1984 after many unsuccessful efforts to have him extradited or deported.

Various right-wing groups, many representing private enterprise, took part in the campaign of destabilization which prepared the ground for the 1973 coup. The military regime, however, banned most political activity of left and right, although pressure from a range of democratic forces has forced an occasional softening of this line. The regime has relied extensively on imprisonment without trial, torture, assassination by death squads and the "disappearance" of political opponents, and tens of thousands have been forced into exile. The ideology of the military regime has been consistently anti-communist, authoritarian and monetarist.

Active organizations

Alianza Chilena Anticomunista (Acha)
Chilean Anti-Communist Alliance

Orientation. Ultra-right death squad

History. This group, also known as *Acción Chilena Anticomunista* or *Acción Cristiana Anticomunista*, killed a left-wing leader of the indigenous Mapuche community in January 1984, assaulted a centrist leader in March of the same year, and carried out other attacks on leftist and centrist politicians. In 1985 it machine-gunned a Mapuche community centre in Temuco. It may draw some of its membership from a paramilitary police force, the *carabineros*. An Amnesty International report in 1986 attributed at least 64 kidnappings to the Acha and similar groups in 1985, and noted the ease with which such groups operated in daylight or during the curfew hours.

Policies. The Acha seeks to discourage opposition activism by means of selective assassinations and assaults.

Grupo Antimarxista (Grapa)
Anti-Marxist Group

Orientation. Ultra-right guerrilla group

History. The Grapa carried out a number of attacks on left-wing targets in 1984.

Grupo 11 de Septiembre
September 11 Group

Orientation. Anti-communist death squad

History. This Group, whose name derives from the date of the 1973 coup, claimed responsibility for the killings of four alleged left-wingers shot in September 1986 as an apparent reprisal for a communist resistance group's near-successful attempt earlier in the month to assassinate Pinochet.

Policies. The Group's anonymous spokesman threatened to kill a left-winger for every person killed by the communist guerrillas.

Movimiento de Acción Nacional (MAN)
National Action Movement

Base. Santiago

Leadership. Federico Willoughby (president); Pablo Rodríguez (leader)

Orientation. Pro-military

History. This small party, formed in 1985, joined with other right-wing groups in the *Acuerdo Democrática Nacional* (Adena—National Democratic Accord), a conservative coalition formed in 1984 and led by Juan de Dios Carmona. Rodríguez had until the late 1970s been national leader of *Patria y Libertad*, a paramilitary fascist group.

Policies. The MAN supports the Pinochet regime which it regards as patriotic and nationalist. It opposes calls for the reopening of the democratic process.

Movimiento Nacionalista Popular (MNP)
Popular Nationalist Movement

Base. Temuco

Leadership. Roberto Thieme (leader)

Orientation. Ultra-nationalist

History. The MNP was established in 1980 after Thieme, who as leader of a neo-fascist grouping called *Patria y Libertad* had supported the 1973 coup, had withdrawn his support from the Pinochet government. In 1980 Thieme was forced to flee to Argentina after a coup plot in which he was implicated was uncovered by the secret police. It is unlikely that the movement has survived in his absence although he has continued to issue statements as head of the MNP.

Policies. The Movement has populist, nationalist and anti-communist policies, and is opposed to the foreign investment strategy of the military government. It has sought support mainly in rural south central Chile.

Defunct organizations

Avanzada: a right-wing monthly journal (Advance) which was published in the early 1980s from a Santiago post office box. It was edited by Guido Poli but was more explicitly pro-Pinochet than Poli's other journal, *Orden Nuevo.*

Comando de Defensores de la Patria: the Fatherland Defenders Commando was an ultra-right death squad active around 1979.

Comando Vengador de Martires (Covema): the Martyrs' Avengers Commando, a death squad, was active in 1980-81, kidnapping and assaulting a number of journalists and students and killing at least one of them.

Falange Chilena: the Chilean Phalanx was a street-fighting group of ultra-right youths which developed within a section of the Christian Democratic movement in the early 1970s. It disappeared by the middle of that decade.

Movimiento contra el Cáncer Marxista: the Movement Against the Cancer of Marxism, another ultra-right paramilitary group, carried out several attacks in 1983-84. No reports of its activities have come to light since 1984.

Movimiento de Unidad Nacional: the National Unity Movement was a right-wing pressure group active in the 1970s.

Partido Nacional Socialista: the Chilean Nazi Party had 20,000 members and a large force of storm-troopers when it was banned in October 1934 by the Salas government. It had been founded in 1932 by Jorge González von Marees. Some of the *"nacis"*, as followers of González were known, were involved with the *Vanguardia Popular Socialista* during the 1940s.

Orden Nuevo: this fascist grouping (New Order), which published a magazine of the same name, was founded in 1969 as *Tacna*, which was also the name of an artillery regiment which participated in Gen. Viaux's coup plot. The *Tacna* group was banned as subversive in 1970, but re-emerged after the Pinochet coup of 1973 and continued to publish its review until at least 1977, under the leadership of Erwin Robertson and Guido Poli.

Patria y Libertad: Homeland and Liberty was a neo-fascist group which was deeply implicated in efforts to subvert the Popular Unity government in 1970-73. Its journal, *Tizona*, was edited by Pablo Rodríguez (see MAN). The group, which had a paramilitary uniform and structure, infiltrated the right-wing National Party, and dominated the Party's security service (the *Comandos Rolando Matus*) as well as sponsoring a clandestine anti-communist guerrilla group called *Proteco*. It was banned for its involvement in an unsuccessful coup in 1973; it never recovered its influence after the Pinochet coup, although its journal remained in existence at least until 1976. Its general secretary, Roberto Thieme, went on to establish the *Movimiento Nacionalista Popular.*

Silo: this illegal nazi grouping, linked to the Argentinian Tacuara group, was violently opposed to the Allende regime.

Other organizations

Minor right-wing groupings which may or may not remain in existence include an affiliate of the Christian Mission to the Communist World (United Kingdom). The Pinochet regime is supported by a large number of foreign groups, including organizations like the American Chilean Council (United States).

Individuals

Franz Pfeiffer: this German nazi, who fled to Chile after the war,founded the *Partido Nacional Socialista Obrero Chileno* (PNSOCh— National Socialist Chilean Workers' Party) in the late 1960s. The Party, which joined the World Union of National Socialists, was particularly close to the *Frente Nacional Socialista Argentino* in the mid-'70s. Pfeiffer edited a clandestine fascist newsletter, *Audacia*, during the Allende era, and after the 1973 coup he published a monthly, *El Telex Urgente*. Although the PNSOCh appeared to have collapsed by the late '70s, Pfeiffer was operating a neo-nazi information service from his home address (Avenida Las Parcelas 5117, Santiago 16) in the early 1980s.

Colombia

capital: Bogotá   **population: 30,000,000**

Political system. The Republic of Colombia has an executive President and a bicameral Congress, both elected for four years by universal adult suffrage. There are 112 seats in the Senate and 199 in the House of Representatives.

Recent history. The political system in Colombia has been dominated for 130 years by the Conservative and Liberal parties, each of which is at present divided into a number of factions. There are also several smaller parties, and guerrilla movements have been active since the 1950s. Since the near civil war of the 1950s, which took place under a succession of military rulers, power has alternated between the main parties, initially under a National Front accord (from 1958 to 1974) and subsequently as the result of free elections.

The evolution of the far right. In the turmoil following the assassination of a left-wing mayor of Bogotá in 1948, President Laureano Gómez assumed dictatorial powers. He was overthrown in 1953 by the more right-wing Gen. Gustavo Rojas Pinilla, whose dictatorship was replaced by a military junta in 1957, leading to the re-establishment of democracy. Rojas later established a right-wing party, the ANAPO, as whose candidate he came close to victory in the 1970 presidential election. The ANAPO lost most of its following in the next few years.

In the early 1980s right-wing death squads were established, under the patronage of drug dealers and their military associates, in order to combat the left-wing guerrilla movements which had become increasingly active in the 1970s. The adoption of an electoral strategy by some of these movements did not halt the killings; the *Unión Patriótica*, the party formed by the leading guerrilla group, lost a number of its leaders to the death squads in 1986-87.

Active organizations

Asociación para la Unificación Latinoamericana
Latin American Unification Association

Orientation. Anti-communist

History. This grouping was formed in the early 1980s as one of several Latin American fronts for the Unification Church (see South Korea), a right-wing sect controlled by Sun Myung Moon.

Policies. The group's ostensible aim is the furthering of political, social and spiritual unity among the Latin American nations.

International affiliations. The Association is also organized in Costa Rica and other Latin American countries.

Escuadrones de la Muerte
Death Squads

Orientation. Ultra-right

History. This generic name is given to the numerous and probably autonomous secret groups of military, police or civilians who kill suspected criminals or left-wingers. It includes several organized groups such as the MAS and the *Legión Aguilas Blancas.* The Squads were responsible for several hundred killings a year in the early 1980s.

International affiliations. Although there are probably no formal links, these groups are the Colombian manifestation of a phenomenon known elsewhere in Latin America, and notably in Chile, Brazil, El Salvador and Guatemala.

Legión Aguilas Blancas
Legion of White Eagles

Orientation. Ultra-right

History. This death squad emerged in September 1984 to threaten the lives of left-wing activists on the grounds that the leftist guerrilla groups were reneging on peace agreements. The group claimed to have "legionnaires" in most large cities.

Muerte a los Secuestradores (MAS)
Death to Kidnappers

Base. Medellín

Orientation. Ultra-right

History. The MAS was founded around 1981 with the support of right-wing military personnel and prominent drug dealers. In October 1981 it was announced in Calí that 200 dealers had set up a fund of more than US$2,000,000 to arm and maintain the MAS.

Of more than 500 killings definitely attributed to the MAS in its first five years, most were of peasant or trade union activists rather than of known guerrillas. Among its best-known victims have been the amnestied leaders of two of the three main guerrilla groups.

After a presidential inquiry in 1982-83, a list published in February 1983 named 163 alleged members of the MAS, including two serving colonels and 57 other soldiers. The inquiry has not resulted in any convictions and the MAS remains active; in 1985 it was responsible for the decapitation of seven peasants involved in a land dispute in the north of the country.

Policies. Although the professed aim of the group is to stamp out left-wing guerrilla organizations responsible for kidnapping, it also functions as a private militia defending the interests of the drug trade.

Defunct organizations

Alianza Nacional Popular (ANAPO): the Popular National Alliance was founded in 1960 as the personal vehicle of Gen. Rojas Pinilla, the former dictator. It initially worked by infiltration of the two main parties and did not receive recognition as a party until 1970, by which time it had moved to the centre-right and had a substantial congressional representation. Rojas narrowly lost the 1970 presidential election to the Conservative candidate, but the ANAPO gained 72 seats in Congress. The party's support had declined drastically by the 1974 elections. It remained in existence in the mid-1980s, under the leadership of Joaquín Mejía, but was regarded as moribund.

Colombia Joven: this group (Young Colombia) was founded in the 1960s by A. Madrid as a "national revolutionary" fascist group, under the slogan "Colombia over all and God over Colombia". It continued in existence at least until 1977.

Movimiento de Renovación Nacional (MRN): the National Renewal Movement was formed in 1977 by Gen. Alvaro Valencia Tovar, who had been dismissed from the army in 1975 amid rumours of a coup. He contested the 1978 presidential election, winning 66,000 votes for a "democratic right-wing" platform emphasising citizen participation and moral renewal. The party and its publication, *Renovación*, appear to have collapsed.

Other organizations

In the late 1970s there was a Colombian affiliate of the UK-based Christian Mission to the Communist World.

Costa Rica

capital: San José   **population: 2,400,000**

Political system. Costa Rica is a stable parliamentary democracy with a popularly elected President and a 57-seat Legislative Assembly. The country maintains a policy of neutrality and has no standing army, although some of its police units receive military training.

Recent history. Costa Rica has enjoyed uninterrupted constitutional government for nearly seven decades, apart from a brief revolutionary episode in 1948-49. Since the start of the contra war against Nicaragua in 1981, Costa Rican politics have been dominated by the issue of whether or not the rebel contra troops should be allowed to operate from Costa Rica. Until the surrender in May 1986 of its commander, Edén Pastora, the ARDE was the main contra force based in Costa Rica; since early 1986, however, the FDN alliance has taken over the southern front.

The evolution of the far right. Apart from the Nicaraguan groups based in Costa Rica, the domestic ultra-right has produced a number of paramilitary offshoots in recent years, the largest being the *Costa Rica Libre* movement. It was estimated in mid-1986 that these groups had a total of 5,000 men under arms.

Journalists injured in the attack have claimed that the 1984 bombing of the ARDE camp in Costa Rica, apparently an attempt on Edén Pastora's life, was carried out by local ultra-rightists co-operating with the Cuban Omega 7 group. They also claimed that the same individuals had attacked the US embassy in San José in an attempt to provoke outrage against Nicaragua. Foreign mercenaries arrested in Costa Rica have claimed to be working for the US-based Civilian Military Assistance group, which supplies military aid to the contra forces.

Active organizations

Asociación para la Unificación Latinoamericana—see under Colombia.

Ejército del Pueblo Costarricense (EPC)
Costa Rican People's Army

Orientation. Ultra-right

History. This guerrilla organization began operations in 1984.

Movimiento Costa Rica Libre
Free Costa Rica Movement

Address. Apartado 5092, Calle 3 bis Avenida 749, no. 788, San José

Leadership. Bernal Urbina

Orientation. Fascist

History. This group was formed in the early 1970s. Its founders included Urbina; Benjamin Piza, who was appointed in 1984 as head of the Ministry of Public Security (and as such, controller of the Civil Guard, an armed urban and border police force); Gonzalo Facio, a former Foreign Minister; an assistant director of one of the country's many right-wing papers, *La Nación*, and various Chamber of Commerce officials. It was led in the mid-1970s by J.M. Estrada.

The group came to public attention in June 1985, when members stoned the Nicaraguan embassy in San José; in December, members attacked a hotel in which participants in a Central American peace march were staying. Piza then had the marchers expelled from the country.

Policies. The group opposes Costa Rica's traditional neutrality, particularly as regards its northern neighbour, Nicaragua.

International affiliations. In the 1970s the Movement was the Costa Rican affiliate of the World Anti-Communist League (see South Korea).

Patria y Verdad
Homeland and Truth

Orientation. Ultra-right

History. This previously-unknown guerrilla group was suspected of having bombed a power line near the Nicaraguan border on June 11, 1985.

Defunct organizations

Partido Nacional Independiente (PNI): shortly after its foundation the strongly anti-communist PNI gained six seats in the 1974 legislative elections. It declined thereafter and was declared in suspension after its failure to contest the 1978 elections, at which time it was led by Jorge González Martén and Alberto Pinto Gutiérrez.

Other organizations

In the late 1970s the UK-based Christian Mission to the Communist World had at least one affiliated organization in Costa Rica.

Cuba

capital: Havana   **population: 10,000,000**

Political system. The Republic of Cuba is governed by a 500-seat National Assembly of People's Power, which is elected by municipal assemblies and which in turn elects a 31-member Council of State. The President of the Council of State is head of state and government. The sole legal party is the Communist Party of Cuba.

Recent history. Cuba became independent in 1902, but some powers were reserved to the United States until 1934. Fulgencio Batista, who had come to power by a military coup in 1933 and was elected President in 1940, retired in 1944 but staged another coup in 1952, establishing a corrupt and brutal dictatorship. A nationalist revolutionary movement, led by Fidel Castro, overthrew the dictatorship in 1959 and established a radical regime which in 1961 declared itself to be communist. Castro remained in power in 1987, and the generally pro-Soviet regime is active in the Non-Aligned Movement, despite giving diplomatic and military support to several Marxist revolutionary movements and, more recently, governments in the Third World.

The evolution of the far right. The Batista coup in 1952 led to seven years of extremely repressive rule, during which most left-wing activists were imprisoned, exiled, killed or forced underground. Following the Castro revolution, the US intelligence services became deeply involved in the efforts of right-wing Cuban émigrés to stage a counter-revolutionary invasion. These efforts culminated in the Bay of Pigs fiasco of April 1961, when a rebel force landed on Cuba with extensive US logistical support, only to be routed by the local militias and killed, captured or forced to withdraw within days. The last Bay of Pigs prisoners were released in 1962 in return for US$53,000,000 worth of medicines and dried milk.

The anti-Castro programme, called Operation Mongoose by the US Central Intelligence Agency (CIA), continued to support émigré guerrilla groups during the 1960s, with small and ineffective landings and sabotage campaigns taking place around 1968-70, as well as occasional air and seaborne attacks. The CIA, apparently acting without government authorization but with the co-operation of Italian-American interests, also became involved in 1961-65 in several plots to assassinate Castro.

Currently active opposition groups are almost exclusively formed by more recent émigrés or second-generation Cubans in the United States, who are known pejoratively as *gusanos* (silkworms) in Cuba; anti-communism, rather than nostalgia for the Batista era, is the most significant factor. The main waves of emigration to the United States were from 1965-73, 1978-79 and April-June 1980, with perhaps 500,000 in all involved. (In recent years there has been a significant flow in the opposite direction.)

The more recent émigré guerrilla groups have carried out numerous armed attacks on Cuban targets, mainly in the United States. Two Cuban fishing boats were machine-gunned near Florida in April 1976; the embassy in Lisbon was blown up some days later, killing two people. In July and August of the same year the Cuban mission to the UN and Cubana airline offices in Barbados and Panama were bombed, and two Cuban diplomats were kidnapped in Argentina.

From 1982 onwards there were reports that Cuban groups were running paramilitary training camps in Florida and elsewhere in the United States with the tacit approval of the Reagan administration.

Active organizations

Alpha-66

Address. 1530 NW 36th Street, Miami, Florida 33142, United States

Telephone. (305) 633 5542

Leadership. Andrés Nazario Sargent (general secretary); Humberto Pérez Alvarado (chief of military operations)

Orientation. Anti-communist political-military group

History. Alpha-66 was founded in Puerto Rico in June 1962 by a group of 66 exiles, led by Eloy Gutiérrez. It has carried out numerous attacks on Cuban property and citizens; in 1970, it landed 13 men in eastern Cuba. Commanded by Vicente Méndez, the group killed five Cuban soldiers before being captured. In the same year it sank two Cuban fishing vessels and held 11 fishermen hostage in an unsuccessful attempt to secure the release of survivors of the Méndez band. In 1981 the group organized another unsuccessful invasion, with five of its members arrested in Matanzas province. Alpha-66 also sponsors radio broadcasts to Cuba and maintains a self-proclaimed government-in-exile.

Policies. The group seeks to liberate Cuba from communism and Soviet domination and to create a new nation based on free enterprise and individual liberty.

Membership. In 1986 the group claimed 5,000 members.

Publications. *Alpha-66*, monthly.

International affiliations. The group is a full member of the World Anti-Communist League (see South Korea).

Asociación de Combatientes de la Brigada 2506
Bay of Pigs Veterans' Association

Address. 1821 SW Ninth Street, Miami, Florida 33135, United States

Leadership. Miguel Alvarez (president); Juan Pérez Franco (chairman)

Orientation. Anti-communist

History. The Association was formed in 1963 by and for ex-members of the *Brigada 2506*, the code-name for the US-trained counter-revolutionary force which staged an unsuccessful invasion of Cuba in 1961. In the mid-1980s this organization was reportedly running guerrilla training camps for Cuban and Nicaraguan right-wingers in the Florida Everglades.

Policies. The Association's long-term goal is the freeing of Cuba from communist rule. In the interim it seeks to raise the awareness of the American public as to the threat posed to them by the Cuban regime, and to maintain the solidarity and welfare of the Bay of Pigs survivors.

Membership. 1,600

Publications. Girón, monthly, named after the Cuban name for the beach on which the force landed.

Comité pro Derechos Humanos en Cuba
Committee for Human Rights in Cuba

Address. Calle General Pardiñas, Madrid, Spain

Leadership. Armando Valladares (president)

Orientation. Anti-communist

History. The Madrid headquarters of the Committee were broken into in early November 1985; Valladares, a poet and former political prisoner in Cuba, claimed that the Cuban embassy had staged the burglary to obtain important documents, but the embassy denied the charge and said that Valladares was a suspected American agent.

Policies. The Committee seeks to denounce and publicize breaches of human rights and political freedoms in Cuba.

Cuba Independiente y Democrática (CID)
Independent and Democratic Cuba

Address. 10020 SW 37th Terrace, Miami, Florida 33155, United States

Telephone. (305) 551 0271

Leadership. Huber Matos (general secretary); Mario Villar Roces

Orientation. Anti-communist

History. In October 1980 a conference of counter-revolutionary groups was held in Venezuela at the instigation of Matos, a former member of Castro's revolutionary forces who had emigrated in 1979 after serving a 20-year sentence for treason. Plans were approved for the destabilization of Cuba in order to create the conditions for a popular uprising against the Castro regime. The CID was founded in 1980 as a coalition of groups favouring this strategy.

In December 1984 Matos was said to be recruiting a 50-strong Cuban detachment to fight alongside the Nicaraguan contra forces. He had previously spent six weeks with the FDN contras in Honduras.

Policies. The CID seeks to denounce the Castro regime at every opportunity, to help in the establishment of a free, democratic and independent Cuba, and to help other countries resist communist subversion.

Membership. In 1985 the CID claimed to have about 100 local affiliates in the United States, mainly in the Florida region.

Cuban-American National Foundation—see Of Human Rights

Junta Patriótica Cubana
Cuban Patriotic Junta

Base. New York, United States

Leadership. Israel Romero (representative)

Orientation. Anti-communist

History. This exile grouping was active in 1985 in lobbying for political asylum for Cuban immigrants.

Movimiento Insurreccional Martí
Martí Insurrectional Movement

Base. Miami, Florida, United States

Leadership. Lázaro Brudelas (leader)

Orientation. Anti-communist

History. The Movement's leader was quoted in 1984 as opposing the normalization of migration between the USA and Cuba and opposing the "persecution" of "freedom fighters in exile".

Policies. The Movement seeks the overthrow of the Communist Party government.

Movimiento Patriótico Cuba Libre
Free Cuba Patriotic Movement

Address. 1635 SW 98th Street, Miami, Florida 33165, United States

Leadership. Carlos Márquez (organizer)

Orientation. Anti-communist

History. The Movement was founded in 1963 and merged in 1976 with the Liberation Committee of Cuba.

Policies. The Movement seeks "to co-ordinate the maximum number of exile organizations in order to present a united front and to exchange and develop ideas on strategy and tactics to be pursued in the struggle for a free and democratic republic of Cuba".

Associated organizations. 50 affiliated exile organizations.

Of Human Rights

Address. Box 2268, Hoya Station, Georgetown University, Washington DC 20057, United States

Telephone. (202) 342 1586

Leadership. Frank Calzón

Orientation. Anti-communist

History. This group was formed in 1975.

Policies. Of Human Rights aims to monitor and denounce repression and abuses of human rights under the communist regime, and to raise the US public's awareness of such matters.

Membership. 1,500 (1985).

Publications. The group produces an annual report on human rights in Cuba as well as various pamphlets and lectures.

Associated organizations. Its founder is also the director of the Cuban-American National Foundation (CANF), an anti-communist lobbying group set up in 1981 with Jorge Mas Canosa as chairman. The CANF contributes to the election funds of US congressional candidates and has hosted speeches by President Reagan and by the then

US ambassador to the UN, Mrs Jeane Kirkpatrick. The CANF claims to be largely reponsible for the Reagan administration's decision to fund Radio Martí, an anti-communist propaganda station which commenced broadcasts from Miami to Cuba in May 1985.

Omega 7

Leadership. Eduardo Arocena (last known leader)

Orientation. Anti-communist

History. This guerrilla organization was founded by anti-communist Cuban émigrés in the United States, and was led by Arocena (also known as Omar). It came under investigation by the New York police and the Federal Bureau of Investigation (FBI) in 1975, and by a joint task force of the two agencies in 1982. It carried out two murders and more than 30 bombings in Miami, New York, New Jersey and Washington in the seven years to 1985, mainly directed at Cuban diplomats and moderate émigrés. After failing to assassinate the Cuban ambassador to the United Nations, the group killed a lower-ranking diplomat at the mission in 1980.

Following President Reagan's assumption of office in January 1981, Omega 7 maintained a nine-month "truce" in the expectation of a harder line being adopted against Cuba. It resumed its efforts with the bombing of Mexican, Soviet and Venezuelan consulates. Arocena was arrested in Miami in July 1983 and charged with murder, handling explosives and conspiracy to murder the ambassador; weapons and bomb components were seized at his house. In November 1984 and May 1985 he was sentenced respectively to life imprisonment for the murder of the diplomat and to 20 years for a number of the bombings.

In April 1984 another suspect in the murder conspiracy, Alberto Pérez, was convicted of criminal contempt of court after refusing to testify to a grand jury. In November 1984 three émigrés on trial for explosives offences were imprisoned after refusing to give evidence about Omega 7. In February 1985 the group bombed the Washington office of the Soviet airline, Aeroflot.

Policies. Omega 7 has sought to gain public attention and support for the anti-Castro cause, and to foster the conditions for an internal rebellion in Cuba, by highly publicized terrorist activity directed at Cuban targets. The group is opposed to any peaceful contacts between the Castro regime and Cuban exiles.

Membership. The FBI estimated in 1985 that the group had no more than 15 active members.

Associated organizations. Omega 7 is believed to have acted under other names including that of *El Condor*, in which name responsibility was claimed for an airliner bombing in 1976 (see below).

Organización para la Liberación de Cuba (OPLC)
Organization for the Liberation of Cuba

Base. Miami, Florida, United States

Leadership. Héctor Fabián (spokesman)

Orientation. Anti-communist

History. In January 1982 the OPLC established clandestine training camps to instruct Cuban exiles in guerrilla warfare. Its spokesman maintained that its activities were not being interfered with by state or federal authorities and that its funding came from wealthy individuals in the Miami Cuban community.

Policies. The OPLC seeks the overthrow of the communist government in Cuba.

Radio Martí—see Of Human Rights.

Representación Cubana del Exilio (RECE)
Cuban Organization for the Representation of Exiles (CORE)

Address. 1784 W Flagler Street, Room 21, Miami, Florida 33165, United States

Telephone. (305) 642 3236

Leadership. Jorge Mas Canosa (director)

Orientation. Anti-communist

History. This pressure group was active from the late 1960s at least until the mid-1980s.

Policies. The group seeks to "inform the free world about the Cuban tragedy" and to raise support and funding for the liberation struggle. It also lobbies the US administration and the Organization of American States to secure more effective action against the Castro regime.

Publications. RECE, monthly.

Associated organizations. Mas is also involved in the Cuban-American National Foundation (see Of Human Rights), and was spokesman of the National Coalition for a Free Cuba, a "political action committee" which donated US$200,000 to President Reagan's re-election campaign.

Defunct organizations

BCOR: this Cuban émigré organization, details of which are unavailable, was in contact with foreign groups belonging to the World Union of National Socialists in the early 1980s. It was based at that time in Union City, New Jersey, United States, but has not responded to requests for information.

Centro Iberoamericano de Enlace Nacionalista (CIEN): The Ibero-American Centre for Nationalist Collaboration, which developed in 1973 from *Joven América* magazine (founded around 1970) and the later *Centro de Enlace Nacionalista* (CEMEN), was an organization led by Aldo Rosado of the *Comandos Libres Nacionalistas* which sought to foster co-operation among Cuban and other Spanish-speaking fascist and anti-communist groups. Around 1976 Rosado established the *Unión Mundial Nacionalrevolucionaria*, which sought to foster links between such groups and the English-speaking and other neo-fascist movements. Both the CIEN, which was in contact with CEDADE and other Spanish nazi groups, and the Union appeared to have dissolved by 1980.

El Condor: this name (The Eagle) was used in claiming responsibility for the bombing of a Cuban airliner off Barbados in October 1976. Seventy-three people were killed. Orlando Bosch, an exile thought to be linked with Omega 7 and the CORU, was one of four men acquitted of involvement by a Venezuelan court in September 1980.

Coordinación de la Organización Revolucionaria Unida (CORU): this guerrilla force was reportedly founded in Chile by Orlando Bosch in 1975, and had as its aim the undermining of links between Cuba and other American nations. It was held responsible for bombing the Cuban embassy in Caracas in 1974 and the airport at Kingston, Jamaica, in 1976.

Cruzada Anticomunista: the Anti-Communist Crusade was a New York-based émigré grouping which published *Latin American News* from 1971 to 1974, and again around 1977.

Cubanos Unidos: Wilfredo Navarra, the leader of this group, sent several boats to the US military base at Guantánamo, Cuba, in August 1981, with the intention of establishing a provisional government on Cuban soil. A tropical storm intervened and the entire expeditionary force had to be rescued by US coastguards.

Fuerza Nueva: a fascist guerrilla group which united in June 1973 with the *Comandos Libres Nacionalistas.*

Hoja de Combate: this periodical (Combat Journal) was published in Florida in the 1970s by Manuel F. Benítez R., a supporter of Batista who had also (through the magazine *Vanguardia*) supported the US presidential campaign of George Wallace.

Movimiento Cubanos Libres: the openly-fascist Movement of Free Cubans was founded in Miami in 1973, but dissolved within three years due to disputes among its leaders, who included Felipe Rivero, Jose Freyre, S.R. Hernández and Horacio Minguillón.

Movimiento Nacional Cristiano: in 1970 this Miami-based group announced that its leader, "Captain" Orlando Lorenzo, had invaded Cuba with several supporters.

Movimiento Nacionalista Cubano: three members of this US-based group were convicted in 1979 of involvement in the murder three years earlier of Orlando Letelier, an exiled Chilean politician. The Nationalist Movement was led by Felipe Rivero and Guillermo Novo, and published *Manifiesto Nacionalista*; it was disbanded in the late '70s, with most of its members joining similar groups. The Movement may have been responsible for *El Nacionalista*, a Cuban right-wing periodical published in Union City, New Jersey, until about 1977.

Partido Nacionalsocialista Cubano: the miniscule Cuban Nazi Party was founded secretly in Miami in 1976, and disappeared shortly thereafter, having produced only a few copies of its journal *Swastica y Palma.*

Vanguardia: this irregular periodical was published from New York from 1968 until the late 1970s, under the direction of Horacio Minguillón, Manuel Benítez and other anti-communist exiles. Similar but unconnected periodicals of the 1970s included *Zig-Zag Libre* (Miami), and *Acción* (El Monte, California; published in support of the *Comandos Libres Nacionalistas* and the *Movimiento Nacionalista Cristiano*).

Other organizations

Other US-based anti-communist exile or support groups active at various times during the past 25 years have included the *Citizens' Committee for a Free Cuba* (Berryville, Virginia), and the apparently unrelated *Citizens for a Free Cuba* (2379 SW 28th Street, Miami, Florida 33133); Henry Arguero's *Comandos Libres Nacionalistas Cubanos* (Free Cuban Nationalist Commandos—PO Box 97, South Ozone Park Station, New York, NY 11420, or PO Box 1132, El Monte, California 91734), a nazi guerrilla group, founded in 1970, which publishes *Nuevo Orden* magazine; the *Committee of Cuban Intellectuals*; the *Cuban Cultural Center*; the *Cuban National Revolutionary Council* (which sponsored the Bay of Pigs invasion and disappeared shortly afterwards); the *Cuban National Socialist Legion*; the *Federation of Cuban Masons*; the *Frente Democrático Revolucionario* (Democratic Revolutionary Front); the *Movimiento Demócrata Cristiano* (Christian Democratic Movement); the *People's Revolutionary Movement*; the *Truth about Cuba Committee* (Box 571, Miami, Florida 33101), the *Union of Cubans in Exile* and the *Veinte de Mayo* (May 20) group.

Cyprus

capital: Nicosia

population: 660,000

Political system. The 1960 republican Constitution provides for power-sharing between the ethnic Greek and ethnic Turkish communities which account respectively for 75 per cent and 23 per cent of the population. However the Constitution and the institutions—presidency, legislature and Cabinet—established under it are able to function only in the south of Cyprus. In the northern part of the island, which is under Turkish military occupation, there is a "Turkish Republic of Northern Cyprus" which is not recognized as an independent state except by Turkey.

Recent history. A guerrilla campaign beginning in 1955, with the aim of ending British colonial rule and uniting Cyprus with Greece, resulted in the establishment of an independent Cyprus in 1960. There followed clashes between the majority Greek-speaking and minority Turkish-speaking communities, and the Turks withdrew from the island's government. The ultra-right Greek colonels' regime sponsored a military coup in July 1974; the resulting Turkish invasion and occupation of northern Cyprus was followed by massive refugee movements in both directions. A de facto government was set up in 1975 in the Turkish zone, which proclaimed itself an independent republic in 1983. Most of Cyprus continues to be ruled by the Greek community's centrist coalition government.

The evolution of the far right. The 1974 coup installed as President Nicos Sampson, an ultra-right leader of the EOKA-B guerrilla group. He was forced to resign within eight days. There has since been little far-right activity among the majority community although there are some far-right Turkish parties.

Active organizations

Milliyetci Türk Partisi
Turkish Nationalist Party

Address. [Via Turkish postal system:] Nicosia, Mersin 10, Turkey

Orientation. Turkish ultra-nationalist

History. This party was formed in 1981 and was led by Ismail Tezer, the founder of the rival Turkish Unity Party. In January 1984 Tezer was one of four founders of a centre-right New Birth Party (*Yeni Dogus Partisi*), which sought the support of Turkish immigrants—as had both Tezer's previous parties. It is not clear whether the new group, which won 9 per cent of the vote and four of the 50 seats in the June 1985 election to the northern assembly, completely replaced the Nationalist Party. Tezer had in any event left the New Birth Party in February 1985, founding a New Turkish Unity Party which failed to win any seats in the assembly.

Policies. The Party has called for the permanent retention of the Turkish presence in northern Cyprus.

Protoporia

Base. Nicosia

Orientation. Anti-communist

History. A delegation representing this group attended a right-wing youth congress in South Africa in 1985. No further information has come to light on its history or policies.

International affiliations. See Youth for Freedom (South Africa).

Türkiye Birlik Partisi
Turkish Unity Party

Address. [Party daily; via Turkish postal system:] 43 Yediler Street, Nicosia, Mersin 10, Turkey

Telephone. [Party daily:] 020-72959

Leadership. Osman Imre (leader); Olgun Pashalar (editor of daily)

Orientation. Turkish ultra-nationalist

History. This party, founded in 1978 by Ismail Tezer (later of the Turkish Nationalist Party, the New Birth Party and the New Turkish Unity Party), established a daily newspaper in 1980. In the following year it won a single seat in the elections to the Legislative Assembly of the de facto regime in northern Cyprus, and in 1982 it joined the de facto government in that area.

Policies. The Party promotes Turkish immigration and the maintenance of a permanent Turkish state on northern Cyprus.

Publications. Birlik, daily, circulation 2,000.

Defunct organizations

EOKA: the National Organization of Greek Combatants fought the UK from 1955 for *Enosis*, or the union of Cyprus with Greece. Its political leader, Archbishop Makarios III, was forced into exile in 1956 but returned in 1959 to become the first President of independent Cyprus in 1960. *EOKA-B* emerged in 1971 as an anti-Makarios group, backed by the Greek military regime, and in July 1974 its then leader, Nicos Sampson—an ultra-rightist who had succeeded Gen. George Grivas—was installed as President in a coup carried out for the Greek regime by the Civil Guard. Sampson was forced to resign eight days later, after a Turkish invasion, and the Greek dictatorship collapsed shortly afterwards; in 1976 Sampson was imprisoned for 20 years. In July 1978 there were allegations that EOKA-B sympathizers, led by Kikis Constantinou, had conspired with foreign agents to stage a right-wing coup in Cyprus.

Czechoslovakia

capital: Prague   **population: 15,500,000**

Political system. The Czechoslovak Socialist Republic consists of autonomous Czech and Slovak states, each with a National Council. A bicameral Federal Assembly elects a President. All candidates for election belong to a National Front consisting of the Communist Party and several smaller groupings.

Recent history. Czechoslovakia was freed from German occupation and its pre-war borders restored in 1945. It became a People's Republic in 1948 and was closely aligned thereafter with the Soviet Union, apart from a brief liberalizing phase which ended with the intervention by Warsaw Pact armies in August 1968.

The evolution of the far right. During the 1930s there was a substantial nazi movement among the German-speaking population of the Sudetenland, in northern Czechoslovakia, as well as native fascist parties. The wearing of the swastika was forbidden by law in March 1932 (leading the Germans to ban the display of the Czechoslovakian flag from March 1934). German pressure resulted in a four-power agreement whereby the Sudetenland was ceded to Germany in 1938, along with other transfers of territory to Poland and Hungary. With the outbreak of war in 1939 the rest of Czechoslovakia was invaded and occupied, and a puppet "Government of Slovakia" was installed under the Hlinka Party. Most of the country's Jews were deported to death camps in Poland. After the war the Sudetenland and other areas were recovered, the German minority was expelled and a communist-dominated regime was installed.

There has subsequently been little evidence of right-wing activity within Czechoslovakia, although resistance to Soviet-style communism surfaced in the 'Prague Spring' of 1968 and again in the Charter 77 and VONS civil rights movements beginning in 1977. There are many right-wing émigré organizations, notably in the United States.

Active organizations

Council of Free Czechoslovakia

Address. 321 E 73rd Street, New York, NY 10021, United States

Leadership. Jiri Horak (secretary)

Orientation. Anti-communist

History. This group was founded by right-wing exiles in 1949.

Policies. The Council opposes the communist regime in Czechoslovakia, works for national liberation and democracy, and monitors and publicizes abuses of human rights.

Membership. 200.

Publications. Monthly newsletter; occasional monographs.

Czechoslovak National Council of America

Address. 2137 S Lombard Avenue, Room 202, Cicero, Illinois 60650, United States

Orientation. Anti-communist

History. Formed in 1918 by Czechoslovakian immigrants, this group has moved over the years from being primarily a cultural and social organization to being concerned mainly with the resettlement and welfare of anti-communist refugees and with denouncing the communist government for abuses of human rights.

Publications. Vestnik, monthly, and internal bulletins.

Czechoslovakian Christian Democracy

Base. Munich, West Germany

Orientation. Anti-communist

History. This group was founded by conservative exiles in 1957. It has members in Europe and in North America.

Policies. Apart from its denunciation of the communist regime in Prague, the group's policies are not dissimilar to those of mainstream Western European Christian democratic parties.

Publications. Demokracie v Exiliu, published in the United States.

Slovak League of America

Address. Box 150, Middletown, Pennsylvania 17057, United States

Orientation. Anti-communist

History. This émigré organization represents anti-communist Slovaks in the United States. Its journal has been edited by Jozef Pauco, ex-editor of the wartime Tiso government paper of the same name; his successor, Michael Novak, is now involved with the Nicaragua Freedom Fund (see Nicaragua). Contributors to the journal have included Stanislaw Kirschbaum, son of the general secretary of Tiso's party.

Policies. The League is staunchly anti-communist and advocates an independent Slovak nation.

Publications. Slovakia

Defunct organizations

Fascist party: a small Czechoslovakian fascist movement developed in the early 1930s under the leadership of a retired general, Gaida. In May 1932 the government prohibited fascist youth associations. Some 30 sympathizers of the movement, led by Kobsenek, staged an unsuccessful coup at Brno in January 1933, leading to Gaida's temporary arrest. The party's 10 seats in parliament were reduced to six in the 1935 general election.

German Revolutionary Committee of Action: formed in March 1934 to circumvent the ban on the German Nazi Party, this coalition, which was led by Dr Otto Strasser's Black Front, espoused "German socialism" and economic and social policies identical with those of the nazis. The Committee's weekly newspaper was entitled *German Revolution.*

National Sozialistische Deutsche Arbeiterpartei (NSDAP): the German Nazi Party, which was organized mainly in the Sudetenland border region, was declared an illegal organization in Czechoslovakia in October 1933, along with the smaller German Nationalist Party. The NSDAP reorganized under other names and was reconstituted after the cession of the Sudetenland to Germany in 1938.

Slovak Clerical (Hlinka) Party: this group, founded by a Catholic priest, Fr Hlinka, and later led by Tiso, formed the supposedly independent Slovak government during the German occupation. It followed nazi orders in all matters and in particular was responsible for the Aryanization policy, which involved the extermination of most of the country's Jews.

Sudetendeutsche Partei: the Sudeten German Party was a nazi formation led from 1935 by Konrad Henlein. It secured 1,400,000 votes and 44 seats in its first general election, that of May 1935, thus becoming the second largest parliamentary bloc. It was absorbed into the NSDAP after the 1938 cession.

Other organizations

Minor anti-communist émigré organizations recently reported as active include the *Canadian Slovak League*; the UK-based *Committee for the Defence of Liberties in Czechoslovakia*, led by a former Foreign Minister of Czechoslovakia, Arthur London; the Christian democratic *Czechoslovak People's Party*; *Europan*, a Brazilian-based Czech exile movement affiliated to the Czechoslovak National Council of America; the *National Committee for the Liberation of Slovakia* (National Press Building, Washington, DC 20004, United States), and the *Slovensky Oslobodzovací Vybor* (SOV—Slovak Liberation Council), based in West Germany (Postfach 200402, 8000 Munich).

Denmark

capital: Copenhagen   population: 5,100,000

Political system. The Kingdom of Denmark, which includes the autonomous Faroe Islands and Greenland, has a constitutional monarch and a unicameral 179-seat Parliament (*Folketing*) which is mostly elected by universal adult suffrage. There is a cabinet system of government.

Recent history. Most recent governments have been centre-right or centre-left coalition or minority governments. The main parties are the Social Democrats, the Conservative People's Party, the Liberals and the Socialist People's Party, which together account for about 75 per cent of the vote.

The evolution of the far right. A number of small fascist movements existed prior to the Second World War, and there were many reports of nazi agitation, notably among the farmers of South Jutland in 1933-34. In 1933 Denmark became the first country to outlaw the wearing of political uniforms, a move quickly copied by Norway, Sweden, the Netherlands, Switzerland and Belgium. Denmark was occupied by nazi Germany from 1940 to 1945, and was incorporated into the Reich, with the NSDAP (German Nazi Party) taking over the existing fascist groups. There has been little recorded fascist acitivity in the post-war era, although the main nazi party, the DNSU, has a high profile internationally.

Active organizations

Dansk Nasjonal Sosjalistisk Ungdom (DNSU)
Danish National Socialist Youth

Address. Postboks 7916, 9210 Aalborg SØ

Leadership. Poul Heinrich Riis-Knudsen (leader)

Orientation. Nazi

History. The DNSU, in existence since the late 1960s, regards itself as the continuation of the original Danish Nazi Party youth group, which was formed in 1934. In July 1984 Riis-Knudsen caused controversy by using the state-owned radio service to call for the deportation of immigrants on the grounds that "race-mixing is threatening our biological heritage". Several days later a hostel for Iranian refugees was besieged by a crowd of right-wing youths.

Policies. The party holds white supremacist, nordicist, anti-semitic and authoritarian views, and seeks to vindicate Hitler, the German Nazi Party and wartime Danish collaborationists.

Publications. Nasjonal Sosjalisten

Associated organizations. The party's printing and publishing company, the Nordland Forlag (Northland Press), operates from the same address. Some publications have borne the imprint DNSUs Forlag.

International affiliations. The DNSU has extensive international contacts, and in the 1970s it became increasingly involved in the World Union of National Socialists (WUNS). It has had particularly close relations with Swedish nazis and with the NSDAP-AO (United States). The Nordland Forlag was reported to have taken over the production of the NSDAP-AO's propaganda after the latter's Austrian and German presses were closed down in 1977.

Fremskridtspartiet
Progress Party

Address. Folketinget, Christiansborg, 1218 Copenhagen K

Telephone. (01) 116 600

Leadership. P.S. Hansen (president); V.A. Jakobsen, Helge Dohrmann

Orientation. Libertarian

History. The Progress Party was founded in August 1972 by Mogens Glistrup, and achieved representation in parliament on an anti-tax platform. Its first electoral trial, in 1973, gave it 28 seats, making it the second-largest parliamentary bloc, but this decreased to 20 seats by 1979 and to 16 in 1981. In the January 1984 general election, which was necessitated by the Progress Party's withdrawal of support from the conservative coalition government, the Party received 120,631 votes (3.6 per cent, and won six of the 175 metropolitan Danish seats in the *Folketing*. One of these went to Glistrup, whose earlier conviction for tax fraud led to his expulsion from the *Folketing* the following month.

Policies. The party advocates the abolition of income tax and of the diplomatic service, and reductions in the volume of legislation and in the size of the civil service.

Membership. 9,000 (1986 estimate).

Publications. Fremskridt, weekly, circulation 3,000.

Greenshirts

Base. Copenhagen

Orientation. Neo-nazi

History. The Danish police arrested 23 members of this group after the murder in October 1985 of a taxi-driver, following threats made to his firm that drivers would die unless the Greenshirts were permitted to broadcast on television a demand for the repatriation of immigrants and refugees. The green shirt as a fascist uniform had previously been used by the Hungarian Arrow Cross movement, the Spanish Escamots and several other groups.

Policies. The Greenshirts are white supremacists opposed to immigration.

Nordland Forlag—see DNSU

World Union of National Socialists (WUNS)

Address. Postboks 7916, 9210 Aalborg SØ

Leadership. Poul Heinrich Riis-Knudsen (commander)

Orientation. Nazi

History. The WUNS was founded in 1962 at the instigation of Colin Jordan, then leader of the National Socialist Movement (United Kingdom). After Jordan's imprisonment on arms charges in the same year, control passed to Lincoln Rockwell of the American Nazi Party; he renamed it the World Union of Free Enterprise National Socialists (and soon renamed his own party the National Socialist White People's

Party). Jordan became merely the commander of the European section of the Union. On Rockwell's assassination in 1967 the command of his party and of the Union passed to Matt Koehl, who resumed the title WUNS. The European section came under the Danish nazi party in the 1970s; however the DNSU leader, Riis-Knudsen, has often been described in recent years as commander of the WUNS, and it is possible that his section has become detached from the US-based WUNS which remains under the control of Koehl's group (now known as the New Order).

Policies. The founding charter, known as the Cotswold Agreements, defined the purpose of the Union as being to "combat and destroy international Jewish communism and Zionist treason and subversion... [to]promote the Aryan race... [and to] accomplish on a world-wide scale the just and final settlement of the Jewish problem".

Membership. Membership of the Union is open only to nazi parties, although individuals may correspond with it. Affiliations and the names of affiliated groups change frequently but the WUNS has some contact with the vast majority of openly nazi parties around the world and with many neo-nazi groupings.

Defunct organizations

Danish Fascist Movement: a meeting in Copenhagen in April 1933, attended by 150 delegates reportedly representing 15,000 supporters, agreed to establish an independent Danish fascist movement to be led by a margarine manufacturer, Andersen. The movement, which rejected class struggle in favour of a community of the people and determined national leadership, held its first public rally in April.

Danmarks Nasjonal-Sosjalistske Arbejder Parti (DNSAP): the National Socialist Workers' Party of Denmark was founded in 1930 and was led at first by a triumvirate of Einar Jorgensen, C.C. Hansen and C. Lembcke, who were succeeded by Fritts Clausen in 1933. It was the most important of the pre-war fascist groups. From 1934 the DNSAP had a women's wing, the *Danske Piger*, and a youth wing, the *Nasjonal Sosjalistisk Ungdom* (NSU), from which the present-day DNSU traces its history. The NSU's two sections were the *Skjoldunge* (Youth Defence Group, for under-14s) and the *Vaebnere* (Shield-bearers, up to 18 years old). The party had an illegal uniform; its emblem was the nordic sunwheel (a cross surmounted by a circle), which remains in vogue among European fascist groups. Its journals were *Nasjonal Sosjalisten* and *Faedrelandet* (Fatherland).

Dansk Folkeparti: the Danish People's Party was formed in 1940 by the unification of Petersen's DSP (incorporating the DNSP) with Wendelin's *Nasjonalt Samvirke* and Johansen's *Nasjonale Genrejsningsparti*. Petersen became leader of the combined party, whose organ was *Sorte Faner* (Black Banner).

Dansk Front: the Danish Front, also known as the *Arbejdfaelleskabet*(Labour Fraternity), was a dissident nazi coalition founded in the late 1930s, under the leadership of the former NSU chief Thorndal.

Dansk Nasjonal Sosjalistisk Parti (DNSP): founded in 1930 by Carl Borg, and fused in 1934 with the fascist *Dansk Sosjalistik Parti* (DSP) of Wilfred Petersen. Petersen remained leader of the party, which retained the name of the DSP.

Dansk Samlings og Korporationsparti: the Danish Corporate Union Party was an Italian-style fascist grouping founded in 1926. Along with many small fascist and nazi groups it formed the *Dansk Front* in the 1930s.

Landbrugernes Sammenslutning: the quasi-fascist Farmers' Alliance was founded in 1931 by Jorgen Schested, and was allied with Clausen's DNSAP.

Nasjonale Blok: a coalition, formed in 1940 by E. Madsen, which included several small nazi groups such as the *Dansk Folkfaelleskabet*(Danish Folk Fraternity) of Sorenson, the *Dansk Nordisk Front* (Danish Nordic Front) of Orla Emil Olsen and the *Danmark for Folket* (Denmark for the People) movement of Jensen, all of which began as splinters from the DNSAP.

Nasjonale Genrejsningsparti: the National Renaissance Party, led by Svend Johansen, joined in the Danish People's Party in 1940.

Nasjonal Sosjalistisk Arbejder Parti (NSAP): the National Socialist Workers' Party was established by Aage Andersen in 1935 as an extremely anti-semitic splinter group of the DNSAP. Its publications included *Kamptegnet* (Battle Cry).

Nasjonalt Samvirke: National Co-operation, a small fascist grouping, was led during its brief existence (1938-40) by K. Wendelin.

National-Socialistische Deutsche Arbeiter Partei Nordschleswig (NSDAPN): the National Socialist German Workers' Party of North Schleswig was founded in 1933 among the ethnic German community in North Schleswig by Jens Moller as an affiliate of Hitler's NSDAP. Although it was prevented by law from adopting a nazi uniform, it had a paramilitary section—the *Schleswigsche Kameradschaft* (SK—Schleswig Comrades League)—modelled on the German SA, as well as a 5,000 member labour front, and youth and women's sections known respectively as the *Deutsche Jugendschaft Nordschleswig* (DJN) and the *Deutsche Mädchenschaft Nordschleswig* (DMN). Moller served for a time in the *Folketing*.

Other organizations

Minor fascist, anti-communist and other right-wing groups reportedly active in recent years include the following: an affiliate of the UK-based Christian Mission to the Communist World; *Conservative Youth* and its affiliate, *Konservatieve Gymnasiaster* (Conservative School Students); the *European Workers' Party*, part of the La Rouche network (see National Democratic Policy Committee, United States); *Foedre Lander*; *Folk og Land* (Land and People) magazine; a tiny *Ku Klux Klan* group (two of whose members were prosecuted for inciting racial hatred in 1983); the *Landsorganisationen Frihed for Nationer-Unge Solidarister* (National Freedom Organization for Young Nationalist Solidarists—Postboks 4, 8361 Hasselager), and the *Vigilante Forum*.

Dominica

capital: Roseau   **population: 76,000**

Political system. Dominica is a republic with a one-chamber House of Assembly, mainly elected by direct popular vote, and a nominally executive President who appoints a Prime Minister as head of government.

Recent history. Dominica became independent within the Commonwealth in 1978. The centre-left Dominica Labour Party (DLP), which had formed the government since 1961, was comprehensively defeated by the conservative Dominica Freedom

Party (DFP) at a general election in 1980. The DFP retained power in the 1985 elections.

The evolution of the far right. There are no native fascist groups in Dominica. A former DLP Prime Minister, Patrick John, was implicated with US fascist groups in a planned invasion and coup d'etat. He was alleged to have recruited mercenaries, including members of the Alabama-based Knights of the Ku Klux Klan (see United States) and of the Canadian Knights of the Ku Klux Klan, but the alleged plot was denounced in March 1981 and John, the Klan leader and others were imprisoned. An apparent coup attempt failed in December 1981. John was acquitted and freed in June 1982, and was elected to the House of Assembly in 1985, while a retrial was pending, as a candidate of the new Labour Party of Dominica (LPD), which included the old DLP.

Dominican Republic

capital: Santo Domingo   **population: 6,250,000**

Political system. The Dominican Republic has an executive President and a bicameral Congress, both elected for four-year terms by compulsory adult suffrage. The 120 members of the Chamber of Representatives are elected under a proportional representation system with multi-seat constituencies, while simple pluralities in single-seat districts elect the 27 senators.

Recent history. A pro-US dictator, Rafael Trujillo Molina, ruled directly or by proxy from 1931 to 1961. A year of centre-left government was terminated by a coup, followed in 1965 by riots and US military intervention. A right-wing government was then installed under Dr Joaquín Balaguer of the Reformist Party (PR), and it was returned to power in the elections of 1970 and 1974. In 1978 and 1982 the centre-left Dominican Revolutionary Party (PRD) was returned to power, but the PR, again under Balaguer, won the 1986 election.

The evolution of the far right. Trujillo's dictatorship, under which opposition was not tolerated, ended with his assassination in 1961. There was a right-wing coup in 1963. Balaguer, although an associate of Trujillo, was less autocratic, but there were some excesses during a counter-insurgency campaign in the mid-1970s. There was another attempted coup in 1978. Fascist and ultra-right groups have little popular support; there are however right-wing conservative parties, including the National Action Party (PAN), the National Salvation Movement (MNS) and the Quisqueyan Democratic Party (PQD).

Active organizations

**Comité Pro Libertate
Freedom Committee**

Address. Apartado 1633, Santo Domingo

Orientation. Anti-semitic

72

History. This small group was in contact with foreign fascist groups in the mid-1980s.

Policies. The Committee is thought to propagate belief in a Jewish conspiracy and opposition to race-mixing.

Grupo Armado Nacionalista Revolucionario (GANR)
Armed Nationalist Revolutionary Group

Orientation. Ultra-right

History. This previously unheard of group bombed the electoral tribunal offices in June 1982, killing five people and injuring 20. Three retired colonels and several civilians were later arrested for questioning.

Ecuador

capital: Quito   **population: 9,500,000**

Political system. The Republic of Ecuador has an executive President, a Vice-President and a unicameral 57-seat Congress, all elected for four-year terms.

Recent history. The coastal region's Liberal Party (PL) was in power for several decades until a minority Conservative Party (PC) government, which gained most of its support in the highlands, was formed in 1956. A new PL regime was overthrown in 1961, but the President, Dr José María Velasco Ibarra, returned to office in 1968 after a period of unstable government. In 1970 Velasco assumed dictatorial powers to deal with an economic crisis, but he was overthrown again in 1972; democracy returned in 1979. The centre-left government then installed gave way to a centre-right one and, after 1984, to a new conservative regime under the Social Christian Party (PSC). That government has had stormy relations with the congressional left and has also faced military unrest.

The evolution of the far right. The electoral participation of the far right is hindered by registration requirements including the need to show a minimum membership of 1.5 per cent of the electorate across 10 of the 20 provinces. Established right-wing conservative parties include the Democratic Institutionalist Coalition (CID), the PC, the National Republican Party (PNR), the National Velasquista Party (PNV—founded by the late ex-President), the Nationalist Revolutionary Party (PNR—founded by the Vice-President who staged a coup against Velasco in 1961) and the governing PSC. There is a tradition of right-wing attitudes among the military, expressed in coups in 1963 and 1972 and in occasional attempts and plots since then, but ultra-right political organizations have not gained a significant popular following.

Active organizations

Círculo Ecuatoriano de Amigos de Europa (CEDADE)
Ecuadorian Circle of Friends of Europe

Leadership. Carlos Cornejo

Orientation. Nazi

History. This branch of the Spanish-based CEDADE was organized in Quito in the mid-1970s. Several of its members were arrested in a murder investigation in January 1978.

Policies. Like the parent group, this organization has classic national socialist policies on economic and political matters, is anti-semitic and preaches a non-nordicist white supremacism.

International affiliations. See CEDADE (Spain, Argentina, France and elsewhere).

Defunct organizations

Partido Acción Revolucionaria Nacionalista Ecuatoriana: the Ecuadorian Nationalist Revolutionary Action Party was active in the 1970s, espousing a nationalist and anti-communist philosophy, but it failed to secure popular support.

Other organizations

Other organizations active in Ecuador in recent years have included an affiliate of the British-based Christian Mission to the Communist World.

El Salvador

capital: San Salvador   **population: 5,000,000**

Political system. The Republic of El Salvador has an executive President and a Legislative Assembly, both elected by universal adult suffrage. The President is assisted by a Vice-President and a Cabinet.

Recent history. El Salvador has had an extremely unstable political history with frequent military intervention. In 1932 a peasant uprising was suppressed by a military government headed by Gen. Maximiliano Hernández Martínez, with up to 30,000 civilian deaths. There followed a succession of right-wing military regimes, some installed after fraudulent elections and all allied with the landed oligarchy. In the 1960s and '70s their instrument of government was the pro-military National Conciliation Party (PCN).

In 1980 a civilian-military coalition including the centrist Christian Democratic Party (PDC) came to power as left-wing guerrilla activity and official and unofficial counter-measures increased in intensity. A right-wing coalition won elections boycotted by the left in 1982, by which time over 30,000 had died in three years of war. The fighting went on and there were widespread abuses of human rights.

The PDC's José Napoleón Duarte, who supported a negotiated peace, won a clear victory over Maj. Roberto D'Aubuisson, leader of the ultra-right ARENA, in a presidential election in 1984. Duarte remained in power, with substantial US support, in 1987. The guerrilla war was continuing, with over 50,000 deaths recorded by end-1986.

The evolution of the far right. The 14 families controlling most of El Salvador's agricultural base have traditionally relied on the armed forces and on private paramilitary groups to defend their position. The 1932 uprising and massacre made a deep impression on the national consciousness; the main guerrilla coalition now active takes its name from the leader of the peasants at that time, Farabundo Martí, who was himself killed by Hernández' forces. In the current war there have been countless reports of arbitrary killings, torture and other abuses of civilians by the regular military and by militias in zones affected by guerrilla activity (as well as counter-claims of atrocities by guerrilla forces).

After 1961 the main right-wing political party was the PCN, which remains in existence but was overtaken in terms of votes in the early 1980s by D'Aubuisson's ARENA. There have been, and are, a number of smaller and more radical right-wing parties, including the PAISA, which broke away from the PCN. Right-wing conservative parties not dealt with here include the Democratic Action Party (PAD), an anti-communist grouping formed in 1981 by René Fortín Magaña, and the Salvadorean People's Party (PPS), formed in 1966 by business interests.

Ultra-right death squads, which many believe to be merely fronts for military or police operations, have been active since the 1970s. Their best-known action was the assassination in 1980 of Mgr Oscar Arnulfo Romero y Galdames, the Archbishop of San Salvador, an originally conservative churchman who had become increasingly outspoken on the questions of poverty, oppression and injustice. The death squads' activities reached a peak in 1983, with a concerted campaign of executions of agrarian and trade union leaders in an attempt to prevent a land reform opposed by the ARENA. Academics, lawyers, students and clerics have also been threatened, kidnapped, tortured and killed in large numbers by the squads, as have workers and peasants with no known political affiliation. Deaths attributed to the squads declined to 39 in the second half of 1984, but rose to 81 in the first half of 1985. Government and judicial investigations of the squads and their activities have generally failed to produce convictions except in a few cases where the victims were United States citizens.

Active organizations

Alianza Anticomunista Maximiliano Hernández Martínez
Maximiliano Hernández Martínez Anti-Communist Alliance

Orientation. Ultra-right death squad

History. This group (also known as the *Brigada Anticomunista Maximiliano Hernández Martínez*), named after the the President (1931-44) who suppressed the 1932 rebellion, began its activities in 1979. In November 1980 it killed six leaders of a left-wing coalition, the FDR. In 1982 it published a death list naming 34 local and foreign journalists.

After a period of silence, the Alliance reappeared in November 1984 to announce that it had allied with the CDM death squad.

Policies. The group seeks to eliminate or intimidate left-wing leaders.

Associated organizations. See *Comando Domingo Monterrosa.*

Alianza Republicana Nacional (ARENA)
National Republican Alliance

Base. San Salvador

Leadership. Maj. Roberto D'Aubuisson Arrieta (honorary president); Alfredo Cristiani (leader); Mario Repdaelli (general secretary)

Orientation. Ultra-right

History. This party was formed in 1981 by Salvadorean right-wingers, several of whom, including the then leader, D'Aubuisson, were alleged to be closely connected with military-controlled death squads including that responsible for the murder of Archbishop Romero. D'Aubuisson had been arrested in May 1980 on suspicion of planning a right-wing coup on behalf of his *Frente Amplio Nacional* (FAN—National Broad Front); in March 1981, after explicitly calling for such a coup, he went into temporary exile. The FAN received 430,205 votes (29.1 per cent, the second-highest share) and 19 of the 60 seats in the 1982 election to the Constituent Assembly, of which D'Aubuisson became President. Although the ARENA sought a military solution to the guerrilla war, it entered into a pact in August 1982 with right-wing and centrist parties, including the Christian Democrats, in order to end a legislative stalemate. At least two ARENA deputies have been killed by left-wing guerrillas since 1983.

D'Aubuisson came second in the two-stage presidential election of March and May 1984, with 46.4 per cent of the final vote, having moderated his stance during the campaign in an effort to distance himself from the paramilitary right. Later in 1984 the party formed an alliance with the National Conciliation Party (PCN), jointly winning 25 of the 60 seats in the 1985 Legislative Assembly election. In late 1984 the party split, with one faction forming the *Patria Libre* grouping. In September 1985 D'Aubuisson stood down as leader but was elected to his present position; it was reported in 1987 that he had decided to resign that post and retire from party politics.

Policies. The ARENA has opposed large-scale land reform and has condemned labour and agrarian activists, and their clerical and lay sympathizers, as communists. It is strongly pro-military and anti-communist, extending its definition of communism to take in anything to the left of the Christian Democratic government. It is also ultra-nationalist and is opposed to any compromise or negotiation with the guerrilla opposition.

Associated organizations. The ARENA is very close to the PAISA, a right-wing splinter group of the PCN; however, D'Aubuisson formed an alliance with the more moderate bloc of the PCN for the March 1985 elections.

International affiliations. It was reported in 1985 that D'Aubuisson was to head a political institute being established by the World Anti-Communist League (see South Korea).

Bloque Antiguerrillero del Oriente (BAGO)
Eastern Anti-Guerrilla Bloc

Orientation. Ultra-right death squad

History. The BAGO was formed in 1980, its first major action being the killing of 14 alleged guerrillas on September 24 of that year. It carried out several other killings and bombings but has been largely inactive in recent years.

Policies. The BAGO, like other death squads, seeks to terrorize left-wing activists and their sympathizers.

Comando Anticomunista Salvadoreño
Salvadorean Anti-Communist Commando

Orientation. Ultra-right death squad

History. This group emerged in February 1984 when it threatened to "execute journalists... who collaborate with the enemies of the republic". It also threatened churchmen who had denounced abuses of human rights.

Comando Domingo Monterrosa
Domingo Monterrosa Commando

Orientation. Ultra-right death squad

History. The Comando was named after a counter-insurgency officer killed in action in Morazán in October 1984. Two months after his death, the group issued a statement threatening to "demolish all communist elements" in the government.

Associated organizations. The group appears to be identical with the *Frente Patriótico Domingo Monterrosa* (Domingo Monterrosa Patriotic Front), which issued a statement in November 1984 condemning peace talks with the guerrillas. See also the *Alianza Anticomunista Maximiliano Hernández Martínez*.

Ejército Secreto Anticomunista (ESA)—see *Partido de Liberación Nacional.*

Escuadrón de la Muerte Nuevo (EMN)
New Death Squad

Orientation. Ultra-right death squad

History. The EMN, founded in 1980, began operations in September of that month. It has carried out numerous shootings, bombings and kidnappings.

Membership. Statements attributed to the group have claimed that it has 3,000 members; this is certainly an exaggeration.

Frente Patriótico Domingo Monterrosa—see *Comando Domingo Monterrosa.*

Movimiento Estable Republicano Centrista (Merecen)
Stable Republican Centrist Movement

Leadership. Juan Ramón Rosales y Rosales (general secretary)

Orientation. Right-wing

History. In 1984 Rosales gained 0.5 per cent of the vote in the first round of the presidential election. The Movement allied with the POP in the following year's Assembly election, but failed to win representation.

Policies. The Merecen presents right-wing nationalist policies sympathetic to the business sector.

Partido Auténtico Institucional Salvadoreño (PAISA)
Salvadorean Authentic Institutionalist Party

Base. San Salvador

Leadership. Dr Roberto Escobar García (general secretary)

Orientation. Ultra-right

History. This party was formed by the right-wing majority of the parliamentary representation of the PCN following the 1982 Constituent Assembly election. It then had nine seats in the Assembly, representing over 160,000 votes. Two of its deputies were, however, assassinated in February and March 1984. Escobar, a retired army colonel, won 1.2 per cent of the vote in the first-round presidential election of 1984. The March 1985 Assembly election reduced the PAISA's representation to one member, who voted with the ARENA.

Policies. The PAISA is a pro-military, anti-communist party, opposed to a negotiated settlement to the guerrilla war.

Associated organizations. It has been allied since its foundation with the ARENA.

Partido de Liberación Nacional (PLN)
National Liberation Party

Leadership. Aquiles Baires (general secretary)

Orientation. Ultra-right

History. The PLN was founded in 1983 to oppose any form of compromise with the left-wing rebel forces.

Policies. The Party believes in a purely military approach to the rebellion and in the complete destruction of left-wing forces.

Associated organizations. The PLN leader has been identified as the commander of the *Ejército Secreto Anticomunista* (ESA—the Secret Anti-Communist Army), a clandestine terrorist organization also known as the *Ejército Salvadoreño Anticomunista*. The ESA, which was formed in 1979, has carried out many attacks on academic, clerical and other activists sympathetic to the left. It has also issued death threats against union leaders, President Duarte and many others.

Partido de Orientación Popular (POP)
Popular Orientation Party

Leadership. Guillermo Trujillo (last presidential candidate)

Orientation. Ultra-right

History. The POP was founded in 1981 by Gen. Medrano, the former commander of the paramilitary *Orden*. It was based mainly on his *Frente Unido Democrático Independiente* (FUDI), the party for which he had gained 10 per cent of the vote in the 1972 presidential election. In the Constituent Assembly election of 1982 and the presidential elections of 1984 the new party's vote was less than 1 per cent. In March 1985 Medrano was assassinated by persons unknown.

Policies. The POP calls for a non-party democracy, property rights, the reversal of land reform and the privatization of the financial sector.

Patria Libre
Free Fatherland

Leadership. Hugo Barrera (leader)

Orientation. Anti-communist

History. Until 1984 Barrera was deputy leader of the ARENA, but he left that party after the failure of its 1984 election campaign in which he had been D'Aubuisson's vice-presidential running mate.

Policies. The party's policies are in most respects the same as those of ARENA, the principal differences apparently arising from personality issues.

Vanguardia
Vanguard

Address. Calle Arce 1286, 3er piso no. 12, San Salvador

Orientation. Ultra-right

History. This magazine was circulating among foreign fascist groups, including members of the World Union of National Socialists, in the mid-1980s. It did not respond to a request for information and may be defunct.

Defunct organizations

Frente Político Anticomunista (FPA): despite its name (Anti-Communist Political Front), the FPA was a purely military grouping, one of the many death squads which have been active since the mid-1970s. Little has been heard of this particular group since its formation in May 1979. Other anti-communist groups active in recent years have included *Acción Democrática* and the *Movimiento Anticomunista Nacional* (MAN).

Orden: this grouping, the full name of which was *Organización Democrática Nacional* (the acronym means "order" in all its senses), was formed in 1968 by Gen. José Alberto Medrano, founder of the National Intelligence Agency, as a landowner militia to assist the regular security forces in containing the guerrilla threat. It was officially encouraged until its dissolution in the aftermath of the 1979 coup against President Carlos Humberto Romero. Medrano, whose Independent United Democratic Front (FUDI) held seats in the Assembly from 1974 to 1976, went on to form the POP (see above). The name *Orden* has been used since 1979 by death squads which may or may not be composed of former militiamen.

Organización para la Liberación del Comunismo (OLC): the Organization for Liberation from Communism killed four left-wing leaders and bombed Catholic institutions in 1980.

Unión Guerrera Blanca (UGB): the White Warrior Union (the name of which has also been reported as *Unión de Guerreros Blancos*) killed several allegedly left-wing Catholic priests, mainly of the Jesuit order, in 1977 and 1979, and on August 16, 1979, it massacred 16 garage mechanics in San Salvador.

Fiji

capital: Suva   **population: 680,000**

Political system. Fiji is a Commonwealth member with the UK sovereign, represented by a Governor-General, as head of state. The bicameral Parliament has 52 elected Representatives and a 22-seat appointive Senate. The House of Representatives appoints the Prime Minister, who chooses a Cabinet.

Recent history. After a century as a British possession, Fiji became independent in 1970 under an Alliance Party government. That party, based in the indigenous Fijian population, remained in power until it lost the 1987 elections to the National Federation Party, representing the substantial minority of Indian descent (giving rise to a military coup by Fijians).

The evolution of the far right. The ethnic basis of the two largest parties has prevented the emergence of a right-left dichotomy, although the strongly pro-Fijian policies of the small Fijian Nationalist Party (formed in 1974 by Sakeasi Butadroka) have tended to foster anti-Indian sentiment, and the party has accordingly been accused of racism. The only ultra-right group to have emerged is the Fiji Youth Anti-Communist League, formed in the early 1980s as a very small affiliate of the Asian People's Anti-Communist League (see Taiwan) and thus of the World Anti-Communist League (see South Korea). Another small anti-communist grouping is affiliated to the Christian Mission to the Communist World, which is based in the United Kingdom.

Finland

capital: Helsinki **population: 4,900,000**

Political system. The Republic of Finland has a 200-seat unicameral four-year parliament, the *Eduskunta*, elected by universal adult suffrage using a system of proportional representation. An indirectly elected President has executive powers, which are exercised through a Prime Minister and Council of State.

Recent history. Since gaining independence from Russia in 1917-20, Finland's external policy has been dominated by the question of relations with the Soviet Union, with which it was at war in 1939-40 and 1941-44. Although it has remained a neutral member of the Western system since a punitive peace treaty in 1947, Finland has been careful to maintain good relations with the Soviet Union which accounts for more than a quarter of its trade and adjoins its long eastern border. Internally there has been a succession of short-lived coalition governments, mainly of the centre-right and the centre-left.

The evolution of the far right. The small pre-war fascist movement planned a coup in December 1931, but the plot was discovered. The Lapuan movement, led by Gen. Wallenius, staged an unsuccessful revolt and was banned in 1932. After losing a short war with the Soviet Union in 1939-40, the Finnish government, under President Ryiti, joined the Axis in 1941 and participated in an invasion of the Soviet Union. Some 30,000 Finns—mainly supporters of the quasi-fascist People's Patriotic Movement (formed in 1932)—joined the Wiking and Nordland divisions of the German SS. A separate peace was made in 1944 and territorial and financial penalties were exacted by the Soviets in a treaty three years later. There has been little ultra-right activity since the war, partly because of a term of the peace treaty with the Soviet Union which obliges the Finnish authorities to suppress fascist and anti-communist formations. Four such groups were banned in 1977.

Active organizations

Kansallinen Demokraattinen Puolue (KDP)
National Democratic Party

Address. Postboks 41, 00510 Helsinki

Leadership. Pekka Sili Siitoin (leader)

Orientation. Nazi

History. The KDP was formed around 1982 by Siitoin, following his release from prison after serving a sentence in connection with the activities of the defunct Patriotic People's Front. He was in contact with World Union of National Socialists parties in the early 1980s.

Policies. The party has mainstream nazi policies.

Publications. Steelkryss.

Defunct organizations

Isanmaallinen Kansanrintama: the Patriotic People's Front, a small ultra-right grouping, was banned along with three similar groups in November 1977. In 1977-78 its leader, Pekka Siitoin, was involved in arson attempts against two left-wing publications; in the following year he was sentenced to five years' imprisonment, but he was released early and founded a new nazi grouping, the KDP. Five of his associates were imprisoned for shorter terms. The movement's symbol was a reversed swastika. Its international contacts included the Spanish CEDADE group and various West European nazi movements with which it attended the Dixmuide rallies in Belgium.

Lapuan National Patriots movement: this pre-war grouping, founded in 1930 as an anti-communist, Christian and nationalist farmers' association, was led by Gen. Wallenius, former Chief of the General Staff, and by Koivosto, Kosala, Somersalo, Susitaival and Sario; it had some support from mainstream conservatives. It sought the prohibition of communist movements and communist propaganda, and secured legislation to that effect after elections in 1930. It engaged in violent tactics including the kidnapping and beating of opponents; in 1930 it abducted the President, Stahlberg. By late 1931 the movement was generally regarded as anti-democratic and fascist in character.

The movement initially supported the conservative Sunila government formed in 1931, but staged an unsuccessful uprising in late February 1932, involving a mass march on Helsinki. Meetings of the movement (and of two smaller ultra-right groups) were prohibited from March 14, and the paramilitary wing of the movement was outlawed on March 24. Further legislation in May 1933 prevented the formation of other fascist paramilitary groups. The political party of the Lapuan National Patriots remained in coalition with the conservatives until the general election of 1933.

In the post-war era, the nearest equivalent to the movement has been the *Suomen Maaseudun Puoloe* (SMP—Finnish Rural Party), a strongly anti-communist but non-fascist party founded in 1959. The SMP, then led by Veikko Vennamo—a refugee from Karelia—won 18 seats in the 1972 parliamentary elections, but suffered splits and electoral setbacks thereafter. It almost recovered its original strength, winning 17 seats in 1983 (under the leadership of Pekka Vennamo), by which time it had moderated its stance to the extent that it was able to join the Social Democrats and other parties in a coalition government.

France

capital: Paris   **population: 54,400,000**

Political system. France is a parliamentary democracy with universal adult suffrage. The executive President is directly elected for a seven-year term, while the Prime Minister is appointed from the majority grouping in the parliament. There is a 491-member National Assembly, whose members are elected on a proportional representation system for a five-year term, and a 317-member indirectly elected Senate, with a nine-year term. The main administrative division is the department, of which there are 96 in mainland France; there are several overseas departments (mainly in the Caribbean) and overseas territories (mainly in the Pacific).

Recent history. Since 1945 France has had two constitutions; the period of the Fourth Republic (1945-60) was characterized by frequent changes of government among conservative and socialist coalitions, while in the Fifth Republic (created under de Gaulle in 1960) the President has greater executive powers, and successive governments of a right-of-centre nature held power until the 1981 elections. There has been little organized political violence apart from the student and worker uprising of 1968 and the efforts of returned settlers to resist or avenge the granting in 1962 of Algerian independence. The current (1987) government is headed by a Socialist Party president whose term has overlapped with the election of a right-wing majority in the National Assembly.

The evolution of the far right. Before the Second World War there was a lengthy tradition of nationalism, ultra-conservatism and racism, notably anti-semitism, in France. The most organized of the far-right groupings in the 1930s were the paramilitary *ligues*, the best-known of which were the *Jeunesses patriotes*, the *Croix de feu* and the *Action française*, elements of which were involved in serious rioting in 1934 and later supported the collaborationist Vichy government established by Marshal Pétain after the defeat by Germany in 1940. (The Vichy territory was occupied by Germany in 1942.) Other right-wing groups, including nazi and fascist movements, emerged in the 1930s or during the occupation.

During and after liberation in 1944 a large number of French fascists and other suspected collaborators were executed, but right-wing elements survived and two distinct tendencies have existed down to the present day: a violent, clandestine neo-fascist element, and an ultra-conservative, nationalist element. The former tendency has been represented at various times by, for example, the settler movements opposing Algerian independence or the more recent FANE group, while the latter includes *Action française* and Catholic ultra-orthodox groupings.

In recent years the distinction has blurred, with the rise of an overtly racist political party, the *Front national* led by Le Pen. This has been the only far-right grouping, apart from the Poujadist movement of the 1950s and '60s, to gain significant electoral support, including 11 per cent of the total vote in the 1984 European Parliament elections and a slightly lower share in the March 1986 general election (with local support reaching as much as 22.5 per cent of the vote in Marseilles). In 1986 it won 35 seats in parliament. Most of the country's far right groups participate in the annual Joan of Arc Day parade in mid-May, with about 15,000 attending the 1985 event.

As in the UK, West Germany and elsewhere, there is a fascist element among the violent "skinhead" gangs of the larger cities, notably Paris and Nice, some of which are associated with particular football clubs. Right-wing terrorist activity in the 1970s and '80s has included a number of bombings, mainly of Jewish and immigrant targets, and several killings. (For details of anti-Basque terrorism in France, see Spain.)

Active organizations

L'Action Française—see *Restauration nationale*.

Alliance générale contre le racisme et pour le respect de l'identité française et chrétienne—see *Chrétienité-solidarité*.

Association des amis du socialisme français et de la commune
Association of Friends of French Socialism and of the Commune

Address. 5 rue Las Cases, Boîte Postale 18, Paris 7

Orientation. Ultra-right

History. This group, active in the mid-1980s, appears to be a front for or a close associate of the nazi FNE.

Policies. The Association promotes "pre-Marxist" socialism and "pre-De Gaulle" nationalism.

Associated organizations. See *Faisceaux nationalistes européens*.

Association des combattants de la union française (ACUF)
French Union Combatants' Association

Base. Paris

Orientation. Right-wing ex-servicemen's group

History. This pressure group succeeds the earlier *Front national des combattants* (FNC), founded by Jean-Marie Le Pen in 1957 as part of the *Algérie française* movement. Several ACUF members were candidates for Le Pen's *Front national* in the 1978 Assembly elections. The Association represents ex-servicemen and is closely allied to the main ex-paratroop organization, the National Union of Paratroopers, with which it shares premises and some officers.

Policies. The Association is nationalist and strongly anti-communist.

International affiliations. The Association is the leading component of the French chapter of the World Anti-Communist League (South Korea).

Association entreprise moderne et libertés—see *Entreprise moderne et Libertés*.

Association des jeunes pieds-noirs
Young Settlers' Association

Orientation. Right-wing

History. This organization of French settlers returned from Algeria took part in the 1985 Joan of Arc Day parade, an annual ritual dating back to 1909 and involving virtually all national or Paris-based nationalist, Catholic fundamentalist, monarchist and ultra-rightist groups in France. The parade takes place in May in Paris, from the Place de la Concorde to the Place des Pyramides.

Policies. The Association regards the granting of Algerian independence as a betrayal of French nation interests and of the white settler population.

Association Liberté pour Rudolf Hess
Free Rudolf Hess Association

Address. Boîte Postale 140, 75226 Paris Cédex 05

Leadership. Pierre Morel

Orientation. Nazi

History. In 1984-85 this group, which was founded early in 1981, held numerous demonstrations calling for the release of Hitler's imprisoned deputy.

Associated organizations. Publicity material and advertising would suggest that the group is a front for the *Faisceaux nationalistes européens*, but it is supported by other nazi groups.

International affiliations. There are "Free Hess" movements or committees in most Western European countries, most being merely fronts for nazi parties.

Association Pétain-Verdun
Pétain Verdun Association

Orientation. Ultra-right

History. This group placed a full-page advertisement in *Le Monde* in July 1984. It took part in the 1985 Joan of Arc Day rally.

Policies. The group seeks the posthumous rehabilitation of Marshal Pétain, who led the collaborationist Vichy government during the war.

Associated organizations. The Association works in collaboration with an Association to Defend the Memory of Marshal Pétain.

Bakounine-Gdansk-Paris-Guatemala-Salvador

Orientation. Apparently anti-Soviet guerrilla group

History. This group carried out 16 bombings, mainly in Paris and mainly of targets connected with the Soviet Union, Poland or the arms industry, between December 1981 and February 1983. No-one was injured. The group, which may have been inspired by anarchist rather than right-wing ideology, may now be defunct.

La Bretagne réelle—Celtia

Address. 44 rue Philippe Lemercier, 22230 Merdrignac, CCP 754-82 Rennes

Leadership. Jacques Quatreboeufs (editor)

Orientation. Right-wing regionalist

History. This group's magazines carried exchange advertising in 1980 for the neo-nazi *Devenir européen* group.

Policies. The group promotes Breton nationalism.

Publications. *La Bretagne réelle*, 10 per year, campaigning magazine; *Cahiers de la Bretagne réelle*, quarterly, special topics; *Celtia*, every two months, "Celtic philosophy".

CAUSA

Base. Paris

Leadership. Yves Cygnac (leader)

Orientation. Anti-communist

History. This Korean-based pressure group opened an office in Paris in 1986.

Policies. The group seeks to defend Western values, to oppose communist ideology and to publicize specific anti-communist causes.

Associated organizations. The ex-wife of *Front national* leader J.-M. Le Pen has claimed that CAUSA provides a significant share of FN funds; several FN officials attended the opening of the Paris office. See also CIRPO.

International affiliations. See CAUSA-International (South Korea), which is closely linked to Sun Myung Moon's Unification Church. There are CAUSA groups in several Western countries. Cygnac represented CAUSA at the 1986 World Anti-Communist League conference (see South Korea).

Centre national des indépendants et paysans (CNIP)
National Self-Employed and Small Farmers' Association

Address. 106 rue de l'Université, 75007 Paris

Telephone. (1) 4705 4964

Leadership. Philippe Malaud (president); François-Xavier Parent (general secretary); Michel Junot

Orientation. Right-wing

History. This group was founded in 1948 by pre-war *ligueur* René Coty (see *Solidarité française*) and Roger Duchet as the *Centre national des indépendants* (CNI), an umbrella group for right-wingers. It adopted its present name a few months later on absorbing the agrarian conservative *Parti républicaine de la liberté*. It took part in several conservative governments between 1951 and 1962.

In 1958 Jean-Marie Le Pen, later to become the most important post-war ultra-right leader, was elected to the National Assembly as one of 120 successful CNIP candidates, but the Association split soon afterwards over De Gaulle's Algerian policy and it was reduced to a very minor role from 1962.

Following its October 1984 conference the CNIP allied itself with the right-wing student group, GUD, in the MNR. The electoral influence of the CNIP in recent years is a matter of some debate; in the 1982 cantonal elections, for example, it claimed to have won more than 100 of the 2,000 seats, whereas the national press put the figure at fewer than 20. This may be due to CNIP members standing as the candidates of other right-wing groups.

Policies. The CNIP is not a fascist or extreme right-wing group but it has often had prominent right-wingers among its membership. It has pro-family, authoritarian, anti-immigration, nationalist and anti-communist policies. It supports co-operation between right-wing parties and condemned the refusal of the national leaderships of the mainstream conservative UDF and RPR parties to approve of local deals with the *Front national* in the 1985 and 1986 elections.

Membership. 25,000.

Publications. *Le Journal des Indépendants*, weekly, circulation 40,000.

International affiliations. Liberal and Democratic Group (European Parliament).

Cercle européen des amis de l'Europe (CEDADE)—see *Devenir européen*(below) and CEDADE (Spain).

Cercle national entreprises et libertés—see *Entreprise moderne et Libertés*.

Chrétienité-solidarité
Christianity Solidarity

Leadership. Romain Marie (real name Bernard Antony; president)

Orientation. Right-wing

History. This network of local committees, also referred to as the Catholic Solidarity Movement, was founded in the early 1980s by the editor of the right-wing journal *Le Présent*. It took part in the 1984 and 1985 Joan of Arc Day rallies. In 1986 Marie/Antony sued journalists of *Le Monde* for reporting grossly anti-semitic statements made by him at a meeting organized by *Fraternité française* in 1983. He lost the case and was himself convicted of inciting racial hatred.

Policies. The group espouses fundamentalist Catholic moral precepts and authoritarian political positions. It is part of the "integrist" movement which supports the rebel archbishop Marcel Lefebvre (see Switzerland).

Associated organizations. Several Solidarity activists are associated with the FN; Marie/Antony himself was a successful FN candidate in the 1984 European elections. The movement encourages its members to become militants in existing right-wing parties and does not participate as such in electoral politics. Similar ultra-right Catholic fundamentalist groups include the *Conseil de la maintenance catholique française*, led by Dr Doublier-Villette, and *Renouveau catholique*. Marie/Antony is also president of a smaller group, the *Alliance générale contre le racisme et pour le respect de l'identité française et chrétienne* (AGRIF—General Alliance against Racism and for Respect for France's Christian Identity).

Club des amis d'Alphonse de Chateaubriant
Club of Friends of Alphonse de Chateaubriant

Address. Boîte Postale 350-16, 75768 Paris Cédex 16; or 16 rue de Texonnieras, 87270 Couziex

Leadership. Franck Peyrot (director)

Orientation. Ultra-right

History. The Club (also known as the Club Alphonse de Chateaubriant) was founded around 1978 to perpetuate the memory and the ideas of Chateaubriant, a right-wing author.

Associated organizations. Peyrot is an editorial associate of *Devenir européen*; the activities of the group have also been reported approvingly in the journal of the nazi *Faisceaux nationalistes européens*.

Club Charles Martel
Charles Martel Club

Orientation. Anti-immigrant guerrilla group

History. This organization, also known as the *Groupe Charles Martel*, was named after the leader of the French army which defeated an Arab invasion at Poitiers in 732. It has bombed two Algerian consulates— that in Marseilles in December 1973, when four people were killed, and that in Paris in May 1980. It claimed responsibility for another bombing in Marseilles in 1983, and bombed the Paris offices of the left-of-centre *Jeune Afrique* magazine on 15 March 1986.

Policies. The Club exists to oppose what it terms "the frightening African invasion" of France.

Club de l'horloge
Clock Club

Leadership. Jean-Yves Le Gallou (general secretary)

Orientation. New right "think tank"

History. This organization was founded in order to provide a forum for discussions among the intellectuals of France's far right, particularly in the field of public administration. Its activities include the organization of conferences and debates on national identity and other topics of interest to the right.

Policies. The Club is ultra-nationalist, anti-immigrant and anti-socialist. It opposes the concept of a multi-cultural society and advocates a "French first" approach in all spheres.

Associated organizations. The Club is close to the leadership of the *Front national*, although it has members in the RPR and other conservative and ultra-right formations. It was initially sympathetic to GRECE but disapproved of that group's increasingly anti-American stance.

Columne 88 Heil Hitler
Column 88 Heil Hitler

Orientation. Neo-nazi guerrilla group

History. This group was one of three which claimed responsibility for the bombing of a Paris cinema in March 1985 during an annual Jewish film festival. Eighteen people were wounded.

Comité flamand de France
Flemish Committee of France

Address. 9 rue Jeanne d'Arc, 59370 Mons, Baroeul

Orientation. Flemish nationalist

History. This group, which is ostensibly concerned with the preservation of the Flemish language and culture in the Belgian border zone, was in contact in the early 1980s with at least one neo-nazi group (*Devenir européen*).

Policies. The Committee's main goal is to secure the teaching of Flemish in state schools in the border region.

Associated organizations. Other French Flemish groups which co-operated with the Committee in the early 1980s were *het Reuzekoor*, the *Menschen Lyk Wyder* and the *Cercle Michel de Swaen*, or *Michiel de Swaenkring* (villa Vlaanderen, rue de l'Eglise, Bierne, 59380 Bergues).

Comité national des Français juifs
National Committee of Jewish French People

Base. Paris

Leadership. Jean-Charles Bloch

Orientation. Anti-communist

History. The Committee was founded in October 1986 by Bloch, a retired scientist, and Robert Hemmerdinger, a *Front national* member of the Paris regional council.

Policies. The declared aim of the Committee is to fight communism and Islam.

Associated organizations. No evidence has come to light of any other pro-FN Jewish groups. There are, however, anti-communist groups, including one—*Judaïsme et liberté*—which is equally opposed to the Communist Party and the Front. Its founders in 1985 were Claude-Gérard Marcus and Lucien Finel, elected representatives of the RPR and the UDF respectively.

Comités d'action républicaine (CAR)
Republican Action Committees

Leadership. Bruno Mégret (president); Jean-Claude Bardet-Apremont

Orientation. Right-wing conservative

History. The CAR movement was established shortly after the socialist victory in the 1981 presidential election, and at first declared its intention not to participate directly in electoral politics. Mégret was an RPR candidate in Yvelines in that year's legislative elections. In December 1985, however, the group formed an electoral alliance with the *Front national*, under the slogan *Rassemblement national*, and Mégret led a departmental list of the FN in the March 1986 legislative elections; the imposition of his candidature by the central leadership on the local FN, making him in French political jargon a *parachutiste*, caused a split in the local party.

Policies. The CAR seeks to foster co-operation among mainstream and extreme right-wingers.

Associated organizations. Mégret also heads the *Confédération des associations républicaines*.

Commandos de France contre l'invasion maghrébine
French Commandos against the North African Invasion

Orientation. Anti-Arab guerrilla group

History. This organization (often referred to as *Commandos de France*) claimed responsibility for three bombings of Arab businesses in Toulon and Marseilles on the night of 1-2 May, 1986. On 12 June it bombed two shops and a tourism office in Fréjus and Draguignan which were selling tickets for a concert in aid of *SOS-Racisme*. One person was injured. The death in Toulon on 18 August of four members of SOS-France, who were transporting a bomb (similar to those used by the Commandos) when their car exploded, was followed by a halting of the Commandos' activities, suggesting an overlap of personnel. Among the dead was Claude Noblia, the SOS-France leader and thus possibly the leader of the Commandos. Documents found at Noblia's home detailed plans for the launch of a political-military movement to be called *Renouveau national* (National Renewal), while explosives were found at premises connected with another of the dead.

Bernard Bagur, the president of the Toulon branch of the *Maison du para* and a member of SOS-France, called for the burial of the four with military honours, but he was arrested for illegal possession of arms a few days after the explosion.

Policies. The group seeks to deter immigration from Algeria, Morocco and Tunisia.

Associated organizations. The Commandos may be linked to SOS-France.

Confédération des associations républicaines (CODAR)
Confederation of Republican Associations

Leadership. Bruno Mégret (president)

Orientation. Right-wing conservative

History. The CODAR allied itself with the *Front national* in November 1985. The Confederation's leadership included several independent right-wing public representatives as well as an FN central committee member and two prominent right-wing journalists (Yann Clerc, editor of the weekly *Valeurs actuelles*, and Dominique Jamet, a leader-writer with the *Quotidien de Paris*).

Policies. The CODAR was founded as an alliance of right-wing opposition clubs, many of whose members supported the RPR rather than the FN.

Associated organizations. Mégret is also president of the *Comités d'action républicaine* (CAR).

Conférence internationale des résistants dans les pays occupés (CIRPO)
International Conference of Resistance Movements in Occupied Countries

Base. Paris

Leadership. Pierre de Villemarest

Orientation. Anti-communist

History. This organization, established by de Villemarest—a former intelligence officer and writer   was active in the mid-1980s.

Policies. The group seeks to raise support and funding for anti-communist guerrilla armies and nationalist political movements in communist-ruled and other countries, including the USSR, Cuba, India and South-East Asia.

Associated organizations. The committee of the CIRPO includes a *Front national* member of the National Assembly. The group has contacts with the French CAUSA.

International affiliations. The CIRPO attended the 1986 World Anti-Communist League conference (see South Korea). Among groups which it supports are various East European émigré movements and the Khalistan movement for a Sikh homeland in India.

Contre-réformation catholique
Catholic Counter-Reformation

Base. Paris

Orientation. Catholic fundamentalist

History. This organization was represented in the 1985 Joan of Arc Day rally of right-wing groups.

Policies. The group represents traditionalist or "integrist" tendencies among France's 45,000,000 Roman Catholics. It rejects what it regards as the heretical alterations to Church attitudes and rituals following the Second Vatican Council.

Devenir européen
Europe's Future

Address. 1 rue du Rhône, 44100 Nantes

Leadership. Yves Jeanne (director); Goulven Pennaod (editor of journal)

Orientation. Neo-nazi

History. This organization was formed in 1978 by Jeanne, a former OAS activist, leader in the 1960s of the *Parti national socialiste français* and political associate of Françoise Dior (see below), and Robert Yver, who left the group in 1981. A member of the group, Christian Le Bihan, blew himself up on the night of 3-4 June, 1985 , while attempting to bomb the courts at Guingamp (Côtes-du-Nord). He had until 1980 been active in *Strollard ar Vro*, the Country Party (also known as the Breton National European Federalist Party; now the *Parti pour l'organisation de la Bretagne libre*).

Policies. The group holds national socialist views, which, however, it terms *ethniste-socialiste*, based on a "scientific" racism; it maintains that it is not a right-wing organization. It opposes Judaism and freemasonry and actively promotes pagan beliefs based on Nordic mythology; it holds festivities to mark solstices, the feast of Beltane and so on.

Publications. Le Devenir européen, every two months (and occasional special issues).

Associated organizations. Among many French fascist, regionalist and racist groups with which this group is in contact are the FNE, *La Bretagne réelle—Celtia*, the *Club des amis d'Alphonse de Chateaubriant*, the *Comité flamand de France*, the *Front de libération des Gaules* and *Facettes*.

International affiliations. The group has particularly close relations with the youth-oriented Spanish nazi group, *Círculo Español de Amigos de Europa* (CEDADE), and with its French offshoot, the *Cercle européen des amis de l'Europe* (also known as CEDADE). The main French branches of CEDADE in the early 1980s were one in Provence which produced the publication *Projèts et références* (Boîte Postale 361, 13609 Aix en Provence) and another (Boîte Postale 69, 84100 Orange) which ran a mail-order book service. *Devenir européen* is also in correspondence with other pan-Europeanist fascist groups such as the *Nouvel Ordre Européen*(Switzerland), and attends the fascist rallies at Dixmuide (Belgium).

Diffusion de la pensée française (DPF)
Centre for French Thought

Address. Chiré en Montreuil, 86190 Vouillé, or Boîte Postale 92-18, Paris 18

Leadership. Jean Auguy (director); Henry Coston (founding editor)

Orientation. Conspiracy theorist

History. This right-wing publishing organization was founded in the 1950s and remained active in the early 1980s.

Policies. A particular concern of the DPF is the identification and denunciation of freemasons throughout French society. It is also anti-semitic and anti-communist.

Publications. Lectures françaises, monthly, and occasional special issues.

Associated organizations. There is exchange advertising with other right-wing groups, notably the neo-nazi *Devenir européen*. Auguy also directs the ultra-right publishing house *Éditions de Chiré*.

Entreprise moderne et libertés
Modern Enterprise and Liberties

Address. 78 avenue Raymond-Poincaré, 75116 Paris

Leadership. André Dufraisse (founder)

Orientation. Ultra-right

History. In September 1984 Dufraisse, the Paris secretary of the *Front national*, created this (formally independent) group to organize right-wing businessmen and professionals in support of the FN. (The name of the association is often incorrectly reported as *Cercle national entreprises et libertés* or as *Association entreprise moderne et libertés*.)

Policies. The policies of the group are those of the *Front national*, although it is particularly interested in those aspects of policy which have a direct bearing on industrial, commercial and professional matters. It seeks to provide the party with professional expertise in the areas of organization, administration and policy formation.

Membership. 800 (mid-1985).

Publications. Esprit d'entreprise, monthly newsletter.

Associated organizations. The association works partly through a network of *cercles professionels* covering particular professions and *cercles interprofessionels* covering geographic areas, with various *cercles sectoriels* at national level. Not all members belong to the FN.

Europe jeunesse
Young Europe

Address. 91 bis rue de la Div. Leclerc, Linas, 91310 Montlhery

Leadership. Raymond Ferrand (director)

Orientation. Neo-fascist

History. This group was active in 1986, organizing summer camps and other youth-oriented activities.

Policies. The group seems to advocate a pan-European imperialism based on white supremacist ideas.

International affiliations. Advertising for the group has appeared in European ultra-right magazines including *Scorpion* (Great Britain).

Europe, notre patrie
Europe, Our Homeland

Address. Boîte Postale 512-02, 75066 Paris Cédex 02

Orientation. Neo-fascist

History. This group was in correspondence with several other French neo-fascist groups in the early 1980s.

Facettes
Facets

Address. Boîte Postale 15, 95220 Herblay

Orientation. Right-wing

History. This magazine carried exchange advertising in the early 1980s for the neo-nazi *Devenir européen* group.

Faisceaux nationalistes européens (FNE)
European Nationalist Fasces

Address. 28 rue Jean Moinon, 3ème étage droite, 75010 Paris, or c/o Notre Europe, Boîte Postale 76, 75462 Paris Cédex 10

Leadership. Marc Fredriksen (founder); Michel Faci; Claude Domino (editor of journal); Louis Jeancharles, A. Pirucchi

Orientation. Neo-nazi

History. The FNE was created as the direct successor to the nazi FANE (*Fédération d'action nationale européenne*) when the latter group was banned. The FANE was formed by Fredriksen in 1966 from the *Cercles Charlemagne* and *Action occidentale*, both splinter groups of *Occident*. It attracted a significant and violent following among neo-fascists.

Because of its increasing association with political violence, the FANE was banned by the French government in September 1980, but was reorganized immediately as the FNE. Both Fredriksen, who served a prison sentence in 1980-81 for incitement to racial hatred, and Faci are former members of the *Front national*; another FNE associate, Charles Pettit, was a minister in the Vichy government.

Several members of the FANE/FNE have been convicted of offences including the illegal possession of arms, but not of major crimes attributed to the group, such as the murder of four people in the bombing of a synagogue in the rue Copernic in October 1980 (an attack also attributed to Palestinian groups).

Policies. The FANE and the FNE have adopted white supremacist, authoritarian, anti-semitic policies based on national socialism. Although it does not use the swastika as its main symbol the group openly proclaims its nazi orientation and organizes Hitler birthday parties.

Membership. The FANE claimed to have fewer than 300 members in 1980.

Publications. *Notre Europe*, monthly bulletin, address as above; previously published from Boîte Postale 45, 75961 Paris Cédex 20.

Associated organizations. The FNE maintains good relations with a variety of French fascist and racist groups, and its journal reports the activities of the entire ultra-right including the *Front national*.

International affiliations. Both the FANE and its successor have cultivated links with a wide range of neo-nazi and ultra-right groups around Western Europe, including the EPE and *Euro-forum* (Belgium). One of Fredriksen's principal supporters has been Alex Oumow, who has contacts with British fascists. In 1981 a British nazi leader, Tony Malski, was reported to have acquired detonators from a Paris FANE member, Vietnamese-born Yan Tran Long (in whose apartment a Spanish fascist terrorist, Juan Martínez, was arrested in 1983). FANE and FNE delegations have attended the annual Belgian *Ijzerbedevaart* fascist rallies, and from the early 1980s the FNE has attended the biennial meetings of the Swiss-based *Nouvel ordre européen*.

Fédération professionelle indépendante de la police (FPIP)
Independent Professional Police Federation

Base. Paris

Leadership. Serge Lecanu (general secretary)

Orientation. Ultra-right

History. This right-wing trade union was formed in the late 1970s, and by 1983 represented some 3 per cent of police officers in France.

Policies. Lecanu has called for "a strong regime, based on the concepts of order and nationhood, and spurning all decadent humanitarian theories".

Associated organizations. The FPIP is very close to the *Front national*; Le Pen has appeared at many FPIP rallies, while many FPIP men belong to the FN's *service d'ordre* (paramilitary guards).

Fraternité française
French Brotherhood

Base. Paris

Orientation. Ultra-nationalist

History. A member of this group, who was also a prospective parliamentary candidate for the FN and a member of *Chrétienté-solidarité*, was convicted of inciting racial hatred after a Brotherhood rally in October 1983.

Policies. The Brotherhood opposes immigration and pursues nationalist and authoritarian policies.

Front des étudiants nationalistes—see *Renouveau nationaliste.*

Front de libération des Gaules
Gaulish Liberation Front

Address. 163 boulevard Edouard Vaillant, 93300 Aubervilliers

Leadership. Pierre de la Crau (leader)

Orientation. Celtic fascist

History. The Front was founded in the late 1970s.

Policies. It seeks to blend Celtic mysticism with contemporary ultra-right ideology to produce an elitist and racist philosophy.

Publications. Triscèle.

Associated organizations. In 1980 the Front announced plans for the creation of the *Ordre sol dur* (Order of the Hard Ground), a chivalrous band of pagan Knights Templar who would devote their lives to practical and theoretical work towards the construction of a Celtic nation. Membership was to be open to members of other far-right groups.

Front national (FN)
National Front

Address. 11 rue Bernouilli, 75008 Paris

Telephone. (1) 4602 1194

Leadership. Jean-Marie Le Pen (president); Jean-Pierre Stirbois (general secretary); Jean-Marie Le Chevallier (director); Bruno Gollnisch (policy co-ordinator)

Orientation. Extreme right-wing

History. Possibly the largest ultra-right political party in Western Europe, with the exception of the Italian MSI, the Front was founded by Le Pen on Oct. 5, 1972. Its name recalled that of a pre-war fascist alliance. Many of its founding members came from existing ultra-right groups, and they included former supporters of the Vichy regime and of the OAS. The FN was relatively unimportant during the 1970s, gaining only 2.5 per cent of the vote for its 100 candidates in the legislative elections of 1973 and 0.7 per cent in the 1974 presidential poll (with Le Pen as its candidate). The FN scored only 3 per cent in the 1978 legislative elections, in which it had 108 candidates, but it benefited more than its main rival, the PFN, from the phenomenal growth in the popularity of the extreme right in the early 1980s. The FN's strategy from around 1980 was to present itself more and more as a party of the conservative right, rather than of the militant quasi-fascist fringe. That approach brought the extreme right its first electoral success in 25 years when, in late 1983, Stirbois won a local council by-election in Dreux by allying the FN with the local section of the mainstream conservative RPR.

The FN won 10.9 per cent of the vote and 10 seats in the 1984 European Parliament elections. (One of its successful candidates, Gustave Pordea, was later alleged by the *Matin de Paris* and by the British *Sunday Times* to be a Romanian spy who had bribed his way onto the FN slate.) The FN won 8.7 per cent in the first round of the regional council elections in March 1985. (It withdrew most of its candidates in the second round to avoid splitting the right-wing vote in constituencies with a large left-wing vote.) At the end of 1985 it suffered a minor split, with some members forming a rival *Front d'opposition nationale.*

The FN went on to gain 35 of the 577 seats in the parliamentary elections of March 1986 (although one of its members subsequently decided to sit as an independent); in some *communes* in the south, its share of the vote touched 27 per cent, compared with a national average of 9.7 per cent. It received a total of 2,705,838 votes, many of which came from working-class areas hitherto loyal to the Communist Party, and opinion polls showed that it had managed to make its preoccupations with immigration, unemployment and law and order into important electoral assets. It also secured 130 seats on regional councils. In all its electoral outings it has performed best in the three south-eastern departments of Var, Bouches-du-Rhône and Alpes Maritimes.

Although the party originally intended to support the Prime Minister, Jacques Chirac, in the 1988 presidential election, it withdrew its support in May 1986 after a dispute about electoral reforms. Later in 1986 Le Pen was arrested briefly at a New York airport and had a handgun confiscated. In September 1986 he was reported to have decided to stand for the presidency himself in the 1988 election, and was collecting the necessary 500 signatures from public representatives.

Most of the FN's candidates in 1986 were solid middle-class individuals with no record of fascist activism, although some had interesting pasts—Roland Gaucher (also known as Joseph Goguillot), editor of the weekly *National Hebdo*, had been a leading member of a collaborationist youth group, the *Jeunesses nationales populaires*, during the war; Pierre Sergent had been sentenced to death in the early 1960s for his role in the OAS, and later went on to join the CNIP; Pierre Ceyrac was a "Moonie"; Bernard Antony (also known as Romain Marie) founded the ultra-right daily *Le Présent* and the *Chrétienté-solidarité* group.

The party leader, Le Pen, was active in the 1940s in the Union of Independent Intellectuals (UII), which sought an amnesty for collaborators, and in the royalist National Restoration movement; he also founded a right-wing magazine, *Étudiants*. He served in the Parachute Regiment in Indo-China (1954) and Algeria (1956-57), and has been involved in numerous libel cases against newspapers and broadcasting organizations which stated that he took part in the torture of Algerian prisoners. During the 1950s he was active in the Poujadist movement (being elected to the National Assembly in 1956 on the list of the Poujadist *Union de défense des commerçants et artisans*—UDCA), and later in the *Front national des combattants* (part of the French Algeria movement) and in the CNIP. In the following decade he remained active in the Algerian settler movement and supported the presidential ambitions of the right-wing leader Jean-Louis Tixier-Vignancourt, a candidate in 1965.

Having founded the FN in 1972, Le Pen befriended a millionaire alcoholic and drug addict who died suddenly in 1976, leaving him a château and a fortune. The circumstances of the death led to a public trading of insults in 1985 between Le Pen and a close colleague, Dr Jean-Maurice Demarquet, who was the millionaire's physician and was, like Le Pen, a former Poujadist deputy and Algeria veteran. Le Pen has criminal convictions, inter alia for selling nazi propaganda. In March 1986 he was found guilty of making anti-semitic remarks and was ordered to pay damages to France's leading anti-fascist group, the LICRA.

The Front's members have included the late Claude Noblia, who left it to found SOS-France; like several other FN members, he was involved in violent attacks on immigrant families and political opponents. These attacks increased in frequency during 1984-85, and in the March 1986 election campaign an FN activist serving in the French army murdered a Socialist Party member in a Paris suburb. Pierre Bousquet, a founder-member, had served in the Waffen SS and in 1978 stated that the Second World War had been started by the Jews. He left the party in 1982 on the grounds that it was too moderate. Jean Roussel, an FN regional councillor, was fined in March 1985 for inciting racial hatred. In July 1985 four FN members blew up a bar in Annecy; the leader of the group, Jean-Pierre Chatelain, had bombed a Communist Party office in Annemasse (Haute-Savoie) earlier in the month.

Policies. The Front espouses nationalist and populist policies, not dissimilar to those of the 1950s Poujadist movement (although Poujade himself has denounced Le Pen as "an adventurer"); it has been careful to distance itself from the paramilitary far right, and has condemned attacks on immigrants. Nevertheless it is widely accepted that the policies of the FN have encouraged, rather than merely reflected, the xenophobic attitudes behind such attacks.

The FN calls for strong support for the police, the introduction of the death penalty for terrorism and drug trafficking, the reduction of trade union rights, the halting of all immigration, the removal of work permits from immigrants, changes to the nationality laws and deportation of immigrant convicts. The party, and Le Pen in particular, dislikes being referred to as racist or fascist. It is not opposed in principle to collaborating in government with centre-right parties, although the mainstream conservatives have generally avoided dealings with the FN and have been criticized by Le Pen as "decadent".

The FN is opposed to the independence movement in the overseas territory of New Caledonia, where the party withdrew from local elections in favour of Gaullist candidates in 1985. It also opposes the Corsican autonomist movement and has voted with the Gaullists in the regional assembly (in elections to which it gained 9 per cent of the vote in 1984). It links its anti-immigrant policies to the unemployment issue.

It was reported in late 1986 that a split was developing within the party between a purist "old guard" which sought to promote the party as an independent force and a "modern" faction which sought to create a broad coalition of right-wing parties led by Le Pen, with the FN itself playing a smaller role.

Membership. About 65,000 (1986 claim, compared to 30,000 in 1984 and 50,000 in 1985).

Publications. The official party monthly is *Le National*, but the de facto party organ is the *National Hebdo*, a technically independent weekly newspaper, with whose unsophisticated approach Le Pen was reportedly in disagreement in late 1986. In January of that year the editor, known as Roland Gaucher, had been heavily fined and, most unusually, sentenced to ten days' imprisonment (suspended for five years) for a gross libel on a member of the *Conseil d'Etat*.

The party is also supported by the daily *Le Présent*; other right-wing publications sympathetic to the FN or to its policies include *Rivarol, Minute, Aspects de la France* and *le Crapouillot.* In 1985 the party started a daily telephone message service called "Radio Le Pen". A party member and deputy for Marseilles, Gabriel Domenech, edits the local daily *Le Méridional*, which has twice been successfully sued for large amounts (in 1953 and 1986) after alleging that a leftist "reign of terror" followed the liberation of Marseilles.

Associated organizations. FN congresses have been stewarded by members of the PFN (which broke away from the FN in 1974 and has subsequently maintained an intermittently friendly rivalry), and by members of the MNR, the FNE and *Oeuvre française*. In 1984 it set up its own stewarding organization, the *service d'ordre*, under Roger Holeindre, a former OAS activist (who had been Tixier-Vignancourt's bodyguard in 1965 and was a founding member of the FN).

Young supporters of the FN form the *Front national de la jeunesse*(FNJ), some of whose members have been involved with more radical neo-fascist groups. A minor organization founded by and containing numerous FN supporters is SOS-France. The party is close to right-wing pressure groups such as the *Club de l'horloge* and GRECE, and to right-wing policemen in the FPIP. It has many sympathizers in other right-wing business and professional associations such as the SNMPI (which is usually associated with the conservative RPR, although the SNMPI president, Gérard Deuil, was a supporter of Pétain) and the CID-UNATI, and in 1984 the FN created its own business support group, the *Entreprise moderne et libertés* association.

In November 1985 the FN received the support of the hitherto non-aligned *Confédération des associations républicaines* (CODAR), whose leader, Bruno Mégret, was also president of the *Comités d'action républicaine*(CAR); the CAR itself allied with the FN in December 1985 to form an electoral alliance called the *Rassemblement national.*

International affiliations. The FN members sit in the European Parliament as the largest component of the Group of the European Right, which also involves the Italian neo-fascist MSI (whose general secretary, Giorgio Almirante, has attended several FN meetings as a guest of honour), the Greek EPEN and, as an individual member, the right-wing Ulster Unionist, John Taylor. In November 1986 Le Pen toured Asia, being received by President Aquino of the Philippines but not by the Japanese premier, Nakasone. He also met anti-communist groups including the *Kokusai Kyosho Rengo* (Japan) and others in Hong Kong and South Korea.

Front national de la jeunesse—see *Front national* and also FNJ (below).

Front d'opposition nationale (FON)
National Opposition Front

Leadership. Roger Palmieri (honorary president); Hugues d'Alauzier (chairman); Jean-André Nourigeon (policy director); Jean-Michel Luciani

Orientation. Ultra-right

History. The FON was founded in Corsica in October 1985 and formally constituted at a meeting in Blois (Loir-et-Cher) on Nov. 11, by ex-members of the *Front national* whose principal grievance with the FN leadership was the manner in which the general secretary, Stirbois, had designated candidates for the 1986 legislative elections. Palmieri is a vice-president of the Corsican Assembly; he resigned from the FN after a fellow vice-president was chosen as an FN candidate for the National Assembly. D'Alauzier, a Vaucluse industrialist, is a veteran right-winger who joined the FN in early 1984 after a period as vice-president of the CNIP. Nourigeon is a former RPR activist who joined the FN in 1985. The FON announced its intention of presenting National Assembly candidates in about 40 departments in March 1986. In the event it fielded only six departmental lists, which scored from 0.6

per cent (Maine-et-Loire) to 2.4 per cent (Corse-du-Sud). The Gironde list included Pierrette Le Pen, the estranged wife of the FN leader.

The formation of the FON followed the creation in October of a "vigilance committee" of dissident FN members in Vaucluse, under the leadership of Dr Jean-Maurice Demarquet, who announced his intention of transforming it into a *Rassemblement national de salut public* open to non-FN members; his group was expected to join the FON in 1986.

In April 1986 the first FON congress was held in Paris, with only 45 delegates (supposedly representing "several thousand" followers).

Policies. The FON's policies are virtually identical with those of the FN, concentrating on immigration and security issues. It regards the FN as having abandoned the fight against "Marxism and freemasonry" by becoming just another parliamentary party.

Groupe parlementaire d'amitié France-Afrique du Sud
France-South Africa Parliamentary Friendship Group

Address. Assemblée Nationale, Paris

Leadership. Albert Brochard (president)

Orientation. Pro-South African

History. This parliamentary grouping had official status within the French National Assembly until 1981, when its recognition was withdrawn in favour of a study group on "the problems of apartheid". However, the right-wing victory in the general elections of 1986 was followed in June by the reformation of the group by Brochard, a deputy of the mainstream conservative UDF party, and the restoration of recognition. The UDF itself condemned apartheid but did not interfere with Brochard's activities.

Policies. In an interview Brochard maintained, among other things, that the Western media was involved in "disinformation" on South Africa; that Oliver Tambo, the leader of the African National Congress, was a colonel in the Soviet security agency, the KGB; that South Africa had made considerable progress in the fifteen years to mid-1986, in that, for example, blacks had the right to get on the same buses as whites; and that he was personally opposed to apartheid.

Groupe Union-Défense—see *Renouveau nationaliste*.

Groupement de recherche et d'étude pour la civilisation européenne (GRECE)
Group for Research and Studies on European Civilization

Address. 13 rue Charles Lecocq, 75737 Paris Cédex 15

Leadership. Alain de Benoist (editor, *Nouvelle École*); Pierre Vial (editor, *Eléments*); Mircea Eliade, Hans Eysenck, Konrad Lorenz, Roger Pearson (patrons)

Orientation. New right "think tank"

History. Like the *Club de l'horloge*, GRECE functions as a forum for the intellectual right. It was founded in 1968 by a group of French right-wing intellectuals, several of whom were in more activist right-wing groups such as Europe-Action and the *Fédération des étudiants nationalistes*(FEN) in the mid-1960s. These included de Benoist, Vial, the Nordicist Jean Mabire, Jean-Claude Rivière, Jean-Claude Valla (the first general secretary of GRECE) and Dominique Venner, an admirer of pre-war fascist leader Drieu La Rochelle. Its patrons have included Arthur Koestler and other well-known academics from Europe and North America, some of whom have no known racist connections, and racists such as Pearson (see Council for Social and Economic Studies, United States). De Benoist, then using the pseudonym Fabrice Laroche, was a contributing editor of Pearson's *Western Destiny* in the mid-1960s.

Policies. GRECE provides a platform for right-wing interpretations of social, economic, racial, cultural, genetic and historical topics. It rarely comes close to endorsing fascist or white supremacist ideas in an open manner, and specifically opposes fascist terrorism, but it provides an intellectual forum in which elitist, pan-Europeanist and quasi-fascist ideas are developed. GRECE is anti-egalitarian, anti-American, anti-Soviet and pro-authoritarian, and regards the Judaeo-Christian tradition as decadent and debilitating.

Publications. *Nouvelle École*, glossy quarterly owned by de Benoist but published in support of GRECE (from Boîte Postale 129, 75326 Paris Cédex 07); *Eléments*, in-depth single-topic per issue monthly; *Études et Recherches*, official journal, irregular.

Associated organizations. GRECE publishes books through a company called Copernic; *Panorama des idées actuelles* (Panorama of Contemporary Thought) is a quasi-academic conservative journal published from the same address and edited by Prof Jean Varenne.

International affiliations. GRECE has been represented at late 1970s gatherings of the World Anti-Communist League (see South Korea), but appears to have no current formal international affiliations except through its *comité de patronage*. It has several foreign imitators, including *Scorpion* (United Kingdom) and *Vouloir* (Belgium).

L'Immonde
The Unworldly

Address. Ce Cedias, Boîte Postale 4, rue Las Cases, 75007 Paris

Orientation. Ultra-right

History. This journal was circulating among foreign far-right groups, including at least one beloning to the World Union of National Socialists (see Denmark), in the mid-1980s.

Judaïsme et liberté—see *Comité national des Français juifs.*

Lectures françaises—see *Diffusion de la Pensée Française.*

Légitime Défense
Legitimate Defence

Leadership. François Romerio (president)

Orientation. Ultra-right

History. The president of this group was in 1984 appointed by Jacques Chirac, then Mayor of Paris and currently (1987) Prime Minister, to serve on a civic Committee for the Prevention of Delinquency.

Policies. Legitimate Defence advocates a vigilante approach to the problem of inner-city lawlessness, and demands the restoration of the death penalty.

Membership. 15,000 to 20,000 (1983 estimate).

Librairie française
French Bookshop

Base. Paris

Leadership. Jean-Gilles Malliarakis (director)

Orientation. New right

History. The *Librairie* is France's leading new right bookseller, promoting ideas akin to those of GRECE. In March 1985 Malliarakis, the leader of the MNR, organized a conference in Paris of prominent European new right figures.

International affiliations. Typical of the foreign groups with which this operation has contact is the British magazine *Scorpion*.

Ligue Mondiale Anti-Communiste—see *Association des combattants de l' Union Française*, CAUSA, and CIRPO (above); and World Anti-Communist League (South Korea).

Maison du para
Para House

Orientation. Right-wing ex-paratroopers' organization

History. This organization held a joint demonstration with SOS-France on July 14, 1986, to oppose a concert in Var in aid of the anti-fascist group *SOS-Racisme*. A representative of the *Maison* was reported to have said that no further concerts of that type would be tolerated in France. The president of its Toulon branch, Bernard Bagur, was arrested on arms charges shortly after four SOS-France members blew themselves up in August 1986.

Associated organizations. See SOS-France.

Militant

Leadership. Patrick Chabaille (general secretary); Pierre Pauty (editor in chief); Pierre Bousquet

Orientation. Neo-fascist

History. Militant developed in 1981 as a clandestine dissident group within the *Front national*, the members of its *comités de soutien*(support committees for its journal) seeking to preserve the ideological purity of the FN against the pressures expected to result from its increasing electoral success. Some Militant sympathisers left the FN to found the *Parti nationaliste français*, while the rest of the group continued to function secretly until breaking away from the FN to establish an independent organization in January 1986. Militant leaders accused Le Pen of courting notabilities and of associating with Jews and Arabs.

Policies. The movement presents "popular nationalist" policies varying little from those of the FN. Its main preoccupations are immigration control and racial purity, being rather more explicit on the latter point than the parent party; it regards the "white European race" as under threat. It seeks the repeal of the *loi Pleven* of 1972 which outlawed racial discrimination, and of other measures forbidding the defence of wartime collaboration and removing the statute of limitations in respect of crimes against humanity.

Publications. Militant.

Minute

Address. 49 avenue Marceau, 75016 Paris

Leadership. Jean-Claude Goudeau (managing editor)

Orientation. Right-wing

History. Minute, which was founded in 1962, has become the largest-selling right-wing weekly magazine in France. One of its leader-writers, the former OAS member François Brigneau, was one of the founding members of the *Front national* in 1972; he later left *Minute* to join a similar publication, *Le Présent.*
In April 1985 the offices of *Minute* were bombed by the left-wing *Action directe* group.

Circulation. 300,000.

Associated organizations. The journal is very close to the PFN, one of the main far-right parties.

Mouvement nationaliste révolutionnaire (MNR)
National Revolutionary Movement

Base. Paris

Leadership. Jean-Gilles Malliarakis (leader)

Orientation. Solidarist

History. This organization, which is often called the *Mouvement national révolutionnaire,* has drawn its membership from a number of older far-right groups, such as the CNIP, the PFN and the student group GUD. Members of the MNR have been associated with acts of political violence; in October 1980, the group was held responsible for a bombing which injured a tourist in Paris. The MNR has provided stewards for rallies of the FN and participated in the 1985 Joan of Arc Day parade, where it was reported to have had a following comprised mainly of skinheads and black-jacketed youths.

Policies. The Movement has adopted neo-fascist and anti-immigrant policies. It describes itself as "solidarist", i.e. opposed to the class struggle.

Associated organizations. Malliarakis also runs the *Librairie française.* Some members of the MNR were involved in the formation in 1981 of *Renouveau nationaliste.*

International affiliations. Members of the MNR have attended recent Dixmuide rallies (the annual Belgian and European fascist and nationalist gatherings).

Mouvement de restauration nationale—see *Restauration nationale.*

Notre Europe
Our Europe

Address. 13 rue de la Machine Outil, 59600 Maubeuge

Leadership. Jean Buzas (leader)

Orientation. Nationalist

History. This group (which is not to be confused with the FNE, whose journal is called *Notre Europe*) was active in 1986.

Policies. The group espouses extreme French nationalist policies.

Publications. Kultura.

Nouvelle Acropole
New Acropolis

Leadership. Fernand Schwartz (leader)

Orientation. Neo-fascist

History. This group was founded in the 1960s by an Argentinian ultra-rightist; Schwartz took over as leader in 1973. The group has a paramilitary command structure.

Policies. The group is active mainly in developing cultural activities with a neo-fascist bias and in fostering contacts between ultra-right groups around the world.

Nouvelle action royaliste
New Royalist Action

Address. 17 rue Croix des Petits-Champs, 75001 Paris

Leadership. Bernard Renouvin (leader)

Orientation. Monarchist

History. This group was formed in 1971(as *Nouvelle action française*) as a moderate splinter group of the *Restauration nationale*, the main post-war manifestation of the old *Action française*. Its leader contested the 1974 presidential election, securing 0.2 per cent of the vote, and the party's eight candidates in the 1978 National Assembly elections likewise secured insignificant support. Renouvin was unable to secure enough nominations for the 1981 presidential election.

Policies. The group seeks the restoration of the French monarchy and opposes both communism and unrestrained capitalism. Its other policies are approximately centre-right. It is a French nationalist group which, unlike other royalist groups, condemns the wartime collaborationism of the Vichy regime.

Publications. Royaliste, six per year, circulation 10,000.

Objectif: survie
Objective: Survival

Address. Boîte Postale 331, 37303 Joué les Tours

Leadership. Olivier Devalez (founder)

Orientation. Survivalist

History. The survivalist movement which developed in the United States in the aftermath of the Vietnam War is a right-wing paramilitary tendency which predicts and prepares for the collapse of civilization as we know it, whether by nuclear conflagration or by domestic subversion; its adherents wear combat gear and practise shooting and living rough. *Objectif: survie*, the first French manifestation of this tendency, is a magazine founded in 1983 on the model of the British *Survivalist*.

Policies. The magazine promotes survivalist concepts, strategies and techniques, and the sale of equipment and literature.

Publications. Objectif: survie, monthly; manuals and books.

Associated organizations. Devalez is associated with the nazi FNE, which has recommended his magazine to its members.

Oeuvre française
French Labour

Leadership. Pierre Sidos (leader)

Orientation. Ultra-right

History. This semi-clandestine grouping was formed by Sidos in 1968, and was based on his earlier *Jeune Europe* grouping. Some of its members have acted as security stewards at meetings of the *Front national*. It participated in the 1985 Joan of Arc Day parade, and has also (along with the FN and the PFN) attended the *amitié française* rallies organized by fundamentalist "national Catholic" groups.

Policies. The group is pan-Europeanist and admires the Pétain regime. However, it seeks to distance itself from overtly nazi groups such as the FNE.

Associated organizations. French Labour has co-operated with the MNR and *Militant*; in 1983 several of its members joined the *Parti nationaliste français*. It has also been close to the *Association des combattants de l'Union française*, and through it to the French affiliates of the World Anti-Communist League (see South Korea).

Pardes—see *Totalité.*

Parti démocrate française (PDF)
French Democratic Party

Base. Paris

Orientation. Right-wing opposition

History. This party was founded in 1982.

Parti des forces nouvelles (PFN)
New Forces Party

Address. 7 boulevard de Sebastopol, 75001 Paris

Leadership. Roger Giraud (general secretary, member of collective leadership); Jack Marchal, Roland Hélie (other members of collective leadership)

Orientation. Right-wing opposition

History. This party was formed on Nov. 11, 1974, by former leaders of the neo-fascist *Occident* movement, which was banned in 1969 and became the *Ordre nouveau* under the leadership of Alain Robert; after the latter group was also banned, in mid-1973, virtually all its supporters joined Le Pen's new *Front national*. Disappointed by the poor showing of the FN in the 1973 legislative elections, and seeking to present a forward-looking image in contrast to the perceived preoccupation of the FN with the past, the *Ordre nouveau* men, including Robert, left that party at the end of 1973, founding *Faire front* (Form a Front) which became the PFN a year later.

The PFN overtook the FN in terms of support and was probably the leading ultra-right party until the phenomenal surge in the FN vote in the early 1980s. The main spokesman of the PFN until a reorganization in 1982 was Pascal Gauchon, a well-known historian. In 1977 the PFN co-operated with the RPR in municipal elections; in 1978, after the failure of talks on a joint FN-PFN list, the parties stood separately in the legislative elections, with the PFN's 89 candidates winning 1.1 per cent to the

FN's 0.3 per cent. Although there was initial agreement on a joint list in the 1979 European poll, the PFN eventually presented its own list, led by Jean-Louis Tixier-Vignancourt, a 1965 ultra-right presidential candidate (who had on that occasion secured 5.3 per cent in the first round). The FN, which regarded the PFN move as a betrayal, called for abstention from voting, and the PFN's 81 candidates, standing as the *Union française pour l'eurodroite des patries* (French Union for a European Nationalist Right), won only 1.3 per cent. Neither party could gather enough signatures from elected representatives to present a joint or separate candidate in the 1981 presidential election. The June legislative elections saw Le Pen winning more votes than Gauchon, causing a leadership crisis in the PFN.

Under its new collective leadership, the PFN sought after 1982 to become the "cutting edge of the new opposition", but by late 1984 the Party was virtually defunct, with much of its membership having defected to the CNIP (which recruited Robert), the FN or the MNR. There were no PFN candidates in the 1984 European elections. Philippe Cocagnac, the leader of the PFN's school student group, was among a group of neo-fascists arrested in possession of petrol bombs during a demonstration in Paris in June 1984.

Policies. The PFN opposes immigration and calls for authoritarian government to enforce law and order and introduce a new approach to economic planning. It is generally regarded as more militant or extreme than the FN and does not seek to ally itself with mainstream conservative parties, having abandoned a policy of entryism (infiltration of larger parties) in 1983.

Publications. Pour une force nouvelle, six per year. The Party is supported by *Minute* newspaper.

International affiliations. The PFN enjoyed a particularly close relationship with the Italian MSI until the MSI allied with Le Pen's rival *Front national* in the European Parliament. It has also been allied with the Spanish *Fuerza Nueva* and has been in contact with the Australian National Action group.

Parti nationaliste français (PNF)
French Nationalist Party

Base. Paris

Orientation. Ultra-right

History. The PNF was formed as the result of a split in the larger *Front national* in December 1983, with some of its members coming from what was then a secret FN faction known as *Militant* (now a separate organization). Other members were drawn from *L'Oeuvre française* and the MNR. The PNF participated in Joan of Arc Day parades from 1984, and in the annual Dixmuide (Belgium) rallies organized by the Flemish fascist and nationalist groups.

Policies. The Party has ultra-nationalist, authoritarian and anti-immigrant policies.

Parti pour l'organisation de la Bretagne Libre (POBL)
Party for the Organization of a Free Brittany

Orientation. Libertarian nationalist

History. The POBL was formed in 1983 from *Strollard ar vro*, the Country Party (or Breton National European Federalist Party), which was itself derived from the *Mouvement pour l'organisation de la Bretagne* (MOB), founded in 1957.

Policies. The POBL describes itself as "neither of the left nor of the right"; it opposes both capitalism and socialism as well as centralism and cultural uniformity; it supports individual and collective self-determination, and in particular advocates Breton separatism.

Parti ouvrier européen
European Labour Party

Base. Paris

Leadership. La Roucheist

Orientation. Ultra-right

History. The Paris headquarters of this party was bombed on 7 April, 1986, by a group called Black War.

Policies. The party is in sympathy with the aims of Lyndon LaRouche's National Democratic Policy Committee, which is to say that it espouses a complicated and improbable conspiracy theory.

International affiliations. See National Democratic Policy Committee (United States). The party was originally organized under the same name in West Germany, where it is now known as Patriots for Germany; in Italy it is the *Partito Operaio Europeo*.

Partisan Européen
European Partisan

Address. Boîte Postale 41, 34502 Beziers

Orientation. Pan-Europeanist

History. This right-wing bulletin was in circulation in 1986.

Policies. The philosophy of the magazine is close to that of the GRECE, with a greater emphasis on European unity.

Le Présent

Address. 5 rue d'Amboise, 75002 Paris

Leadership. Bernard Antony (publisher)

Orientation. Ultra-right

History. This daily newspaper was founded by Antony, also known as Romain Marie, who became a *Front national* Euro-MP in 1985. It was described in a European Parliament report as carrying frequent racist and anti-semitic material. In late 1986, however, it dispensed with the services of its director and most consistently anti-semitic columnist, François Brigneau (who wrote under the pseudonym Mathilde Cruz). Brigneau had previously been associated with the rival *Minute* magazine and was a founding member of the FN.

Policies. The paper supports the Catholic fundamentalist "integrist" movement, of which Antony is a leading member (see *Chrétienité-solidarité*), and calls for strong government. It is opposed to abortion (and was successfully sued in 1985 by three doctors whom it had accused of carrying out abortions in order to sell foetuses for experimentation).

Associated organizations. The paper is sympathetic to, but independent of, the FN.

Provence Liguirie

Address. 34 bvd Jean Jaurès, 06300 Nice

Leadership. Jean-Claude Rivière (editor)

Orientation. Ultra-right

History. This monthly magazine is produced by Rivière, a professor at Nantes University who was suspended in July 1985, and later boycotted by students and colleagues, for his central role in the *affaire Roques* (see Henri Roques).

Policies. The magazine promotes historical revisionism, nationalism and right-wing political concepts.

Rassemblement national—see *Comités d'action républicaine.*

Recours (association de rapatriés)
Recourse (Returned Settlers' Association)

Base. Paris

Orientation. Colonialist

History. This organization was active in 1984-85.

Policies. The group, which usually capitalizes its name (*RECOURS*), seeks to represent the interests of former settlers in French overseas possessions. It also takes an interest in present-day controversies regarding the remaining possessions, and in the case of New Caledonia it opposes the Kanak independence movement.

Renouveau nationaliste
Nationalist Renewal

Orientation. Fascist

History. This organization was formed in 1981 after the voluntary dissolution of the *Groupe Union-Défense* (GUD—Union and Defence Group), which had been formed in the late 1970s as a student and youth grouping and had allied itself loosely with the PFN. Ex-members of the GUD established the new group along with individual members of the MNR, the FEN and the FNJ.

Policies. The group seeks to foster co-operation among right-wing nationalist organizations.

Publications. The GUD's organ until 1981 was *Présence Occidentale--Publimag* (94 boulevard de Sébastopol, 75003 Paris).

Résistance International
Resistance International

Leadership. Jean-François Revel

Orientation. Anti-communist

History. Resistance International was founded in 1985 as a co-ordinating group for supporters of various anti-communist political and guerrilla movements, principally in the Third World.

Associated organizations. Revel is also a member of the board of *Liberté sans frontières* (LSF), a pressure group created in 1985 by *Médecins san frontières* (MSF), which was founded in 1971 to provide medical assistance in areas of the Third World where conflict prevented the functioning of state medical services. Although the MSF is generally regarded as a non-partisan humanitarian organization, the LSF is associated with the French new right; another board member, Jean-Claude Casanova, is linked with the US new right journal *Commentary* and with the anti-Soviet Committee of Intellectuals for a Europe of Liberties.

International affiliations. Resistance International is very similar to the US-based Democratic International, founded around the same time.

Restauration nationale
National Restoration

Address. 10 rue Croix des Petits-Champs, 75001 Paris

Telephone. (1) 4296 1206

Leadership. Guy Steinbach (general secretary)

Orientation. Right-wing opposition

History. This movement was organized in 1947 by ex-members of *Action française*. The *Ligue d'action française* was founded in the 1920s as a Catholic fundamentalist pressure group, but was denounced by the French Church in 1926 and by the Pope in 1927. Its treasurer, Berger, was assassinated in May 1925. Led by Charles Maurras and Léon Daudet, it was the principal right-wing organization in pre-war France, and its members, known as *ligueurs*, joined in anti-semitic rioting in 1934; it claimed 60,000 members at the time. Its vice-president was Baron de Lessus, and the leader of its student section was Pierre Pujo, who remains active in the movement. In February 1936 the organization was banned after several violent incidents, but it remained in existence. Maurras was imprisoned in May 1936 for advocating the assassination of left-wing leaders in the event that France went to war with fascist Italy. During the Second World War the movement supported the collaborationist Vichy regime.

It reorganized in 1947, as the National Restoration Movement (MNR), by which name it is still known, and began to publish its current journal. An early recruit was Jean-Marie Le Pen, now the leader of the FN, who was arrested in 1948 while selling the journal at a monarchist rally. This movement is the oldest of the right-wing groupings which participate in the annual Joan of Arc Day parades.

The movement has not participated in electoral politics. In 1971 the movement divided, with its more progressive wing forming what is now the *Nouvelle action royaliste*.

Policies. A royalist group supporting the pretension of the Comte de Paris, the movement also has an array of right-wing nationalist and anti-socialist policies. It seeks to vindicate the wartime collaborationism of *Action française*.

Publications. Aspects de la France, weekly, edited by Pierre Pujo.

Rex solidarité nationaliste révolutionnaire
Rex Revolutionary Nationalist Solidarity

Base. Quimper

Orientation. Neo-nazi

History. The name of this group is probably derived from the Belgian Rexist movement. The French group was first reported as active in 1984.

Policies. In 1984 the group distributed tracts denouncing "the myth of the gas chambers", which would place it in the international historical revisionist (or Holocaust denial) movement.

Associated organizations. The group has the approval of the nazi FNE.

Rivarol

Address. 9 passage des Marais, 75010 Paris

Orientation. Right-wing

History. This literary, political and satirical weekly magazine was founded in 1951, and was edited by Maurice Gaït until his death in 1981. It has become one of the main journals of the French right.

Policies. The magazine promotes the unity of right-wing nationalist forces.

Circulation. 45,000.

Associated organizations. *Les Amis du Rivarol*, a possibly defunct readers' group which has organized seminars and rallies attracting a broad spectrum of conservative and fascist support.

Service action civique (SAC)
Civic Action Service

Leadership. Pierre Debizet (general secretary)

Orientation. Gaullist paramilitary group

History. The SAC was founded in 1958 as a semi-clandestine security group serving the Gaullist movement; it became involved in political violence, directed in 1959-63 mainly against supporters of the OAS. From 968, when it started to recruit members of *Occident*, the SAC's actions were mainly against the left and (particularly in the 1970s) against regionalist movements. During the 1970s President Pompidou purged the SAC of some 7,000 members allegedly involved with fascist groups or with organized crime.

Six ex-members were imprisoned in 1985 for the July 1981 murder of the Marseilles SAC leader and five members of his family. The apparent intention was to stop the man testifying about the involvement of the ultra-right in various criminal activities.

In view of this and other cases, the SAC was banned by the government in July 1982. By that time it was already moribund and there is no evidence that it continues in existence.

Associated organizations. The SAC founded an ultra-right university student group, the UNI.

SOS-France

Leadership. Bernard Bagur (president)

Orientation. Ultra-nationalist, white supremacist

History. SOS-France was legally registered in Var on Feb. 6, 1986 by its founding president, a 44-year-old ex-*pied-noir* and former *Front national* European Parliament candidate, Claude Noblia. It was regarded as a right-wing response to the formation of the anti-fascist *SOS-Racisme*.

Noblia, who had been in hiding for some months as an anti-immigrant bombing campaign built up in the south of France, was killed when a car blew up in Toulon near former *SOS-Racisme* offices on the night of 17-18 August. Three other SOS-France members died with him, including the vice-president, Yvon Ricard; their funeral became a major ultra-right gathering. Police reportedly thought that the group was a front for the *Commandos de France contre l'invasion maghrébine*. Bagur, who immediately assumed the presidency of SOS-France, was arrested later in August for the illegal possession of a gun.

Policies. The declared objective of the group is "to assist, defend and ensure justice for those who suffer discrimination, hatred or violence because of their status as French citizens". It has been particularly active in opposing *SOS-Racisme* as an "anti-police and anti-French" organization.

Activities. The group was responsible for a sticker and tract campaign in the summer of 1986 parodying an *SOS-Racisme* campaign. It also organized a meeting to oppose an *SOS-Racisme* concert on 17 July.

Membership. The group had about 50 members in August 1986, mainly *Front national* supporters and ex-paratroopers.

Associated organizations. See *Commandos de France contre l'invasion maghrébine*, which may or may not be linked with SOS-France. The group has collaborated with *La Maison du para*, in which Bagur holds an important office. The *Front national* denies any connection with the group.

Totalité
Totality

Address. Boîte Postale 47, 45390 Puisseaux; has also been published from Boîte Postale 141, 75263 Paris Cédex 06

Leadership. Georges Gondinet (editor)

Orientation. Fascist

History. This magazine was founded around 1979 by Gondinet, who is politically close to the GRECE while remaining an admirer of the Italian fascist thinker Julius Evola (most of whose works are devoted to explaining and developing the differences between fascism and national socialism). Gondinet runs the Pardes publishing house from the same address; it produces many Evola titles and several other journals of interest to the right.

Publications. *Totalité*, quarterly of variable extent and price; *Rebis*, on sexual politics; *L'Age d'or*, on mystical topics; *Kalki*, on warrior castes.

L'Union et cercle légitimiste
Legitimist Union Circle

Orientation. Right-wing

History. This body was represented at the 1985 Joan of Arc Day celebrations.

Union des intellectuels indépendants (UII)
Union of Independent Intellectuals

Leadership. Claude Adam (organizer)

Orientation. Ultra-nationalist

History. This group was active in the aftermath of the Second World War in a campaign for clemency for collaborators. One of its members at that time was Jean-Marie Le Pen. In 1985, when Le Pen—then leader of the *Front national*—was being accused of having tortured prisoners in the Algerian war, the UII issued a statement calling on the then defence minister, Charles Hernu, to speak out in defence of the reputation of the army and of Le Pen as an army veteran.

Policies. The UII works for unity between the many right-wing nationalist formations.

Associated organizations. The then vice-president of the UII was responsible for the formation for the Free Rudolf Hess Association.

Union national interuniversitaire (UNI)
National Inter-University Union

Orientation. Far right

History. This right-wing student group was set up by the Gaullist movement in 1968 and was active in the 1980s in opposing the Mitterrand government. Ô

Policies. The UNI groups students sympathetic to both right-wing conservative and neo-fascist politics.

Associated organizations. The UNI has reportedly had links with the right wing Gaullist *Service action civique* and with the *Front national*. It has also co-operated closely with the conservative RPR and has links with the UII, the *Club de l'horloge* and other organizations.

International affiliations. The UNI, which has been affiliated to the Union for Freedom (the French section of the World Anti-Communist League—see South Korea), received US$575,000 in the fiscal year 1984-85 (i.e. April 1984 to March 1985) from the US government-sponsored National Endowment for Democracy. This was the second largest payment to a Western European group, the largest being US$830,000 paid to the French anti-communist trade union federation, *Force ouvrière*. A further US$125,000 was disbursed in France and US$1,800,000 in other West European countries, with almost US$15,000,000 distributed elsewhere.

Volks Unis—National Socialisme
United Volk—National Socialism

Orientation. Neo-nazi guerrilla group

History. This group was one of three which claimed responsibility for the bombing of a cinema during a Jewish film festival in 1985 (see Column 88 Heil Hitler).

Defunct organizations

Association française pour la défense de la culture: an anti-communist organization which was the French affiliate to the Korean-based World Anti-Communist League (WACL) until the early 1980s.

Breiz Atao: Brittany Forever, a regionalist party founded in 1919, collaborated with the Nazi occupation forces in 1940-44. It failed to achieve significant devolution of power to the region, discredited the Breton cause and disappeared after the war (although its leader, Yann Goulet, ran a Committee for Free Brittany from Ireland); it was not until the mid-1960s that new Breton separatist movements emerged.

Brigades révolutionnaires françaises: the BRF (French Revolutionary Brigades) kidnapped a left-wing journalist for about a week in April-May 1982 in an unsuccessful attempt to force the government to adopt anti-communist policies in domestic and foreign affairs. Later in 1982 the group also bombed the home of the left-wing writer Régis Debray, and issued threats to the left in general.

Cahiers européens: this right-wing journal of the late 1960s and early 1970s was directed by François Duprat, who also wrote for *Défense de l'occident* (see *Occident*), and by Alain Renault. Duprat became a founding member of the *Front national* in 1972, and was killed by an unexplained car bombing in 1978.

Camelots du Roi: one of the *ligues* involved in serious riots early in 1934, this monarchist grouping led by Maxime Réal del Sarte had fewer than 1,000 members. It was banned in February 1936.

Centre des études évoliens: this small grouping was formed in the mid-1970s by admirers of the ideas of an Italian fascist theoretician, Julius Evola. A similar organization was the *Centre d'Études Doctrinales Évola*, based in Villemomble and active in the late 1970s and early 1980s.

Centre d'études nationalistes: an ultra-right publishing house of the 1960s, based in Monsecret-Orne, it published the works of (among others) René Pellegrin, a veteran of the PPF and the LVF who became involved with the neo-nazi *Devenir européen* group just before his death in 1980.

Cercle nationale et socialiste européen: a small nazi grouping active around 1963-64.

Colère des legions: the Anger of the Legions group appeared in November 1981, when it was one of several organizations claiming responsibility for a raid on a military arms depot. Nothing more was heard of the group and the arms were recovered by the police some weeks later.

Comité pour le peuple français: the Committee for the French People was founded in the mid-1970s as a fascist "cultural" group led by Thierry Colombo, who was imprisoned in May 1981 for withholding information about the murder in 1976 of a suspected police informer by two of Colombo's associates.

Commandos delta: the first group to use this name was an OAS unit whose leader, Roger Degueldre, was executed on 6 July 1962. The name was revived by a fascist guerrilla group (also known as the *Organisation delta* or simply as Delta) which killed an Algerian community leader in Paris in December 1977. It went on to kill an Egyptian communist in Paris in May 1978, and bombed his house and that of a French communist in mid-1980. In 1981 it sent a parcel bomb to the editor of *Le Monde*, and in 1983 it claimed responsibility for a bombing in Marseilles. The later Delta also used the name Commando Marco Tutti, after a captured Italian terrorist.

Croix de feu: the Fiery Cross was a fascist group of war veterans active in the 1930s. It was involved in the so-called *ligues* riots in February 1934, soon after its formation. Its leader was Col. de la Rocque. The group differed from nazism and Italian fascism principally on the racial question; de la Rocque maintained that France, "the great assimilator", had no need of race doctrines, and presented the *Croix de feu* as a "movement of national reconciliation". In 1934 it claimed 35,000 full members, organized in a paramilitary command structure, and 130,000 official supporters. Later in 1934 it formed an alliance with the larger *Jeunesses patriotes* and the UNC. By December 1935 it claimed to have 712,000 members. Its paramilitary wing was dissolved after several street clashes, and in June 1936 the *Croix de feu* itself was banned, but regrouped as the *Parti social française*.

Éditions Copernic: a publishing house responsible in 1980 for the works of at least one neo-nazi, Pierre Zind of *Devenir européen.*

Elsass-Lothringer Partei: the Alsace-Lorraine Party was formed under the German occupation as a successor to the 1930s *Jungmannschaft* autonomist group of German-speaking Alsatians. The leader of both groups was Hermann Bickler, who was arrested in 1939 along with other right-leaning Alsatian autonomist leaders on suspicion of plotting against state security. Bickler's colleagues included three deputies to the National Assembly—Rossé, Stürmel and Mourer—and Dr Spieler, as well as Dr Karl Ross, who was shot for treason in 1940. Freed under the German occupation, Bickler became an enthusiastic collaborator with the occupation regime and supported the conscription of Alsatians into the Wehrmacht. After the war he went to live in Italy where he remained active in the Alsatian autonomist and neo-fascist cause into the late 1970s. (The status of Alsace, which has a German-speaking majority, has not been seriously contested since the war, although a few right-wing guerrilla groups have emerged from time to time.)

Elsässische Kampfgruppe Schwarze Wolfe: the Black Wolf Fighting Group of Alsace (sometimes called the *Loups noirs* in the French press) was an autonomist paramilitary group active in the early 1980s among the ethnic German population of the region. After three bombings in 1981 which were claimed by the *Kampfgruppe,* five of its members were sentenced in July 1982 to terms of imprisonment.

Entente internationale anti-communiste: this forerunner of the World Anti-Communist League (see South Korea) was based in France from its foundation in 1924 until its dissolution around 1952 or '53. Its affiliates included anti-communist groupings in several European countries.

Étudiants: this student magazine, which described itself as "against Gaullism and for a European nation", was founded in 1949 by Jean-Marie Le Pen, later the leader of the *Front national.* It disappeared in the early 1950s.

Europe-Action: an ultra-right magazine founded in the mid-1960s, *Europe-Action* was run by Alain de Benoist and others then involved with the *Federation des étudiants nationalistes,* a right-wing student grouping which published *Cahiers universitaires,* and who were subsequently active in GRECE. The magazine had a supplement entitled *Nouvel observateur européen.*

*Fédération d'action nationale européenne—*see *Faisceaux nationaliste européens.*

Fédération des contribuables: the Taxpayers' Federation was a pre-war ultra-right grouping.

Francistes: a fascist group which had about 8,000 members by late 1935. It was prohibited along with similar groups in June 1936.

Front national: the original body of this name, which has no direct connection with the present-day FN, was an alliance formed in 1934 by the *Jeunesses patriotes,* the *Solidarité française* and *Action française.*

Front national pour l'Algérie française (FNAF): formed in 1959 by M. Soustelle, this body supported the *pied-noir* insurrection against the French government. Jean-Marie Le Pen was a leading member.

Front national des combattants (FNC): an *Algérie française* grouping; see *Association des combattants de l'union française.*

Front national de la jeunesse: this National Youth Front, not connected with the *Front national* youth wing, claimed responsibility for the bombing of the Paris to Moscow train in April 1980.

Gringoire: founded in 1928, this weekly journal was the leading publication of the racist and anti-semitic right throughout the 1930s, its print run reaching a peak of 640,000 in 1936.

Groupe action-jeunesse: one of the first ultra-right groups to define itself as "solidarist", meaning that it rejected the class struggle in favour of a nationalist solidarity of capital and labour, this movement developed in the early 1970s and disappeared by the middle of that decade, most of its members having joined the *Front national*. A leading figure in the movement was Jean-Pierre Stirbois, who in 1980 became the FN's general secretary and Le Pen's deputy. The name of the group was used to claim responsibility for the petrol-bombing of a pacifist office in Paris in June 1981; the message described the group, which is thought to be unconnected with the original movement, as opposed to "cosmopolitanism and internationalism" (code words used by neo-fascists to describe a supposed Jewish conspiracy).

Groupe 204: nazi tracts bearing the name of this ephemeral grouping circulated in Strasbourg, Marseilles and Chateauroux in early 1981.

Groupe Peiper: this group (named after Col. Joachim Peiper, an SS war criminal assassinated in France in 1976) has carried out several bombings of Jewish and immigrant properties, and was one of several groups claiming responsibility for the bombing of a Paris cinema on March 29, 1985, during a Jewish film festival. It is also known as the Peiper Vengeance Group or Frankreich-Peiper Group.

Groupe de résistance armée contre l'immigration: leaflets in the name of an Armed Resistance Group against Immigration, signed by "Gen. Aume", were widely circulated in 1983, but no further evidence of the group's existence has come to light.

Groupes nationalistes révolutionnaires: the GNR (Nationalist Revolutionary Groups) were established by François Duprat in the late 1970s as a network of neo-fascist clubs. Most of the Groups disappeared around 1980 as a result of Duprat's death, but at least one (in Le Havre) survived until 1982 by merging its activities with those of the local branch of the FNJ, the youth wing of the FN.

Gwenn ha Du: this Breton separatist guerrilla group, whose name means Black and White, was active in the 1930s. It sought funding and support from the German Nazi government.

Heimatbund: the Homeland League was formed in the University of Strasbourg in 1924 by right-wing ethnic German students from Alsace-Lorraine. It established contact with the German Nazi Party and with similar groups in the Czechoslovakian Sudetenland in 1925, became a non-student pressure group in 1926, and built up a significant following in the region.

Heimdal: an ultra-right regionalist cultural-political magazine published in Normandy from the late 1970s to the early 1980s; its offices were raided by the police in 1980.

Honneur de la police: this group (Honour of the Police), which was active from 1979, was implicated in the bombing of the car of a trade unionist and in the murder of an ex-prisoner. In 1981 a death threat was sent in its name to the socialist Interior Minister.

Item: a right-wing magazine published in the mid-1970s, it attracted contributions and subscribers among a variety of nationalist and neo-fascist groups.

Jeune Nation: an ultra-right grouping founded in 1951 by the Sidos brothers, it was banned in 1958 but regrouped immediately as the *Parti nationaliste*. Offshoots of the group included the *Association des Vikings* (later the PPNS) and *Europe-Action*.

Jeunesses patriotes: this fascist youth league claimed 300,000 members by mid-1934, although press sources gave a figure of 90,000. Its leader was M. Taittinger. Deputies representing the group sat with the royalists, forming a bloc of five after the 1932 election, and they supported the conservative Tardieu government. Around 1934 the league joined the *Front national* coalition. By June 1936, when it was banned, it claimed to have about 200,000 members.

Jungmannschaft—see *Elsass-Lothringer Partei.*

Justice Pieds-Noirs: Settler Justice; a guerrilla group formed by former settlers in Algeria, including members of UDIFRA; in 1975 the group carried out several bombings in the Vars region.

Landespartei: an autonomist movement of German-speaking Alsatians, this party was active in the 1930s.

Légion des volontaires français contre le bolchevisme: the LVF (Legion of French Volunteers against Bolshevism) was an army recruited from among French collaborators by the German occupation administration. It was organized in 1941 and was promoted by Marcel Déat, leader of the RNP. It fought mainly on the Russian front, although it was also active in Tunisia in 1942-43.

La Mangouste: The Mongoose was the name used by a group which admitted the bombing of three ultra-left premises in Toulouse in May 1981.

Mouvement de libération de l'Europe: this neo-nazi group was founded by French supporters of the imprisoned West German fascist leader, Manfred Roeder; it published a bulletin from a Paris box number in 1980-81.

Mouvement national Citadelle: a fascist grouping of the 1940s which developed into the *Parti socialiste français.*

Mouvement national socialiste: this nazi group was reportedly active around 1980, although it failed to make a significant impact.

Mouvement populaire français: the fascist MPF (French Popular Movement) was founded by Charles Luca in 1958 as a successor to the banned *Phalange française.*

Nouvel ordre européen: the French section of the fascist NOE (New European Order), which still exists as an international group based in Switzerland, was led in the late 1950s and the 1960s by Josseaume, Binet, Jeanne and Cavallier. The French participation in the NOE is currently through the FNE.

Nouvelle front nazi française: the NFN (New Nazi Front) reportedly emerged in 1981 as an offshoot of the FANE (most of which regrouped as the FNE).

Nouvelle génération fasciste: the Fascist New Generation announced its existence with a statement in early 1981 to the effect that Adolf Hitler was God. It threatened several prominent Jews in the south of France. The statement carried a runic symbol used by the banned FANE (see FNE) and also by several other European and North American fascist and nordicist groups.

Nouvelle voix d'Alsace-Lorraine: a magazine published around 1980 in support of the autonomist movement of Alsace-Lorraine; among its contributors was at least one leading member of the neo-nazi *Devenir européen* group, namely Pierre Zind.

Occident: this neo-fascist group, which had paramilitary leanings, was formed in the mid-1960s and outlawed in 1969, with its leadership immediately forming the *Ordre nouveau.*

Odessa: this name, derived from the acronym of a secret group of German veterans of the SS, has been used occasionally by French right-wing groups from the 1960s. The most recent use of the name was by a group which bombed the home of a well-known "nazi hunter", Beate Klarsfeld, in the early 1980s.

Ordre et justice nouvelle: New Order and Justice bombed a left-wing printing company in Marseilles in August 1980, wounding 17 people.

Ordre nouveau: New Order was a neo-fascist paramilitary group formed in 1969 after the banning of *Occident*. Several of its members, including its leader, Alain Robert (now of the CNIP), went on to join the FN in 1972-73 and the PFN in 1974. *Ordre nouveau* was banned and apparently ceased to exist in June 1973 after incidents following a rally against immigration.

Organisation de l'armée secrète: the OAS (Secret Army Organization) was the best-known of the numerous right-wing groupings set up by, and mainly comprising, former French settlers in Algeria, who felt that the mainland, and in particular Gen. de Gaulle, had betrayed the national interest in giving Algeria its independence. The main OAS campaign lasted from 1958 to 1962, but its veterans was responsible for numerous attempts on the life of Gen. de Gaulle before it disappeared in the early 1970s. OAS members went on to found a variety of ultra-right groupings. The history of the Organization has been the subject of numerous books and articles.

Organisation pour la libération de la France: the OPLF (Organization for the Liberation of France) bombed a mosque in Romans, in south-eastern France, in May 1982.

Parti fasciste d'action révolutionnaire: the Fascist Revolutionary Action Party bombed a Paris courthouse on March 11, 1980.

Parti national socialiste française: this overtly nazi grouping was formed in 1963 and was led by Yves Jeanne. It collapsed soon after the leader's arrest in 1964. Jeanne went on to found the *Devenir européen* magazine and group.

Parti populaire français: the PPF was a nationalist revolutionary party formed in 1936 by Jacques Doriot, a former communist.

Parti proletarien national-socialiste: the PPNS evolved in the 1960s from the *Association des Vikings*. It was an overtly nazi grouping which affiliated to the World Union of National Socialists (see United States and Denmark).

Parti social français: the PSF (French Social Party) was founded in June 1936 by Col. de la Rocque as a successor to the *Croix de feu*, which was banned. It failed to retain the massive support of the earlier organization, possibly because of its commitment to constitutional politics.

Parti social national français: the PSNF was founded in 1933 by Sean Hennessy, a deputy and former ambassador. Its "social nationalist" philosophy, which it contrasted with both fascism and national socialism, was anti-communist, anti-democratic and anti-republican. It had a syndicalist economic programme based on co-operation between capital and labour, and was pro-militarist, racist and ultra-nationalist. The party did not survive the war.

Phalange française: the French Phalanx was a fascist party founded in October 1955 and having as its president Charles Luca (a nephew of the fascist leader Marcel Déat—see LVF and RNP) and as its general secretary Henri Roques (see below) who was then using the pseudonym Henri Jalin. It was banned, together with its monthly journal *Fidelité*, in May 1958; Luca went on to found the MPF. The Phalanx was essentially a continuation of the *Parti socialiste français*, which was itself a successor to the *Mouvement national Citadelle*.

Rassemblement anti-juif de France: this uncompromisingly anti-semitic grouping was founded in 1934 by Darquier de Pellepoix, editor of *La France enchaînée*, and Henri-Robert Petit; the former went into exile after the war, while the latter, after serving a long sentence for collaboration, remained active on the ultra-right, joining the FNE in his senescence in the mid-1980s.

Rassemblement national populaire (RNP): this collaborationist grouping was led from 1940 to 1945 by Marcel Déat, a fascist who is remembered mainly for his recruiting work for the LVF, a volunteer SS battalion. Its journal was *L'Oeuvre* and its youth affiliate was the *Jeunesses nationales populaires* (JNP), one of whose members, Roland Gaucher, is currently a leading figure in the *Front national*.

Solidarité française: a fascist *ligue* of the 1930s, this group, led by René Coty of the cosmetics family, claimed to have about 2,000 active and 180,000 supporting members in 1934. By June 1936, when it was prohibited, it reportedly had 20,000 active members and was affiliated to the *Front national*.

Union de défense des commerçants et artisans (UDCA): the Union for the Defence of Tradesmen and Artisans, founded by Pierre Poujade in 1956, rapidly became France's leading ultra-right party, winning 11.5 per cent of the vote in that year's legislative elections. No fewer than 52 Poujadist candidates were elected, including Jean-Marie Le Pen, now leader of the *Front national*, and Jean-Maurice Demarquet, who led the Poujadist *Union et fraternité française* parliamentary bloc. The poor organization of the UDCA led to an equally rapid decline and to numerous defections to the more established right-wing parties, so that by January 1957 there were only 36 Poujadist deputies, and in June 1958 only 29. The platform of the UDCA was fairly similar to that of the modern FN, concentrating on law-and-order issues and on French nationalism; it was opposed to the Algerian independence movement, with both Le Pen and Demarquet signing up as volunteers in parachute regiments.

Union de défense des interêts des Français rapatriés: the UDIFRA (Union for the Defence of the Interests of French Repatriates) was formed in 1965 as a *syndicat de choc* by Roger Piegts, brother of OAS activist Claude; many UDIFRA members were implicated in the activities of *Justice pieds-noirs*. Its members included Claude Noblia, who went on to found SOS-France.

Union et fraternité française—see *Union de défense des commerçants et artisans*.

Viking: a white supremacist and Nordicist magazine published from 1948 by Alain Mabire, who later changed its name to *Heimdal*. It gained a Europe-wide circulation.

Other organizations

Among the vast number of fascist, racist, ultra-nationalist, anti-semitic and other right-wing groupings which have been reported as active in France in recent years are the following, most of which may well be defunct: *Action Populaire* (Popular Action), a corporatist social credit group led by Janpier Dutrieux (operating through the *Mouvement Populiste Européen*, Boîte Postale 30, 75462 Paris Cédex 10); the *ADMP*; *Alternative* magazine; *Les Amis de Gustave le Bon* (34 rue Gabrielle, 75018 Paris), which publishes the works of a 19th-century racist; the *Amis de Robert Brasillach* (Jeanne Barthelemy, Le Rochafon, 74560 Monnetier-Mornex), a group founded in Switzerland in 1948 to perpetuate the memory of a French collaborationist writer; *Anti-Hernu* (a probably obsolete pressure group opposed to a former Socialist cabinet minister); the Catholic fundamentalist *Association St. Pious V*; the Nordicist *Association des Vikings de France*; and the fascist magazine *Balder*.

The *Centre de culture européene (CLODO)*, founded in 1983 and claiming to be a death squad composed of police officers; the *Cobra Information* group, set up in 1982 by the FNE and similar groups to support "nationalist political prisoners" (and run by Antoine Bouveret from Boîte Postale 1917, 37000 Tours); the *Comité clandestin des résistants métros* (Guadeloupe), a settlers' guerrilla group which opposes the independence movement in one of France's Caribbean departments; the anti-crime, pro-police *Comité d'entente pour le réveil français* (CERF—Committee of Understanding for a French Revival), which publishes *L'Entente* from Boîte Postale 35, 13254 Marseilles Cédex 06; the anti-communist *Comité international contre la repression* (International Committee against Repression); the *Comité pour l'ordre moral*; the *Comité de repression antimarxiste*; the *Comités de défense Charles Martel*; the *Confédération française du travail* (French Confederation of Labour), a right-wing trade union group; *Confidentiel* bulletin; and the *CSL*.

Défense de l'occident magazine, and the *Comités défense de l'occident* (Defence of the West Committees); the quasi-fascist *Défi* magazine, edited by Odin Rossignol (impasse des Colibris, Le Taillan Médoc, 33320 Eysines), who also leads the *France demain* group (founded in 1972) and the *Comités génération nouvelle*; *Douar Breiz*, a fascist-linked Breton regionalist magazine edited by M.A. Keruel (10 rue du Champ de Foire, 22530 Mur de Bretagne); *L'Éclair* (Lightning), a clandestine nazi magazine first published in 1983; *Écrits de Paris* journal; a large number of fascist publishing houses and commercial publishers of fascist or right-wing books, including *Éditions Debresse* and *Éditions de la Vieille Taupe* (an "alternative" publishing house which has published material supporting Faurisson's gas-chamber theories); the *Encre noir* group, a right-wing guerrilla group, allegedly consisting of police, formed around 1983; *Escadron Noir* magazine; *Europe 2000* magazine, a pan-European publication founded in 1983 for regionalists and ethnic nationalists (Boîte Postale 113, 75563 Paris Cédex 12), and *Europe uni* (United Europe).

The *Fédération autonome des syndicats de la police*, possibly superseded by the FPIP; the *Fédération générale des travailleurs*; the anti-socialist *Fédération des unions royalistes de France*, led by Jean de Beauregard, which has not participated in elections since the mid-1970s and may be defunct; *La Flamme* magazine; two Corsican anti-independence guerrilla groups, *France-Résurrection* (founded 1983) and the *Front d'action nouvelle contre l'indépendence et l'autonomie* (Francia, founded 1977); the *Front des étudiants nationalistes*; the *Front de libération nationale française* (FLNF—French National Liberation Front), an anti-semitic group which emerged around 1980; deputy Jean Fontaine's right-wing conservative *Front militant départmentaliste*, founded in 1981 and seeking to maintain French control of Réunion; and the *Front uni d'Hainaut*.

The *Groupe autonome national socialiste*, whose existence was revealed in a communiqué issued after solstice celebrations in June 1983, and also in leaflets found on three skinheads who attacked a Saudi diplomat in May 1986; the *Groupe Condor*; the *Groupe nationaliste européene*; the *Groupe Orly*; the *Groupes nationalistes révolutionnaires*, possibly the same as the *Groupes nationales révolutionnaires*; the *IOTA* group of M. Bianconi; *Jeune nation solidariste*; the *Jeune taupe* (Young Mole, an ecologist magazine which had a small ultra-right following around 1980); *Lettres de Roeder*, a possibly-defunct bulletin from a German nazi criminal, translated and published in the early 1980s by M. Loubet (Boîte Postale 277, 75827 Paris 17); the *Librairie des Deux Mondes* (Two Worlds Bookshop) and the *Librairie Grégori*; the *Ligue des combattants français contre l'occupation juive* (League of French Fighters against the Jewish Occupation); and the *Lynx Club*, Argenteuil.

The *Mouvement justicialiste*, based on the Argentinian Peronist movement and led by Jacques Bourcelot; the *Mouvement oxydant*, possibly a successor of the *Occident* movement banned in 1969 (see above); the fascist-social creditist *Mouvement populiste français*, publisher of *France populiste* magazine, edited until 1983 by Janpier Dutrieux (see *Action Populaire*) and thereafter by Nadège Carpentier (Boîte Postale 1077, 59011 Lille Cédex; editorial office at 57 rue Boucher de Perthes, 59800 Lille); the *Nantes renouveau jeunesse*, a non-party fascist group formed in 1981 by local activists of the FJ, the FNJ, the FEN and the FNE to publish the monthly *Fanal* magazine (edited by Alain Larmet, CLR, Boîte Postale 778, 44209 Nantes Cédex); the fascist *National-Provence* journal; the *Nouvel ordre social*; *Nouvelles éditions latines*, which (under Fernand Sorlot, who died in 1981) has published editions of Hitler's *Mein Kampf*; *Ordre et tradition*; the *Ordre noir* (Black Order); *Paroles françaises* journal; the *Parti proletarien national-socialiste*; the *Parti socialiste français*(founded as the *Mouvement national citadelle*); *Pays réel*, a royalistmagazine; *Peste brune* (Brown Plague) magazine; *Peuple et Nation*, a "national-revolutionary" magazine edited by Denis Charles (Boîte Postale 67, 69397 Lyon Cédex 3); and the *Presse de la Cité* publishing house, which has produced fascist titles.

Radio Monte Carlo, which was banned in 1981 for broadcasting material from FNE member Jean-Pierre Chapelle (who has since been imprisoned for inciting racial hatred); *Refus* magazine, founded in 1983 ("for a socialist, nationalist, revolutionary order"); *La Revue d'étude des relations internationales*; the *Revue internationale des problèmes du nationalisme*, a fascist theoretical journal; *Rot un Wiss* (Red and White), a fascist Alsatian monthly (Boîte Postale 132, R14, 67004 Strasbourg); *Sécurité, tranquillité et ordre publique* (STOP), a vigilante group in Tourcoing (near Lille); the *Syndicat national de la presse indépendante* (an umbrella group for publishers of right-wing journals), at 26 rue Volembert, 95100 Argenteuil; *Terre et foi* (Land and Faith) magazine; the *Union des Français de bon sens* (UFBS—Union of Frenchmen of Good Sense), an anti-trade union party founded in 1977 by industrialist Gérard Furnon; the *Union française de solidarité* (Boîte Postale 11, 44210 Pornic), which promotes co-operation among right-wing nationalist groups; *Union et liberté* and the French section of the German Viking Youth, the *Jeunesses wikings*.

Individuals

Françoise Dior: a perfume heiress who was deeply involved in the financing and organizing of nazi activities in the United Kingdom in the early 1960s, Dior has been imprisoned in France and Britain for offences including conspiracy to burn synagogues. She remained active in French and British ultra-right circles and joined the UK Conservative Party's Paris branch. In 1984 she was reported to be associating with the ousted Webster faction of the British National Front and with the Hancock family of racist printers and publishers.

Robert Faurisson: the best known "revisionist" historian in France (the term adopted by those who seek to rewrite history from a far-right perspective, sometimes by maintaining that the nazi massacre of European Jews never took place), and one of the half-dozen most prominent revisionists in the world (others being Arthur Butz in the United States, Wilhelm Stäglich in West Germany, Ernst Zündel in Canada, David Irving in the UK and Ditlieb Felderer in Sweden). A lecturer at the University of Lyons, he was involved in the Nantes controversy of 1985-86 (see Henri Roques), was a contributor to *Rivarol* magazine and was on the editorial committee of the Institute of Historical Review (United States). A well known newspaper cartoonist produced a comic book in 1986 (under his pen-name of Konk) supporting Faurisson's theories and claiming that the gas chambers never existed.

Yann Moncomble: a conspiracy theorist who publishes his own material denouncing the machinations of the Trilateral Commission and other groups (from Boîte Postale 24, 27330 La Neuve Lyre).

Georges de Nantes: the abbé Georges of Nantes became increasingly involved in ultra-right activities in the early 1960s, leading to his suspension *a divinis* by the Vatican in 1966 (a measure which prevented him from exercising priestly functions). He continues to be active in the integrist (Catholic fundamentalist) movement, denouncing reformism in the Church as treason and heresy, and has a large personal following among the secular ultra-right; he calls for a monarchy or dictatorship as the best form of government for France. He is associated with *Rivarol* magazine.

Marc-Henri Nabe: this anti-semitic writer has appeared on television to praise the nazi genocide programme.

Henri Roques: a revisionist historian and former general secretary of the fascist *Phalange française*, his fraudulent doctoral thesis attempting to disprove the murder of Jews in Nazi gas chambers was sustained by an ad hoc "jury" of revisionists at the University of Nantes on 15 June, 1985, but after considerable public controversy the acceptance was annulled by a government minister in July 1986, mainly on the grounds of procedural irregularities in his enrolment, supervision and adjudication. (The first French "revisionist", much admired by Roques, was Paul Rassinier, active in the early 1960s.)

René Woerly: a neo-nazi implicated in a number of attacks in Alsace, he stood in the March 1985 local elections; the mayors of the canton of Villé refused to organize the count unless his candidature were forbidden.

New Caledonia

capital: Nouméa   **population: 62,000**

Political system. The Overseas Territory of New Caledonia is governed by a High Commissioner appointed by the French President and, in most internal matters, by a 42-seat popularly elected Territorial Assembly which appoints a Council of Ministers led by a President. Some powers are devolved to regional councils.

Recent history. The political process has been dominated since the late 1970s by the independence movement representing most of the native Melanesian (Kanak) population, and an opposing movement mainly representing the settled (*caldoche*) and immigrant (*métro*) French communities. A referendum in 1985, following serious communal violence, may lead eventually to a form of "independence-association" which will involve a Kanak-dominated government and French control of defence and external relations.

The evolution of the far right. Some French colonists have turned to the metropolitan French ultra-right, and in particular to the *Front national* of Le Pen, for support in their resistance to the independence movement, which they liken to that in Algeria in the 1950s. By no means all parties which oppose independence are of the radical right; the main parties in favour of either the status quo or an upgrading to departmental status are grouped in the RPCR, which is allied to the mainstream conservative RPR in the metropolis (but has on occasion co-operated with more right-wing forces), while a pro-autonomist coalition opposed to independence, the FNSC, has an approximately centre-left ideology.

Active organizations

Front calédonien (FC)
Caledonian Front

Orientation. Ultra-right

History. The FC was founded in 1981 by Justin Guillemard, who defected to the RPCR in 1983 and was succeeded as party president by Claude Sarran, who had been imprisoned for three months after attacking the National Assembly building in mid-1982. In 1984 the FC supported the FN in the European elections but ran its own list in the Territorial Assembly elections, gaining limited support.

In February 1985 the FC staged a provocative "picnic" at Thio, leading to clashes with Kanaks, and on Feb. 21 expulsion orders were issued against five of its members or sympathisers, including Sarran, his vice-presidents Michel Reuillard and Alain Dagostini, and Emile Lebargy, president of the territorial branch of the right-wing *Union national des parachutistes.*

Policies. The FC represents French immigrants who are broadly in sympathy with the racial and social attitudes of the metropolitan FN but who seek to organize autonomously within the territory.

Membership. 300 (1985 claim).

Front national de la Nouvelle-Calédonie (FN)
National Front of New Caledonia

Leadership. François Néoéré (secretary); Roger Gaillot, Alain Camille

Orientation. Ultra-right

History. The FN was organized in New Caledonia in the late 1970s in response to the increasing influence of the Kanak independence movement and to suggestions that a socialist government in France might be willing to concede the Kanak demands. In the June 1984 European Parliament election, in which its list was supported by the FC, the FN secured 15.7 per cent of the territory's votes; in the November 1984 elections to the Territorial Assembly the FN won 2,379 votes (6.1 per cent) and secured one seat. One of its members, Gaillot, is Mayor of the important town of Thio and a member of the Territorial Assembly; Néoéré is a Kanak chief and leader of the *Regroupement de la cause de la paix* (Pro-Peace Group).

Policies. The New Caledonian FN supports the policies of the metropolitan party, with an emphasis on resistance to any change in the territory's status.

Membership. Rallies held by the FN have been attended by 3,000 or more supporters.

Other organizations

Mouvement pour l'ordre et la paix: the MOP (Movement for Order and Peace), which may be defunct, was founded in 1979 as an anti-independence pressure group based in the French settler community. In January 1980 the killing by a policeman, who was allegedly a MOP member, of a Kanak youth led to considerable inter-communal tension.

Federal Republic of Germany

capital: Bonn   **population: 61,770,000**

Political system. The Federal Republic of Germany (West Germany) is a parliamentary democracy created in 1949 in the parts of Germany occupied upon Hitler's defeat in 1945 by the three Western allies. The two legislative chambers are the 45-seat *Bundesrat*, whose appointed members represent the 10 states and the West Berlin enclave, and the 520-seat *Bundestag* elected by universal adult suffrage. There is a non-executive President and the federal government is headed by the Chancellor, who is the leader of the parliamentary majority.

Recent history. Power has since 1949 alternated between the Social Democratic Party and the Christian Democrats, apart from periods of coalition involving both parties separately or together. The Christian Democrats were in power in 1987, in coalition with the Christian Social Union.

The evolution of the far right. The history of Adolf Hitler's National Socialist German Workers' Party (NSDAP or Nazi Party), of smaller fascist groups (the *Alldeutsche Verband*, the *Deutschnationale Volkspartei*, the *Reichslandbund*, *Stalhelm*, the Bavarian People's Party, its Iron Watch, and so on), and of the Third Reich itself, is amply documented elsewhere, and we are concerned here exclusively with the post-war era.

As the home of national socialism, Germany has had little difficulty in sustaining a range of ultra-right political parties and groups since the end of the Second World War, despite constitutional, legislative and administrative obstacles to fascist activities. Although in the East German territory occupied by the Soviet Army most captured Nazi war criminals were summarily dealt with, in the West many former Nazis were allowed a significant role in administrative arrangements set up under Western occupation.

One of the issues around which far-right groups have organized has been that of clemency for the minority of war criminals who were imprisoned. The best-known case, now that most of the prisoners have died or been released and rehabilitated, is that of Rudolf Hess, Hitler's deputy, who remains in Spandau Prison at the insistence of the Soviet Union although the Western powers have come to the view, long advocated by neo-nazis, that he should be freed. Another manifestation of revanchism has been the formation of "old comrades' associations" representing former soldiers in the *Schutz-Staffel* (SS) and other Nazi forces. Reunions of these groups have since the mid-1970s caused frequent protests in West German towns, with, for example, veterans of the *Totenkopf* and other SS Divisions being refused permission to meet in Bad Harzburg in 1984, in Oberaula in 1985 and in Detmold in 1986, after anti-nazi demonstrations in those and previous years. There has been, and may still be, an international network called Odessa (*Organisation der Ehemaligen SS-Angehörigen*) consisting of, and serving, former SS members and other war criminals seeking to evade discovery and prosecution.

A third factor in the growth of the ultra-right, especially in the northern cities, has been racism directed at foreign contract workers— *gastarbeiter*—who were recruited, mainly from Turkey, until the rise in unemployment in the 1970s. Immigration is now discouraged and incentives are offered to immigrants wishing to return to their countries of origin. Some conservative politicians are also seeking to restrict the right to political asylum. "Skinhead" violence against Turks, and reciprocal violence, are frequently reported; several neo-nazi skinhead gangs have organized around football clubs. Some of their number were jailed in July 1986 for beating a Turkish man to death in Hamburg the previous December. The main centres of skinhead activity are Hanover and Hamburg. The immigrant communities, and especially the Turks, have

. themselves formed numerous ultra-right groups, which are generally not concerned with German politics.

There appears to have been little interest in pan-Germanism since the defeat of the Third Reich. German communities expelled from Silesia by the Polish authorities, and from the Sudetenland by the Czechs, following the territorial adjustments at the end of the war, did not in the main support irridentist movements or become involved in fascist activity. However a Silesian exile organization became involved in a controversy affecting the Christian Democratic Chancellor in 1984-85.

The West German state has monitored the ultra-right more closely and more publicly than most other Western nations, in view of legal restrictions on groups deemed hostile to the democratic constitution; these measures, applied also to left-wing organizations, have ensured the availability of reliable historical data on the far right through the annual Interior Ministry reports on subversion. According to the 1986 report the country had 23,500 extreme right-wingers, of whom 1,400 were classed by the state as neo-nazis, meaning essentially that they did not conceal their admiration for Hitlerite national socialism; most of the remainder were members of the National Democratic Party (NPD), a party of the radical right which many observers would also classify as neo-nazi although it eschews the swastika and other symbols of Nazism. The 1985 report listed 34 organizations with a total of 22,000 members, who had carried out 74 known violent crimes; that for 1984 listed 16 groups. In 1983 there were 20,300 extreme rightists, including 1,400 neo-nazis, and 78 acts of violence, compared with 19,000, 1,300 and 70 respectively in 1982.

There was a large number of neo-nazi crimes in the late 1970s and early 1980s, including the bombing of the Munich Oktoberfest beer festival on Sept. 26, 1980, with 13 deaths (including that of the bomber) and 219 people wounded. This period also saw the formation and growth of the *Wehrsport gruppe Hoffmann* and several similar neo-nazi paramilitary groups.

Evidence of the persistence of anti-semitic attitudes in mainstream German parties is found infrequently nowadays. In 1986 a Christian Social Union (CSU) member of parliament, Hermann Fellner, commenting on a compensation award to former slave labourers, said that Jews were "quick to step forward when money rattles in German tills". The CSU's coalition partner, the CDU, admitted in 1986 that its West Berlin branch had funded neo-nazi groups, allegedly with a view to dissuading the nazis from taking part in elections.

Active organizations

Aktion Oder-Neisse—see German Nationalist Party

Aktion Unpolitische Schulen
Non-Political Schools Action

Base. Bielefeld

Orientation. Anti-communist

History. Leafleting activities of this pressure group were reported in the neo-nazi press in 1984.

Policies. The group appears to be mainly concerned with combating an alleged Marxist influence in West German schools.

Aktionsfront Nationaler Sozialisten—Nationaler Aktivisten (ANS-NA)
National Socialists' and Nationalist Activists' Action Front

Address. Postlagerkarte AO 18753, Hamburg 80

Leadership. Michael Kühnen (leader)

Orientation. Nazi

History. The ANS-NA was formed by Kühnen, a former member of the West German armed forces, on his release in 1982 from a three-year prison term for promoting nazi beliefs. It followed unreservedly nazi policies, to the extent of adopting a black uniform. Among its recruits were former members of the *Wehrsportgruppe Hoffmann* and of Friedhelm Busse's nazi People's Socialist Movement of Germany (VSBD).

Several members of the ANS-NA, including its deputy leader, Arndt-Heinz Marx, were arrested in 1983 and 1984, and charged inter alia with torturing a dissident member. Kühnen fled to France in 1984 after being charged with inciting racial hatred and producing nazi propaganda. The Front, which had over 260 known members, was banned at that time and may now be defunct.

Policies. The Front advances classic nazi policies including anti-semitism based on a Jewish conspiracy theory, authoritarianism, white supremacism and German nationalism.

Associated organizations. The ANS has probably been superseded by the *Freiheitliche Arbeiterpartei*, although it was reported in September 1984 that some ANS-NA members were planning the creation of a *National-Europäische Union*.

Anti-Bolshevik Bloc of Nations—see under United Kingdom.

Antikommunistische Vereinigung
Anti-Communist Alliance

Base. Pinneberg

Leadership. Matthias Pagel

Orientation. Neo-nazi

History. The Alliance was first reported active in early 1984. It may be a successor to an earlier *Antikommunistisch Front*.

Policies. It appears to be a neo-nazi organization, although its public activities stress opposition to communism.

Membership. 20 active members (mid-1984).

Publications. *Pinneberger Beobachter*.

Associated organizations. The group has a paramilitary section called the OST.

Aufbruch
Rising

Address. Postfach 582, 5750 Menden 1

Orientation. Neo-nazi

History. This magazine was published in 1986.

Policies. The journal describes itself as "national revolutionary". It opposes "the ethnic genocide of one-worldism", a terminology which suggests belief in the fascist theory that Jews promote "world government" and racial inter-breeding. It also opposes immigration and egalitarianism.

Publications. Aufbruch, monthly.

August 13 Working Group

Leadership. Wolf Quasner

Orientation. Anti-communist

History. In July 1986, close to the 25th anniversary of the construction of the Berlin Wall, this group presented to the media an East German taxi driver who claimed to have crossed illegally to the West in a car containing three tailor's dummies disguised as Soviet officers. West German police dismissed the tale as a publicity stunt, maintaining that the car contained four dummies.

Activities. The Group maintains a museum near "Checkpoint Charlie", a main crossing-point from East to West Berlin.

Die Bauernschaft—see Kritik Verlag.

Borussenfront
Borussia Front

Base. Dortmund

Leadership. Siegfried Borchardt (leader)

Orientation. Nazi

History. This football gang, associated with Borussia Dortmund soccer club, was responsible for racist chants and assaults on mainly Turkish immigrant spectators at numerous games. "SS Sigi" Borchardt was imprisoned for one year in 1984 for his role in the gang.

Burgerinitiative Deutsche Arbeiterpartei—see *Freiheitliche Arbeiterpartei.*

DESG-Inform

Address. Postfach 110 702, 6100 Darmstadt

Orientation. Libertarian

History. This right-wing libertarian journal aims to appeal to a wide range of disaffected youth by concerning itself with ecology and other issues hitherto monopolized by the left and centre-left. The journal was founded by the *Deutsch-Europäische Studiengesellschaft* (DESG—German-European Studies Society).

Policies. Recent issues of the journal have focused on "alternative groups" concerned with environmentalism, "national revolution", regionalism and the European new right.

Publications. DESG-Inform, monthly; *Junges Forum*; booklets.

International affiliations. The journal has exchange advertising arrangements with foreign ultra-right publications including *Scorpion*(United Kingdom).

Deutsche Bürgerinitiative
German Citizens' Initiative

Address. 3579 Schwarzentorn, Knull, Richberg

Leadership. Manfred Roeder (*Reichsverweser*, or Reich administrator)

Orientation. Neo-nazi

History. This organization, formed in 1971, is one of many groups or publications founded since the war by Roeder (born in 1930), a former officer in the Nazi air force who practised as a lawyer until he was disbarred in the late 1970s. It was originally based in Buffalo, New York (United States). Roeder has often been arrested or imprisoned for his activities; while he was serving sentences for incitement to hatred and for anti-constitutional activities in 1976 and 1977, his supporters formed a protest group called *Komitee Freiheit für Roeder* (Roeder Freedom Committee).

In June 1981 Roeder was sentenced to 13 years' imprisonment as the intellectual leader of the *Deutsche Aktionsgruppen* (German Action Groups), which, under the operational leadership of Raimund Hörnle (who was sentenced to life imprisonment), had bombed refugee hostels in 1980, killing two residents. Also sentenced were Sybille Vorderbrügge (life imprisonment) and Dr Heinz Colditz (six years). Roeder's wife, who lives in the United States, is a frequent guest at Aryan Nations functions there; at least one journal in the United States was founded specifically to support Roeder's activities in West Germany.

The *Aktionsgruppen* were probably identical with the *Deutsche Aktionsfront*, which had claimed responsibility for attacks including the bombing of an exhibition on concentration camps in February 1980.

Policies. The group promotes fascist and pan-German nationalist ideas. It supports the confederal "Europe of the nations" concept adopted by very many West European fascist groups (whereby each ethnic group— including minorities such as the Bretons, the Croats and so on—would constitute a state).

Publications. Bulletins in German and English called *Deutsche Bürgerinitiative*.

International affiliations. See *Teutonic Unity* (United States). Roeder's support group in France is the *Mouvement de libération de l'Europe*.

Deutsche Frauenfront
German Women's Front

Address. Robert-Bunsen-Strasse 10, 6090 Rüsselheim

Leadership. Andrea Korn (leader)

Orientation. Neo-fascist

History. The Front was founded in 1983 as a coalition of ultra-nationalist and neo-nazi women.

Deutsche Freiheitsbewegung der Bismarck-Deutsche
German Freedom Movement of Bismarck Germans

Base. Munich

Leadership. Otto Ernst Remer (leader)

Orientation. Nazi

History. Remer, a former SS general involved in foiling the Stauffenberg plot on Hitler's life, was released shortly after the war and established the neo-fascist Socialist

Reich Party in 1948. In 1951 a fascist paramilitary group which he had established was banned, but his party won 15 seats in *Landtag* elections in Lower Saxony. In 1952, after two criminal convictions, he moved to Egypt and later to other Middle East countries, where together with Austrian war criminal Alois Brunner (see Syria) he became involved in the international arms trade. Remer later returned to West Germany, serving a brief prison sentence in 1954, and supported the defunct German Rights Party. In 1983 he established his present organization, which has little popular support.

Policies. Remer opposes the US military presence in West Germany and calls for national reunification and pan-German patriotism. He advocates an anti-American alliance between the German and Russian peoples.

Associated organizations. Remer's writings have appeared in the publications of the *Unabhängige Nachrichten* organization, and have also been published by the Verlag K.W. Schütz, a nazi propaganda press in Oldendorf.

International affiliations. His main US ally is H. Keith Thompson, formerly of the American Renaissance Party and now an associate of Willis Carto's Liberty Lobby. Remer has participated in the annual fascist rallies at Dixmuide in Belgium, and has close links with French nazis formerly in the FANE. He has also claimed to have Arab support.

Deutsche Volksunion (DVU)
German People's Union

Leadership. Dr Gerhard Frey (chairman)

Orientation. Neo-fascist

History. The DVU has sponsored speaking tours of West Germany by the British revisionist historian David Irving. Frey announced on March 6, 1987, in Munich, the formation of the *Deutsche Volksunion/Liste D*, as a new party, and claimed to have over 3,000 membership applications.

Policies. The DVU has anti-semitic, white supremacist and neo-fascist policies.

Membership. It was reported to have over 1,000 members, mainly in southern Germany, in the early 1980s. At the time of the formation of his new party in March 1987, Frey said that the *Volksunion* itself would continue, as before, as an umbrella organization which currently claimed 16,000 members.

Publications. Deutsche National-Zeitung.

Associated organizations. The DVU has worked through organizations such as the *Aktion Deutsche Einheit* (AKON—German Unity Action) and the *Volksbewegung für Generalamnistie* (VOGA—People's Movement for a General Amnesty).

Deutsches Einheitsbewegung
German Unity Movement

Address. Postfach 911 268, 3000 Hanover 91

Leadership. Ingeborg Winkler (contact)

Orientation. Nationalist

History. This group was in correspondence with foreign nazi groups in 1984.

Policies. The group appears to advocate the reunification of Germany and the reconstitution of the Reich.

Europäische Arbeiterpartei—see Patriots for Germany.

Freiheitliche Arbeiterpartei (FAP)
Free German Workers' Party

Leadership. Martin Pape (chairman); Michael Kühnen

Orientation. Nazi

History. The FAP was formed in 1984 after the banning in December 1983 of ex-soldier Kühnen's previous organization, the *Aktionsfront Nationaler Sozialisten—Nationaler Aktivisten* (see above). That group, formed in 1982, had about 260 members at the time of its prohibition. The *Burgerinitiative Deutsche Arbeiterpartei* (BIDAP—Citizens' Initiative for a German Workers' Party), founded by Kühnen in February 1984, seems to have merged with the FAP, although its initial aim was reportedly the production of campaign materials for all ultra-right groups. In April 1984 Kühnen fled Germany to avoid prosecution, handing over control of his operation to his deputies Thomas Brehl and Christian Worch.

During 1984 the FAP absorbed the *Nationaler Bund Rhein-Westfalen*(NBRW) of Jürgen Mosler, a former member of the ANS and of the BIDAP.

The FAP has a following among the skinhead gangs of Hamburg and Hanover. Some 40 anti-nazi demonstrators and FAP members were arrested after violent clashes at an FAP rally in Stuttgart in mid-1986. Later in 1986 there were reports of an ideological struggle within the FAP between hard-liners supporting Kühnen, who had returned to serve a 3-year prison sentence imposed in January 1985 for distributing nazi propaganda, and Pape, who was said to represent a populist Strasserite tendency. (Arnd-Heinz Marx, a former ANS-NA member, was sentenced along with Kühnen to 2 years.)

Policies. The FAP is a traditional nazi party with a platform closely modelled on that of Hitler's NSDAP. It follows the confederalist "Europe of the nations" policy popular among European fascist groups.

Publications. In 1984 Kühnen started a magazine, *Die Neue Front*, which sought to rally support for a new far-right party through the creation of "readers' groups" around the country. It claimed to have 44 groups, with 600 members, by the end of the year.

Freiheitverein Hansa
Hanseatic Freedom League

Base. Hamburg

Orientation. White supremacist

History. This street-level fascist group was involved in anti-immigrant demonstrations in Hamburg in the mid-1980s. It may be linked with a *Hansa-Band* active around 1980.

German Nationalist Party

Address. PO Box 1057, Trenton, New Jersey 08608, United States

Leadership. Dwight B. McMahon (US representative)

Orientation. Nazi

History. The Party was formed in 1964 as *Aktion Oder-Neisse*, whose name referred to the post-war German-Polish border (rejected by pan-Germanists for its incorporation of Silesia in Poland); and it adopted its present name around 1983. It has functioned mainly as a point of contact between West German and German-American fascists, facilitating the exchange of propaganda materials, and it also seeks to explain the German nazi cause to the general US public.

Policies. The Party seeks the restoration of the pan-German Reich and an end to Holocaust reparations; it opposes communism, race-mixing and liberalism.

International affiliations. The Party has contacts with many US and foreign nazi groupings.

Hamburger Liste für Ausländerstopp
Hamburg List for a Halt to Foreigners

Address. Postfach 52 01 49, 2000 Hamburg 52

Orientation. Anti-immigrant

History. This group was registered as a political party in 1984.

Policies. It seeks legislation to prevent the influx of immigrants.

Hilfsgruppe Nationalistische Gefangenen (HNG)
Aid Group for Nationalist Prisoners

Address. c/o Christian Worch, Böhmerweg 21, 2000 Hamburg 13

Leadership. Henri Beier (honorary president); Christa Goerth (director); Wolfram Mook (assistant director)

Orientation. Neo-nazi

History. The HNG was formed in Frankfurt in 1980.

Policies. Its purpose is to provide moral support for those whom it regards as political prisoners held for their nationalist beliefs or for actions in furtherance of nationalist causes; to campaign for clemency and ultimately for the release of all such prisoners, and to provide assistance for prisoners' families.

Membership. 150 (1985).

Associated organizations. The HNG is not affiliated to a particular party but draws most of its support from those groups, such as the FAP, whose members most frequently find themselves in prison.

International affiliations. A similar group exists in Belgium.

Initiative Ausländerruckfuhrung
Foreigner Repatriation Initiative

Base. Bremen

Orientation. Anti-immigrant

History. Founded in 1984, the Initiative has participated in demonstrations against refugee and "guest worker" immigration. It succeeds similar groups active in the 1970s, such as the *Initiative für Auslander-Begrenzung* (Foreigner Limitation Initiative) and *Ausländer-Stop*. It may be linked to the *Aktion Ausländerrückführung—Volksbewegung gegen Überfremdung und Umweltzerstörung* (Action for the Repatriation of Foreigners—People's Movement against Foreign Infiltration and Environmental Destruction), led around 1983 by A.-H. Marx (Postfach 70 03 51,

54 Hanau 7), who is probably the Arnd-Heinz Marx who was sentenced to 2 years' imprisonment in January 1985 for producing propaganda for the outlawed ANS-NA.

Policies. The group opposes black and "Third World" immigration and calls for a programme of repatriation.

International Society for Human Rights

Base. Frankfurt

Leadership. Iwan Agrusow (founder); Robert Chambers (general secretary)

Orientation. Anti-communist

History. The Society was founded in West Germany in 1972 by anti-communist émigrés from Eastern Europe, including Agrusow, a former member of the Russian fascist NTS (see Soviet Union). Its chairwoman, Cornelia Gerstenmaier, resigned in 1976 after the Society was discredited by its spurious allegations that the Soviet Union was using slave labour to build a gas pipeline.

In the mid-1980s the Society became increasingly identified as an apologist for the South African regime's illegal occupation of Namibia. The South African ambassador was a guest of honour at the Society's annual meeting in Frankfurt in March 1986, as was Arturo de Fonseca, a representative of the Mozambican MNR. Later in March it held a conference in London on human rights in Namibia, concentrating on unsubstantiated allegations of the abuse of refugees by the SWAPO liberation movement. The conference was organized by its United Kingdom branch, which is chaired by David Atkinson (a Conservative Party Member of Parliament, and of the British-South Africa Parliamentary Group) and run by Harry Phibbs (of the Federation of Conservative Students).

Policies. The Society is primarily concerned with denouncing abuses of human rights under left-wing regimes.

Konservative Aktion
Conservative Action

Leadership. Ludek Pachmann (leader)

Orientation. Ultra-right

History. This group was formed in 1981 by Pachmann, a former Czechoslovakian chess champion. Other prominent members include Gerhard Löwenthal, a well-known television commentator, and Prof Golo Mann, an historian.

The concerns of the group have moved gradually from nationalism and opposition to immigration, towards an open identification with fascism. In June 1983 serious rioting followed a Conservative Action rally in Berlin. It organized a rally in November 1985, partly in order to call for the release of Rudolf Hess; an elderly man was reported to have died of a heart attack during scuffles outside the meeting.

Policies. The group seeks to halt the "decline of the German nation", which it attributes to the presence of non-white immigrants and to the availability of abortion. It also forms part of the national movement to free Rudolf Hess, and has called for the readoption of the full version of the *Deutschlandlied* national anthem, including the "*Deutschland über alles*" lines dropped after the war.

Membership. The group claims to have 45,000 members.

Kritik Verlag
Critic Press

Address. 2341 Mohrkirch, Krämersteen

Leadership. Thies Christophersen (editor)

Orientation. Nationalist

History. This publishing company was producing a range of right-wing material in the early 1980s. Christophersen, a former SS member, is a leading historical revisionist, responsible for Holocaust-denial works such as *The Auschwitz Lie*. In 1976 he was convicted in Denmark of publishing nazi propaganda; he received a nine-month sentence in West Germany in 1981 for a similar offence, but evaded arrest until 1983.

Publications. *Die Bauernschaft* (The Peasantry), a right-wing ruralist "patriotic journal" circulating among German and foreign nazis in 1984-85.

Liberation Commando Rudolf Hess

Orientation. Neo-nazi guerrilla group

History. A bomb was set off by this group on Oct. 23, 1986 in the offices of Spandau prison, West Berlin, which housed Rudolf Hess, the last surviving member of the wartime Nazi leadership. The release of Hess, convicted in 1946 and moved to Spandau in 1966, had long been a demand of West German and other neo-nazi groups, and had increasingly been advocated by non-nazi politicians; of the four powers controlling West Berlin only the Soviet Union continued in 1987 to maintain that Hess should remain in prison for life. After the death of Hess in August 1987, aged 93, neo-nazis were involved in demonstrations at his funeral.

In an earlier incident two West German neo-nazis had in February 1985 forced their way into the prison's driveway to give nazi salutes and shout slogans calling for Hess's release.

Nation Europa
European Nation

Address. Postfach 670, 8630 Coburg

Orientation. Neo-nazi

History. Founded in the late 1940s by Arthur Erhardt, a former SS officer, this magazine achieved a wide circulation among West European fascists and was an important platform and point of contact for surviving nazi and fascist leaders from Germany, Britain, France and elsewhere. In the 1960s Ehrhardt was a contributing editor of *Western Destiny*, a journal published by leading US racist Roger Pearson (see Council for Social and Economic Studies, United States).

Policies. The magazine promotes the widest possible degree of collaboration among nationalist and fascist groupings in West Germany and Western Europe.

Associated organizations. *Nation-Europa-Freunde*, readers' groups.

International affiliations. The magazine does not appear to be linked with similarly named groups or journals in France or Belgium.

Nationaldemokratische Partei Deutschlands (NPD)
National Democratic Party of Germany

Address. Postfach 2881 (Rötestrasse 4), 7000 Stuttgart 1

Leadership. Martin Mussgnug (president)

Orientation. Neo-nazi

History. The NPD was founded in 1964 by Adolf von Thadden and other former supporters of the Hitler regime. In the *Bundestag* elections of 1965 it won 2 per cent of the vote and in 1969 won 4.3 per cent; its support declined through the 1970s, and in 1983 it won only 91,095 votes (0.2 per cent of the total). It never secured representation at federal level, although it won over 50 seats in seven *Landtag* elections in the late 1960s.

A split in the NPD in 1967 resulted in the formation of the National People's Party. Von Thadden resigned as leader at a party congress in 1971, but the NPD survived and remains in existence as probably the largest ultra-right party in Germany. In late 1981 Heinz Lembke, a member of the NPD and associate of Manfred Roeder, was arrested and committed suicide; evidence which he had given led to the discovery of 31 arms caches.

In 1985 a leading official of the party was arrested for espionage on behalf of East Germany. In the same year an anti-fascist demonstrator was accidentally killed by police at a demonstration against the NPD; the police were later reported to have called for the banning of the NPD. In the 1984 elections to the European Parliament the group won 0.6 per cent of the vote, and in the 1985 Saarland Diet elections it won 0.7 per cent, a share which it held in the 1987 general election.

Sixteen party sympathizers, and two anti-fascists, were arrested in Herne in May 1986 after violence during an NPD congress. There had been serious street violence at other NPD congresses and rallies, notably in Frankfurt in September 1985 (when one protestor was killed), in Fallingbostel in October 1983, in Bochum in May 1983, in Nuremberg in March 1982 and in Philippsthal, near the East German border, in June 1980.

Policies. The NPD, which does not accept its widespread description as a neo-nazi party, calls for an end to immigration and for the reunification of West and East Germany. It also espouses strong law-and-order policies and an aggressively anti-communist foreign policy.

Membership. It was reported in 1985 to have 15,000 members. Another press report a year later suggested that the party was in decline, having 6,000 or fewer paid-up members.

Publications. Klartext, monthly; *Deutsche Stimme.*

Associated organizations. The Party has a youth branch, the *Junge Nationaldemokraten* (JN), which claims 6,000 members; there is also a *Nationaldemokratische Schülergemeinschaft* for school students and a *Nationaldemokratischer Hochschulbund* in the universities. The existence in the armed forces of an illegal *Nationaldemokratischer Soldatenbund* has also been reported. At least two NPD members have been tried for crimes committed in the name of the *Braunschweiger Gruppe*.

Nationale Volksfront
National People's Front

Base. Rüsselheim

Orientation. Neo-nazi

History. The Front was founded in 1984. No other information is available.

Publications. *Eiserne Front*.

Nationalsozialistische Deutsche Arbeiterpartei - Auslandorganisation (NSDAP-AO)—see United States.

Organization der Ehemaligen SS-Angehörigen (Odessa)
Organization of Former SS Members

Orientation. Nazi

History. This organization, which may now be defunct, was established in the closing stages of the war as a means of securing the futures of war criminals belonging to the SS, an elite section of the Nazi forces, which was declared in the Nuremburg trials to be a criminal rather than a military organization. Details of its membership and activities are not widely known, but it is believed to have assisted many ex-SS men to settle in South America and elsewhere with adequate funds to purchase new identities, immunity from state harassment and a means of subsistence. It is thought to have relied on the support of local nazi and neo-nazi groups throughout the world, and was based in Madrid.

A leading figure in the Odessa network, Hans-Ulrich Rudel, was instrumental in finding Josef Mengele—the Auschwitz "Angel of Death"—a new home in Paraguay, where the Stroessner dictatorship granted him full citizenship (revoked in the 1970s after international protests). Rudel, an unrepentant nazi who died in late 1982, had been involved with Otto Skorzeny in organizing Odessa and in 1953 was associated with Dr Walter Neumann's neo-nazi coup plot in West Germany; he was subsequently involved in the *Deutsche Reichspartei*, a precursor of the NPD.

Patriots for Germany

Address. Adolfsallee 17, 6200 Wiesbaden

Leadership. Helga Zepp-LaRouche (leader); Anno Hellenbroich (deputy leader); Paul Goldstein, Warren Hamerman

Orientation. LaRoucheist

History. This group was launched in 1986 by the Lyndon LaRouche organization, which is centred on the National Democratic Policy Committee (United States). The group is essentially a reorganized version of the German section of the European Labor Party (*Europäische Arbeiterpartei— EAP*), founded in Germany in late 1974 by Helga Zepp Ljustina, who had founded the European Labor Committees in Dusseldorf in 1973 as the first LaRoucheist organization in Europe. (She married LaRouche in 1977.)

The EAP won 0.1 per cent of the vote in the federal elections of 1976; in 1983 it won 15,000 votes. In mid-1986 Patriots for Germany won 11,300 votes (0.3 per cent) in the Lower Saxony *Landtag* elections. Among its supporters in Germany are Gen. Paul Albert Scherer, who was dismissed for criminal activities while head of military intelligence in 1977, and Adml. Adolf Zenker, a war veteran and post-war naval commander.

The ideological peculiarity of the group is reflected in the fact that the EAP was listed by the German counter-intelligence service as a Soviet front until 1976. In the 1980s, despite its increasing identification as a quasi-fascist movement, the movement has received no attention from the service. (Coincidentally, the head of the service from 1983 to 1985 was Herbert Hellenbroich, brother of Anno and brother-in-law of the head of an academy linked to the EAP.)

The substantial means of the group and its associates in West Germany and elsewhere are said to come from public donations and subscriptions. The parent body in the United States has derived much of its income, according to the US Federal Bureau of Investigation, from a massive fraud perpetrated against credit-card holders.

Policies. Like its parent body, the group espouses a painfully complex conspiracy theory of world history, with LaRouche cast as leader of the progressive forces in the political, economic and social fields, and most prominent statespeople identified as drug dealers, crypto-communists, nazis, homosexuals, CIA agents, KGB agents or any combination thereof. (In the 1970s the EAP called the then leader of the Social Democrats, Willy Brandt, a CIA agent; he won a US$10,000 libel award.) The group also favours European unification, the rapid development of the Third World, based on nuclear power, and the "Star Wars" space weaponry plans, and it opposes the Soviet Union, the Club of Rome, the Trilateral Commission, Jewish bankers, the drugs trade and the environmentalist Green party.

Membership. 250 to 300 (government estimate, 1984); 2,000 (press estimate, 1986).

Publications. The group contributes to LaRouche's *Executive Intelligence Review,* which is published in the United States and the United Kingdom, and to *Fusion,* which supports the European Labor Party.

Associated organizations. Zepp-LaRouche also heads the Hanover-based Schiller Institute, which was founded in 1984, supposedly in order to foster links between West Germany and the United States. The group's publishing house, also based in Wiesbaden, trades as *Spuren und Motive.* LaRouche's New Solidarity International Press Service is also represented in West Germany, and the group also runs the Club of Life, founded in the early 1980s, and the *Private Akademie für Humanistische Studien,* founded in 1977.

International affiliations. Patriots for Germany maintains links with the European Labor Party groups in Belgium, Denmark, France, Italy and Sweden, and describes itself as a "co-thinker" of the National Democratic Policy Committee (United States).

Radio Free Europe/Radio Liberty (RFE/RL)

Address. Headquarters: 1201 Connecticut Avenue NW, Washington, DC 20036, USA; *studios*: Munich

Telephone. Headquarters (Washington): (202) 457 6900

Leadership. Eugene V. Pell (president of RFE-RL); Malcolm S. Forbes Jr (chairman of broadcasting board); Prof Nicholas Vaslef (Radio Liberty director); Gregory Wierzynski (RFE director)

Orientation. Anti-communist

History. Radio Liberty and its sister station, Radio Free Europe, were founded in 1949 and 1951 as secret tools of the US Central Intelligence Agency (CIA) at the height of the Cold War, with the aim of broadcasting propaganda to the Soviet Union and Eastern Europe. They were originally run by front organizations called the National Committee for a Free Europe and the American Committee for Liberation from Bolshevism. The CIA link, long suspected, was admitted in the early 1970s, when the stations were reorganized. During the early 1980s there developed a struggle within the stations' staff between hard line anti-communist émigrés, including some accused of anti-semitic and anti-democratic attitudes, and those favouring an appearance of moderation and independence. About 75 per cent of the staff of the radio stations are drawn from the East European émigré communities.

Both Radio Liberty and Radio Free Europe are now overt, rather than covert, tools of the US government, since both, though nominally forming a private corporation, are controlled by a US staff reporting to a Board for International Broadcasting appointed by the US President. The funding for both stations (US$168 million proposed for 1987) comes from the US budget, with a small amount also coming from private sector donations.

Radio Liberty broadcasts full-time to the Soviet Union in a number of languages, including Russian. Its programming includes both "news" programmes consistent with the foreign policy of the USA and feature material. Radio Free Europe broadcasts to other Eastern European countries, their combined total being over 1,000 hours per week in 21 languages.

Policies. The stations seek to ensure that US policy and Western influence reaches the Soviet and other East European populations.

Publications. Apart from their broadcasting output the stations jointly produce a number of bulletins and situation reports on Soviet and East European affairs.

Die Republikaner
The Republicans

Base. Bavaria

Leadership. Franz Schönhuber (leader); Harald Neubauer (general secretary)

Orientation. Right-wing nationalist

History. This grouping was formed in November 1983 by Ekkehard Voigt and Franz Handlos, both defectors from the *Bundestag* bloc of the conservative Christian Social Union (which dominates Bavarian politics and is allied at national level with the more centrist Christian Democratic Union). In early 1984 the *Bürgerpartei* (Citizens' Party) of Baden-Württemberg, led by Hermann Joseph Fredersdorf, merged with the Republicans.

In October 1986 the Republicans gained 342,000 votes, 3 per cent, in their first electoral test, the elections for the Bavarian Diet. Their leader is a former television personality sacked after revelations about his wartime SS membership; the party was described by the influential Swiss *Neue Zürcher Zeitung* as "heir to the NPD, the *Deutsche Volksunion*" and other right-wing groups.

Policies. The Republicans' election campaign opposed immigration, the grand bourgeoisie, asylum-seekers, the European Communities, trade unions and foreign "guest workers", and advocated pan-German nationalism and eventual reunification, law and order and right-wing social and economic policies.

Membership. The party claims 4,000 members, 80 per cent in Bavaria.

Publications. The general secretary of the party is a former editor of the *National-Zeitung*, a right-wing paper which supports the Republicans' philosophy.

International affiliations. The party compares itself to the French *Front national*.

Der Schulungsbrief
Educational Newsletter

Address. Box 21, Reedy, West Virginia 25270, United States

Leadership. Georg Dietz (editor)

Orientation. Nazi

History. This bulletin, which first appeared in Berlin in 1980, is produced by a German-American nazi group which imports and exports nazi propaganda, mainly from the USA to West Germany.

Policies. The bulletin follows traditional national socialist ideas.

Publications. Der Schulungsbrief, mainly directed at West German readers; *Liberty Bell*, for US readership.

Associated organizations. The bulletin is published by the US-based *NSDAP-Reichsleitung in Exil.*

International affiliations. Like the NSDAP-AO, this group appears to co-operate with the World Union of National Socialists and with what is now the New Order party (United States).

Silesian Compatriots' Association

Leadership. Herbert Hupka (chairman)

Orientation. Nationalist

History. This organization was formed by ethnic Germans forced to leave Silesia when that region was incorporated into Poland at the end of the war. It is not a fascist group but its ultimate goal of re-establishing German control over Silesia is one which has the support of most West German fascist groups and the more nationalist elements in the mainstream parties. In 1983 the then Interior Minister of West Germany, Zimmermann, made a speech to the effect that the "German problem" was not confined to East and West Germany, and referring to the "expulsion and dispossession" of the Silesian Germans, thereby occasioning a diplomatic protest from Poland. In 1984-85 the group became embroiled in a controversy involving the Christian Democratic Chancellor, Helmut Kohl, whose sympathy with the Silesian cause led in 1984 to Soviet charges of irridentism, i.e. a desire to recover the territory. East German and Bulgarian leaders cancelled planned visits to West Germany in September 1984, and in November the Foreign Minister, Hans-Dietrich Genscher, was forced by pressure from within the Christian Democratic Party to cancel a planned visit to Poland. Kohl accepted an invitation to address the Compatriots' Association congress in June 1985, as the first Chancellor to do so, but in return the Association had to agree to tone down its slogan from "Forty years of banishment: Silesia remains ours" to "Forty years of banishment: Silesia remains our future in a Europe of free peoples". In January 1985 the Association's magazine published a controversial article by Thomas Finke describing a fictional West German drive to reconquer Silesia and to "liberate" much of Eastern Europe. Another article described as treasonable the acceptance (by treaty, in 1970) of the Oder-Neisse line as the permanent boundary between Poland and Germany. Despite criticism from the Social Democratic opposition, which described Kohl's contact with the Association as harmful to West Germany's foreign relations, the Chancellor duly addressed the congress in June, but his speech was was disrupted by young neo-nazis.

Policies. The Association seeks to defend the interests of Silesian Germans and their descendants, and hopes ultimately for the reincorporation of Silesia in a united German nation.

Publications. The Silesian.

Stosstrupp Nagold
Nagold Shock Troop

Orientation. Neo-nazi

History. The Troop was founded in 1984 by former members of Michael Kühnen's ANS-NA. Some of its members, who were mostly aged in the early twenties, were arrested in January 1985 in a series of raids in Baden-Württemberg, in which the police also seized arms and nazi propaganda produced by this group and by the similar *Stosstrupp Renchen* and *Karlsruher Front* groups.

Policies. It has white supremacist and national socialist policies.

Publications. Der Angriff (The Offensive).

Thule

Leadership. Pierre Krebs

Orientation. Right-wing

History. Krebs addressed a March 1985 conference of European new right groups. The gathering, in Switzerland, was organized by the *Cercle Proudhon.* No further information is available on Thule, which is thought to be a publishing company.

Unabhängige Arbeiterpartei - Deutsche Sozialisten (UAP)
Independent Labour Party - German Socialists

Address. Postfach 10 38 13 (Bergmühle 5), 4300 Essen 1

Leadership. Erhard Kliese (chairman)

Orientation. Neo-fascist

History. The UAP was founded in January 1962.

Policies. The Party opposes communism and capitalism, and also claims to be anti-fascist although its policies resemble those of many fascist groups; it seeks German reunification within a federal Europe, the reorganization of the economy on "German socialist" lines, and the reintroduction of military conscription.

Membership. 2,700 adult members; 3,100 youth members.

Publications. Reichs-Arbeiter-Zeitung, monthly, circulation 5,000.

Associated organizations. The Party's youth wing is called the *Blaue Adler Jugend* (Blue Eagle Youth).

Unabhängige Nachrichten (UN)
Independent News Service

Address. Postfach 400 215, 4630 Bochum 4

Leadership. Hans W. Schimmelpfeng, Eberhard Engelhardt, Werner Gebhardt, Dr Hans Riegelmann, Emil Maier-Dorn, Helmut Dieterle, others (main contributors)

Orientation. Neo-nazi

History. This organization was established in the late 1970s to disseminate nazi and racist propaganda under the guise of an independent news agency service. Its publications, which are widely circulated mainly among West European fascist groups, include ad hoc news releases and a bulletin. (The organization may be linked with a Prof Hagen Prehl of Bochum, whose name appeared on a European nazi address list in the early 1980s.)

Policies. The aim of the UN is to provide the widest possible access to fascist ideas and positions, which would otherwise be denied a hearing in the "liberal" mainstream media.

Publications. Most UN publications are monthly A5-sized broadsheets entitled *Unabhängige Nachrichten* or *Unfreie Nation* with a subtitle to indicate the subject matter.

Associated organizations. The group gives extensive coverage to several neo-fascist groups in West Germany and elsewhere, such as Remer's *Deutsche Freiheitsbewegung*; the anti-immigrant *Aktion Deutschland den Deutschen* (Germany for the Germans Action Group, Postfach 1566 (GD), 6940 Weinheim); *Kreis Heilbronner Bürger* (Postfach 2443, 7100 Heilbron); Udo Walendy's revisionist history press; the *Deutsche Rechtsschutzkreis* and the *Unabhängige Freundreskreise* (both at the same address as UN).

Unabhängiger Wählerkreis Würzburg
Würzburg Independent Voters' League

Base. Würzburg

Orientation. Neo-nazi

History. This group was banned by the Bavarian Interior Minister in 1984 on the grounds that it was a reincarnation of another fascist group, the AAR, which had been banned in December 1983. It is not clear whether the group is connected with the ultra-right Independent Voters' Association which arose in Schleswig-Holstein before the 1987 general election.

Policies. The stated purpose of the group, which may be defunct, was to provide a non-party forum for discussions among right-wing electors.

Uwe Berg Verlag

Address. Tagendorfer Strasse 6, 2096 Toppenstedt

History. This publishing company was selling old and new national socialist books and memorabilia in the early 1980s.

Verlag für Volkstum und Zeitgeschichtsforschung
History and Nationality Studies Press

Address. Hochstrasse 6, Postfach 1643, 4973 Vlotho

Leadership. Udo Walendy

Orientation. Historical revisionist

History. This publishing house, run by leading German revisionist Walendy, was active from the early 1980s.

Policies. The Press's publications seek to demonstrate that the Holocaust was a myth, and otherwise to further a pro-nazi interpretation of recent history.

Publications. The main output of the firm is a series of booklets under the imprint *Historische Tatsachen* (Historical Facts).

International affiliations. Walendy is an editorial advisor to the US Institute for Historical Review.

Volkssozialistische Bewegung Deutschlands - Partei der Arbeit (VSBD-PdA)
People's Socialist League of Germany - Party of Labour

Address. Brunhildenstrasse 28, 8014 Neuberg, Munich

Leadership. Friedhelm Busse (leader)

Orientation. Nazi

History. This group was founded by Busse in 1971 as the *Partei der Arbeit* after a split in the NPD; it adopted its present name in 1975. In 1980 a member, Franz Schubert, left to form the *Volkssozialistische Gruppe*; in December, while attempting to smuggle arms from Switzerland, he killed two Swiss border guards and then killed himself. Busse (who was born in 1929 and arrived as a refugee from East Germany in 1953) was imprisoned for six months in 1981 for inciting racial hatred.

The VSBD-PdA was banned, and the homes of many of its supporters raided, in January 1982, three months after the death of two members and the arrest of three, including Busse, during an attempted bank robbery. The trial of these three and of two other VSBD-PdA members, including one Frenchman, opened in June 1983; all received lengthy prison sentences and the VSBD-PdA may now be defunct.

Policies. The group has put forward straightforward national socialist policies, emphasising extreme anti-semitism.

Membership. In 1981 the VSBD-PdA reportedly had 40 members in Bavaria and about 50 elsewhere in West Germany. By early 1982 its membership was reportedly 120.

Publications. *Der Bayerische Löwe* (The Bavarian Lion); *Der neue Beobachter* (The New Observer), edited by J. Brandt.

Associated organizations. The youth branch of the VSBD-PdA is the *Junge Front*. A splinter group, the *Volkssozialistische Bewegung Hessens*, led by Wolfgang Koch, printed a new version of Goebbels' propaganda paper, the *Völkischer Beobachter* (National Observer), in Britain around 1980.

International affiliations. Among foreign nazi groups with which the VSBD-PdA has been in contact was the FANE (France), now superseded by the FNE, and other groups in France, Belgium, the United Kingdom, Canada, Austria, Italy and Switzerland.

Wehrsportgruppe Hess
Hess Military Sports Group

Orientation. Nazi

History. This group, named after Hitler's imprisoned deputy, was one of those claiming responsibility for the Berlin disco bombing in 1986 which prompted the US government to stage its air raid on Libya.

Wehrsportsgruppe Hoffmann (WSG Hoffmann)
Hoffmann Military Sports Group

Leadership. Karl-Heinz Hoffmann (founder and leader)

Orientation. Neo-nazi paramilitary group

History. Hoffmann (born in 1938) founded the group in 1974 as a training organization for ultra-right militants, and based it in a castle near Erlangen. He was convicted of assaulting students in 1977 and of wearing a Nazi uniform in 1979.

The group was banned as subversive in January 1980, and quantities of arms were captured in police raids. After a series of neo-nazi crimes including the September 1980 bombing of the Munich beer festival, in which two of the group's members were implicated, Hoffmann was arrested but was later released; with a dozen of his followers he moved to Beirut (Lebanon) and became involved with Palestinian guerrillas. The group was known there as the *WSG-Ausland*.

(Of those who went to Lebanon, Franz Joachim Bojarsky and Klaus Hubel were arrested in Italy in January 1982, and arms were seized; Odfried Hepp, who had also belonged to the Young Nationalists group, was arrested in France in 1985 with two others in connection with attacks carried out in the name of the Lebanese-based Palestinian Liberation Front. In February 1987 Hepp was extradited to West Germany on charges arising from bank robberies and attacks on US military installations in 1982.)

Hoffmann was arrested again in June 1981 but was eventually acquitted on June 30, 1986, after an earlier trial had been aborted, of inciting the murder of a Jewish publisher and another person killed in 1980 by Hoffmann's lieutenant, Uwe Behrendt (who apparently killed himself in Lebanon in 1981). Hoffmann was, however, sentenced to 9 years' imprisonment for offences including forgery, illegal possession of arms and the kidnapping and torture of one of his followers. An accomplice, Franziska Birkmann, was sentenced to six months. The group is probably now inactive.

Policies. In a 1977 interview Hoffmann said, "I am not interested in today's democracy in Germany... A dictatorship with the right man in charge can do anything for a people."

Membership. The group had at one time as many as 800 members, according to the security police; other sources placed its maximum strength at less than 500.

Publications. *Kommando*

Associated organizations. Among the many neo-nazi paramilitary groups which were formed along the lines of the WSG Hoffmann were the *Wehrsportgruppe Erhardt* (probably named in honour of the post-war nazi leader Arthur Erhardt), the *Wehrsportsgruppe Nordland*, the *Wehrsportsgruppe Ruhrgebiet* (two of whose members, including former NPD youth leader Joachim Grönig, were imprisoned on arms charges in July 1981) and the *Wehrsportsgruppe Schlageter*. The WSG Hoffmann was supported by the *Freundeskreis zur Forderung der Wehrsportsgruppe Hoffmann* (Circle of Friends for the Promotion of the WSG Hoffmann).

Weltbund gegen Geschichtsverfälschung
World Union against the Falsification of History

Leadership. Carlus Baagoe

Orientation. Historical revisionist

History. As part of the international historical revisionist movement, the Union, which was active in 1984, has produced materials denying the facts of the Nazi Party's programme for the extermination of European Jewry.

Policies. The group argues that a Jewish conspiracy has succeeded in creating the "Holocaust myth" in order to discredit nationalism, and that steps must be taken to set the record straight.

Weltunion der Nationalsozialisten—see World Union of National Socialists (Denmark and United States).

Wiking Jugend
Viking Youth

Address. Brockenberg 5a, 519 Stolberg

Leadership. W. Nahrath

Orientation. Nazi

History. A sort of scouting organization for national socialists, this group was formed in West Germany in the 1970s and quickly spread to other Western countries. It remained active in the mid-1980s.

Policies. The group organizes camps and indoctrination activities for under-25-year-olds on a non-party basis.

International affiliations. There have been more or less successful attempts to establish Viking Youth branches in Australia, Belgium, France, the Netherlands, New Zealand, Norway, South Africa, Spain and Switzerland.

Wir Selbst
We Ourselves

Address. Postfach 168, 5400 Koblenz

Orientation. National revolutionary

History. This ultra-nationalist journal, the name of which may be derived from that of the Irish republican group *Sinn Féin*, was being published in the mid-1980s.

Policies. The journal opposes "US and Soviet imperialism" and calls for a strong, reunified Germany in a neutral Europe.

International affiliations. The journal circulates widely among foreign fascist groups.

Defunct organizations

Aktion Neue Rechte: the ANR (New Right Action) was formed in the early 1970s and was active at least until the early 1980s. It had neo-nazi policies and was in contact with the World Anti-Communist League (see South Korea) under the League's then pro-fascist leadership in the 1970s.

Bewegung Drittes Reich; the Third Reich Movement was a hitherto-unknown, and possibly non-existent, group in whose name responsibility was unconvincingly claimed for the murder in May 1981 of the Hesse economics minister, H.-H. Karry, who was generally believed to have been killed by the ultra-left Revolutionary Cells.

Das Braune Bataillon: this nazi magazine (The Brown Battalion), which apparently derived its name from the colour of the uniform of the pre-war SA group of Nazi Party street fighters, was produced in 1979 by Henry Beier and Wolfgang Koch, who were consequently imprisoned for 18 and 13 months respectively in May 1980.

Braunschweiger Gruppe: five members of the Brunswick Group, founded in 1977 as a paramilitary organization along the lines of the WSG Hoffmann, were imprisoned for terms ranging up to 5 years in February 1981 for causing explosions in Hanover in October 1977 and for arms offences. The longest sentence went to the group's leader, Paul Otte.

Bürgeraktion gegen Chaos: founded in August 1981, this ultra-right youth group sought to mobilize the "silent majority" against a left-wing squatters' movement which had occupied buildings in Berlin.

Deutsche Artgemeinschaft: the German Race Society was formed after the war by Dr Wilhelm Kusserow, a former SS officer who adopted the Odinist philosophy espoused by nazi leader Erich Ludendorff. In the late 1960s Kusserow was associated with the Northern League (see Netherlands), as was the nazi race theorist Hans Günther.

Deutsche Partei: the DP (German Party) was a conservative grouping based in Lower Saxony within which an ultra-nationalist fringe became increasingly influential in the 1950s and '60s.

Deutsche Reichspartei: the DRP (German Reich Party) was one of the most important formed by nazi revivalists in the post-war years. Established in 1946, mainly by supporters of the old German Nationalist Party, as the *Deutsche Rechtspartei* (German Right Party), it contested the 1949 parliamentary elections in an alliance with the *Deutsche Konservatieve Partei* (DKP), jointly securing five seats with 1.8 per cent of the vote. It maintained its support at around 1 per cent nationally until its dissolution in 1965; its membership was never greater than 10,000. The leader of the DRP was Adolf von Thadden, leader from 1967-71 of the NPD, and its US representative was H. Keith Thompson (of the American Renaissance Party), who was reported to be assisting ex-SS Gen. Otto Ernst Remer's efforts to establish a new German nazi party in the mid-1980s (see *Deutsche Freiheitsbewegung*).

Gesellschaft für Freie Publizistik: the GFFP (Society for Free Journalism) was affiliated to the South Korean-based World Anti-Communist League in the late 1970s.

Heidelberg Circle: a group of right-wing academics who produced an anti-immigration manifesto in the early 1980s.

Kampfbund Deutscher Soldaten: the German Soldiers' Fighting League was founded in the late 1970s by Erwin Ernst Schönborn, who was deported from Austria in February 1982.

Nationalsozialistische Antikomintern-Jugend: the National Socialist Anti-Comintern Youth was founded in 1979 by Volker Heidel, who received a ten-month prison sentence in October 1980 for issuing nazi propaganda.

Nordische Zeitung: this neo-nazi newspaper was published in the late 1960s and early 1970s by Norbert Seibart, who joined the Northern League (see Netherlands) along with other leading German fascists.

Sozialistische Reichspartei: the SRP (Socialist Reich Party) was a fascist group formed in 1949 by ex-members of the DRP, including Remer (see *Deutsche Freiheitsbewegung*). By 1950 the SRP, with 10,000 members, was the largest ultra-right grouping, but it was banned, along with its *Reichsfront* auxiliary grouping, in 1951-52.

Volkisch-Nationaler Solidaritätsbund: this small fascist grouping, formed in 1981 or '82 by Horat Helmut Gebhard, joined Kühnen's ANS-NA in August 1983.

Wirtschaftliche Aufbau-Vereinigung: the WA-V (Economic Reconstruction Union) was one of the first neo-fascist parties in Germany; it secured 12 seats with 2.9 per cent of the vote (in Bavaria) in the 1949 federal elections.

Wolfspack—Sturm 12: a Koblenz-based nazi "defence sports group" founded in January 1983 and banned in April, by which time it had only seven members.

Other organizations

A vast number of ultra-right groupings, often with but a handful of members, appear and disappear every year in West Germany, and few dissolutions are reported unless they result from state action. It would not be possible to list in this chapter every group which has been active in the post-war era, nor to distinguish with certainty between those which are active and those which are defunct. The following list mentions a selection of groups which are not definitely known to be defunct, covering a spectrum of concerns from anti-communism to racism and outright nazism, and concentrating on those which have more recently been reported as active.

Action Front for National Priorities; *Aktion Deutsche Einheit*(Akon—Action for German Unity); *Aktion Deutscher Osten* (Action for the East of Germany), active around 1979; *Aktion Deutsches Radio und Fernsehen*(German Radio and Television Action), which sought to counter an alleged left-wing bias in broadcasting; *Aktion Junge Rechte* (Young Right-Wing Action, active around 1979); *Aktion Oder* (possibly the same as *Aktion Oder-Neisse*—see German Nationalist Party); *Aktionsfront der Nationalisten*(Nationalists' Action Front); *Aktionsgemeinschaft Nationales Europa*(European National Action Society), active around 1980; *Aktionsgemeinschaft Nationaler Sozialisten* (National Socialists' Action Society), active at least until 1979; *Aktionskomitee Peter Fechter* (active around 1979); the *All-German Fighting Group*; the *Alster-Gesprachkreis* (Alster Discussion Group), active around 1979; *Amnesty National*, a pressure group working around 1980 for nationalist and fascist "political prisoners"; *Anti-Holocaust-Aktion*, which denied the facts of the genocide against Jews and sought to counter "Holocaust propaganda"; the *Antikomintern Jugend*, active in the late 1970s, which around 1980 was also known as the *National Sozialistische Antikomintern-Jugend*; the *Arbeitskreis Deutscher Sozialismus*(German Socialism Working Group, "German socialism" being an early euphemism for Nazism); the *Arbeitskreis für Lebenskunde der Ludendorff-Bewegung* (Biology Working Group of the Ludendorff Movement, and the associated *Bund für Gotterkenntnis* (Religious Knowledge League); the *Arbeitskreis Südwest*; the *Arbeitskreis Volkstreuer Verbände* (AVV—Working Group of Ethnically Loyal Groupings) and its subsidiary, the *Freundeskreis für Jugendarbeit im AVV* (Circle of Friends for Youth Work in the AVV).

Belsen Scene; the *Bio-political League*; *Black Rebel*, a nazi magazine published from England by Gerhard Töpfer; the *Braune Hilfe Gau Nordmark*; the *Brown Action Front*; the *Bund Albert Leo Schlageter*, active around 1979, which may be the same as the Albert Schlageter Action Group; the *Bund Deutscher Nationaler Sozialisten* (League of German National Socialists), active around 1980; the *Bund für Deutsche Einheit—Aktion Oder-Neisse*, probably the same as the group which became the German Nationalist Party; the *Bund für Deutsche Wiedervereinigung* (German Reunification League); the *Bund Hamburger Mädel* (Hamburg Lasses' League); the *Bund Heimattreuer Jugend* (Patriotic Youth League); the anti-immigrant *Bund RePatria*; the *Bureau for International Monarchist Relations* (Bahnhofstrasse 35, 7102 Weinsberg); the *Bürgergemeinschaft Hamburg* (Hamburg Citizens' Society); the late 1970s *Bürgerinitiative für die Todesstrafe, gegen Pornographie und Sittenverfall* (Citizens' Initiative for Capital Punishment and against Pornography and Moral Turpitude); the *Bürgerinitiative gegen Terrorismus und Fünf-prozent-Klausel* (Citizens' Initiative against Terrorism and the Five Per Cent Clause, i.e. the electoral law restricting parliamentary representation to parties gaining more than five per cent of the vote); the *Bürgerinitiative zur Wahrheitspflege* (Citizens' Initiative for the Protection of the Truth), and the *Bürger- und Bauerinitiative*(Citizens' and Peasants' Initiative).

The *Committee for the Extermination of Aliens*; the *Deutsch-Arabische Gemeinschaft* (German-Arab Society); the *Deutsch-Nationale Verteidigungsorganisation* (National German Defence Organization); the *Deutsch Völkische Gemeinschaft* (German National, or Racial, Society) and the *Deutsch Völkische Jugend*; the *Deutsche Akademie für Bildung und Kultur*(German Academy for Learning and Culture); the *Deutsche Aktionsfront*, formed around 1980; the *Deutsche Aktionsgemeinschaft für Nationale Politik*(German Action Society for National Policies, or for Nationalist Politics); the *Deutsche Arbeiterfront* (DAF—German Workers' Front) and the *Deutsche Arbeiterjugend* (publishing *Deutscher Kurier* until it was banned in 1983); the *Deutsche Arbeitskreis Witten*; the *Deutsche Block*; the *Deutsche Division für Naturpolitik*; the *Deutsche Freiheitsbewegung*, probably Remer's grouping, which called in 1983 for a German-Russian alliance (Allgäuerstrasse 1, 8954 Ebenhofen); the *Deutsche Gesellschaft für Erbegesundheitspflege* (German Association for the Protection of the Health of our Heritage); the *Deutsche Kulturegemeinschaft* (German Cultural Society); the *Deutsche Volksfront*; the *Deutsche Volkspartei*; *Deutscher Bewegung für Demokratie und Volks- und Umweltschutz* (German Movement for Democracy and Protection of the People and the Environment); the *Deutscher Freundeskreis* (Circle of German Friends); the *Deutsches Kulturwerk Europäisch Geistes* (German Cultural Work for the European Spirit); *Deutschland in Geschichte und Gegenwart* (Germany Yesterday and Today), and the *Deutschnational Volkspartei* (People's Party of the German Nation).

Editions Askania (3067 Lindhorst), a firm which in 1979 published the memoirs of Alsatian fascist leader Hermann Bickler; *Europa Korrespondenz* magazine; the *Europäische Kameradschaft* (European Comradeship Group); the *European Freedom Movement*, associated with Manfred Roeder; the *European National Union*; the *Europäische Volksbewegung* (European People's Movement), a probably-defunct Roeder front of the early '80s; *Fanfare* magazine, published from 1981 by H. Pauken of Mayen; the *Freiheitlicher Rat*(Freedom Council); the *Freiheitsbewegung Deutsches Reich* (German Reich Freedom Movement); the *Freikorps Saudi Arabia* and the *Freikorps Adolf Hitler*, which were in contact with Palestinian groups around 1978; the *Freundeskreis Denk Mit*; the *Freundeskreis Dicherstein Offenhausen*; the *Freundeskreis Filmkunst*; the *Front of National Soldiers*; *Gäck* magazine; *Gaeta*, a prisoners' support group; the *Gemeinschaft Ostdeutscher Grundeigentümer—Notverwaltung des Deutschen Ostens* (Society of East German Landowners—Provisional Government of Eastern Germany), and the *Landerrat der Notgemeinschaft des Deutschen Ostens* (States' Council of the Emergency Grouping of Eastern Germany); the *German Christian Association*; the *German Social Movement*; *Germania International*, and the possibly unconnected *Kulturring Germania*; the *Germanische Gemeinschaft* (Teutonic Society); the *Gesamtdeutsche Aktion* (All-German Action); the *Gesellschaft fur Biologische Anthropologie, Eugenik und Verhaltenforschung* (Association for Biological Anthropology, Eugenics and Behaviouristics), and the *Gesellschaft für Philosophische Studien*(Association for Philosophical Studies).

The *Hanau Group*; the *Hans Seidal Foundation*; the *Hansa-Band* (possibly linked to the *Freiheitverein Hansa*); the *Harting* group; a large number of veterans' groups, including the *Hilfsgemeinschaft auf Gegenseitigkeit der Soldaten der Ehemaligen Waffen-SS* (HIAG—Mutual Assistance Society for Soldiers of the Former Waffen-SS), publishing *Der Freiwillige*; the *Hilfsgemeinschaft Freiheit für Rudolf Hess* and the *Kampfbund Freiheit für Rudolf Hess*; the pro-apartheid *Hilfskomitee Südliches Afrika* (Aid Committee for Southern Africa) and the similar *Germany-South Africa Association*; the *Hochschulgruppe Pommern* (Pomeranian University Group); *Die Innere Front*, a journal; *Innere Sicherheit* (Internal Security); the *Jugendbund Adler* (Eagle Youth League); the *Jugendpresseverband Nordrhein-Westfalen* (North Rhine-Westphalia Youth Press Club); the *Junge Garde*; the *Junge Nationalsozialisten*; the *Junge Nationalsozialistische Deutsche Arbeiterpartei*; the *Jungnationalisten*, an NPD youth group led by Klaus Krause, and the *Jungstalhelm* (Steel Helmet Youth) named after a pre-war fascist group.

The *Kameradenkreisen* (Comrades' Circles); the *Kampfbund Horst Wessel*, named after an early Nazi "martyr"; the *Kampfgemeinschaft das Deutsches Nationalen Sozialismus*; the *Kampfgruppe Grosser Deutschland*(Greater Germany Fighting Group); the *Kampfgruppe Priem*; the *Kampfgruppe Schwarzwald* (Black Forest Combat Group); the *Kampfgruppe Zündel*, possibly named in honour of the Canadian-based fascist publisher Ernst Zündel; the *KLA*; the *Kommando* group; various unsuccessful *Ku Klux Klan* groups;

the *Legion Afrika*; the *Legion Kondor Kameradschaft*, founded by veterans of the Luftwaffe volunteers who fought for Franco in the Spanish war; the *Militanten Nationalsozialisten Regensburg*; the *MUT-Freundeskreis*, publishing *MUT* magazine (Postfach 1, 2811 Asendorf, or Postfach 20, 3091 Asendorf); a possibly fictitious *National Democratic Front for the Liberation of West Germany*, which claimed responsibility for bombing a British Army barracks in 1987; the *Nationale Deutsche Arbeiterpartei* (NDAP—German National Workers' Party) and the *Nationaldemokratische Arbeiterpartei*, the latter having merged in 1981 with the VSBD; the *Nationale Front* and the *Nationale Volksfront*; the *National-Europäische Union*; *Nationalrevoluzionäre Aktion* and Dieter Stockmeir's *Nationalrevoluzionäre Arbeiterfront*; several small groups simply calling themselves *Nationalsozialistische Deutsche Arbeiterpartei* after Hitler's *NSDAP*, including one led around 1980 by Wilhelm Kraus; the *NSDAP-IEM*; the *Nationalsozialistische Freiheitsbewegung* (National Socialist Liberation Movement); the *NS-Gruppe Schwarzwald* (Black Forest Nazi Group) and the *NS-Gruppe Wübbels*, the latter probably descended from the *NSDAP-Gruppen* of the mid-'70s; the *Nationalsozialistische Kampfgruppe Ostwestfalen-Lippe*(Eastern Westphalia—Lippe National Socialist Fighting Group); the *Nationalsozialistische Partei Deutschlands*; the *Nationalsozialistische Revoluzionäre Arbeiterfront* (NSRAF) of Gerhard Töpfer, and Albert Brinkman's probably-defunct *NS-Kurier*, published from the United States in the late 1970s.

The *Naturpolitische Volkspartei*; the *Neues Nationales Europa* (New Europe of the Nations) group; the *Nordischer Ring*; *Politischer Informations-Club*; the *Revolutionary Cells—Bruno Basic Section*; the *SA-Sturm 8 Mai*; the *Sache des Volkes—Nationalrevolutionäre Aufbau Organisation* (People's Cause—National Revolutionary Development Organization); *Samisdat Publications*, run from Canada by Ernst Zündel; the *Schillerbund—Deutscher Kulturverband*, named after the same writer who inspired the LaRoucheist Schiller Institute; the *Schutzbund für das Deutsche Volk* (German People's Defence League); the *Schwarzer Adler* (Black Eagle); the *SDAJ*; the *Soldatenkameradschaft Hans Ulrich Rudel*, a veterans' group named after a Luftwaffe pilot active in the neo-nazi movement; the *Soziale Demokratische Union*; the *Stahlhelm-Kampfbund für Europa* (Steel Helmet Fighting League for Europe), formed in 1951 and named after the 1918-33 *Stahlhelm* fascist group; the *Stille Hilfe Deutschland* (Silent Help for Germany); the *Storm Frankfurt* (effectively the Frankfurt section of the WSG Hoffmann); the *Sturmgruppe 7*; the monarchist *Tradition und Leben*(Tradition and Life) group, publishing *Erbe und Auftrag* (Bahnhofstrasse 35, 7102 Weinsberg), which has a significant following in the United States; the *Unabhängige Arbeiterpartei—Deutsche Sozialisten* (Independent Workers' Party of German Socialists); the student fascist *Unabhängiger Schülerbund*; the *Unabhängiger Wählerkreis—Arbeitskreis für Wiedereiningung und Volksgesundheit* (Independent Voters' Circle—Working Group for Reunification and National Wellbeing); the *Unabhängiges Zentrum Deutschlands*; the *Verein der Freunde des Deutschen Eisenbahn* (Union of Friends of the German Railway); the *Vereiningung Verfassungstreuer Kräfte*(Union of Constitutionalist Forces); the *Vertriebenen und Teilen der Union*(Partitioned and Dispossessed of the Union); the *Volkisch-Nationaler Solidaritätsbund*; the revisionist *Volksbewegung gegen Antideutsche Greuellügen* (People's Movement against Anti-German Atrocity Lies); the *Volksbund Deutscher Ring*; the *Volkssozialistische Deutsche Partei— Nationalrevolutionäre Bewegung*; the *Volkssozialistische Einheitsfront*(People's Socialist Unity Front); the *Volkssozialistische Gruppe*, active around 1980; *Der Weg* and *Die Wende* magazines, the latter (Postfach 1633, 5810 Witte) aimed at children; the *Werewolf Group*; and the *Zyklon-B Group*, named after the poison gas used in the concentration camp gas chambers.

Individuals

Rudolf Koch: this schoolteacher gained some notoriety in 1986 when he received a suspended prison sentence for telling pupils that the nazi Holocaust never happened and for making racist statements.

Ingeborg Schulte: together with Hans-Günther Fröhlich, Schulte produced a board game in 1983 called *Jew Don't Get Angry.* Samples were sent to Jewish organizations. The theme of the game was the extermination of the Jewish prisoners in each of six concentration camps. There followed a trial for incitement to racial hatred and in 1984 Schulte received a suspended prison sentence.

Dr Wilhelm Stäglich: a retired judge, he is an editorial advisor to the US-based Institute for Historical Review, which exists to deny the facts of the Holocaust. He has been convicted in West Germany of distributing anti-semitic material including his book *The Auschwitz Myth.*

Greece

capital: Athens   population: 10,000,000

Political system. Greece (the Hellenic Republic) has a unicameral legislature, whose number of seats varies between 200 and 300. This body, the *Vouli*, is elected by universal adult suffrage, and elects an executive President who in turn appoints a Prime Minister.

Recent history. Greece was occupied by nazi Germany during the Second World War, which was followed by a bloody four-year civil war between communists and pro-Western monarchists. A period of instability led to a military coup in 1967; the monarchy was abolished after another coup in 1973, but after the failure of the new regime's Cypriot policy a civilian government was installed in 1974 and a democratic republican Constitution was adopted in 1975. Greece elected its first socialist government in 1981, and re-elected it in 1985.

The evolution of the far right. There was very little fascist activity in pre-war Greece, although anti-semitic incidents occurred, notably at Salonika in 1931, and there was a right-wing military coup in 1936. There were right-wing monarchist and anti-communist movements. Greece was under Axis occupation during part of the Second World War, which was followed by a civil war in which right-wing monarchist forces defeated communists. Several ultra-right groups were active in the post-war era, including a clandestine military movement which attempted a coup in 1951 and conspired almost continually thereafter until the conditions for a successful takeover were present. A left-wing deputy was assassinated by right-wingers in 1963, and 11 ultra-right groups were banned in July 1964.

The April 1967 coup was supported by right-wing officers in the armed forces, with Col. Giorgios Papadopoulos as the leading figure. He became Prime Minister in December 1967, Regent in March 1972 and President in June 1973. The so-called "colonels' regime" was overthrown in a second coup in November 1973 and Papadopoulos was later tried and in 1975 was imprisoned for life for treason (a death sentence having been commuted). Various military conspiracies were uncovered in 1974-75. The French ultra-right leader, Jean-Marie Le Pen, attempted to visit Papadopoulos in prison in 1984, but he was refused entry. A conference of European right-wing parties, which was to have involved Le Pen, was banned by the Greek government in September 1986.

Active organizations

Ceniaio Ethnikistiko Kinema (ENEK)
United Nationalist Movement

Address. Filolau 147, Pangrati, Athens

Leadership. Nicholas Michaloliakos

Orientation. Nazi

History. This overtly-national socialist organization was active at least from 1981, when it entered into contact with foreign fascist groupings including the League of St George (United Kingdom) and the FNE (France).

Publications. Golden Dawn

EPEN
Greek National Political Society

Base. Athens

Leadership. Giorgios Papadopoulos (leader)

Orientation. Ultra-right

History. This party was formed in 1984 as the personal vehicle of the imprisoned ex-dictator, who was unable to stand for office because of the nature of his sentence. In 1984 it won one of Greece's 24 seats in the European Parliament. In its first general election, that of June 1985, it secured only 0.6 per cent of the poll (some 39,000 votes).

Policies. The EPEN advocates authoritarian government, nationalism and "Hellenic Christian ideals".

Membership. Some 5,000 people reportedly attended the meeting in January 1984 at which the party was launched.

International affiliations. The EPEN's sole Euro-MP sits with the Group of the European Right, which also includes 10 members of the French National Front, five of the Italian Social Movement and John Taylor of the Ulster Unionist Party.

Ethnikon Metapon
National Front

Address. 42 Odos Panepistimiou, Athens

Leadership. Stefanos Stefanopoulos (founder)

Orientation. Right-wing conservative

History. The Front was founded in October 1977 by Stefanopoulos, a former Prime Minister. It secured 6.8 per cent of the vote and four seats in that year's parliamentary election, but declined rapidly thereafter; it did not take part in the 1981 election and may now be extinct.

Policies. The Front espoused nationalist policies and sought inter alia an amnesty for imprisoned participants in the colonels' regime and the restoration of the monarchy.

4th of August Movement

Address. Makedonias 148, TT251, Thessalonika

Leadership. Demetrios Mylonas (leader); M. Michaelidis

Orientation. Nazi

History. The Movement, which takes its name from the date of the 1936 coup, was involved in numerous acts of violence in the aftermath of the colonels' regime; several of its members were arrested in 1977. Its leader in the 1970s was Kostas Pleuris, assisted by Demetrios Kapsalas and Nicolas Metaxas. The Movement remained active in the mid-1980s.

Policies. The Movement follows traditional national socialist policies. It seeks to make Greece the guardian of Europe against the "cruel and sub-human hordes" of Turks, Mongols and Asiatics.

International affiliations. The Movement is in contact with member parties of the World Union of National Socialists (see Denmark and United States).

Defunct organizations

National League of Greek Officers: one of several clandestine groupings of pro-coup elements to emerge in the aftermath of the colonels' regime, the League was active briefly in 1975.

New Order: this ultra-right group, linked with the similarly named Italian group banned in 1973, was active as a pro-government paramilitary organization in the final years of the military regime. In 1974, along with about two dozen groups formed by the ultra-right during military rule, it was granted provisional registration as a political party but it failed to participate in mainstream politics.

Organization to combat communism: the formation in Athens of a non-party anti-communist front was reported in March 1933.

Organization for National Recovery (or Restoration): more than 40 bombs were set off by this group in Athens on Dec. 17, 1978, in honour of the memory of a policeman killed two years earlier who had allegedly been employed as a torturer by the military regime.

Sacred Bond of Greek Officers: the IDEA was one of several ultra-right military fraternities established during the Second World War. One of its leaders was Giorgios Papadopoulos, who was involved in an unsuccessful coup attempt in 1951 and who led the 1967 coup and subsequent military government.

Other organizations

Other groups reportedly active on the Greek radical right in recent years have included the following: *Areioi*; *Axaioi*; the *Civil Defence Group*; *Demokratiki Enosis* (Democratic Union); *Ethnike Koinike Drave*; *Ethniki Laiko Komma*; the *National Democrats*; the *National Shock Group*; the *National Socialist Front*; the *Nationalist Patriots' Group*; the *New Anti-Communist Crusade*; the *X Group* and the *Young Militants' Group*.

Individuals

Dr John Phrantzes: the Greek correspondent of *The Spotlight*, journal of the anti-semitic Liberty Lobby (United States).

Guatemala

capital: Guatemala City   **population: 8,500,000**

Political system. The Republic of Guatemala has an executive President and a 100-seat Legislative Assembly, both directly elected by universal adult suffrage.

Recent history. Guatemala has been governed since independence in 1838 mainly by military dictators, mostly of the right. A progressive government was overthrown by US and local forces in 1954, and the next elected President was also deposed by a coup in 1963. Subsequent governments were installed by elections, some characterized by fraud and violence, in 1966, 1970, 1974 and 1978, but the 1982 presidential election was followed by a coup. There was widespread political violence in the 1970s and early '80s, with up to 60,000 people, mainly peasants and workers, killed by right-wing death squads, government forces and left-wing guerrillas.

Several attempted coups in 1982-83 culminated in the August 1983 overthrow of the military President, Efraín Ríos Montt, by a rival military faction. Democratization followed by means of Constituent Assembly elections in 1984, which were won by right-wing parties, and presidential and legislative elections in November 1985, won by the Christian Democratic Party.

The evolution of the far right. The 1954 coup installed a right-wing government under Col. Carlos Castillo Armas, who was assassinated three years later. That of 1963 installed Col. Enrique Peralta Azurdia of the right-wing National Liberation Movement (MLN), who ruled by decree until 1966. From the early 1960s right-wing paramilitary groups were used as part of an official strategy to combat left-wing influences among the peasantry and working class. The Méndez government of 1966-70 saw the establishment of at least three such groups. From 1970 the MLN was back in power, and right-wing death squads began a concerted campaign against urban and rural radicals. It was widely believed that successive MLN regimes under Gens. Carlos Araña Osorio and Kjell Laugerud García encouraged and protected the death squads, which were thought to have close links with the security forces.

The violence reached a peak in 1981 under Gen. Fernando Romeo Lucas García, who was elected to the presidency in 1978. The left withdrew from electoral politics and Gen. Ríos Montt seized power in 1982, after inconclusive presidential elections. Congress, the Constitution and all political parties were suspended. Despite the General's professed willingness to introduce reforms and to seek a dialogue with the left, killings and abuses of human rights continued, and the government lost much of its support due to Ríos Montt's increasing reliance on a small group of advisors and on a fundamentalist Protestant sect.

Gen. Oscar Humberto Mejía Victores overthrew the regime in 1983 and once again promises of reform were accompanied by continuing rural and urban terrorism mainly involving government and right-wing forces. The MLN, in coalition with the Authentic Nationalist Centre (CAN), won the largest number of seats (but not of votes) in the Constituent Assembly election of 1984, but the 1985 elections showed a substantial decline in support for the extreme right.

Active organizations

Ejército Secreto Anticomunista (ESA)
Secret Anti-Communist Army

Orientation. Ultra-right death squad

History. The ESA was founded in 1976 and has carried out a very large number of assassinations; the Jesuit order claimed in 1980 that the ESA had killed 3,252 leftists, peasant leaders, students and others during the first ten months of 1979. The group has from time to time published death lists naming supposed communists and subversives.

Policies. The ESA and similar groups seek to diminish support for the left by the annihilation of those whom it identifies as left-wingers and by intimidating others into exile or into silence.

Associated organizations. The ESA is widely regarded as the military wing of the MLN, led by Mario Sandóval Alarcón.

International affiliations. A group of the same name, and using similar tactics, was operating in El Salvador in the early 1980s.

Frente de Unidad Nacional (FUN)
National Unity Front

Leadership. Col. Enrique Peralta Azurdia, Gabriel Girón Ortiz

Orientation. Ultra-right

History. The FUN was formed in 1977, but became important only after it was joined in 1978 by Peralta, leader of the 1963 coup, who had come second in the 1978 presidential election as the MLN candidate. The party contested the 1982 election as part of the centre-right coalition which won the largest number of votes; in 1984, however, it contested the Constituent Assembly elections in its own right, but its sole representative, Santos Hernández, almost lost his seat when he was found to be illiterate. He was recruited by the MLN but was assassinated some weeks later.

The FUN gave its support to Sisniega of the PUA in the 1985 elections.

Policies. The FUN is nationalist, anti-communist and in favour of private enterprise.

Movimiento de Liberación Nacional (MLN)
National Liberation Movement

Address. 5a Calle 1-20, Zona 1, Guatemala City

Leadership. Mario Sandóval Alarcón (leader)

Orientation. Ultra-right

History. The MLN was formed in 1960, but derives from the *Movimiento de Liberación* which carried out the US-backed coup of 1954. In 1963 it staged a coup (under Col. Peralta, now of the FUN), and in 1970 and 1974 it won presidential elections for Col. (later Gen.) Carlos Araña Osorio and Gen. Kjell Laugerud García. Peralta lost the 1978 election and Sandóval, who had been Laugerud's vice-president (and an enthusiastic supporter of the World Anti-Communist League—see South Korea), lost that of 1982. The party supported the Ríos Montt coup but turned against the resulting ultra-Protestant regime, with some members forming the PUA.

In 1984 the MLN allied itself with Araña's new party, the centre-right *Central Auténtica Nacionalista* (CAN), and later with the PID, another centre-right grouping which had supported MLN candidates in 1970 and 1974. It contested the 1985 elections with the support of the PID, winning 6.3 per cent of the vote and six seats in the Assembly (while the PID had an identical share of votes and seats and the CAN, the leadership of which had passed to Mario David García, had 6.3 per cent but only one seat).

Policies. The MLN was in power during the build-up of the death squad campaign in the 1970s. It is closely identified with the death squads' goal of eliminating urban and rural left-wing opposition, and has described itself as "the party of organized violence". The party professes authoritarian and strongly anti-communist policies.

Membership. 95,000.

Associated organizations. Of the many Guatemalan right-wing guerrilla groups, the MLN is particularly identified with the ESA and the EM. The party leadership does not publicly accept that there is any connection. The MLN is also close to the Guatemalan section of the World Anti-Communist League (see South Korea), and Sandóval has attended at least one recent WACL congress (in the United States, in 1985) despite the purge of ultra-rightists from the Latin American regional WACL.

Nueva Derecha
New Right

Orientation. Ultra-right

History. This grouping appeared in 1984. It does not appear to have achieved a significant popular following.

Policies. The group is thought to represent right-wing industrialists and businessmen. In 1985 it gave its support to the MLN leader, Sandóval, in the presidential elections.

Partido de Unificación Anticomunista (PUA)
Anti-Communist Unity Party

Leadership. Leonel Sisniega Otero (leader)

Orientation. Ultra-right

History. The PUA was founded in 1983 by Sisniega, who had been a leading member of the MLN until his deportation in 1982 for allegedly planning a coup against the Ríos Montt regime. The PUA attracted the support of former MLN supporters opposed to the Protestant fundamentalism of the regime. In the 1984 Constituent Assembly elections the PUA gained a single seat.

The PUA contested the 1985 elections with Sisniega as its presidential candidate and with the support of the FUN and of the *Movimiento Emergente de Concordia* (Emerging Movement for Harmony, led by Francisco Gordillo); it secured 1.9 per cent of the vote and no seats.

Policies. The PUA is staunchly anti-communist and has authoritarian and pro-military policies.

Death squads

As noted above, political assassination has been employed by the Guatemalan right wing since the early 1960s, often with the tacit support, if not the actual direction and funding, of successive MLN and military regimes. Although the recent democratization and subsequent measures (including the disbandment in 1986 of a secret police force) were expected to reduce the frequency of death squad killings, some groups have remained active. It is difficult to say with certainty when or whether any of these groups have become defunct, as new death squad names appear and old ones reappear at frequent intervals. The proliferation of names among right-wing Guatemalan guerrilla groups, as compared to the relatively few leftist groups, does not necessarily mean that the guerrilla right has more people under arms than has the left; it arises rather from strategic and tactical considerations.

Firstly, it is the practice of right-wing groups to assume new names from time to time, in order to evade detection and to disguise the fact that many of their members are drawn from the regular security forces, whereas left-wing groups have sought to stress their individual and collective strength and their historical continuity by keeping to the same names. (As may be seen from the list below, the actual names adopted by right-wing groups are often colourful, intimidatory and individualistic, whereas the left has traditionally opted for names stressing the organized, popular, revolutionary and militant nature of their organizations.)

Another factor is that the chosen strategy of the right-wing death squads—selective or random assassination of individuals identified with problematic organizations or sectors of the population—causes them to adopt hit-and-run tactics, with small strike forces operating independently, while the left's prolonged popular war strategy dictates the formation of large forces with unified command structures.

150

Apart from the ESA (see main entry above), names used during recent years by death squads have included the following: *Banda de los Buitres* (Band of the Vultures); *Banda de los Halcones* (Band of the Hawks); *Banda del Rey* (The King's Band); *Los Centuriones* (The Centurions); *Comando Anticomunista del Sur* (CAS—Southern Anti-Communist Commando, founded 1980); *Consejo Anticomunista de Guatemala* (CADEG—Guatemalan Anti-Communist Council, formed in the late 1960s); *Escuadrón de la Muerte* (EM—Death Squad, often used generically rather than of a specific organization); *Frente Anticomunista del Nororiente* (FANO—North-Eastern Anti-Communist Front, founded 1980); *Fuerzas de Acción Armada* (Armed Action Forces, active in 1979); *Juventud Organizada del Pueblo en Armas* (JOPA—Organized Youth of the Armed People, formed in March 1980); *La Mano Blanca* (The White Hand, formed in 1970 by Gen. Manuel Sosa Avila—who was assassinated in 1985—and close to the MLN); *Milicias Obreras Guatemaltecas* (MOG—Guatemalan Workers' Militia, formed March 1978); *Movimiento Anticomunista Organizado* (MANO—Organized Anti-Communist Movement); *Nueva Organización Anticomunista* (NOA—New Anti-Communist Organization, founded in the late 1960s); *Nueva Organización Antiterrorista* (NOA—New Anti-Terrorist Organization, formed 1982); *Ojo por Ojo* (An Eye for an Eye, active from the early 1970s); *Orden de la Muerte* (Order of Death); *Organización Cero* (Zero Organization); *El Rayo* (The Thunderbolt); *La Sombra* (The Shadow), and *Unión Guerrera Blanca*(UGB—White Warrior Union).

Other organizations

Other right-wing organizations active in Guatemala since the late 1970s include a section of the UK-based Christian Mission to the Communist World, and the *Centro de Estudios Económicos-Sociales* (Apartado Postal 652, Zona 4, Guatemala City).

Honduras

capital: Tegucigalpa   **population: 3,800,000**

Political system. The Republic of Honduras has an executive President, appointed by the party winning most votes in elections (held every four years) to the unicameral 82-seat National Assembly.

Recent history. In the present century the leading political forces have been the Liberal Party of Honduras (PLH) and the conservative and pro-military National Party (PN). A period of military rule, beginning in 1963, ended with the installation of a PLH government in 1982, although the armed forces retain considerable de facto power. A left-wing insurgency, accompanied by right-wing death squad activity and harsh military repression, has continued throughout the 1980s; the conflict in neighbouring Nicaragua has also had a profound effect on Honduran politics due to the use of bases within Honduras by the US-backed right-wing "contra" rebel forces.

The evolution of the far right. Liberal governments elected in 1954 and 1957 were overthrown by right-wing military coups, and the military regimes of 1963-81 pursued consistently right-wing policies. Outside the PN and the armed forces the most important movements on the right have been the paramilitary groups which developed in the 1970s and 1980s in response to leftist guerrilla activity.

Active organizations

Asociación para el Progreso en Honduras (APROH)
Association for Progress in Honduras

Leadership. Gen. (retd) Gustavo Alvarez Martínez (leader); Miguel Facussé (vice-president); Oswaldo Ramos Soto (secretary)

Orientation. Anti-communist

History. The APROH was formed in January 1983 by right-wing army officers and businessmen. It was banned in November 1984 after the arrest in the USA of associates of Alvarez on charges of drug smuggling and conspiracy to assassinate President Roberto Suazo (the PLH leader). As commander-in-chief of the Honduran armed forces until his dismissal in March 1984 at the request of colleagues, Alvarez had strengthened the military alliance with the United States and had been an enthusiastic supporter of the Nicaraguan contras.

Policies. The APROH originally declared itself to be a non-political civic group concerned with attracting foreign investment to Honduras.

Associated organizations. The APROH reportedly received US$5,000,000 on its foundation from the Iglesia de Unificación, the Honduran affiliate of the anti-communist "Moonie" organization based in South Korea.

La Mano Blanca
The White Hand

Orientation. Ultra-right death squad

History. This group, which is modelled on and possibly connected with similar organizations elsewhere in Central America (notably in Guatemala, where there is an identically named group), issued death threats against alleged left-wing activists in the 1970s and 1980s, and carried out a number of killings.

Policies. The purpose of the group is to eliminate or intimidate its political opponents.

Defunct organizations

CAUSA: a Honduran branch of this international anti-communist movement, which is closely linked with Sun Myung Moon's Unification Church, was established in Honduras in 1982-83, along with a branch of the Church itself; no reports of its activities have subsequently come to light. The Church was repeatedly denounced by the press and by the Catholic hierarchy in late 1983 and was believed to have made little impact in Honduras.

Movimiento Anticomunista Hondureño: this group, known as Macho, was an ultra-right paramilitary tendency formed in the late 1970s.

Hungary

capital: Budapest   **population: 10,600,000**

Political system. Hungary is a People's Republic with a popularly elected, unicameral 352-seat National Assembly. The Assembly in turn elects a collective presidency and a Council of Ministers. The People's Patriotic Front, dominated by the communist Hungarian Socialist Workers' Party (HSWP), has a monopoly of political power.

Recent history. Hungary was liberated in 1944, and in 1948 the two leading political parties, the communists and the social democrats, united to form the Hungarian Workers' Party. The party, which became the HSWP in 1956, followed a pro-Soviet line, apart from a period of liberalization in the immediate post-Stalin era. The country has been stable and peaceful since the suppression by Soviet and Hungarian forces of civil disturbances in 1956.

The evolution of the far right. There was a significant fascist and anti-semitic movement in the 1920s and '30s, the main group being the Arrow Cross movement. An anti-Jewish measure known as the *numerus clausus* law was enacted in 1925. In November 1931 a coup plot was discovered which reportedly involved activists of both the ultra-right and the ultra-left, their alleged objectives including the kidnapping of 1,500 wealthy Jewish citizens and the destruction of synagogues. Anti-semitic agitation increased throughout the 1930s, despite modest legislative measures taken to curb the fascist movement; it was particularly prevalent in the universities, where from 1933 Jewish students were obliged to sit at the rear of the lecture halls and were forbidden to converse with non-Jews. Assaults on Jewish students increased in frequency from 1935.

The pro-fascist government allied Hungary with Nazi Germany in the late 1930s, and made territorial gains in the 1938-39 partitioning of Czechoslovakia. Hungary became a member of the Anti-Comintern Pact in 1939. Although the pro-German National Socialist Party was banned in February 1939, strongly anti-semitic legislation was enacted in May of that year. Hungary entered the war on the Axis side in 1941. The alliance was terminated by the Hungarian side in 1944, but German troops remained in occupation until the liberation.

Many fascist activists went into exile, and the main émigré fascist grouping still active is based in Australia. The communist regime established in 1945 has been relatively stable; intra-party faction fighting of 1955-56 falls outside our brief. Some anti-communist guerrilla activity, associated with the right-wing Catholic Church led in Hungary by Cardinal Mindszenty, occurred in 1956 but was suppressed by government and allied forces; a new wave of exiles reinforced the external opposition.

Active organizations

Cardinal Mindszenty Foundation—see United States.

Co-ordinating Committee of Hungarian Organizations in North America

Address. 4101 Blackpool Road, Rockville, Maryland 20853, United States

Orientation. Anti-communist

History. This non-fascist grouping was created in 1965 as an alliance of several refugee groupings.

Policies. The Committee seeks to further "the ideals of the 1956 Revolution".

Hungarian Freedom Fighters Federation of the USA

Address. Box 3091, Washington, DC 20010, United States

Telephone. (202) 234 8021

Leadership. Dr Andras H. Pogany

Orientation. Anti-communist

History. The Federation was formed in 1958.

Policies. It seeks the overthrow of the Hungarian communist government and its replacement with a pro-Western system.

International affiliations. This body is affiliated to the World Federation of Hungarian Freedom Fighters, also known as the Hungarian Freedom Fighters' World Federation Inc., now based at the same address (formerly in Union City, New Jersey).

Hungarist Movement

Address. c/o B. Kantor, PO Box 125, Merredin, Western Australia 6415

Leadership. Bela Kantor (leader)

Orientation. Nazi

History. The Hungarist Movement sees itself as the direct descendant of the Hungarist, or Arrow Cross, movement founded in Hungary in the 1930s and led during the Second World War by Ferenc Szalasi, who was executed as a war criminal in 1946. It is now strongest among Hungarian émigrés in Australia; in the late 1960s and early '70s, under Ferenc Megadja, it was linked with the National Socialist Party of Australia (NSPA), and to a lesser extent with the rival Australian National Socialist Party. It urged Hungarians settled in Australia to vote for NSPA candidates in local and state elections, and translated propaganda material into Hungarian.

Policies. The Movement espouses ultra-nationalist, authoritarian, racist and anti-communist ideas and attempts to defend the record of the wartime collaborationist movement, and especially of Szalasi. Its publicity materials speak of the "red plague" and of the "decadence of the democratic system"; it denies that the Holocaust of Jews and other opponents of nazism ever took place, and calls for world-wide anti-Jewish solidarity.

Publications. *Perseverance*, monthly, published in Australia in English, Hungarian, Spanish and French editions.

Ut és Cêl

Address. Box 614, Fairfield, New South Wales, Australia

Orientation. Ultra-right

History. This journal was circulating among Australian and other Hungarian exile communities in the 1970s and early 1980s. It may now be defunct following the death in 1981 of its long-serving editor, Ferenc Megadja.

Associated organizations. The publication has served as an internal organ of the Hungarist Movement.

Defunct organizations

Arrow Cross (Hungarist) movement: the Hungarian fascist movement which developed in the early 1930s came into increasing conflict with the authorities. In September 1933 the wearing of the swastika was outlawed, whereupon the main fascist movement, led at that time by Mesko, adopted a green shirt as its uniform and crossed arrows as its badge. Adherents of the movement collaborated with Axis forces during the Second World War. Remnants of the movement exist in Australia (see above) and elsewhere.

Other organizations

Émigré groupings active since the 1970s, but which may be defunct, include the following: the *Hungarian National Council* (125 East 72nd Street, New York, NY 10021, United States); *Fighter* magazine, published by a Cleveland, Ohio (United States) section of the Hungarian Freedom Fighters; the pro-Hungarist *Hungaria Szabadsagharcos Mozgalom Lapja*, a US-based grouping led in the late '70s by Maj. Tibor and publishing *Szittyakürt* magazine; the *Independent Hungarian Freedom Fighter Federation*(3967 Tyler, Gary, Indiana 46408, United States); the *Szabad Magyareag* newspaper (Box 174, New York, NY 10001, United States).

Iceland

capital: Reykjavík   **population: 240,000**

Political system. The Republic of Iceland has a nominally executive President, but effective power is held by a Prime Minister and Cabinet appointed from the parliament which, like the President, is elected for a four-year term by universal adult suffrange. For most purposes the parliament (*Althing*), which had 60 members at the time of writing, sits as two chambers.

Recent history. Iceland has formed part of the Western alliance since the Second World War, having become independent from Denmark in 1944. It has been ruled since 1959 by centrist and left-of-centre coalitions.

The evolution of the far right. The radical right has had no perceptible impact on Icelandic politics since the war. Apart from the group mentioned below, the only relevant organization which appeared to be active in the early 1980s was an affiliate of the British-based Christian Mission to the Communist World.

Active organizations

National Sozialistiski Islonzki Verkamanna Flokkurinn (NSIF) National Socialist Icelandic Workers' Party

Address. Postholf 10240, 130 Reykjavik

Orientation. Nazi

History. This very small party was reported as active in the early 1980s. Two of its members were killed, allegedly by left-wingers, in early 1981.

Policies. The Party is a mainstream national socialist formation with Nordicist and anti-semitic views.

Publications. Dagenning.

India

capital: New Delhi   **population: 780,000,000**

Political system. The federal Republic of India has a non-executive President, a 244-seat upper house (the *Rajya Sabha*), a 544-seat lower house (the *Lok Sabha*) and a cabinet system of government led by a Prime Minister. Most members of the lower house are elected by direct popular vote, while the upper house and the President are indirectly elected.

Recent history. India became independent in 1947, losing some of its territory to what is now Bangladesh and Pakistan. Its political life has subsequently been dominated by the Congress Party, and more specifically by the Nehru family which has provided the only three Prime Ministers to date.

The evolution of the far right. There has been little organized far-right activity in India, although there have been many instances of authoritarian, repressive and arbitrary rule and of racism at local and national level. Some ethnic autonomist, cultural or religious groups not covered here have been active in local campaigns with racist undertones, for example in opposing Muslim settlement in Assam or that of Bengalis in Tripura. Some Sikh and Hindu organizations have aligned themselves with international anti-communist movements. There is a small Islamic fundamentalist movement, based in Kashmir, which falls outside the scope of the present study as do Sikh and Hindu movements per se. The term "national socialist" is used with non-fascist connotations in the name of at least one Indian group.

Active organizations

Akhil Bharat Hindu Mahasabha

Address. Hindu Mahasabha Bhawan, Mandir Marg, New Delhi 110001

Leadership. Vikram Narayan Savarkar (president); Gopal Godse (general secretary)

Orientation. Right-wing Hindu

History. This party was founded in 1915 as an Indian nationalist group, and its sympathizers adopted a red-shirted uniform and a hard line pro-independence stance during the 1930s. The brother of the party's current general secretary was responsible for the assassination of Mahatma Gandhi in 1948. The party was represented in the lower house of the national parliament from 1952 to 1967, and has also held seats in state assemblies.

Policies. The party regards Indiaas a Hindu nation and regards non-Hindus as threatening to the nation's identity and cohesion. It has right-wing economic and social policies.

Membership. Over 2,000,000 (1985 claim).

Associated organizations. The party's outlook is sympathetic to that of the RSSS. Other radical right-wing anti-Islamic Hindu movements influenced by the RSSS include the *Jan Sangh* (or *Bharatiya Jana Sangh*; Indian People's Union), founded in 1951and led by Balraj Madhok, and the *Bharatiya Janata* Party (Indian People's Party), founded in 1980 by former *Jan Sangh* members who had affiliated in 1977 to the larger *Janata* Party.

Anand Marg
Path of Eternal Bliss

Base. Bihar

Leadership. Prabhat Ranjan Sarkar (leader); Sarveshwarananda Avadhoot (general secretary)

Orientation. Right-wing Hindu

History. This political-religious sect was founded in 1955. Sarkar was arrested in 1971 after the killing of six defectors from the group. It was banned in 1975-77 because of its alleged involvement in political violence, and eight members were convicted of murder in 1976; five, including Sarkar, were freed on appeal. In 1977-78 its followers in Australia and Thailand were held responsible for the bombing of several Indian diplomatic targets, killing two people, and for plotting to bomb other targets. In 1982 the West Bengal state government initiated a judicial inquiry into violence connected with the sect after 17 followers had been lynched for allegedly kidnapping children.

Policies. The "progressive utility" theory of Sarkar provides the socio-economic basis of the group's philosophy, while its religious side concentrates on the worship of Kali, the Hindu goddess of destruction.

Membership. In the late 1970s the group claimed to have 1,900,000 adherents in India and about 400,000 abroad.

Associated organizations. Anand Marg is generally regarded as controlling the international Proutist political movement.

International affiliations. Most of the group's foreign adherents appear to be in the United Kingdom, Australia and the United States.

Khalistan National Organization

Base. London, England

Leadership. Dr Jagjit Singh Chohan ("Prime Minister of Khalistan")

Orientation. Sikh separatist

History. The agitation for a separate nation-state for the Sikhs of the Punjab is not of itself an ultra-right movement, and its origins and development are not covered here. However, some sections of the movement have had contacts with foreign right-wingers, including this group, which was founded in 1972 as the National Council of Khalistan.

Publications. Pro-Khalistan journals published in London with right-wing or racist content include *Des Pardes*, which has denounced the British Afro-Caribbean community as consisting of "muggers and buggers"; the *Punjab Times*, which has advertised military training courses for young Sikhs; and the *Khalistan News*, journal of the Organization, which has had commercial and personnel links with a group of pro-South African magazines covering African affairs.

International affiliations. Jagjit Singh represents a self-proclaimed government-in-exile in a Paris-based group supporting mainly anti-communist guerrilla movements, the CIRPO (see France). He has also received the support of the right-wing Republican US senator, Jesse Helms.

Rashtriya Swayam Sewak Sangh (RSSS)
National Union of Selfless Servers

Leadership. M.S. Golwalkar (leader)

Orientation. Right-wing Hindu

History. The RSSS, the name of which has also been reported as *Rashtriya Seval Sangh* (RSS), was founded in 1925 by Dr K.B. Hedgewar, who was succeeded as leader by Golwalkar in 1940. It was banned for a year after the assassination in 1948 of Mahatma Gandhi, and again in 1975-77, and from 1968 government employees were forbidden to join it. In the early 1970s, in 1978-79 and in the mid-1980s it was regarded as having provoked serious violence against Muslims in various parts of India.

Policies. The RSSS leader has stated that Islam, Christianity and communism are alien to India and threaten its stability as a basically Hindu nation (some 83 per cent of the population follow that religion).

Membership. Reliable figures are not available; it claimed 300,000 adherents in 1970, and anything up to 10,000,000 in the late 1970s. The current figure may be in the region of 1,000,000.

Associated organizations. See *Akhil Bharat Hindu Mahasabha* and *Vishawa Hindu Parishad.*

Universal Proutist Revolutionary Party

Orientation. Right-wing Hindu

History. This group was founded in the early 1970s as part of the movement led by Prabhat Ranjan Sarkar of the *Anand Marg* sect. It was banned along with the sect in 1975-77, and during 1977-78 it was held responsible for bombings in Australia and elsewhere, including the destruction of an Air India jet with over 200 deaths on Jan. 1, 1978.

Policies. The Party's beliefs are based on the "progressive utility" (hence "prout") theories of Sarkar.

Associated organizations. See *Anand Marg.*

Vishawa Hindu Parishad (VHP)

Leadership. Hasmukh Viji Shah (spokesman)

Orientation. Radical Hindu

History. The VHP is an international Hindu cultural organization with a strong presence in the United Kingdom, where it was accused in 1986 of having close connections with the Indian ultra-right, particularly the RSSS, and with the assassin of Mahatma Gandhi.

Policies. The VHP describes its aim as the securing of social reforms including the abolition of dowries and of untouchability.

Associated organizations. The group concedes that RSSS members were involved in its foundation, but points to the involvement of supporters of the Congress Party and other mainstream formations as evidence that it is not of the extreme right.

Defunct organizations

Northern World: this white supremacist and anti-semitic periodical was founded and published in Calcutta in 1956 by Roger Pearson, a tea planter who moved in the mid-1960s to the United States (where he now heads the Council for Social and Economic Studies). Despite being published in India it achieved a considerable circulation among American and European fascists.

Individuals

Bimal Kanti: the Indian correspondent of the Liberty Lobby's anti-semitic journal, *The Spotlight* (United States).

Indonesia

Political system. The Republic of Indonesia is governed by a People's Consultative Assembly, which consists of a 460-seat, mainly elected House of Representatives, acting as a legislature, and another 460 appointed and indirectly elected members. The executive President, elected by the Assembly, appoints a Cabinet.

Recent history. The Netherlands East Indies won its independence as Indonesia in 1949, after three years of Japanese occupation followed by a four-year war with the Dutch. The nationalist leader, Dr Sukarno, established a dictatorship with a pro-Chinese foreign policy. In 1967, after a communist uprising was bloodily suppressed, power passed to Gen. Suharto, who became leader of the monolithic ruling party, the Golkar, and established a right-wing and military-controlled government.

The Suharto regime occupied East Timor, formerly a Portuguese colony, in 1975, and remains at war with the left-wing nationalist Fretilin movement. There is another low-intensity insurgency in Irian Jaya, where the OPM movement seeks union with Papua New Guinea. Suharto remained in power in 1987.

The evolution of the far right. A native fascist movement was founded in the then Dutch colony in mid-1933. The movement sought the establishment of an independent fascist state of Java under the Panembahan Senopati dynasty. It did not gain a popular following. Indonesia was occupied by Japan in 1942 and liberated in 1945. In the post-war era the Sukarno dictatorship and the ensuing right-wing military regime under Suharto have been the only significant right-wing movements, apart from Muslim fundamentalism which falls outside the scope of this work.

In March 1981 an airliner with 55 passengers on board was seized by five men at Bangkok airport. Apart from demanding a cash ransom and the liberation of 84 political prisoners, the hijackers were also reported to have called for the expulsion of all Jews from Indonesia. No further information has come to light as to the reason for the latter demand, which was not granted.

Active organizations

Sekber Golongan Karya (Golkar)
Joint Secretariat of Functioning Organizations

Base. Jakarta

Leadership. Gen. Suharto (president); Gen. Sudharmono (chairman)

Orientation. Right-wing

History. The Golkar was founded in 1964 under the Sukarno regime as an alliance of pro-government professional and commercial groupings. It was reorganized in 1971 by Suharto, whose authoritarian "New Order" policies it helped to develop and implement. At present the party, which is funded by the state, holds 461 of the 920 Assembly seats, including 246 of the 460 in the House of Representatives.

Policies. The Golkar supports the military-controlled government and the state-sponsored *Pancasila* philosophy, which has a nationalist and monotheist basis.

Republic of Ireland

capital: Dublin   **population: 3,600,000**

Political system. The Republic of Ireland, which comprises the 26 Irish counties not ruled by Britain, has a bicameral parliament consisting of a non-executive President; a lower house—*Dáil Eireann*—with 166 deputies (TDs) elected by universal adult suffrage, and a 60-seat senate with limited powers. The *Taoiseach*, who is the majority leader in the *Dáil*, heads a cabinet.

Recent history. Power has alternated since the 1930s between a populist nationalist party, *Fianna Fáil*, and a Christian Democratic party, *Fine Gael*, the latter often relying on the support of the small Labour Party. Both main parties have their origins in the civil war of the early 1920s. The state has been relatively untouched by the conflict in the north-east of the island, although most of its political parties advocate, with greater or lesser degrees of enthusiasm, the reunification of Ireland, which was divided in 1921 with the creation of Northern Ireland. Political discourse is dominated by economic and social policy; the state has a very large foreign debt and is attempting to liberalize its legislative and constitutional positions on sexual and family matters.

The evolution of the far right. Anti-semitism was rife in Ireland in the early years of the century; there were pogroms in Limerick and Cork in 1904. The Jewish population has now almost disappeared due to emigration and assimilation.

During the heyday of European fascism Ireland produced its own version, a blue-shirted paramilitary movement which later merged with what is now the centre-right *Fine Gael* party (of whom the term "Blueshirt" is still used pejoratively). The leader of the Blueshirts, Gen. Eoin O'Duffy, took a small contingent to Spain during the Civil War, where he lost more men to disease and boredom than to enemy action. The movement disappeared before the Second World War, although there remains a right-wing fringe within *Fine Gael*. Ireland was neutral during the war, and there was a certain amount of German Nazi espionage and sabotage activity directed against the United Kingdom, but this in the main made use of republican rather than fascist networks.

The rest of the far right in Ireland has organized almost exclusively around Catholic fundamentalism, and there have been numerous anti-communist, anti-modernist, anti-liberal movements down to the present day. Some of these groups concentrate on single issues, such as abortion, and are not listed below. Apart from those groups working within mainstream Catholicism, there is a small following in Ireland for Archbishop Lefebvre's rebel "integrist" tendency (see Switzerland), which regards the Catholic Church as having been taken over by communists and freemasons. The Mother Superior of the main group of Lefebvrist nuns, the Carmelite Order of the Holy Face, is Frances O'Malley, an Irishwoman.

There are very few Eastern-bloc émigrés in Ireland, and no known organizations representing émigrés, although there has been a Free Czechoslovakia Society and some Irish fascist and anti-communist organizations have been in contact with émigrés elsewhere. In June 1979 a Serbian separatist hijacked a flight from New York to Ireland as a publicity stunt. At least one Nazi war criminal, Pieter Menten of the Netherlands, moved to Ireland after the war; he was extradited and imprisoned in the late 1970s.

Almost alone in Western Europe, Ireland has no legislation prohibiting incitement to racial hatred, a fact which has made it an entrepôt for dealers in fascist propaganda.

Active organizations

CAUSA

Address. c/o J. Keating, Kiora House, Greystones, Co. Wicklow

Leadership. Jim Keating (organizer)

Orientation. Anti-communist

History. This offshoot of the US-based CAUSA group held a meeting in Dublin in September 1986 in support of the Nicaraguan contras. One of its organizers, Keating, was previously involved with a leading nazi in other Irish anti-communist groups such as the Irish Council for European Freedom.

Policies. The group opposes the spread of communism on the grounds that it represents a threat to family life and freedom.

Membership. Some 30 people were reported to have attended the meeting of 13 September 1986.

Publications. Keating's personal organ, *Clarion*, has since the early 1970s promoted the policies now followed by CAUSA.

Associated organizations. The *Sunday Tribune* (Dublin) reported that many of the group's members were active in "conservative Catholic groups such as Family Solidarity".

International affiliations. See CAUSA and Unification Church (United States).

Christian Community Centre (CCC)

Address. 22 Merrion Square, Dublin 2

Leadership. T.C. Gerald O'Mahony (director)

Orientation. Fundamentalist Catholic, anti-communist

History. The CCC was established in the early 1970s by O'Mahony, a solicitor, and is run by him from his offices. He started a radio station on Oct. 1, 1984.

Policies. The Centre seeks "to counteract secular atheism" and to promote Catholic teaching on faith and morals. It also opposes communism.

Publications. O'Mahony runs a pirate radio station, Christian Community Radio, from his offices, broadcasting religious and anti-communist material twice daily.

Associated organizations. O'Mahony has also operated as the Community Consultative Council and as Community Co-operation.

International affiliations. O'Mahony has collaborated with émigré and similar organizations such as the Irish Czechoslovak Society in publicity stunts intended to embarrass Eastern European governments, as in an appeal to deliver a religious statue to Lithuania.

Family Solidarity

Address. 34-35 South William Street, Dublin 2

Leadership. Michael Lucey (chairman); Des McDonald (secretary); Eugene Long (administrator); John O'Reilly

Orientation. Conservative Catholic

History. Family Solidarity was organized in 1984 by activists of the anti-abortion Pro-Life Amendment Campaign (PLAC), and has been involved in campaigns against abortion, sex education and divorce.

Policies. This group seeks to defend conservative Catholic teachings on family life and moral issues against what it perceives as a liberalizing and secularizing tendency in modern Ireland.

Membership. The annual meeting in November 1986 was attended by 200 delegates.

Associated organizations. Some Family Solidarity members are active in CAUSA.

National Socialist Irish Workers' Party (NSIWP)

Address. c/o 69 Eugene Street, Dublin 8 (an unoccupied accommodation address)

Leadership. Commander John T. Kane (name used by leading spokesman); Michael J. McGrath (Chief Lieutenant, Kilkenny Unit)

Orientation. Nazi

History. The NSIWP was established around 1970 by the late "Commander" Terence A. Byrne and an associate called Webb, and functioned from a mailing address (at 4 St. Brendan's Cottages, Dublin 4). Among its early members was a Belgian SS veteran living in Ireland. Around 1975-76 a splinter group, using the same name, was led by an ex-soldier, Colum Tarrant (or O Tóráin; 9 Dartry Road, Rathgar, Dublin). The latter organization appeared to have disbanded by 1977, with Tarrant joining a short-lived nationalist party called *Aontacht Eireann*. In 1983 a member of the NSIWP, Private Michael McAleavey, murdered three Irish Army colleagues in Lebanon. By 1986 the main party appeared to be leaderless; its main spokesman, who uses the name Kane, is widely believed to be a man living in Warrenpoint, in Northern Ireland.

The party is organized in district units, the most active of which outside the capital is based in Kilkenny and is also known as the National Socialist Party (NSP); under the latter name the party has applied for registration to the Clerk of the *Dáil*. The NSIWP and the NSP do not admit to being the same organization but the evidence is compelling.

Policies. In a manifesto issued in the name of the NSP the party described its aims as the establishment of "one Celtic National Socialist State; the supremacy of the white Celtic race; a strong Commander of State". Its members also speak of Ireland's "Jewish problem" and of the need to "smash Zionism"; it seeks the expulsion ("repatriation") of non-white people, and opposes "satanic perversions" such as homosexuality.

Publications. The NSIWP produces numerous stickers with fascist slogans—"Keep Ireland White", "Hitler is the Future" etc. The original periodical later taken over by Tarrant's faction, the *Irish Worker*, appears to be defunct, although *The Phoenix*, which became the organ of the NSIWP-NSPUK, is still published as the party monthly.

Associated organizations. The British sister party of the NSIWP is the National Socialist Party of the United Kingdom; the two are commonly referred to together as NSIWP-NSPUK. During the late 1970s Tarrant's faction of the NSIWP, which was not linked with the NSPUK, was associated with numerous other right-wing groups such as the Free Rudolf Hess Committee, the Irish Council for European Freedom, the National Movement and the Free Czechoslovakia Committee; it also traded as Irish Worker Publications and as Revisionist Books, and its youth group was called the Michael Collins Youth (after a civil war general). An interview with an NSIWP spokesman has been reprinted in the magazine of the Ulster Volunteer Force (a loyalist paramilitary group in Northern Ireland).

International affiliations. The lack of any legislation in Ireland which would hinder the production and distribution of racist literature has allowed the NSIWP to produce magazines, leaflets and other material which has circulated freely among fascist groups and sympathizers in other countries, mainly in Western Europe. Both NSIWP groups sought affiliation in the 1970s to the World Unon of National Socialists (see Denmark and United States). An associate of the NSIWP, Raymond Hughes (286 Swords Road, Santry, Dublin 9), was in close contact with the defunct British Movement, the main UK fascist party, in the late 1970s. Around 1981-82 the NSIWP was reportedly involved in safe-housing a German nazi wanted for terrorist offences, Gerhard Töpfer, who now resides in London.

Defunct organizations

Army Comrades Association (ACA): the first and best-known of the names adopted by Gen. Eoin O'Duffy's 1930s fascist "Blueshirt" movement, the ACA was set up by Commandant Ned Cronin in February 1932 as a pressure group representing veterans of the Free State Army. Its main aim was to fight communism "or any disguised form of it", in which category it placed the remnants of the Irish Republican Army guerrilla group. The first president of the movement was Col. Austin Brennan, replaced in August 1932 by Col. Thomas F. O'Higgins, who was succeeded by O'Duffy, a former police commissioner, in July 1933. The ACA, which claimed 30,000 members, adopted its blue-shirted uniform in April 1933 and was banned in July, but continued in existence by changing its name to National Guard; when the latter group was banned in August it became the Young Ireland Association, which in turn became the League of Youth within four days of the banning of the Association in December. The Irish fascist movement merged briefly with mainstream conservatism when the United Ireland Party, or *Fine Gael*, was created late in September 1933 with O'Duffy as its first president. O'Duffy was eased out of the leadership in 1934 and left the League of Youth in 1935 to form a short-lived and explicitly fascist National Corporative Party, which had a green-shirted uniform. The League, under Cronin, collapsed soon afterwards. O'Duffy was a delegate to the International Fascist Congress at Montreux in December 1935, and returned to Ireland with a group from Vidkun Quisling's Norwegian fascist movement. In 1936, at the instigation of the Catholic Primate of Ireland, O'Duffy formed the *Bandera Irlandesa*, a small squad which had a short and undistinguished campaign on the fascist side in the Spanish Civil War. The main fascist newspaper in Ireland in 1933-35 was *The Blueshirt*.

Carraig Books: this mail-order bookselling operation was established in the 1970s in Blackrock, Dublin, by Alfred Day, a former follower of the British fascist leader, Oswald Mosley. It was linked informally with Tarrant's NSIWP and supplied racist, fascist and ultra-right literature, much of it imported from the USA, throughout Ireland and Britain.

National Movement: this group was founded in the 1960s by Limerick window-dresser John Buckley, Dublin postman A.L. Price, and octogenarian retired soldier, Commandant W.J. Brennan-Whitmore. It had contacts in several British and other fascist groups, and its members sported black shirts and swastika armbands. Its journals, *The Nation* (Dublin) and *Nationalist Worker* (Limerick), espoused national socialism, racism and anti-communism. In 1970 some 25 Movement activists staged a march to welcome a South African rugby team to Ireland. In the same year it became involved in a campaign, led by Steve Coughlan, to close down a Maoist bookshop in Limerick. The Movement faded away during the 1970s, and may have merged with Tarrant's faction of the NSIWP around 1977.

Nationalist News: a monthly magazine published around 1977 by Colum Tarrant (see NSIWP), the *News* consisted largely of reprints from the journals of foreign racist and facists groups such as the *South African Observer* and *The American Mercury*. It called for Irish reunification and independence, and opposed alleged left-wing control of the media and an alleged "secret and evil" world-wide Jewish conspiracy. It ceased publication around 1978; in 1980 Tarrant became secretary of the Irish-Arab Association, and he has subsequently been active on the fringes of various British fascist groups.

Other organizations

Other right-wing groupings recently reported as active in Ireland include the Christian Social Party (10 Lower Abbey Street, Dublin 1), led by Harry Richards and Eoin O Maille. In May 1987 Alan G. Glenhill, a long standing member of the NSIWP living in Warrenpoint (Northern Ireland), was active on behalf of a National Workers' Party, which may be a new name for the NSIWP or a faction thereof.

Israel

administrative capital: Tel Aviv
(Jerusalem is claimed as the capital)

population: 4,000,000
(excluding occupied territories)

Political system. The State of Israel is governed by a unicameral parliament, the 120-seat Knesset, which elects a non-executive President as head of state. The Prime Minister, who must command a parliamentary majority, heads a Cabinet. Only Israeli nationals may stand for election or vote in elections to the Knesset. Competing for recognition with the State of Israel is the Palestine Liberation Organization (PLO) which, with its associated bodies, represents the indigenous and largely dispossessed Arab population of the territories occupied *de jure* and *de facto* by Israel.

Recent history. The State of Israel was proclaimed in 1948, following the termination of the British mandate over the mainly Arab territory of Palestine. The founders of the state, who belonged to the Zionist movement (which sought a permanent "homeland" for Jews), intended it primarily as a refuge for Jews who had suffered decades of discrimination, assault and persecution in Europe, culminating in the nazi Holocaust of 1940-45. The aspirations of the Zionist movement brought it into conflict with the native Arab population of Palestine, and several wars involving Israeli and pan-Arab forces have led to the present position whereby most Palestinian Arabs live outside the territory in refugee camps or elsewhere, mainly in neighbouring Arab states, while a minority remains under Israeli rule, despite suffering numerous legal, social and economic disadvantages.

The Israeli state has occupied expanses of neighbouring territory and has failed to gain the recognition of any Arab state other than Egypt. It has relied heavily on the financial and material support of the United States, with which it is closely aligned in foreign policy. Most Israeli governments have been coalitions of large centre-left or centre-right secular parties with smaller parties, many of the latter being influenced by fundamentalist Judaism.

Since its foundation in 1964, the PLO has sought international recognition as the sole legitimate representative of the Palestinian people. It has suffered frequent faction-fighting and was severely disabled by its losses in the Lebanese conflict in the early 1980s.

The evolution of the far right. There is a continuing debate, particularly among the Marxist left, as to whether the mainstream of the Zionist movement, which is largely a response to anti-Jewish racism, is itself racist in its depiction of the Jewish people as the chosen race of God and as the sole rightful heir to the territories occupied for many centuries by the Palestinian Arabs. Without taking a position on that question, the writer has dealt here only with those Zionist movements which profess open and unashamed anti-Arab racism or which pursue expansionist ideologies designed to extend the Jewish occupation of non-Israeli territory; those which seek a condominium or other accommodation of Arab rights are excluded from consideration. The best-known modern expression of the extreme Zionist tendency is Meir Kahane's *Kach* movement.

Conversely, there are many, particularly in Jewish and Zionist organizations around the world, who would depict the Palestinian struggle against the State of Israel, and any opposition to Zionism, as essentially anti-Jewish and comparable to nazism. Again the author does not wish to take a position on that question, and has investigated only those Arab organizations which appeared to have direct links with fascist groups or causes. The main Palestinian organization, the PLO, has a socialist ideology but undoubtedly contains some anti-Jewish members; it has published a book by one Ahmed Hussain which denies that the nazi Holocaust took place.

The treatment of the State of Israel is particularly problematic in a work of this nature and it must be pointed out that the inclusion of particular organizations, some of which have a notable record of active opposition to fascist movements, does not imply that the organizations concerned are to be regarded as fascist in any scientific sense of the word. On the other hand, the exclusion of most Arab groups is likely to annoy those who perceive a vast overlap at what might be called the interface between anti-Zionist and anti-semitic organizations. The criterion which the author has tried to apply is whether it would be reasonable for users of this work to expect the inclusion of a particular group by analogy with groups outside the Middle East conflict.

Active organizations

Kach
Thus

Address. 11 Agripas Street, Jerusalem

Telephone. (02) 247202

Leadership. Rabbi Meir Kahane (leader)

Orientation. Ultra-Zionist, anti-Arab

History. This party was founded in 1977 by Kahane, formerly a New York rabbi, who had in 1968 founded the fiercely anti-nazi, anti-Palestinian and pro-Zionist Jewish Defense League in the United States, before moving to Israel in 1972. Kahane has frequently been in trouble with the Israeli authorities for advocating the expansion of Israel, particularly into the occupied territories. The party gained 25,907 votes in the 1984 elections to the Knesset, and won one seat (for Kahane).

Policies. The group advocates the expulsion of the Arab population from all territories occupied by Israel, and opposes social or sexual contacts between Arabs and Jews. It maintains that no non-Jew has a right to Israeli citizenship. *Kach* has been described by left-wing Israelis as a Jewish fascist movement.

International affiliations. Committee for the Jewish Idea; Jewish Defense League (United States).

Palestinian Liberation Front

Leadership. Abu Abbas (leader)

Orientation. Anti-Zionist

History. This faction of the Palestinian liberation movement has had contacts with at least one known European fascist.

International affiliations. Odfried Hepp, a West German neo-nazi who was sought by police in connection with bombings of Jewish and American targets in West Germany and France in 1981-82, was described by Abu Abbas as "a friend... a militant anti-imperialist and anti-Zionist", in an interview in the Paris daily *Libération* in 1985. Hepp was arrested in Paris in 1985 at an apartment used by the supposedly left-wing Lebanese Armed Faction.

Defunct organizations

Jewish Armed Resistance Strike Unit: a US-based guerrilla group associated with Kahane's Jewish Defense League; it planted bombs at the UN building in New York in 1978.

Jewish Underground: this organization was responsible for a series of attacks on West Bank Arabs in 1980-84, in which several people were killed. Of 26 members imprisoned for their crimes, 23 had been released by March 1987, when the remaining three, who had been given life sentences, had their penalities commuted by the Israeli President to 24 years' imprisonment.

Redemption of Israel: led by Yoel Lerner, a former Kahane associate, this group was broken up in 1978 after allegedly plotting a terrorist campaign against Arabs.

TNT: a Jewish anti-Arab terrorist group active in the occupied territories in the early 1980s; its name derived from the Hebrew for "terror against terror".

Other organizations

Other Zionist ultra-nationalist and expansionist organizations active in recent years include *Gush Emunim* (Bloc of the Faithful, led by Rabbi Moshe Levinger; encourages Jewish settlement of occupied zones); *Agudat Israel* and *National Religious Party* (ultra-orthodox); *Herut* (right-wing Zionist); Matzad (Religious Zionism Party; for territorial expansion), Shas (Sephardic Torah Guardians; ultra-orthodox); *Tehiya* (Zionist Revival Movement; for permanent settlement of occupied territories); and *Tzomet*(Renewed Zionism Party; similar aims).

Italy

capital: Rome   population: 57,000,000

Political system. Italy is a parliamentary democracy with an indirectly elected non-executive President and a directly elected bicameral Parliament, consisting of a 315-seat Senate and a 630-seat Chamber of Deputies. (Some additional senators are appointed or sit ex officio.)

Recent history. From the end of the war until the general election of 1963 Italy was ruled by the centre-right Christian Democratic Party (DC). It has subsequently been ruled by a succession of coalition and minority governments, led in the main by DC Prime Ministers.

The evolution of the far right. The leader of the Fascist Party, Benito Mussolini, became Prime Minister in 1922 and by 1926 was dictator. The history of fascist rule up to 1943, including the alliances with Franco in the Spanish Civil War and with Hitler in the Second World War, is well documented elsewhere, and the listings below refer only to the post-war period.

Mussolini's regime was dissolved along with the Fascist Party in July 1943, and the subsequent German occupation of Italy ended with the Allied victory of April 1945, whereupon Mussolini was killed. Subsequent legislation made any attempt to reconstitute the Fascist Party, under any name, a criminal offence.

There was little overt fascist activity in the immediate post-war era, and it was not until 1963 that the extreme right gained significant electoral support. The leading ultra-right party, the MSI-DN, was winning about 7 per cent of the parliamentary vote by the early 1980s. Outside Parliament a number of far-right terrorist organizations such as the Armed Revolutionary Nuclei (NAR) and New Order emerged in the 1970s, and several right-wing coup conspiracies were uncovered, starting with the De Corenzo plot of 1964 and generally involving members of the secret services and high-ranking military officers acting in collusion with neo-fascists. In the mainly German-speaking autonomous region of the South Tirol, ceded by Austria after the First World War, there was a neo-nazi bombing campaign in the 1960s.

Major fascist crimes in recent years have included the bombing of a crowded bank in Milan in 1969, the intention being to blame the left and to destabilize society to the point where a coup would succeed; the bombing of the Italicus international express train in 1974, for which four fascists went on trial in 1985; the killing of eight anti-fascists at a rally in Brescia in 1974; the bombing of Bologna railway station (with 85 deaths), in 1980, and the bombing of the Naples-Milan train in December 1984, killing at least 15 people. In early 1981 details became known of a clandestine masonic lodge, P-2, which had apparently orchestrated far-right activity in co-operation with organized crime. There were a number of trials of fascists, including former military and secret service officers, in the early 1980s. The secret services engineered the escape from Italy in August 1977 of a German war criminal, Herbert Kappler.

Active organizations

Il Borghese

Address. Via Regina Margherita 7, 20122 Milan

Telephone. (02) 592 966

Leadership. Mario Tedeschi (editor)

Orientation. Extreme right-wing

History. This weekly magazine, founded in 1950, is the largest-selling far-right periodical in Italy.

Diorama Letterario
Literary Survey

Address. Via dell'Oriolo 20, Casella Postale 1364, 50100 Florence

Leadership. Marco Tarchi (editor)

Orientation. New right

History. This review has been produced since the early 1980s by a "new right" publishing house, La Roccia di Eric, which also produces books on themes of interest to the right.

Policies. The review concentrates mainly on literary and cultural matters, which it interprets from a right-wing perspective.

International affiliations. It has been advertised in a British ultra-right journal, *The Scorpion*.

Edizioni di Ar

Address. Via Patriarcato 34, Padua

Orientation. Ultra-right

History. This publishing house, founded in 1963 by neo-fascist activist Giorgio Freda, who has served many years in prison on suspicion of complicity in terrorism, has produced a variety of titles on political, social and cultural issues, viewed from the extreme right.

Publications. Books produced by the firm include translations of the *Protocols of Zion* and of the works of racist theoreticians including Gobineau and Codreanu.

Elemente
Elements

Address. Via Ansaldi 1612, 18038 San Remo

Orientation. Ultra-right

History. This review was being published in the mid-1980s.

Policies. Elemente is concerned with a range of topics of interest to the extreme right.

Associated organizations. Elemente is owned by a publishing house called Edizioni il Labirinto, based at the same address.

Ludwig

Orientation. Ultra-right terrorist

History. At least 15 killings were carried out in the name of this group in the seven years before the arrest in 1984 of Marco Furlan and Wolfgang Abel, of Verona. They were each sentenced to 30 years' imprisonment in February 1987; there had been no Ludwig attacks since their capture and it is likely that the group had no other members.

The group's victims, mainly in Italy but also in Bavaria, included customers of a pornographic cinema, priests, a homosexual and a drug addict; most were beaten and stabbed, suggesting that the name in which attacks were vindicated was derived from the 19th-century German writer, Otto Ludwig, who advocated the clubbing to death of sinners. Messages to newspapers from Ludwig were in a Germanic script and bore a swastika; there is no other evidence that the crimes were inspired by a specifically national socialist ideology.

Policies. The apparent intention of the group, which may now be defunct, was to terrorize those whom it regarded as degenerates into mending their ways.

Movimento Sociale Italiano—Destra Nazionale (MSI-DN)
Italian Social Movement—National Right

Address. Via della Scrofa 39, 00186 Rome

Telephone. (06) 654 3014

Leadership. Pino Romualdi (president); Giorgio Almirante (general secretary, leader); Alberto Giovannini (publications director); Pino Rauti, Franz Maria d'Assaro

Orientation. Neo-fascist

History. The MSI was organized between 1946 and 1948 as a successor to the outlawed Fascist Party of Mussolini. It has contested local and national elections, starting with the 1948 elections in which it gained only six seats in the Chamber of Deputies. During the 1950s and '60s it maintained its representation at about two dozen seats; in 1972 it allied with the Italian Democratic Party of Monarchist Unity, the alliance being called the *Destra Nazionale*, and jointly gained 56 seats. The MSI-DN was created with the formal merger of the allies in the following year, but the new party was reduced to 35 seats in the 1976 elections.

Despite the defection of 17 of its deputies to a non-fascist grouping, the *Democrazia Nazionale*, in 1976-77, the MSI won 30 seats in the 1979 elections, and gained over 2,500,000 votes in the lower-chamber elections of 1983 (6.8 per cent of the total), winning 42 seats. It simultaneously gained 18 Senate seats (as against 13 in 1979), with 7.3 per cent of the vote. It was thus the fourth largest parliamentary party. In 1985 five MSI candidates, including Almirante and Romualdi, were elected to the European Parliament.

Many MSI youth section members or ex-members have been involved in ultra-right terrorism, mainly through the *Nuclei Armati Rivoluzionari* (NAR) or *Terza Posizione*. An MSI deputy, Sandro Saccucci, fled the country in 1976 while being investigated for involvement in the *Ordine Nuovo* terrorist group and in the killing of a Communist Party member. An MSI member, Giuseppe Misso, was alleged by the Italian police to have taken part in the planning of the December 1984 massacre on the Naples-Milan train (see NAR), and to have led the central Naples Camorra (a Mafia-like criminal fraternity). Misso's MSI branch was reportedly disbanded by the leadership for excessive violence.

Almirante, a former member of Mussolini's Cabinet, was the subject of arrest warrants in Italy in 1986 for a breach of the 1952 law against reconstituting the Fascist Party and for involvement in the 1972 escape of a right-wing terrorist, Carlo Cicuttini (see *Ordine Nuovo*). Both the Italian and the European Parliaments have waived the immunity from prosecution to which membership entitled him.

Policies. The MSI follows Mussolini's policies of ultra-nationalism, authoritarianism, economic planning, a corporate state and anti-communism, with less emphasis on anti-semitism than, for example, the German neo-nazi parties.

Membership. The party claims about 400,000 members, which would almost certainly make it the largest ultra-right organization in Europe. Its youth section, FUAN, is much smaller.

Publications. Until 1984 the MSI published a daily newspaper, *Il Secolo d'Italia*, which had a circulation of 12,000 when financial difficulties forced it to close.

International affiliations. The MSI sits in the European Parliament as part of the Group of the European Right, which includes the French *Front national*, the Greek EPEN and John Taylor of Northern Ireland. The Movement also has friendly relations with many other far-right parties in Europe. Although the MSI was prevented by the moderate leaders of the UK section from attending the 1973 congress of the World Anti-Communist League (see South Korea), the Movement was subsequently recognized as the Italian chapter of the League and Almirante attended its congresses in the late 1970s; the League has since attempted to reduce its fascist connections. Elements of the MSI attend the annual Diksmuide fascist rallies in Belgium. There have been MSI branches in some overseas Italian communities, including those in Australia and the United Kingdom.

Partito Operaio Europeo (POE)
European Labor Party

Orientation. LaRoucheist

History. The POE was founded in 1986 as the Italian branch of an international network of political parties and pressure groups controlled from the United States by Lyndon LaRouche.

Policies. As with all LaRouche operations, it is difficult to be precise about the ideological orientation of the POE. The central belief of the LaRouche network is that there is a massive world-wide conspiracy involving reactionary establishment figures ranged against enlightened progressive forces, with the LaRouche groups in the vanguard of the latter movement. The group's actions and alliances make it possible to define it as a radical right-wing group, although it seeks on occasion to present itself as the sole legitimate force of the left.

International affiliations. See National Democratic Policy Committee (United States) and its affiliates in France, West Germany and elsewhere.

Defunct organizations

Anno Zero: a small fascist terrorist group active in the early 1970s.

Association for the Protection of Italians: an Italian nationalist guerrilla group active in the South Tirol, it carried out eight bombings in 1979 to mark its opposition to the autonomy movement supported by the German-speaking local population (and by Austrian and local fascist groups). A similar group active in 1979-80 called itself the Italian Fighters for Alto Adige.

Associazione Internazionale per la Cultura Occidentale: the International Association for the Defence of Western Culture was one of the two Italian affiliates of the South Korean-based World Anti-Communist League (WACL) in the 1970s, the other being the *Istituto Nazionale di Studi Politici ed Economici* (National Institute for Political and Economic Studies).

Avanguardia Nazionale: a neo-fascist terror group founded in the late 1960s, reportedly by Stefano delle Chiaie of the *Ordine Nuovo*, who fled the country after being implicated in the unsuccessful coup led in 1970 by Valerio Borghese. The

National Vanguard carried out several gun and bomb attacks, and in 1976 one of its leaders, Pier Luigi Concutelli, (who had been involved with anti-Basque terror groups in Spain), used a Spanish police machine-gun to kill a Roman judge who was investigating right-wing terrorism. Some members of the National Vanguard were reportedly active in Lebanon in the early 1980s. Many sources report that delle Chiaie was involved in the 1980 Bologna massacre; he was extradited from Venezuela to Italy in 1987, after some years spent in Chile and Bolivia.

Befreiungsausschuss Südtirol: the South Tirol Liberation Committee was a guerrilla group which carried out numerous bombings in the late 1950s and in the 1960s in pursuit of its demand for the reincorporation of the South Tirol into Austria, which had ceded it in the aftermath of the First World War. Its best-known member was Norbert Burger, who went on to lead the neo-nazi National Democratic Party in Austria despite having been sentenced to life imprisonment *in absentia* by an Italian court in 1970.

Democrazia Nazionale: National Democracy was a right-wing party which was created by a split in the parliamentary bloc of the MSI-DN in December 1976. The new party, which was led by Ernesto de Marzio, renounced fascism in favour of ultra-conservative policies, and gained the support of 17 of the 35 MSI deputies and of nine senators; it was wiped out in the 1979 elections.

Edizioni Barbarossa: this publishing house produced some influential "national revolutionary" texts in the early 1970s. Its directors were Marizio Murelli and Giancarlo Rognoni.

Fronte dalla Gioventù: the Youth Front was responsible for bombing left-wing premises in the early 1970s.

Fronte Nazionale: the National Front was a neo-fascist group which conspired to stage a coup between 1969 and 1972. Its leader was Prince Junio Valerio Borghese, who died in Spain in 1974 while another coup plot was being investigated. A Front member, Augusto Cauchi, organized the *Ordine Nuovo* in the early 1970s after his release from a five-year prison sentence for attempting to reorganize the Fascist Party. Around 1976 Cauchi fled to Spain where he was reportedly involved with local ultra-right groups and with other fugitives including Stefano delle Chiaie; Cauchi and delle Chiaie have been identified in some press sources as the leaders of a shadowy organization called the Fascist International.

Giovane Italia: a clandestine right-wing terrorist group, reportedly consisting of ex-members of the MSI, it was active in the early 1970s.

Istituto Nazionale di Studi Politici ed Economici—see *Associazione Internazionale per la Cultura Occidentale.*

Movimento di Azione Rivoluzionaria (MAR): some 55 associates of Carlo Fumagalli, the leader of this fascist guerrilla group, were sentenced with him in 1978 to terms of imprisonment for involvement in the *Rosa dei Venti* coup plot and in other right-wing terrorist conspiracies in the early 1970s.

Movimento Popolare Rivoluzionario (MPR): this fascist terrorist group emerged in 1980.

Nuclei Armati Rivoluzionari (NAR): the Armed Revolutionary Nuclei, led by Gilberto Cavallini and Giuseppe "Guisva" Fioravanti, carried out several bombings, killings and armed robberies in the late 1970s and early 1980s. Other prominent members were Allesandro Allibrandi (killed by the police in Rome in 1981), Fabrizio Zani and Francesco Mambro. The NAR acted as the military wing of a ruralist, Strasserite tendency called the *Terza Posizione* or Third Position. Fioravanti, now one of the *penitenti* or informers who have featured in large-scale terrorist trials, has been charged with involvement in the August 1980 bombing of Bologna railway station, in which 85 people were killed. Formerly a well known child television performer, Fioravanti has alleged that the right wing and the Mafia collaborated in the 1980 assassination of the President of the Sicilian regional assembly. Other crimes in which the NAR has been implicated include the following: in 1979, two bombings in Rome; in 1980, the assassination of an ultra-left activist, a public prosecutor and a policeman, and the bombing of a Communist Party office in Naples; and in 1981, the killing of another policeman.

Several of its members went to Britain and to Lebanon after the Bologna massacre and some joined the National Front (see United Kingdom), helping a dissident faction to remove a leading member, Martin Webster, from the national directorate. Supporters of *Terza Posizione* in the United Kingdom may be contactable via BMC Kursaal, London WC1V 6XX. Those in Lebanon were reportedly involved with the Phalange. Other members fled to Bolivia, where some became involved with the *Novios de la Muerte* gang controlled by a Nazi war criminal.

A number of former NAR members, and other right-wing terrorists who denied NAR membership, were tried on terrorist charges in 1984-85. Among those convicted of organizing an armed gang were Massimo Morsello (sentenced to 10 years' imprisonment), Marinella Morsello (two years, eight months), Roberto Fiore (nine years), Stefano Tiraboschi (eight years, two months) and Marcello de Angelis (six years), all resident in the United Kingdom but apparently not extraditable; most were wanted for other crimes. Serena Depisa, wanted for an armed robbery, was extradited from the United Kingdom in 1986. About a dozen other Italian fascists remained in the United Kingdom. Four Italian-based NAR members were imprisoned in 1984 for the 1980 killing of a Bologna prosecutor who had been investigating the ultra-right.

A fascist activist, Luciano Petrone, carried out a major bank robbery in Marbella, Spain, in 1983, and was in contact with NAR members in London prior to his extradition to Italy on murder charges. After the bombing of the Naples-Milan train in December 1984, in which 15 people were killed, investigators alleged the involvement of the Neapolitan Camorra and of Mafia bankers connected to the NAR.

In May 1985, 53 NAR members were sentenced to terms ranging from 18 months to 20 years for murders, robberies and bombings between 1977 and 1981. Another trial in Milan resulted in the sentencing of 27 members of the NAR in November 1986.

Ordine Nuovo: New Order, founded in the late 1960s by Pino Rauti, formerly of the MSI, and led by Stefano delle Chiaie, Marcello Soffieti, Augusto Cauchi, Mario Affatigato and others, was a fascist terrorist group mainly active in the early 1970s. A leading member, Vincenzo Vinciguerra, was implicated in a car-bombing at Peteano in 1972 which killed three policemen. The bombing, which was blamed at the time on leftist groups, was reportedly part of an ultra-right conspiracy to create the conditions for a military coup.

Carlo Cicuttini, variously reported to be a member of the NAR, the MSI, *Ordine Nuovo* or the *Avanguardia Nazionale*, went abroad soon afterwards, allegedly with the help of a 20,000 payment from Giorgio Almirante, leader of the MSI; he was arrested in Spain in late 1972 but was freed. After Cicuttini was reportedly involved in an attempted airliner hijack it was alleged that he had also taken part in the Peteano bombing. In 1986 the Italian authorities recommended extradition proceedings in Spain, a petition in 1982 having been rejected on the grounds that his alleged offences were political. Cicuttini and other Italian fugitives in Spain and in the south of France were alleged to have assisted the *Grupos Antiterroristas de Liberación* (GAL) and other right-wing terrorist groups in their fight against the Basque separatist movement.

Delle Chiaie fled to Spain around 1975, and was also involved with the Spanish ultra-right in the following two years. After the Order was banned in 1973 (following the conviction of 30 of its estimated 600 members for reconstituting the Fascist Party) the movement reappeared as *Ordine Nero* (Black Order). Under that name it was held responsible for the murder of eight people at an anti-fascist demonstration at Brescia in May 1974, and of the bombing of the Rome-Munich train three months later, in which 12 people were killed. Other bombings in November killed one person.

Rauti started a fortnightly journal, *Línea*, around 1980 in support of the MSI-DN, which he had rejoined around 1970. A train bombing near Florence which killed at least 15 people in December 1984 was claimed by telephone callers to be the work of the *Ordine Nero*, although other groups also claimed responsibility and it had been generally supposed that the *Ordine* had ceased to exist.

Propaganda Due (P-2): this masonic lodge, whose existence became known in early 1981, causing the resignation of the government, had about 1,000 members in various positions of power and influence in Italian political, military, intelligence, media, financial and criminal circles. It was shown to have been involved in many political and financial scandals, including at least one right-wing plot to overthrow the government after destabilization by means of terrorist activities. It was implicated in the collapse of the Banco Ambrosiano, a major bank with Vatican connections, in mid-1982; there were allegations that many millions of dollars were channelled to right-wing groups and governments, notably in Latin America. The head of the bank, P-2 member Roberto Calvi, died in London in June 1982 in what may have been a suicide.

The P-2 "grand master", Licio Gelli, escaped from prison in Switzerland in 1983 and fled to Uruguay. In December 1985 he was charged *in absentia*, along with 14 others including secret service officers, with involvement in the 1980 Bologna massacre. By June 1986 there were 19 defendants, including three alleged to have planted the bomb.

Quex: this national revolutionary magazine was produced in the early 1980s by Sergio Latini and others.

Rosa dei Venti: Compass Points was a clandestine conspiracy in the early 1970s which was preparing for a right-wing military coup. In 1973 the authorities discovered a 2,000-name death list belonging to the group, and in 1974 its alleged financial backer, Andre Mario Paiggio, was arrested.

Solstitium: this magazine ("Solstice") was a vehicle in the late 1970s and early '80s for ultra-right intellectuals.

Squadre Azione Mussolini: the SAM was a small fascist terrorist group discovered and broken up in 1974.

Squadre Nazi Armate: the Armed Nazi Squads bombed the home of a prominent Jew in Livorno in February 1980.

Tirol: this guerrilla movement arose in the South Tirol in 1980 in support of the demand for self-determination for the formerly Austrian region. It carried out several bombings of property in the region in late 1980, late 1981 and late 1982.

Other organizations

Minor groupings and publications which have been reported as active on the Italian extreme right during the past decade include the following, most of which may well be defunct: Giovanni Oggero's fascist *Association Europe-Islam*, publishing *Jihad* in the early 1980s (Casella Postale 160, 10064 Pinerolo, Turin); the *Black Cell of Lucca*; the *Centro di Ricerca Bio-Politica* (Bio-Political Research Centre); the *Centro Librario di Contrainformazione* (Counter-Information Book Centre); the *Centro Studi Evoliani* in

Genoa, and its affiliate in Montreal, Canada, founded in 1976 by V. de Cecco (formerly of Unità Italica, a Canadian section—1964-71—of *Ordine Nuovo*); the *Circulo Culturale di Amici de Europa Knut Hamsun* (Knut Hamsun Cultural Centre of Friends of Europe, formed in Rome in 1978); the magazines *Construiamo l'Azione, Corrispondenza Europea l'Alternativa* and *Dimensione Cosmica*; many publishing houses including *Edizioni All'Insegna del Veltro* (possibly defunct since the imprisonment in 1981 of Claudio Mutti), *Edizioni Arktos* (associated with the Association Europe-Islam), *Edizioni Atanor* (part-financed by the P-2 masonic lodge), *Edizioni Europa, Edizioni Nerbini* (producing various fascist titles around 1983-84), *Edizioni Okha, Edizioni Thule* and the pro-Evola nazi firm *Edizioni Viking; Eowyn* magazine; *Europa Nazione* (Europe A Nation); *Fare Fronte* magazine; *La Fenice* and *Nuova Fenice* magazines; the *Fiume Liberation Organization*; the *Fronte Nazionale de Liberazione (National Liberation Front),* which was created in 1977 with the supposed aim of conducting a clandestine struggle against the secret services.

The *Gruppi de Ricerca Ecologica* (Ecology Research Groups); *La Legione; Lotta di Popolo* (The People's Struggle); *Lotta Europea, Lotta Politica* and *Lotta Popolare; La Mosca Bianca* magazine; the *MPON* and the *MTR*; the *National Labour Party*; the MSI-linked *National Parachutists' Association*; the *National Socialist Party*; the *Nuclei Sconvolti per la Sovversione Urbane* (Clandestine Nuclei for Urban Subversion); the prison-based *Nucleo Prigioneri Rivoluzionari Nuovo*, formed in Sardinia in 1980; *Osare* (To Dare); *Per l'Onore d'Italia* (For Italy's Honour); the *Popolo di Sicilia in Piedi; Relazioni* journal; *Soccorso Nazionale* (National Assistance), aiding fascist prisoners (Paola Bezicheri, secretary, presso Studio Bezicheri, 2 via Broccaindosso, 40100 Bologna); the *Unione Socialista Nazionale* (National Socialist Union), a probably extinct grouping led around 1978 by F. Donini and affiliated to the New European Order (see Switzerland); and *La Voce delle Fogne* magazine.

Japan

capital: Tokyo   **population: 122,000,000**

Political system. Japan has an Emperor as non-executive head of state. Legislative power is held by a bicameral parliament (the *Kokkai*, or Diet), consisting of a 511-seat House of Representatives and a 252-seat House of Councillors, both elected by universal adult suffrage. A Prime Minister, elected by the Diet, appoints a Cabinet.

Recent history. Following its defeat in the Second World War Japan adopted a democratic Constitution in 1946, retaining the Emperor (whom many outside Japan continue to regard as a war criminal), but renouncing war and the theory of the Emperor's divinity. The country regained its sovereignty in 1952. Political power has been virtually monopolized by the Liberal Democratic Party (LDP, or *Jiyu-Minshuto*), a conservative grouping, since its formation in 1955. The country is a major element of the Western alliance and has a very strong economy based on manufacture.

The evolution of the far right. Japan's pre-war ultra-right included a traditionalist reactionary movement and a European-style nazi party founded in 1932 by a faction of the social democratic party. The coming to power of the Japanese fascist movement, and the country's role in the Axis during the Second World War, are well documented elsewhere, and we are concerned here only with post-war movements. Most such movements have been militaristic and Emperor-worshipping; a typical case was that of novelist Yukio Mishima's private army, which dissolved after its leader's suicide in 1970 following the failure of his call for a military coup. Two gunmen belonging to a similar group were arrested in August 1984 after seizing the judge who had ordered their eviction from their headquarters. In 1985 the strength of all radical right-wing groups was estimated at 120,000, with up to 5,000 of these affiliated to some 50 extremist and paramilitary groups. In January 1986 almost 140,000 right-wingers, many in paramilitary uniforms, attended a celebration of the 60th anniversary of the accession of Emperor Hirohito.

The large-scale rehabilitation of war criminals and pre-war ultra-rightists led to a significant right-wing influence in mainstream conservative parties, including the LDP. One of the main financiers of the LDP was Yoshio Kodama, a founder in 1931 of the reactionary Patriotic People's Mass Party, who amassed a fortune in China during the war; he was a central link in the Lockheed bribery scandal which erupted in the 1970s. He died in 1984. A co-founder of the Mass Party was Riyoichi Sasakawa, who described himself in the 1970s as "the world's richest fascist"; in the aftermath of the war he and Kodama had shared a cell with Nobusuke Kishi, who like them was under investigation for war crimes. In 1958 Kishi became an LDP Prime Minister. The present LDP Prime Minister, Yasuhiro Nakasone, who has been a leading advocate of increasing the status of the Emperor, was forced to apologize for his remark in September 1986 that the general level of intelligence in the United States was lowered by the presence of black, Puerto Rican and Mexican minorities.

Racism persists in mainstream Japanese thinking, and is directed mainly against the substantial ethnic Korean minority population. Another non-racial minority which suffers discrimination is the group of families designated as "unclean" because of their traditional occupations; this group has difficulty in obtaining ordinary employment or in intermarrying with the majority.

Active organizations

Kokusai kyosho rengo
International Union for Victory over Communism

Base. Tokyo

Leadership. Osami Kuboki (president)

Orientation. Anti-communist

History. This Japanese chapter of the World Anti-Communist League (see South Korea) was founded in 1968 by associates of Sun Myung Moon, a religious leader and tax criminal (see Unification Church, South Korea). The organization provided US$30,000 for the 1985 WACL conference in the United States. Kuboki, who attended the 1986 conference in Luxembourg, is also the leader of the "Moonie" organization in Japan. He is a close associate of the LDP Prime Minister, Nakasone, who, like ex-Prime Minister Kishi—a practising Moonie—interceded with President Reagan in 1985 an attempt to secure the early release of Moon from a US prison where he was serving a sentence for fraud.

Policies. The WACL, in Japan as elsewhere, seeks to support and publicize anti-communist causes around the world. It works partly through student groups and other anti-communist and nationalist organizations.

Membership. The Union's claim to 7,500,000 members has not met with universal credence.

Publications. Sekai nippo (Daily World).

International affiliations. In late 1986 the organization hosted J.-M. Le Pen, leader of the French ultra-right *Front national*, on a visit in which he also met LDP leaders.

Defunct organizations

Political Federation of Japanese People: this right-wing anti-communist party contested the 1983 partial elections to the upper chamber, but it failed to gain representation and appears to have become extinct.

Tatenokai: the Shield Society was a small but fanatical right-wing sect led by the writer Yukio Mishima until his suicide by ritual disembowelment in 1970.

*Youth League for the Overthrow of the Yalta and Postdam Structures:*two members of this group, which sought the revision of the punitive treaties imposed on Japan at the end of the war, joined with two ex-members of the *Tatenokai* in holding hostage several leaders of a business federation in Tokyo on March 3-4, 1977.

Other organizations

Small ultra-right groups reportedly active in recent years include the *Defence Youth League*, the anti-semitic *Middle East Problems Research Centre* run by Masami Uno, the *Showa Restoration League* and the *Young Men's Thought Research Institute*. There is also a Japanese section of the Christian Mission to the Communist World (see United Kingdom).

Individuals

Individual right-wing activists of particular importance who are not known to have links with the above organizations include Aisaburo Saito, an LDP member of the

Diet, who has written a book entitled *The Secret Jewish Power of World Control*, and Toru Kawajiri, a "revisionist historian" who has maintained that the true number of Jewish casualties in the Nazi Holocaust was 200,000.

Kampuchea

capital: Phnom-Penh   population: 6,000,000

Political system. The People's Republic of Kampuchea, formerly Cambodia, and known in 1970-75 as the Khmer Republic and in 1976-79 as Democratic Kampuchea, is at present ruled by a popularly elected National Assembly, a Council of State, and a Council of Ministers led by a Prime Minister. The sole legal political force is the Kampuchean United Front for National Construction and Defence, the main component of which is the communist Kampuchean People's Revolutionary Party (KPRP).

Recent history. The government of Prince Norodom Sihanouk, which followed a broadly socialist line, was overthrown in 1970 by a right-wing military faction led by his Prime Minister, Lon Nol. Sihanouk combined with a communist guerrilla movement, the Khmer Rouge, to form a resistance movement and a government-in-exile; over five years of civil war the Khmer Rouge became increasingly powerful, and it seized complete control after the military regime collapsed in 1975. Sihanouk was installed as head of state but he resigned in 1976. The Khmer Rouge government, under Pol Pot, applied its policies for radical social change with extreme force; perhaps 1,000,000 citizens died over three years.

A rival communist group, the KPRP, developed in the mid-1970s and invaded the country in 1978, with substantial Vietnamese support. It won power in 1979. That regime, under Heng Samrin, remains in place in 1987 while the Khmer Rouge-Sihanouk coalition, in an uneasy alliance with a non-communist rebel movement, is maintaining a guerrilla campaign in various parts of the country. This anti-Vietnamese alliance continues to function as a government-in-exile and it has received widespread international recognition.

The evolution of the far right. Cambodia, as it then was, was under Japanese occupation during the Second World War. A puppet government was established under Son Ngoc Thanh, who led a right-wing coup plot in 1957 and was in exile until returning as Prime Minister in the Lon Nol regime of 1970-75. That right-wing government enjoyed little popular support and its followers are not a significant element of the current anti-communist forces. Within the opposition alliance's "Government of Democratic Kampuchea" the main non-communist element is Sihanouk's National Liberation Movement of Kampuchea (Moulinaka), while the most right-wing element is the Khmer People's National Liberation Front (KPNLF). The latter group was founded in France in 1979 and is led politically by Son Sann, a former Prime Minister, and militarily by Sat Sutsakhan.

The term *Khmers Serei* (Free Khmers) was originally applied to anti-communist bands recruited by the South Vietnamese government in the mid-1960s to raid Viet Cong bases inside Kampuchea. Elements of these groups supported the 1970-75 right-wing Lon Nol regime, and conducted occasional raids from Thailand against the ensuing Khmer Rouge regime. After the Vietnamese invasion of 1978 the term was applied loosely to a range of non-communist opposition forces including the KPNLF and Sihanouk's personal following in the Moulinaka (as distinct from his joint effort with the Khmer Rouge). Other such forces included the Khmer People's National Liberation Armed Forces, founded in 1979 by a former Lon Nol regime officer; the short-lived Liberation National Government of Kampuchea, formed in 1979 and led by Van Saren; and the National Liberation Movement led by In Sakhan, which has effectively merged with Sihanouk's group.

In the mid-1980s at least one European fascist group was in contact with a National Liberation Front of Cambodia (FLNC-PNK), presumably a *Khmer Serei* formation. It was based in Thailand (202-3 Namirat Road, Prasal, Surim), the contact being Mme. Pensiri Soudsempom. No further information on this group has come to light.

Republic of Korea

capital: Seoul   **population: 40,000,000**

Political system. The Republic of Korea (generally known as South Korea) has an executive President, chosen by a popularly elected Electoral College, who appoints a Prime Minister and cabinet. A 276-seat National Assembly is partly elected and partly appointed.

Recent history. The Republic came into existence in 1948, and was ruled until 1960 by the authoritarian and corrupt Syngman Rhee. This period included a war with its northern neighbour, the (communist) Democratic People's Republic of Korea, in 1950-53. A military coup in 1961 installed President Park Chung Hee, after whose assassination in 1979 another coup gave effective power to the army commander, Gen. Chun Doo Hwan, who assumed the presidency in 1980 and was confirmed in office for a seven-year term by indirect election in 1981. Legislative elections in 1981 and 1985 resulted in large majorities for the government party. The Rhee, Park and Chun regimes, despite their intermittent adoption of democratic forms and institutions, have been characterized by uncompromising and sometimes violent repression of dissent.

The evolution of the far right. Korea was ruled by Japan from 1910 until the end of the Second World War in 1945. The southern part of the peninsula, which was liberated by Western forces while the Soviet Union liberated the north, has subsequently been ruled by anti-communist regimes supported by the United States and other Western powers. The present leadership is particularly close to the World Anti-Communist League and has provided its headquarters. Under successive post-war governments political parties have frequently been banned, demonstrations forcibly broken up, democratic opposition leaders imprisoned or exiled, and martial law imposed.

Active organizations

CAUSA-International

Base. Seoul

Leadership. Bo Hi Pak (leader)

Orientation. Anti-communist

History. This organization, which has affiliates in several Western countries, has close links with Sun Myung Moon's Unification Church and with the Korean Central Intelligence Agency.

Policies. The group seeks to defend Western values and individual freedom, and to oppose communist totalitarianism.

Associated organizations. See Unification Church.

International affiliations. See individual chapters of CAUSA (France, Ireland and elsewhere). The organization is close to the World Anti-Communist League, also based in South Korea, and to the International Federation for Victory over Communism (Japan).

Democratic Justice Party (DJP)

Address. 155-2 Kwanhoon-dong, Chongo-ku, Seoul

Telephone. 720-8771

Leadership. Chun Doo Hwan (president); Ro Tae Woo (chairman); Yi Han Tong (general secretary)

Orientation. Right-wing conservative

History. The DJP, founded in 1981 as the political organ of the Chun regime, is the successor to President Park's Democratic Republican Party. It was granted 151 of the 184 directly elected seats in the National Assembly after elections held in 1981, and 87 after the 1985 elections, in which its share of the vote was stated to be 35.3 per cent. The allocation of extra seats assured it of an overall majority on both occasions.

Policies. The Party is extremely conservative and pro-military. It is effectively the personal vehicle of President Chun Doo Hwan.

Membership. The DJP claims 1,000,000 members.

Associated Organizations. The Party supports the World Anti-Communist League, partly through massive donations of public funds.

Unification Church

Base. Seoul

Leadership. Sun Myung Moon (founder); Yung Suk Choi (president)

Orientation. Anti-communist

History. This cult was established in the early 1970s. It gained a wide international following, particularly among the youth of the United States and Western Europe, but was in decline in the 1980s following the imprisonment of its leader for tax fraud in the USA.

Policies. The Church functions as a religious cult, allegedly using indoctrination methods designed to instil total obedience to Moon. As a result of its emphasis on Moon's personality the sect is usually known as "the Moonies". Its theological orientation is somewhat difficult to define, apparently relying on a fusion of Christian and Eastern beliefs. A feature of the sect's practices is the holding of mass marriage ceremonies, at which couples who may never have met are chosen and married to each other by Moon.

Associated organizations. The group is fiercely anti-communist and is openly associated with CAUSA-International and its foreign affiliates; it is less overtly linked to the World Anti-Communist League and its affiliates.

International affiliations. The Church is active in most Western countries. See particularly Unification Church (United States).

World Anti-Communist League (WACL)

Address. Freedom Center, San 5-19, Changchung-dong, Chong-ku, CPO Box 7173, Seoul

Telephone. 252-4597

Cables. WACLSEC SEOUL

Leadership. Gen. John K. Singlaub (USA; honorary chairman); Prof. Woo Jae-Seung (South Korea; general secretary); David Finzer (head of youth wing)

Orientation. Anti-communist

History. The WACL, possibly the most important far-right network in the world, was founded in Taiwan in 1967 after contacts in 1966 between the Asian People's Anti-Communist League (see Taiwan) and the Anti-Bolshevik Bloc of Nations (ABN—see United Kingdom). Among its founders were the late Ukrainian émigrés Lev Dobriansky and Yaroslav Stetsko, and Kuomintang Central Committee member Ku Cheng-kang, who became its honorary chairman "for life". It was dominated for many years by East Europeans and Asians, the former by and large providing the ideology and the latter the funding.

In the early 1970s the group attracted the support of anti-semitic and fascist organizations in a number of countries, notably in Latin America, a trend encouraged by the WACL's then leadership. This led to tensions with mainstream conservative affiliates, including the British section which tried to exclude fascists from the 1973 (7th) annual convention in London, although Raymundo Guerrero, head of the fascist-dominated Mexican section, was then chairman of the League. The convention was cancelled by the leadership and Geoffrey Stewart-Smith withdrew his British group (see *East-West Digest*), which was replaced as the local affiliate by the anti-semitic British League of Rights. The US section, the American Council for World Freedom, withdrew for the same reason in 1975, and was replaced by the Council on American Affairs, led by well-known racist Roger Pearson, who chaired the League's 11th annual conference in Washington in 1978. Among fascists and anti-semites in attendance were Giorgio Almirante of the Italian MSI, William Pierce of the US National Alliance, Eric Butler of the Australian League of Rights, and members of the US Liberty Lobby; others present included two US Republican Party senators, Jake Garn and James McClure; Ivor Benson, a South African anti-semite; and representatives of the French group, GRECE.

In-fighting between pro- and anti-fascist factions continued into the 1980s, and surfaced at the 1980 conference in Geneva and the 1983 conference in the European Parliament building in Luxembourg. There was something of a purge in 1983-84 and the current leadership, which was installed at the 17th annual conference in San Diego, California, in 1984, denies any fascist associations. A former US army general dismissed for insubordination by President Carter, Singlaub, took over the chair; he is a key figure in many US right-wing groupings. The League's 18th annual conference took place in Dallas, Texas, in September 1985, and the 19th in Luxembourg in September 1986.

The supreme organ of the WACL is the annual conference. There is a 15-seat Executive Board (elected by a Council, which in turn is elected by the Conference) with representatives of the larger member organizations. The funds of the League are derived mainly from the South Korean government, which was paying at least US$120,000 per year in the mid-1980s, and from fees paid by member groups, which accounted for about US$17,000 per year. Member groups are responsible for the costs of WACL conferences, with that in 1985 costing about US$380,000. The youth wing of the movement was originally the Mexican-based World Youth Anti-Communist League (Youth-WACL), which was disbanded because of fascist penetration, and was replaced in 1986 by the Young Conservative Foundation (based in the United States), which has changed its name to the World Youth Freedom League.

Policies. The League describes its objectives as fighting communist totalitarianism and upholding human rights. It became particularly active in the mid-1980s in support of counter-revolutionary movements such as the Nicaraguan *contras*, and to a lesser extent the guerrilla oppositions in Afghanistan, Laos, Kampuchea and Angola. It was an important conduit for private and possibly covert official funding of the *contras*. From 1986 it was hoping to collaborate with Western intelligence agencies in anti-communist propaganda and "psychological warfare".

Membership. The League has six regional groupings, 11 international, 93 national and seven associate member organizations. Some of these are merely groups of individuals sympathetic to the WACL, while others are parties or pressure groups active in national politics. The Latin American regional group was expelled in the early 1980s for its fascist links (see CAL, Mexico) and was replaced by a very similar grouping (see Fedal, Paraguay). The North American Regional WACL (NARWACL), dominated by Pearson's Council on American Affairs, was likewise taken over under Singlaub's leadership by the US Council for World Freedom. Another regional grouping, the Organization for African Freedom, may be inactive. The Middle East grouping is known as the Middle East Solidarity Council. Other groups affiliated to the WACL include the Asian Christian Association and the World Christian Anti-Communist Association, both based in Taiwan, and the Asian Youth Anti-Communist League, which can be contacted via Freedom Center.

Publications. Freedom Digest, quarterly; *WACL Newsletter*, monthly. The WACL also holds bimonthly seminars on communism and produces circulars, booklets and other material.

International affiliations. See FNLA (Angola); Tradition, Family and Property (Brazil); Alpha-66 (Cuba); CAUSA, CIRPO, WACL (France); Anti-Bolshevik Bloc of Nations, British League of Rights, Crown Commonwealth League of Rights, *East-West Digest*, European Council for World Freedom, WACL (United Kingdom); CAUSA (Ireland); MSI (Italy); CAUSA-International, Unification Church (South Korea); Femaco (Mexico); Fedal (Paraguay); Roumanian Freedom Front (Romania); Seychelles National Movement (Seychelles); Asian People's Anti-Communist League (Taiwan); American Council for Peace through Strength, Civilian Military Assistance, Council on American Affairs, *Eagle*, Heritage Foundation, *Soldier of Fortune*, US Council for World Freedom, Western Goals, World Youth Freedom League (United States).

Other important "national units" of the League exist in Taiwan, Saudi Arabia, Japan, Bahrain, Oman, the United Arab Emirates and Hong Kong. There are also chapters in Australia, in Austria, in Belgium and Luxembourg (combined), in Bolivia, Canada, Chile, Colombia, Costa Rica, Denmark, the Dominican Republic, Ecuador, El Salvador, West Germany, Greece, Guatemala, Haiti (possibly defunct), India, Indonesia, Iran (probably defunct), Jordan, the Lebanon, Macau, Malaysia, Nepal, Norway, Pakistan, Panama, Paraguay, the Philippines, Singapore, Sri Lanka, Sweden, Switzerland, Thailand and Turkey, with expatriate organizations representing Bulgaria, Byelorussia, Croatia, Lithuania, Latvia, Romania and the Ukraine. See also CAL, FEMACO, *Los Tecos* and the White Hand (Mexico); the League is also in contact with Nicaraguan *contra* groups, the MNR of Mozambique and other anti-communist guerrilla movements.

The League has had friendly relations with the Reagan White House, through Lt.-Col. Oliver North until his dismissal in the Iran-Nicaragua scandal of 1986-87, and also through the President himself, who sent a lengthy message of "warm greetings" to the 1985 conference. It has been suggested that the League was used as a conduit for secret US government funding of *contras*.

Defunct organizations

Democratic Republican Party: the political party of the Park dictatorship, the DRP was formed in January 1963 and dissolved, along with all other parties, in 1980. It has effectively been superseded by the Democratic Justice Party.

Lebanon

capital: Beirut

population: 3,200,000

Political system. The Republic of Lebanon has a directly elected 99-seat National Assembly which appoints a non-executive President. The President appoints a Prime Minister and Cabinet. The nominal term of a parliament is four years, although it has not been possible to hold elections since 1972 due to the present civil conflict.

Recent history. Lebanon became independent in 1941-44, since when there have been occasional clashes between militias representing various Muslim and Christian factions. The outright civil war which started in 1975 was continuing in 1987.

The evolution of the far right. Right-wing forces in Lebanon have traditionally arisen from within the Christian communities, while the local Muslims and their allies in the Palestinian refugee camps have generally identified with the left (although a right-wing Muslim militia, the Lebanese Revolutionary Party, was active in the late 1970s). The main right-wing force is the fascist-influenced Phalange, led by the Gemayel family and recruited from the Maronite Catholics who form the greater part of the Christian portion (43 per cent) of the population. Right-wing Maronite forces without a fascist influence include the *Bloc National* of Raymond Eddé, which has sometimes allied itself with the Phalange.

Active organizations

Phalanges Libanaises—Al Kata'eb
Lebanese Phalange

Address. PO Box 992, place Charles Hélou, Beirut

Telephone. 338230

Telex. 42245

Leadership. Elie Karame (leader); George Saadé (deputy leader); Joseph Saadé (general secretary)

Orientation. Right-wing

History. This grouping was founded in 1936 and led by Pierre Gemayel, a right-wing Maronite Christian. The last elections to what was then the Chamber of Deputies (now the National Assembly), held in 1972, gave it seven seats. In the early 1970s it became increasingly involved in fighting with the Palestinian *fedayeen* guerrillas, and in 1975 the fighting, centred on Beirut, developed into full-scale civil war. Along with other right-wing forces, the Phalange accepted the support of Israel, which invaded Lebanon in 1978 and again in 1982-85. By 1980 the Phalange had established control over a wide area, including that hitherto controlled by another right-wing Maronite group, the *Parti libéral national*(PLN—National Liberal Party) of ex-President Camille Chamoun; the Phalange and the PLN formally merged at this point, creating a 17-seat parliamentary bloc. An allied militia, the South Lebanon Army of Maj. Saad Haddad (since succeeded by Maj. Antoine Lahad), controlled much of southern Lebanon with the backing of Israel.

The military commander of the Phalange, Bashir Gemayel (son of Pierre), was assassinated in 1982 shortly after his election, but before taking office, as President of Lebanon; the presidency passed to his brother, the less militant Amin Gemayel. In

1983 the Phalange lost territory in the Chouf mountains to the Muslim Druze militias.

The fascist origins of the Phalange are not emphasised in its current political activity but there have been frequent reports since the mid-1970s of the participation of European fascists in its paramilitary activities. Groups mentioned in this context have included the Italian *Nuclei Armati Rivoluzionari* and the West German *Wehrsportsgruppe Hoffman*.

Policies. The Phalange was influenced at the time of its formation by European fascist ideologies. It has evolved into a nationalist and democratic party, but elements within it have maintained links with fascist groups.

Membership. About 90,000.

Publications. *Al-Amal*, Arabic daily, circulation 45,000, editor Georges Omeira; the party also controls two radio stations.

Associated organizations. The Phalange is the major component of the Lebanese Front alliance led by Dory Chamoun of the PLN and including other right-wing Christian parties and militias. In September 1982 the Front's forces were held responsible for the massacre of several hundred Palestinian refugees in camps in Beirut.

International affiliations. The Phalange has received extensive Israeli financial and military support for its assaults on Palestinian forces.

Defunct organizations

Cedar Guardians: a right-wing Christian militia active north of Beirut in the late 1970s, it was led by Said Akl. In 1979 it was involved in clashes with the PLN's militia. Other right-wing Christian militias active at this time included the *Organization of Revolutionaries of the North* and the (pro-PLN) *Tiger Militia*, with non-military right-wing groups including the *Maronite League*.

Libya

capital: Tripoli   **population: 3,600,000**

Political system. Libya, or the Socialist People's Libyan Arab Jamahiriya as it is formally known, is governed by a system of popular congresses and committees led by the 1,112-member General People's Congress and its 20-member executive, the General People's Committee.

Recent history. Since a coup d'état in 1969 the de facto head of state and government has been Col. Muammar al-Gaddafi, whose revolutionary teachings are contained in the "Green Book". Gaddafi has advocated pan-Arab unity against Israel and its Western allies and has attempted to unite Libya with several other states. His government has given vocal and practical support to many Palestinian, third world and other guerrilla movements, as a result of which he has been vilified in the Western media and has been the target of American economic sanctions and military attack.

The evolution of the far right. Although there is no evidence of fascist activity inside Libya, there have been claims that the Gaddafi regime has given financial or other support to fascist groups in Western countries, including the Call of Jesus Christ group in Spain and the National Vanguard in Australia. There were also claims by the losing faction that Libyan funding had been provided to the "Strasserite" faction which assumed control of the National Front in the UK at the end of 1983. The Libyan government has hosted the anti-semitic leader of the Nation of Islam (see United States).

Opposition movements within the country, such as the National Front for the Salvation of Libya which staged an unsuccessful coup in 1984, or the Libyan Baathist Party, do not appear to have a definite radical right-wing orientation; nor do external groups such as the Manchester-based Libyan Constitutional Union, the Libyan Democratic Movement, the Cairo-based Libyan National Association or the Khartoum-based Libyan National Salvation Front.

Liechtenstein

capital: Vaduz   **population: 26,000**

Political system. The Principality of Liechtenstein, a constitutional monarchy, has a 15-seat parliament (the *Landtag*) elected by adult citizens. Female suffrage, only recently introduced at national level, has not yet been introduced for communal elections in four of the 11 communes. Liechtenstein has a special economic and diplomatic relationship with Switzerland, which it borders.

Recent history. The dominant political party since the late 1920s has been the conservative Progressive Citizens' Party (FBP), which has formed the government apart from a period from 1970-74, when it was replaced by the centrist Patriotic Union (VU), and the period from 1978 to date (1987), when it has been the minority partner in a coalition with the VU.

The evolution of the far right. The native tradition of conservatism has been reflected in the rejection until 1984 of attempts to extend the franchise for national elections to women. There has, however, been no evidence of ultra-right activity in the Principality since the 1930s, apart from its use since the late 1970s as the postal address of what may be a Swiss-based historical revisionist operation. The Documentary Series Establishment, using a Liechtenstein address (Postfach 121, 9494 Schaan), has produced anti-semitic literature and recordings for distribution throughout Western Europe. It is possible that the absence of relevant legislation makes the Principality attractive to distributors of such material.

Luxembourg

capital: Luxembourg-Ville **population: 366,000**

Political system. The Grand Duchy of Luxembourg is effectively a parliamentary democracy ruled by a Council of Ministers answerable to a directly elected 64-seat Chamber of Deputies. The Grand Duke, as constitutional head of state, is assisted by a Council of State with some legislative powers.

Recent history. Luxembourg was dominated by the Social Christian Party (PSC) from 1919 to 1974, apart from the wartime German occupation. After five years out of government the PSC returned in 1979 as part of a centre-left coalition.

The evolution of the far right. Luxembourg was under Nazi occupation from 1940 to 1944, and was formally incorporated in the Reich in August 1942; some 12,000 citizens were conscripted into the German forces, giving rise to a present-day pressure group (the *Enrolés de Force*) which seeks compensation. There was very little fascist activity either before or after the occupation.

Active organizations

Ligue Mondiale Anti-Communiste
World Anti-Communist League (WACL)

Leadership. Gen. Robert Close

Orientation. Anti-communist

History. The joint Belgium and Luxembourg chapter of this important international anti-communist pressure group (see South Korea) hosted the 19th conference of the group in Luxembourg-Ville in Sepember 1986. It had also held the 1983 conference.

Policies. The League seeks to promote anti-communist causes and to defend Western values.

Mexico

capital: México DF

population: 80,000,000

Political system. The United Mexican States form a federal republic with a National Congress of 64 Senators and 400 Deputies, elected by universal adult suffrage—with an element of proportional representation in the case of the Chamber of Deputies. There is a powerful executive President, directly elected for a six-year term.

Recent history. Political power has been monopolized since 1929 by a vast and monolithic party now known as the Institutional Revolutionary Party (PRI). The PRI is ideologically heterogeneous, but is generally regarded as following a progressive and non-aligned foreign policy coupled with a conservative domestic policy; the professed ideology of the party is approximately social democratic.

The evolution of the far right. Since the dictatorship of Porfirio Díaz (from 1876 to 1910), and the ensuing revolutionary upheaval, Mexico has been governed by nominally liberal and progressive regimes with occasional periods of reactionary governmental or opposition activity. There were substantial clerical-fascist (*cristero*), nazi (*camisas doradas*—goldshirts) and quasi-fascist (*sinarquista*) movements in the 1920s and '30s. Anti-semitic groups became increasingly active from 1930, and were involved in riots, notably in Mazatlán, in 1933. After a lull in their activities due to the war (in which Mexico joined the Allies in 1942) they reappeared in 1954 and in the 1960s. Due to the absence of any legal obstacles, Mexico became an important centre for the production of anti-semitic literature. An increase in anti-semitic activity was reported in 1974, accompanied by threats to Jewish businesses from a "National Liberation Front".

There have been right-wing elements in the PRI, which came to the fore in the presidencies (*sexenios*, from their duration) of Gustavo Díaz Ordaz (1964-70) and Luis Echeverría Alvarez (1970-76). Student riots during the Olympic Games in 1968 were violently repressed by a combination of state and ultra-right forces, with an unknown number of deaths and injuries. A similar incident occurred on the feast of Corpus Christi in 1971. Right-wing militias known as the *Brigada Blanca*, the *Halcones* and the *Tecos* were formed in the 1960s and '70s, often with at least the tacit approval of local PRI authorities.

The conservative movement in Mexico is now represented mainly by the National Action Party (PAN), which showed some anti-semitic tendencies in the mid-1940s but is now a right-wing Christian democratic party. *Sinarquismo* now operates through the Mexican Democratic Party (PDM). There is also a right-wing, anti-communist Catholic traditionalist movement; a secular anti-communist movement typified by the Mexican Anti-Communist Federation (Femaco); and a right-wing paramilitary tendency, now virtually defunct but typified by the student *porro* gangs and the remaining *Tecos*. The *porros*, like their labour movement counterparts, the *charros*, often arose in the 1970s as anti-socialist groupings tolerated by and sometimes linked unofficially with governmental or academic authorities or with individual employers or employers' groups. Rightist death squads were held responsible for at least two killings in 1984, involving a journalist and an amnestied guerrilla leader.

Active organizations

Federación Mexicana Anticomunista (Femaco)
Mexican Anti-Communist Federation

Address. Avenida 8 de julio 428, 44910 Guadalajara, Jalisco

Leadership. Raymundo Guerrero

Orientation. Anti-communist

History. The Femaco was founded in 1967.

Policies. The Federation opposes all forms of communism and socialism and seeks to defend free enterprise and Western values against Marxist subversion.

Publications. The Femaco is supported by *Réplica* magazine, published since the late 1960s in Spanish and English editions (by José Chávez Chávez, Avenida de las Américas 132, Guadalajara; tel. 151575).

Associated organizations. A group close to the Femaco is the MIN (which may stand for National Independence Movement; based at Apartado Postal 131, Guadalajara).

International affiliations. The Femaco was formerly the Mexican affiliate of the World Anti-Communist League (see South Korea), but was expelled in the early 1980s for reasons set out below (see *Confederación Anticomunista Latinoamericana*).

Partido Demócrata Mexicano (PDM)
Mexican Democratic Party

Address. Edison 89, Colonia Tabacalera, México 1 DF

Leadership. Gumersindo Magaña Negrete (president); Roberto Picón Robledo (secretary)

Orientation. Ultra-conservative

History. The PDM was established in 1971 but gained most of its membership in the late 1970s. It is a creation of the *Unión Nacional Sinarquista* (UNS), a "synarchist" or quasi-fascist movement which developed in Guanajuato state in 1937. The movement was originally led by Helmut Schreiter, Feliciano Manrique, José Antonio Urquiza, Luis Belmont, Salvador Abascal and others. In 1941 the UNS was granted permission to establish a model settlement in the Baja California peninsula, and it organized a "long march" of a couple of hundred of its claimed 1,000,000 peasant sympathizers. Its first attempt to function through a political party structure ended with the prohibition of the *Partido de la Fuerza Popular* (Popular Force Party) in 1949. It continued to exist through the 1950s and '60s, undergoing a major reorganization in 1966, but did not reappear on the national political scene until the 1970s. It organized the PDM but continued to exist in its own right at least until the early 1980s.

The PDM was registered as a political party in 1978 and won ten seats in the Chamber of Deputies in its first electoral outing in 1979. It went on to win 1.9 per cent of the vote in the 1982 presidential election, and gained eight seats in the simultaneous congressional election. In 1985 it won 12 seats.

Policies. The PDM has abandoned fascist rhetoric and now presents itself as a radical conservative party, based on Catholic morality, pluralism and industrial co-ownership. Its policies are in line with those of the UNS, whose "general statutes" define its "supreme goal" as "the implementation in Mexico of a Christian social order". Both the PDM and the UNS are anti-communist and ultra-nationalist.

Membership. The PDM claims 450,000 members.

Publications. *El Demócrata*, circulation 30,000.

Associated organizations. In January 1983 the PDM joined the larger, mainstream conservative National Action Party (PAN) in the Democratic Action for Electoral Rescue (ADRE) alliance.

Los Tecos

Base. Autonomous University of Guadalajara, Jalisco

Orientation. Nazi

History. This clandestine terrorist grouping is typical of the right-wing student gangs, or *porros*, active in a number of university campuses, and is also active outside the university. This group was suspected of involvement in the 1968 massacre of protesting students. The Guadalajara University, founded in 1935, has always been a centre of radical right-wing activity.

The involvement of the *Tecos* in the Mexican Anti-Communist Confederation, and through it in the World Anti-Communist League (see South Korea), began in the early 1970s, causing several non-fascist affiliates to drop out of the League. The new US-based leadership of the League severed the connection in the early 1980s. The *Tecos* also dominated the WACL's youth section, Youth-WACL, since replaced by the Young Conservative Foundation (see World Youth Freedom League, United States). It has been reported that a core group of the *Tecos*, known as *la Mano Blanca* (The White Hand), has operated as a co-ordinating body for Central American death squads.

Policies. The current activities of the *Tecos* and similar groups consist mainly of assaults on left-wing students and organizations. In the heyday of the group in the early 1970s it protested against reforms in the Catholic Church and against alleged freemasonic and Jewish conspiracies.

Unión Nacional Sinarquista—see *Partido Demócrata Mexicano.*

Defunct organizations

Brigada Blanca: the White Brigade was an unofficial right-wing militia active in the late 1970s. It was held responsible for the kidnapping of several hundred ex-prisoners and alleged left-wing activists, and for the torture of some of its victims. Members of a federal police force were widely thought to control the group.

Camisas Doradas: the Gold Shirts or *Acción Revolucionaria Mexicanista*, a national socialist formation led by Gen. Nicolás Rodríguez (a former follower of Pancho Villa), became involved in strike-breaking and in anti-semitic rioting in various parts of Mexico in the early 1930s. The organization was banned in December 1935 after serious street clashes with the communists, and Rodríguez fled to the United States.

Centro Anticomunista: founded in Guanajuato in 1936 by Helmut Oskar Schreiter, a German Nazi immigrant; this was one of the fore-runners of the *Unión Nacional Sinarquista.*

Centro Patronal de la Comarca Lagunera: the Laguna Regional Employers' Centre was one of the first of many right-wing organizations which emerged to oppose the radical policies of the populist president Lázaro Cárdenas in the 1930s. Others founded in this period, few of which lasted into the 1940s, included the *Centro Patronal del Distrito Federal* (the capital city's employers' centre, which co-ordinated many other right-wing groups), the *Confederación de la Clase Media* (Middle-Class Confederation), the *Confederación Patronal de la República Mexicana* (another employers' organization), the *Partido Social Demócrata*, the *Unión Nacionalista Mexicana* and the anti-semitic *Comité Nacional pro-Raza* and *Liga de Defensa Mercantil.*

Círculo Democrático Mexicano: the Mexican Democratic Circle was a vehemently anti-socialist and somewhat anti-semitic grouping active from about 1967 until the late 1970s; it was particularly opposed to Archbishop Sergio Méndez Arceo and other progressive members of the Catholic clergy. Among its leading members were Ruben Mendoza Heredia and Rodrigo García Treviño; its journal was *Impacto*.

Comité Renovador Universitario: the University Renewal Committee (also known as the *Frente Renovador Universitario* or *Frente Renovador Estudiantil*) was one of many anti-communist groups which had an ephemeral existence around 1968-70, their main purpose being to expose alleged communist subversion of the student movement. This particular group, which published *Resumen* magazine, was led by Gustavo de Anda. A similar group was the *Frente Universitario Mexicano* (Mexican University Front), led by Alvaro Flores Rico and linked to the PRI; others were the *Comité Mexicano de Orientación Popular* (Mexican Committee of Popular Orientation), led by Alfredo Kawage Ramia, the *Comité Nacional de Orientación Cívica* (National Civic Orientation Committee) and numerous student groups with names such as Committee of Non-Compromised Preparatory Students or Committee of the Authentic Student Body.

Conciencia Joven: Young Consciousness, active in the mid-1970s, was a "racist, hierarchical and idealist" grouping, producing a magazine of the same name and led by Vitela, Salmas and Novo, and in contact with many foreign fascist groups. It professed a co-operativist variant of fascism. Its symbol was virtually identical to that of the Hungarian Arrow Cross movement.

Confederación Anticomunista Latinoamericana: the Anti-Communist Confederation of Latin America (CAL) was the regional affiliate of the World Anti-Communist League (see South Korea) in the 1970s. It had affiliates representing each of the 20 Latin American republics by the time of its second congress (in Rio de Janeiro, Brazil, in 1974). The third congress was held in Asunción, Paraguay, in 1977. The CAL was based at the offices of its Mexican constituent, the Femaco, led by Raymundo Guerrero, who was chairman of the WACL for a time in the early 1970s. The secretary of the CAL was Prof Rafael Rodríguez López of Guadalajara. The CAL was expelled from the WACL in the early 1980s because of its acceptance of anti-semitic groups and its alleged connections with Central American death squads, mainly through the paramilitary *Tecos* group and its secret central unit, the *Mano Blanca* (White Hand). However, the CAL's replacement as the WACL regional body—the Fedal (see Paraguay)—was reported to have essentially the same membership.

Cristero movement: a Northern Mexican peasant movement fiercely opposed to the anti-clericalism of the government party in the 1920s; it was involved in a virtual civil war in 1926-29.

Despertar—Cooperativismo; a journal and grouping formed in 1974 by J.L. Ontiveros (later of *Año Cero*) and M. de la Isla, it advanced co-operativist fascist ideas similar to those later adopted by *Conciencia Joven*. It was ultra-nationalist, racist and anti-communist, put forward a masonic conspiracy theory and spread the ideas of European fascist thinkers such as the Italian Julius Evola.

Editorial Epoca: a publishing house in Mexico City which produced a range of anti-semitic works, including those of Ford and Hitler and the *Protocols of Zion*, in the late 1970s.

Editorial Jus: a publishing house which produced *cristero* books and the works of the Romanian anti-semitic author, Traian Romanescu, in the 1960s and '70s. It also maintained a right-wing bookshop in Mexico City.

Frente Constitucionalista Mexicano: an anti-communist group active in the late 1960s and early 1970s, it was led by Pedro Antonio Flores.

Los Halcones: the Falcons were a right-wing guerrilla group which attacked a student demonstration in June 1971, with police connivance, killing an unknown number of the students. The group was banned after protests.

Las Legiones: a semi-secret anti-communist organization founded in 1935 by Salvador Abascal; it became *La Base* in 1936 and in the following year was merged into the *Unión Nacional Sinarquista*, of which Abascal became a national leader. Abascal remained active in anti-communist causes for more than 40 years, and in the late 1970s he was running a right-wing Catholic "integrist" publishing house, *Editorial La Tradición*, in México.

Liga Nacional: the National League was the first recorded anti-semitic organization in Mexico. Founded in 1930, and originally known as the National League Against Chinese and Jewish Penetration, it secured the temporary support of two deputies, business leaders and two national newspapers, but it failed to secure its goal of anti-semitic legislation and faded away in the late 1930s.

Movimiento Universitario Renovador de Orientación: the MURO (the acronym means The Wall), or University Movement for a New Orientation, was a student *porro* movement which began in 1963 as a clerical-fascist group and was active as an anti-communist pressure group at least until the early 1970s. The MURO functioned partly as a co-ordinating group for local *porro* movements such as the *Frente Estudiantil Mexicano* (based in the Federal District, and especially active in 1973) and the *Federación Estudiantil de Jalisco* (active in the Jalisco state university since the 1940s).

Partido Comunital Progresista: the PCP (Communal Progressive Party) was one of several parties founded in the 1970s, led by and mainly consisting of Alfonso González Marckez of Puebla.

Partido Justicialista Mexicano: the PJM (Mexican Justicialist Party), another González group, was named after the Argentinian Peronist party and was active in 1978.

Partido Laborista Mexicano: a Mexican manifestation of the Lyndon LaRouche operation (see National Democratic Policy Committee, United States), the PLM was active through *Comités Laborales* and a journal called *Solidaridad* in the late 1970s. The Mexican branch of the movement also operated through New Solidarity International Press Service (NSIPS), which had offices in Venezuela and Colombia but was controlled by the New York-based Campaigner Publications (the name used in the late 1970s by LaRouche's *Executive Intelligence Review* operation—see United States).

Vanguardia Nacional: the National Vanguard (or *Vanguardia Nacionalista Mexicana*), another anti-semitic pressure group, was active from 1938 and was strongly influenced by European fascism. Together with similar groups—the *Juventudes Nacionalistas* of Humberto Tirado and the *Partido Nacionalista Cívico Femenino* (a women's anti-communist party)—it was in regular contact with the German embassy in Mexico. With other anti-semitic and pro-fascist groups, it was suppressed after Mexico's entry into the war on the Allied side in 1942.

Other organizations

Minor right-wing organizations active in the past ten to fifteen years have included the following: *Adalid*, an anti-semitic integrist journal published from Guadalajara in the late 1970s; the *Alianza Popular Anticomunista* (Popular Anti-Communist Alliance); *Año Cero* (Year Zero), a little-known Evolian co-operative fascist group and review formed in 1977 by J.L. Ontiveros; the *Asociación de Padres de Familia* (Parents' Association), a right-wing Catholic moralist pressure group; the *Coalición Nacional de Agrupaciones Anticomunistas* (National Coalition of Anti-Communist Groupings); the *Cruzada Regional Anticomunista* (Regional Anti-Communist Crusade); *Evangelismo Sin*

Fronteras (Evangelism without Frontiers), a fundamentalist Christian anti-communist group led by Roberto Porras Mainas and linked to foreign groups such as the Christian Mission to the Communist World; the *Frente Anticomunista de México* (Anti-Communist Front of Mexico); the *Frente Nacional de Conciliación* (National Conciliation Front); the *Frente Revolucionario de Afirmación Civil* (FRAC, Revolutionary Front for Civic Affirmation), founded in 1961 by the right-wing PRI ex-president (1946-52) Miguel Alemán; *Hoja de Combate* (Combat Bulletin), published by Catholic ultra-rightist Salvador Abascal (see *Las Legiones*, above); the *IAP*; the *Movimiento Nacionalrevolucionario Hispanoamericano*, a nazi group founded in 1974 (and almost certainly defunct); the *porro* grouping, *Movimiento Organizado Democrático Universitario*; a short-lived *Partido Nacional Anticomunista* (National Anti-Communist Party); *Patria Nueva* (New Fatherland), an ultra-right bookselling operation started around 1975; *Trento* (Trent), a journal representing the rebel "integrist" movement within the Catholic Church, whose leader, Archbishop Lefebvre (see Switzerland), was denied entry to Mexico in 1977; and the *Unidad Liberal Benito Juárez* (Benito Juárez Liberal Group).

Individuals

Salvador Borrego: a prolific anti-semitic author and publisher (based at Lisboa 48, México 6 DF), he was particularly active in the 1970s.

Arturo Ramírez: the Mexican correspondent of *The Spotlight*, journal of the anti-semitic Liberty Lobby (United States). He may be associated with a small publishing house, *Ramírez Editores* (M. Azuela 227, México DF), which published a Spanish edition of *Mein Kampf* in the late 1970s.

Mozambique

capital: Maputo   **population: 13,000,000**

Political system. The People's Republic of Mozambique is governed by the sole legal political party, the former liberation movement Frelimo, through a People's Assembly, an executive President and a Council of Ministers.

Recent history. Following a guerrilla war from 1964-1974, Mozambique gained independence from Portugal in 1975 under the presidency of Frelimo leader Samora Machel, who remained in power until his death in an unexplained plane crash in South Africa in 1986. The independence years have been marked by a continuing war between government forces and the anti-communist guerrilla movement, the MNR, which is backed by South Africa and other Western powers.

The evolution of the far right. The MNR has been the only substantial and effective right-wing force since the achievement of independence.

Active organizations

Movimento Nacional da Resistência (MNR or MNRM)
National Resistance Movement

Leadership. Afonso Dlakama (commander and president); Evo Fernandes (general secretary); Arturo Janeior da Fonseca (secretary of external relations); Armando K. Gumbe, Jorge Correia (European representatives)

Orientation. Anti-communist guerrilla group

History. This guerrilla army, also known as *Resistência Nacional Moçambicana* (Renamo), was established in what was then Rhodesia in 1975. Its forces, funded, armed and trained initially by the Smith regime in Rhodesia and from 1980 by South Africa, have been active in various parts of Mozambique since independence but stepped up their campaign in 1981, harassing the Mozambican Army, destroying crops and installations, and providing intelligence and cover for South African military operations against Mozambique. There has been massive disruption of internal and external trade.

The MNR is thought to be based in Malawi, although the government there claimed in 1982 to have dismantled all MNR camps. It has established field headquarters in central Mozambique but has had difficulty in holding these against government offensives. The movement also has representative offices in Portugal. South Africa, which continued to provide clandestine support to the MNR, was involved in attempts to negotiate a ceasefire in 1984-85, but as of March 1987 the fighting was continuing.

Policies. The movement seeks the overthrow of the existing Marxist government and its replacement by a pro-Western regime.

Membership. The MNR is thought to have several thousand men under arms, with many more in reserve.

Publications. The main organ of the MNR is its radio station, *Voz da Africa Livre* (Voice of Free Africa).

International affiliations. Following the signature of a non-aggression pact between Mozambique and South Africa in 1984, the Pretoria regime claimed that it had ceased to provide support to the MNR. Nevertheless the movement is still thought to rely extensively on South African funding, whether through official or other channels. It also receives support from former colonists and exiled opposition politicians in Portugal. During a visit to Washington in August 1986 Correia met Patrick Buchanan, then one of President Reagan's most senior advisors, and also signed an agreement with Ndabaningi Sithole of Zimbabwe. The MNR maintains an office in West Germany. Gumbe represented the group at the 1986 conference of the World Anti-Communist League (see South Korea).

Defunct organizations

Frente Unida Moçambicana (Fumo): this anti-communist grouping was established in 1974 by Portuguese business interests, and moved its base to Portugal after independence. In 1980 it was reportedly attempting to organize an anti-Frelimo army independent of the MNR, but nothing seems to have come of these efforts.

Namibia

capital: Windhoek   **population: 1,200,000**

Political system. Namibia is occupied by the South African regime, which has appointed an Administrator-General who exercises de facto power. The South African authorities have staged restricted elections for parliamentary-style assemblies which are not recognized internationally.

Recent history. Namibia, then known as South-West Africa—the name still used by the South African regime—was occupied by Germany in 1884. In 1920 the League of Nations gave the South African government a mandate to administer the territory, and in 1946 South Africa applied unsuccessfully to the United Nations for permission to annex it.

The South-West African People's Organization (SWAPO) launched a campaign for independence in 1958, and in 1966 began an armed struggle through the People's Liberation Army of Namibia (PLAN). In the same year the UN terminated the South African mandate, but subsequent legal and diplomatic efforts to oblige South Africa to withdraw have had no discernible effect. Internal racially segregated political structures established by the South African regime have not been recognized by SWAPO, which is regarded by the UN as the authentic representative of the Namibian people. South African forces based in Namibia have frequently invaded and bombed neighbouring Angola, allegedly in pursuit of or in pre-emptive strikes against SWAPO forces.

The evolution of the far right. Coverage is not given here to all groups which participate in political structures created by South Africa; the present book restricts its coverage to those which actually defend the South African occupation, oppose independence and/or profess racist ideologies. Parties thus excluded, but which participate in the South African structures, include the Democratic Turnhalle Alliance (and its 11 constituent parties), the Action Front for the Preservation of Turnhalle Principles (dominated by the South African-linked National Party), the Labour Party of South West Africa, the Liberal Party, the Namibia Christian Democratic Party, the Namibia Independence Party, the Organization for the Interests of German-Speaking Southwesters and the Rehoboth Liberation Front. The de facto government, its organs and its foreign representation are likewise excluded from this work.

Apart from the South African-style white racist movement, classic nazi ideology has found expression in the country mainly through the pre-war organizations of the substantial German minority, which in the 1930s formed one-third of the 30,000-strong white population. The main nazi party was briefly represented in the whites-only parliament. In August 1933 the Legislative Assembly outlawed political uniforms, nazi propaganda and the boycotting of Jewish businesses; more severe action, including the expulsion of nazi leaders, was taken in the following year.

Active organizations

American Anti-Terrorism Institute

Address. 910 17th Street NW, Suite 320, Washington, DC 20006, United States

Orientation. Pro-South African

History. This Institute, effectively part of the South African lobby in the United States, was founded in 1980.

Policies. The primary function of the Institute is to spread the message that SWAPO is a Soviet-backed terrorist organization whose aims and activities represent a threat to the security interests of the United States.

Der Deutsch-Sudafrikaner
The German South African

Address. Postfach 223, Swakopmund

Leadership. W.R. Schirmer (publisher)

Orientation. White supremacist

History. This journal was being published in the early 1980s.

Policies. It presents white supremacist and anti-democratic ideas from the viewpoint of the German-speaking section of the white population of Namibia.

Herstigte Nasionale Party (HNP)
Reconstituted National Party

Address. Sanlam-Gebaude 218, Bulowstrasse, Postfach 2455, Windhoek

Leadership. Sarel J. Becker (leader)

Orientation. White supremacist

History. The ultra-right HNP was organized by supporters of the South African party of the same name, of which this group is essentially a subsidiary. It won 5,781 votes (1.8 per cent of the total vote) and one seat in the "National Assembly" elections held by the South African occupation administration in 1978. Most of its support comes from the German and Afrikaans-speaking communities.

Policies. The HNP seeks the integration of Namibia into South Africa under an apartheid system. Its policies on this and on other matters are identical with those of the South African parent group.

International affiliations. See HNP (South Africa).

International Society for Human Rights—see West Germany.

Wit Weerstandsbeweging
White Resistance Movement

Orientation. White supremacist

History. Little has been heard of this guerrilla group since it destroyed the Windhoek offices of the SWAPO in June 1979.

Policies. The Movement seeks to preserve white minority rule and the link with South Africa.

Defunct organizations

Deutsche Bund: the German League, led by Dr Schwieterung, was the main pre-war nazi movement, and had the support of a large proportion of the German settler population. It had basically the same policies as the Nazi Party in Germany, and was modelled on that party, even calling its youth section the *Hitlerjugend*. It resisted the administration of the region as a province of South Africa and sought increased autonomy and stronger ties with Germany, the colonial power before the First World War.

In July 1933 Capt. von Losnitzer, leader of the Hitler Youth, was expelled from the territory, and the movement was temporarily banned. In August 1933 and April 1934, in attempts to control the activities of the *Bund*, the parliament of South-West Africa, dominated by white men of British and Dutch descent, passed legislation restricting nazi activities and propaganda and banning the use of political uniforms (although an exception was made for the Hitler Youth, as for two scouting organizations). The *Bund*'s representatives withdrew from the Parliament in protest in the following month. The boycott continued until October 1934, when the nazi movement was outlawed, but the German community then formed an Economic League to take up the nazi seats in parliament. In November Major Weigal, the German officer commanding the nazi stormtroopers, was expelled, and the nazi offices in Windhoek were closed.

The Netherlands

capital: Amsterdam   **population: 14,450,000**

Political system. The Kingdom of the Netherlands is a hereditary monarchy with a bicameral parliament, the States-General, consisting of a 75-seat, indirectly elected First Chamber and a 150-seat Second Chamber directly elected using a form of proportional representation. Executive power is held by a Prime Minister and Council of Ministers responsible to parliament.

Recent history. Since liberation in 1945 the Netherlands has had a series of coalition governments, involving a variety of Catholic, Protestant, liberal and social democratic parties. These governments have pursued centre-right or centre-left policies and have frequently collapsed due to internal differences.

The evolution of the far right. There was a significant nazi movement in the 1930s; in September 1933, however, the wearing of political uniforms or badges was outlawed. The Netherlands was occupied by Nazi Germany during the Second World War, and a collaborationist regime was established. Local fascist groups such as the NSB provided a recruiting ground from 1940 for the Dutch-speaking SS Westland regiment, also recruited in the Flemish community in Belgium. The ultra-right has not been a major factor in post-war politics although an anti-immigration movement developed in the 1970s.

Active organizations

Amajuba Bulletin

Address. Postbus 1293, Gronigen

Orientation. Neo-fascist

History. This English-language periodical was being published in the mid-1980s. It was part of a bookselling and merchandising operation.

Policies. It concentrates on right-wing analyses of events in Europe and South Africa.

Centrum Partij (CP)
Centre Party

Address. Postbus 670, 2500 CR The Hague

Telephone. (070) 46 93 80

Leadership. Drs N. Konsa (chairwoman); D. Jegers (secretary)

Orientation. Right-wing and racist

History. The CP was formed in March 1980, partly by ex-members of the fascist NVU such as Robert Boot (the CP's first secretary). It contested local elections without success in 1980, and won only 12,000 votes in the 1981 general election, but in 1982 it gained over 68,000 votes (0.8 per cent) and one seat in the elections to the second chamber. Its successful candidate, the then CP chairman Hans Janmaat, and his deputy (and leader of the CP's "defence courses") Nico Konst, were involved in controversy in 1983 arising from their positions as teachers in the state educational system. In 1984 the Party won 10 per cent of the vote in the Rotterdam council elections, securing eight seats. There have been violent incidents at some CP rallies, including 70 arrests and the burning of a hotel in Leerdam in early 1986.

Policies. The main Centre Party policy is total opposition to black immigration. It also espouses law and order and other right-wing policy concerns, although it claims to be "neither of the right nor of the left".

Membership. 4,000.

Publications. *Centrumnieuws*; *Middenweg*

Associated organizations. The youth wing of the party is the *Jonge Centrum Democraten*. Organizations with which it co-operates or where there has been an overlap in membership include the *Wetenschappelijk Bureau Prof. G. van der Leeuw* and anti-immigrant groups such as the *Ekologiese Beweging*(which publishes *Bewust* magazine and whose chairman, Alfred Vierling, became Janmaat's parliamentary assistant), the *Groene Partij* (not to be confused with the progressive ecologist *De Groenen* movement), *Nederland voor de Nederlanders*, *Referendum-Nederland* and the *Vereninging tot Behoud van het Nederlandse Volk*.

De Levensboom

Address. Kluizenaarsweg 1, 6881 BS Velp

Orientation. Ultra-right

History. This publishing and bookselling operation was active in the mid-1980s.

International affiliations. Foreign publications in which this service has advertised include *Euro-forum* (Belgium).

Nationaal Jeugd Front (NJF)
National Youth Front

Address. Postbus 43314, The Hague; or Postbus 10366, 1001 EJ Amsterdam

Orientation. Neo-fascist

History. This group attended the 1983 Diksmuide rally organized by the Belgian fascist movement. It functions as the youth wing of the NVU. In April and May 1983

the name of the NJF was used, probably spuriously, in claiming responsibility for three bomb attacks on a Pacifist Socialist Party office in Tilburg.

Publications. Opmars, monthly. The group is almost certainly also the publisher of the *NJF-Nieuws*.

Nederlandse Volksunie (NVU)
Dutch People's Union

Address. Postbus 10366, 1001 EJ Amsterdam

Leadership. Joop G. Glimmerveen (president); F. Zoetmulder (secretary); Et Wolsinck

Orientation. Ultra-nationalist

History. The NVU, founded in March 1971, took part in elections from 1974 onwards. In 1977 it won 33,000 votes (0.4 per cent) in the Second Chamber elections. It received legal recognition as a political party in April 1979 despite moves to ban it because of its extremist positions. Glimmerveen, who has convictions for inciting racialism, was in May 1981 deposed as leader of the NVU by a more moderate conservative faction led by Berendregt, but he regained the presidency in 1983 (after he had formed a separate organization the *Jongers Front Nederland*).

Policies. The NVU opposes black immigration and supports the political unity of the Netherlands with Germany and other northern European countries.

Associated organizations. See *Nationaal Jeugdfront*. The NVU has recruited members from or lost members to a wide variety of other right-wing groupings, including the *Boerenpartij*, the *Binding Rechts*, the *Centrum Partij* and the *Viking Jeugd*. A leading member, J.W. van der Meulen, has been associated with the *Viking Jeugd* and broke away from it around 1979 to form the *Commando Paul Klomp*. The NVU has sponsored the *Rudolf Hess Vrij* committee.

Publications. Wij Nederland.

International affiliations. The Union has particularly close connections with the Belgian Institute for European Studies. One of its leading members, R. Raes, has been associated with Belgian fascist groups, including *Were Di*, *Voorpost* and the *Vlaamse Volksunie*.

Northern League

Address. Postbus 1796, Amsterdam

Leadership. Jan Kruls (secretary)

Orientation. Fascist

History. This group was established in 1958 by US-based anthropologist Roger Pearson (see Council for Social and Economic Studies, United States) and Scottish teacher Alistair Harper, who were then editor and associate editor respectively of *Northern World*, a Nordicist and anti-semitic journal with an international circulation. Among prominent members or supporters of the League have been Ray Bamford, John Bean and Ted Budden of the United Kingdom; American Ku Klux Klan leader Ernest Sevier Cox; veteran British fascist Oliver Gilbert; Hans Günther, a West German nazi race theorist; H.B. Isherwood, a British racist pamphleteer; nazi leader Colin Jordan and Peter Ling of Column 88 (UK); ex-SS officer Wilhelm Kusserow of the *Deutsche Artgemeinschaft*; Swiss racist leader James Schwarzenbach; Norbert Seibart, of the German *Nordische Zeitung*; Martin Webster, then of the British National Front and now in Our Nation, and W.P. Zeilmaker (Netherlands).

The heyday of the League was in the late 1960s and early '70s, when it held major conferences in Brighton (England), but it remains in existence in the mid-1980s and held a conference in Utrecht in 1984. Its present leader, Kruls, was active in the NSB and the Fatherland Club as a pre-war plantation owner in the East Indies. He later moved to England and was active for a time in the National Front.

The League's emblem is the *tryfoss* rune, a swastika-like symbol.

Policies. The original and continuing purpose of the League was to provide a cultural and political forum for people of "all Teutonic nations", to further appreciation and understanding of their common heritage. In practice it has functioned as a point of contact for members of a variety of fascist and racist groups in Western Europe.

Publications. The journal of the League, *Northlander*, no longer appears regularly. It has been supported by G. van der Ven's Dutch-language *Europa Post*.

Associated organizations. Among many Dutch groups which have or have had Northern League connections are the NVU, the *Boerenpartij*, the *Viking Jeugd*, the *Nationaal Jeug Front* and the *Centrum Partij*. H. Kilinkenberg, an SS veteran and League member, is a leading member of the *Boven de Veertig* society.

International affiliations. Little is known of the present state of the League or of its foreign affiliates. These are, however, known to include the League of St. George (United Kingdom), which shares the Northern League's aims.

Defunct organizations

Cultural Future of the Netherlands: the headquarters of this group was raided by the police in March 1984 and arms and other materials were seized. Five members were arrested. According to reports the group was opposed to immigration and had been involved in at least two attacks on Arabs.

Fatherland Club: a wartime collaborationist organization.

National Socialist Union (NSB): this pre-war fascist party, which was organized throughout Holland and in the Dutch East Indies (now Indonesia), collaborated with the German occupation administration. Many of its members joined locally recruited Waffen-SS forces.

Other organizations

Other right-wing groupings active in the Netherlands in recent years include the following (some of which may be defunct): *Binding Rechts* (Co-operation on the Right), founded in Apeldoorn in 1968, led by E.J. Harmsen and including many ex-members of the libertarian *Boerenpartij* (Farmers' Party) and of the NVU; the *Bond Nederland-Israel*; the racist *Ekologiese Beweging* (Ecological Movement), which is led by E. Vleer-Jagerman and Drs A.J.C. Vierling, and its splinter groups the *Volksnationaal Front* (led by B. Bronk and A. Roos) and *Communisme Nooit*; the *Fascisties Bevrijdingsfront*(Fascist Liberation Front), which along with three other groups—J.W. van der Meulen's *Commando Paul Klomp*, J.J.G. van Spengen's *Mutua Fides* (Mutual Trust) and the *Vapan*—arose from the *Viking Jeugd*, the Dutch affiliate of the German-based *Wiking Jugend* (a neo-nazi scout group); *Interdoc* (the International Centre for Documentation and Information); the fascist *Jongers Front Nederland* (Holland Youth Front—Postbus 962, 2501 CZ The Hague), founded in 1981 by Joop Glimmerveen after he was temporarily deposed as leader of the NVU; the *Oud Strijders Legioen*, comprised of veterans of the Nazi armed forces; the *Sint-Maartensfonds* (a nazi veterans' group—see Belgium); *Storm* magazine (published by ex-NVU member M. Clabou, and including among its contributors Joop Glimmerveen); the "Moonie" Unification Church (see South Korea), which operates in the Netherlands as the *Verenigingskerk* and through a front called the Federation for World Peace; and *Voorpost-Nederland* (related to the Belgian *Voorpost*), which publishes *Revolte*. There is also a Netherlands affiliate of the World Anti-Communist League (WACL—see South Korea), which attracts a broad spectrum of right-wing support. The small Socialist Party (SP) has been accused, particularly in 1983, of having a racist attitude to immigrant communities.

New Zealand

capital: Wellington   **population: 3,300,000**

Political system. The Dominion of New Zealand is a constitutional monarchy with the UK sovereign as head of state. There is a 95-seat House of Representatives elected by universal adult suffrage, and a Cabinet headed by a Prime Minister.

Recent history. Political power has alternated between the conservative National Party and the social democratic Labour Party, with the latter party forming the government after the 1984 and 1987 elections.

The evolution of the far right. New Zealand has been relatively free of fascist agitation, although there have been a number of right-wing conservative fringe organizations.

Active organizations

Democratic National Party

Address. PO Box 45-031, Lower Hutt

Orientation. Ultra-right

History. This white supremacist organization was active in the late 1970s and early 1980s. Its name has also been reported as New Zealand Democratic Nationalist Party.

Nationalist Workers' Party (NWP)

Base. Wellington

Orientation. Ultra-right

History. This group was formed in the early 1980s. In March 1984 it was suspected of involvement in the bombing of a trade union hall, in which the caretaker was killed.

Policies. The NWP has white supremacist and authoritarian policies.

International affiliations. The Party is particularly close to the Australian National Action movement.

New Zealand League of Rights

Leadership. Bill Daly (national director)

Orientation. Anti-semitic, white supremacist

History. This group, descended from the Australian League of Rights, was active in 1985-86.

Policies. The international League of Rights movement promotes belief in a Jewish conspiracy for world domination.

International affiliations. Through the Crown Commonwealth League of Rights (see United Kingdom) the League is linked to similar organizations in Britain, Canada, Australia and the United States.

New Zealand Phalanx

Address. 49 McAnalley Street, Manurewa; or PO Box 23-215, Papatoetoe, Auckland

Orientation. Neo-fascist

History. This group was in contact with foreign fascist groups in the late 1970s and early 1980s. It did not respond to a questionnaire and may be defunct. The Manurewa address, which was that of the Phalanx in the early 1980s, was used in the mid-1970s by the New Zealand Commonwealth Alliance, a white supremacist grouping chaired by Ronald Keen; it is possible that the two groups have merged.

Society for the Protection of Individual Rights (SPIR)

Leadership. Pat Hunt (spokesman)

History. In 1985 this group (which has also been named in reports as the Society for the Protection of the Rights of Individuals, SPRI) was involved in promoting sporting links between New Zealand and South Africa.

White People's Alliance

Address. PO Box 20-132, Christchurch 5

Orientation. White supremacist

History. The Alliance, which was active in the early 1980s, may include former members of the New Zealand National Front, a late 1970s Christchurch-based offshoot of the British National Front. Its Post Office Box number is that used in the 1970s by the National Socialist Party of New Zealand.

Policies. The Alliance is strongly opposed to non-white immigration.

Defunct organizations

Heed: this extremely anti-communist journal, which sought to provide a platform for "patriotic opinion", was launched in 1976 by Larsen and Crawford as a bi-monthly. It ceased publication shortly thereafter.

National Socialist Party of New Zealand: founded in 1969 by Durward Colin King-Ansell (also known as Colin Ansell), who had been imprisoned in 1968-69 for damaging a synagogue, the NSPNZ virtually disappeared after its leader's disastrous performance in a television chat show in 1970, following which he went to Australia and became involved in both small nazi parties active there (the NSPA and the ANSP). His deputy was a burglar, Errol James Silvester, and the party secretary was called

Benstead. The party organ was the *Observer*. In 1978 King-Ansell was reportedly leading a National Socialist White People's Party (NSWPP), which was affiliated through the World Union of National Socialists to the US party of the same name.

Other organizations

Other relevant groupings reportedly active during the past decade include the following: *British Israel World Federation* (part of the British Israel movement—see United Kingdom); a section of the UK-based *Christian Mission to the Communist World*; *Truth* magazine; a branch of the German-based *Viking Youth* nazi scouting movement, and the *White People's Alliance*.

Nicaragua

capital: Managua   **population: 3,000,000**

Political system. Under a Constitution drafted in 1985-86, to come into effect in 1987, Nicaragua has an executive President and a 90-seat National Assembly, both elected by universal adult suffrage.

Recent history. A prolonged revolution succeeded in 1979 in overthrowing the corrupt and despotic regime of the Somoza family. A broad-based junta took office, but the main revolutionary force—the left-wing Sandinista National Liberation Front (FSLN)—gradually extended its control over government institutions, a process accelerated by the development of a counter-revolutionary guerrilla campaign openly supported after 1981 by the United States government. Despite the disruption caused by the fighting, elections were held in 1984, with the FSLN winning the presidency and almost two-thirds of the seats in the new legislature. The opposition armies, known as *contras*, continued their campaign, especially along the Honduran border, into 1987.

The evolution of the far right. The complete upheaval produced by the revolution destroyed the main right-wing party—Anastasio Somoza's National Liberal Party—and most other far-right parties and pressure groups. Since 1979 the right-wing *contra* movements, and their political structures (which, at present, are embryonic), have consisted of three strands, which are becoming less easily distinguishable: the first comprises survivors of Somoza's National Guard (the *somocistas*), the second, disaffected middle-class and ecclesiastical figures not particularly identified with the Somoza regime, and the third, now almost extinct, consists of the small band (led until mid-1986 by Edén Pastora) of ex-Sandinistas and other anti-Somoza elements who turned against the revolution when it became clear that the FSLN was to dominate the government.

The United States, acting mainly through the Central Intelligence Agency (CIA), has expended considerable energy and money in an effort to create and maintain political and military co-ordination of the opposition groupings. The foundation in 1985 of the UNO alliance was the most significant result of that pressure. The US has also been more directly involved in the fighting, with the CIA mining Nicaraguan ports in 1984. US government funding of the *contras* probably began with

US$19,000,000 provided by the National Security Council and paid through third countries (including El Salvador, Guatemala, Argentina and Honduras) in 1981. About US$61,000,000 was disbursed in 1982-84. The US Congress has authorized most of the funds received to date by the *contra* armies, including US$27,000,000 in "humanitarian" aid in 1985 (although there was a temporary suspension of official payments in 1984-85). Despite revelations of drug dealing and the embezzlement by *contra* leaders of millions of dollars of earlier US funding, and despite a ruling in June 1986 by the International Court of Justice that the US involvement in the *contra* war was illegal, the Reagan administration persuaded Congress to authorise in August 1986 a US$100 million military training and supplies package to assist the *contras*. The war had by that time caused about 26,000 casualties, including some 15,000 deaths.

Official US funding was supplemented in 1984-86 by a secret government operation diverting to the *contras* income from the illegal sale of weapons to Iran, and by US pressure on friendly governments in the Middle East and elsewhere to supply arms or money. The US policy is motivated by President Reagan's analysis of Nicaragua as "a country held captive by a cruel clique of deeply committed communists at war with God and man" and as a threat to the security of the United States. The administration generally describes the *contra* movements as "the resistance" and as "freedom fighters".

Various private groups, such as the US Council for World Freedom, the "Soldier of Fortune" mercenary group, Civilian Military Assistance and Citizens for America have also been supplying funds, material and other support to the *contras*. *Contra* sources put this support at US$1,500,000 per month by late 1984. The *contras* also receive the support of the World Anti-Communist League (see South Korea) and its European affiliates, while two British nazis are prominent in recruiting mercenaries to help them. Foreign governments which are known to have provided funds include those of Argentina, Venezuela, Saudi Arabia, Taiwan, Israel and Brunei.

All of the *contra* movements are based outside Nicaragua, the majority of their troops being in Honduras and Costa Rica and the majority of their leaders in Miami and New Orleans in the US. In early 1987 their strength was variously estimated at between 15,000 and 20,000 men, of whom only a few thousand were engaged in fighting at a given moment. Within Nicaragua there are now no active legal far right groups, although elements of the press and the Catholic Church have at times adopted positions sympathetic to the right, and anti-Sandinista conservative and liberal parties remain in existence.

At the time of writing the US governmental and private sponsors of the *contra* movements were embroiled in congressional and media investigations of what was inevitably dubbed the Irangate scandal; partly as a result of the scandal, there were serious disputes within the movements, and the entries below may not take full account of the leadership changes and other matters arising from such disputes. It must be noted in particular that Alfonso Robelo and Arturo Cruz, hitherto leading figures in the more "moderate" of the *contra* groupings, appeared by mid-April 1987 to have withdrawn, perhaps temporarily, from the positions and movements ascribed to them below, in both cases as a result of differences with their right-wing rival Adolfo Calero.

Active organizations

Alianza Revolucionaria Democrática (ARDE)
Democratic Revolutionary Alliance

Leadership. Alfonso Robelo Callejas (political leader); Fernando Chamorro Rapaccioli (also known as El Negro; military commander); Adolfo Chamorro (also known as Popo)

Orientation. Contra

History. The ARDE was founded in San José (Costa Rica) in September 1982 as a coalition of contra guerrilla and political groups; its first military commander, Edén Pastora (see FRS), was a defector from the Sandinistas. It commenced guerrilla operations on the southern front in May 1983, co-ordinating its main offensives in September and December with those of the northern FDN.

Although the ARDE claimed responsibility for the mining of Nicaraguan ports in February 1984, this was later proven to be the work of the CIA. Two months later the ARDE seized the town of San Juan del Sur for four days, leading to the closure of its Costa Rican offices after a diplomatic protest from Nicaragua. The presence of ARDE bases and occasional allegations of croos-border incursions (in both directions) continued to sour relations between Nicaragua and Costa Rica in the following years.

Pastora resigned the command in October as a result of the ARDE's alliance with *somocistas* in the FDN; his disagreement with that policy was widely held to be the reason for an attempt on his life some months earlier. He left the *contra* campaign altogether in May 1986. ARDE's military activities have continued, mainly along the Costa Rican border.

Policies. The ARDE called initially for the holding of elections and for the withdrawal of Cuban military advisors from Nicaragua. The ARDE claims to oppose the "totalitarianism" of the present-day FSLN while respecting the memory of Augusto Sandino, the revolutionary leader of the 1930s from whom the term "Sandinista" derives, and calling for profound social and economic reforms.

Membership. The original components of the ARDE coalition were the FRS, the MDN, Rivera's Misurasata and the UDN-FARN; by 1986 the membership consisted of the FTN (a *contra* trade-union federation based in Costa Rica), the MDN, the UDN-FARN, the anti-Rivera Misurasata faction, the FSDC and the small *Solidaridad de Trabajadores Cristianos* (STC—Christian Workers' Solidarity, led by Donald Castillo).

Publications. The ARDE operates a radio station, *Voz de Sandino*.

Associated organizations. The ARDE and the FDN announced a formal alliance in July 1984; in September they combined with Misura to form the UNIR grouping. In June 1985 this grouping joined the CDN to form the UNO coalition; tensions have reportedly arisen within the ARDE as to the degree of military control which the UNO leadership should exercise over its components.

Asamblea Nicaragüense de Unidad Democrática (Anude)
Nicaraguan Assembly of Democratic Unity

Base. Costa Rica

Leadership. José Dávila Membereno

Orientation. Contra

History. The Anude was formed in September 1982 by non-*somocista* right-wing émigrés.

Policies. Dávila has called for the violent overthrow of the Sandinista regime by a united opposition front.

Associated organizations. In August 1985 the Anude helped to found the BOS alliance. Dávila leads the *Frente de Solidaridad Demócrata Cristiana* (FSDC), a right-wing émigré faction of the PSCN (the Nicaraguan Social Christian Party).

International affiliations. In 1983 the group claimed to have offices in Costa Rica, Venezuela and Europe, and to have contacts in the Honduran armed forces.

Bloque Opositora del Sur (BOS)
Southern Opposition Bloc

Base. Costa Rica

Leadership. Alfredo César Aguirre, José Dávila Membereno (leaders)

Orientation. Contra

History. The BOS was formed in August 1985 by Edén Pastora (see FRS) and other non-*somocista* exiles including the leadership of the ARDE. By mid-1986 it appeared to be in some disarray, with most of its commanders favouring greater co-operation with the UNO's guerrilla forces—which included the FDN. Pastora and his allies had rejected the inclusion of any *somocista* elements. In March 1986 the BOS announced its agreement to form a common front with the UNO, leaving Pastora somewhat isolated. The ejection of Pastora from the ARDE leadership in May strengthened the political and military alliance of BOS and its constituents with the UNO groupings.

Policies. The BOS has called for the unification of *contra* forces subject to certain conditions including equal status for the various groups.

Membership. The announcement of the formation of the BOS was made in the names of various *contra* groupings, including *Rescate y Conciliación Nacional* and the ARDE.

International affiliations. The BOS has protested that its members have not received a fair share of the US funding of the *contra* movement.

Central de Trabajadores Nicaragüenses—see CDN.

Committee for a Free Nicaragua (CFN)

Base. London, UK

Leadership. David Hoile (founder)

Orientation. Pro-*contra*

History. A Labour Party member of the UK Parliament alleged in October 1986 that this organization, led by a member of the Federation of Conservative Students who worked as research assistant to a Conservative Party MP, was responsible for recruiting mercenaries to fight alongside the *contras* in Nicaragua. Hoile had in May 1985 visited *contra* bases on the Honduran border, along with Michael Waller, who is national secretary of the US-based Young Americans for Freedom (and is also an employee of the pro-*contra* Council for Inter-American Security).

In December 1986 Hoile, together with Waller, Mark Gordon and others, organized a "Conference for a Free Nicaragua" in London. The meeting, the funding of which was secret, was addressed by Arturo Cruz of the UNO and by associates of the US Heritage Foundation, and was attended mainly by European conservative youth groups.

Policies. The group exists to oppose what it terms the Sandinista dictatorship, and to espouse and publicize the cause of the contras.

Confederación de Unificación Sindical—see CDN.

Consejo Superior de la Empresa Privada—see CDN.

Coordinadora Democrática Nicaragüense Ramiro Sacasa (CDN)
Ramiro Sacasa Democratic Co-ordinating Body of Nicaragua

Leadership. Dr Eduardo Rivas Gasteazoro (president); Dr Arturo José Cruz, Adán Fletes, Pedro Joaquín Chamorro

Orientation. Pro-*contra*

History. The CDN was founded in July 1981 as an alliance of the main internal conservative opposition groups. It withdrew from the Council of State in March 1984, alleging abuses of human rights, and boycotted the November elections in which Cruz had been its prospective presidential candidate.

Policies. The CDN sought at first to persuade the government to enter into negotiations with the *contra* forces and to carry out various political reforms. It has subsequently adopted political positions close to those of the *contras*, while retaining a presence within Nicaragua.

Membership. The founding members of the CDN were the PSCN, the PCDN, the PLC, the *Partido Social Demócrata* (PSD, a right-wing social democratic group led by Wilfredo Montalván), the *Consejo Superior de la Empresa Privada* (Cosep, an employers' federation), and the *Confederación de Unificación Sindical* (CUS) and *Central de Trabajadores Nicaragüenses* (CTN; right-wing trade unions). By mid-1985 it consisted of the *Partido Social Cristiano Nicaragüense* (PSCN, the main Christian Democratic party); the *Partido Liberal Constitucionalista* (PLC, a centre-right faction which broke away from Somoza's PLN), the PSD and a minority faction of the *Partido Conservador Demócrata* (PCD or PC, this faction led by Mario Rappaccioli and Miriam Argüello).

Associated organizations. After holding discussions with leaders of the ARDE, the FDN, the FPS and Misura in early 1985, the CDN joined those groups to form the UNO coalition in June.

Coordinadora de la Oposición Nicaragüense: see MDN.

Ejército de Liberación Nacional (ELN)
National Liberation Army

Base. Honduras

Leadership. Pedro Ortega (also known as Juan Carlos; leader)

Orientation. Somocista

History. The ELN was formed in 1979 by ex-members of Somoza's National Guard. Its reported operations have been confined to the north-eastern border area. The ELN may have merged with a larger force in view of the lack of recent news of its activities.

Policies. It is one of the most right-wing of the *contra* armies.

Membership. Between 4,000 and 6,000 (1980 claim).

Federación de Trabajadores Nicaragüenses—see ARDE.

Frente Revolucionario Sandino (FRS)
Sandino Revolutionary Front

Orientation. Contra

History. This group was formed by Edén Pastora Gómez, who under the *nom de guerre* of Comandante Cero was a popular and daring leader of the FSLN guerrilla forces. After the revolution, when it became clear that he was not to hold a senior post in the new government, Pastora moved to a position of outright opposition to the Sandinistas, and in 1981 he fled to Costa Rica where he announced the formation of the FRS as a fighting force to take on the FSLN.

After an increasingly ineffective campaign along Nicaragua's southern border, Pastora decided in May 1986 to stop fighting and in June he was granted political asylum in Costa Rica. In August 1986 a US State Department report to Congress acknowledged that "a senior figure" in the FRS leadership had been engaged in drug trafficking on a massive scale. The Front may have disbanded.

Policies. The FRS seeks the overthrow of the Sandinista government and the establishment of a democratic non-socialist state.

Associated organizations. The FRS was a founding member of the ARDE alliance but was reported to have withdrawn from it in 1984 in protest at its association with the FDN. Pastora nevertheless maintained contact with the ARDE, the BOS and other *contra* groups until his retirement.

Frente de Solidaridad Demócrata Cristiana— see ARDE and Anude.

Fuerzas Armadas Revolucionarias Nicaragüenses—see UDN-FARN.

Fuerzas Democráticas Nicaragüenses (FDN)
Nicaraguan Democratic Forces

Base. Honduras

Leadership. Adolfo Calero Portocarrero (C.-in-C.); Enrique Bermúdez (military commander); Indalecio Rodríguez (head of civilian services)

Orientation. Somocista

History. The FDN (the name of which is frequently rendered in the singular, *Fuerza Democrática Nicaragüense*) was formed in November 1981 by right-wing business interests and commenced guerrilla activities along the northern border in 1982. It was joined in 1983 by Calero, a kinsman of Somoza and leader of the PCD, who was named by the FDN as "president in exile". It became, and remains, the largest and most effective of the *contra* armies, having suffered and inflicted thousands of casualties in the five years from 1982. Its major offensives to date have been launched in December 1982, August and December 1983, March 1984 and July and November 1985, with sporadic raids, including aerial and seaborne attacks, in the intervening months.

In October 1985 five alleged members of the FDN were arrested in Managua on terrorist charges. It has continued its rural campaign, without major advances since late 1985.

Policies. The goal of the FDN is "to liberate [the Nicaraguan]people from Marxist totalitarianism".

Membership. Estimates of its strength vary from about 10,000 to 30,000.

Associated organizations. The FDN began as a military alliance of the Misurasata, the UDN and the *Legión 15 de Septiembre* (a *somocista* group founded in 1979), but it now functions as a single organization with a four-man directorate.

In July 1984 the FDN allied with the other main *contra* formation, the ARDE, causing a split in the latter organization; in September this alliance became the UNIR coalition. In June 1985 it became a major part of the UNO, a broad *contra* alliance created at the instigation of the United States.

International affiliations. The FDN has from 1982 received substantial logistic and financial support from the CIA and from private agencies in the United States. It has also reportedly received official support from the governments of Argentina, Guatemala, Israel, Taiwan and Venuezuela.

Human Development Foundation

Address. 444 Brickell Avenue, Miami, Florida, United States

Orientation. Pro-*contra*

History. This organization, which is apparently controlled by a Panamanian company unconnected with the identically named Foundation based in West Palm Beach, Florida, was created in 1984 to gather funds for *contra* movements. It solicits donations from private individuals and companies in a manner which circumvents the provisions of the US Neutrality Act.

Policies. Newspaper advertisements represent the Foundation as a humanitarian organization concerned with assisting refugees from "communist dominated Nicaragua".

Jeane Kirkpatrick Task Force—see Nicaragua Freedom Fund.

Kisán
Nicaraguan Indigenous Communities Union

Base. Honduras

Leadership. Diego Wykliffe (leader)

Orientation. Contra

History. This political-military group was formed in September 1985 at a meeting of about 900 Nicaraguan Indians from the Miskito coast. It has reportedly been responsible for the forcible relocation to Honduras of about 9,000 Indians.

Policies. The group maintains that the Atlantic coast indigenous communities have suffered at the hands of the Sandinista government.

Associated organizations. The main body of *Kisán* is an affiliate of the UNO *contra* alliance, although factions within it have defected to the Nicaraguan government-sponsored *Misatán* group.

International affiliations. It reportedly sought US$300,000 in US government funding in 1985-86.

Legión 15 de Septiembre—see FDN.

Misura

Orientation. Contra

History. This group, founded in Honduras in July 1982 by Steadman Fagoth Müller (a former member of the Council of State) as *Guerrilla Miskito*, consists of Sumo and Rama Indians from the Miskito region on Nicaragua's Atlantic coast. It conducted a low-intensity guerrilla war against Sandinista forces independently of other *contra* groups until it joined the UNIR alliance in August 1984.

In January 1985 Fagoth was deported from Honduras after the failure of a Nicaraguan extradition request prompted by the kidnapping of 23 Sandinista troops. He returned to lead the group but was arrested by his men in August after allegedly betraying secrets.

Membership. 3,000 under arms (1985 estimate).

Associated organizations. The group is amember of the UNIR and has supported the political demands of the CDN.

Misurasata

Leadership. Joaquín Suazo Jessy, Guillermo Espinoza, Rafael Zelaya (leaders)

Orientation. Contra

History. This faction broke away in late 1984 from the larger group of the same name (founded in 1982 and led by Brooklyn Rivera) in protest at the main body's decision to leave the ARDE *contra* grouping and to seek negotiations with the Sandinista government. It continued to fight the guerrilla campaign begun in 1982 by *los Astros*, the military wing of Rivera's group.

Policies. Misurasata claims that the Sandinistas have persecuted the Sumo and Rama Indians and Creoles of the east coast.

Associated organizations. See ARDE.

Movimiento Anticomunista Nicaragüense (MAN)
Nicaraguan Anti-Communist Movement

Orientation. Contra

History. The MAN emerged in mid-1985, when it kidnapped and later released a group of US Christian activists and journalists on the Costa Rican border.

Movimiento Democrático Nicaragüense (MDN)
Nicaraguan Democratic Movement

Leadership. Alfonso Robelo Callejas (leader); Fabio Gadea Mantilla

Orientation. Contra

History. The MDN was founded in April 1978 by businessmen who sought the resignation of the Somoza government and an end to the civil war. In July of that year it joined an opposition broad front, and it was represented in the first post-revolutionary government. It soon came into conflict with the FSLN and withdrew from the Council of State after the banning of a rally in November 1980.

In November 1981 the MDN declined to co-operate with the conservative PSCN and PSD parties in seeking negotiations with the FSLN, and in June 1982 Robelo left Nicaragua after his property was forfeited for subversive activities. After becoming involved in street clashes with the Sandinistas, the MDN became a founding member of the ARDE *contra* grouping in December 1982.

Policies. The MDN represents the non-*somocista* middle class section of the *contra* movement.

Associated organizations. Apart from the ARDE, the MDN is a member of a moderate *contra* alliance, the *Coordinadora de la Oposición Nicaragüense* (CON—Co-ordination of the Nicaraguan Opposition), a Costa Rican-based coalition which it co-founded in March 1985 with the PSCN, the PCD, the mainstream liberal *Partido Liberal Independiente* (PLI) and the *Movimiento Social Democrático* (MSD).

Nicaragua Freedom Fund

Base. United States

Leadership. William Simon (chairman); Michael Novak, Midge Decter (members of executive board)

Orientation. Pro-*contra*

History. This Fund was established in May 1985 under the chairmanship of Simon, a former US Treasury Secretary. Novak is a Slovak émigré (see Slovak League of America, under Czechoslovakia) and former member of the board responsible for Radio Liberty (see West Germany), an anti-communist propaganda operation. Decter is well known as an opponent of the women's movement. Other supporters of the Fund include Sun Myung Moon's Unification Church (see South Korea), and former US ambassadors Clare Luce Booth and Jeane Kirkpatrick—in whose honour a new *contra* group, the Jeane Kirkpatrick Task Force, was named in October 1984. (That 800-man group—also known as the Task Force Jeane Kirkpatrick—was reportedly in difficulties in mid-1986 after its commander, Gerardo Martínez, was dismissed for exposing corruption among the higher leadership.)

Policies. The purpose of the Fund is to supply "humanitarian" aid to the Nicaraguan contra groups. Its initial fund-raising target was US$14,000,000.

Partido Conservador Demócrata—see CDN and CON.

Partido Liberal Constitucionalista—see CDN.

Partido Social Cristiano Nicaragüense—see CDN and CON.

Partido Social Demócrata—see CDN.

Rescate y Conciliación Nacional de Nicaragua
Nicaraguan Rescue and Conciliation

Leadership. Alfredo César Aguirre (leader); Lionel Poveda

Orientation. Contra

History. This group was founded in October 1983 as Recovery of the Original Nicaraguan Revolution, adopting its present name in 1984. Aguirre, a former president of the Nicaraguan Central Bank, had been living in exile since mid-1982. The group is political rather than paramilitary.

Policies. This non-*somocista* group regards the FSLN regime as a Marxist dictatorship.

Associated organizations. In August 1985 it was a co-founder of the BOS alliance.

Solidaridad de Trabajadores Cristianos—see ARDE.

Unidad Nicaragüense para la Reconciliación (UNIR)
Nicaraguan Unity for Reconciliation

Leadership. Alfonso Robelo Callejas, Adolfo Calero Portocarrero, Steadman Fagoth Müller (leaders)

Orientation. Contra

History. The formation of this alliance of *contra* groups, announced on Sept. 5, 1984, followed months of pressure from the United States for the unification of the political and military leaderships of the movements. It has been superseded for the present by the formation of the UNO but may remain in formal existence.

Membership. The groups forming the UNIR were the ARDE and the FDN (which had already been co-ordinating their activities for some months) and Misura.

Unión Democrática Nicaragüense—Fuerzas Armadas Revolucionarias Nicaragüenses (UDN-FARN)
Nicaraguan Democratic Union—Nicaraguan Revolutionary Armed Forces

Leadership. Fernando Chamorro Rappaccioli (leader)

Orientation. Contra

History. The UDN was formed by conservative non-*somocista* businessmen opposed to the Sandinista revolution; the FARN, its military wing, carried out numerous guerrilla operations along the Honduran border from 1980. The movement was one of the founding members of the FDN in 1982, and of the broader ARDE coalition thereafter; Chamorro succeeded Edén Pastora as military commander of the ARDE following that group's alliance with the FDN.

Policies. Although some founders of the UDN opposed the Somoza regime in 1978-79, and despite the movement's stated opposition to the return of a right-wing dictatorship, it has been prepared to form tactical alliances with *somocista* groups in order to pursue an effective guerrilla campaign.

Membership. The movement claimed to have 2,000 members by the end of 1980, and to have 600 under arms in Honduras in 1981.

Unión Nicaragüense de la Oposición (UNO)
United Nicaraguan Opposition

Base. New Orleans, United States

Leadership. Arturo Cruz (political director); Alfonso Robelo, Adolfo and Mario Calero (military leaders); Eveno Valdivia (general co-ordinator)

Orientation. Anti-communist political-military grouping

History. This alliance of *contra* movements was formed on June 12, 1985, largely at the instigation of the Reagan administration, to provide the rebel armies with a coherent political-military strategy and an efficient means of allocating money and supplies. In that capacity it effectively superseded the UNIR.

Membership. The main members of the UNO are the ARDE, represented by Robelo; the CDN, represented by Cruz, and the FDN, represented by the Caleros; each of these consists of alliances of other groups.

International affiliations. The UNO represents the *contra* movement in its relations with many foreign private and governmental institutions. Mario Calero addressed the 1986 conference of the World Anti-Communist League (see South Korea) on its behalf. The UNO is involved in soliciting and channelling funds and matériel for the *contra* war, including about US$400,000 and two helicopters received in 1985-86 from the US Council for World Freedom. Cruz attended the December 1987 pro-*contra* rally organized in London by members of the Federation of Conservative Students (United Kingdom) and the Heritage Foundation (United States).

Defunct organizations

Fuerzas Armadas Anticomunistas: the Farac (Anti-Communist Armed Forces) carried out sabotage activities in the immediate aftermath of the Sandinista revolution. Seven of its members were imprisoned in August 1980, since when there have been no reports of its activities.

Fuerzas Armadas Democráticas: the FAD (Democratic Armed Forces) were founded in 1979 by Carlos García Solorzano, an intelligence officer under the Somoza regime who was imprisoned in May 1980 for conspiring against the Sandinistas. His successor, Bernardino Larios, another Somoza officer who had served briefly in the first post-revolutionary government, was imprisoned in September; a Spanish diplomat in contact with the FAD was expelled in October, and in November the group's financial backer, Jorge Salazar Argüello, was shot dead in a confrontation with police.

Movimiento Tercera Vía: the M3V (Third Way Movement) was a *contra* guerrilla group founded in Costa Rica in October 1983 with the aim of opening an internal third front to complement the northern FDN campaign and that of the ARDE in the south. It was led by Abelardo Taboada, Luis Riva and others, including Sebastián González who has been identified in US reports as a major drug dealer, and it was said to have 300 members in 1984. Little has been heard of it since late 1985 and it has probably been assimilated into one or other of the larger groups.

Partido Liberal Nacional: the PLN (National Liberal Party) was the political organ of the Somoza dictatorship. It collapsed in 1979.

Salvación Internacional de Nicaragua del Comunismo: the SINC (Nicaraguan International Rescue from Communism) carried out guerrilla operations in Costa Rica in 1980-81, including an attack on a pro-Sandinista radio station and the hijacking of an airliner.

Norway

capital: Oslo   **population: 4,200,000**

Political system. The Kingdom of Norway has a directly elected and normally unicameral parliament, the 155-seat *Storting*, which in effect appoints a Prime Minister who heads a State Council, or Cabinet. The hereditary monarch has only nominal executive powers.

Recent history. Following its liberation in 1945, Norway was governed by the Labour Party until 1965, and thereafter by alternating centrist coalitions and minority Labour administrations until the Conservatives established a minority government in 1981. This was followed in 1983 by another centrist coalition and eventually by a Labour government installed in 1985.

The evolution of the far right. During the period of Nazi occupation, from 1940 to 1945, Norway was governed by a fascist puppet government led by Vidkun Quisling. Popular repudiation of the collaborationist era has ensured that no substantial fascist group has developed since the war, although the non-fascist Progress Party has gained significant electoral support and a small neo-nazi movement arose in the mid-1970s. A left-wing bookshop in Tromsø was bombed in March 1977. Two nazi guerrilla groups were broken up in 1981-82, but there are still a number of small fascist and racist parties and pressure groups. Legislation forbidding private paramilitary groups was used for the first time against the Norwegian-German Army in 1981, and the armed forces announced new measures to prevent infiltration by political extremists.

In 1978 details were published for the first time of a secret military-controlled organization, apparently in existence since the 1940s, which held arms and other matériel in readiness for conducting guerrilla and sabotage activities in the event of an invasion. Concern was expressed that the corps was a potential threat to state security, but no evidence of right-wing influence was produced.

Active organizations

Nasjonalisten
Nationalists

Address. Post Box 5331, Majorstven, Oslo

Leadership. Erik Blucher

Orientation. Neo-fascist

History. This group is the successor to the *Norsk Front* (Norwegian Front), also led by Blucher, which was active in the 1970s when it entered into contact with the World Anti-Communist League (see South Korea). The present non-nazi leadership of the WACL has ceased to correspond with the Front.

Publications. The *Norsk Front* publication was *Attakk* (distributed from Post Box 104, Skoyen, Oslo 2).

International affiliations. Blucher has had dealings with British ultra-rightists including Martin Webster and the Hancock family and has been banned from entering Great Britain. He attended the 1983 and 1984 *Ijzerbedevaart* rallies of Flemish fascists and nationalists at Diksmuide (Belgium).

Nasjonalt Folkeparti (NF)
National People's Party

Base. Oslo

Leadership. Jan Ødegård (president); Olav Hoass, Henrik Bastian Heide

Orientation. Nazi

History. In 1984 NF leader Ødegård, party ideologist Hoass and party founder Heide were arrested with two others for incitement to racial hatred; all five were found guilty, with the party leader receiving a 10-month prison sentence. Eleven members of the NF, including Ødegård, were arrested in June 1985 in connection with the bombing of an Oslo mosque. A quantity of arms and explosives was also seized by police.

Policies. The NF follows classic national socialist policies with an emphasis on anti-semitism and Nordic racial supremacy.

Publications. Nordic Order, an English-language magazine co-published with other Scandinavian fascist organizations.

International affiliations. The NF has close ties with Danish and Swedish nazi groups.

The Paladin Press/Norway

Leadership. Ole Christian Olstad (co-owner)

Orientation. Right-wing

History. This publishing company was set up in 1985, apparently as an offshoot of the US publishing company of the same name. Like its US counterpart, it specializes in titles dealing with survival techniques, guerrilla warfare, mercenary soldiering and other paramilitary topics. Olstad, one of the three founders, is thought to be sympathetic to the *Nasjonalt Folkeparti*, and has worked in Lebanon for Saad Haddad's South Lebanon Christian Militia.

International affiliations. See Paladin Press (United States).

Defunct organizations

Nasjonal Samling: the National Union was an ultra-right group active in the late 1970s and early '80s.

Norsk Front: see *Nasjonalisten*.

Norwegian-German Army: a nazi guerrilla group founded in 1980 by an army sergeant, Espen Lund, the Army was broken up by police and its arms, explosives and documents seized after the killing of two dissident members in 1981. Lund, who claimed to have been acting under the instructions of the German nazi group Odessa (see West Germany), was sentenced in January 1982 to 18 years' imprisonment together with Johnny Olsen (also 18 years) and Jon Charles Hoff (12 years). The three were aged between 19 and 20.

Organization against Detrimental Immigration to Norway: this white supremacist pressure group was active around 1980.

Vigilante: a nazi guerrilla group which attacked left-wing demonstrations between 1979 and 1982; one of its members, Johnny Olsen, was imprisoned in 1982 in connection with Norwegian-German Army activities. Explosives stockpiled by the group were found by police.

Other organizations

Of other Norwegian right-wing groups active in the past 10 years, the most important is the libertarian *Fremskrittspartiet* (Progress or Progressive Party), founded in 1973 as Anders Lange's Party; it is mainly an anti-tax pressure group, and currently has about 10,000 members, led by Carl Hagen. In 1981 it secured 4.5 per cent of the vote and four seats in the *Storting* election, but in 1985 its shares fell to 3.1 per cent and two seats. Other relevant organizations include an affiliate of the UK-based Christian Mission to the Communist World, the *Moderat Ungdom* (Moderate Union); the *Norwegian Anti-Communist League* (affiliated to the WACL—see South Korea), the *Norwegian Democratic Party*, the *Norwegian Social Movement* and the *Ungdommens Heimerven*.

Individuals

Tor Petter Hadland: a Norwegian ultra-rightist with extensive international contacts, he is at present based in Sweden where he is associated with the BSS. In 1985 he was arrested in Finland and imprisoned for eight months for disrupting a Nobel Peace Prize award ceremony with a bomb hoax.

Oman

capital: Muscat   **population: approximately 2,000,000**

Political system. The Sultanate of Oman is ruled by decree by the Sultan, assisted by an appointed Cabinet and Consultative Assembly. There are no political parties.

Recent history. The present (1987) Sultan, Qaboos bin Said, seized power in a coup in 1970. Like his father and predecessor, Sultan Said bin Taimur, Qaboos has maintained conservative domestic policies and strongly pro-Western foreign policies, and has relied on British military support to maintain his regime.

The evolution of the far right. The authoritarian rule of the Sultans has prevented the emergence of local political organizations. Oman does, however, have a well-funded chapter of the World Anti-Communist League (see South Korea), which contributed US$10,000 to the League's conference expenses in 1985.

Pakistan

capital: Islamabad   **population: 96,500,000**

Political system. The Islamic Republic of Pakistan is governed under a 1973 Constitution amended by the present military President to give him extensive powers. There is provision in the Constitution for a bicameral parliament.

Recent history. The Dominion of Pakistan was created in 1947 when the Indian Empire was dissolved; it then included what is now Bangladesh, which became independent after a war in 1971. Pakistan became a republic in 1956, and was ruled by military men from 1958 to 1971. Zulfiqar Ali Bhutto became President of what remained of the country after the 1971 war, and after serious internal disorders a military coup in 1977 installed the present head of state, Gen. Zia ul-Haq, who has ruled by martial law and suppressed most opposition.

The evolution of the far right. The Islamic fundamentalism which has led some opposition groups and the current government to adopt anti-democratic positions falls outside the scope of the present work. Some Islamic fundamentalist groups, such as *Jamaat-i-Islami* (the Islamic Assembly), have very right-wing social and economic policies. There are no known secular far-right organizations within Pakistan, but some Islamic organizations have entered into contact with foreign right-wing groups. The Christian Mission to the Communist World (see United Kingdom) has a small Pakistani affiliate.

Many anti-communist guerrilla organizations from neighbouring Afghanistan (see separate chapter) have their headquarters in Pakistan, mainly in the North-West Frontier province, which has over 2,000,000 Afghan refugees.

Active organizations

World Muslim League

Base. Karachi

Leadership. Dr Inamullah Khan (secretary general)

Orientation. Islamic

History. In 1981 this organization paid for the sending of two anti-semitic books, *Anti-Zion* and *The Six Million Reconsidered*, to every member of the UK Parliament, in order "to correct many wrong notions about the Jews". It also provided a grant to a US anti-semitic author, William Grimstad, and has expressed support for the US fascist organization, Liberty Lobby.

International affiliations. See Historical Review Press (United Kingdom) and Liberty Lobby (United States). Khan is a leading figure in the World Anti-Communist League (see South Korea), and is thought to have secured Saudi funding for the WACL through his position as advisor to the Saudi royal family.

At the time of writing it was not possible to establish whether Khan's organization was the same as the Saudi Arabia-based Muslim World League (*Rabitat al-Alam al-Islami*), founded in 1962 and dedicated to the promotion of Islamic unity and solidarity.

Panama

capital: Panamá   **population: 2,175,000**

Political system. The Republic of Panama is governed by a popularly elected unicameral Legislative Assembly consisting of one representative from each of 67 polling districts. There is an executive President, who in practice serves at the pleasure of the commander of the National Guard, and who is assisted by two Vice-Presidents and a Cabinet.

Recent history. Panama was created at the instigation of the United States in 1903. Its political history was unstable until a coup in 1968 which installed a populist nationalist regime under Col. Omar Torrijos Herrera, commander of the National Guard. Despite the creation of a new legislature and the appointment of civilian Presidents, effective power rested with Torrijos until his death in 1981. There have since been several changes of President and Guard commander, with each of the regimes pursuing policies more conservative than those of Torrijos.

The evolution of the far right. Conservative movements were active before and after the ten-year suspension of political parties from 1968, but there have been few extreme right-wing groupings.

Defunct organizations

Frente Nacional de Panamá: the FNP (Panama National Front), led by Abraham Crocamo, was allegedly behind a right-wing coup plot whose existence was announced in October 1979. Among alleged supporters of the plot were foreign mercenaries and leaders of the *Partido Panameñista* of ex-President Arnulfo Arias Madrid, a conservative anti-communist formation which remained in existence (as the *Partido Panameñista Auténtico*) in the mid-1980s. There were several arrests in connection with the alleged plot and Crocamo sought refuge in Venezuela.

Paraguay

capital: Asunción   **population: 3,600,000**

Political system. Paraguay is formally a representative democracy with a popularly elected executive President and a bicameral National Congress. The 60-seat Chamber of Deputies and the 30-seat Senate are elected under a system which gives two-thirds of the seats in each chamber to the largest party, with the remaining seats divided among other parties in proportion to their share of the vote.

Recent history. Gen. Alfredo Stroessner Mattiauda seized power in a coup in May 1954. He has since governed as a dictator, despite the existence of a formally democratic Constitution. There are frequent waves of repression of dissidents, most of whom belong to the Radical Liberal (centrist) or *Febrerista* (social democratic) parties. A vast proportion of the population has been forced into exile for political or economic reasons, and the General and his family enjoy virtually unchallenged control of the country and its wealth.

The evolution of the far right. Paraguay's tradition of rule by dictatorship dates back to 1814. In modern times the main right-wing organization has been the Colorado Party, which won a civil war in 1947-48. Since taking power in 1954 Stroessner has used the Colorado Party as his personal vehicle, declaring himself the victor as the Colorado candidate in elections in 1958, 1963, 1968, 1973, 1978 and 1983. Arbitrary arrest and detention without trial, torture, "disappearances" and censorship are commonplace. The Colorados have participated in the activities of the World Anti-Communist League (see South Korea) and hosted its 1979 congress.

Under Stroessner, Paraguay has achieved some notoriety as a haven for Nazi war criminals, including Dr Josef Mengele of the Auschwitz death camp, who was given citizenship (revoked after international protests). A more recent right-wing refugee was Anastasio Somoza, the former dictator of Nicaragua, who settled in Paraguay in 1979 but was assassinated by unidentified, possibly left-wing Argentinian, guerrillas in 1980.

Some politicians have taken part in the "elections" organized by the Colorados and have been granted seats as the "opposition" in the National Congress; most genuine opposition groupings are unable to meet the conditions for participation in the processes, while others qualify but decline to take part. Officially recognized "opposition" groupings are regarded by some as collaborators with what is often termed a fascist regime, but they have been excluded from consideration in the present work as they profess non-fascist ideologies.

Active organizations

Asociación Nacional Republicana—Partido Colorado (ANR-PC)
National Republican Association—Colorado Party

Base. Asunción

Leadership. Alfredo Stroessner (leader); Dr Juan Ramón Chávez (president); Dr Sabino Augusto Montanaro (vice-president); Mario Abdo Benítez (secretary)

Orientation. Ultra-right

History. The Colorado Party, as the ANR is known from the red banner adopted as its symbol in the 19th century, is at present very much the vehicle of Gen. Stroessner, who staged a coup in 1954. Its main leader in the 1940s was Gen. Higinio Morínigo, who was identified with an ultra-right faction called the *Guión Rojo*; he assumed the presidency of Paraguay in 1940 following the death of the Liberal incumbent, and pursued a nominally neutral but pro-Axis policy during the Second World War. Morínigo's forces won the civil war of 1947, but in 1948 the *Guión* turned against him and installed Natalicio González as President. Stroessner's coup followed six years later.

The party has undergone frequent purges to ensure that it remains loyal to Stroessner, leading to the creation of several dissident Colorado parties of centrist ideology. In the early to mid-1980s, as the question of succession to the septuagenarian dictator became increasingly urgent, there developed a supposedly pro-Stroessner "populist" tendency among younger Colorados within the ANR-PC, in opposition to the hard line "traditionalist" tendency which was preparing for the imposition of an equally authoritarian successor.

Policies. The Party has extremely conservative domestic and foreign policies emphasizing the need for vigilance against communist aggression and subversion. It depends largely on a highly developed personality cult encapsulated in the slogan "Peace, Order and Progress with Stroessner".

Membership. Membership of the Colorado Party is compulsory for public employees, whose subscriptions are deducted from their salaries. Total membership in the mid-1980s was about one third of the population.

Publications. Patria, daily, circulation 8,000; *La Voz del Coloradismo*, networked radio programme.

International affiliations. The party supports the Paraguayan chapter which hosted the 1979 congress of the World Anti-Communist League (see South Korea) and now provides the secretariat for the WACL's Latin American regional organization, the Fedal.

Federación Democrática de América Latina (Fedal)
Federation of Democratic Latin American Groups

Base. Asunción

Leadership. Dr Carlos Barbieri Filho (Brazil); Adolfo Granada Campos (Paraguay)

Orientation. Anti-communist

History. The federation was established in the early 1980s as the Latin American regional organization of the World Anti-Communist League (WACL—see South Korea), in succession to the *Confederación Anticomunista Latinoamericana* (CAL—see Mexico), which was discredited by its links with Mexican and Central American fascist groups and death squads. Most CAL members simply transferred their affiliation to the Fedal, and the personnel is little changed—Barbieri, for example, was vice-president of the CAL.

The headquarters for the Fedal were provided by the active Paraguayan chapter of the WACL, which is led by Granada Campos and receives financial and political backing from the Stroessner dictatorship. The CAL had held its third congress in Paraguay in 1977, and the WACL met there in 1979.

Policies. The Fedal promotes individual freedom and Western values, and opposes all manifestations of totalitarian communism.

Membership. The group has affiliates based in or representing most Latin American countries.

International affiliations. See WACL (South Korea). Latin American affiliates include Tradition, Family and Property (Brazil) and the UNO (Nicaragua).

Peru

capital: Lima   **population: 19,500,000**

Political system. The Republic of Peru has a bicameral, mainly elected, National Congress compromising of an 180-seat Chamber of Deputies and a Senate consisting of (i) 60 regional representatives and (ii) former Presidents of constitutional regimes. Ordinary members serve for five years and the ex-Presidents for life. An executive President, popularly elected by absolute majority, and two Vice-Presidents also serve five-year terms.

Recent history. Peru was under military rule in 1948-56 and 1968-80. The dominant political parties have been the social democratic APRA, which was illegal for all but three years between 1931 and 1956, and the conservative Popular Action (AP), founded in 1956. The AP won the presidential and congressional elections of 1980 and the APRA those of 1985. An insurgency led by the Maoist *Sendero Luminoso* (Shining Path) has been under way since 1980.

The evolution of the far right. Peru has had no significant ultra-right movements, with its military and civilian governments following conservative, populist or centre-left policies. The current insurgency has led to the employment of occasionally brutal tactics by both sides, with alleged massacres of civilians by guerrillas and of guerrilla sympathizers by the armed forces.

Active organizations

Movimiento Nacional Socialista del Perú (MNSP)
National Socialist Movement of Peru

Address. Sánchez Cerro 2134, Apartado 11517, Lima 11

Leadership. E. Basurto Carbonell

Orientation. Nazi

History. This small group was in contact with foreign nazi parties in the early 1980s, and has been recognized since 1981 as the Peruvian section of the World Union of National Socialists (see United States and Denmark).

Policies. It is thought to follow mainstream national socialist policies.

Publications. *El Avance*, and *Trinchera-88* (Trench 88), whose name reflects the fact that the initial letters of Heil Hitler are the eighth in the German alphabet (although not in the Spanish alphabet).

Other organizations

Right-wing parties and movements active in recent years include the following: *Movimiento Cívico Nacional 7 de Junio* (June 7 National Civic Movement), which contested the 1985 presidential election; the *Movimiento Democrático Peruano* (Peruvian Democratic Movement), active in the late 1970s; the fascist *Movimiento Poder Blanco* (M-88—White Power Movement); the *Partido Avanzada Nacional* (National Advance Party), formed in 1984, and the ultra-nationalist *Tradición y Acción para un Perú Mayor* (Tradition and Action for a Greater Peru).

The Philippines

capital: Quezon City (Manila)   **population: 57,000,000**

Political system. The 1973 Constitution, which was never fully implemented under the Marcos regime, has been superseded by a new Constitution devised by and legitimizing the Aquino government installed in 1986. The new order provides for a popularly elected executive presidency and a Congress.

Recent history. Although independence was gained in 1946, the Philippines remained firmly under the control of United States business interests and was disrupted by political violence throughout its first two decades. In 1965 Ferdinand Marcos, leader of the *Nacionalista* Party, was elected President, and he was re-elected in 1969.

In 1972 Marcos declared martial law, suspended Congress, imprisoned opposition leaders and began to rule by decree, supposedly in order to deal with small communist and Islamic guerrilla movements. He altered the Constitution in 1973 to remove a limit on his incumbency and remained in power until February 1986, using occasional dubiously conducted referendums and elections to extend his rule. Marcos amassed a great personal fortune and much of the economy was run by his family and associates.

In 1983 an exiled leader of the democratic opposition, Benigno Aquino, returned to the country and was immediately shot dead, possibly on government instructions. Popular revulsion at the murder led to the formation of a united opposition, which in 1986 (after another controversial election process) staged a largely peaceful rebellion supported by elements of the armed forces. Marcos was overthrown. A broad-based democratic government, led by Aquino's widow and initially including a number of former Marcos allies, has ruled the country since then.

The evolution of the far right. The Philippines was under fascist occupation from 1942 until the defeat of Japan in 1945. In the post-war era the most significant ultra-right organizations were the private armies maintained by a number of big landowners; these were disbanded after Marcos' election in 1965, although semi-official militias created in the 1970s remained in place until early 1987, having a total membership estimated at 10,000. During the Marcos regime a number of right-wing death squads operated under the patronage of senior police and armed forces officers. Their "salvagings", or executions, accounted for several hundred deaths in the late 1970s and early '80s.

Since the "people power" rebellion of 1986 the main focus of right-wing activity has been clandestine conspiracy against the Aquino government. Some conspirators aim at the restoration of Marcos, while others merely seek a return to his right-wing and corrupt style of government. A Marcos associate, Arturo Tolentino, attempted a coup in July 1986, and at least two other coup plots have been discovered. Public demonstrations during 1986 indicated that the Marcos restoration movement had the support of at least 30,000 citizens.

Active organizations

Kilusan Bagong Lipunan (KBL)
New Society Movement

Leadership. Manuel García (interim chairman); José Rono (general secretary)

Orientation. Right-wing

224

History. The KBL was formed by Marcos in 1978, mainly from his supporters in the *Partido Nacionalista.* It thereby became the government party and was officially accorded majorities in subsequent elections held for the legislature and the presidency. The 1986 revolution effectively destroyed the party, which had been led by Imelda Marcos, wife of the dictator.

The main successors to the pre-revolutionary KBL are this group, using the same name and led by the KBL general secretary, and the apparently larger and more moderate *Partido Nacionalista ng Pilipinas*(PNP), founded in March 1986 by Blas Ople.

Policies. The KBL policies include anti-communism and support for free enterprise and Western values.

Defunct organizations

Partido Nacionalista (PN): the original party of this name was formed under US rule in 1907, and split in 1946 between centrists, who formed the Liberal Party, and right-wingers, who retained the name. This was Marcos' party when he came to power in 1965, and it supported his authoritarian, corrupt and vigorously anti-communist rule. In 1978 Marcos formed the KBL but the PN survived as a coalition of anti-Marcos right-wingers. It split in 1981 between a majority faction led by José Laurel and a minority led by José Roy. In 1982 the main faction joined the pro-Aquino opposition coalition, and in 1986 the main PN, then led by Renato Cayetano, recruited many former KBL members. The modern-day PN is not sufficiently identified with the far right to require fuller treatment here.

Other organizations

Smaller radical-right groupings recently active in the Philippines include the *Tadtad* (Chop-Chop) cult, a 2,000-member eclectic religious sect with extreme anti-communist tenets. In March 1987 members of *Tadtad* in southern Davao reportedly decapitated an alleged communist and drank his blood. Of the semi-official vigilante movements mentioned above, the more active in mid-1987 included *Alza Masa*, or Masses Arise, led by local police chief Col. Franco Calida, which was active in Davao City in mid-1987, while a *Citizens' Anti-Communist Army* was active on the central island of Cebu and was influenced by ex-rebel Pastor Alcover's *National Movement for Freedom and Democracy.*

Poland

capital: Warsaw   **population: 37,400,000**

Political system. Poland is a socialist republic, whose supreme authority is the 460-seat parliament, the *Sejm*, which is elected by universal suffrage and which in turn elects a 17-member Council of State, led by a President.

Recent history. The occupation of Poland by German and Soviet forces in 1939 marked the beginning of the Second World War. Since liberation in 1945 the main political party has been the communist Polish United Workers' Party, which adopted its present name in 1948. The communist-dominated government faced internal crises in 1948, 1956, 1970, 1978 and 1980-84, the last period resulting from the formation, activities and suppression of the labour-based Solidarity movement. A military government under Gen. Wojciech Jaruzelski was installed in 1981; this regime, which had undergone a number of changes including Jaruzelski's election as President, was still in power in 1987.

The evolution of the far right. There was a small nazi movement in Poland in the 1930s, with anti-semitic incidents being reported at most Polish universities in late 1931 and late 1932. A short-lived nazi National Radical Party appeared in 1934. (The German Nazi Party was organized in the then Free City of Danzig—now Gdansk, and part of Poland.) Right-wing groups have not been permitted to organize within Poland since the war. However, there has been evidence of underground anti-communist activity, partly conducted with the assistance of Western intelligence agencies and Polish émigré groups, which have attempted to exploit the emergence of the Solidarity independent trade movement, especially after the declaration of martial law and prohibition of Solidarity in December 1981.

An anti-communist "government in exile" established in 1941 continues in existence, with a base in London; it is not considered sufficiently active or important for inclusion here. There are also exiled Christian democratic and social democratic political parties, and a large number of émigré organizations, (particularly in the United Kingdom, the United States and France), which are only incidentally anti-communist, their main concerns being cultural, social and welfare matters.

Active organizations

Anti-Communist Confederation of Polish Freedom Fighters Inc. (ACCPFF)

Address. 18 Boardman Street, Salem, Massachusetts 01970, United States

Telephone. (617) 744 6710

Leadership. Jozef Mlot-Mroz (president)

Orientation. Fascist

History. The ACCPFF was founded in 1953 as the Alliance of Friends of the Polish Village, and adopted its present name some years later. It is generally known as the Polish Freedom Fighters (PFF), and has adopted as its badge a cross and sword. In 1984 the Confederation opened a fund for the erection of a memorial to Polish soldiers massacred in Katyn forest, allegedly by the Red Army (although the Soviet version is that the massacre was carried out by Germans).

Policies. The Confederation is extremely anti-semitic, regarding Jews as spreading communism and undermining Christianity through their alleged control of the mass media.

Membership. 1,700 (1985).

Publications. *SOS USA*, monthly (formerly *SOS USA Ship of State*); *Tribune of Enslaved Nations*, monthly.

Associated organizations. The group is in contact with many Polish exile and non-Polish fascist organizations. Its Katyn fund was publicized by the racist Mountain Church (United States).

Confederation for an Independent Poland (KPN)

Leadership. Robert Leszek Moczulski (leader)

Orientation. Anti-communist

History. This group was founded in 1979, and was financed by anti-communist émigré organizations. Moczulski, who had previously led a Movement for the Defence of Human and Civil Rights (formed in 1977), was arrested in 1980 and, together with three other KPN members, was convicted in October 1982 of conspiracy to overthrow the state, but he was released in August 1984 as part of a general amnesty. Also freed were his deputies, Tadeusz Stanski and Romuald Szeremietiew. Five Confederation members, including Moczulski, were arrested at a meeting in March 1985. The KPN had been involved in the formation of Solidarity in 1981.

Policies. The KPN is nationalistic and anti-Soviet. In January 1985 it called for the "annihilation" of the communist system and for the holding of free elections. It also called for the withdrawal of Poland from the Warsaw Pact and for the return of territory ceded to the Soviet Union.

Membership. The March 1985 meeting was attended by no more than ten people.

Polish Council of Unity in the United States

Address. 2238 Decatur Plaza NW, Washington, DC 20008, United States

Leadership. Stefan Korbomski (chairman)

Orientation. Anti-communist

History. The Council was founded in 1958.

Policies. The Council seeks the liberation of Poland from communist rule and the creation of a free democratic nation.

Associated organizations. It is the Polish affiliate of the Assembly of Captive European Nations, an emigré coalition based in the United States.

Defunct organizations

Armed Forces of Underground Poland: eight members of this group received prison sentences ranging from two to 25 years after an incident in February 1982 in which a Warsaw policeman was killed.

Club for a Self-Governing Republic—Freedom, Justice, Independence: this group was formed in late 1981 by Jacek Kuron, formerly leader of the KOR. It was anti-communist and anti-Soviet, calling for the formation of new political parties and for the assertion of national sovereignty. The Club was immediately suppressed by police but Kuron continued to advocate a "co-ordinated attack on all centres of power and information" with the aim of overthrowing the government.

Danzig Nazi movement: there was a substantial national socialist movement among the ethnic German majority in what was then the free city of Danzig, now the Polish city of Gdansk, in the 1930s. The movement was essentially a branch of Hitler's NSDAP. By 1933 the Nazis had secured 38 of the 72 seats in the Danzig Diet, and their government, led by Rauschning, applied policies more or less identical to those of the German parent party, although at first there was no official persecution of Jews. The movement supported the German invasion of Poland and the subsequent German war effort. At the end of the war few ethnic Germans remained in the city and this nazi movement did not reappear.

National Radical Party (NRP): a national socialist party organized in April 1934 by young members of the main opposition grouping, the National Democrats; it was banned by the Interior Minister, Pieracki, in June 1934, leading to his assassination by NRP "greyshirts" on the following day. The party was completely suppressed by September, with dozens of its leaders arrested.

Polish Home Army of Resistance: four members of this guerrilla group seized hostages in the Polish embassy in Berne (Switzerland) for three days in September 1982, in an unsuccessful attempt to force the lifting of martial law in Poland.

Polish National Socialist Party: this pro-German formation, based in Silesia and Vilna, was dissolved in June 1934 after it had hosted a visit by Goebbels, Hitler's Propaganda Minister.

The Solidarity Episode

Mention is made here of the history of the independent trade union *Solidarnosc* or Solidarity, not as an organization which would itself meet the criteria for inclusion in this directory, but because of the importance of its challenge to the regime and the extent to which capital was made from this by organizations of the radical right.

Solidarity was founded in September 1980 as a national all-industry non-communist trade union movement, uniting several local workers' groups. (Organizations involved in setting up Solidarity included KOR, the Social Self-Defence Committee led by Jacek Kuron, which dissolved itself in September 1981.) Solidarity quickly attracted a substantial following among many sectors of Polish society, its membership reportedly reaching about 10,000,000. An agricultural version of Solidarity was formed in December 1980.

Although it was initially tolerated by the state, and recognized in negotiations, Solidarity became increasingly involved in strikes and other confrontational activities over working conditions, wages, prices and political questions. The Council of State decided at the end of 1981 to suppress it as part of emergency measures including the creation of the martial law government led by Gen. Jaruzelski. Its founder, Lech Walesa, and other leaders were imprisoned; some 10,000 arrests were reported, with most of those concerned being released after ashort time but some being detained for up to three years. Martial law was revoked in December 1982 and a new trade-union system was introduced in 1983.

After the prohibition of Solidarity some individuals associated with Solidarity, including Walesa, were involved in attempts to maintain the organization and its clandestine publications and radio station. There have been reports of the reappearance of Solidarity banners and leaflets within Poland, and an underground opposition movement continues to use its name. From London and New York respectively Solidarity publishes *Voice of Solidarity* and *Solidarnosc Bulletin*, and its activities are sustained by dozens of Solidarity support groups in Western Europe and North America.

Portugal

capital: Lisbon   **population: 10,150,000**

Political system. Portugal is a democratic republic governed by a President, who appoints a Prime Minister heading a Council of Ministers, and by a unicameral 250-seat Assembly of the Republic. Both President and Assembly are subject to direct election, the former for a five-year term and the latter for four years.

Recent history. The right-wing Caetano government, successor to Salazar's quasi-fascist regime, was overthrown in 1974 by a left-wing military coup. After a period of turmoil, which saw the virtual dissolution of Portugal's overseas empire (apart from Madeira, the Azores— see below—and Macao), an Assembly and a President were elected in 1976. There has since been a succession of centre-left and centre-right coalition and minority governments.

The evolution of the far right. Dr António de Oliveira Salazar, who became Prime Minister in 1932, established a right-wing dictatorship strongly influenced by Mussolini's corporatist ideas. A one-party state was constituted under the leadership of Salazar's National Union. The regime remained neutral and survived the Second World War, continuing with its quasi-fascist policies until the retirement of the dictator in 1968. By then the country had become embroiled in revolutionary wars in several of its colonies, most of which gained independence immediately after the 1974 coup which deposed Salazar's heir, Dr Marcello Caetano. Salazar's party was disbanded after the coup and ultra-right groups have subsequently had little success in Portugal.

Legislation in 1978 prohibited the promotion of fascism or of violence against democratic institutions or national unity, with lengthy prison sentences for infringements.

Active organizations

Círculo Europeo de Amigos de Europa (CEDADE-Portugal)
European Circle of Friends of Europe

Address. Apartado 672, 4011 Oporto Codex

Leadership. Luis Filipe Baião (leader)

Orientation. Nazi

History. CEDADE-Portugal, like its counterparts in Spain and elsewhere, is a youth-oriented national socialist grouping. It was first reported active in the early 1980s and is based in Oporto.

Policies. The movement has traditional national socialist economic, social and racial policies, combined with a nostalgia for the Salazar era. It is openly anti-semitic and anti-communist and organizes paramilitary camps.

Publications. Alternativa.

Associated organizations. A CEDADE leader was arrested in 1984 along with members of the now-defunct *Movimento Nacionalista*. In the same year CEDADE organized a joint "Free Rudolf Hess" demonstration (demanding the release of a German war criminal) along with the *União Nacional*.

229

International affiliations. The group is an offshoot of the *Círculo Español de Amigos de Europa*, based in Barcelona; there are CEDADE groups in several other countries, including France, Ecuador and Argentina. The Portuguese group is also in contact with other fascist groups, notably the French FNE.

Edicões Ultimo Reduto
Last Stronghold Editions

Address. Apartado 598, 4009 Oporto Codex

Leadership. J. Campos

Orientation. Fascist

History. This Oporto company was the leading Portuguese fascist pqblishing house in the 1980s. One of the firm's directors was arrested along with members of the *Movimento Nacionalista* in 1984.

Policies. The firm has been described as a front for a Portuguese nazi party.

Publications. Ultimo Reduto, monthly.

Futuro Presente
Future Present

Address. Rua de São Nicolau 71 2 E, 1200 Lisbon

Orientation. New right

History. This magazine was founded around 1980.

Policies. It espouses authoritarian and elitist new right ideas similar to those advanced by the French GRECE movement.

Mocidade Patriótica
Patriotic Youth

Address. Apartado 162, 2700 Amadora

Orientation. Fascist

History. This group was almost destroyed by a series of arrests in the early 1980s, including that of its then leader, Arlindo Miguel Figueiras, who was imprisoned in 1983 for fascist agitation. The group nevertheless remained active in the mid-1980s.

Policies. The organisation appears to be motivated by nostalgia for the Salazar era.

Publications. Vanguardia Nacional (formerly *Renovação*).

Associated organizations. It has co-operated with CEDADE-Portugal and with another ultra-right group, the *Círculos Nacionalistas*, in demonstrations and other public activities.

Ordem Nova
New Order

Address. Rua Logistas 46, 1800 Lisbon

Leadership. Felipe (contact)

Orientation. Fascist

History. This semi-clandestine organization, which was active in the mid-1980s, is probably the same as the identically named group which was in contact with CEDADE and with the French *Devenir européen* nazi group in 1980-81, but was based in Portugal's second city (Apartado 489, 4008 Oporto).

Policies. The group has white supremacist and fascist social and economic policies.

Publications. Vanguarda.

Partido da Democracia Cristão (PDC)
Christian Democratic Party

Address. Rua Passadiço 28-2, Lisbon

Leadership. Santos Ferreira (general secretary)

Orientation. Right-wing conservative

History. The PDC was founded in Lisbon shortly after the 1974 coup by former supporters of the Salazar regime. It was prevented from participating in the 1975 elections but in those of 1976 it gained 0.5 per cent of the vote. In 1980 it allied with the *Frente Nacional* and the PDP to contest a general election, but their combined vote was less than 20,000. The PDC contested the 1985 general election in its own right, but secured only 0.7 per cent of the poll.

Policies. The PDC has nationalist and ultra-conservative policies.

União Nacional
National Union

Orientation. Fascist

History. The Union, which sees itself as a successor to Salazar's party, emerged in Lisbon and Oporto in the early 1980s.

Policies. It is ultra-authoritarian and has corporatist and white supremacist policies.

Associated organizations. In 1984 the group co-operated with CEDADE-Portugal.

Defunct organizations

Accão Nacional Popular: Salazar's *União Nacional* adopted this name in 1970. It had formed the government since 1932, and was the sole legal party under the 1933 corporatist Constitution. Its ideology was at first closely modelled on Italian fascism, but it professed neutrality during the war. In the post-war period it continued to follow ultra-right and anti-communist ideas, and no opposition was permitted until a brief period of liberalization in 1969-70. Its last leader, Caetano, was overthrown in the 1974 coup, and the party was disbanded, although a modern fascist movement has revived the original name.

Movimento Nacionalista: this small fascist group, active from the late 1970s to the early '80s, published the periodical *A Rua* (The Street). In March 1980 it launched a short-lived *Frente Nacional* (National Front), which allied itself with the PDC and the PDP in that year's general election but failed to win representation. Twelve of its supporters were arrested in 1984 along with followers of CEDADE-Portugal.

National Syndicalist Movement: this blue-shirted paramilitary party, which sought to create a Portuguese blend of fascism and national socialism, was founded in February 1933 by Dr Rolão Preto, with the Conde de Monsaraz. Its badge was a Maltese cross.

Its leaders were "invited" to join Salazar's party in 1934 and declined; they were deported to Spain in July of that year.

Partido da Derecha Portuguesa: formed in June 1977 as the *Movimento Independente de Reconstrução Nacional* (MIRN—Independent Movement for National Reconstruction), this right-wing anti-communist group became the PDP (Party of the Portuguese Right) in October 1978. Its leader, Gen. Kaulza Oliveira de Arriaga, had been a colonial military commander. In 1980 it allied with the *Frente Nacional* and the PDC to contest the general election, without success.

Other organizations

Among the less important right-wing groups active in the past two decades are the following, many of which are likely to have disbanded: *Accão Nacionalista Revolucionário* (Revolutionary Nationalist Action); *Aginter Press*; an affiliate of the British Christian Mission to the Communist World; the *ELA*; the *Legião Verde* (Green Legion); the *Grupos de Accão Nacionalista* (Nationalist Action Groups); *Macao* (the Anti-Communist Commando Movement); the *Paladin Group*; the moribund *Partido Popular Monárquico* (Popular Monarchist Party) of Gonçalo Ribeiro Telles, which has traditionally represented an authoritarian and anti-democratic tendency but which has in recent years adopted an ecologist platform; and the magazine *Resistência*.

Individuals

Fernando do Canto e Silva: the Portuguese correspondent of the leading US anti-semitic journal, Willis Carto's *The Spotlight* (see Liberty Lobby, United States).

Juan Fernández Krohn: a Spanish-born priest of the ultra-right Catholic fundamentalist "integrist" movement, he attempted in May 1982 to assassinate the Pope during the latter's visit to Portugal.

Azores Islands

Political system. Two years after the 1974 revolution in Portugal, the Azores were granted a form of autonomy with their own assembly and budgetary powers. They remain under a Portuguese-appointed governor.

Recent history. The current (1987) governor, João Mota Amaral, supports increased autonomy, including the introduction of a separate Azores flag and anthem. This has led to problems with the Portuguese garrison, which from mid-1986 was refusing to recognize the new symbols. The centre-right regional government has opposed metropolitan Portuguese governments involving the Socialist Party.

The evolution of the far right. After the Portuguese revolution of 1974 there developed an extreme right-wing secessionist movement, which declined after the 1976 concessions. Since 1979 the movement has reportedly received the support of Libya. The current governor has denied suggestions that he is still sympathetic to the separatists, whom he supported in 1974-75.

Active organizations

Frente de Libertação dos Açores (FLA)
Azores Liberation Front

Leadership. José de Almeida (leader)

Orientation. Right-wing secessionist

History. The independence movement in the Azores, formed in mid-1975, opposed the left-wing metropolitan administration and the activities in the Azores of left-wing parties. It accepted the autonomy provisions of the 1976 Constitution but has been involved in occasional violent protests thereafter. According to the regional government the FLA had very little popular support by late 1986.

Policies. The FLA is fiercely anti-communist and right-wing in its social and economic policies, but reportedly receives the support of Gaddafi's Libya on the grounds that it is an anti-colonialist movement.

Associated organizations. In the mid-1970s the FLA was in contact with a similar anti-communist autonomist movement in Madeira, known as the *Frente de Libertação do Arquipélago de Madeira* (FLAMA—Madeira Archipelago Liberation Front). That movement became dormant after the concessions granted in the 1976 Portuguese Constitution.

Romania

capital: Bucharest   **population: 23,000,000**

Political system. The Socialist Republic of Romania has a 369-seat Great National Assembly elected by universal adult suffrage for a five-year term; it in turn elects an executive President, a Cabinet and a State Council. The sole legal party is the Romanian Communist Party (PCR).

Recent history. Since the proclamation of the Republic in 1947 the PCR has formed the government, at first under Gheorghe Gheorghiu-Dej and, since 1965, under Nicolae Ceaucescu. The PCR has since 1965 been relatively independent of the Soviet Union, while remaining a member of Comecon and of the Warsaw Pact.

The evolution of the far right. There were three large and some smaller fascist organizations in the 1930s, the most important of which was the Iron Guard. The Guard supported the German-backed dictatorship under Gen. Antonescu which took Romania into the Second World War in 1940 as a member of the Axis. Soviet forces liberated the country in 1944 and disbanded the Iron Guard.

There have been no organized right-wing parties in the country since the war, although Iron Guardist movements survive in émigré communities. In late 1986 there was a report that a synagogue in Buhusi, in the north, had been burnt down by masked men; this was the first recorded anti-semitic attack since the wartime pogroms. There have been occasional allegations of discrimination against the ethnic minorities, and particularly the Hungarian community.

Human rights activities in Romania, although supported by foreign ultra-right groups, fall outside the scope of this work, as does the exiled anti-communist Social Democratic Party, which is based in Paris. There was a small unofficial trade union movement in the late 1970s.

Active organizations

Legion of St. Michael

Orientation. Fascist

History. This network of ex-Iron Guard members and supporters is represented among most Romanian exile communities. There is a substantial overlap in membership with the Roumanian Freedom Front.

Policies. The group seeks the overthrow of the Romanian communist government.

Roumanian Freedom Front

Leadership. Dr Const-Radu Budisteanu (leader)

Orientation. Fascist

History. This émigré grouping, which has had several other names, represents sympathizers and former members of the Iron Guard.

Policies. The Front is anti-communist and pro-Western.

Associated organizations. Several Front leaders are also active in the Legion of St. Michael.

234

International affiliations. The Front has members in several Western countries, including the United States, the United Kingdom and Spain. It has received recognition as the Romanian chapter of the World Anti-Communist League (see South Korea), and is also in a WACL affiliate, the Anti-Bolshevik Bloc of Nations (see United Kingdom). It maintains contact through the ABN with other East European émigré groups.

World Union of Free Romanians

Base. London, UK

Leadership. Ion Ratiu (director)

Orientation. Anti-communist

History. This émigré organization received publicity in mid-1986 for its claims, denied by the Romanian authorities, that women in Romania were subjected to frequent gynaecological examinations at their workplaces in order to encourage them to breed.

Policies. The Union opposes the communist government in Romania and seeks to expose offences against human rights.

Defunct organizations

Agrarian Party: also known as the Goga Fascist Party, after its leader, this group won seven seats in the July 1932 general election, increasing its representation by one in the following year.

Anti-Semitic Party: this party, led by Cuza, won 11 of the 387 seats in the 1932 parliamentary election, but in 1933 it was reduced to nine seats.

Iron Guard: this pre-war fascist movement was led by Corneliu Codreanu, and held five seats in parliament in 1932. A liberal government which came to power in November 1933 banned fascist organizations; a supporter of the movement assassinated the Prime Minister, Ion Duca, in December, whereupon a more specific order banned the Guard itself and forbade its candidates to take part in parliamentary elections. Codreanu went into hiding but was arrested in March 1934. The president of the movement, Prof Cristescu, was assassinated in 1939, whereupon the Guard killed the Prime Minister, Armand Galinescu. The movement supported the Antonescu dictatorship during the war. A Guard sympathizer accused of war crimes, Archbishop Valerian Trifa of the Romanian Orthodox Church in the United States, was ordered to be deported in 1986 after the Israeli authorities had sought his extradition. He applied unsuccessfully for refuge in Switzerland and, according to some reports, Romania. His case was publicized by US nazi groups, including the New Order. Apart from the movements mentioned above, there are groups of Romanian exiles who describe themselves as the Iron Guard, or as the Iron Guard in Exile (the latter movement led by Jianiu Danieleau).

Saudi Arabia

administrative capital: Jeddah   **population: 10,600,000**

Political system. Saudi Arabia is a monarchy with no legislature or political parties. The monarch rules in accordance with Islamic law and with the non-binding advice of a Council of Ministers.

Recent history. The current (1987) monarch, King Fahd, is a member of the family which has ruled much of the Arabian peninsula throughout the present century. The Kingdom of Saudi Arabia was proclaimed in 1932, and exploitation of its vast petroleum reserves in the post-war period laid the basis for the country's enormous wealth. The country has generally been stable politically, apart from isolated incidents such as the assassination of King Faisal in 1975 and the seizure of the Grand Mosque in Mecca by Islamic fundamentalists in 1979.

The evolution of the far right. The ruling family has traditionally governed in an autocratic manner, following ultra-conservative and anti-communist domestic and foreign policies, and opposition is not tolerated. The government has provided possibly millions of dollars in funding to foreign right-wing causes, including the World Anti-Communist League (see South Korea) although Saudi funding of the WACL declined in the early 1980s). It has also funded the World Muslim League (see Pakistan), which has been involved in some anti-semitic activities, and there were reports in the mid-1980s that it was assisting the Nicaraguan *contra* guerrilla movements.

Seychelles

capital: Victoria   **population: 65,000**

Political system. Since 1979 Seychelles has been a one-party state with a directly elected executive President and a one-chamber National Assembly with 23 directly elected and two appointive seats.

Recent history. Seychelles was a British colony until achieving independence in 1976. The corrupt and unpopular conservative regime of President James Mancham was overthrown in a coup in June 1977, and Albert René, leader of what is now the Seychelles People's Progressive Front, became President. René's socialist regime follows a non-aligned international policy.

The evolution of the far right. Right-wing opponents of René have financed coup attempts involving foreign mercenaries on numerous occasions, including November 1979, November 1981, October 1982 and November 1983.

Active organizations

Seychelles Democratic Party

Base. London, UK

Leadership. David Joubert (leader)

Orientation. Anti-communist

History. This party was formed in London in October 1985 by Joubert, formerly a government minister in Seychelles.

Policies. It seeks the overthrow of the socialist government.

Seychelles National Movement

Base. London, UK

Leadership. Paul Chow (leader); Robert Firchot

Orientation. Anti-communist

History. This organization was founded in London in 1984 by right-wing opposition leaders who had since 1979 also controlled a clandestine internal opposition organization, the *Mouvement pour la Résistance*. Its founders had sponsored a coup attempt in November 1981 in which a group of 44 mainly South African mercenaries, led by "Mad Mike" Hoare, attempted to storm the airport. Several of the mercenaries served prison sentences after escaping to South Africa. The Movement's co-founder, Gerard Paul Hoareau, who had fled to London after the 1981 coup attempt, was assassinated there in November 1985.

The Movement has the support, but not the active involvement, of the deposed President Mancham.

Policies. The Movement seeks the overthrow by any necessary means of the "illegal and repressive" René government.

Membership. The group claimed to have 100 members in Britain and 250 in Australia in late 1985.

International affiliations. Chow represented the Movement at the September 1985 congress of the World Anti-Communist League (see South Korea), to which the Movement had affiliated in 1984.

Defunct organizations

Seychelles Liberation Committee: a Paris-based right-wing exile group founded in 1979, it appeared to have become extinct by 1984.

Seychelles Popular Anti-Marxist Front; an anti-communist exile movement active in the early 1980s, it was based in South Africa but denied involvement in the 1981 coup attempt launched from there.

Singapore

capital: Singapore City   **population: 2,600,000**

Political system. The Republic of Singapore has a unicameral 79-seat directly elected Parliament, which appoints a non-executive President. Government is led by a Prime Minister and Cabinet.

Recent history. Singapore gained independence in 1965, after a century spent mainly under British colonial rule. The country has been dominated by Lee Kuan Yew's People's Action Party (PAP), founded in 1954, which has followed a generally pro-Western foreign policy and has enacted tough anti-subversion legislation directed at the small left-wing element of the opposition. Most non-government parties represent ethnic minorities.

The evolution of the far right. There is little evidence of right-wing activity outside the PAP, which falls outside the scope of this work. There is an active chapter of the World Anti-Communist League (see South Korea) and of the Christian Mission to the Communist World (see United Kingdom).

Individuals

Tseng Chou-Koo: the Singapore correspondent of the Liberty Lobby's anti-semitic paper, *The Spotlight* (see United States).

South Africa

administrative capital: Pretoria   **population: 29,000,000**

Political system. South Africa is governed by a complex Constitution giving effective power to its minority white population, which through a parliament elects the executive President; there are parallel but ineffective institutions purporting to represent other sectors of the population.

Recent history. Since becoming a republic in 1961, South Africa has been ruled by the white minority's National Party with the necessary assistance of an extensive security apparatus. The white population consists of over 2,500,000 Afrikaners (of Dutch origin) and slightly fewer of other (mainly British) origins, and there has traditionally been some antagonism between these blocs. The black, Asian and "coloured" (mixed race) population forms more than a dozen major ethnic groups, with left-wing elements among them tending to play down the ethnic differences and conservatives stressing them.

The principal organization of the mainly black resistance to the regime has been the illegal African National Congress (ANC), which with its military wing *Umkhonto we Sizwe* has achieved widespread international recognition as the legitimate representative of the South African people. Other opposition groupings, tolerated to a greater or lesser degree, have functioned, including the broad-based United Democratic Front (UDF) formed in 1983. The increasing difficulty of defending the state against the majority population obliged the government to impose emergency laws in 1985, providing for press censorship, the prohibition of virtually any kind of opposition political activity and the introduction of internment without trial.

The evolution of the far right. The South African state with its premise that white people are naturally superior to blacks, has throughout its existence been a repository and breeding-ground for racist and fascist ideology. There is also a long history of anti-Jewish thought. The ideological underpinning of minority rule has been the concept of apartheid, or the separation of the various ethnic communities, supposedly in order that each may develop at its own pace and within its own traditions; most outside observers see apartheid as a means of maintaining white control over the country's resources and political system.

The principal organs of the white supremacist movement have been the National Party (NP) and its semi-clandestine ally, the *Broederbond*. There have also been a number of smaller and more strident racist organizations, mostly in and around Pretoria. In recent years some elements within the white community, including the present NP leadership, have sought to deflect the pressure for radical change in South Africa by making certain concessions to the non-white communities, and this has given rise to a reactionary tendency exemplified by the paramilitary AWB and the parliamentary HNP and Conservative Party.

An important element of the apartheid regime's strategy has been the fostering of nominally independent "homelands", or Bantustans, where black people may be assigned "citizenship" according to ethnic identity, and where they may have to live if their labour is not needed elsewhere. The "governments" of these "states" are, by definition, formed by individuals willing to work with the apartheid system, although many of them express distaste at apartheid; black resistance groups generally oppose the governments of these "states", which have consequently required mechanisms for controlling the people resident within their "borders". There have arisen a number of vigilante organizations to fulfil this function, often by means of murder and intimidation, and similar groupings have developed in non-"independent" black areas to defend local elites. Although generally referred to as right-wing, they often lack formal structure or ideology, and so most are outside the scope of this book. These groupings include the *Fathers* group in the Crossroads squatter camp near Cape Town; the Zulu *Amabutho* of Umlazi township, in Durban; the *Mbhokoto* group, now reportedly suppressed, in the "KwaNdebele homeland"; the followers of "President" Sebe of the "Ciskei homeland"; and elsewhere the A-Team, the Pakhatis, the Green Berets and so on.

The *Inkatha* movement, followers of Chief Mangosuthu Buthelezi of the "Kwazulu homeland", and opposition parties which work within the existing political structure, while themselves opposing apartheid or advocating reforms such as federalism or power-sharing, are not included here. To classify such organizations as "far right", on the grounds that they recognize the apartheid state, would be too broad a definition for the present work, not just in respect of South Africa but as to other states with corrupt or exclusive power structures.

Active organizations

Afrikaner Volkswag—see *Volkswag*.

Afrikaner Weerstandsbeweging (AWB)
Afrikaner Resistance Movement

Leadership. Eugene Terre Blanche

Orientation. Neo-nazi, Afrikaner nationalist

History. The AWB (the acronym is pronounced locally in the Afrikaans manner, *ah-vay-bay*) was founded in 1973 by Eugene Terre Blanche (also spelt Terre'blanche, Terre' Blanche or Terreblanche; born in 1943 as Terblanche; a farmer, and a former police bodyguard to Prime Minister J.B. Vorster) and six others at a meeting in Heidelberg, in the Transvaal. In 1978 the group was responsible for an assault on a non-fascist historian, Prof Floors van Jaarsfeld, who was tarred and feathered for suggesting that the celebration of the "Day of the Covenant"—the anniversary of the defeat of the Zulus by the Afrikaners—should be discontinued. In 1982 arms were captured in raids on AWB premises and Terre Blanche arrested, with eight other members; he received a suspended prison sentence for terrorism in 1983. Two other AWB members who were imprisoned for 15 years had conspired to release syphilis-infected rats in Sun City, the sex-and-gambling complex in the "homeland" of Bophuthatswana.

Despite, or perhaps because of, publicity concerning the convictions, the movement became more popular among Transvaal whites, and in 1983 it began to disrupt meetings of the ruling National Party, resulting in an inconclusive police investigation into its activities. It achieved considerable international publicity in May 1986 when it forcibly took over a meeting which was to have been addressed by the South African Foreign Minister, Pik Botha. The subsequent AWB rally became the first white gathering in South Africa to be broken up by police using teargas.

It was announced in October 1986 that the AWB had renounced the use of violence against the South African state, and that President Botha, while regarding the movement as "un-Afrikaner", had accordingly agreed to meet Terre Blanche for discussions on topics including the prohibition on police membership of the AWB and the proposals, rejected by the AWB, for a multi-racial legislature in Natal and Kwazulu.

The AWB has adopted as its symbol a three-armed device which most press observers liken to the swastika, but which the AWB says has biblical origins.

Policies. Terre Blanche has advocated the disenfranchisement of Jews, and advanced a Jewish conspiracy theory. However, the movement at present concentrates on opposing what it contrives to see as the liberal racial policies of the government of South Africa. Terre Blanche maintains that he is not a nazi nor a racist, but a nationalist who he loves his *volk*, the Boers, and his *vaderland*, i.e. the 19th-century Boer republics. He has stated that if a black revolution begins in South Africa, "there will be a white force under the AWB that will fight back... [and] implement a white people's state", the *Boerevolkstaat*. He has dismissed democracy as a "British-Jewish system" and called for the dissolution of the existing political parties. AWB members are reportedly encouraged to infiltrate the South African armed forces.

Membership. Estimates of the movement's membership in mid-1986 ranged from 50,000 to 100,000. A joint AWB, Conservative Party (CPSA) and *Herstigte Nasionale* Party (HNP) rally at the Voortrekker monument in 1986 was attended by about 9,000 people. Membership is restricted to white Christians.

Associated organizations. The movement has a brown-shirted paramilitary wing, the "Storm Falcons". It was reported in 1983 that the movement had successfully applied for the registration of a White People's State Party, but it does not appear to have made use of that body. The AWB has co-ordinated its activities with those of the HNP and the CPSA. There have been suggestions, so far resisted by Terre Blanche, that the three should merge. Unity talks were held with the Conservatives early in 1986. The AWB also controls the *Brandwag* vigilante group.

Anglo-Afrikaner Bond

Address. PO Box 143, Belleville, Cape Town 7350

Orientation. White supremacist

History. This organization was founded in the 1970s.

Policies. It works for political unity between the English- and Afrikaans-speaking sections of the white population.

Publications. *AAB-Report*, monthly.

Brandwag
Sentinel

Orientation. White supremacist

History. This network of vigilante organizations, an offshoot of the *Afrikaner Weerstandsbeweging* (AWB), was formed in the early 1980s. Andries Treurnicht, the Conservative Party leader, said in March 1985 that he was "satisfied that the organization is not militant and will operate totally within the law". In July 1986 the AWB suspended a *Brandwag* organizer, ex-security police colonel Arthur Cronwright, for saying that the *Brandwag* would train children as young as 10 in the use of arms.

Associated organizations. See AWB.

Broederbond
Brothers' Union

Leadership. J.P. de Lange (chairman)

Orientation. White supremacist

History. The *Broederbond*, a semi-secret society of Afrikaner men, was founded to counter British discrimination against the Boers in colonial times. Although functioning semi-secretly, it has been a powerful force in South African politics since the Second World War. A former chairman of the *Broederbond*, Andries Treurnicht, resigned from it in June 1984 after forming the Conservative Party; another, Carel Boshoff, leads the *Voortrekker* youth movement. Most of the current South African Cabinet, including President Botha, are members of the society.

Policies. The society seeks to ensure the survival of the Afrikaner culture and of Afrikaner political power in South Africa. To that end it has supported minimal compromises with other sections of the population, including the 1983 constitutional changes. It was alleged in February 1987 that the *Bond* was discussing internally the possibility of an eventual transition to democracy in South Africa, albeit with special status for the white minority.

Associated organizations. The *Bond* is closely identified with the National Party, and is sometimes referred to as the NP's "think tank". It has consequently come in for severe criticism from more right-wing white organizations such as the HNP and the AWB.

Conservative Party of South Africa (CPSA)
Konserwatiewe Party van Suid-Afrika (KPSA)

Leadership. Dr Andries P. Treurnicht (leader); Dr Ferdie Hartzenberg (deputy leader); A.C. van Wyk (general secretary)

Orientation. White supremacist

History. The Conservative Party was formed in March 1982 after the expulsion from the ruling National Party of some members who opposed what they perceived as a liberalizing tendency. The main support for the Conservatives came from the Afrikaners of the rural Transvaal, many of whom supported the National Conservative Party of Connie Mulder. Other groups incorporated in the new party were *Aksie eie Toekoms* (Action for Our Future), led by Prof Alkmar Swart, and the South Africa First Campaign of Brendan Willmer. The party leader, Treurnicht, is a former National Party cabinet minister and a former chairman of the powerful *Broederbond* organization.

In May 1983 the CPSA contested three by-elections as a test of strength against the National Party; two of its members, originally elected as NP candidates, lost their seats, but Treurnicht was returned to the House of Assembly. In June 1984 the party, in an alliance with the *Afrikaner Weerstandsbeweging* and the *Herstigte Nasionale* Party, defeated the National Party in a provincial council by-election in Potgietersrus. By mid-1985 the Conservatives held 18 of the 178 seats in the parliament. Parliamentary by-elections in October 1985 saw the Conservatives greatly increase their vote in three NP constituencies.

For the 1987 white elections the Conservative Party recruited several prominent white right-wingers as its candidates, including Gen. Hendrik van den Bergh, who had been in charge of the main intelligence agency (then called the BOSS—Bureau of State Security) in the 1970s.

Policies. The Conservative Party seeks to return to the traditional "separate development" theory of apartheid, and opposes concessions to the black population. The ideological sophistication of the party may be exemplified by a delegate at the August 1985 annual conference, who said that blacks were childlike creatures whose lives revolved around sex and who were incapable of thinking ahead. Unlike the HNP, the Conservatives do not advocate the removal of official status from the English language, and propose the creation of "coloured" and Indian homelands.

Associated organizations. There have been suggestions that the party should merge with other far-right groups, with which it has staged joint activities. In March 1986, following talks, Treurnicht issued a statement approving of the activities of both the AWB and the *Brandwag* group. Later in 1986 unity talks were held with the HNP and, separately, with the AWB, with a view to forming either an ad hoc or a permanent alliance before the 1987 whites-only elections. Treurnicht has been associated with the *Volkswag* movement but has severed his connection with the *Broederbond*.

Federation of the Covenant People

Address. PO Box 830, Honeydew 2040

Orientation. White supremacist

History. This grouping is part of the international movement often known as "British Israel".

Policies. It maintains that the white people of north-western Europe, and their "kith and kin" in the former colonies, are the chosen race of God. The movement finds most of its recruits in the Protestant churches and usually has an anti-communist and millenarian bent, with undertones of racism and anti-semitism.

International affiliations. The movement is based in Britain but has adherents elsewhere, notably in Canada and Australia.

242

Herstigte Nasionale Party (HNP)
Reconstituted National Party

Address. PO Box 1888, Pretoria 0001

Leadership. Jaap A. Marais (chairman, leader); Louis F. Stofberg (general secretary); Gert Beetge (deputy chairman)

Orientation. White supremacist

History. The HNP was founded by Dr Albert Hertzog in October 1969 to co-ordinate numerous small organizations to the right of J.B. Vorster's National Party, representing that political standpoint from which it is possible to regard as *verligte* (enlightened, or liberalizing) the policies of the National Party leadership. Its founders, representing the rival *verkrampte* (sound) tendency, had been expelled from the NP's parliamentary group, and failed to retain their seats at subsequent elections.

Beetge, a trade-union leader, denounced as "Jewish propaganda" a television film about the Holocaust shown in 1985. Stofberg, who succeeded Beetge as HNP general secretary, won the constituency of Sasolburg, in the Orange Free State, from the National Party in parliamentary by-elections held in October 1985. He said that his election "heralded the resurrection of the Afrikaner nation as a free and independent entity". A 1986 by-election in Klip River resulted in an increased HNP vote but the NP retained the seat.

Policies. The HNP advocates "Christian nationalism", Afrikaner supremacy, the removal of official status from the English language, the strengthening of apartheid based on the homelands policy, and immigration control favouring whites.

Publications. *Die Afrikaner*, weekly; edited by Z.B. du Toit. It claims a circulation of 15,000.

Associated organizations. The HNP has staged joint activities with the *Afrikaner Weerstandsbeweging* and the Conservative Party, and has held unity talks with the Conservatives.

International affiliations. The HNP is organized under the same name in Namibia (which it calls South-West Africa). It has extensive international links with white supremacist and ultra-right organizations including National Action (Australia).

Mbhokoto

Orientation. Right-wing vigilante group

History. The *Mbhokoto* was established to support the "government" of the "homeland of KwaNdebele", a region 50 miles north-east of Pretoria. Piet Ntuli, as "Minister of Home Affairs of KwaNdebele", effectively controlled the organization until his assassination, by persons unknown, in mid-1986. The "Cabinet of KwaNdebele" thereupon decided to disband the group, in what was thought to be a gesture to factions within the local elite opposing the "independence" on offer from Pretoria and supported by Ntuli.

Movement for the Liberation and Protection of White South Africa

Orientation. White supremacist

History. In February 1986 this group issued a threat against the British anti-apartheid campaigner, Peter Hain, then planning a visit to South Africa, to the effect that its members would risk "the gallows" to punish him for having "humiliated South Africa into the ground".

National Forum

Address. PO Box 1564, Krugersdorp 1740

Leadership. Ivor Benson (leader)

Orientation. Anti-semitic

History. Benson was formerly a mainstream press journalist in South Africa and in Britain (for the *Daily Telegraph* and the *Daily Express*), and was also a press censor in Rhodesia under the illegal Smith regime. In the early 1960s he was a contributing editor of *Western Destiny*, the journal of racist anthropologist Roger Pearson (see Council for Social and Economic Studies, United States). He founded the Forum in the 1970s.

Policies. The Forum promotes belief in a Jewish conspiracy and in white supremacy.

Publications. Behind the News, monthly.

International affiliations. The Forum is the South African chapter of the World Anti-Communist League (see South Korea). Benson is the South African correspondent of the US Liberty Lobby's anti-semitic journal, *The Spotlight*; he is associated with the Crown Commonwealth League of Rights (see United Kingdom), and spoke at its 1985 conference.

National Party of South Africa (NP)
Nasionale Party van Suid-Afrika (NP)

Address. PO Box 6308, Johannesburg 2000

Leadership. P.W. Botha (leader)

Orientation. Conservative, white supremacist

History. The National Party has been the ruling party and the main political organ of the white minority in South Africa since 1948. The party was founded in 1912 by Gen. J.B.M. Hertzog, who broke away from the ruling South African Party (SAP) over the principle of a separate Afrikaner identity. It joined a coalition government in 1924 and was the largest parliamentary party from 1929. In 1934 it fused with the SAP to form the United Party (UP), although a minority faction under Dr D.F. Malan formed a Purified National Party which came to power in 1948 (as the Reunited National Party) after recruiting a large number of UP supporters. From 1953 the NP has held an absolute majority in the white assembly. Its leaders have included Hendrik Verwoerd, who was assassinated in 1967; John Balthazar Vorster, during whose leadership various ultra-right elements broke away in 1969 to form the *Herstigte Nasionale* Party; and the current State President of South Africa, P.W. Botha, during whose leadership a similar split in 1982 resulted in the formation of the Conservative Party.

During the 1970s, and particularly under Botha in the early 1980s, the NP leadership moved away from the Verwoerdian notion of permanent apartheid in favour of a very gradual transition towards sharing power with non-white communities—a shift of position expressed in Botha's exhortation "adapt or die". The changes he offered in a constitutional reform in 1983, based on the notion of "co-responsibility" leading eventually to some variant of democracy, were insufficient to meet the demands of the black majority, but enough to enrage the neo-nazi right which began to disrupt National Party meetings. By mid-1985 the NP was facing a serious challenge from more right-wing elements in parliamentary by-elections. As of early 1987 the National Party remained in power.

Policies. While its raison d'être is the preservation of white rule in South Africa, the NP professes the goals of raising living standards for black and white alike and of fostering the independence of black nations. It supports equal status for English- and Afrikaans-speaking whites, although its power base remains largely in the Afrikaner community. The current leadership is described in South African terms as "enlightened" (*verligte*), in contrast to the hard line racist (*verkrampte*) factions which have mostly defected to the CPSA or the HNP.

Membership. 1,000,000.

Publications. Daily newspapers which support the NP include *Die Burger* and *Oosterlig* (Cape Province), *Die Volksblad* (Orange Free State), *Beeld*, *Die Transvaler* and *Die Vaderland* (Transvaal).

Associated organizations. See *Broederbond.*

Patria
Fatherland

Address. PO Box 705, Belleville, Cape Town 7530

Leadership. Johan Dipenaar (editor)

Orientation. White supremacist

History. This periodical was circulating among foreign fascist groups, including member organizations of the World Union of National Socialists (see United States and Denmark), in the early 1980s.

Society of Orange Workers

Orientation. White separatist

History. This organization was formed in 1980. It has selected certain areas, such as the community of Morgenzon 200 km east of Johannesburg, as "growth points" for its model communities.

Policies. The Society promotes the idea that whites have become too dependent on black labour and that the best hope for the survival of white South Africa is the development of completely separate white communities, even if this means whites doing actual physical work.

Membership. The Society claimed 2,000 members in early 1986.

South African Observer

Address. Box 2401, Pretoria

Leadership. S.E.D. Brown

Orientation. White supremacist

History. This monthly racist and anti-semitic periodical, established in the early 1970s, enjoyed a wide foreign circulation in the early 1980s.

Policies. It espouses right-wing nationalist and white supremacist ideas.

South African Patriot

Address. PO Box 6019, Durban 4000

Orientation. White supremacist

History. This magazine, which broadly supported the HNP, was established around 1979 by Irishman John Hiddlestone and Englishman John Harvey, both former members of the British National Front and recent immigrants to South Africa. Hiddlestone returned to Northern Ireland in 1983 after a financial dispute, and later denied accusations that he was working as a police informer. The *Patriot* was still being published in the mid-1980s.

United Christian Action

Orientation. Anti-communist

History. This group staged a memorial service in Pretoria on the third anniversary of the bombing there by the ANC of the air force headquarters, in order to "draw attention to the fact that the ANC is a terrorist organization". It may be the South African affiliate of the Christian Mission to the Communist World, a UK-based organization.

Volkswag
People's Watch

Leadership. Prof Carel Boshoff

Orientation. White supremacist

History. This body (also known as the *Afrikaner Volkswag*) was founded in May 1984 by Conservative Party sympathizers and others as the cultural arm of the Afrikaner supremacist movement. Boshoff, who also leads the *Voortrekker* movement, is reported to believe that the Volkswag should co-ordinate all Afrikaner cultural groups. In 1985 a leading member of *Volkswag*, Dr Theo Schumann, called for the organization of a campaign to expose "the fable" of the nazi Holocaust, which he said was invented by "Jewish monetary powers".

Membership. A 1985 *Volkswag* conference was attended by more than 1,000 delegates.

Voortrekkers
Scouts

Leadership. Prof Carel Boshoff (chief leader); Jan Oelofse (chief secretary)

Orientation. White supremacist

History. This Afrikaner youth organization is divided into a hard-line faction led by Boshoff—a former *Broederbond* chairman—and a *verligte*("enlightened", or moderate) faction led by Oelofse. Boshoff was re-elected as leader in July 1985, despite a controversy over his simultaneous role as leader of the *Volkswag*. The supreme organ of the movement is its congress, held every four years.

Wit Kommando
White Commando

Orientation. White supremacist guerrilla group

History. This group was formed in May 1980 with the principal aim of opposing what it regarded as the appeasement policies of the National Party government. In 1981 Massimo (Max) Bollo, a member of the National Directorate of the South African National Front, and Fabio Miriello were convicted of several bombings carried out against various black, anti-apartheid and pro-government targets and claimed as the work of the Commando. Bollo, then 42, was released in November 1985 and deported to Italy after serving part of his sentences, which totalled 52 years. There have been no recent reports of the Commando's activities and it may be defunct.

Youth for Freedom

Orientation. Anti-communist

History. This organization held a conference of right-wing youth groups in Johannesburg in July 1985. The cost of the gathering, estimated at R250,000, was borne by anonymous South African and US business interests. Among those who addressed the meeting—which included sessions on disinvestment in South Africa, Marxism, free enterprise and security— were Gerald Ludi and Michael Morris, former spies for the South African police; Vladimir Sakharov, a former KGB agent; a former US Ambassador to the United Nations and a US national security advisor. The meeting agreed to form a "liberty and democracy international alliance".

Associated organizations. The 1985 conference was hosted by the National Student Federation of South Africa.

International affiliations. Organizations attending the 1985 conference included the British Schools' Old Boys Society (Uruguay); the Federation of Conservative Students (United Kingdom); *Protoporia* (Cyprus); and others from Nicaragua, Afghanistan and elsewhere. At the time of writing it had not been possible to ascertain whether the group was the same as the International Youth for Freedom group which contributed US$30,000 to the costs of the 1985 conference of the World Anti-Communist League (see South Korea).

Defunct organizations

African Gentile National Socialist Movement: this nazi group was founded in Cape Town in October 1933, and its anti-semitic propaganda was the subject of several protests by members of parliament, including Jan Smuts, and by Jewish leaders.

African-German Cultural Society: this nazi front group was established in 1933, with Gen. Herzog as its patron and Werner Schmidt of Pretoria as president. It had offices in Munich headed by a German diplomat.

Afrikaner Ossewabrandwag (Afrikaner Ox-Wagon Guards): a heavily armed pro-Nazi grouping active in the Transvaal during the Second World War, this body fomented an Afrikaner rebellion (Operation Weissdorn) against the Smuts government, with the objective of bringing South Africa over to the Axis side. Its activists included J.B. Vorster and P.W. Botha, both of whom later became National Party heads of government.

Afrikaner Party: a white supremacist formation which was represented in parliament in the late 1940s.

Aksie Eie Toekoms: Action for Our Future was an Afrikaner racist group founded in February 1981 by Prof Alkmaar Swart. In early 1982 it merged into the Conservative Party.

Council of Europeans: founded in Pretoria in 1931, this body existed to combat "negrophilism", and sought to remove "natives" from urban areas to "homelands". The principal difference between its policies and the NP's later Bantustan strategy was the explicitly sexual motivation of the Council.

Hitler Youth: Capt. von Losnitzer, leader of this German-sponsored grouping which drew most of its membership from the German community in South West Africa, was expelled from South Africa in July 1934, and the movement was banned as subversive.

National Conservative Party: this breakaway group formed in 1979 by National Party hardliners including Cornelius (Connie) Mulder, a former Cabinet Minister, was superseded by the Conservative Party of South Africa, formed in 1982.

South Africa First Campaign: a pressure group of English-speaking white supremacists, the Campaign, formed in the late 1970s by Brendan Willmer (former youth leader of the British nazi National Youth League), joined the Conservative Party in March 1982. Willmer, who had also been very active in the Save Rhodesia Campaign and in the pro-apartheid Civic Action League, was required to leave South Africa in March 1983.

South African National Front: the SANF was established in the early 1970s by racist activists including Ray Hill, who later had a change of heart and infiltrated and disrupted the British ultra-right on behalf of *Searchlight*, an anti-fascist magazine. Max Bollo, a member of the Front's National Directorate, was imprisoned in 1981 and later deported for his role in the terrorist activities of the *Wit Kommando*. He was in contact with the New European Order (see Switzerland).

South African Party: the SAP was the ruling party of the white minority until 1924, when it was ousted by a coalition of the National Party (which had broken away from it in 1912-14) and the Labour Party. It allied itself with the NP in 1933 and merged with it a year later.

To the Point: an ultra-conservative publication funded secretly by the South African government in the 1970s, its wide foreign circulation made it one of the more effective of the propaganda weapons exposed in the 1979 "Muldergate" scandal. It had an international edition published from the Netherlands by British staff.

Other organizations

Minor groups active in South Africa in recent years, and others on which insufficient information has come to light, include the following: *African Outlook*, a white supremacist magazine established around 1974; the *Christian League of Southern Africa*, mainly active in propaganda campaigns in United Kingdom; *Dolphin Press*; *Der Handwerker* (The Artisan), a fascistic newsletter published from Johannesburg by A. Martin; *Hit Back* journal; the *Legion Afrika*; the *Ruiterwag*; the *Sons of England Patriotic and Benevolent Society*, for immigrants; the South African Institute for the Study of Conflict; *A Vanguarda*, a racist journal founded in the 1970s by white refugees from newly-independent Angola; the *Verkrampte Party*, which opposed any compromise in the apartheid policies; the *White People's State Party*, and the *White Rhino Club* (PO Box 11795, Marine Parade, Durban), which has policies similar to those of the *South African Patriot*. External organizations concerned with South Africa have included the *Scottish-South African Union* (United Kingdom), whose most prominent associate is Nicholas Fairbairn MP, and *South African Scope*, a newsletter (655 Madison Avenue, New York, NY 10021, United States).

Spain

capital: Madrid   population: 38,000,000

Political system. Spain is a constitutional monarchy governed by a Prime Minister and Cabinet representing the majority bloc in the bicameral parliament, the *Cortes Generales*. The Constitution is democratic and there are few restrictions on political activity. Several regions have devolved governments, although in the Spanish part of the Basque country (which also extends into France) there is agitation, backed by revolutionary violence, for independence. Spain also controls some territory in North Africa, consisting mainly of the enclaves of Ceuta and Melilla (on the Moroccan coast), and lays claim to Gibraltar, a British-controlled peninsula on the south coast.

Recent history. A military rebellion and civil war in 1936-39 installed the 40-year dictatorship of Generalissimo Francisco Franco y Bahamonde, who was ideologically close to the Italian and German fascists, although remaining neutral in the Second World War. Since Franco's death in 1975, there have been stable and liberalizing governments, directed successively by the centre-right and the centre-left, and at least three right-wing coup attempts have been foiled by the security forces. By far the largest political force is the Socialist Party.

The evolution of the far right. The long tradition of racism and xenophobia in Spain, dating from the expulsion of the Jews and Muslims in 1492, is expressed nowadays mainly in regard to the native population of about 300,000 gypsies and the immigrant communities of (mainly Portuguese and Moroccan) seasonal and other low-paid workers. There have been frequent reports of assaults on gypsies, including the destruction by mobs of gypsy camps in Andalucía in 1984 and July 1986.

A right-wing dictatorship under Gen. Primo de Rivera, from 1922 to 1929, was followed by the establishment of a republic, dominated by left-wing forces. A substantial fascist movement existed in Spain in the 1930s, as well as a right-wing agrarian movement and a clericalist movement which came into conflict with the left. There was also a monarchist movement which staged a revolt, led by Gen. Sanjurjo and centred on Seville, in August 1932; a similar plot was uncovered in May 1933. In March 1933 fascist propaganda was outlawed by the republican government. In July of that year there were over 500 arrests in connection with an anti-republican plot reportedly involving pro-Italian fascists, syndicalists (followers of a fascist movement led by the ex-dictator's son) and monarchists. All of these groups supported Franco's revolt, which started in the Moroccan outposts in 1936 and ended, after 500,000 deaths, in 1939, with victory for the rebels.

The principal source of support for modern right-wing movements is nostalgia for the Franco era. The sole legal political party under Franco—the *Falange*—was dissolved in 1977, but the right rapidly regrouped into several smaller parties which enjoyed some support among the armed forces and the paramilitary Civil Guard. At least three military coup plots have come to light—the Galaxia conspiracy of 1978, the *Almendros* or F-23 plot involving an assault on the *Cortes* by police colonel Antonio Tejero's forces in February 1981, and the Cervantes or Mars conspiracy led by Tejero's associate, army general Jaime Milans del Bosch, in October 1982. All three movements were apparently motivated by a desire to restore a *franquista* dictatorship. Each of the plots, and in particular that of Tejero (who became an idol of the far right) was supported by some retired and serving military officers, fundamentalist Catholics opposed to the liberalization of social legislation, neo-nazi organizations and others of both conservative and fascist tendencies. All the plots were frustrated by loyal forces and many of the conspirators received lengthy prison sentences. Annual rallies have been held by right-wing groups on the November anniversary of Franco's death, with the tenth in 1985 attracting some 50,000 people, including Italian fascists.

Basque separatist guerrilla activity has produced a right-wing response in the form of Spanish nationalist death squads. The activities of these groups increased significantly and spread into southern France during the early 1980s. Italian fascist terrorists, several of whom had taken refuge in Spain, became involved in these groups.

Other Spanish ultra-right groups include a Catholic fundamentalist ("integrist") movement, sections of the *Carlista* monarchist movement (although there is also a progressive monarchist tendency, most of which has accepted the present King), and a few nazi groups, the largest of which, the CEDADE, is well known outside Spain.

After the Second World War Spain accepted a number of fugitive Italian, German and other war criminals, including SS general Leon Degrelle of Belgium, who was given refuge and Spanish citizenship despite having been sentenced to death for his crimes. Several of those concerned still live in Spain.

Active organizations

El Alcázar

Address. Edificio Astygi, San Romualdo 26-3, Madrid 17

Telephone. 754-1245

Leadership. Antonio Izquierdo Ferigela (editor)

Orientation. Far right

History. This right-wing daily newspaper was founded in 1936, during the three-month siege of the Francoist stronghold of the Alcázar, as the principal organ of the nationalist cause. Its circulation is mainly among Francoist veterans and the modern ultra-right, and its columns were used for coded communications in connection with the Tejero coup plot of 1981. In June 1983, after the confirmation of sentences passed on the conspirators, *El Alcázar* became the focus of a protest campaign by right-wing army officers, whose letters calling for clemency for Tejero and his associates appeared at frequent intervals in the paper. In September 1983 the general commanding the traditionally right-wing Seventh Military Region of Valladolid expressed his sympathy for the plotters, causing the Socialist government to remove him from his post.

Circulation. 95,000.

Associated organizations. The paper is published by Diarios y Revistas S.A. (DYRSA). Its editor and several of its senior staff are leading members of the Francoist *Juntas Españoles* party, which was organized by readers of the paper in 1984-85.

Alianza Apostólica Anticomunista (AAA)
Apostolic Anti-Communist Alliance

Orientation. Anti-communist

History. This guerrilla organization emerged in late 1976 and was responsible for several violent attacks on left-wing organizations and individuals in the late 1970s and early '80s. Its most notorious action was the "Atocha massacre" in January 1977 of five socialist lawyers in Madrid; several *Fuerza Nueva* members, including José Fernández, received lengthy prison sentences for that attack. There have been few reports about the organization since late 1980 and it may have disbanded.

Policies. The AAA opposes regionalism, separatism and communism, and has denounced the existence of a masonic conspiracy against Spain. It has sought to kill or intimidate individuals associated with the democratization process, including members of post-Franco governments, and other liberal and left-wing activists.

Alianza Apostólica Antigua (AAA)
Old Apostolic Alliance

Orientation. Anti-communist

History. This group was reported to have issued a death threat against a communist senator in November 1985.

Associated organizations. The group may be identical with the other AAA.

Batallón Vasco Español (BVE)
Spanish Basque Battalion

Orientation. Ultra-right death squad

History. The BVE appeared on May 24, 1978, when it claimed responsibility for killing a taxi-driver in the Basque province of Guipuzcoa. It carried out numerous assassinations of alleged members or supporters of the Basque guerrilla group, the ETA, over the following years; in 1980 alone it was held responsible for about 20 killings. One of its members was arrested in March 1981 in the south of France, where the BVE had conducted several operations including at least three murders. It has not been active of late and may have been superseded by the GAL.

Policies. The BVE seeks to exterminate or intimidate supporters of the Basque nationalist cause.

Associated organizations. Information circulating among foreign nazi movements in the early 1980s gave the address of a Barcelona man as contact for this group and for the *Gruppe Peiper*, a nazi guerrilla organization named after German war criminal Joachim Peiper.

Centro Unitario Nacional Socialista
National Socialist Unity Centre

Address. Apartado 14.010, Barcelona

Leadership. Ramón Bau (leader)

Orientation. Nazi

History. The Centre was established by Bau in 1984 as a means of co-ordinating the activities of the various Spanish nazi groups with those of other, primarily Western European, groups.

Policies. The Centre's publications advance traditional national socialist views on all matters and advocate co-operation between nazi groups.

Publications. *Mundo NS* (NS World).

Associated organizations. Bau is a leading member of the main Spanish nazi group, CEDADE, and the Centre uses the CEDADE post office box number. The Centre is thought to be linked with a Falangist publication, *Patria y Libertad* (Fatherland and Liberty).

International affiliations. The Centre exchanges publications with many foreign groups, including the French FNE.

Círculo Español de Amigos de Europa (CEDADE)
Spanish Circle of Friends of Europe

Address. Apartado 14.010, Barcelona

Leadership. Ramón Bau

Orientation. Nazi

History. The CEDADE (or Cedade), which is almost invariably known by its acronym, was formed in 1965 by fascists, including fugitive Italians and Germans and Spanish veterans of the *Blaue Division* (see below). After the collapse of the Franco regime it became the largest and most active fascist group in Spain. The CEDADE youth group, the JNR, was suspected of involvement in at least one murder (of a communist) in April 1979, some days after the group had staged a celebration of Hitler's birthday. Several of its members were arrested after an arms seizure.

The emblems used by CEDADE are the Celtic cross (a cross surmounting a circle) and an eagle device borrowed from the *Falange*. Its principal activities include camping, the production and distribution of propaganda, demonstrations and social events such as Hitler birthday celebrations.

Policies. It pursues classic national socialist policies (anti-semitism, white supremacism, anti-communism, authoritarianism, nationalism, corporatism), with an unusual emphasis on youth; it has a regular turnover of its leadership to replace those over about 40 years of age. It has adopted an ecological policy. It regards the main ultra-right parties, such as *Fuerza Nueva*, as bourgeois formations. It promotes eugenics and euthanasia and, in common with many other fascist groups, advocates the construction of a "Europe of nationalities" based on racial, cultural and liguistic units.

Publications. Cedade, monthly. Most of the local branches have their own bulletins, which have included *Cruz Solar* (Sun Cross), *En Marcha* (On the March), *Halcón* (Hawk), *Tizona* (Firebrand), *Ataque* (Attack; all Madrid), *Walhalla* (Albacete), *Waffen* (Seville), *Revolución Nacional* (Valencia), and so on.

Associated organizations. See *Centro Unitario Nacional Socialista* and *El Guardián*. Local CEDADE groups have often adopted different names, often also used for their journals, such as *Año Cero* (Year Zero—Alicante) and *Hijos de Castilla* (Sons of Castile—Madrid). The CEDADE youth movement is the *Juventud Nacional-Revolucionaria* (JNR—National-Revolutionary Youth), based in Barcelona (and also known as the *Juventudes Nacional-Revolucionarias*), which publishes *Joven Europa* (Young Europe) magazine.

International affiliations. The very extensive international contacts of this group include most of the active West European nazi and fascist groups, as well as a number of North American and Latin American groups. It has sister organizations in France, Ecuador, Argentina, Portugal and elsewhere, all using the acronym CEDADE, and has particularly close relations with the French groups FNE and *Devenir européen* and with the Portuguese *Ordem Nova*. It is a regular guest at the Belgian fascist movement's Diksmuide camps. The *Frente Femenino* women's group of CEDADE corresponds with similar groups abroad, such as the Italian-based *Eowyn— Alternative Femminili*.

Coordinadora de Fuerzas Nacionalistas
Co-ordinating Group of Nationalist Forces

Leadership. Col. Carlos Meer de Ribera

Orientation. Francoist

History. This clandestine organization was established by right-wing military and civilian leaders in 1985. Meer was arrested in May 1986 while allegedly organizing the transfer of funds from Libya for the Spanish ultra-right; the incident, with other similar occurrences, led to considerable friction between the two countries. Meer claimed to be a long-standing personal friend of the Libyan leader, Col. Gaddafi. The Spanish government, which had earlier permitted the use of its airspace for a US air raid on Libya, accused the Gaddafi government of collaborating with terrorist acts against Spain.

Policies. The Group seeks the unification of ultra-right forces with a view to re-establishing an authoritarian and anti-democratic regime. One of its leading members, José Antonio Assiego, has stated his opposition to both capitalism and communism, opting for "the third way".

Associated organizations. One of the main organizations associated with the Group is the National Labour Force, led by Assiego and Enrique Romero Gómez (formerly of the *Central Obrera Nacional Sindicalista*).

Falange Española de las Juntas de Ofensiva Nacional-Sindicalistas (Falange Española de las JONS)
Spanish Phalanx of the Boards of the National-Syndicalist Offensive

Leadership. Diego Márquez Jorillo (leader)

Orientation. Fascist

History. This grouping, which regarded itself as the direct continuation of the Francoist movement of the same name (which was banned in 1977), contested the 1979 general elections in the *Unión Nacional* alliance (with *Fuerza Nueva*). The alliance obtained only one seat. In 1982 the *Falange* was unable to field any candidates in the general election and it may well have dissolved in the mid-1980s.

Policies. The grouping's policies included authoritarianism, anti-communism, fascist socio-economic doctrines and opposition to regionalist and separatist movements.

Frente Nacional
National Front

Base. Madrid

Leadership. Blas Piñar (leader)

Orientation. Francoist ultra-right

History. This party was launched in late 1986 by Piñar, a former leader of the *Fuerza Nueva*.

Policies. The party projects itself as an alternative to the democratic system.

Frente Nacional de la Juventud
National Youth Front

Address. Via Layetona 17, Barcelona

Orientation. Fascist

History. This organization, founded in 1978, was in contact with various Spanish and foreign nazi groups in the early 1980s. Its leader, Juan Ignacio González, was assassinated by leftists on Dec. 12, 1980.

Publications. Patria y Libertad (Fatherland and Liberty)

Fuerza Nueva (FN)
New Force

Address. Mejía Lequerica 8, Madrid 4

Telephone. 445-9000

Leadership. Manuel Ballesteros (editor of weekly journal)

Orientation. Francoist

History. This party was set up by a leading Francoist politician, Blas Piñar, in 1976, just before the dissolution of Franco's *Falange*, which it sought to replace. Several of its members were convicted of murders committed in 1977 in the name of the AAA death squad.

The FN won only a handful of votes in the 1982 elections and the majority faction of the party declared its dissolution in November of that year. Piñar went on to found the *Frente Nacional*, but the rump of the *Fuerza Nueva*, based around the party journal, appears to have maintained an independent existence without achieving any political impact.

Policies. The FN opposed the democratization of Spain and seeks a return to the authoritarianism and order of the Franco era, which it contrasts with the subversion, debauchery and decadence of the present day.

Publications. Fuerza Nueva, weekly.

Associated organizations. The youth wing of the FN is called *Fuerza Joven* (Young Force).

International affiliations. In 1978 the FN was party to a meeting in Madrid which established a "Euro-Right" union also incorporating the Italian MSI-DN, the French PFN and GUD and an Argentinian fascist leader, Curuchet. The alliance failed to achieve anything and it has effectively been superseded by the European Parliament grouping which includes the MSI-DN, the *Front national*, the Greek EPEN and the Irishman John Taylor. The *Fuerza Nueva* appears to have very limited international contacts at present.

Fundación Nacional Francisco Franco
Francisco Franco National Foundation

Orientation. Francoist

History. This institution was established in the late 1970s to perpetuate the memory and the philosophy of the late dictator. It has published a number of books and tracts.

Fundamentos
Essentials

Address. Apartado 45.024, Madrid 28080

Leadership. José Redondo (editor)

Orientation. New right

History. This magazine was in circulation in 1986.

Policies. Like the French *Eléments*, the magazine expounds authoritarian, elitist and anti-American "new right" ideas.

Grupos Antiterroristas de Liberación (GAL)
Anti-Terrorist Liberation Groups

Orientation. Nationalist death squad

History. This organization was set up in 1983 as a right-wing Spanish nationalist response to the activities of the Basque separatist guerrilla movement, *Euskadi ta Askatasuna* (ETA). Few details of its structure and leadership have come to light despite numerous trials of low-ranking members; a Spanish industrialist, Víctor Manuel Navascués, was acquitted of being a leader of the GAL in December 1985 after a trial in which he was defended by a right-wing lawyer, Angel López Montero (who had led the unsuccessful defence of Tejero in the 1981 coup trial).

The GAL has assassinated a number of suspected ETA members in both Spanish and French territory, although its activities have been concentrated in the French part of the Basque country. By May 1986 a total of 31 deaths had been attributed to it, including at least eight French citizens and about 20 Basque activists or refugees; at least eight of the killings were acknowledged mistakes.

There have been persistent reports of the involvement of fugitive Italian neo-fascist terrorists in the activities of the GAL, although most of the few dozen members arrested to date have been Spanish or French, including some ultra-right activists and some common criminals.

Associated organizations. Precursors and associates of the GAL include the *Batallón Vasco Español*, the *Grupos Armados Antimarxistas* and both of the organizations using the acronym AAA. A similar group, the *comando Jaizubia*, was set up in 1984 and was integrated into the GAL command shortly afterwards; two of its members were imprisoned for murder in December 1985.

Among the Basque and Spanish left, the GAL is unequivocally regarded as a mercenary arm of the Spanish security services; there is conclusive evidence that at least some members of the group have acted under police direction. It also appears from court cases, interviews and other sources that GAL assassins have had access to both Spanish and French police intelligence sources and official documents, and that large sums of money were paid for at least some of the killings.

Grupos Armados Españoles (GAE)
Armed Spanish Groups

Orientation. Ultra-right death squad

History. The Groups began a campaign of assassination and intimidation against Basque separatists in 1979. They lost three members killed by ETA guerrillas in January 1980, and they killed five Basques in the same month. Their activities extended outside Spain on Sept. 18, 1980, when they claimed responsibility for the killing of a Basque refugee in Biarritz, in the south of France. Little has been heard of them since that date.

Policies. The Groups have sought to undermine the Basque separatist movement by killing some of its supporters.

Gruppe Peiper—see *Batallón Vasco Español*.

El Guardián
The Guardian

Base. Valencia

Leadership. José Miguel García (editor)

Orientation. Nazi

History. This monthly publication was started in 1984.

Policies. It follows the nazi policies of the CEDADE, of which García is a prominent member.

Guerrilleros del Cristo Rey
Warriors of Christ the King

Orientation. Ultra-right death squad

History. This counter-terrorist group was active from the early 1970s, i.e. the last years of the Franco regime. In the mid-1970s, with the assistance of fugitive Italian neo-fascists, it conducted a bombing and shooting campaign against the Basque separatist movement. Its leader at that time was Mariano Sánchez Covisa. It has been inactive for some time.

Iglesia Cristiana Palmariana de los Carmelitas de la Santa Faz
Palmar Christian Church of Carmelites of the Holy Face

Base. El Palmar de Troya

Leadership. Clemente Domínguez (pope)

Orientation. Catholic ultra-right

History. This schismatic movement developed within the Roman Catholic Church in the late 1970s, centred on supposed apparitions at the village of El Palmar de Troya. It came into increasing conflict with the Catholic hierarchy and effectively became independent in 1976. Domínguez, leader of the sect, proclaimed himself Pope in 1977, and has proceeded to ordain a large number of bishops and priests. In December 1985 it failed to win legal recognition as a church, which would have won it important fiscal concessions.

Policies. The sect subscribes to ultra-right political positions, and has proclaimed the sainthood of José Antonio Primo de Rivera, Francisco Franco, Luis Carrero Blanco and other dead fascists. It has prophesied the salvation of the world by Blas Piñar (see *Frente Nacional*) and Gen. Pinochet of Chile.

Associated organizations. The Church runs a religious order, which has also been denied official recognition, called the Religious Order of Carmelites of the Holy Face in the Company of Jesus and Mary.

International affiliations. Among countries in which the Palmar sect has a following are Ireland, Portugal and United Kingdom.

Juntas Españolas
Spanish Boards

Base. Madrid

Leadership. Antonio Izquierdo Ferigela (acting general secretary)

Orientation. Francoist

History. This movement was founded on June 21, 1985, and is probably the largest Francoist party to be formed since the defeat of *Fuerza Nueva* at the 1982 general election. Moves to organize the party began in November 1984 and were led by Pablo Ortega Rosales, an economist.

Policies. The party regards left-wing terrorism as the greatest threat to the Spanish nation and supports extreme counter-measures. Many members of the party favoured the various post-Franco coup attempts, and at a party rally in October 1986 insults were directed at King Juan Carlos, who is closely identified with the democratization process.

Publications. Izquierdo edits the ultra-right daily newspaper, *El Alcázar*, with which several other leading members of the *Juntas* are associated.

Juntas Españolas de Integración
Spanish Integration Boards

Leadership. Federico Silva Muñoz, Fernández de la Mora

Orientation. Francoist

History. This party was founded in September 1984 by Muñoz (a former minister in a Franco cabinet) and other veterans of the *Falange* and *Fuerza Nueva* parties.

Policies. The party seeks to offer an alternative to the democratic system, i.e. the reconstruction of an authoritarian state.

International affiliations. The party reportedly sought to model its policies and strategies on those of the French ultra-right leader, Jean-Marie Le Pen.

Juntas Revolucionarias Nacionalsindicalistas (JRN)
National-Syndicalist Revolutionary Boards

Address. Apartado de Correos 289, Oviedo

Orientation. Fascist

History. This organization was active in the mid-1980s. It may be a successor to the *Juntas de Acción Nacional Sindicalistas*, which emerged in late 1977 and was led by veterans of the *Falange* labour movement.

Policies. It seeks to revive the original national syndicalist movement based on the ideas of Primo de Rivera and Franco.

Lucha por la Libertad de Melilla
Struggle for the Freedom of Melilla

Orientation. White supremacist

History. This movement developed among the ethnic Spanish population of the North African enclave of Melilla in response to fears of a Moroccan takeover. In June and July 1986 it was involved in demonstrations and disturbances in the enclave in which a number of people were injured. In earlier incidents, notably in November 1985, journalists and others regarded as sympathetic to the Arab community had been assaulted. (The Arab population comprises 27,000 out of the total of 75,000; only 7,000 of the Arabs had been granted Spanish citizenship by mid-1986.)

Policies. The movement seeks the strict application of a new Spanish nationality law, which would lead to the disenfranchisement and possible deportation of a very large proportion of the Arab population of Melilla.

Membership. The movement appears to have about 300 active supporters.

Llamada de Jesu Cristo
Call of Jesus Christ

Leadership. Faisal Hanna Joudi (leader)

Orientation. Anti-semitic guerrilla group

History. The 10 known members of this group were arrested in France and Spain in January and May 1986. It was reported that the group, founded in Lebanon in 1978, had bombed the Air France office in Lisbon after a member was arrested and recruited by the French intelligence service; that it had attempted to bomb a Paris synagogue, and that it was planning a bank robbery and a bombing campaign against Jewish and US targets in Spain and Portugal. Its members included Spanish, Lebanese, Syrian, Jordanian and Portuguese nationals.

Policies. The reported goal of the group was the expulsion of Israeli occupation forces from the Christian holy places in Jerusalem.

International affiliations. The group was alleged by the Spanish authorities and by its (Lebanese) leader to be in receipt of funds from Libya, 15 of whose nationals had earlier in the year been expelled from Spain for alleged subversive activities. It was reportedly founded in the Greek Catholic community in Lebanon.

Solidaridad Española (SE)
Spanish Solidarity

Leadership. Antonio Tejero Molina (leader)

Orientation. Fascist

History. This party was founded in 1982, following the failure of a coup attempt led by Tejero, then a lieutenant-colonel in a national police force, on Feb. 23, 1981. The attempt, which was code-named *Almendros* (Almond Trees) and is now popularly referred to as "F-23", had the support of a number of right-wing military and police officers, but most of the security forces rallied behind the democratic government and the King. Tejero, who had seized control of the *Cortes* while it was in session, was captured and imprisoned. His party contested the 1983 general election, securing 25,000 votes.

A prominent member of the party, Carlos Jiménez Palanca (who had been expelled from the *Falange* for violence), was one of several right-wingers involved in an attack in 1984 on a Catalan theatre group in Granada. Other activists include Tejero's brother Ramón, and José Castro Ortega.

Policies. The party seeks to reverse the liberalization of Spanish society to return to the authoritarian state imposed by Franco.

Defunct organizations

ATE: this grouping, whose name derives from the reversal of the acronym of the main Basque separatist guerrilla group, used the slogan "*Antiterrorismo contra la ETA*". It was active in 1976-78 and carried out several attacks on separatist and left-wing targets.

CEDA: this right-wing agrarian movement of the 1920s and '30s was widely regarded as a clerical-fascist party. It had parliamentary representation (94 seats in the February 1936 general election), and one of its leaders, Gil Robles, was for a time Minister of War. Its youth section was the JAP. By the mid-1930s the CEDA had about 100,000 followers. It was allied with the traditionalist Agrarian Monarchist movement.

Central Obrera Nacional Sindicalista: the National-Syndicalist Workers' Confederation, a Francoist trade union group, was formed around 1980 by José Antonio Assiego, formerly prominent in the *Fuerza Nueva*. Assiego was linked with all three coup plots discovered in the post-Franco era and was imprisoned for a year in 1982 on arms charges. In May 1986 Assiego was leading a Libyan-backed group called the National Labour Force, which was linked to the *Coordinadora de Fuerzas Nacionalistas*.

Comandos Antimarxistas: this death squad was active in the late 1970s. In 1979 it set fire to a Communist Party building in Valladolid, killing two people.

Comando Jesús García: an ultra-right group which issued a statement in 1980 threatening to burn down the retail outlets of a news magazine; several such fires did take place but may not have been the work of this one group.

División Azul—Blaue Division; the Blue Division was a volunteer force of Spanish fascists which fought alongside the Axis forces in the Second World War. Veterans of the Division maintained contact and they were organizing annual memorial masses for Hitler in Barcelona and Madrid as recently as 1968.

Movimiento Nacional: the National Movement was a coalition based on the sole legal political party during the Franco dictatorship, the *Falange Española Tradicionalista y de las Juntas de Ofensiva Nacional-Sindicalistas*(Spanish Traditionalist Phalanx of the Boards of the Nationalist Trade Union Offensive). The *Falange* and the JONS were originally separate movements, both founded in the early 1930s, but they united in February 1934 under the leadership of José Antonio Primo de Rivera, son of the 1920s dictator. The *Falange* originally included a green-shirted paramilitary wing known as the *Escamots*, and membership of the united movement was at first restricted to those under 45. In later years the party uniform was a blue shirt. The manifesto of 1934 described the movement as "for national unity, direct action and economic revolution; against communism and parliamentarianism". By March of that year the movement claimed 400,000 members.

The movement supported Franco's rebellion and formed a major part of the rebel forces in 1936-39, being thereafter the party of Franco's dictatorial government. In 1937 the *Falange* absorbed most other conservative parties, and in 1938 Franco was adopted as leader (Primo de Rivera having been executed in 1936). Under Franco's regime Spain remained officially neutral during the Second World War, although the dictatorship was in sympathy with the Axis. In 1943 the party militia, which had been modelled closely on the Italian MSVN, was disbanded.

In the post-war era the regime moderated its tone to present a right-wing conservative image; while suppressing domestic opposition with some brutality, in foreign affairs it generally followed a pro-US line. The *Falange*, and thus the National Movement, were dissolved by decree in April 1977, after Franco's death. (The name is, however, used by one of the many parties formed by Francoists after the dissolution of the original *Falange*.)

Renovación Española: Spanish Renewal was a monarchist party led in the early 1930s by Antonio Goicochea. At a rally in Madrid in July 1935 it defined itself as a reactionary fascist party (in contrast to the "revolutionary fascism" of Primo de Rivera). It sought the construction of a corporate state under the pretender, Don Juan.

Spanish Catalan Battalion: a little-known group briefly active in 1981, it was opposed to the autonomist movement in Catalonia. It may have been linked to the equally obscure *Partit Nacionalsocialista Català* (PNSC— Catalan National Socialist Party), founded in 1978, but the use by the latter group of the Catalan language would suggest otherwise. A right-wing Catalan anti-separatist group was responsible for a forest fire at Montserrat, the historic capital of the region, in mid-August 1986.

United International Secret Revolutionary Cells: this group, possibly a front for a Cuban émigré guerrilla organization, bombed a Cuban airline office in Madrid in 1976.

Other organizations

Minor right-wing groupings active in the post-Franco era, and groupings on which insufficient information is available, include the following: *L'Abet Negre*, a Catalan ecologist journal linked with the nazi group CEDADE; *Acción Democrática Española* (Spanish Democratic Action); *Acción Social Cooperativa* (Co-operative Social Action); *Arriba* (Upwards) magazine; a section of the *Carlista* monarchist movement, most of which has taken a progressive line; a section of the UK-based *Christian Mission to the Communist World*; the *Confederación Nacional de Excombatientes*, a large Civil War veterans' group which organizes the Franco commemorations; *Edelweis* group, which was said in a European Parliament debate (in January 1985) to be run by homosexuals and to recruit youths aged between 10 and 16 for paramilitary activities; a large number of publishers of fascist and right-wing literature, including *Ediciones Bausp* (of Barcelona, run by Ramón Bau of CEDADE), *Ediciones Huiguin*, *Editorial Aztlán* (hispanist), *Editorial Graal* (linked to CEDADE), and *Editorial Occidente* (possibly an Argentinian firm); the *Ejército de Liberación Española* (Spanish Liberation Army), which carried out several bank robberies and bombings of left-wing offices before being broken up by police action in 1980; *Enlace* (Link) magazine; the *Grupo Intelectual Antimarxista Español*; the *Guardia de Franco*. The *Juventud Falangista*, probaby the youth branch of one of the *Falange* factions; the *Juventudes Vikingos* (Viking Youth), a Spanish affiliate of the West German *Wiking-Jugend* nazi scout group (two of whose members, Walther Matthai and Miguel Boria, were arrested on arms charges in 1983); the *Legion of the Archangel Michael* (three of whose members were arrested in Alicante on arms charges in late 1983); the *Movimiento Falangista de España*; *Orden Nuevo*, linked to other Western European fascist New Order groups; the *Organización Internacional para la Defensa de los Europeos*, a fascist front organized in 1978 to publicize murders of whites in Zaïre; the nazi *Partido Nacional Socialista Español*; *Pueblo* (People) magazine; *Rojo y Gualda* magazine; the *Unión de Patriotas Españoles* and the *Unión del Pueblo Español*. There is also a mostly unorganized anti-Islamic Spanish nationalist movement in the Ceuta and Melilla enclaves (see also *Lucha por la Libertad de Melilla*). The publications of many fascist groups and publishing houses in other Spanish-speaking countries, particularly Argentina, also circulate in Spain.

This listing is by no means exhaustive; a great many short-lived and localized organizations sprang up in the aftermath of the dictatorship. It can be said with certainty that fascist and other ultra-right groups are very much fewer and weaker now than a decade ago.

Individuals

Juan Domingo Martínez Lorenzo: amember of a paramilitary group connected to the *Falange*, he was imprisoned briefly in the late 1970s after a murder, moved to France, and was rearrested on new charges in 1984 in an apartment belonging to a member of the FANE (France).

Marqués de Villaverde: one of the leading figures of the "old guard" of the Francoist establishment, the marquis is a frequent guest at major right-wing rallies such as the annual commemorations of the dictator's death. Other such figures are *Carmen Franco* (daughter of the Generalissimo), *Antonio María de Oriol y Urquijo, Raimundo Fernández Cuesta, José Utrera Molina* and *Pilar Primo de Rivera*, none of whom are particularly active in party politics apart from Utrera (who is closely involved with the *Juntas Españolas de Integración*); Fernández was in the late 1970s leader of a now defunct *Histórico* faction of the *Falange*.

Sweden

capital: Stockholm   **population: 8,340,000**

Political system. Sweden is a constitutional monarchy with a popularly elected 349-seat unicameral parliament, the *Riksdag*, seats in which are allocated mainly on a constituency basis using a form of proportional representation. There is a highly developed multi-party committee system which ensures that most issues are debated and settled before coming to the floor of the *Riksdag*.

Recent history. Sweden has been neutral since the early 19th century and has been dominated since the early 1930s by the Social Democratic Labour Party, which has formed the government for all but six years, either qlone or in coalition. The party's leader, Olof Palme, was assassinated in 1986 while serving as Prime Minister; apart from that incident, the country has enjoyed almost unparalleled freedom from political violence.

The evolution of the far right. Sweden's neutrality before and during the Second World War was partly due to the absence of a significant fascist movement (although it was considered necessary to ban political uniforms in August 1933). There has been little evidence of organized right-wing activity since the war apart from that of the Nordic Reich Party. In 1951 a conference in Malmö attempted to establish a Fascist International to co-ordinate the activities of surviving pre-1945 fascist leaders with the emerging neo-fascist movements of Western Europe; that function was assumed by the New European Order (see Switzerland).

In 1985 it was reported that a Swedish neo-nazi group was selling cassette tapes purporting to contain a message from war criminal Josef Mengele, who was later reported to have died in Brazil in the early 1980s. There is also a Maoist organization, the Communist Party Marxist-Leninist (Revolutionaries) or KPML(r), which has expressed racist and anti-gay views in its periodical.

Unorganized right-wing activity consists mainly of skinhead gangs, which have been involved in numerous violent attacks on immigrants. In April 1984 five skinheads were arrested while staging a "Free Rudolf Hess" demonstration outside the Soviet Embassy in Stockholm. An incident in mid-1986 resulted in the murder of a young man attempting to protecd child from a racist attack by skinheads.

There is a Croatian émigré community in Sweden which has been involved in Ustasha attacks on Yugoslavian diplomats. Right-wing groups also exist in the substantial Turkish community.

It has recently been suggested that a secret right-wing faction which arose in the early 1970s within the now disbanded 03 section of the Swedish intelligence service was behind the 1986 assassination of Olof Palme. The section had reportedly engaged in infiltration and disruption tactics against Swedish and foreign left-wing groups until 1973. No firm evidence has emerged to support the association with Palme's death. (See also European Labor Party and European Nationalist Union.)

Active organizations

Bevara Sverige Svenskt (BSS)
Keep Sweden Swedish

Base. Stockholm

Leadership. Leif Zeilon

Orientation. Racist

History. The BSS was established in the late 1970s as an umbrella grouping for racists in other political groups. Among its most prominent members and associates are Gösta Berquist, a leading Malmö fascist; Christopher Jolin, a conservative writer; Nils Mandell, formerly of the NRP and the Independent National Socialists; Rolf Pettersson, director of Open Forum radio station and a collaborator of revisionist historian Dietlieb Felderer; and Norwegian immigrant Tor Petter Hadland, who has extensive foreign contacts. BSS supporters have been held responsible for numerous acts of harrassment and intimidation of immigrants and for the disruption of meetings on immigration and anti-fascism.

Policies. The BSS opposes non-Nordic immigration to Sweden, partly on the grounds that immigrants are supposedly more likely to take part in criminal activities. It does not openly advocate fascist ideas on other issues, as part of its strategy to attract mainstream conservative support.

Associated organizations. The group has a number of front organizations, including the Open Forum community radio station, started in 1980 in the Taby district of Stockholm; the Swedish Society for Social Research, and a group called Nordic Freedom. There have been at least three prosecutions of Open Forum broadcasters under anti-racist laws, and there have been attempts to withdraw its licence.

Bible Researcher

Address. Marknadsvagen 289, 2 tr, 183.34 Taby, Stockholm

Orientation. Anti-semitic

History. This group published historical revisionist material, principally in the Holocaust denial field, in the early 1980s.

Associated organizations. The group has connections with Dietlieb Felderer and the BSS. A similar group, Jewish Information, operates from the same address, giving the telephone number (08) 768 1398.

Europese Arbetarepartiet
European Labor Party

Leadership. Michael Ericson

Orientation. LaRoucheist

History. This Party (also translated as European Workers' Party) is the Swedish section of the international network headed by Lyndon LaRouche's National Democratic Policy Committee (United States). In March 1986 Ake Lennart Viktor Gunnarson, who had been associated with the party in 1984-85, was arrested on suspicion of involvement in the Palme assassination, but he was released without charge a few days later. The Party had conducted a campaign against Palme whom it denounced, on less than conclusive evidence, as "a homosexual drug pusher".

Policies. As with any LaRouche operation, it is difficult to describe this group's policies in the context of a serious non-fiction work. In short, it propounds a complex conspiracy theory wherein most international statesmen, and the Queen of England, have important and nefarious roles. While presenting itself as a left-wing movement, the LaRouche network is almost unanimously regarded as a quasi-fascist tendency. It is vehemently anti-communist and strongly in favour of the US space armaments plan.

Publications. The Party promotes the La Roucheist publication *Executive Intelligence Review* (see United States).

International affiliations. The Party operates in France (as the *Parti ouvrier européen*, led by Jacques Cheminade) and is associated with other LaRoucheist groups in West Germany (such as the Schiller Institute, led by LaRouche's wife Helga Zepp, and Patriots for Germany) and the United States.

Nordiska Rikspartiet (NRP)
Nordic Reich Party

Address. Postbox 162, 152.01 Strangnas

Leadership. Lars Göran Assar Oredsson and Vera Oredsson (leaders); Staffan Winlöf (Action Group Leader)

Orientation. Nazi

History. This small nazi party was formed in 1956. Several of its members have been involved in violent incidents in recent years, including a lurid murder case in November 1983. Winlöf, leader of a paramilitary youth section known as the RAG, was convicted of arms offences in 1984. Ten members of the party, including Winlöf, were attacked in the small town of Växjö by a crowd of 3,000 citizens in April 1985. They managed to take refuge in a public lavatory but were flushed out and forced to leave town.

Winlöf moved to Helsingborg, where a ten-strong party rally in September 1985 was attacked by 1,000 townspeople, and he was again forced to flee the town. In 1986 it was reported that members of the Gothenburg branch had been imprisoned for terrorism, and that Winlöf and five others were facing a variety of charges in Växjö.

Policies. The party opposes immigration and demands a "Sweden for the Swedes". It has also opposed vivisection and has attempted to raise funds from animal lovers. It is openly nazi and defends the German Nazi Party and its Swedish collaborators.

Publications. *Solhjulet* (The Sunwheel); *Nordisk Kamp* (Nordic Struggle).

Associated organizations. It was reported in early 1984 that Assar Oredsson was the leader of a Scandinavian Cultural Organization, which was described as a front for a neo-nazi party called the Scandinavian National Party.

International affiliations. Winlöf reportedly belongs to an international fascist network known as Legion Omega.

Sveriges Nationella Forbund
Swedish National League

Address. Postbox 7071, 200.42 Malmö

Orientation. Fascist

History. This group became active in the mid-1970s. In 1978 it was visited by Roger Pearson, then a leader of the World Anti-Communist League (see South Korea), with a view to its becoming the local affiliate of the WACL. In the event the non-fascist faction which assumed control of the WACL in the early 1980s terminated the connection.

International affiliations. One of the League's leaders, Lars Hedengard, has been associated with the World Union of National Socialists (see Denmark).

Defunct organizations

Independent National Socialists: a traditional nazi group founded and led in the 1970s by Nils Mandell, formerly the Stockholm leader of the NRP and later a leading member of the BSS.

New Nazi Party: the only recorded action of this party was a flyposting exercise in the southern town of Olofström in March 1979, which advocated racial purity and threatened a new *Kristallnacht* pogrom against immigrants.

Other organizations

Other Swedish right-wing groupings include the *Nysvenska-Rorelson*, a non-party nationalist association based in Malmö (Amiralsgaten 12.511), and the *Swedish Party*, a fascist group formed in 1986 which has been in contact with the British National Front. Palme's assassination was stated in anonymous letters to the press have been the work of a *European Nationalist*(or *National Socialist) Union*, but little credence was given to the claim.

Individuals

Dietlieb Felderer: a "revisionist historian" who produces newsletters and other publications denying the reality of the nazi Holocaust, Felderer was thought to have been involved in the establishment of the Open Forum radio station (see BSS), and is a political associate of Open Forum's director, Rolf Pettersson. Felderer was sued in 1985 by an Auschwitz survivor who won damages of US$5,250,000 in a US court. His principal publication is *Revisionist History Magazine*, published from his home in the Taby suburb of Stockholm. He is also an editorial advisor of the US-based Institute for Historical Review. His works have been published in translation by Ediciones Bausp, linked to the Spanish nazi group CEDADE.

Switzerland

capital: Berne   **population: 6,500,000**

Political system. Under the 1874 Constitution Switzerland is a democratic state with a Federal Council serving as a Cabinet. The President of the Federal Council and of the Swiss Confederation is elected annually by a bicameral Federal Assembly, consisting of a National Council with 200 directly elected members and a Council of States with 46 members elected by various methods to represent the 26 autonomous territorial divisions (mainly cantons).

Recent history. The current prosperity and stability of the country are widely attributed to its neutrality, which has been universally respected since 1815, and to the 30-year-old tradition of coalition government by centrist (social democratic, liberal and Christian democratic) parties. Most political discourse at a national level is conducted on or through referendums on a variety of policy issues.

The evolution of the far right. Switzerland's policy of neutrality preserved it from fascist aggression during the 1939-45 war, despite its contiguity with four fascist-ruled countries. There had been a small Nazi movement among the German-speaking community in the 1930s, but uniformed political movements were outlawed in May 1933. (In August of that year there was a border incursion by German Nazi Party stormtroopers, leading to a formal protest.)

In more recent times Switzerland has not had any substantial overtly fascist movement, despite, or perhaps because of the cultural and ethnic diversity of its population; however, in recent years there has been a movement in both the francophone and the German-speaking communities (which together account for some 94 per cent of the total) opposing immigration. The other principal focus of right-wing activity is Lefebvre's Catholic traditionalist movement, whose influence is felt in most Western countries.

In December 1980 a German ultra-rightist, Frank Schubert, killed two Swiss border guards and himself after attempting to smuggle arms out of the country. Some other German movements have used Swiss addresses for propaganda distribution. Some local or cantonal agitations, such as the pro- and anti-Jurassic movements, which might be regarded as right-wing, have been excluded from the present work.

Active organizations

Cercle Proudhon
Proudhon Circle

Base. Geneva

Leadership. Pascal Junoud (organizer)

Orientation. New right

History. The *Cercle* held a conference in March 1985 at which representatives of GRECE (France), *Scorpion* (United Kingdom), *Thule* (West Germany) and other "new right" and "national-revolutionary" groups and publications exchanged ideas on the question of a European identity.

Policies. As is the case with other new right groups, this organization is seeking to develop alternative forms of expression and action to the outmoded and anachronistic positions of neo-fascism. It is an elitist and intellectual grouping rather than a political movement.

Courrier du continent
Continental Bulletin

Address. Case Ville 2428, 1002 Lausanne

Orientation. Fascist

History. This publication was circulating in the early 1980s. It may be linked to Gaston Amaudruz (its address being that used in the early 1980s by the New European Order).

Policies. It seeks to maintain communication between a range of West European right-wing groups.

Lefebvrist movement

Base. Ecône

Leadership. Archbishop Marcel Lefebvre (leader); Fr Franz Schmidberger (chief administrator)

Orientation. Catholic ultra-right

History. This schismatic movement, which has to date avoided a complete breach with the Roman Catholic Church, developed in opposition to the liturgical reforms and associated liberalization measures arising from the Second Vatican Council in the 1960s. Lefebvre, who as superior general of the Holy Ghost Fathers was one of the Church's most senior missionaries, regarded the changes as heretical and refused to abandon the 400-year-old Tridentine rite of the Mass. He became the focus of a world-wide reactionary "integrist" movement within the Church and from about 1969, despite repeated pleadings and disciplinary action by the Vatican, he has built up a large and well-funded operation centred on a seminary at Ecône and offices at Rickenbach, in north-western Switzerland. The present (1987) Pope, John Paul II, has adopted a conciliatory attitude towards Lefebvre but has not been able to impose his authority on the movement.

Unlike the more radical clerico-fascist sect at Palmar de Troya (Spain) the Lefebvrist movement has refrained from consecrating bishops or setting up Lefebvre as an anti-pope, steps which would mark the final rupture with Rome. It has, however, ordained priests and established religious and secular orders, seminaries and other institutions.

Policies. Most of Lefebvre's followers advance the thesis that the Roman Catholic Church has been taken over by a heretical conspiracy, which some would identify as masonic, Jewish, communist, satanic or any permutation thereof. The movement promotes traditional moral values, strict adherence to ancient Catholic rites and practices (including the exclusive use of Latin in the liturgy), anti-communist and ultra-right political positions and the rejection and reversal of ecumenism and progressive social ideas within the Church. It places greater reliance on prophesy, penance, divine right and other fundamentalist concepts that does the mainstream Church.

Membership. No figures are available for the membership of the movement, operating as it does within the structures of the Roman Catholic Church. It has, however, been estimated that the movement has the active support of less than 0.1 per cent of the world's 760,000,000 Catholics, i.e. something over 500,000 individuals. The strength of support for the positions advocated by Lefebvre, individually or as a whole, is impossible to quantify but it includes several bishops and other prominent lay and ecclesiastical figures, such as the abbé Paul Aulagnier, leader of the French section of the movement, and Bishop Antônio de Castro Meyer of Brazil. The movement had in 1984 some 135 priests ordained by Lefebvre, and 70 "houses" and seminaries around the world.

Associated organizations. Among the many organizations of the Lefebvrist movement, some of which parallel identically named groups remaining under the authority of Rome, is the Society of St. Pius X, formed by Lefebvre in the late 1960s and having Fr Schmidberger, a German, as its superior general since Lefebvre's retirement from the post in 1983. The Society has members in most Western European countries, Mexico, South America and elsewhere and includes the *Fraternité sacerdotale saint Pie X*(Priestly Fraternity of St Pius X). National political parties with which the integrist movement is particularly identified include the *Mouvement conservateur* (Switzerland) and the *Front national* and allied groups (France).

Mouvement d'action politique et sociale (MAPS)
Political and Social Action Movement

Leadership. Luc de Meuron (president)

Orientation. Ultra-right

History. The MAPS was founded in October 1977 as a successor to the *Mouvement national d'action républicaine et sociale*, which arose in the mid-1970s as a francophone splinter group of the SRB.

Policies. The MAPS opposes immigration as a threat to national and local identity, and promotes free enterprise and traditional moral values.

Mouvement conservateur et libéral
Conservative and Liberal Movement

Leadership. André Luisier, Guy Genoud, Roger Lovey, Roger Pitteloud, René Berthod

Orientation. Ultra-right

History. The *Mouvement conservateur* (as it is usually known) developed in the canton of Valais (Wallis) in early 1985 as a pressure group within the main Christian democratic party, the CVP-PDC, in which Genoud and Lovey held important cantonal positions. Pitteloud and Berthod are respectively the prefect and the deputy prefect of Valais. Many of the Movement's followers are sympathetic to the "integrist" Catholic fundamentalism of Archbishop Lefebvre.

Policies. The Movement may perhaps be viewed as a reversion to the right-wing and confessional origins of the CVP-PDC, which was founded in 1912 as the Conservative Party with an exclusively Roman Catholic following, but which currently has a centrist "social Christian" outlook. Through the *Nouvelliste* (see below) the founders of the Movement have expressed their rejection of "anti-Christian ideologies". For the present it has declared its intention of working within the CVP-PDC for the adoption of more right-wing policies, rather than of establishing a rival party, although the general secretary of the CVP-PDC (Hans Peter Fagagnini) has denounced the Movement in the strongest terms as representing the "bacillus" of extremism.

Publications. The Movement has the support of the canton's right-wing Catholic newspaper, the *Nouvelliste et feuille d'avis de Valais* (published by Luisier's Imprimerie Moderne SA, rue de l'Industrie, 1950 Sion). The same newspaper had in 1935 described Mussolini as "*l'homme de génie de la race latine*".

International affiliations. The Movement is in complete sympathy with the *Front national* (France), whose leader, Le Pen, visited the canton in 1985 at the invitation of the *Renouveau rhodanien* society (to which many of the Movement's sympathizers belonged).

Nationale Aktion für Volk und Heimat (NA)—Action nationale (AN) National Action for People and Homeland

Address. Postfach 59, 8956 Killwangen

Telephone. (056) 711974

Leadership. Rudolf Keller (central president); Fritz Rötlisberger (first vice-president); Fritz Stalder (second vice-president); Anita Wilhelm (secretary)

Orientation. Conservative, anti-immigration

History. National Action was founded in the canton of Zürich in 1961, and has most of its strength there and in Berne among the German-speaking section of the population. The party contests local and federal elections, and has gained enough signatures to force the holding of three referendums on immigration. In 1970 it gained 46 per cent support for its policy of forcible deportation of immigrants in a referendum on the "Schwarzenbach initiative", named after the NA's founder, James Schwarzenbach (see SRB). Intiatives on similar issues were also rejected in 1974 and 1981. The NA has been represented in the National Council in 1967-70, when Schwarzenbach held its one seat, and from 1971, when it won four seats.

It has become the leading party of the Swiss right, with about 9 per cent support in opinion polls in 1986-87 (compared with about 3-4 per cent in the early 1980s), and the "nationalist" bloc which it forms with Vigilance and the SBR gained five of the 200 seats in the National Council elections of 1983. In the following year it played host to the French ultra-right leader, Jean-Marie Le Pen, who spoke at rallies in Freiburg, Geneva, Lausanne and Zurich; although the Geneva government prohibited a personal appearance in March 1985, he appeared on television stations in western Switzerland later in the year, causing some controversy. (The Geneva authorities also prevented the broadcasting of a Le Pen speech in January 1986.) In 1985 the NA won 16 of the 100 seats in the Lausanne assembly, and also scored 15 per cent or more in elections in Berne, Geneva and Zurich, although elsewhere—in Aarau, for example (where it stood in alliance with the SRB as *Nationale Aktion und Republikaner*)—its support was less than 5 per cent.

The most senior of its deputies, Valentin Oehen, who had been president of the party from 1972 to 1980, left to form the Liberal Ecologist Party in April 1986; he maintained that hardline anti-immigrant activists in the party, led by Markus Ruf and Rötlisberger, had given the party a "simplistic, racist and extremist" image. In the same year *Nationale Aktion* won 21 seats in cantonal elections.

In the June 1986 party congress Keller, representing a less extremist faction within the party, won the presidency, but in order to present a united front the next most senior post went by agreement to Rötlisberger. Keller succeeded Hans Zwicky, who had held the post since 1980.

Policies. The main aim of the party is the restriction of immigration, including that of refugees and of employees of international organizations. It also espouses neutrality, environmentalism, law and order and individual rights.

Membership. At least 5,000 members, mainly from German-speaking communities.

Publications. *Volk und Heimat*, circulation 7,000; a French edition, *Peuple et patrie*, sells about 1,000.

Associated organizations. The party is allied to the Vigilance group of Geneva, and has formed electoral alliances with the SRB. It has, however, rejected the possibility of any alliance with the nazi NSP, which, like the SRB, originated as a splinter group of the NA.

National-sozialistische Partei (NSP)—Parti national socialiste (PNS)
National Socialist Party

Base. Zürich

Leadership. Ernst Meister (leader)

Orientation. Nazi

History. This party was founded in August 1985 by Meister, a former cantonal vice-president of the National Action party, from which he had resigned in 1983.

Policies. The NSP-PNS is an overtly nazi party, in contrast to the National Action party's racist conservative image. It is particularly opposed to immigration.

Nouvel Ordre Social (NOS)
New Social Order

Address. Case Postale 249, 1211 Geneva 6

Orientation. Fascist

History. The NOS was active in the early 1980s.

Policies. It professes white supremacist, pan-European nationalist ideas.

Publications. *Rat noir* and *The Black Rat* (part comic-strip magazines); *Avant Garde.*

Associated organizations. The NOS is almost certainly the francophone counterpart of the *Volkssozialistische Partei,* with which it shares a post office box number.

Ökologische Freiheitliche Partei [der Schweiz]—Parti écologiste libéral
Liberal Ecologist Party [of Switzerland]

Leadership. Valentin Oehen (founder)

Orientation. Ultra-right

History. This group was founded on Aug. 30, 1986, by Oehem, formerly a leader of *Nationale Aktion,* a xenophobic right-wing grouping in the federal parliament.

Policies. The new party places less emphasis on immigration control than on ecological issues.

Activities. The Party planned to fight federal elections in 1987.

Membership. It claims about 1,000 members, mostly drawn from the German-speaking community.

Le Pamphlet
The Pamphlet

Base. Lausanne

Leadership. M. Paschoud (editor)

Orientation. Ultra-right

History. This "confidential bulletin" received considerable publicity in August and September 1986 when Mariette Paschoud, a regular contributor and the wife of its editor, publicized her support for the "thesis" whereby the revisionist historian Henri Roques (see France) was awarded a bogus doctorate for denying the existence of gas chambers in the nazi concentration camps. The public interest in her utterances arose from her appointments, since withdrawn, as a high school teacher and as a captain and military judge in the Swiss army.

Policies. The bulletin carries a range of articles interpreting current affairs and history from an ultra-right standpoint.

Schweizerische Republikanische Bewegung (SRB)—Mouvement républicain Suisse (MRS)
Swiss Republican Movement

Address. Busenhardstrasse 9, 8704 Herrliberg

Leadership. Franz Baumgartner (leader)

Orientation. Anti-immigrant

History. The SRB was founded in 1970 by Dr James Schwarzenbach, who as the sole parliamentary representative of the *Nationale Aktion* (which he had founded in 1961) had come to national prominence during an anti-immigration referendum campaign in 1968-70. In the 1971 general election the SRB gained seven seats, which from 1973 were allied with the four seats of the NA. Schwarzenbach and three other SRB members resigned from its parliamentary bloc in 1974, and the movement went into decline; it held only four seats in the 1975 elections, falling to one in 1979 and 1983.

Policies. The SRB campaigns mainly on the immigration issue, but is also concerned with protecting the interests of small businesses.

Associated organizations. Since 1973 the SRB has been allied with the NA. It is also ideologically close to the Vigilance movement, which is the main ultra-right group in the French-speaking population of Geneva, whereas the SRB draws most of its support from German speakers in the same canton.

Terrorism Research Associates

Base. Zürich

History. A former South African police spy, Michael Morris (who was active in the University of Cape Town until 1979), attended a right-wing youth conference in South Africa in July 1985 and announced that he was working for this body.

Activities. This group apparently carries out research on "international terrorism".

International affiliations. See Youth for Freedom (South Africa).

Vigilance

Base. Geneva

Leadership. Arnold Schlaepfer, Mario Soldini

Orientation. Ultra-right

History. This group, known colloquially as *Les Vigilants*, was founded in Geneva in 1964 and has been represented on the city council of Geneva since 1967 and in the cantonal assembly since the 1970s. It won 12 of the 80 seats contested in the October

1985 elections to the cantonal assembly, bringing its total representation to 19 of the 100 seats; however, Schlaepfer failed to gain election in the following month to one of the seven seats on the canton's executive council.

Policies. The group bases its electoral platform on opposition to immigration, refugee settlement and criminality.

Associated organizations. Vigilance, which exists only in Geneva, is closely linked to the federally organized *Nationale Aktion* party, and co-operates with the NA's Geneva section (led by Mary Meissner) and with the SRB.

Volkssozialistische Partei
Popular Socialist Party

Address. Case Postale 249, 1211 Geneva 6

Orientation. Fascist

History. This German-speaking Swiss nationalist party arose among the students of Geneva university in the early 1980s.

Policies. It professes an approximately national socialist ideology.

Associated organizations. The Party has close links with the *Nouvel ordre social.*

International affiliations. It has established contact with several member parties of the World Union of National Socialists (see Denmark).

Defunct organizations

Corporative Party: this grouping formed part of the parliamentary opposition in the mid-1930s.

Faschistischen Föderation Schweiz: the Swiss Fascist Federation was formed in the early 1930s but failed to achieve a widespread following. In 1935 it formed an electoral alliance with the Conservative Party (now the centrist CVP-PDC) in Valais; the right-wing tendency of the Party in that canton is now represented in the *Mouvement conservateur.*

Front national: the National Front (or *Frontenbewegung*) was a fascist movement active in the 1930s. In 1935 it gathered 35,000 signatures for a petition seeking to reform the Constitution by enhancing the autonomy of the cantons vis à vis the federal government.

New European Order: the NOE (as it was generally known, from the French version of its name—*Nouvel ordre européen*) was an international network of neo-fascist groups, latterly including Italian terrorist organizations. The Order was founded in Zürich in 1951 at a meeting attended by representatives of several foreign groups. It held congresses to co-ordinate the platforms and activities of neo-fascist parties in Paris (1952), Hanover (1954), Lausanne (1956, 1960 and 1962), Milan (1958, 1965 and 1967), Barcelona (1969) and Lyon (1972). Other NOE congresses have taken place from time to time thereafter, with the 15th being held in Barcelona in April 1981. Among parties and movements which belonged to or were associated with the NOE were CEDADE (Spain), *Nouvel ordre* (France), *Ordem Nova* and *Quarta Frente* (Portugal), the *Hilfsgemeinschaft Freiheit für Rudolf Hess* (Society for the Freedom of Rudolf Hess, Merzhausen, West Germany) and numerous Italian, Canadian, Croatian, British, West German and other groups. It was run in the 1970s by Gaston Amaudruz of Lausanne. It was reportedly involved in securing sanctuary in England for a number of Italians after the Bologna bombing of 1980. The policies of the Order were based on eugenics and ecology; it had subsidiary organizations including (from 1969) a Quebec-based Higher Institute for Psychosomatic, Biological and Racial Sciences and several Action Committees dealing with particular topics. By the early 1980s the importance of the NOE had declined and it is now thought to be defunct.

Opposition to the Alien Invasion: this grouping was established in the 1960s by James Schwarzenbach, an anti-immigration activist who also edited a right-wing newspaper, *Der Republikaner*. Schwarzenbach became a member of the international racist co-ordinating body, the Northern League (see Netherlands), and led the NA in 1961-70 and the SRB in 1970-74.

Other organizations

Among other organizations recently reported as active on the right of the political spectrum in Switzerland are the following: the *Chabeuillards*, a paramilitary movement in the Valence region which announced a "crusade" against socialism; the *Comité de solidarité avec Giorgio Freda* (a support group for an Italian fascist prisoner); the *Jeunesses nationales-démocratiques* (National Democratic Youth); the *Nationalen Basis Schweiz*, and a branch of the *Viking Youth* nazi scout group (see West Germany).

Syria

capital: Damascus   **population: 10,200,000**

Political system. The Syrian Arab Republic has a popularly elected 195-seat People's Council and an executive President, similarly elected, who appoints Vice-Presidents, a Prime Minister and a Council of Ministers.

Recent history. Since independence in 1946 most Syrian governments have been installed by military coup, with the last in 1970 beginning the present regime of Gen. Hafez al-Assad. Assad has governed with the assistance of a pan-Arabist socialist party, *Baath*, and has been declared the victor, by massive majorities, in presidential elections held in 1971, 1978 and 1985. Apart from palace intrigues leading to government reshuffles and the exile of rivals, the only serious internal threat to Assad's rule has come from Islamic fundamentalists who staged a bloodily suppressed uprising in 1982.

The evolution of the far right. Apart from the illegal conservative Muslim Brotherhood, which falls outside the scope of this work, there appear to be no right-wing organizations in Syria. However, there have been frequent reports that Baathist governments, beginning with that of Amin al-Hafiz (1963-66), have provided protection and employment to a notorious Austrian nazi war criminal, Alois Brunner. Brunner was involved in arms trading together with the West German nazi, Ernst Otto Remer, in the 1960s, and to have been implicated in a neo-nazi plot to murder the leader of the World Jewish Congress. He was reported to be still living in Damascus, as George Fischer, in 1985.

Taiwan

capital: Taipei   **population: 19,000,000**

Political system. Taiwan, or the Republic of China as it calls itself, consists mainly of a large island off the Chinese coast but officially regards itself as the seat of government for all of China. There is a National Assembly, most of whose thousand members are lifetime appointees, and this Assembly elects an executive President; the main legislative body is the 364-seat Legislative *Yuan*, also dominated by life members.

Recent history. The island of Taiwan was occupied in 1949 by followers of Gen. Chiang Kai-shek's *Kuomintang* (KMT) Party, which had lost the civil war in China to the Communist Party of Mao Zedong. The *Kuomintang*, or Nationalist, forces established a government in Taiwan and have continually asserted that it was the true Chinese government, while the People's Republic of China in turn has claimed dominion over Taiwan. With the economic and military (and, until recently, diplomatic) support of Western powers, the Taiwan regime has developed a strong economy, making the island the world's twentieth largest exporter by 1980.

Internal politics are distorted by the leading role accorded to surviving members of the last all-China Nationalist administration; the native Taiwanese, although forming the vast majority of the population, have a very limited say in government and have led the illegal opposition movements. The KMT remains in power; Chiang Kai-shek was President until his death in 1975 when he was succeeded by his son, Chiang Ching-kuo.

The evolution of the far right. The Taiwanese regime has always been stridently anti-communist; it was instrumental in founding the World Anti-Communist League (see South Korea) and remains one of its major sponsors. The KMT remains the largest, and the only effective, political party and there have been violent assaults on opposition movements. Civil rights have been suspended since 1948 in accordance with the regime's view that it, as the legitimate government of all China, is faced with an insurrection which has gained temporary control over part of the national territory, to wit the entire mainland. The regime executed many of its opponents in the 20 years after its establishment in Taiwan, and there are still many hundreds of political prisoners.

One of the few political parties, the China Democratic Socialist Party, was founded in 1932 as the National Socialist Party, but it has never professed fascist ideology and is currently a moderate right-wing formation.

Active organizations

Asian People's Anti-Communist League (APACL)

Address. 8th Floor, 100 Hengyang Road, Taipei; or PO Box 22992, Taipei

Leadership. Dr Han Lih-wu (leader)

Orientation. Anti-communist

History. The APACL was established in 1954. In 1966 it joined with Eastern European émigré organizations in forming the World Anti-Communist League (WACL—South Korea).

Policies. The group aims to counter communist subversion in Asian countries and to educate the Asian public as to the threats posed by communism and socialism.

Publications. Asian Outlook

Associated organizations. The League's youth section is the Asian Youth Anti-Communist League. Within Taiwan the League is close to the *Kuomintang*, which provides its secretariat and much of its funding.

International affiliations. The APACL is a regional section of the WACL, which is based in South Korea and has affiliates in most Western countries. The APACL itself has affiliates or branches in many Asian and Pacific countries.

Committee for a Free China (CFC)

Address. PO Box 65012, Washington, DC, United States

Telephone. (202) 223 8596

Leadership. Dr Ray S. Cline (president); Dr Walter H. Judd (chairman)

Orientation. Pro-KMT

History. The CFC was formed in 1972 as the Committee of One Million, and adopted its present name in the mid-1970s. Judd is a former Republican member of the US House of Representatives, while Cline is a retired intelligence officer.

Policies. The Committee lobbies US government and media organizations in favour of the defensive, economic and diplomatic interests of the Taiwan regime, and against those of "Red China".

Publications. The China Letter, every two months.

Associated organizations. The CFC is supported by many Chinese-American organizations, most of which have a mainly social or cultural function. It is also associated with the Student Committee for a Free China (see World Youth Crusade for Freedom, United States). Another Committee for Free China existed in Madison, Wisconsin, in 1974.

[Chung-kuo] Kuomintang (KMT)
Nationalist Party [of China]

Address. 11 Chung Shan South Road, Taipei

Leadership. Gen. Chiang Ching-kuo (chairman); Tsiang Yien-si (general secretary)

Orientation. Right-wing anti-communist

History. The KMT (also commonly transliterated as *Kuo-min-tang* or *Kuo Min Tang*) was founded in 1894, as the *Hsing Chung Hui*, by Dr Sun Yat-sen and adopted its present name in 1919. It became the ruling party of a united Chinese Republic in 1928, under Chiang Kai-shek, the leader of the right wing of what had hitherto been a broad-based movement. Although both the KMT and the rival forces of Mao Zedong's Communist Party resisted the Japanese invasion of Manchuria in 1931, and remained at war with Japan until 1945, the KMT maintained friendly relations with other fascist countries; in 1934 it appointed an Italian fascist to a teaching post at Sun Yat-sen University in Canton, with a view to developing fascist policies applicable to the Chinese situation.

The KMT was overthrown by Communist forces in 1949 after a long civil war. Chiang and his followers fled to Taiwan and formed the "government of the Republic of China", which continues in existence in 1987 under Chiang's son. Elections to legislative bodies, which are of limited significance in view of the predominance of lifetime appointees, are invariably won by the KMT with overwhelming majorities.

Only KMT or independent candidates are permitted to stand in the infrequent elections to the Legislative *Yuan*.

Policies. The Party seeks to recover mainland China from the Communist government, to promote democracy and free enterprise, and to maintain the national culture, goals which comprise the "Three Principles"of KMT ideology as enunciated by Chiang Kai-shek.

Membership. The Party claims more than 2,000,000 members.

Publications. Chung-yang Jih-pao (Central Daily News), party journal, founded in China in 1928. Many other newspapers and periodicals support the KMT.

Associated organizations. The KMT has since 1947 effectively controlled the anti-communist Young China Party and the China Democratic Socialist Party, which are the only other parties permitted by the Taipei regime.

International affiliations. The KMT, through the APACL, was a prime mover in the establishment of the World Anti-Communist League (see South Korea), which it continues to support through the Taiwan chapter of the League. In 1985 the Taiwan chapter subscribed about US$70,000 to WACL funds.

World Christian Anti-Communist Association (WCACA)

Address. 8th Floor, 53 Jen Ai Road, Sec. 3, Taipei

Leadership. Lee Shih-feng (leader)

Orientation. Anti-communist

History. This group was founded in the 1970s.

Policies. It seeks to unite and co-ordinate the work of various national and international Christian organizations which oppose communism and, in some cases, attempt to provide a Christian ministry to communist countries or to members of communist movements.

International affiliations. The WCACA is affiliated to the WACL (see South Korea).

Defunct organizations

Free Pacific Association: this pressure group, formed by Taiwanese elements in New York (United States), sought to combat and expose communist influence in the entire Asia-Pacific region and to ensure continued governmental and public supportt in the USA for an aggressively anti-communist foreign policy, including support for Taiwan. It was particularly active in the 1960s and '70s.

Individuals

Joseph Yu-jui Ku: the "Free China" correspondent of *The Spotlight*, anti-semitic journal of the Liberty Lobby (United States).

Thailand

capital: Bangkok   population: 52,000,000

Political system. The Kingdom of Thailand has a constitutional monarch, a Cabinet system of government and a bicameral National Assembly consisting of a directly-elected 324-seat House of Representatives and a 243-seat appointive Senate.

Recent history. Thailand has been under direct or disguised military rule for much of the present century. Several of the military regimes have originated in coups (which succeeded in 1932, 1933, 1947, 1957, 1976 and 1977) and most have followed right-wing authoritarian policies, often involving the suspension of civil rights. The current government, led by Gen. Prem Tinsulanonda, has been in power since 1980 and has the support of a right-wing majority in the Assembly (although centrist forces made important gains in the elections of July 1986).

The government has been engaged, particularly since the late 1960s, in contesting a left-wing insurgency, which has declined in intensity since the early 1980s. In this effort the government is assisted by the drastic powers granted it under a 1952 act for the suppression of communism.

The evolution of the far right. Field Marshal Pibul Songgram was involved in right-wing coups in what was then Siam in 1932 and 1933. In 1938 he became Prime Minister (and was behind the adoption of the name Thailand in 1939). He was an admirer of the fascist *Führerprinzip* (leadership principle) and collaborated with the Japanese invasion in 1941, declaring war on the Allies. His puppet government was ousted in 1944 but a coup in 1947 reinstated him as Prime Minister. He followed strongly anti-communist policies until his overthrow in another coup in 1957.

A martial law regime under Field Marshal Sarit Thanarat dissolved all political parties in 1958; his successor (1963-73), Gen. (later Field Marshal) Thanon Kittikachorn, also ruled by martial law apart from a short period (1968-71). A series of constitutional governments was followed in October 1976 by a right-wing coup installing Adm. Sa'ngad Chaloryoo, whose revolutionary council reimposed martial law and ruled at first through a civilian Cabinet and from October 1977 directly, with Gen. Kriangsak Chomanan as Prime Minister. In 1978 that regime promulgated a Constitution, under which the premiership passed in 1980 from the right-winger Kriangsak to the centre-right Gen. Prem. In 1987 Prem remained in office, having survived attempted coups in 1981 and 1985; from 1983 he has governed with the support of a right-wing coalition in the National Assembly.

Several Kampuchean anti-communist organizations are based inside the Thai borders, but have little influence on domestic politics. Thai forces have frequently clashed along the border with Vietnamese forces supporting the Kampuchean government.

Thailand's active section of the Asian People's Anti-Communist League (see Taiwan) is also affiliated to the World Anti-Communist League (see South Korea).

Active organizations

Chart Prachathippatai
National Democracy Party (NDP)

Leadership. Gen. Kriangsak Chomanan (leader); Ob Vasuratana (general secretary)

Orientation. Right-wing

276

History. The NDP was formed by Kriangsak and others in September 1981 on the basis of the *Seritham* party, which had supported him as Prime Minister in 1977-80. He had been appointed Prime Minister as Supreme Commander of the Armed Forces and as the candidate of a revolutionary council of military leaders, but remained in office for some time after the dissolution of the council in mid-1979. The NDP was supported on its formation by 49 Representatives, but it was reduced to 15 seats in the 1983 elections.

It aligned itself with the Prem government as one of four parties in the ruling coalition, but in September 1985, following an abortive coup, Kriangsak was arrested and charged with sedition, as were several other senior officers including one serving Deputy Supreme Commander. Ob thereupon resigned his cabinet post as Minister of Industry.

Policies. The NDP has right-wing authoritarian policies.

Muanchon
Mass Party

Leadership. Capt. Chaloem Yubamrung (acting leader)

Orientation. Right-wing

History. This Party, founded in January 1985 by dissident members of both government and opposition parties, may be a successor to the Mass Line Party formed in the mid-1970s by Maj.-Gen. Sudsai Hasdin (see Red *Gaurs*), who served in the early 1980s as one of several Ministers to the Prime Minister's Office under Gen. Prem. The Party has no representation in the National Assembly.

Policies. The Mass Line Party followed ultra-right anti-communist policies.

Prachakorn Thai
Thai Citizens' Party

Leadership. Samak Sundaravej (leader); Samak Sirichan (general secretary)

Orientation. Right-wing

History. The Party, founded in 1979 (when it gained 32 seats in the House of Representatives), won 36 seats in the 1983 elections to the House, thereby becoming the fourth-largest formation in the National Assembly and the third-largest element of the ruling coalition. The July 1986 elections reduced its representation to 24 seats.

Policies. The Party is authoritarian in outlook, anti-communist and strongly monarchist.

Associated organizations. The Party is linked with right-wing military elements and with extra-parliamentary anti-communist groups.

Prachaseri
Free Democrats

Leadership. Dr Watana Khieovimoi (leader); Somsak Sertakorn (general secretary)

Orientation. Ultra-right Buddhist

History. This party was formed around 1980 by Watana, previously the leader of the *Nawapon* paramilitary group. In 1983 it won a single seat in the elections to the House of Representatives.

Policies. The *Prachaseri* movement follows extreme nationalist and pro-military policies.

Thai People's Party

Leadership. Capt. Somwong Sarasart (leader); Dr Salai Sookapantpotaram (general secretary)

Orientation. Right-wing

History. The Party was founded in 1979. Although it has failed to win election to the House, one independent Representative elected in 1983 subsequently aligned himself with the Party.

Policies. The Party has extreme right-wing, pro-military, authoritarian and monarchist policies.

Defunct organizations

Nawapon: a 500,000-member Buddhist movement which followed militant anti-communist policies, the *Nawapon*, led by Watama (see *Prachaseri*), was involved in destabilizing political violence in the months before the 1976 coup. These activities included attacks on left-wing politicians and the storming of a Bangkok university campus, with at least 40 students killed in the latter incident. The movement was widely held to be controlled by right-wing military officers and their civilian financial backers.

Red Gaurs: the Gaurs or Red Bulls, a fascistic paramilitary group of students, took part in numerous assaults on left-wing forces, including the massacre of students in 1976 and the bombing of the offices of the social democratic New Force Party in the same year. Its leader, Maj.-Gen. Sudsai Hasdin, went on to form the Mass Line Party (see Mass Party).

Turkey

capital: Ankara   **population: 49,000,000**

Political system. Under the Constitution of 1982, Turkey is a republic with a unicameral Grand National Assembly which elects an executive President. The current President, however, is the head of the military-dominated National Security Council, which assumed power after a coup in 1980.

Recent history. Turkey remained neutral for all but the closing stages of the Second World War. The armed forces have played a major role in national politics since a coup in 1960; a wholly civilian government was installed in 1973, but another coup in 1980 installed the present regime, which banned political activity and in 1981 declared all political parties to be dissolved.

The 1982 Constitution envisages a gradual reversion to democracy, but there are restrictions on the formation and activities of political parties, only three of which were authorized in time for the Assembly elections of November 1983.

The evolution of the far right. Since the introduction of competitive party politics in 1946 the two strands of radical right-wing activism in Turkey have been an Islamic fundamentalist tendency, typified by the National Salvation Party, and a secular ultra-right, typified by the National Action Party. There has also been a number of fascist paramilitary groupings such as the Grey Wolves, and right-left violence became a major problem in the late 1970s.

The ban on political activities imposed by the military regime in 1980 has resulted in the disappearance of most of these groups, although some managed to regroup under new names after the restrictions were relaxed in 1983. The military regime was held responsible for widespread abuses of human rights, including torture and extra-judicial killings, especially in 1981-83, when tens of thousands were arrested for alleged political offences. Legislation in 1983 forbade the organization of parties which advocated communism, dictatorship or the desecularization of the state.

The Armenian and Kurdish nationalist movements, which have carried out many attacks on Turkish institutions at home and abroad, particularly in the 1970s and '80s, are outside the scope of this work, as are most right-wing Islamic fundamentalist formations such as the Welfare Party, the West German-based Turkish Islamic Cultural Association and the defunct *Milli Selamat Partisi* (National Salvation Party), Muslim Brotherhood Union and Turkish Islamic Army death squad.

Active organizations

Bozkutlar
Idealist Hearth Youth Movement (Grey Wolves)

Leadership. Col. Alparslan Türkes (leader)

Orientation. Fascist guerrilla group

History. This paramilitary organization, which arose as a youth wing of the National Action Party, was very active in the late 1970s, when it carried out a large number of political assassinations in Turkey. It was reported to have used drug smuggling to finance its activities. It was banned and largely suppressed after the 1980 coup, and Türkes was imprisoned until April 1985 (when he was freed on health grounds), but the organization remained active in the Turkish émigré communities of Western Europe. In April 1987 over 200 Wolves associates, including Türkes (who received only a token sentence), were found guilty of subversion, with five receiving death sentences and 11 life imprisonment.

A Grey Wolves supporter, Mehmet Ali Agca, who had escaped from prison in Turkey (having been convicted of murdering a newspaper editor in 1979), shot and wounded Pope John Paul II in Rome in May 1981. Two other alleged Wolves activists were arrested in Switzerland for complicity in the attempt. Agca has at different times claimed to be Jesus Christ and a Bulgarian secret agent.

Another activist, Alliosman Egbir, failed to answer to bail in London in March 1985 while facing arms charges there; he was also wanted for two murders in Turkey. Also in March, two members were sentenced to death in Turkey for killings in the late 1970s; three more were sentenced to death in July and another seven, from the Bursa region, were similarly sentenced after a mass trial in December of 143 members, 86 of whom received prison sentences. (No executions have taken place since 1984.)

Policies. The Grey Wolves specialized in the murder of left-wing politicians and trade union leaders in the period leading up to the coup. Its policies were those of the National Action Party.

Defunct organizations

Büyük Ülkü Dernegi: the Great Ideal Society was a paramilitary group linked with the NAP and active in the mid- to late 1970s.

Confederation of Nationalist Trade Unions: the MISK was a right-wing labour grouping whose leader, Faruk Akinci, was imprisoned in 1979 for two murders. The MISK was banned after the 1980 coup.

Milliyetçi Harekat Partisi: the neo-fascist National Action Party (NAP), led by Col. Alparslan Türkes, was founded in 1948 as the Republican Peasant Nation Party. It sought the establishment of a Greater Turkey reincorporating some areas of the Ottoman Empire. It won one seat in the National Assembly in 1969, three in 1973 and 17 in 1977. In 1979 it lent its support to a conservative Justice Party (JP) minority government; its leaders and several hundred of its members were imprisoned after the 1980 military coup, at which time it claimed to have 300,000 members, including a large paramilitary wing. One of its followers, Mahil Sivgin, subsequently became deputy chairman of the Motherland Party, which was founded by Turgut Ozal in 1983 and won a majority in the Assembly elections of that year. Sivgin was removed from his post in April 1985.

Organization for the Liberation of Enslaved Turks: a right-wing terrorist group active in the late 1970s, associated with a similar group called the Turkish Lightning Commandos.

Ülkü Yolu: the Idealistic Path was a violent fascist youth grouping active in the late 1970s, when it was responsible for murdering some two dozen alleged left-wingers. It was banned and several of its members prosecuted by the military regime.

Other organizations

Other right-wing organizations active during the past 10 to 15 years, many of which have probably been disbanded, include the following: the *Banner Party*; the pro-NAP *Federation of Turkish Idealist Associations*(based in the emigrant communities in West Germany and elsewhere); the *New Prosperity Party*, led by Ahmet Tekdal; *Noble* (or Supreme) *Duty Party*, founded in 1983 by Aha Vefa Karatay; the *Tranquillity Party*; *Turk-Bir*; *Turk Ocagi Dernegi*; *Turk Yar*, and the *Turkish Federation in Germany* (West (Germany).

Union of Soviet Socialist Republics

capital: Moscow   **population: 280,000,000**

Political system. The Union of Soviet Socialist Republics is a federation of 15 states with a bicameral federal legislature, the Supreme Soviet, and a collective presidency. The Chairman of the Supreme Soviet heads a Council of Ministers. Political power is monopolized at federal level by the Communist Party of the Soviet Union (CPSU), and by its constituent parties within each of the Union Republics.

Recent history. The CPSU has undergone a number of ideological and leadership changes since the Second World War, with an overall tendency to a relaxation of the authoritarian and sometimes arbitrary rule associated with Josef Stalin (party leader from 1922 to 1953), developing into a relatively more relaxed and open style of government favoured by the present (1987) leader, Mikhail Gorbachev, installed in 1985.

The evolution of the far right. There is a very old tradition of anti-semitism in what is now the Soviet Union, but the 1917 revolution ended the large-scale pogroms and officially sanctioned discrimination which were its most frequent organized expression. Early anti-semitic groups included the Alliance of the Russian People, active around the turn of the century. Although the communist leadership has consistently denounced anti-semitism and denied that it is prevalent in Soviet life, there have been frequent reports of the appearance of anti-Jewish material even in party publications, mainly under the guise of anti-Zionism, and many external pressure groups have alleged routine discrimination against Jews in economic and political affairs. The UK newspaper *The Guardian* reported in May 1987 that an organized anti-semitic movement, known as *Pamyat* (Heritage), had emerged in the Soviet Union. (Internal and foreign pressure groups advocating Jewish rights, especially in regard to emigration, are not considered to fall within the scope of this study.)

Right-wing groups have been able to organize openly in Soviet territory only during the period and within the area of the Nazi occupation, that is, in the western republics from 1941-44. Substantial Nazi volunteer and auxiliary forces were recruited among the populations of the Baltic states of Estonia, Lithuania and Latvia (which had been independent under anti-communist regimes and had fascist and national socialist groups until they were annexed by the Soviet Union in 1940), and also in the Ukraine and Byelorussia.

The Soviet Union lost about 20,000,000 war dead and suffered enormous material damage. Captured war criminals and collaborators were summarily dealt with and the right-wing groups survived only among the émigré communities. Domestically, there have been several cases of nationalist agitation and other dissident activity since the war, few of which, although supported by external anti-communist groups, fall within our terms of reference. There is no legal internal opposition group. Émigré organizations are listed below rather than under the country in which they are based, except for those (e.g. the Anti-Bolshevik Bloc of Nations, in the United Kingdom) which include non-Soviet émigré groups.

An effort has been made to distinguish between internal and external pressure groups which are solely concerned with human rights issues (and which are therefore excluded from this work) and pressure groups which publicize human rights issues in the context of or in association with broader anti-communist campaigns (which are included). This distinction is not always easily made, particularly in the case of internal groups on which information may be limited, and such groups are listed with "errors and omissions excepted". The *samizdat* publishers, unregistered churches and religious rights groups, Helsinki Accords monitors, unofficial peace and detente groups, left-wing and intra-party opposition, psychiatric abuse activists and unofficial trade union movements are specifically excluded, as are individual opposition activists, unorganized nationalist agitations, exiled Christian democratic and social democratic parties and the small "legations" in London which purport to represent the legitimate governments of the Baltic states.

Active organizations

Americans for Due Process (ADP)

Base. New York, United States

Leadership. Rasa Razgaitis (director)

Orientation. Anti-communist

History. The ADP was formed by American citizens, mainly of Baltic and Ukrainian birth or descent, in the mid-1980s. It was instrumental in forming the Coalition for Constitutional Justice and Security, an umbrella organization with similar aims which had 90 affiliated émigré groupings in mid-1987 (and was led by Mari-Ann Rikken).

Policies. It seeks to defend war crime suspects from extradition to the Soviet Union and from the use of Soviet-supplied evidence; many of its members seek the disbandment of the Office of Special Investigation— the US government body which investigates war crimes—and the termination of such investigations.

Americans for Human Rights in the Ukraine (AHRU)

Address. 43 Midland Place, Newark, New Jersey 07106, United States

Orientation. Anti-communist

History. This group, consisting mainly of first- and second-generation Ukrainian immigrants, was active in the mid-1980s.

Policies. It seeks to expose and denounce abuses of human rights in the Ukraine and to work for an independent and democratic Ukrainian state.

Anti-Soviet Society

Address. Alternative Bookshop, Covent Garden, London, England

Leadership. Brian Micklethwaite (organizer); Chris Tame, Mark Taha

Orientation. Anti-communist

History. The Society was established in the early 1980s by supporters of one of the main fascist émigré groups, the NTS. Taha was reported by *Searchlight* magazine in 1984 to have been involved with mercenary recruitment in 1981, and with British ultra-rightists in the Nationalist Self-Help Group and the National Front. Tame's Libertarian Alliance (United Kingdom) is very closely linked with the Society and has also had Taha as a member.

Policies. The Society seeks to foster opposition in Britain to the foreign and domestic policies of the Soviet government.

Publications. The Society produces a journal and occasional pamphlets, one of which, published in 1983, was entitled *In Defence of Mercenaries.*

Associated organizations. See NTS. The Society is based in the libertarian Alternative Bookshop, a fact which led to a split in the Libertarian Alliance between pro- and anti-NTS factions.

Association for a Free Russia

Address. London, England

Leadership. Nicolai Tolstoy (president); Nicholas Bethell, Alan Tyrell (patrons); George Miller (chairman of executive bureau)

Orientation. Anti-communist

History. This organization, which was founded in the 1970s and originally based in Paris, staged a fringe meeting at the 1986 conference of the Federation of Conservative Students (see United Kingdom), at which Tolstoy (ibid) reiterated his allegation that ex-Prime Minister Harold Macmillan had been guilty of war crimes. Steve Nicholson, vice-chairman of the FCS, was also on the platform. Two of the Association's patrons are British Conservative members of the European Parliament.

Policies. The Association supports Russian nationalism and opposes the Soviet state and government.

Associated organizations. The Association is linked through Miller with the NTS, to whose Free Russia Fund it donated 800 in 1982.

Association for the Liberation of Ukraine

Address. 136 Second Avenue, New York, NY 10003, United States

Leadership. Valentyn Koval (president)

Orientation. Anti-communist

History. This society of Ukrainian émigrés and their descendants, which has been based in New York at least since the early 1970s, remained active in the 1980s.

Policies. It promotes Ukrainian nationalism and anti-communist ideas, and advocates a pro-Western revolution in the Ukraine.

Publications. Various journals.

Baltic American Freedom League

Address. Box 29657, Los Angeles, California 90029, United States

Leadership. Avo Piirisild (president)

Orientation. Anti-communist

History. The League was founded in 1981.

Policies. It seeks to raise public awareness in the United States about what it terms the Soviet occupation of the Baltic states, to monitor human rights abuses and to foster support for the nationalist cause in the states.

Publications. Baltic Bulletin, every two months; *Alert*, approximately monthly.

Baltic World Conference

Address. 243 East 34th Street, New York, NY 10016, United States

Leadership. Julijs Kadelis (spokesman)

Orientation. Anti-communist

History. The Conference was formed in 1972 as a coalition of groups representing about 1,000,000 descendants of, and first-generation, immigrants to the United States from the Baltic republics (Lithuania, Estonia and Latvia) now incorporated into the Soviet Union. In July 1985 the Conference organized a two-day "tribunal" in Copenhagen and a cruise on the Baltic to publicize allegations against the Soviet government concerning the "illegal occupation and Russification" of the republics. Demonstrations were held in several Scandinavian cities. The episode strained relations between the Soviet government and those of Sweden, Finland and Denmark.

Policies. The Conference rejects the incorporation of the Baltic states in the Union and calls for their separate independence. In the short term it fosters co-operation between organizations representing Balts in exile.

Associated organizations. Groups affiliated include the Supreme Committee for the Liberation of Lithuania, the World Federation of Free Latvians and the Estonian World Council, all based in the United States. There is an overlap in membership with the Joint Baltic-American National Committee. Other US-based organizations with similar goals, which may or may not be formally linked to the Conference, include the Baltic Women's Council and the United Baltic Appeal.

Byelorussian Congress Committee of America

Address. 85-26 125th Street, Queens, New York 11415, United States

Leadership. John J. Kosiak (president)

Orientation. Anti-communist

History. The Committee arose in 1951 at the initiative of recent immigrants from Byelorussia.

Policies. It is a nationalist formation which seeks "the liberation of Byelorussia from Soviet occupation".

Publications. Byelarusskaya Dumka, two per year; various books and tracts.

International affiliations. The Commitee may be in contact with a Canadian-based Federation of Free Byelorussian Journalists, on which no information is available.

Byelorussian Liberation Front

Base. Cleveland, Ohio, United States

Leadership. John Shimchich (president)

Orientation. Anti-communist

History. The Front was formed in the late 1950s.

Policies. It seeks the "liberation" of Byelorussia and its independence from the Soviet Union.

Publications. Baracba, irregular.

Associated organizations. Other Byelorussian-American groups with a similar political orientation include the Byelorussian-American Association, the Byelorussian-American Women's Association, the Byelorussian-American Youth Organization and the White Ruthenian American Relief group.

Committee for a Free Lithuania

Address. 71-67 58th Road, Maspeth, New York 11378, United States

Leadership. Dr Bronius Nemickas (chairman)

Orientation. Anti-communist

History. This body, formed in 1951 as the Lithuanian Consultative Panel, adopted its present name a year later.

Policies. It works for an independent non-communist Lithuania and for the survival of the Lithuanian culture.

Associated organizations. The Committee represents Lithuania in the Assembly of Captive European Nations (United States). In 1974 the Committee shared an address (29 West 57th Street, New York, NY 10019) with a Committee for a Free Estonia and a Committee for a Free Latvia.

Congress of Russian Americans

Base. United States

Orientation. Anti-communist

History. This organization, which is one of the larger of the many organizations representing Russian immigrants to the United States and Americans of Russian descent, held a conference in St. Petersburg, Florida, in May 1983. The Congress received a telephone greeting from President Reagan, who said that the Russian people had suffered under communist rule and that his government did not confuse the Soviets with the Russian people.

Policies. The Congress promotes Russian culture and nationalism and opposes the communist regime.

Publications. Bulletin, monthly.

Cossack-American Citizens' Committee

Address. Box 1095, Grand Central Station, New York, NY 10163, United States

Leadership. Dr W. Glasgow (chairman)

Orientation. Anti-communist

History. The Committee was founded in the early 1960s.

Policies. It is extremely anti-communist and anti-Russian, advancing the case for an independent Cossack state (principally consisting of the Ukraine).

Publications. The Committee produces several journals, in English and Ukrainian.

Associated organizations. It is closely associated with the Supreme Cossack Representation in Exile, founded in 1947 (and currently led by Ivan Ivanovich Bezugloff).

Joint Baltic American National Committee

Address. Box 432, 400 Hurley Avenue, Rockville, Maryland 20850

Leadership. Gunars Meierovics (chairman)

Orientation. Anti-communist

History. The Committee was founded in 1961 as a co-ordinating body for three small Baltic groups.

Policies. The Committee seeks self-determination for the Baltic peoples.

Membership. The member organizations are the American Latvian Association, the Estonian American National Council and the Lithuanian American Council.

Associated organizations. It is affiliated to the Baltic World Conference and the World Federation of Free Latvians.

Latvian Youth Association

Address. 98 Wokingham Road, Reading, Berkshire, England

Leadership. Ivar Sinka

Orientation. Anti-communist

History. The Association was formed among first and second-generation Latvians settled in Great Britain.

Policies. The group regards the Soviet regime in Latvia as unlawful and protests at alleged Russification and human rights abuses. It supports Latvian nationalism and defends the state's cultural and linguistic identity.

Lithuanian-American Community of the USA

Base. Philadelphia, Pennsylvania, United States

Orientation. Anti-communist

History. This group was formed in the late 1940s or early '50s.

Policies. It opposes the "occupation" of Lithuania, publicizes human rights issues, works for the survival of the national language and culture and co-ordinates its activities with those of like-minded organizations.

Associated organizations. There are upwards of 100 Lithuanian-American organizations, most of which have social, cultural or benevolent functions while remaining generally sympathetic to the anti-communist policies of this group.

Lithuanian Information Center

Base. New York, United States

Orientation. Anti-communist

History. The Center was opened around 1980.

Policies. It compiles and disseminates information on civil rights and political matters relating to Lithuania, with particular emphasis on political prisoners, religious persecution and opposition movements.

Lithuanian National Foundation

Address. 1611 Connecticut Avenue NW, Suite 2, Washington, DC 20009, United States

Orientation. Anti-communist

History. The Foundation is one of the most senior of the emigré groupings, having been established in 1922.

Policies. It advocates self-determination for Lithuania and seeks to expose human rights abuses there.

Associated organizations. The Foundation is regarded as a front for the activities of the Supreme Committee for the Liberation of Lithuania.

Narodno Trudovny Soyuz (NTS)
People's Labour Union

Bases. West Germany; London, England

Leadership. George Miller (British representative); Boris Miller (British publications director); George Bonafede (head of foreign relations)

Orientation. Anti-communist

History. The NTS, also known as the Alliance of Russian Solidarists, was founded in 1930 by anti-communist emigrés in Belgrade. It was based in Nazi Germany during the war and was to have participated in the government of Nazi-occupied Soviet territory, but disagreements arose. The NTS co-operated with the Germans in the raising of a conscript army from Soviet prisoners-of-war and deserters, under the command of Gen. Vlasov. After the war it helped Western intelligence to place agents in the Soviet Union. The Union, which has many members in Britain and the USA, now claims to support clandestine anti-communist publications inside the Soviet Union.

In the 1970s Boris Evdokimov, a journalist, was active in the Leningrad NTS and in the SMOT, an illegal labour organization which occasionally calls for strikes and other agitation. His son, Ratislav, was charged with NTS and SMOT activities in 1983. Also in 1983 Valery Senderov was sentenced in Moscow to four years' imprisonment and five years' internal exile after admitting NTS membership and activities in support of the SMOT. He had also published one of several illegal *samizdat* journals, the *Chronicle of Current Events*, in the 1970s. Later in the same year Edward Chick, a Briton, was expelled from the Soviet Union for smuggling NTS publications.

Policies. The NTS is completely opposed to the Soviet state and professes Russian nationalism and anti-communism. It seeks to rehabilitate the memory of wartime collaborators.

Membership. About 1,000 outside Russia.

Publications. *Possev*, quarterly. George Miller is the editor of *Soviet Labour Review*, a London-based anti-communist magazine which in 1984-86 received over US$100,000 from the US government-sponsored National Endowment for Democracy through a semi-secret Russian Research Foundation based in New York. A *Review* associate, Simon Clark, also edits a right-wing student magazine, *Campus* (United Kingdom).

Associated organizations. See Anti-Soviet Society and Association for a Free Russia. The NTS publishing house is called Possev (Possev-Verlag, Flurscheideweg 15, 6230

Frankfurt am Main 80, West Germany). The group also runs a propaganda fund called the Free Russia Fund.

Organization of Ukrainian Nationalists (OUN)

Base. London, England

Orientation. Ultra-right

History. The OUN, led by Stepan Bandera and Yaroslav Stetsko, was the main fascist group in the wartime Ukraine. Many of its members enlisted in volunteer divisions of the German army. Stetsko became in 1941 the Prime Minister of the Nazis' puppet regime in the Ukraine, was briefly imprisoned by the Germans as a result of a jurisdictional dispute, and later fled the country with Bandera to found the Anti-Bolshevik Bloc of Nations (ABN—see United Kingdom). Bandera was killed soon afterwards, possibly by Soviet agents, but Stetsko remained active in émigré groups until his death in 1986.

The OUN retains a significant following among Britain's Ukrainian population, although it now emphasizes Ukrainian nationalism and anti-communism rather than overt fascism. It claims to have a following inside the Ukraine and has reportedly assisted in the infiltration of Western agents into the Soviet Union.

Policies. The OUN promotes Ukrainian culture, nationalism and anti-communism, and opposes the Soviet government and in particular what it sees as the domination and Russification of the Ukraine.

International affiliations. Members of the OUN were among those present at the London launch of Lyndon LaRouche's *Executive Intelligence Review* (see United States). Through the ABN the OUN is represented in the World Anti-Communist League (see South Korea), whose 1986 conference was addressed by Stetsko.

Obschcherossisky Monarkhichesky Front
All-Russian Monarchist Front

Address. c/o S.S. Ziloti, 65 East 96th Street, New York, NY 10128, United States

Telephone. (212) 722 0994

Leadership. S.S. Ziloti (secretary)

Orientation. Imperialist

History. The Front was formed in 1958 to co-ordinate the work of monarchist organizations of Russian émigrés in the United States, Australia, Europe and Latin America.

Policies. The Front is fervently anti-communist and seeks the restoration of imperial Russia.

Publications. Nasha Strana, weekly; *Znamia Rossiya*, monthly; various journals and pamphlets.

Ukrainian Congress Committee of America

Address. 203 Second Avenue, New York, NY 10003, United States

Leadership. Ignatius Bilinsky (president); Dr Lev Dobriansky (chairman)

Orientation. Anti-communist

History. This émigré organization, formed around 1940, has a substantial membership among the US Ukrainian community. Its chairman was appointed by President Reagan as US ambassador to the Bahamas. Its magazine publishes frequent articles vindicating the wartime collaborationism of the Organization of Ukrainian Nationalists. Its editorial board included Yaroslav Stetsko (see OUN) until his death in 1986.

Policies. The group is Ukrainian nationalist, regarding the Ukraine as being under Russian occupation. It is also staunchly anti-communist.

Publications. Ukrainian Quarterly; Ukrainian Bulletin. The Committee also runs a Ukrainian National Information Service.

Associated organizations. Captive Nations Committee (United States); World Congress of Free Ukrainians.

International affiliations. The Committee's chairman was a co-founder of the World Anti-Communist League (see South Korea).

Vyriausias Lietuvos Islaisvimano Komitetas
Supreme Council for the Liberation of Lithuania

Address. c/o Lithuanian National Foundation, 1611 Connecticut Avenue NW, Suite 2, Washington, DC 20009, United States

Leadership. Dr C.K. Bobelis (president)

Orientation. Anti-communist

History. The Council was founded in 1943.

Policies. It works for "the restoration of national sovereignty" in Lithuania and produces anti-communist propaganda materials.

Publications. Elta (Lithuania), in various languages; other materials distributed through the Elta Information Service at the same address.

Volya

Address. London, England

Leadership. Terry Liddle

Orientation. Anti-communist

History. This journal, which describes itself as an information bulletin on Soviet and East European affairs, was published in 1985-86.

World Association of Estonians

Address. 243 East 34th Street, New York, NY 10016, United States

Orientation. Anti-communist

History. The Association was founded in 1941.

Policies. The aims of the group are to fight communism and to maintain links between Estonian refugee and cultural organizations.

Associated organizations. Among New York-based bodies with which the Association is in contact are Estonian Aid and the Estonian-American National Council.

World Federation of the Cossack National Liberation Movement of Cossackia

Address. 21 South Western Highway, Blauvelt, NY 10913, United States

Leadership. Nicholas Nazarenko (leader)

Orientation. Anti-communist

History. The Federation was formed in the early 1970s by the amalgamation of at least two Cossack groups.

Policies. It seeks the "liberation" of "Cossackia", an area consisting mainly of the Ukraine, from what it sees as Russian occupation. Unlike most such groups, the Federation seeks to influence American politics; most of its members appear to support the Republican Party, within which they campaign for a strongly anti-communist foreign policy and increased military spending.

Membership. About 12,000.

Associated organizations. The Federation belongs to the Captive Nations Committee (United States).

World Federation of Free Latvians

Address. Box 16, 400 Hurley Avenue, Rockville, Maryland 20850, United States

Leadership. Dr Olgerts Pavlovskis (president)

Orientation. Anti-communist

History. The Federation was founded in 1960.

Policies. It works for the national independence of Latvia and against human rights abuses.

Membership. 150,000 (1985 claim).

Publications. Latvija Sodien, annual.

Associated organizations. American Latvian Association; Joint Baltic-American National Committee; Baltic World Conference.

Defunct organizations

Action Front for the Liberation of the Baltic Countries: this émigré guerrilla group bombed three Soviet offices in Paris in April 1977.

Ban the Soviets Coalition: an umbrella group of émigré and native anti-communist organizations which campaigned for the exclusion of the Soviet Union from the 1982 Los Angeles Olympic Games (an effort rendered unnecessary by the Soviet boycott).

Belarus Brigade: this fascist death squad was active in Byelorussia during the Nazi occupation. Its leader, Radislaw Ostrowsky, settled after the war in the United States.

Danganas Vanagi: a Lithuanian exile group active in Australia in the 1960s and '70s, during which time it was associated with the Australian Nationalist Workers' Party (later the Australian National Socialist Party).

Estonian Union of Frontists: this group, based on veterans of the counter-revolutionary struggle of 1917-22, attempted a coup in Estonia in March 1934, after which it was banned together with the Association of German Knights and other fascist groups. The main fascist leaders in Estonia in the 1930s were Gen. Larka and

Sirk, a lawyer. From 1935 the right-wing conservative government, based on the agrarian party of Pats and Laidoner, adopted elements of fascist ideology. After the German invasion a puppet government was formed under Hjaelmer Mae; several thousand Estonians served in SS units, including the Estland division, and in other German army and auxiliary forces.

Ivan Petrov Group: this US-based group of fascist Russians campaigned from 1962 to the late 1970s under the slogan "Communism is Jewish"; it maintained that the Soviet Union was under Jewish occupation and that communist movements around the world functioned as tools or as dupes of a Jewish conspiracy. It was probably a forerunner of or an alternative name for the Committee of Russian Slaves of Jewish Communism (see below).

Latvian fascist movement: the pre-war nazi movement in Latvia consisted mainly of the *Ugunkrust* (Fiery Cross), which changed its name to *Perkonkrust* (Thunder Cross) and was initially led by Zelmin. It was fiercely nationalistic and organized on paramilitary lines, having a grey shirt as its uniform. It was banned in March 1933, but quickly reappeared and split in 1934 between factions led by Dr Neumann and Pastor Sass. In 1934 a right-wing coup installed Ulmanis as dictator (or *Vadonis*).

The movement was closely allied with the German Nazi movement and supported the invasion of the Soviet Union and the Baltic states. Paul Reinhardts, a Foreign Minister in Gen. Danker's fascist puppet government during the wartime occupation (and now based at the Latvian "legation" in London and living in Gravesend, Kent), reportedly recruited for Nazi death squads and ran a slave labour office which was responsible for the deportation of 280,000 Jews. Up to 146,000 Latvian men served in the German army or in local auxiliary units, including by 1945 an entire army (the Sixth, composed of the Lettland and Latvia divisions).

Lithuanian Auxiliary Volunteer Police Battalions: about 8,000 Lithuanians participated in the 20 Battalions (*Schutzmannschaften*) formed by the German authorities in 1941-42, and generally under the command of German police reserve officers. Many of these units were involved in atrocities directed against Lithuanian and Soviet Jews, resistance fighters and ordinary civilians. Some of their members, such as Antanas Gecevicius (Gecas) of 3 Moston Terrace, Newington, Edinburgh, Scotland, subsequently took up residence in Western countries. In 1984 the US Justice Department began denaturalization proceedings against Matthew Katin, who lied about his participation in a *Schutzmannschaft* in order to gain entry to the United States.

Supreme Committee of the National Movements of Estonia, Latvia and Lithuania: this organization was founded in the Soviet Union in 1977 by a Lithuanian nationalist, Viktoras Petkas, who was imprisoned in 1978.

Tautinakai: the Lithuanian Nationalist Party, led by Smetona, deposed the fascist regime instituted in a 1926 coup by Prof Woldemara; the Smetona party also followed fascist ideas, and was represented at the 1934 International Fascist Congress at Montreux. It remained in power until the 1940 annexation by the Soviet Union, and supported the later German invasion; some 5,000 of its sympathizers joined the Waffen SS in 1944.

Ukrainian Liberation Front: this group bombed a Soviet airline office in Luxembourg in November 1980.

Ukrainian National Army: this body was established in 1941 as a volunteer SS division under the command of Obergruppenführer Shandruk, the highest-ranking non-German in the SS. In 1986 surviving members of the Army were involved in the funeral in Britain of Yaroslav Stetsko, who was "Prime Minister" of "Free Ukraine" at the time of the Army's formation.

Other organizations

Among lesser-known anti-communist and nationalist groups active in Soviet émigré communities in recent years are the following, all based in the United States unless otherwise stated: the *American Association of Crimean Turks*; *Americans for Congressional Action to Free the Baltic States*(based in the 1970s at Box 77048, Los Angeles, California 90007); the *Baltic Women's Council* (195 Linwood Avenue, Bogota, New Jersey 07603); the *Chicago Latvian Community Center*; the *Committee for the Defence of Persecuted Orthodox Christians*; the fiercely anti-semitic *Committee of Russian Slaves of Jewish Communism* (Box 927, Union City, New Jersey 57013), which published *Borba* magazine in the mid-1970s and may be a successor to the Ivan Petrov Group; the *Cossack Combatants' Association* (Box 323, Blauvelt, New York 10913; the *Estonian National Council* (Box 226, Claremont, California 91701), which used to publish the *Newsletter from Behind the Iron Curtain*; the *Georgian National Alliance*; the *Latvian Information Bulletin* (4325 17th Street NW, Washington, DC 20011); the *Order of Russian Imperialists' Union* (65 Blakeman Place, Stratford, Connecticut 06497); the *Organization for the Defense of the Four Freedoms of the Ukraine* (Box 304, New York, NY 10003); the *Russian Anti-Communist Organization*, active in the 1970s in New York; the *Russian Immigrants' Representative Association in America*, publishing the *Voice of Americans of Russian Origin* and sharing an office with the *American Russian Aid Association* (349 West 86th Street, New York, NY 10024).

The *Samizdat Bulletin* (PO Box 6128, San Mateo, California 94403); *Smoloskyp*, the *Organization for the Defense of Human Rights in the Ukraine*(PO Box 6066, Patterson Station, Baltimore, Maryland 21231; *or* 25 Rodd Street, Sydney, New South Wales 2143, Australia; *or* PO Box 153, Station T, Toronto, Ontario M6B 4A1, Canada); the *Turkestanian American Association* and its *Auxiliary Youth League*; the *Ukrainian Academy of Arts and Sciences*(200 West 100th Street, New York, NY 10025); the *Ukrainian-American Civic Center* (845 N. Western, Chicago, Illinois 60600); the *Ukrainian American Hetman Association* (8827 Joseph Camp Street, Hamtramack, Michigan 48200); the *Ukrainian American Youth Association* (also based in Hamtramack); the *Ukrainian Information Service* (200 Liverpool Road, London N1 1LF, United Kingdom); the *Ukrainian Youth Association* (961 Weathersfield Avenue, Hartford, Connecticut 06100); and the *Association of Ukrainians in Great Britain* (more moderate than the OUN).

Individuals

Vladimir Bukovsky: this former internal opposition activist emigrated in 1976. He has been involved with the anti-socialist Freedom Association (United Kingdom) and has attended at least one congress of the World Anti-Communist League (South Korea), in 1983. He also participated in demonstrations connected with the Baltic World Conference event in Scandinavia in 1985.

Vladimir Sakharov: a former KGB agent in the Middle East, he defected in 1972 and later wrote a book entitled *High Treason*. He attended a right-wing youth congress in South Africa in 1985.

Alexander Solzhenitsyn: a writer and former internal opposition activist, he emigrated in 1974 and has since been prominent in anti-communist agitation. His activities are well documented elsewhere.

Nicolai Tolstoy: see Great Britain.

United Arab Emirates

capital: Abu Dhabi   **population: 1,300,000**

Political system. The United Arab Emirates (UAE), a group of seven sheikhdoms, has a federal system of government, headed by a Supreme Council of Rulers which appoints a federal Cabinet; within the sheikhdoms each ruler has almost absolute power. There is an appointive Federal National Council which has some legislative functions.

Recent history. The UAE became independent in 1971 after more than a century as a group of autonomous British protectorates. There have been occasional tensions in federal-sheikhdom relations, but the state has survived and prospered due to its vast oil reserves.

The evolution of the far right. No federal or local political parties are tolerated. Apart from the generally authoritarian and militaristic conduct of the government, the only recent evidence of right-wing activity is the formation in the 1970s of a chapter of the World Anti-Communist League (see South Korea). In 1985 the UAE chapter contributed US$10,000 towards the holding of a WACL conference in the United States.

United Kingdom

capital: London   **population: 56,500,000**

Political system. Great Britain, together with Northern Ireland, forms the United Kingdom, a constitutional monarchy. Great Britain consists of England, Scotland and Wales, which for most purposes are integrated although some separate institutions and political parties exist. The United Kingdom has a cabinet system of government and the Parliament is bicameral, with an elected lower house and a mainly-hereditary, partly-appointive upper house, known respectively as the House of Commons and the House of Lords. The United Kingdom has a small number of remaining overseas territories and possessions.

Recent history. Power has tended to alternate between the Conservative Party and the Labour Party, with a minor role played by the Liberal Party. Since 1979 a right-wing Conservative government has been in power, with Margaret Thatcher as Prime Minister.

The evolution of the far right. The information below refers to Great Britain unless otherwise stated. Prior to the Second World War, Oswald Mosley's British Union of Fascists gained a small urban following.

Since the war the principal preoccupations of the ultra-right have been resistance to the dismantling of the British Empire and its transformation into the commonwealth, and, more recently, to the increase in Britain's black population, which arose mainly as a result of immigration from colonies and independent Commonwealth countries in the 1950s and 1960s. Upon the brief return of Mosley from self-imposed exile in 1958, there were race riots in the Notting Hill area of London and elsewhere. By the late 1960s the right had regrouped and the National Front (NF) was formed by a number of smaller parties. There was also, and still is, a considerable right-wing and racist fringe element in the Conservative Party, although perhaps not significant in the context of its claimed membership of about 2,000,000.

Encouraged by the racist anti-immigration pronouncements of a senior Conservative member of parliament, Enoch Powell, the NF and like-minded organizations took to the streets in 1969, and by the mid-1970s they had built up a significant electoral following. Adverse publicity arising from racist violence, and other factors including the emergence of an anti-racist movement, resulted in a falling away of electoral support and by 1986 far-right candidates were performing badly in every election which they contested at local or national level.

Several splits in the National Front, the collapse in the early 1980s of the overtly nazi British Movement, and the adoption by the Conservative Party of ever more hard line stances on immigration and social policy, weakened the extra-parliamentary far right to the point where it commanded support almost exclusively among skinhead thugs and football hooligans. Nevertheless racist violence, including occasional murders, continued into the mid-1980s, with frequent suggestions that the police in major cities were insufficiently diligent in prosecuting offenders. In 1984, for example, the Home Office recorded more than 7,000 racial attacks, very few of which resulted in criminal proceedings. Persistent allegations of anti-black bias in the police and other public bodies gave rise to rioting in several urban areas in the 1970s and 1980s.

A number of war crime suspects and other anti-communist refugees from Eastern Europe settled in Britain shortly after the Second World War. In 1948 investigations into war criminals effectively ended, although in 1987 there were moves to reopen some cases, particularly in relation to 17 named individuals.

Active organizations

Action Society

Address. Nash House, Fishponds Road, London SW17

Leadership. Jeffrey Hamm (organizer); Robert Row (editor)

Orientation. Mosleyite

History. The Action Society is the latest in a series of post-war Mosleyite movements, having taken over from the Union Movement in 1978. Its leader, Hamm, was Mosley's private secretary for some time before the fascist leader's death in 1980. The Society is open to members of other fascist groups.

Policies. The Society follows a pan-Europeanist line, calling for the creation of a new power bloc comprising Western Europe and the white-ruled countries of the old Commonwealth (including South Africa).

Publications. Action (sometimes rendered Action!), irregular.

International affiliations. There is a similarly named sister organization in the United States.

Anti-Bolshevik Bloc of Nations (ABN)

Address. Holland Park, London; *also at* Zeppelinstrasse 67, 8000 Munich, West Germany

Orientation. Anti-communist

History. This group was set up in Munich in 1946 by Yaroslav Stetsko, who had been Prime Minister of the Germans' puppet regime in the Ukraine in 1941, and Stepan Bandera, the leader of the collaborationist Organization of Ukrainian Nationalists. It was intended as an umbrella group for the political activities of numerous East European anti-communist émigré groups; it was a founding member of the World Anti-Communist League (WACL—see South Korea), but was out of favour with the mid-1980s leadership of WACL on account of the wartime record of many ABN activists.

The 1985 ABN conference was held in London. Stetsko remained chairman of the ABN until his death in 1986, and the group remained under Ukrainian domination.

Policies. The ABN seeks to publicize and denounce abuses of civil rights in communist countries, and to educate the public about the shortcomings of communist regimes and the threat to individual freedom posed by the communist bloc.

Publications. Stetsko was on the editorial board of the *Ukrainian Quarterly* (see Soviet Union).

Associated organizations. The ABN has friendly relations with several British anti-communist groups, and with Conservative Party members of parliament such as Sir Frederick Bennett, Stefan Terlezki and John Wilkinson.

International affiliations. The ABN retains a strong presence in West Germany. It has an International Youth Committee, which includes representatives of non-East European groups such as the Young Monday Club (the youth branch of the Monday Club—see below). It remains an active component of the World Anti-Communist League (WACL—see South Korea), and of the European Freedom Council (which may be the same as the European Council for World Freedom—see below). Émigré groups represented in the ABN include those of the Ukraine, Romania, the Baltic states, Russia and other East European countries. There is an ABN support group in the United States.

Bloomfield Books

Leadership. Donald A. Martin (proprietor)

Orientation. Anti-semitic

History. This bookselling operation was established by an Australian anti-semite who went on to found the British League of Rights.

Publications. The firm distributes a wide range of anti-semitic and anti-communist literature, including the Tsarist forgery *The Protocols of the Learned Elders of Zion* and a number of Holocaust-denial titles produced by "revisionist historians". It also supplies white supremacist material.

British Friends of Ulster—see Northern Ireland below.

British Israel movement

Orientation. Anglo-Saxon supremacist

History. The British Israel movement evolved in the 19th century, perhaps as a theological justification for the dominant imperialist and anti-semitic ideology. It appears to gain most of its support from conservative members of the Church of England and other Protestant churches. It has split into at least two organizations—the British Israel World Federation and the Covenant People's Fellowship—neither of which could be described as right wing per se, but both of which espouse ideas attractive to anti-semites and white supremacists.

Policies. The movement maintains that Anglo-Saxons are the "lost tribe of Israel" and the chosen people of God; the Jews are either impostors or mistaken in their beliefs. Although some of its adherents develop this notion into a cult of white supremacy, others are content to limit the political connotations of the belief to a "proof" of the divine right of the English monarchy.

Associated organizations. The movement has sympathisers in many right-wing groups, including Kenneth R. McKilliam in the British National Party. Similar groupings active in recent years have included the Society for Proclaiming Britain is Israel (SPBI).

International affiliations. The theology of the British Israel movement has reappeared in the United States in a more extreme form as the Christian Identity movement. The mainstream British Israel movement is represented in the white Commonwealth countries and in South Africa.

British League of Rights (BLR)

Leadership. Donald A. Martin (founder, national director); A.S. Battams; Dr C. Geoffrey Dobbs; Dr Kitty Little

Orientation. Anti-semitic, white supremacist

History. The BLR was founded in 1970 as an offshoot of the Australian League of Rights. In 1974 it became the British chapter of the World Anti-Communist League, and administered the WACL's then European regional section, the League for European Freedom; however, it was expelled from the WACL in the early 1980s, under the new Singlaub leadership, as being too anti-semitic.

The "patron" of the BLR was the late Air Vice-Marshal Donald Bennett, a wartime bomber commander in charge of the Pathfinder squadron, who was briefly a Liberal member of parliament in 1945 and a Liberal candidate in 1945 and 1950. Bennett was also associated with WISE, the National Front, a defunct anti-communist New Liberal Party, the anti-EEC Safeguard Britain Campaign and British Independence Movement, and other ultra-right groups. In 1979 Bennett stood in the European Parliament elections, securing 6 per cent of the vote in the Cotswolds constituency as a United Anti-Common Market candidate.

Policies. At least a large proportion of League members appear to believe in Jewish conspiracy theories. The League itself is anti-communist and advocates close links between white Commonwealth countries. It opposes the European common market and black immigration to Britain.

Publications. *On Target*, monthly bulletin. The BLR also distributes a wide range of anti-communist and anti-semitic literature, including the *Protocols of the Learned Elders of Zion*, various Holocaust denial titles and the memoirs of fascist leaders.

Associated organizations. The BLR has a long-standing connexion with Lady Birdwood, publisher of *Choice*, who became general secretary of the BLR in the 1970s. Don Martin's bookselling operation is Bloomfield Books; he is also a supporter of a Tory fringe racist group, WISE. The League has a close relationship with the British Housewives' League (BHL), which publishes *Home* from Martin's address; the BHL's associates include Victoria Gillick, a former anti-immigration activist now prominent in the "pro-life" movement. The BLR is also in frequent contact with the fundamentalist anti-communist Christian Affirmation Campaign (CAC), which was founded in 1974 by Bernard Smith and publishes *Open Eye* magazine.

International affiliations. Through the Crown Commonwealth League of Rights, the British League is linked with groups in Canada, Australia and New Zealand. Martin is one of two British correspondents of *The Spotlight*, published by the anti-semitic Liberty Lobby (see United States), the other being C. Gordon Tether, formerly of the *Financial Times*. The BLR also has contacts in other countries, notably South Africa.

British Movement (BM)

Base. Hillside View, Linthwaite, Yorkshire

Leadership. Stephen Frost (leader)

Orientation. Nazi

History. The BM, which purports to be a revival of the defunct British Movement led by Michael McLaughlin, appeared in late 1985, when it began to publish leaflets using a Huddersfield post office box number. Other semi-autonomous groupings of BM supporters exist around the country.

Policies. Frost's movement advances the white supremacist and national socialist policies of the old BM.

British National Party (BNP)

Address. Seacroft, 52 Westbourne Villas, Hove, Sussex

Leadership. John Hutchyns Tyndall (chairman); Richard Edmonds (interim leader)

Orientation. Neo-nazi

History. The BNP, not the first right-wing party to use that name, was founded in April 1982 by Tyndall, who had a record of fascist activism dating back to the late 1950s, when he joined the White Defence League (WDL). In 1959 he was convicted of threatening behaviour. He was prominent in the former British National Party in 1960-62, before breaking away, with Colin Jordan, to form the National Socialist Movement (NSM). Tyndall and others were imprisoned later in 1962 for arms offences arising from the activities of Spearhead, the paramilitary wing of the Movement.

In 1964 Tyndall formed the Greater Britain Movement (GBM), which abandoned overt nazism and joined with other groups in 1967 to become the National Front (NF). He rapidly came to dominate the Front and was its leader from 1972 to 1975 and again from 1976. In June 1980 he left to form the New National Front (NNF), marking the final split between Tyndall and his long-time associate, NF activities organizer Martin Webster, whose private life was a source of some dissension within the NF. The activities organizer of the NNF was Dave Bruce. It dissolved and regrouped as the BNP in 1982.

The BNP contested 53 constituencies in the general election of June 1983, securing a negligible share of the vote. It has contested several parliamentary by-elections, also with a notable lack of success. The Party, which was severely damaged in 1982-84 by an anti-fascist infiltrator, is particularly strong in London, Bradford and Leicester. From late 1986 the BNP had friendly relations with the NF Support Group, one of the larger factions of the NF.

Prominent members of the BNP include David Bruce (Enfield), John Wood (Sheffield, Yorkshire), John Coakley Boyce (formerly of the FCS), Eric Brand (Edinburgh) and Ernest Wright (Scotland). Colin Jordan, widely regarded as the father of Britain's post-war nazi movement, has written in its journal. A BNP supporter, Bruno Clifton, was in October 1986 moved from his Welsh Office civil service post after publicity concerning his racist views. In published letters he had called the nazi Holocaust a "myth" and had complained of "creeping communism, multi-racialism and alien cultures". Another leading member, Malcolm Skeggs (formerly on the Directorate of the NF), had earlier in 1986 been dismissed from his post as a librarian after using his employers' equipment for BNP purposes.

A number of the 1,500-odd BNP members have criminal convictions for offences connected with right-wing activities. Tyndall and a colleague, John Morse, were sentenced to 12 months' imprisonment in July 1986 for incitement to racial hatred through the party journal; half of the sentence was suspended on appeal. The party's Leeds organizer, David Owens, was serving a sentence for a similar offence in 1987, while four BNP members in Bristol had been convicted and fined in 1986. (Edmonds, of Lewisham, was appointed interim leader while Tyndall served his sentence; in September, however, he was charged with causing criminal damage, along with two other BNP members, to a bust in London of Nelson Mandela, the imprisoned black South African leader.) The editor of the BNP's youth journal (and former bodyguard of Tyndall), Anthony Lecomber (also known as Tony East or Tony Wells), was jailed for three years in November 1986 after a bomb which he was transporting exploded in his car near the offices of the ultra-left Workers' Revolutionary Party. He had several previous convictions for violence.

Three BNP members were charged with assault and public order offences after disrupting a trades council meeting in Gateshead in February 1987. Six BNP members were fined heavily in the same month for violence at a Remembrance Day ceremony in York in the previous year.

Policies. The policies of the BNP are essentially those espoused in the 1970s by the National Front, namely total opposition to black immigration and a supposed "Zionist" conspiracy, and support for white supremacy and capital punishment. The Party regards the present Front leadership as politically unsophisticated. A BNP spokesman described the Party in early 1987 as "not the yobbos and hooligans the public think we are".

Publications. The party organ is the *British Nationalist*. It is also supported by *The Patriot*, edited by Stuart T. Millson (formerly of Essex University Conservative Association). *Young Nationalist* is the BNP youth journal; it has also produced a broadsheet under the title *New Frontier*. *Spearhead* is Tyndall's own monthly, published since the 1960s, formerly in support of the NF but now supporting the BNP (although publication was suspended during Tyndall's imprisonment).

Associated organizations. *The Patriot* is published by Millson's Restorationist Right Press.

Campaign for the Return of Capital Punishment (Recap)

Leadership. Neil Lynn (organizer)

History. Recap, founded in 1986, came to public attention in 1987 when it threatened to oppose the re-election of a Conservative member of parliament opposed to capital punishment. Lynn, a former officer of the Cambridge Conservative Party and, in the 1970s, of the nazi British Movement, has obtained a letter of support from the Conservative Party chairman, Norman Tebbit.

Policies. Recap campaigns for the reintroduction of hanging for a range of crimes.

Candour Publishing Company

Address. Forest House, Liss Forest, Hampshire GU33 7DD

Telephone. (073 082) 2109

Leadership. Rosine de Bounevialle (editor)

Orientation. Neo-fascist

History. *Candour* magazine was founded in 1953 as a platform for a broad range of right-wing views by pre-war British Union of Fascists member A.K. Chesterton, cousin of the writer G.K. Chesterton. It was originally the organ of the League of Empire Loyalists, which Chesterton brought into the National Front in 1967, when he became the first chairman of the Front. He left shortly afterwards, taking *Candour* with him; he died in 1973 and was succeeded as editor by de Bounevialle, who had joined the League in 1956 and who formed the racist British Resistance movement in 1980.

De Bounevialle's home, from which the company is run, has been a venue for far right gatherings and training camps. Recent contributors to its columns have included Colin Jordan, the veteran nazi leader, while advertisers include John Tyndall's BNP.

Policies. The magazine has promoted anti-semitic and white supremacist views, and in particular belief in a Jewish conspiracy for world government.

Publications. *Candour*, monthly.

Centre for Historical Review (CHR)

Base. East London

Leadership. Robert Young (pseudonym of Martin Webster; director); David Durrant

Orientation. Historical revisionist

History. This Centre, which was formed by Our Nation leader (and former National Front leader) Martin Webster, has since 1983 published *Holocaust News* from a PO Box rented by Durrant, a National Front member.

Policies. The *News* maintains that the Nazi Holocaust did not happen and attempts to demonstrate this by publishing calculations on the burning rates of gas crematoria and other such studies.

Associated organizations. The paper has been sold through the NF but is not formally connected with the party.

International affiliations. The CHR has had dealings with the Institute for Historical Review (United States).

Choice

Base. London

Leadership. Lady Birdwood

Orientation. White supremacist

History. This anti-immigration broadsheet is published by the dowager Lady Birdwood, a well-known figure on the British ultra-right who has played a key role in bringing together the Conservative Party right wing and fascist movements.

Policies. The broadsheet is concerned mainly with opposing black immigration into Britain, but also advocates other right-wing policies, notably on law and order and on the trade unions.

Associated organizations. Birdwood has had a long association with the anti-semitic British League of Rights and with the anti-union Self Help Organization, and was present at the 1985 European launch of *Executive Intelligence Review* (see United States).

International affiliations. Birdwood was active in the World Anti-Communist League until it expelled the British League of Rights.

Coalition for Peace through Security

Base. London

Orientation. Against nuclear disarmament

History. This group has taken part in many activities designed to counter or disrupt events organized by the Campaign for Nuclear Disarmament (CND) and other peace groups. In August 1986 it was expelled from the UN International Year of Peace Council for trying to disrupt a long-distance walk by a CND leader.

Policies. The Coalition maintains that the possession of nuclear weapons has been the most effective guarantee of Britain's security against external threats.

Activities. A regular and typical Coalition tactic is the placing of loudspeakers and banners giving pro-nuclear messages near CND rallies.

Associated organizations. The Coalition is close to Lady Olga Maitland's Families for Defence group.

Combat Publications Ltd

Address. 2-3 Claremont, Hastings, East Sussex TN34 1HA (unoccupied accommodation address)

Leadership. Anthony Hancock (printer); Christopher Nielsen, Kurt Saxon (pseudonyms of editor)

Orientation. Survivalist

History. This ultra-right organization publishes a survivalist magazine and a selection of books on guerrilla warfare, assassination and survivalism.

Publications. *Hardcore Survival*, a semi-pornographic survivalist magazine.

Associated organizations. The telephone number given for *Hardcore Survival*—(0825) 4707—is that of the Hancock family's print works at 17 Bell Brook Industrial Estate, Uckfield, Sussex, suggesting that Combat Publications is a front for their operation (see Historical Review Press). A company which advertises in the magazine uses the name Edelweiss Survival Supplies, suggesting a connection with Ian Souter Clarence of the defunct Column 88 nazi paramilitary group.

International affiliations. The publications sold by the firm appear to be produced mainly in the United States.

Conservative Party

Address. 32 Smith Square, London SW1P 3HH

Telephone. 01-222 9000

Leadership. Margaret Thatcher (leader); Norman Tebbit (chairman)

Orientation. Mainstream conservative with far-right fringe

History. This party (formally known as the Conservative and Unionist Party, and popularly known as the Tory Party), founded in 1870, is one of two which have dominated British political life since the 1920s, the other being the Labour Party. Although not itself a radical right-wing party, the Conservative party has always had a substantial fringe element of racists and quasi-fascists. The philosophy of the party leadership, and the perceived position of the party itself, has latterly veered from the relatively liberal policies of the era of the Heath government (1970-74) to the fairly hard line monetarist policies pursued by the present (1987)leadership, which has formed the government since 1979. We are concerned here not with the party as such, but with evidence of far-right attitudes within it.

The Tory right. Within the Conservative party in the 1980s two parallel streams have co-existed—the minority "wet" (implying spineless) liberal tendency, and the majority "dry" or "sound" right-wing. Further to the right than the "dry" leadership of Thatcher and Tebbit there is a tendency which has much in common with the American libertarian new right, espousing not only such mainstream policies as the privatization of public enterprises and services, but also a much more for-reaching dismantlement of the welfare system and the gradual reduction of the role of the state to a structure concerned solely with defence, social control and foreign policy. This tendency includes both organizations and individuals.

There are several right-wing ginger groups operating within but organizationally separate from the party, the oldest and largest of which is the Monday Club. "Think tanks" supplying the ideological and theoretical groundings for right-wing policies include the Adam Smith Institute and the Centre for Policy Studies. A party youth organization, the Federation of Conservative Students, came under the sway of the radical right in the early 1980s to the extent that it was often in conflict with the senior leadership and was deprived of party funding in 1986. There are also a number of right-wing groups whose membership includes Conservative activists, although the groups themselves are not regarded as part of the Conservative "family"; these include WISE, Tory Action, the Coalition for Peace through Security and Families for Defence.

Piers Merchant, a Newcastle-upon-Tyne Conservative MP, was alleged in the 1983 election campaign to have been involved in the early 1970s with the fascist National Democratic Party, and to have served as an NDP election agent. He denied the allegations. Harvey Proctor, until May 1987 the Conservative MP for Billericay, has a long history of right-wing activism and has participated in the Monday Club's Halt Immigration Now Campaign, WISE and other bodies close to the National Front. His political career was interrupted in mid-1987 by his conviction for sexual offences. Other MPs associated with WISE include Nicholas Winterton and Harold Soref. Lord Henry Plumb, a Conservative Member (and since Jan. 20, 1987, the President) of the European Parliament (MEP), was in early 1987 guest of honour at a London function of the Group of the European Right, which includes the Italian MSI-DN and the French *Front national*.

A number of Conservatives have at one time or another been members or supporters of the National Front, including: Charles Bond, an NF parliamentary candidate in 1974 and 1979, and a member of the National Front Constitutional Movement (NFCM) in the early 1980s, now chairman of the Conservative Party in Barking (Essex); Janice and David Izzard; Trevor Wade; Bernard Ward; and Tom Finnegan. Two leading Tories in Southend (Essex), Frank Paveley and Donald Collard, have in the past been associated with the NF, the (Mosleyite) Union Movement and the National Socialist Movement.

The Conservative Party leadership has repeatedly condemned fascist presence or influence within its ranks, and Conservatives have criticized and sued journalists and others who have made allegations on such matters. A 1984 BBC television programme on ultra-right infiltration of the Party resulted in two MPs, Neil Hamilton and Gerald Howarth, forcing the BBC to retract statements about them and to pay damages, although a contributor to the programme refused to withdraw his statements, and the two MPs eventually dropped their actions against him and were required to pay his legal costs.

Crown Commonwealth League of Rights

Leadership. Eric Butler (president); Don Martin, Ron Gostick, Bill Daly

Orientation. Anti-semitic

History. This group held its fourth conference in London in November 1985.

Policies. The Crown Commonwealth League of Rights seeks to co-ordinate the activities of its constituent organizations in white Commonwealth countries.

Membership. Membership is by group affiliation rather than on an individual basis.

Associated organizations. Members are the British League of Rights and the national Leagues of Rights of Australia, Canada and New Zealand.

International affiliations. The League is associated with like-minded organizations in non-Commonwealth countries, such as Liberty Lobby and the Noontide Press (United States). Its main South African correspondent is Ivor Benson.

Economic League Ltd

Address. First Floor, Asphalte House, Palace Street, London SW1E 5HQ

Telephone. 01-834 0038

Leadership. Jack Winder (director of research)

Orientation. Anti-union

History. The League, founded in 1919 by former military intelligence officers, is one of the oldest right-wing conservative groups still active in Britain, and, with an annual income approaching £1,000,000, it is one of the richest. Its activities are obscured by an obsessive secrecy, but it is generally believed to operate a blacklist of trade union and left-wing political activists and to provide advice and assistance for employers in conflict with unions. In late 1986 it issued a report which attacked extremism of both right and left, specifically condemning the National Front as a threat to public order. In 1987 a police investigation following television allegations found no evidence that the League had improper access to police files.

Membership. Many large and medium-sized private-sector companies subscribe to the League's services. In 1987 the League had about 60 full-time staff in its London and provincial offices, as compared with 123 in 1980.

Publications. Notes and Comments.

English National Party (ENP)

Address. 76 Lock Chase, Blackheath, London SE3 9HA

Telephone. 01-852 0627

Leadership. Ray Shenton (national organizer); N.A. Clarke (secretary)

Orientation. Ultra-right

History. The ENP was formed in the 1970s and has contested several by-elections without success.

Policies. It espouses ultra-nationalist and authoritarian policies. It advocates the repatriation of all immigrants in England, including the Scots, Welsh and Irish.

Publications. ENP Newsletter

Associated organizations. The Save England Crusade operates from the same address.

European Council for World Freedom (ECWF)

Leadership. John Wilkinson MP (chairman)

Orientation. Anti-communist

History. This organization, also known as the European Freedom Council, contributed US$20,000 to the 1985 conference expenses of the World Anti-Communist League (see below and South Korea).

Policies. The Council is a regional organization of the WACL and shares the anti-communist aims of the parent body.

Families for Defence

Address. 1 Lincoln's Inn Fields, London WC2

Leadership. Lady Olga Maitland (chairman)

Orientation. Right-wing conservative

History. This group, established as Women and Families for Defence, was in August 1986 expelled from the Council organizing the UK events marking the United Nations International Year of Peace, on the grounds that the group had engaged in "disruptive" activities. The Campaign for Nuclear Disarmament (CND) had earlier resigned from the Council in protest at the presence of Maitland's group.

Policies. The group was set up to attempt to counter the arguments advanced by the CND and other groups in favour of British abandonment of nuclear weapons.

Publications. Deter, quarterly.

Federation of Conservative Students (FCS)

Leadership. John Bercow (last officially recognized chairman, non-right wing); Steve Nicholson (vice-chairman); Harry Phibbs, Mark Dingwall, David Hoile, Steven Morrison, Paul Masson, A.V.R. Smith (apparent leaders of right wing)

Orientation. Right-wing conservative

History. This body, which was established as a student section of the Conservative Party, was nominally under the control of party headquarters although the actions and pronouncements of several of its leadership—dominated in the mid-1980s by a "dry" or "sound", i.e. very right-wing libertarian, tendency—met with disfavour from party leaders. In 1985 there was a three-month suspension in Conservative Party funding of the FCS during an inquiry into acts of hooliganism at its annual conference.

Right-wingers led by Phibbs suggested in an August 1986 FCS publication that a former Conservative Prime Minister, Harold Macmillan (later the Earl of Stockton), was a war criminal in that he was involved in the transfer to the Soviet Union and Yugoslavia of numerous Cossack and Croat prisoners. The article, based on an interview with Nicolai Tolstoy, led to a renewed confrontation with Conservative leaders, who disowned the publication, and to the forced resignation of Phibbs as editor of *New Agenda*. Bercow's support for these measures led to his censure by the right-dominated FCS national committee.

Two of the more overtly racist members of the FCS, Stuart Millson and James Coakley-Boyce, defected to the British National Party in 1986. Neil Mason and Miles Hempsall, FCS members from Nottingham University, were banned from their campus in early 1986 for painting nazi slogans including "Death to Jews".

In November 1986 the Conservative Party announced plans to replace the then 2,000-strong FCS with a non-elected student representative body, the Conservative Collegiate Forum, which Bercow agreed to lead. It was not clear whether the right-wingers would attempt to maintain the FCS as an independent pressure group, possibly under the title Conservative Students, or would divert their efforts to working within the Forum or other official party youth groups.

Policies. Among causes which the right wing of the FCS has adopted in recent years have been support for the Nicaraguan anti-government contras (with whom some FCS members went "on patrol"), and for the government of Gen. Pinochet in Chile; opposition to the Anglo-Irish agreement of 1985, and to sanctions against South Africa; and support for immigration control and for the virtual abolition of state ownership or control of industry and social services.

Publications. Focus; New Agenda. The positions of the FCS right wing were supported by a magazine, *Campus*, published by Peter Young and edited from 1983 by Simon Clark, who is associated with the Russian émigre group NTS and with the Media Monitoring Unit. Phibbs has announced plans to publish from May 1987 a magazine to be called *New Right*.

Associated organizations. See Western Goals; Association for a Free Russia (under Soviet Union). Libertarians controlling the FCS were reported in late 1986 to be planning a takeover of the Conservative Party's main youth group, the Young Conservatives, at present dominated by the rival "wet" or liberal faction.

International affiliations. An FCS delegation attended a right-wing "Youth for Freedom" conference in South Africa in 1985. Right-wing leaders of the group have established links with the FDN *contra* group (see Nicaragua). The Federation forms part of European Democratic Students, of which Morrison was executive director in 1985. In 1986 the Heritage Foundation (see United States) sponsored a visit to Washington of right-wing FCS leaders; the group has also had dealings with what is now the World Youth Freedom League (United States). The International Youth Year Conference held in Jamaica in 1985 but funded by the US State Department was attended by an FCS delegation which formed a right-wing "Liberty Caucus" to co-ordinate its activities with other groups. The FCS has also had close links with the National Student Federation of South Africa.

Foreign Affairs Publishing Company

Address. 139 Petersham Road, Petersham, Richmond, Surrey TW10 7AA

Telephone. 01-948 4833

Leadership. Geoffrey Stewart-Smith

Orientation. Anti-communist

History. Geoffrey Stewart-Smith, who became a Conservative MP in 1970, formed this company in 1965 to publish his anti-communist newsletter, *East-West Digest*. Subscribers to the newsletter became members of a Foreign Affairs Circle. The Circle supported the formation of the World Anti-Communist League (see below and South Korea), and became its British section; however, Stewart-Smith's alarm at the penetration of the League by fascists and anti-semites led him to try to restrict participation in the 1973 congress of the League, which his organization was to host. The WACL leadership thereupon cancelled the congress, leaving Stewart-Smith with vast personal debts, and the Circle withdrew from the League shortly afterwards. Stewart-Smith's deputy in the Circle, Ian Greig, was at the time the chairman of the "Counter-Subversion Section" of the right-wing conservative Monday Club.

Policies. The company's publications seek to expose and oppose internal communist subversion and the external communist threat to the Western democracies.

Publications. East-West Digest, fortnightly.

Fourth World Review

Address. 4 Abercorn Place, London NW8

Leadership. John Papworth (editor)

Orientation. National revolutionary

History. This neo-fascist journal was founded in 1985.

Policies. The journal's policies are akin to those of the Italian *Terza Posizione*: ultra-nationalist with a ruralist element.

Associated organizations. In October 1985 the journal was represented at a conference held by the ultra-right Iona and Scorpion groups.

Freedom Association

Base. London

Leadership. Brian Crozier, Norris McWhirter

Orientation. Anti-communist, right-wing conservative

History. This group, founded in 1975 as the National Association for Freedom (NAFF), has funded a number of court cases aimed at contesting the rights and privileges of the British trade union movement. Its more prominent supporters have included Jill Knight MP, industrialist Sir Frank Taylor, state security writer Robert Moss (who is associated with Crozier's Institute for the Study of Conflict), Lord Harris (now of the Institute of Economic Affairs), Michael Ivens (of the free-market pressure group, Aims of Industry), and John Gouriet, who led its legal team in cases such as that against the postal workers' union (which sought to boycott South African mail) and that in support of the strike-bound Grunwick photographic laboratory. The Association adopted its present name in 1980. In 1987 it became involved in a controversy over the banning of a television programme about the Zircon intelligence-gathering satellite; the Association tried to force the state to begin prosecutions against journalists and others.

Policies. The Association claims to stand for individual freedom and the rule of law, and to oppose totalitarianism.

Publications. Free Nation, edited by Philip van der Est.

Historical Review Press

Address. c/o 19a Madeira Place, Brighton, West Sussex

Leadership. Alan and Anthony Hancock

Orientation. Ultra-right

History. This company is responsible for publishing a large quantity of racist and fascist material. In 1981 it received funding from the World Muslim League (see Pakistan) to enable it to send anti-semitic books to Members of Parliament. In 1986 the company appeared to be operating through Combat Publications Ltd, producing survivalist material.

The proprietors, Alan Hancock (also known as Grenville Stuart) and Anthony Hancock (also known as Anthony Madeira, Mr Wilson or M. McLaren B.A.), father and son, are prominent British fascists, the father having been involved in the Union Movement in the 1940s and '50s and in the Racial Preservation Society and the Conservative Party in the 1960s. He joined the National Front after its formation in 1967 and his hotel in Brighton was in 1970-71 the centre for international fascist gatherings involving the Northern League. He has subsequently been responsible for printing a wide range of NF and League of St. George publications. His son Anthony is particularly involved in the revisionist history side of the family business.

Publications. Among titles produced by the Press is one of the most widely distributed publications of the "revisionist history" movement (which denies the facts of the nazi Holocaust), a 1974 booklet entitled *Did Six Million Really Die?* by former National Front deputy leader Richard Verrall. Other titles include *Anti-Zion* and *The Six Million Reconsidered*, by American nazi William Grimstad. Periodicals printed by the Hancocks, not necessarily trading as the Historical Review Press, have included *National Front News, Spearhead, Bulldog* and the *League Review.*

International affiliations. The Hancocks' address has been used by the Institute for Historical Review (United States), at least until the Verrall royalties issue arose in 1985; by leading members of the Norsk Front (Norway) and the National Front (France), and by associates of Italian terrorists.

Imperium Press

Address. PO Box 40, Wakefield, Yorkshire; *editorial office* 90 Chantry Road, Lupset, Wakefield

Leadership. Eddy Morrison, K. Boyer

Orientation. Fascist

History. This organization was established at the end of 1986 in order to publish *Truth* magazine. Morrison had previously been active in a range of ultra-right groups including the National Action Party, the National Front, the National Democratic Freedom Movement and the British Movement.

Policies. *Truth* propounds white supremacist and anti-semitic ideas.

Iona

Address. BCM Iona, London WC1N 3XX

Leadership. Richard Lawson (leader)

Orientation. Ultra-nationalist

History. The leader of Iona was formerly a leading member of the National Front and subsequently of its short-lived splinter group, the National Party. He founded a magazine called *Heritage and Destiny* in the late 1970s, and formed Iona around 1983.

Policies. Iona describes itself as an independent cultural society for British nationalists.

Associated organizations. Lawson writes for *Scorpion* magazine, with which Iona held a joint conference on strategy in 1985. He has recently been associated with the National Front Support Group faction.

League of St. George

Address. 9-11 Kensington High Street, London W8 5NP

Leadership. Keith Thompson

Orientation. Neo-fascist

History. The League was established in 1974 by individuals associated with the Mosleyite Union Movement as an umbrella group for an elite of ultra-right activists. It established extensive international links and attracted a significant following among members of most British fascist and racist organizations. Its main leaders in the early 1980s were Thompson, Steve Brady and Mike Griffin (currently leader of the Michael Collins Association), who were reportedly involved in "safe-housing" a group of Italians in 1981. The League went through a financial and organizational crisis in 1983-84 and lost much of its membership.

Policies. The League acts as a non-party forum for the exchange of ideas and contacts among British and foreign—mainly West European— fascists. The group advocates the deportation from Britain of blacks, and a variety of other policies associated with the pre-1980 National Front, including capital punishment. Unlike most British ultra-right groups it has supported the Irish nationalist cause rather than the Northern Ireland loyalists, although Brady has links with loyalist gangs. The League is also anti-semitic and anti-communist, and promotes nordicism and Odinist paganism.

Publications. National Review (formerly *League Review*), every two months.

Associated organizations. Of the main British fascist groups, the League is perhaps closest to Tyndall's British National Party, although it has members in several other groups. Contributors to its journal include Colin Jordan, formerly of the National Socialist Movement.

International affiliations. Among foreign groups with which the League corresponds are the Hungarist Movement (based in Australia; see Hungary); the Belgian VMO; the Spanish CEDADE, and numerous French, West German and Scandinavian organizations.

Libertarian Alliance

Address. c/o Alternative Bookshop, Covent Garden, London

Leadership. Chris Tame

Orientation. Libertarian

History. The Alliance was formed in the early 1980s. Around 1984 it split between an anti-fascist faction, which called itself the Libertarian Alliance Ltd (and published *Free Life* journal), and this faction, also known as the Libertarian Alliance International.

Policies. Libertarianism is an ill-defined political philosophy the central tenet of which is opposition to the power of the state over the individual. It has thus managed to appeal both to left-wing anarchists and to ultra-rightists.

Publications. New Libertarian.

Associated organizations. The Alliance has since the early 1980s had a close relationship with the Russian émigré group, NTS, through Tame's membership of the Anti-Soviet Society (see Soviet Union). It operates from the Alternative Bookshop, which sells a variety of political publications and is managed by Tame.

International affiliations. The Alliance is in contact with several like-minded groups, especially in North America.

Liverpool Newsletter

Address. 17 Hadassah Grove, Lark Lane, Liverpool L17 8XH

Leadership. Anthony Cooney (editor)

Orientation. Anti-semitic

History. This journal has been published since 1959.

Policies. It promotes belief in a Jewish conspiracy to control the world.

Associated organizations. Among contributors to the *Newsletter* are George Kennedy Young, better known as leader of Tory Action. Cooney has also contributed to *Scorpion* magazine.

Mankind Quarterly

Address. 1 Darnaway Street, Edinburgh EH3 6DW

Leadership. Dr Roger Pearson (editor and publisher); Lt.-Col. Robert Gayre of Gayre and Nigg (founder)

Orientation. Racist

History. This journal presents as academic essays the views of racists and eugenists from around the world. Its editor has long been a leading figure on the racist right in the United States. In 1984 he was using a testimonial letter from President Reagan in promotional mailings for the journal. The founder, a close associate of Pearson, lives on the Isle of Man. He has been active in this field since 1939, when he visited the nazi race theorist Hans Günther in Berlin before writing *Teuton and Slav on the Polish Frontier*. After the war he became a professor in an Indian university and was involved with the Candour League and the Racial Preservation Society. He was editor of the *Quarterly* from 1960 until handing over to Pearson in 1978.

In one article in the magazine, a Mr Kiamran Halil referred to an "adage" that "the brain of the negro is contained in one single pip of the fig", and gave details of how to detect an individual's black ancestry of up to one-sixteenth degree. Halil, a British civil servant, brought a libel case against the *Guardian* for allegedly portraying him as a racist. The case was settled out of court in December 1986, with the *Guardian* withdrawing the alleged libel.

Prominent individuals who have been associated with the magazine or its advisory board include the late Ruggles Gates, a racial geneticist; Prof. Otmar von Verschauer, an associate of Josef Mengele; and Prof. Hans Eysenck, a well-known psychologist.

Associated organizations. Gayre became a member of the committee of WISE, a racist pressure group, in 1983.

International affiliations. See *Journal of Social, Political and Economic Studies* (United States). Pearson was a co-founder of the Northern League (see Netherlands).

Media Monitoring Unit (MMU)

Orientation. Right-wing conservative

History. This organization, funded by right-wing business interests in the Confederation of British Industry, issued a report in November 1986 which alleged left-wing bias in television current affairs reporting. The report was compiled by Julian Lewis, who is associated with the Freedom Association and with groups opposing nuclear disarmament, and Simon Clark, a Federation of Conservative Students right-winger who launched *Campus* magazine and is also associated with the Russian émigré group NTS (see Soviet Union).

International affiliations. The MMU is comparable to the Accuracy in Media organization (United States).

Monday Club

Address. 51-53 Victoria Street, London SW1

Orientation. Right-wing conservative

History. The Monday Club is a right-wing pressure group operating within, but organizationally independent of, the Conservative Party. In the early 1970s it organized a Halt Immigration Now Campaign (HINC), and it has remained in the forefront of efforts to strengthen the party's anti-immigration policies.

Among its leading members have been several Members of Parliament including George Gardiner, Harvey Proctor, Gerald Howarth and Neil Hamilton; members of various racist pressure groups, including George Kennedy Young of Tory Action (who unsuccessfully opposed the less extreme Jonathan Guinness in a divisive chairmanship election in 1973); and Conservatives who went on to join rival right-wing parties, including Stuart Millson (head of the Club's student section in the early 1980s), now of the British National Party, and many who joined the National Front or its offshoots.

Policies. The main concerns of the Club are immigration and law and order, although it has taken stands on most areas of party policy and was previously identified particularly with support for Ian Smith's regime in Rhodesia.

Publications. Monday News

Associated organizations. The youth branch, known as the Young Monday Club (YMC), was led in 1986 by Adrian Lee, Paul Masson, A.V.R. Smith and others. It had links with Western Goals UK and with Tradition, Family and Property.

International affiliations. The Monday Club's overseas contacts include former Rhodesian Prime Minister Ian Smith, who addressed a Club dinner in London in 1986. The YMC is affiliated to the Anti-Bolshevik Bloc of Nations (see United States).

National Action Party (NAP)

Orientation. Nazi

History. The Party was formed by Eddy Morrison, Kevin Randall and other committed nazi activists in the early 1980s. Morrison, whose career on the far right included spells in the British Movement, the National Front, the National Democratic Freedom Movement (circa 1974), a 1970s version of the British National Party, the New National Front, the current British National Party and the short-lived (1982) Anti-Communism Movement, was expelled around 1986, and was succeeded by

Randall. The NAP's membership has probably not exceeded 200 and its journals, *National Action* and *Combat*, have not appeared for some time.

Policies. The Party preaches traditional national socialist views on race, nationalism, the "Jewish conspiracy", the economy and other matters. It lays considerable emphasis on physical opposition to the left. On questions of morality the Party journal has stated that "nature never meant men to have sexual relations with other men, nor women either".

Associated organizations. In the mid-1980s the Party established a Nationalist Self-Support Group, whose leader, Adrian Wiltshire (formerly the British agent of the World Union of National Socialists - see Denmark), later defected to the National Front.

National Front (NF)

Address. 50 Pawsons Road, Croydon, Surrey CR0 2QF

Telephone. 01-684 0271

Leadership. Nick Griffin (chairman); Graham Williamson (deputy chairman); Derek Holland, Michael Walker, Pat Harrington

Orientation. Neo-fascist

History. The NF was founded in 1967 by leading members of several far right groups, including the League of Empire Loyalists (LEL), the Racial Preservation Society (RPS) and the British National Party (BNP). Its name recalled that of the National Front Movement, an ultra-right grouping of 1952.

Among prominent early members or supporters of the Front were its first chairman A.K. Chesterton, cousin of the writer G.K., ex-editor of the British Union of Fascists' *Blackshirt* and leader of the LEL; John Bean, former leader of the BNP; Oliver Gilbert, a pre-war member of the Imperial Fascist League; H.B. Isherwood, a prolific racist pamphleteer, and Jan Kruls, a Dutch fascist who went on to lead the Northern League (see Netherlands), in which some NF members participated.

Chesterton was forced out of the NF in 1971, but remained active on the right as editor of *Candour* until his death in 1973. He was succeeded as chairman by John O'Brien. The Front rapidly came to be dominated by John Tyndall and his associate Martin Webster, both of whom had been active in the Greater Britain Movement and, prior to that, in the National Socialist Movement and in its paramilitary offshoot, Spearhead, in connection with which Tyndall had served a prison term. Tyndall became chairman of the NF in 1972, while Webster became his deputy as national activities organizer. Tyndall's personal organ, a monthly also called *Spearhead*, was published in support of the NF in the 1970s and was effectively the party's theoretical journal, whereas *NF News* was the party newspaper.

The Front contested 10 parliamentary constituencies in the general election of 1970, 54 in February 1974 and 92 in October of that year. (It has also contested many by-elections, generally securing a higher vote than in general elections; in West Bromwich in May 1973, it received 16 per cent of the vote, saving its deposit for the only time in its history, as compared to the less than 4 per cent won in most other instances.) It suffered the first of several serious splits in 1975-76, when a number of leading members, including the late John Kingsley Read, Ted Budden and Dave McCalden, first seized control of the NF (Read becoming leader in place of Tyndall in 1974) and later broke away to form the short-lived National Party, leaving the Front under the control of Tyndall and Webster. Soon afterwards another prominent member, Anthony Reed-Herbert, left to form the British Democratic Party (BDP).

In the 1979 general election the NF contested 303 seats, obtaining a minimal share of the vote in the face of a determined campaign by the newly-organized Anti-Nazi League. Another split in 1979 led to the formation by Paul Kavanagh and Andrew Fountaine of a more moderate National Front Constitutional Movement (which became the Constitutionalist Movement, and later the Nationalist Party). Tyndall left in 1980 after a dispute with Webster, forming the New National Front and eventually the British National Party; he was succeeded as NF chairman by Andrew Brons, who was to remain in office for six years. In 1983 the Front was able to field only 60 parliamentary candidates. Webster was ousted in 1983-84 by an anti-homosexual faction assisted by Italian neo-fascist fugitives, and he formed a grouping called Our Nation. The Front gained considerable publicity in 1984-85 as a result of a dispute concerning Harrington, whose registration as a student at North London Polytechnic led to a long confrontation with anti-fascist students. In 1985-86 the NF came under the influence of a faction, including Harrington, which sought to develop it into a revolutionary nationalist movement along the lines of the Italian *Nuclei Armati Rivoluzionari* (NAR); that faction had evolved around a Strasserite ideological journal, *Rising*, in 1983-85.

Yet another split developed during 1986, partly over the involvement in Front activities of Italian terrorists, and in early 1987 there were two competing factions within the party. The dominant Griffin-Holland faction, which gained complete control in mid-1986, was attempting to create a three-tier structure for the party, with an elite of "political soldiers", a middle layer of "supporting members" and a bottom tier of street activists, and to develop a revolutionary ruralist Strasserite ideology modelled on that of the NAR. During 1986 this faction established a new secret headquarters for the Front (PO Box 41, Norwich, Norfolk; telephone 0603 400501), while maintaining the London address for postal purposes and as a bookshop (although they were considering the closure of their premises there in mid-1987). A rival faction, known as the National Front Support Group (NFSG), led by Steve Brady, Joe Pearce and others, offered a more traditional non-military approach. The Griffin group regards the NFSG as part of a state-sponsored plot to destroy the NF, while the NFSG portrays the "official" NF leadership as incompetent and adventurist. (Although the Support Group is seeking to regain control of the NF, rather than to establish a rival organization, and is numerically superior, it is mentioned separately below for the convenience of readers.)

The heyday of the Front was in the early 1970s, when it co-operated with members of the Conservative Party and its fringe group, the Monday Club, in campaigns against black immigration. It remains the largest fascist group in Britain but it has lost most of its electoral support and much of its membership. The age and class profile of the membership has also undergone a transformation; whereas in its early years it attracted many middle-aged, middle-class right-wing Conservatives, it now consists almost exclusively of unemployed skinhead thugs in their early twenties. It is the only fascist group since Mosley's British Union of Fascists which has achieved widespread public recognition.

Street violence has been a frequent feature of NF marches and rallies, three of which (in 1974, 1977 and 1979) have been followed by serious rioting. Over the years very many members and supporters of the NF, which has an enthusiastic following among skinheads and football hooligans, have been imprisoned for offences ranging from violence to gun-running and incitement to racial hatred.

Although it would not be practical to list here all the individual NF members implicated in serious crimes, the following selection of recent cases may be representative: Andrew Robertson (Glasgow), imprisoned in March 1987 for 12 years for conspiring to supply arms to the Ulster Defence Association; Kevin Turner (Consett), a local NF organizer and leader of a punk band called Skullhead, imprisoned in early 1987 for four years for assault with a beer glass; Phil Andrews and Richard

Baggeley, imprisoned in December 1986 and January 1987 respectively for assaulting a policeman and threatening behaviour; Paul Johnson, a former NF Directorate member who sent hoax bombs through the post (in the name of a spurious December 12th Group); Andrew Nichols, convicted in December 1986 of having offensive weapons outside a left-wing meeting; Joe Pearce, who served six months in 1985-86 for inciting racial hatred; Peter Wakeham, who was convicted in 1980-86 of assault, criminal damage, breach of the peace and other offences; Eddie Whicker, convicted of criminal damage; Paul Smith, convicted in September 1986 of assault; Colin Todd (Newcastle organizer) and two supporters, all convicted of possessing offensive weapons in July 1986; James Speed and David Manners, convicted of assault in June 1986; Colin Crouch, convicted of threatening behaviour in the same month; Blackburn organizer John Ellison, imprisoned in March 1986 for six years for unlawfully killing a rival football fan; Mark Andrew Ericson-Rohrer, convicted in November 1985 of carrying an axe on a demonstration; James Fennesey and Darren Langeland, imprisoned in the same month for assaulting police officers.

The early history of the Front is covered in considerable detail in Martin Walker's 1977 book, *The National Front*, while more recent developments are monitored, along with other news on other fascist groups, in the anti-fascist magazine *Searchlight*.

Policies. In 1986 the Front was describing itself as "Britain's only patriotic political party", professing a "distributist" economic philosophy opposed to both capitalism and communism, and a nationalist and populist ideology supposedly based on the ideas of G.K. Chesterton, Hilaire Belloc, William Morris and William Cobbet. It denies that it is a nazi organization, although many of its leading members have nazi associations, while the party's current policies have been likened to those of populist nazi Gregor Strasser and to the "third position" ruralism developed in the 1970s by Italian fascists. Rather than use traditional nazi terminology, the Front has pioneered the use of code words such as Zionists, cosmopolitans or aliens (for Jews) and one-worldism or international Zionism (for a supposed Jewish conspiracy for world domination). The NF continues to espouse the deportation of non-whites from Britain, which it describes as the repatriation of immigrants; it also supports the Loyalists of Northern Ireland (where it has a small presence—see Ulster National Front). It calls for the return of capital punishment for a variety of crimes and for UK withdrawal from multilateral institutions, principally the European Communities and the UN.

Membership. The current membership of the Griffin faction of the NF is probably in the low hundreds; only 80 attended its 1986 annual general meeting. The total number of active sympathisers of the Front—those who regularly participate in its activities—probably exceeds 5,000, compared with almost 20,000 in the early 1970s.

Publications. National Front News, party organ, monthly, circulation 10,000; *Nationalism Today*, every six weeks; *Bulldog*, YNF organ, every two months; *New Nation*, quarterly ideological journal. Of these publications only *NF News* was being produced by the Griffin faction from late 1986, while it also produced occasional issues of a journal called *New Dawn*, possibly as a permanent successor to *Bulldog*. There is also an *NF Members' Bulletin*. Local NF publications have included the *Newcastle Patriot*, *South London News* and the *Islington Nationalist*.

Associated organizations. The Front's bookselling operation has traded as Nationalist Books, from the same address, although there were reports in late 1986 that sales had declined dramatically in the context of the intra-party feuding and that it was to begin trading as Burning Books (using the slogan "books that the state would like to burn"). The party's youth organization is the Young National Front (YNF), led from its foundation in 1977 until 1985 by Joe Pearce (who has several criminal convictions arising from his NF activities) and thereafter by Michael Fishwick. Other NF subsidiary organizations have included the NF Trade Unionists' Association (or

Group), the NF Colour Party, the Nationalist Education Group, the Solidarity with the Miners Campaign (in 1984) and the Unemployed Activists' Group. The NF sponsors a music organization called White Noise, whose racist skinhead bands include Skullhead (led, until his imprisonment, by Kevin Turner), Above the Ruins (led by Nicola Crane and linked with *Scorpion* magazine) and Skrewdriver (led by Ian Stuart, recently released from prison). Some of these bands have also appeared in events organized in the name of Rock Against Communism. The party has run a drinking club, the Excalibur Club, which appears to be defunct, and it has also established ad hoc trading companies such as NF Properties, Leachouse Ltd and Benjuya Ltd.

National Front Support Group (NFSG)

Address. PO Box 230, Worthing, West Sussex BN14 8EG

Leadership. Martin Wingfield, Ian Anderson, Andrew Brons, Joe Pearce, Steve Brady, Tom Acton, Paul Nash

Orientation. Neo-fascist

History. The NFSG evolved in 1986 as a movement within the National Front opposed to the revolutionary strategy of the Griffin-Holland faction which assumed control in that year, and also to the involvement of Italian terrorists such as Roberto Fiore in the Front's affairs. Most leaders of the NFSG have previously held high office within the NF, including three former chairmen of the Front (Wingfield, Anderson and Brons).

The NFSG is currently competing with the Griffin faction for control of the Front, and eventually hopes to assume sole ownership of the National Front name and resources. There was an apparent attempt to assassinate Anderson in July 1986 with a car-bomb. *Searchlight*, the British anti-fascist magazine, speculates that the NFSG is seeking reunification with John Tyndall's BNP, which arose from a split in the Front. In January 1987 Pearce contested the Greenwich parliamentary by-election on behalf of the NFSG (using the designation National Front); he secured 103 votes.

Policies. The NFSG describes itself as a "radical nationalist" movement, in contrast with the "revolutionary nationalist" outlook of the rival faction. It has much in common with the other faction on the questions of white supremacy and belief in a Jewish conspiracy.

Membership. The exact membership of the Group is very difficult to determine, but it would appear in April 1987 to have the support of perhaps 60 per cent of the 300 or 400 core members of the Front. Among important branches which have given their support to the NFSG are those in Birmingham and much of the Ulster National Front (Northern Ireland).

Publications. Vanguard, monthly, edited by Acton; *The Flag*, occasional, edited by Wingfield and Anderson.

National Socialist Action Party (NSAP)

Address. BCM Box 2047, London WC1 3XX; based in South Oxhey, near Watford

Leadership. Tony Malski (leader)

Orientation. Nazi

History. The NSAP was formed around 1982 by Malski and Phil Kersey, both former British Movement members. In 1981 Malski was reported to have been in contact with European fascists, including members of the FANE (France), to discuss the launching of a bombing campaign in Britain. In mid-1986 a Dundee (Scotland) member of the NSAP, Graham Paton, was convicted of sending fascist propaganda and a concealed razor blade to an anti-apartheid activist.

Policies. The NSAP, which advocates the construction of paramilitary units, follows a traditional national socialist ideology.

Publications. European, monthly (publication suspended).

Nationalist Self-Help Group—see National Action Party

New Patriotic Movement (NPM)

Base. Mayfair, London

Leadership. Hamish Robertson (organizer)

Orientation. Ultra-right

History. The NPM was founded in January 1987, when it held rallies in Manchester and London.

Policies. It has campaigned in London against Haringey local council's policy of introducing positive images of homosexuality into the school curriculum, and against a Soviet visit; in Manchester it has supported the Chief Constable's condemnation of homosexuality.

Associated organizations. The NPM is thought to be a front of the 'Moonie' sect, i.e. the Unification Church, several of whose members— including the head of CAUSA UK, its local political wing—have been identified as NPM activists. It has also operated as the Parents and Concerned Citizens of Haringey.

November 9th Society

Address. 49a Park Street, Horsham, Sussex

Leadership. Terry Flynn (also known as A. Ryan; leader); Colin Parkin

Orientation. Nazi

History. This uniformed paramilitary organization was established in the mid-1980s, taking its name from the date of Hitler's "bierkeller putsch" of 1923. To date its main activity has been in spreading fascist graffiti and propaganda. Membership of the Society costs £3 per year, which "carries the right to wear a uniform in private".
Margaret Sibbert, wife of the Society's Milton Keynes-based leader, was imprisoned in 1986 for six months for attacking butchers' shops in furtherance of an "animal rights" campaign directed mainly against kosher and halal practices.

Policies. The Society describes itself as "a classless national socialist organization" and promotes the ideals of Hitler and the German Nazi Party.

Publications. Britain Awake, monthly.

Associated organizations. The Society is thought to be connected with the British White Race Defence Commandos.

Our Nation

Address. BCM Box 5106, London WC1N 3XX

Leadership. Martin Webster (leader)

Orientation. Neo-fascist

History. This group was formed by Webster some months after his expulsion in 1984 from the National Front.

Webster (born in 1943) was expelled from the Young Conservatives and joined the League of Empire Loyalists, an ultra-right group which sought to denounce the decolonization policies of the Conservative and Labour parties. In 1962, after a brief period in the British National Party, he joined the National Socialist Movement (NSM), led by Colin Jordan. His article entitled "Why I am a nazi", published in an NSM journal and referring to "the chill north wind flaunting the swastika banner", and his much-quoted reference to "forming a well-oiled nazi machine" both date from this period.

In 1964 Webster followed John Tyndall out of the NSM and into the Greater Britain Movement (GBM). Although he had escaped prosecution over the NSM's Spearhead paramilitary unit, Webster was imprisoned later in 1964 for an assault on President Jomo Keyatta of Kenya. In 1967 the GBM merged with other groups into the National Front, and Webster became a full-time official of the NF in 1969, remaining its national activities organizer throughout the 1970s despite constant opposition arising partly from his abrasive manner and from his sexual proclivities. In 1980 he finally ended his association with Tyndall, who was expelled from the NF, but Webster's position became increasingly difficult in the face of a conspiracy by youthful Strasserites backed by Italian terrorists. In December 1983 he was dismissed as organizer, and in February 1984 he was expelled from the party.

Our Nation has failed to win a significant following, and has been unable to open a planned office in central London. Among its members or associates have been John Donegan, formerly of the NSM; Denis Pirie, formerly of the NSM and Column 88; Joy Page of WISE; Anthony Hancock of the Historical Review Press, and synagogue arsonist Françoise Dior, a perfume heiress deeply involved in the British nazi movement in the early 1960s and subsequently French representative of the World Union of National Socialists.

Policies. Our Nation functions as a forum for ideological exchange among anti-semites and fascists.

Membership. About 60 (early 1986).

Publications. Our Nation

Associated organizations. The group was reported in 1985 to be planning the launch of an Institute of Contemporary Nationalist Studies (ICONS).

Regionalist Seminar

Address. 3 Asquith Court, Eaton Crescent, Swansea, Wales

Leadership. David Robyns (secretary)

Orientation. Federalist

History. The secretary of this group, which has claimed to have the support of established regionalist parties including *Mebyon Kernow*(Cornwall) and *Plaid Cymru* (the Welsh nationalist party), has written for an English ultra-right magazine, *Scorpion.* The group was founded in the mid-1980s.

Policies. The Seminar campaigns for a federal Britain with parliaments for each of several English regions as well as for Scotland and Wales.

Publications. The Regionalist, half-yearly.

Rucksack 'n' Rifle

Address. 12 Abbott Street, Wrexham LL11 1TA, North Wales

Leadership. Michael McLaughlin (proprietor)

Orientation. Survivalist

History. This shop was opened by McLaughlin after his resignation as leader of the openly-nazi British Movement (BM).

Policies. The shop supplies literature, crossbows, knives and other equipment for the British survivalist movement.

Publications. *The Survivalist*

Associated organizations. McLaughlin continues to sell nazi propaganda through the British Patriot Publications operation which he established while leader of the BM. For details of other British survivalist groups, see Soldier of Fortune Ltd.

Salisbury Review

Leadership. Roger Scruton (editor); Philip Moss (managing editor)

Orientation. Right-wing conservative

History. The *Review* was formed by members and supporters of the Conservative Party in order to provide a forum for the development and dissemination of radical right-wing ideas. It takes its name from the 3rd Marquis of Salisbury, who resigned from the government in 1866 to protest at the enfranchisement of working-class men through a Reform Act. Most of the *Review*'s founders were connected with Peterhouse College, part of Cambridge University, and had belonged since 1977 to a loose grouping of traditionalist Conservatives.

The *Review* achieved considerable publicity in 1984-86 through the publication of articles by a Bradford schoolteacher, Ray Honeyford, which were attacked as racist in their critique of the multi-cultural education policies pursued by many English education authorities. After a protest campaign led by parents of his pupils, Honeyford was persuaded to resign his post in return for a substantial financial settlement. The *Review* was at first published independently, its producers being known as the Salisbury Group; in 1984-86 it was published for the proprietors by the Longman publishing group, and then (from April 1986) by the Sherwood Press.

Policies. The *Review* has advanced a number of right-wing, authoritarian and traditionalist Tory policies on race, immigration, nationalism, education, the economy, law and order and other issues.

Publications. *Salisbury Review*, quarterly.

Save Britain's Heritage

Address. 68 Battersea High Street, London SW11 3HX

Telephone. 01-228 3336

Orientation. Nationalist

History. This group was active in 1986.

Associated organizations. The group has advertised in *Scorpion* magazine.

The Scorpion

Address. BCM 5766, London WC1N 3XX

Leadership. Michael Walker (editor); Dominic Hampshire, Seamus Skelly, Bob Hoy (assistant editors)

Orientation. New Right

History. This magazine was founded in 1981 as the *National Democrat* and adopted its present title in 1985. Most of those associated with it were previously involved with the National Front (NF), the National Party (NP) or other British or (in Hoy's case) US fascist groups. During Walker's membership of the NF (until 1984) he gave accommodation to fugitive Italian terrorist Roberto Fiore, who played a key role in realigning the NF with Strasserite ideology (and was involved with Walker in a travel firm, Heritage Tours).

The magazine presents itself as an intellectual and cultural platform for the British radical right, its lengthy articles demanding a vocabulary far in excess of that required by, for example, the publications of the NF. Among contributors to *The Scorpion* have been Anthony Cooney of the *Liverpool Newsletter*; Richard Lawson, formerly of the NF and the NP; Paul Matthews, who as editor of the defunct *Rising* magazine was deeply involved with Fiore in reshaping the NF, and Peter Peel, associated with the British National Party.

Policies. The magazine is "individualist" and "anti-totalitarian", claiming to reject fascism as well as communism. The tenor of the articles suggests an anti-democratic, elitist and white supremacist orientation, expresssed in terms of concern for order and for "Western civilization". It proposes a "European Imperium" (as advocated by Italian fascist theoretician Julius Evola), independent of both Russia and America.

Publications. The Scorpion, about three per year.

Associated organizations. The magazine is linked closely but informally to the Iona group. A fascist rock band, Above the Ruins, has used Walker's box number in their advertising material.

International affiliations. The Scorpion appears to be modelled closely on the publications of the French new right group, GRECE, reference to which is made several times in each issue. Advertising and other material indicate that the editor is in contact with a variety of European neo-fascist and ultra-conservative groups.

Scottish Loyalists

Base. Glasgow

Leadership. Wally Gemmell, Alec Walker

Orientation. Unionist

History. In 1987 this group was reported to have a substantial following among Scottish supporters of Northern Ireland loyalist groups.

Policies. The group, which is "founded on the Bible", seeks to "smash the scum off the street". It supports the two leading Northern Ireland loyalist paramilitary groups—the UDA and the UVF—and it vehemently opposes the Irish Republican Army.

Associated organizations. See various Northern Ireland groups, including British Friends of Ulster.

Self Help Organization (SHO)

Leadership. Lady Birdwood; Edward Martell

Orientation. Ultra-right

History. The SHO from time to time offers its services to break strikes or otherwise attack trade union power. In particular it has claimed to have facilities to print a non-union daily paper in the event of a strike closing down the rest of the press.

During the coal strike in 1984 it canvassed its supporters for funds to buy a small working mine in Wales, with the intention of inciting the National Union of Mineworkers to picket the premises so that the SHO could apply for the judicial confiscation of the union's funds.

Policies. The Organization regards trade unions as over-privileged and as a threat to democracy and individual freedom. It seeks to challenge union power and to support anti-union initiatives.

Associated organizations. Birdwood has contacts in a wide range of right-wing and racist groups.

Soldier of Fortune Ltd

Address. 4-5 The Arches, Villiers Street, London WC2

Telephone. 01-930 5559

Leadership. Timothy Danvers (proprietor)

Orientation. Survivalist

History. This shop, which opened in the mid-1980s, was one of the first British manifestations of the survivalist cult which was established in the post-Vietnam USA. The shop deals in books, magazines, weaponry and equipment connected with survivalism and guerrilla and mercenary warfare. It also deals in racist and fascist propaganda material, for which purpose it runs a book club in order to circumvent race relations legislation. Among titles in which it deals are *Mein Kampf*, *The Death Dealer's Manual* and *Incendiaries and Sabotage*. Its proprietor has known pro-nazi and anti-semitic tendencies.

Policies. The survivalist cult is based on the premise that society is in imminent danger of collapse, and its (mostly white, male and extremely right-wing) followers prepare themselves for commando-style subsistence and self-defence. Adherents of the cult include real and pretend mercenaries and a large proportion of neo-nazis.

Associated organizations. Survivalist booksellers, equipment merchants and groups in the United Kingdom include the following (not all of which are necessarily pro-fascist): Apex Adventure, The Old Surgery, St. James Street, Ludershall, Andover, Hampshire; Breakaway (run by Mick Tyler), 17 Hugh Thomas Avenue, Holmer, Hereford HR4 9RB; The Challenge Company (Wales) Ltd, The Adventure Centre, Y Dolydd, Llanfyllin, Powys SY22 5LD; the Combat Survival School, PO Box HP18, Leeds L56 3PR; the Combat Training Team of Croydon (not ultra-right); the ECTT, Unit FF4, New Buildings, Price Street, Birmingham B4 6JZ; Escape and Evasion Advertising Exchange, London (telephone 01-409 0766); Frontline UK Ltd, 25 Clover Field, Lychpit, Basingstoke, Hampshire; Meridian Expedition, 4 Candacraig Square, Candacraig Estate, Strathdon, Abberdeenshire; the School of Survival, 22 Langland Drive, Hereford HR4 0QG; South Angus Survival, 43 Ogilvy Place, Arbroath, Angus DD11 4DF; Spartan Survival, The Barn, Eleven Steps, Upper Hulme, Leek, Staffordshire; the Special Adventure School, 215 Gunville Road,

Carisbrooke, Newport, Isle of Wight PO30 5LS; Survi Camps, PO Box 2, Cowes, Isle of Wight PO31 8LH; the Survival Adventure School, 46 Lloyd Goring Close, Angmering, Sussex BN16 4LQ; Survival Aids Ltd, Morland, Penrith, Cumbria CA10 3AZ; Survival Skills (run by Jim Aitken), West End Cottage, Star of Markinch, Fife; *Survival Weaponry and Techniques* (SWAT) magazine (edited by Greg Payne), East Hill, Colchester, Essex; Survive International (not to be confused with Survival International, a humanitarian organization), 131 Longfield, Falmouth, Cornwall; *The Survivor* magazine, 1 Rushton Avenue, Sunderland SR2 7TA; WEST, Gatesgarth Bothy, Buttermere, Cockermouth, Cumbria CA13 9XA, and WEST (SW), Arrina, Shieldaign, Strathcarron IV54 8XU; and Yamabushi, 7-9 Lupton Buildings, Whingate Junction, Leeds, Yorkshire.

International affiliations. This shop is named after the leading US mercenary recruitment and survivalist publishing group. Similar phenomena exist in Britain (see Rucksack 'n' Rifle) and in other countries, for example the French publication *Objectif: survie.*

Tory Action

Leadership. George Kennedy Young (leader); John Andrews

Orientation. Ultra-conservative

History. This group was founded around 1977 by Young, who retired in 1961 as deputy head of British foreign intelligence (MI6). He was involved in the 1960s and '70s in a number of right-wing groups, including the Society for Individual Freedom (SIF) and the Monday Club (of which he failed to become chairman in a bitterly-fought election in 1973).

Tory Action has drawn much of its membership from the Monday Club. It was one of the organizations which featured in a 1984 BBC exposé of alleged links between fascist and racist groups and Conservative MPs such as Gerald Howarth (a former SIF employee), Roger Moate, Nicholas Winterton, Neil Hamilton and Harvey Proctor.

Policies. Tory Action works as a pressure group within the Conservative Party, promoting the repatriation of immigrants and other right-wing policies.

Membership. Precise membership figures are not available, but Tory Action probably has several hundred supporters including about a dozen Tory MPs.

Publications. Round Robin.

Associated organizations. Young has also written for the anti-semitic *Liverpool Newsletter.*

Tradition, Family and Property (TFP)

Base. London

Leadership. Huw Shooter

Orientation. Anti-communist

History. The TFP is one of several foreign affiliates of the Brazilian movement of the same name. Its activities to date have consisted mainly of press advertising designed to publicize the threats posed by socialism and communism to individual freedom, the Western way of life and private enterprise. Shooter is a right-wing historian.

Policies. The TFP seeks to undermine support for all left-wing organizations and to expose communist subversion.

Associated organizations. Most of TFP's support in Britain comes from members of the Monday Club and other right-wing Conservative fringe groups.

International affiliations. See TFP (Brazil) and allied groups in Canada, the United States and elsewhere.

Welsh, Irish, Scots, English (W.I.S.E. or WISE)

Address. 76 South Side, Clapham, London SW4 9DG

Telephone. 01-673 6329

Leadership. Joan Mason (leader); Lt.-Col. Robert Gayre of Gayre and Nigg, Brig. Hugh McIntyre, Rev. P.G.K. Manton (committee members)

Orientation. White supremacist

History. This organization, which is best known by its acronym, was established by Mason in 1974 as an anti-immigration pressure group for right-wing Conservatives. Mason was also involved in similar groups such as the Nationalist Assembly, a alliance formed in 1974 by the Immigration Control Association, the Racial Preservation Society and other racist groupings.

WISE remained an obscure fringe group until the early 1980s, when it achieved publicity by having right-wing Conservative MPs such as Harvey Proctor and Nicholas Winterton address its meetings. It was one of the groups featured in the BBC libel case in 1984-86 when Conservative MPs associated with the group persuaded the Corporation to apologize for the suggestion that they were racists. The publicity surrounding the case apparently damaged WISE to the extent that it was able to hold only two or three meetings in the next year.

Policies. WISE opposes black immigration into Britain, calls for the repatriation of settled blacks and seeks to defend white culture against alien influences.

Associated organizations. Gayre, who joined the WISE committee in 1983, is connected with *Mankind Quarterly* (see above). In 1986 Edinburgh University declined his £100,000 endowment of a literary professorship. Members of WISE come from the Conservative Party and from various ultra-right racist groups.

Western Goals UK

Base. London

Leadership. Andrew V.R. Smith, Paul Masson

Orientation. Anti-communist

History. This pressure group was set up in May 1985 by right-wing members of the Conservative Party.

Policies. Like its US counterpart, this group seeks to convince people of the need for massive rearmament against a perceived threat from the Soviet Union. It also supports Nicaraguan, East European and other anti-communist groups.

International affiliations. The group was established as an offshoot of Western Goals (see United States), a lobbying group run by Gen. Singlaub of the World Anti-Communist League. Western Goals may have set up a West German branch in 1987.

World Anti-Communist League (WACL)

Address. c/o Intelligence International Ltd, 17 Rodney Road, Cheltenham GL50 1HX

Telephone. (0242) 517774

Leadership. Peter Dally (British representative)

Orientation. Anti-communist

History. The first British chapter of the WACL, which was then based in Taiwan but is now in South Korea, was established by the Foreign Affairs Circle, a defunct far-right group run by the then Conservative member of Parliament Geoffrey Stewart-Smith. One of the two main founding organizations of the WACL, the émigré-run Anti-Bolshevik Bloc of Nations, was and is based in Britain but functioned as the East European rather than the British section.

After failing to prevent the virtual takeover of the WACL by anti-semitic and fascist groups, the Circle withdrew in 1974 when a British League of Rights front, the League for European Freedom, became the British affiliate. The main WACL activists then were the BLR's Don Martin and Lady Birdwood.

In the early 1980s the new leadership of the WACL, under American general John Singlaub, expelled the BLR and other anti-semitic affiliates. Dally, a journalist, then became its sole British representative. He is associated with Hugh de Courcy's *Intelligence Digest*, which reports international affairs from a far-right perspective. In 1986 de Courcy was associated with the LaRoucheist *Executive Intelligence Review* (see United States).

Policies. The policies of the British chapter are those of the parent organization.

Associated organiations. See Anti-Bolshevik Bloc of Nations; British League of Rights. Conservative MPs who have been associated with WACL activities include Patrick Wall, Jill Knight and Stefan Terlezski.

International affiliations. See the main entry for the WACL (South Korea).

Defunct organizations

Anglo-German Association: established in the 1920s to foster friendship between the peoples of Germany and England, this group lost all its anti-nazi members in 1933 and was regarded thereafter as a pro-Hitler front. It was revived in 1935 as the Anglo-German Fellowship.

Anti-Communism Movement: formed in 1977 as a successor to the Nationalist Assembly, the first organization of this name sought to act as a forum for ultra-rightists. Its leader, Mary Stanton, had been active in various organizations including the extremely anti-semitic *Christian Attack* publishing group, and in anti-immigration pressure groups. The second Movement emerged in 1982 as a London-based street-fighting gang led by Eddy Morrison, later of the National Action Party.

Anti-Communist Commando: this group was led in the mid-1960s by Victor Norris, a satanist whose career on the right was interrupted from 1969 by a prison sentence for sexual assaults on children. The Commando specialised in provoking violence at left-wing demonstrations. During the 1960s Norris also ran an organization called the Salvo Society and was involved with the Friends of Rhodesia group, the National Socialist Group and sections of the Monday Club.

Anti-Communist League: a small right-wing formation active around 1969.

Anti-Paki League: this name was used by racist gangs active in 1984, including one in Harlow (Essex) which was broken up by police after a series of attacks on Asian families.

Association of British People: a Birmingham-based anti-immigration group of the early 1970s, its leader, Broomhall, was later connected with the National Front.

Association of British Ex-Servicemen: formed around 1982 by Kenneth McKilliam, a leading member of the British National Party, the ABEX (whose name parodies that of a Jewish anti-fascist group) faded away after failing to fulfil its promise to supply a vigilante police force for Brixton, a black area of London.

Aurora Promotions: a nazi book distribution service run from Ipswich in 1984 by Steven Blake of the British National Party.

Battle Re-enactment Group: active around 1981, this group, which purported to act merely as a social forum for people interested in recreating Second World War battle scenes, had extreme right-wing members.

Birmingham National Club: a white supremacist pressure group of the 1950s. It may have been linked with the Birmingham Nationalist Book Club run at about the same time by Colin Jordan.

British Aid for the Repatriation of Immigrants: a racist pressure group formed around 1968 by individuals later associated with the National Front.

British Brothers' League: an early anti-semitic anti-immigration movement, it was active in London around the turn of the century.

British Campaign Against Immigration: the BCAI, also known as the British Campaign to Stop Immigration, was founded around 1971 by Bradford councillor Jim Merrick, on the basis of his Yorkshire Campaign to Stop Immigration, active since the late 1960s. It co-ordinated its activities with other right-wing anti-immigration groups in the early 1970s, and in 1975 Merrick joined the National Front.

British Democratic Party: the BDP was a breakaway faction of the National Front. It was formed around 1979 (as the British People's Party, soon renamed) and was led by Anthony Reed-Herbert, a solicitor. The 600-strong BDP collapsed in 1981 following a Granada Television exposure of its involvement in a gun-running conspiracy.

British Empire Union: an anti-socialist outgrowth of the Anti-German Union, which was founded in 1918. The BEU was loosely connected in the early 1930s with the National Citizens' Union led by Capt. A.H.M. Ramsey, a Conservative MP interned during the war, and with Mosley's British Union of Fascists.

British Fascisti: this 1920s-30s group, led by Brig.-Gen. R.B.D. Blakeney, was modelled on the Italian fascist movement, whereas Mosley and Leese looked primarily to the German model. It failed to establish a popular following. A similar group active oin the mid-1920s was the National Fascisti.

British Mercenary Force: a former Congo mercenary styling himself Maj. Douglas Lord claimed in 1968 to have set up a 170-strong group of British mercenaries willing to fight in Asia or Africa.

British Movement: the first right-wing group to use this name was probably that formed in April 1933 by Duncan Sandys and other members of the Conservative Party, to combat "socialism, defeatism and apathy".

British Movement: formed in 1968 by Colin Jordan as a successor to the National Socialist Movement, the BM had as its chairman Michael McLaughlin, who took over as leader in 1974. This overtly-nazi group was, together with the National Front (which it regarded as too moderate) and the League of St. George (with which it differed mainly on the Irish question), one of the three leading fascist groups in Britain in the 1970s. By 1980 it claimed to have 25 branches and a membership of 4,000. It published *British Patriot* (later *Phoenix*), as its monthly organ, and an internal bulletin, *British Tidings.*

The BM was often associated with violence, having its own paramilitary organization, the Leader Guard. Many of its members have criminal convictions; in January 1981 a member, Rod Roberts, was imprisoned for seven years for arson, arms offences and incitement to racial hatred, with six associates receiving lighter sentences. McLaughlin was imprisoned in 1979 and fined in 1983 for Race Relations Act offences; his predecessor, Jordan (who left the BM in 1976), has convictions for paramilitary activities and shoplifting. Two other members were imprisoned in 1986 for a 2,000,000 drug-smuggling plot.

In 1983-84, shortly after changing its name to the British National and Socialist Movement, the group was wound up by McLaughlin on the grounds that it had become an undisciplined rabble. A small number of members have attempted to reorganize the Movement, with little success. McLaughlin is now active in the survivalist movement (see Rucksack 'n' Rifle) and has continued to run the British Patriot Publications mail-order bookselling operation.

British National Party: a group of this name was formed during the Second World War and had as one of its leaders John Webster, who emigrated to become a leader of the Australian ultra-right.

Another BNP was founded in 1960 by an alliance of the League of Empire Loyalists, the White Defence League and the National Labour Party. Among its leaders were John Tyndall and Martin Webster, who formed the Spearhead paramilitary group, causing a split in the Party. It was led in the mid-1960s by John Bean and had as its organ *Combat*; Bean brought his group into the National Front, rejoining Tyndall and Martin Webster, in 1967.

Yet another BNP emerged briefly in the mid-1970s under the leadership of Eddy Morrison, whose varied career on the ultra-right has included spells in the British Movement and the National Front in the early 1970s; the leadership of the National Democratic Freedom Movement; another period in the National Front, and in Tyndall's New National Front and in the new BNP (of which he was youth leader until a conflict with Tyndall); and the leadership in 1982-83 of the Anti-Communism Movement and in 1983-86 of the National Action Party. Morrison's BNP was associated with the League of St. George and various US fascist groups in the World White Nationalist Congress, formed in 1976.

The current BNP, led by Tyndall, is covered in a main entry (above).

British National Youth: this unsuccessful group was formed in 1962 by Colin Jordan and led from 1964 by Brendan Willmer. It aimed to attract a wide range of right-wing youth and was initially sympathetic to national socialism, but by 1965 it had denounced fascism and was in turn denounced by the World Union of National Socialists. It was also known as the National Youth League (NYL). Willmer eventually emigrated to South Africa where he was involved in several racist groups.

British People's Party: a small pre-war ultra-right grouping.

British Union of Fascists and National Socialists: the BUF, as it was usually known (the second part of the name being a late addition), was the personal vehicle of Sir Oswald Mosley, who sat in parliament in the 1920s for the Conservative Party, the Labour Party and then his own New Party. In 1932 he founded the BUF, which with its black-shirted paramilitary groups gained a significant following, particularly in inner-city areas. The Fascists were involved in frequent street battles with Communist Party and other left-wing militants, notably in London and Oxford in 1936, and the Public Order Act then introduced forbade the use of political uniforms. The Union did not survive Mosley's wartime internment, although an unsuccessful successor organization, the British Union of Ex-Servicemen and Women, was created by Jeffrey Hamm, Mosley's secretary, in 1946. Mosley's Union Movement was created in 1948; from 1951 onwards he spent most of his time abroad, although in the late 1950s he returned briefly to head the Union Movement's unsuccessful fascist electoral initiative; he returned to France after losing his deposit in a parliamentary by-election. His followers were subsequently led by Jeffrey Hamm. The Union Movement remained in existence until the late 1970s (despite a split around 1982, leading to the formation of the League of St. George). It was succeeded by the Action Society, still led by Hamm.

Britons Publishing Company: one of the longest-lasting operations of the racist right, this company, founded before the war as part of the Britons Society (formed in 1918 by Dr John H. Clarke), continued to distribute anti-semitic tracts and similar material until the 1960s.

Clarendon Club: a social and political forum which bridged the short distance between ultra-right Conservatives and neo-fascists, the Club staged meetings in 1979-81 which were attended by, inter alios, David Irving and associates of the League of St. George, the British Movement, Column 88 and the National Front.

Column 88: this nazi paramilitary group, which is generally thought to have taken its name from the fact that the letter H is eighth in the alphabet (HH standing for Heil Hitler), was formed in 1970 by ex-members of the National Socialist Movement, and operated clandestinely until the early 1980s. A number of letter-bomb attacks were attributed to the group, which held several training camps for its members. Its leading members included Les Vaughan, Donald Mudie, Peter Ling, also active in the Northern League (see Netherlands), and Ian Souter Clarence, who also formed similar groups called the Viking Commando and Edelweiss. The group was in contact with several foreign nazi organizations, and was particularly close to the Belgian VMO.

Eldon League: a right-wing Conservative Party ginger group of the 1970s.

English Legion: a short-lived fascist group formed around 1944 by John Webster (see BNP).

English People's Liberation Army: this right-wing guerrilla group sent a bomb, which was defused before it could explode, to the Campaign for Nuclear Disarmament in March 1983.

Essential Books: a fascist bookselling operation run from Taunton by John Webster around 1945.

Five Thousand Group: this obscure right-wing organization, also known as the 5,000 Group, was run in Essex by Vic Norris, a nazi satanist with convictions for child molesting, in the late 1960s.

Freedom Group: an anti-trade union campaign formed in the 1950s by Edward Martell, it produced a newspaper, *The New Daily*, on its own presses. It went bankrupt in the 1960s but Martell reappeared in the 1970s in the very similar Self Help Organization.

Friends of Rhodesia: a pressure group of the 1960s and '70s, formed to support the rebel Smith government and including among its membership several agents of that regime.

Greater Britain Movement: the Movement was founded by John Tyndall and Martin Webster in 1964 after they had left Colin Jordan's National Socialist Movement. Seeking to disguise its nazi orientation, it had no contact with the World Union of National Socialists of which Jordan remained European commander. In 1967 the GBM joined the National Front. The Movement was connected with the National Student Front and the Patriotic Party, but not with the Greater Britain Campaign, a fascist pressure group of the 1960s run by Roger Gleaves (also known as the "Bishop of Medway").

Immigration Control Association: the ICA was founded in the early 1970s by Joy Page, and was linked with the Conservative Party (through the Monday Club's Halt Immigration Now Campaign) and with fascist groups such as the National Front and the British Campaign to Stop Immigration. The ICA has effectively been merged into the WISE, in which Page has been a prominent activist.

Imperial Fascist League: the League's leader, Arnold Leese, regarded Mosley's larger British Union of Fascists as insufficiently radical. He set up the League in 1928 and espoused openly anti-semitic policies. He was interned for most of the war but on his release he published a regular anti-semitic bulletin, *Gothic Ripples*, many of whose subscribers led the next generation of fascist parties. Among other leading members of the League was Oliver Gilbert, later a member of the National Front. In the early

1980s Colin Jordan, ex-leader of the National Socialist movement and a close associate of Leese in the immediate postwar period revived *Gothic Ripples* as his personal publication.

Institute of National Studies: a short-lived organization founded around 1984 by Paul Kingsley (see Friends of British Ulster) and John Henden, the Institute published a journal entitled *National Consciousness*, which sought to give an intellectual perspective on "radical, democratic" nationalism. It was associated with a Wessex Study Group.

Integralists: an authoritarian and anti-communist grouping formed around 1970 by White Russian refugee G. Knupfer.

Kent Heritage Group: a cover name used in the mid-1980s by Kent supporters of the National Front.

Ku Klux Klan: several attempts were made in 1964-65 and in the 1970s to organize a British branch of one or other of the US Klan factions.

Law and Order Society: a right-wing Conservative group of the 1970s which campaigned to bring back capital punishment, its leaders included Lady Birdwood (see Self Help Organization) and Peter Bruinvels (a Conservative MP until 1987), who resigned as chairman in mid-1985.

League of Empire Loyalists: this ultra-right group, founded in 1954, was led by A.K. Chesterton, a former Mosleyite activist. It specialized in disrupting Conservative Party events in order to protest against the dismantling of the British Empire by the granting of independence to colonies. The League was incorporated into the National Front in 1967.

The Liberators: in April 1933 a Conservative MP, Edward Doran, announced that he had established a nazi private army under this name. The army was supposedly training secretly in ten English centres and in Belfast; a Parliamentary Liberators Group claimed 40 members. Doran hosted a visit to Britain by a German Nazi Party representative. In May 1933 the North Tottenham Conservative Association expelled Doran.

The Link: a pro-Hitler grouping established in 1937, it was led by Admiral Sir Barry Domville.

National Democratic Freedom Movement: an ineffective fascist party of the 1970s, it was led by Eddy Morrison, later associated with the National Action Party and similar groups, and two nazi satanists, Joe Short and Dave Myatt.

National Democratic Party: the anti-immigration NDP was formed in 1963 by Dr David Browne, and was joined around 1969 by John O'Brien, ex-leader of the Powell for Premier campaign and the British Defence League. O'Brien and most of the membership later joined the National Front, of which he was chairman in 1970-72. The NDP continued in existence, and it has been reported that one of its leading members in 1971 was Piers Merchant, who became a Conservative MP in 1983.

National Front Movement: a small grouping led in 1958 by Andrew Fountaine, later to hold important posts in the British National Party of the 1960s and in the National Front of the 1970s.

National Front Constitutional Movement: the NFCM was founded by Andrew Fountaine in 1979, partly as a result of a dispute over control of a National Front office building. It later changed its name to Constitutional Movement, and eventually to Nationalist Party, before dying out around 1984. The organization's journal was called *Excalibur*. Most of its members rejoined either the NF or the Conservative Party.

National Independence Party: an unimportant grouping led around 1970 by John Davis, and by the late John O'Brien after his departure in 1972 from the National Front leadership. An associated organization was called the Political Independence Movement.

National Labour Party: the NLP was formed in 1958 by John Bean (an ex-member of the League of Empire Loyalists) and Andrew Fountaine. In 1960 it merged with

Jordan's White Defence League to form the British National Party. An identically-named party was active in Ashford (Kent) around 1981.

National Party: a split in the National Front in 1975-76 led to the formation in January 1976 of the NP (or NPUK), which adopted many of the Front's authoritarian and racist policies, proposing in particular the "repatriation" of blacks, while repudiating the outright nazism with which many Front leaders were associated. Among the better-known members of the NP were Richard Lawson, Dave McCalden and Roy Painter. The leader of the Party, John Kingsley Read, later left ultra-right politics and the party ceased to exist in the early 1980s. The Party's merchandising arm traded as Raven Books and its journal was *Britain First.*

National Party of St George: a tiny group based in Reading (Berkshire) around 1970, it eventually merged with the local National Front branch.

National Reorganization Party: the NRP, which published *North Star* magazine, was a late-1970s group based in London and led by Ian Millard.

National Socialist Group: this small paramilitary organization was formed by Dave Courtney and the Olliffe brothers in the late 1960s. It was closely associated with Colin Jordan's nazi British Movement. The NSG was destroyed by several arms convictions but Courtney was still active in the far right in the early 1980s, through a nazi journal called *Loki.*

National Socialist League: a small and ineffective Hitlerite party active from 1937 until its suppression in 1939.

National Socialist Movement: the NSM was an openly-nazi party founded in 1962 by Colin Jordan and other dissident members of the British National Party. Two of its leading members, Martin Webster and John Tyndall, went on to form the Greater Britain Movement and to join the National Front (established in 1967). A paramilitary group associated first with the BNP and subsequently with the NSM, and known as Spearhead, was broken up in the mid-1960s.

Jordan was responsible for the foundation of the World Union of National Socialists (see Denmark and United States) in 1962, and he was commander of its European section throughout the 1960s. In 1968 the NSM became the British Movement. Jordan disappeared from the public eye for some years in the 1970s, but he has re-emerged as editor of *Gothic Ripples,* a newsletter modelled on the fiercely anti-semitic bulletin produced from the late 1940s by Arnold Leese (see Imperial Fascist League).

National Socialist Party: possibly the first use of the term "national socialist" was in the name of this organization, founded in Britain in 1916 by anti-semitic socialist H. Hyndman.

National Socialist Workers' Initiative: the NSWI, established in 1982 and disbanded within months, involved a number of nazi activists, mainly from the League of St. George and including Tony Williams, synagogue arsonist David Thorne, the late Ian Kerr-Ritchie, Tony Malski and Bill Whitbread.

National Student Front: a small nazi organization of the early 1960s, the NSF, led by James McIntyre, produced *New Nation* in support of the National Socialist Movement (and later the Greater Britain Movement). McIntyre was later involved with the League of St George and the NF.

Nationalist Assembly: this umbrella grouping, also known as the National Assembly or Nationalist Alliance, was run by Mary Stanton in 1974-76. Its members included anti-immigration activists such as Joan Mason (see WISE) and outright fascists such as Kenneth McKilliam (see BNP). In 1977 the Assembly became the Anti-Communism Movement.

Nationalist Party: the name adopted around 1982-83 by the remnants of the Constitutional Movement (formerly the National Front Constitutional Movement). It continued to produce the NFCM publication, *Excalibur.*

New Britain Party: a small ultra-conservative party formed in the 1970s and led by Dennis Delderfield, its supporters have included Don Bennett (see British League of Rights), General Sir Walter Walker (see Unison) and a retired bishop, Cyril Eastaugh. In 1980 New Britain absorbed two smaller right-wing groups, the United Country Party (led by television astronomer Patrick Moore) and the Keep Britain United Party. All three parties have contested parliamentary elections, with a notable lack of success, on manifestos calling for capital punishment, nationalism and British withdrawal from the European Economic Community.

New National Front: see British National Party (current version).

New Party: the precursor of the British Union of Fascists, the New Party was founded by Sir Oswald Mosley in March 1931. It presented 24 candidates in the October 1931 general election, gaining 36,000 votes (out of 21,000,000) and no seats.

Powellight: Enoch Powell, then a Conservative MP (and later an Ulster Unionist MP until 1987), gained considerable publicity in the 1960s and 1970s for his predictions of the collapse of public order and the British way of life under the pressure of black immigration. Powellight, a 600-strong anti-immigration pressure group, was formed by Bee Carthew and others specifically to promote Powell's views among Conservatives. A leading member, John Gadd, was imprisoned for ten years for running guns to the Ulster Defence Association. Powellight faded away in the early 1970s. Carthew is currently active in the Conservative Party and WISE.

Racial Preservation Society: the RPS was an anti-immigration pressure group, founded by Jimmy Doyle and Robin Beauclaire of Brighton, which included many Conservative activists. Five of its members were prosecuted in the Lewes trial of 1968 for breaches of the Race Relations Act. In 1967 the RPS united with other groups to form the National Front.

Right Club: this small pro-nazi organization was infiltrated and suppressed by the security service on the outbreak of the Second World War. Its leader, Anna Wolkoff, was imprisoned after a secret trial in 1940.

Spearhead: this nazi paramilitary organization was run in the early 1960s as an elite group within the British National Party, and later in the National Socialist Movement, by Colin Jordan and also by John Tyndall and Martin Webster, who went on to lead the National Front in the 1970s and early 1980s (both having since been expelled—see Our Nation and the current British National Party). Jordan, Tyndall and others were imprisoned briefly in 1962 for organizing Spearhead. The group was broken up by the police and anti-fascist infiltrators in the mid-1960s, with 13 members or supporters including Françoise Dior (see France) receiving convictions for synagogue burnings and other crimes.

The name of the group reappeared as the title of Tyndall's journal, which is published by him in support of whichever party he belongs to at a given time.

SS Wotan 71: little evidence has emerged to suggest that this group, which claimed to be an armed underground nazi cell, had any real existence. It produced a number of fearsome documents in 1976 and 1977 suggesting that it was preparing for a terrorist campaign against left-wingers and minorities, and also used the names SS Wotan 18, Adolf Hitler Commando, Iron Guard and Knights of the Iron Cross. Reports have named David Wilson and Michael Noonan (formerly of the British Movement) as its organizers; an alleged member, also from the British Movement, killed himself early in 1987. The organ of the group was *Adler und Kreuz* (Eagle and Cross).

Standing Committee Against Immigration: this co-ordinating body was set up by the Monday Club in the early 1970s and included representatives of the British Campaign to Stop Immigration, the Immigration Control Association and other groups.

Stormer: this extremely racist comic-strip magazine, aimed mainly at children, was produced by a group of London fascists in the early 1980s. Its title was borrowed from Julius Streicher's *Die Stürmer*, produced in Germany in the 1930s. Bob Edwards, one of its contributors, was imprisoned in 1983 for inciting racial hatred.

Swinton Circle: this London group held several meetings of right-wing Tories and neo-fascists in the early 1980s, with a view to co-ordinating anti-immigration campaigns.

TRU-AIM: Trade Unionists Against Immigration, better known by its acronym, was a 1970s white supremacist group which functioned essentially as a National Front subsidiary.

Union Movement: this post-war Mosleyite organization, now superseded by the Action Society, suffered a split in 1974 leading to the creation of the League of St. George. The Movement, which was founded in 1948 (see under British Union of Fascists above) but only achieved prominence at the time of the 1958 race riots, was led by Jeffrey Hamm, formerly Mosley's secretary. It promoted European unity and eschewed nazi and anti-semitic terminology.

Unison: Gen. Sir Walter Walker, a former Commander of NATO forces, retired in the early 1970s and in 1975 announced the establishment of a right-wing private army designed to break strikes and to prepare resistance to a leftist revolution. Little was heard of the group, variously known as Civil Assistance or Unison, or of the general in later years. He attended the 1983 conference of the World Anti-Communist League.

White Defence League: a racist grouping established by Colin Jordan in 1958, the WDL was based at Arnold Leese House, a London building bequeathed by and named in honour of one of Britain's most active nazis. The WDL was active at the time of the London and Nottingham race riots in 1958.

White Nationalist Crusade: a failed attempt of 1981 to create a broad front of racist organizations. Among those involved in the Crusade was Robert Relf, who had achieved considerable publicity in 1976 by advertising his home as for sale "to an English family only". (Relf had previously been active in various nazi and Ku Klux Klan groups, and in 1982 he attempted to set up a White Power Movement.)

Other organizations

Among other right-wing organizations which have been active in Britain in the past 20 years or so are the following, many of which may now be defunct: the Academic Council for Peace and Freedom, a pro-nuclear lobby whose members include Roger Scruton; the Action Committee; the Action Front for National Priorities; Action on Repatriation; the Action Party; the Adam Smith Institute, a right-wing Conservative "think tank" headed by Peter Young; the Adolf Hitler Commando; the Adolf Hitler League; Aims of Industry (40 Doughty Street, London WC1), also known (1978-80) as Aims and (1975-78) as Aims for Freedom and Enterprise, a right-wing business pressure group founded in 1942 and currently led by Michael Ivens; Albion Press; the probably-defunct Anglo-Rhodesian Society; the Anglo-Saxon Church of Wodan; the Anti-Communism or Anti-Communist League; Oliver Smedley's Anti-Dear Food Campaign; the Antidote Group; the Anti-Immigration Co-ordinating Committee or Standing Committee, a Birdwood front (32a Anselm Road, London SW6); the Leicester-based Anti-Immigration Movement; the Argus British Rights Association, founded in the mid-1960s; the Association of Self-Employed People; Beacon Books; the Birmingham Immigration Control Association; Kenneth McKilliam's anti-semitic Board of Anglo-Saxon Celtic Deputies (PO Box 112, London N22); British Aid for the Repatriation of Immigrants; the British Anti-Common Market Campaign; the pro-Pinochet British Chilean Council; the British Council of Patriots; the British Cultural Group; the British Free Corps; British Heritage; the late-'70s British Independence (or Independent) Movement; the British Non-Immigration Protection Society; the British Patrials Association; British Resistance; British United Industrialists, a conservative group (which in 1978 funded the establishment of the Adam Smith Institute); the British United Party (6 Chudleigh Road, London SE4); the British War Dead League; Britons Against Immigration; the Britons Society, a British Movement offshoot which has revived the name of a minor pre-war fascist group (9 Bank Grove, Little Hutton, Worsley, Lancashire); M. Powell's NF-derived Brittania Party (72 Fountain Street, Birkenhead, Merseyside; or 10 Greenways, Stevenage, Hertfordshire).

The Camberley Group, a secret right-wing faction of the Monday Club; the Campaign against Racial Integration; the Campaign to Free Rudolf Hess; the Campaign for the Return of Capital Punishment, or Recap, one of whose organizers (Neil Lynn) is a former British Movement officer; the Campaign against Revolutionary Violence, an offshoot of Aims of Industry; the Carlton Club; the Catholic Affirmation Campaign, and the related Christian Affirmation Campaign; Causa UK, an anti-communist Unification Church front; the right-wing Conservative Centre for Policy Studies; Chatham Publishing Co.; Ronald King's Christian Centre Party (157 Vicarage Road, London E10 5DV); the Christian League of Southern Africa, a pro-apartheid pressure group targetting churchmen (Box 8959, London WC1V 6XX); the Citizens' Protection Group; Club 88; the Club of 92, a social and political forum for some 70 right-wing Conservative Party MPs; *Co-existence* magazine; the Committee for Nationalist Unity; Common Cause, which seeks to monitor left-wing subversion, and its associated companies and charitable foundation; the Common Market Safeguards Campaign; the Commonwealth Party; the Community for Mutual Aid; elements of the Cornish Nationalist Party and its Greenshirt Youth Movement; the Council of Nationalist Action Groups; Counterblast Films; Covenant Publishing Co., Covenant Books and *The Covenant Message*, all parts of the British Israel movement; the Crime Defence Group; the Crusaders Movement; Current Affairs Press; the Democratic Association; the Newcastle-based Democratic Movement of the early 1970s; Destiny publishing company; *Dreadnought* magazine (Uxbridge), edited by Young Monday Club member Stuart Northolt; the NF-linked East Anglia Forum, and the similar Sussex Forum; Economic Democracy; *Edinburgh Flame* magazine; *Ego* magazine (19 St. Stephen's Gardens, London W2 5QU); the possibly spurious Eleventh Hour Brigade, reportedly a nazi guerrilla group; the English Nationalist Alliance, a late-1970s SS Wotan cover; the English Rights Association, a racist housing action group of the late 1960s; the Enoch Powell is Right group; the European Remembrance and Reconciliation Association.

Fair Play, a white residents' group led by Ralph Harrison and Lady Birdwood; Far and Wide Publishers Ltd, linked with the Freedom Association; the Fascist League; the libertarian Free Society; the Free Speech Defence Campaign; Freedom Blue Cross, a little-known grouping which reportedly sought to assist "nationalist" prisoners and their dependants; the Freedom Leadership Foundation; the Freedom Party; the Friends of Great Britain; the social creditist Future Studies Centre; *Gothic Ripples*, published by Colin Jordan (Thorgarth, Greenhow Hill, Harrogate, North Yorkshire HG3 5JQ); Group 7, linked to Tony Malski's NSAP (Anglesey Road, Oxhey, Watford); Hatchford Films; Heritage Press; the anti-immigration Housewives of Greater Manchester; the Institute for European Defence and Strategic Studies (13-14 Golden Square, London W1), headed by Gerald Frost and partly funded by the Heritage Foundation (United States); the Keep Britain United Party; the Keep London Free Campaign; the Kempler Ring, an obscure mid-'70s group which allegedly sought to infiltrate and disrupt the left; the League for European Freedom; the League of Venturers; the London and Home Counties Tenants' Association (or Federation), run by Joy Page; the London Residents' Association; *Middle East and Mediterranean Outlook* (or *Memo*), an idiosyncratic right-wing news bulletin; the Militant Nationalist Alliance; the Monarchist League; an obscure Kent-based National Alliance; the National Assembly of Anti-Common Market Associations; the National Association of Ratepayers' Action Groups; the National European Party; the National Federation of the Self-Employed; the National People's Party; the National Socialist Co-ordination Group; the National Socialist Liberation Front; the National Socialist Organization; the Moore faction, formed around 1980, of the National Socialist Party of the United Kingdom (NSPUK); the National Youth Movement, part of the British Movement; the Nationalist Centre; Nationalists Against Homosexuality, a phantom anti-Webster grouping within the National Front; the New Centre Party; the New English Klan; the New Liberal Party; Noontide Press; the North European Ring, possibly the same as the Nordic European Ring; the Nuclear Defence League.

John Yeowell's Odinist Committee (10 Trinity Green, London E1), publishing *Raven Banner* and linked with the League of St. George; the Patriotic Party; a British Movement splinter group, the Patriotic Right, founded in 1980 by N. Lewis; Pentacle Books, run by C. Gordon Tether; the Personal Rights Association, publishing *The Individualist*; the Policy Research Associates, a right-wing Conservative think-tank headed by Julian Lewis and linked to the Coalition for Peace through Security; The Quartermaster, a London shop supplying nazi and paramilitary equipment; Radio Enoch; the Ringwood and District Anti-Common Market Group; the Safeguard Britain Campaign; the St Hugh of Lincoln Society 1255; Sanctuary Press, part of the post-war Mosleyite movement; the social-creditist Scottish Monetary Reform Society; the Scottish Rhodesia Society; the Selsdon Group of right-wing Conservative MPs; the Social Affairs Unit; the Social Credit Centre (10 Midhope Way, Filey, North Yorkshire TO14 0DK), and its offshoots including the Christian Council for Monetary Justice and the National Campaign against Inflation; the Social Credit Movement; *Social Crediter* magazine (KRP Publications Ltd, 26 Meadow Lane, Sudbury, Suffolk CO10 6TD), edited by H.A. Scoular; a right-wing Social Democratic Movement predating the mainstream Social Democratic Party; the libertarian Society for Individual Freedom (55 Park Lane, London W14 4LB); the Sons of St George; the NF-linked Southall Residents' Association; *Soviet Analyst*, an anti-communist newsletter produced by Brian Crozier, Robert Conquest and others; the Strays Sanctuary, possibly linked with the mysterious SS Wotan group; Sunwheel Distributors, run by League of St. George member Keith Thompson (Foundation House, 26 Glade Road, Marlow, Buckinghamshire); an NF-linked Sussex Front, active around 1980.

Francis Forsyth's Teutonic Loyalty group; the Thor Guard; the Thule Society; Top Stone Books, part of the British Israel movement; the Torbay Anti-Common Market League; the right-wing conservative Trident Group, formed in the 1970s; Unit Nine; the United Britons' Party; the United National Party; the United Party; the United Reform Party; the Vigilante Immigration Control Association, based in Birmingham; Viking Books; the Viking Cultural Society; the nazi Viking Youth, linked to the German *Wiking-Jugend* and organized in Britain by Paul Jarvis (who has published *Young Folk*, *Viking Youth* and *Viking News* from BCM Thule, London WC1V 6XX); the NF-controlled Waltham Forest Residents' Association; Waterloo Press; the West Country Anti-Common Market League; Western Destiny Publications; the White Defence Committee; the violent Croydon-based White Defence Force (WDF), which emerged in 1982; White Enterprises (PO Box 192, Manor Park, London E12), distributors of racist material; the little-known survivalist White Man's Society; Women against the Common Market; and the Xcentric Club.

Individuals

David Irving: possibly the best known of the British revisionist historians, Irving has written a number of books on various aspects of the Second World War. In June 1984 he was expelled from Austria while giving a lecture tour in which, inter alia, he was maintaining that Hitler's imprisoned deputy, Rudolf Hess, ought to be awarded the Nobel Peace Prize. Irving has been associated with the neo-nazi *Deutsche Volks Unie* (DVU— West Germany) and with the Committee for Truth in History (Austria). Irving has since the late 1970s been attempting to create a broad-based right-wing movement based on his Focus Policy Group and its (defunct) journal, *Focal Point*. He is perhaps best known for claiming that Hitler was ignorant as to the nature of the Final Solution, and for having in 1983 authenticated the so-called Hitler Diaries.

Col. (retd.) David Stirling: a founder of the elite Special Air Service regiment, he has supported a variety of non-fascist right-wing causes and established a putative strike-breakining militia, GB 75 (which merged in the mid-'70s with a similar grouping, True-Mid). In 1986 he was present at the European launch of Lyndon LaRouche's *Executive Intelligence Review* (see United States).

Count Nicolai Tolstoy: a right-wing historian who has alleged that the former Conservative Prime Minister, Harold Macmillan, had been guilty of war crimes in handling the 1945 repatriation of Cossack and Croat prisoners. Support for this allegation in 1986 from the right-dominated Federation of Conservative Students led to a public dispute between the FCS and the senior party leadership.

Northern Ireland

capital: Belfast   **population: 1,600,000**

Political system. Northern Ireland came into existence in 1921 as a semi-autonomous province of the United Kingdom covering that portion of Ireland where a majority of the population wished to remain under British rule. At the time of writing (1987) Northern Ireland is governed directly from London; it is represented in the UK House of Commons by 17 directly-elected members MPs.

Recent history. The region has never enjoyed political or economic stability, due mainly to the existence of a substantial minority population which seeks to reunite it with the rest of Ireland, which now constitutes the Irish Republic. The latest in a series of revolts by sections of the (Catholic, nationalist or republican) minority began with a civil rights movement in 1968, and violent clashes involving security forces as well as members of the majority (Protestant, unionist or loyalist) population. Paramilitary organizations sought to promote or oppose the cause of Irish reunification; moreover, with the increasing involvement of the police (the Royal Ulster Constabulary) and then, from 1969, of the British Army, it was common among republicans in the minority community to identify as Protestant militias such units as the "B-Special" auxiliary police, disbanded in April 1970, and the part-time Ulster Defence Regiment (UDR), which become operational in the same month with a local support role under the Army command.

The evolution of the far right. Some sections of the Loyalist movement in the early part of the present century, particularly the Ulster Volunteer movement, have sometimes been described as precursors of the British fascist movement. Right-wing organizations have tended to operate almost exclusively in the majority community and left-wing organizations among the minority. Pre-war British fascist movements, including the British Fascisti, the Liberators and the British Union of Fascists (BUF), had small sections in Northern Ireland.

The London-based National Front has operated in the province since the 1970s, both independently and through its contact, at community rather than leadership level, with some native groups including the Democratic Unionist Party (DUP) and the Ulster Defence Association (UDA). Indigenous groups which fall within the scope of this book because of their anti-communism or other far-right positions include Tara (a Protestant paramilitary group).

John Taylor, an Official Unionist Party (OUP) member of the European Parliament, has since January 1987 sat with the fascist "Group of the European Right" in the Parliament, thereby allying himself with the Italian MSI, the French FN and the Greek EPEN.

Active organizations

Friends of British Ulster

Address. BM Box 9249, London WC1N 3XX

Leadership. Paul Kingsley

Orientation. Ultra-loyalist

History. This organization, the name of which has also been erroneously reported as British Friends of Ulster, was formed by British supporters of the loyalist cause in late 1985. Kingsley, a full-time officer of the British trade union NALGO, was previously a prominent member of the National Front and, after 1975, of the National Party. The group appears to have most of its support among the Scottish Protestant population. Leading members include ex-NF officer Rev. Brian Green, a London-based associate of Ian Paisley MP.

Policies. At the time of writing the Friends were mainly concerned with offering the maximum resistance to the implementation of the Anglo-Irish agreements of 1985, which gave the government of the Irish Republic a limited advisory role in respect of the administration of Northern Ireland.

Publications. *British Free Press* (Kingsley's personal publication, now probably defunct).

Associated organizations. The publication of the group has carried advertising for a number of racist and ultra-right organizations based in Britain. A demonstration which it organized in Glasgow in 1987 was attended by Harold McCusker MP, a leading member of the Official Unionist Party, and by Peter Robinson MP, deputy leader of the DUP.

Protestant Unionist Party (PUP)

Leadership. George Seawright (leader)

Orientation. Right-wing Loyalist

History. Seawright, then a local councillor representing the DUP and leader of the Portadown-based Ulster Protestant League (UPL), was imprisoned in 1986 for advocating inter alia the incineration of Roman Catholics. On his release he formed the PUP, reviving the name used in 1969-71 by what is now the DUP. Seawright's wife, who contested the council seat vacated on his imprisonment, became the party's first elected representative in January 1987.

Policies. The PUP stands for uncompromising opposition to Irish Republicanism and to the influence of the Roman Catholic Church in Irish and world affairs. Seawright has supported bombing attacks on the Irish Republic.

Associated organizations. Seawright is regarded as sympathetic to Loyalist guerrilla groups including the Ulster Freedom Fighters (linked to the UDA) and the Ulster Volunteer Force. He also has personal and family associations with the National Front.

Tara

Orientation. Right-wing Protestant guerrilla group

History. This organization was founded in the mid-1960s as an anti-communist and anti-Catholic pressure group. It adopted paramilitary tactics by the end of the decade. A former deputy commander of Tara, Roy Garland, said in 1982 that its current commander was William McGrath who in 1981 had been imprisoned for indecently assaulting children while he was manager of the Kincora boys' home. After a period of silence the group re-emerged in 1986, when it threatened what it called "republican" businesses operating in loyalist areas.

Policies. Tara has described itself as "the hard core of Protestant resistance".

Associated organizations. The membership of Tara is reportedly drawn from the Orange Order, with which McGrath has had strong links, although there is no formal connection between the two bodies.

Ulster National Front (NF)

Address. PO Box 40, Belfast BT7 1LY

Leadership. Nick Griffin (UK chairman); John Field (Northern Ireland organizer)

Orientation. Ultra-right

History. The London-based National Front has attempted several times to organize within Northern Ireland. In addition, vociferous support for the resistance of the Northern Ireland Protestants to what it portrays as communist-inspired subversion has been made a central element of NF propaganda in what unionists call "the mainland", i.e. Britain. In 1971-75 the NF organizer in Belfast was Billy Annett, formerly of the (British) National Socialist Group. The party experienced rapid growth in 1974-75 but failed to maintain its momentum into the later 1970s, largely due to splits in the British party.

Some National Front members have been involved in gun-running or other conspiracies to support or supply the UDA through the latter's British branches. In April 1986 the NF's Northern Ireland treasurer, Andrew McLorie, was imprisoned for petrol-bombing the home of a member of the Royal Ulster Constabulary. In July 1986 it was reported in London that Griffin and Field had participated in the takeover by the DUP of Hillsborough, a village in Co. Down which was the focus of loyalist opposition to an inter-governmental accord signed there by the British and Irish Prime Ministers. Peter Robinson, deputy leader of the DUP, denied any knowledge of NF involvement.

In 1986-87 there were reports that the breakaway NF Support Group had won the support of a large section of the Front's Northern Irish membership, including that of the largest branch, at Coleraine.

Policies. The NF's general policies are described in the main UK section above. Of specific importance in the Northern Ireland context are its advocacy of the death penalty for a range of offences including "terrorism" and its support for the union of Great Britain and Northern Ireland.

Activities. The NF has organized some meetings of its own in Northern Ireland, mainly in the eastern counties, but its banners are most frequently seen on cross-party loyalist demonstrations. Many of its skinhead paper-sellers can be seen in the centres of towns such as Belfast and Portadown at weekends.

Publications. Ulster Front Page, irregular.

Ulster Sentinel

Address. PO Box 3, Newtownabbey, Co. Antrim BT37 9ER

Leadership. David Kerr

Orientation. Fascist

History. This magazine has been published since 1976 by Kerr (under the pseudonym of K.B. White), who has been associated with the North Belfast Independent Unionist Association and the DUP.

Policies. The magazine carries articles sympathetic to loyalism, white supremacism and anti-semitism.

Associated organizations. Kerr trades as US Publications. He has written for National Front publications and has been a member of the League of St. George, a British umbrella group for fascist sympathisers.

International affiliations. The magazine has carried exchange advertising for many foreign fascist groups, inclunding CEDADE (Spain), *Balder* and *National-Provence* (France), Amajuba (Netherlands), National Vanguard, Knights of the Ku Klux Klan, John Birch Society and *Richard Cotten's Conservative Viewpoint* (United States), Dolphin Press (South Africa) and a number of affiliates of the World Union of National Socialists (see Denmark and United States).

Defunct organizations

British Fascisti: the first president of this British-based group, formed in 1923, was the Irish peer Lord Garvagh. He resigned in 1924. The group had few other members in Northern Ireland. Another Irish peer, the seventh Marquess of Londonderry, was one of the leading pro-German figures in British society in the late 1930s.

Down Orange Welfare: the formation of this anti-communist private army was reported in the early 1970s. Its commander, Lt.-Col. E.J.A.H. Brush, CBE, of Moira, Co. Down, disappeared from public life after the group failed to gain popular support.

East Antrim Loyalist Front: founded in 1972 by a group closely associated with the UVF, the EALF contacted the British NF in 1973 and held inconclusive talks on amalgamation. It faded away shortly afterwards.

Empirical Publications: this organization, whose address was that of a Lisburn boutique, distributed fascist and racist literature for about two years in the mid-1970s.

Ulster Constitution Party: founded around 1971 by Lindsay Mason, this group effectively merged with the NF when that party expanded its Northern Irish organization in 1974.

Ulster Fascist Movement: this affiliate of Oswald Mosley's British Union of Fascists (see main UK section) was established in Belfast in September 1933. The movement advocated the unification of Ireland as a dominion within a British Empire of fascist nations, and expressed qualified support for the Blueshirt movement in the Irish Free State. W.E.D. Allen, formerly a Conservative member of parliament for Belfast, became one of Mosley's chief lieutenants in the New Party in 1931, and later in the BUF.

Other organizations

Other loyalist organizations which are sometimes regarded as belonging to the radical right include the Orange Order (a Protestant fraternity similar to freemasonry and traditionally linked with the main unionist party), and similar smaller groupings, namely the Apprentice Boys of Derry, the Imperial Purple Institution, the Independent Orange Order and the Royal Black Preceptory.

Both of the principal unionist parties—the Official Unionist Party (OUP), which is regarded as middle-class, and the working-class Democratic Unionist Party—have right-wing fringes. Enoch Powell, a former British Conservative MP associated with the growth of anti-immigrant movements in the 1970s, represented the OUP at Westminster between 1974 and 1987, while several DUP leaders, including party leader Ian Paisley, have reportedly had contacts with the NF.

Protestant paramilitary groups have included the defunct Ulster Special Constabulary Association, Ulster Service Corps and Third Force militias and Protestant Action Force and Ulster Protestant Action Group death squads. Currently-active groups include the Ulster Defence Association (UDA), which is legal, and illegal groups such as the Ulster Freedom Fighters (affiliated to the UDA), the Ulster Volunteer Force (UVF), and the Red Hand Commandos (affiliated to the UVF). The UDA in particular has had extensive contact with the National Front and other British fascist groups; there is a considerable overlap in membership between the British sections of the UDA and the NF, despite statements from the current UDA leadership repudiating fascism. Two Liverpool UDA members—Tommy Thompson, its British leader, and John Gadd—were imprisoned for gun-running in 1975; both had been members of the NF and Gadd was also in Powellight, a defunct racist group. An Edinburgh UDA man gaoled some months later on arms charges was also linked with the NF, as was a Glasgow man, Andrew Robertson, imprisoned on similar charges in 1987. The UVF journal, *Combat*, carried occasional pieces from NF writers in the mid-1970s. There have been persistent reports of co-operation, in arms buying and training, between Ulster loyalist paramilitaries and continental fascist groups such as the Belgian VMO.

Republican groups are rarely regarded as right-wing, despite their nationalist ideologies; the main guerrilla organization, the Provisional Irish Republican Army (IRA), described itself to Irish-Americans in the early 1970s as a "bulwark against communism", but in the course of the 1970s and early 1980s it adopted a socialist ideology.

The Christian Mission to the Communist World (CMCW), a British-based group, has a following among evangelical churches in Northern Ireland and has a Belfast office (119 Marlborough Park South, BT9 6HW; tel. 666267).

Hong Kong

capital: Victoria   **population: 5,700,000**

Political system. The Territory of Hong Kong is administered by the United Kingdom under a lease from China. A Governor appointed by the UK government chooses and heads an Executive Council and a Legislative Council.

Recent history. Apart from the Japanese occupation of 1941-45, Hong Kong has been a British possession since 1842. Its flourishing economy depends in part on low-wage export-oriented manufacturing industries, concentrating in recent years in the high-technology sector, and partly on its importance as a free port and entrepôt for trade with China. It was agreed in 1984 that ownership would revert to China in 1997, although certain concessions were made concerning internal autonomy, the continuation for 50 years of the capitalist economy, and other matters.

The evolution of the far right. The free-market capitalism of Hong Kong has given rise to numerous anti-communist movements, some of which are especially active among immigrants from communist China. The Kuomintang Party (see Taiwan) has many Hong Kong members, and there is a chapter of the World Anti-Communist League (see South Korea) which donated US$10,000 to help stage the 1985 WACL congress in the United States.

United States of America

capital: Washington, DC   population: 238,000,000

Political system. The USA is a federal entity comprising 50 states, each with considerable autonomy, and a capital district. The executive branch of the federal government is led by a President, chosen by an electoral college elected directly for this purpose. The federal government involves a separation of powers between the executive branch, the legislative branch (Congress, which consists of a 100-seat Senate and a 435-seat House of Representatives) and the judicial branch (headed by the Supreme Court). The term of office for the President is four years, for Representatives two and for Senators six years. Under the constitution the expression of extremist views is given wide protection by the First Amendment. The USA has a number of external territories, including Puerto Rico and various Pacific islands.

Recent history. Power has alternated in the present century between the Democratic Party and the Republican Party, which together account for the vast majority of voters and office-holders; there are numerous smaller parties and pressure groups, but the main two are so broad ideologically that most shades of opinion from left-wing liberalism to right-wing racist authoritarianism have found accommodation within both parties. Insofar as there are consistent Republican and Democratic philosophies, the former is somewhat more pro-business and pro-Christian, while the latter is more labour-oriented and secular. Within both parties, the north-east of the country is generally regarded as the home of liberalism while conservatism and the radical right is strongest in the south and west. At the time of writing (1987) the right-wing Republican President, Ronald Reagan, was entering the final two years of his second presidency with a Democratic majority in both houses of Congress.

The evolution of the far right. In a country with relatively recent experience of the extension of white "pioneer" settlement, and of slavery and massive immigration, it is perhaps unsurprising that racist and authoritarian notions have found expression both in mainstream politics and in more militant fringe activity. The most significant extra-parliamentary right-wing activity in the late 19th and early 20th centuries was that of the Ku Klux Klan, a white male secret society (see Knights of the Ku Klux Klan, below). Until the successes of the civil rights movement in the late 1950s and early 1960s, and especially the Voting Rights Act of 1965, many states imposed legislative or de facto restrictions on the voting and other rights of black people; racists favouring these restrictions were to be found in both major parties, but especially in the southern Democratic Party.

Fringe organizations active since the war in advocating the expulsion, disenfranchisement, denationalization, concentration or extermination of non-white, non-Anglo-Saxon or non-Protestant people include several bodies claiming descent from the Ku Klux Klan, as well as numerous neo-nazi parties; racism nowadays most commonly involves anti-black sentiment, but also includes hostility to Hispanics and Asians, and a significant anti-Jewish tendency persists. An anti-racist organization called Klanwatch estimated in 1986 that the total membership of Klan groupings was between 6,000 and 8,000. A Jewish organization, B'nai B'rith, maintains records of anti-semitic vandalism and similar incidents, which show 670 offences against property and 350 against individuals in 1983, rising to 715 and 369 in 1984; there were 115 arrests for anti-semitic offences in 1983. According to B'nai B'rith "organized hate groups" such as Klan or nazi factions were definitely involved in only five of these incidents in the period 1978-84. There are close links between some Klan and nazi groups; in 1979 members of both tendencies co-operated in the massacre of five Communist Workers' Party demonstrators in Greensboro, North Carolina. Criminal charges having failed, various civil court cases arising from the killings were still in progress in 1987.

Within that part of the right not concentrating on racial issues, the main rallying cries have been for the dismantling of the welfare state and/or of most of the government apparatus, as a drain on free enterprise; for the identification and elimination of a supposed external and domestic communist threat to freedom; for the imposition (or "restoration") of strict moral values based on the nuclear family and fundamentalist Christianity; and for the rights of state government as against federal government.

The activities of the far right received increasing media attention in the mid-1980s, partly as a result of several criminal cases. One neo-nazi group, The Order, carried out several armed robberies and forged currency in 1983-84; in 1986 a Wyoming couple, David and Dorris Young, died while attempting to kidnap a group of schoolchildren to raise $300,000,000 for right-wing causes. A "survivalist" movement which developed in the 1970s, mainly among white male Vietnam veterans, regards as inevitable the collapse of the existing social and economic order, whether through a nuclear war or as a result of domestic unrest, and its followers, now numbering tens of thousands, prepare with greater or lesser degrees of urgency for the establishment of self-sufficient and heavily-armed enclaves. In the area of overlap between survivalism and fascism there is a tendency, typified by the Aryan Nations group, which advocates the proclamation of a white "homeland" in the north-western states, either áas an immediate priority or as a "doomsday" plan.

There are literally hundreds of right-wing conservative pressure groups in the United States which have not been included in the present work; among these are the many "political action committees" (PACs) set up to fund the election campaigns of individual right-wing politicians. Anti-communist exile groupings based in the United States, of which there are many, are generally not listed here, but appear under the country of reference (Cuba, the Soviet Union and so on). The large number of ultra-patriotic or "citizenship education" groups are also excluded, unless they have a pronounced right-wing orientation.

The radical right in the United States consisted in 1987 of the following (often overlapping) tendencies: (i) a conservative "new right", associated with the Heritage Foundation and similar groups, and whose prominent advocates included President Reagan himself, Jack Kemp, Richard Viguerie, Paul Weyrich and others; (ii) a fundamentalist Christian right, typified by Jerry Falwell's Moral Majority group; (iii) ultra-conservative and anti-communist pressure groups, including the John Birch Society; (iv) more activist anti-communist groups such as the US Council for World Freedom and various émigré organizations, some of which are involved with foreign guerrilla groups; (v) revisionist historians, most of whom seek to deny the facts of the nazi Holocaust of European Jewry, without openly espousing fascism; (vi) anti-semitic and conspiracy theory pressure groups such as Liberty Lobby, and quasi-fascist parties such as the Lyndon LaRouche organization; (vi) white supremacist groups such as the various nazi parties and Klans, and other groupings opposed to taxes and to federal power; (vii) white paramilitary survivalist groups and nazi guerrilla organizations. There are, of course, some idiosyncratic groups which do not fit easily into any of these categories, but which espouse certain right-wing, racist or fascist ideas. In addition to the organized right, it has been estimated that as many as about 10,000 individual nazi and fascist war criminals found their way into the United States in 1948-52; many are still alive, although very few are openly active in ultra-right politics.

Active organizations

Accuracy in Academia (AIA)

Address. 1275 K Street NW, Suite 1150, Washington DC 20005

Leadership. John Le Boutillier (president)

Orientation. Right-wing conservative

History. This organization was established in 1985 as an offshoot of the Accuracy in Media organization. Members of Accuracy in Academia, many of whom are students often recruited from college Republican clubs, report suspected left-wing lecturers to a central office which produces newsletters and other material.

Policies. The organization seeks to monitor and publicize alleged instances of left-wing or liberal bias among university and college lecturers.

Associated organizations. See Accuracy in Media.

Accuracy in Media (AIM)

Address. 1275 K Street NW, Suite 1150, Washington DC 20005

Leadership. Donald K. Irvine (secretary)

Orientation. Right-wing conservative

History. This pressure group, founded in 1971, uses a network of 35,000 members to document and protest against alleged left-wing bias in the American print and broadcast media.

Publications. AIM Report, six per year.

Associated organizations. See Accuracy in Academia.

Action Society

Address. Box 4357, San Francisco, California 94101

Leadership. Hamilton Barret

Orientation. Fascist

History. This organization was active in the mid-1980s.

Policies. The Action Society is the main US organization of followers of Oswald Mosley, the late British fascist leader.

International affiliations. It has maintained contact with the various post-war Mosleyite organizations in Britain.

Air Commando Association

Leadership. Gen. Heine Aderholt (head)

Orientation. Anti-communist

History. This organization of US military veterans is led by a retired general who served under Gen. Singlaub (see US Council for World Freedom) in Vietnam and is now active in supplying right-wing forces in Central America.

Associated organizations. Aderholt is also linked with the Soldier of Fortune mercenary group. It has not been possible to establish whether the Association is connected with the First Air Commando Association, based at Broderick, California.

America First Committee

Leadership. Art Jones (leader)

Orientation. White supremacist

History. The Committee has been active from about 1985.

Policies. This organization favours a tactical alliance between white racist groups and black racist groups, notably Louis Farrakhan's anti-Jewish grouping.

Associated organizations. Along with other nazi and racist organizations, the Committee was represented at the 1985 Christian Patriots Conference. The Committee is probably not connected with the America First Club, a conservative organization active in Anderson, Indiana, in the 1970s.

American Catholic Committee (ACC)

Address. 127 East 35th Street, New York, NY 10016

Leadership. James J. McFadden (president)

Orientation. Catholic conservative

History. The ACC was formed in 1982.

Policies. Its main concerns to date have been campaigns against the Nicaraguan government and in favour of nuclear weapons.

Membership. 350 (1986).

Associated organizations. The ACC is in sympathy with the American Catholic Conference, a Washington-based grouping which opposes liberalism, and in particular liberation theology, as contrary to Catholic doctrine.

American Coalition for Traditional Values (ACTV)

Base. Washington DC

Orientation. Evangelical conservative

History. The ACTV was formed in the late 1970s as part of the Protestant conservative tendency generically known, after its major component, as the Moral Majority movement.

Policies. The ACTV opposes homosexuality, abortion, pornography, the peace movement, welfarism, immorality, secularism and the Equal Rights Amendment (an unsuccessful initiative to amend the US Constitution to include a clause guaranteeing equal rights for women).

Membership. About 500.

Publications. Washington Report, monthly.

American Council for Free Asia (ACFA)

Address. 214 Massachusetts Avenue NE, Washington, DC 20002

Telephone. (202) 546 3773

Leadership. Gina Jarmin (executive director)

Orientation. Anti-communist

History. The ACFA was formed in 1978 as one of a large number of right-wing pressure groups sponsored by the Heritage Foundation.

Policies. It lobbies in the United States to heighten awareness of communist activities in South-East Asia, and to further the interests of the Taiwan regime, particularly in regard to the restoration of US diplomatic recognition and the resumption of arms sales.

Membership. The Council claimed in 1985 to have 50,000 members.

Publications. Free Asia Report, quarterly.

American Council for Peace Through Strength—see Coalition for Peace Through Strength.

American Defenders (AD)

Address. 1013 West Greenfield Avenue, Milwaukee, Wisconsin 53204

Telephone. (414) 671 5252

Leadership. David Bathke (director)

Orientation. Ultra-right

History. This organization was founded in 1976.

Policies. The organization is against communism, crime, disarmament, government intervention in the economy, external alliances and compulsory desegregation of schools.

American Foreign Policy Institute—see Council on American Affairs.

American Foundation for Resistance International (AFRI)

Address. 500 Fifth Avenue, Suite 1600, New York, NY 10110

Telephone. (212) 302 3303

Leadership. Albert E. Jolis (secretary)

Orientation. Anti-communist

History. The AFRI was founded in 1984.

Policies. It seeks to expose and counter the world-wide communist threat and to provide aid to anti-communist refugees.

American Immigration Control Foundation (AICF)

Address. Box 525, Three Water Street, Monterey, Virginia 24465

Orientation. Anti-immigration

History. This grouping was active from the early 1980s.

Policies. Although it is not an overtly white supremacist organization, the Foundation's policy of opposition on economic and social grounds to immigration, especially from Mexico, has attracted ultra-right support.

Membership. 80,000 (1985 claim).

Publications. Border Watch, six per year.

American Independent Party (AIP)

Address. 8158 Palm Street, Lemon Grove, California 92045

Telephone. (619) 460 4484

Leadership. Eileen M. Shearer (national chairwoman); Tom Goodloe

Orientation. Right-wing populist

History. The AIP was founded in 1968 to support the presidential aspirations of George C. Wallace, a governor of Alabama state who had a reputation for racism in the 1960s (although his posture was modified during the 1970s). The Party was originally based in Montgomery, Alabama, and has had large and autonomous state sections (often known in the 1970s as Wallace for President campaigns, and supported by some members of the Democratic Party) in California, Florida, Georgia, Illinois, Kentucky, Louisiana, Michigan, Nevada, New Jersey, Pennsylvania, Texas, Utah and Virginia.
In 1972 the AIP nominated John Schmitz as its presidential candidate, and in 1976 Governor Lester Maddox (head of its Georgian section). In 1980 its candidate was Congressman John R. Rarick.

Policies. The AIP is anti-communist, and opposes gun control, income tax, abortion and immigration; it supports free enterprise, a strong defence policy and individual liberty.

Membership. 170,000, mostly in California and Georgia.

Publications. Statesman Newsletter, monthly.

American Jewish League against Communism (AJLAC)

Address. 39 East 68th Street, New York, NY 10021

Telephone. (212) 472 1400

Leadership. Roy Cohn (president)

Orientation. Anti-communist

History. The AJLAC has been active since at least the early 1950s.

Policies. It opposes communism on both the domestic and the international front.

Membership. 500.

Publications. Jews against Communism.

Associated organizations. The AJLAC may be related to the American League Against Communism (1200 South Central, Glendale, Calfornia 91202).

American Majority Party

Address. Box 277, Hooksett, New Hampshire 03106

Leadership. Arnold Moltis (leader)

Orientation. Right-wing

History. This minor group was active in 1985.

American Mercury

Address. Box 1306, Torrance, California 90505

Leadership. Robert Kuttner (editor)

Orientation. Fascist

History. This racist and anti-semitic journal was founded in the early 1920s and taken over in 1966 by Kuttner, who had been a contributing editor of *Western Destiny* (see Council for Social and Economic Studies) and who joined Willis Carto's *Spotlight* in the late 1970s (see Liberty Lobby).

Policies. The *Mercury* advances white supremacist views, anti-semitism, anti-communism, states' rights and nationalism.

Publications. American Mercury, quarterly review; *Washington Observer,* monthly bulletin.

Associated organizations. The *Mercury* operation is politically close to the Liberty Lobby.

American National Socialist Party (ANSP)

Address. Box 817, Claremont, California 91711

Leadership. Hale McGee (leader); Dale Gatewood (chief of staff)

Orientation. Nazi

History. This Party, formerly based in Anaheim, California, is an offshoot of the American Nazi Party.

Policies. The ANSP has traditional national socialist policies.

Publications. New Facts.

American Nazi Party

Address. 4375 North Peck Road, El Monte, California 91732

Leadership. Jim Burford (leader)

Orientation. Nazi

History. This group originated in 1968 as a splinter group of the National Socialist White People's Party (now the New Order), and was at first led by James Warner, who had been secretary of the parent party (which was itself then called the American Nazi Party) in the early 1960s. Much of the US press uses the term "American Nazi Party" to refer to all national socialist groupings. The address given above may not be current.

Policies. The Party espouses white supremacist, anti-semitic and authoritarian ideas and venerates Adolf Hitler.

Associated organizations. This party took part in the 1985 Christian Patriots Conference, which also involved the New Order, the America First Committee and various Klan groupings. Some of its members have participated in the activities of the Oklahoma-based National Socialist Movement.

The American Party

Address. Route 2, Box 1072, Roseburg, Oregon 97470

Leadership. Frank Varnum

Orientation. Right-wing

History. This party was formed in the 1970s. It is not linked with the Utah-based American Party of the United States, but may be associated with the American Party based at Pigeon Forge, Tennessee, and the American Party of SW Florida, based at Cape Coral, both of which were active in the mid-1970s. (The Tenessee-based Party, which was led in the mid-70s by Tom Anderson, had a nationalist and anti-communist, but non-fascist, ideology, and published *The New American Voice*, which claimed a circulation of 60,000.)

Publications. The American

American Revolutionary Army (ARA)

Address. 96875-131, Box PMB, Atlanta, Georgia 30315

Orientation. Neo-nazi

History. The ARA was active at least from the mid-1970s until the mid-1980s.

Policies. It believes in the use of revolutionary violence to overthrow what it sees as a decadent and corrupt establishment.

American Security Council (ASC)

Address. Box 8, Boston, Virginia 22713

Telephone. (703) 547 1776

Leadership. John M. Fisher (president); Robert Hanrahan

Orientation. Militarist, anti-communist

History. The ASC (formally the American Security Council Foundation; previously known as the Institute for American Strategy and as the American Security Council Education Fund) was formed in the mid-1950s as a lobbying and educational organization designed to further right-wing foreign policy goals. It was based in Washington DC until the late 1970s. The ASC administers the Coalition for Peace Through Strength, with which it has a joint National Strategy Committee which includes Gen. Singlaub of the US Council for World Freedom and a number of other US associates of the South Korea-based World Anti-Communist League (WACL). Dr

Roger Pearson, a former WACL leader and now leader of the Council for Social and Economic Studies, has had extensive dealings with the Council.

Policies. The Council acts as a right-wing "think tank" on foreign policy, and lobbies for the expansion and strengthening of US military forces to meet an imminent Soviet threat. It also seeks to educate the American public as to the communist threat to liberty and opposes congressional candidates whom it regards as "soft" on national defence issues.

Membership. In 1985 the ASC claimed 330,000 members.

Publications. Washington Report, monthly; occasional monographs; television and radio material.

Associated organizations. Coalition for Peace Through Strength; US Congressional Advisory Board; National Security Speakers' Bureau (all subsidiaries). Several leading members of the group are also connected with Western Goals, a similar lobbying organization. There is some connection between the ASC and the American Foreign Policy Institute, a quasi-academic organization founded in 1968 and based in Washington DC. Similar, but unrelated, organizations include Americans for President Reagan's Foreign Policy, based in Washington and run by Carl Shipley. The ASC used to administer the American Coalition of Patriotic Societies, founded in 1929 and based in New York, but that organization appeared to be defunct by 1987.

American Society for the Defense of Tradition, Family and Property (TFP)

Address. PO Box 121, Pleasantville, New York 10570

Telephone. (914) 241 7015

Leadership. John Russell Spann (president)

Orientation. Anti-communist

History. The American TFP was formed in 1974, some 14 years after the foundation of the first branch of the international TFP network in Brazil.

Policies. The TFP is anti-communist and anti-socialist, and seeks to expose and counter communist infiltration of Western societies. It is also identified with an authoritarian and anti-modernist Catholic fundamentalism.

Publications. Newsletter, monthly; *Bulletin*, quarterly; books and other materials.

Associated organizations. The TFP is believed to have recruited much of the following of the Catholic Traditionalist Movement which was based in New York in the mid-1970s.

International affiliations. The American TFP is linked with other TFP groups in Brazil, Canada, France, Argentina, Bolivia, Chile, Colombia, Costa Rica, Ecuador, Peru, Uruguay, Venuezula, the United Kingdom, Spain and elsewhere.

American White Nationalist Party (AWNP)

Address. Box 14083, Columbus, Ohio 43214

Orientation. Nazi

History. The AWNP was active from about 1973, and was a member of the White Confederacy alliance which was led by the National Socialist Movement.

Policies. It espouses white supremacist, anti-semitic and national socialist policies.

Associated organizations. This ANWP is probably the same as that operating in the mid-1970s in Davenport, Iowa, and as the American White Nationalists Party in Toledo, Ohio.

Anti-Communist Committee (ACC)

Address. PO Box 1832, Kansas City, Missouri 64141

Leadership. Jack N. Stone (executive officer)

Orientation. Anti-communist

History. The Committee was founded in 1972, and merged in 1978 with the Citizens' Constitutional Committee (CCC). It engages in publishing, research, seminar organizing and other activities.

Policies. The ACC opposes domestic communism, monitors the external communist threat and US preparedness, and assists anti-communist refugees. It fosters co-operaton among all US anti-communist groups.

Membership. About 1,000.

Publications. Bulletin, quarterly.

Associated organizations. The ACC may be the same as the identically named group which operated from Bellflower, California, in the mid-1970s, publishing *Memo USA* magazine.

Anti-Communist League of America (ACLA)

Address. 3100 Park Newport, Suite 101, Newport Beach, California 92660

Leadership. John K. Crippen (executive secretary)

Orientation. Anti-communist

History. This organization is a direct continuation of the American Anti-Communist League, founded in 1938. In the mid-1970s the ACLA was based at Park Ridge, Illinois.

Policies. It opposes communist subversion in the United States and supports foreign anti-communist movements and governments.

The Appalachian Forum

Address. PO Box 1992, Pittsburgh, Pennsylvania 15230

Leadership. John Bright

Orientation. Ultra-right

History. The Forum was established in the early 1980s as a bookselling operation serving the far right.

Aryan Nations

Address. Box 382, Hayden Lake, Idaho 83835

Leadership. Rev. Richard Girnt Butler

Orientation. White supremacist, neo-nazi

History. This body was established by Richard Butler, Louis Beam and others as the secular wing of the Church of Jesus Christ Christian. A group of members led by Robert Mathew and Gary Yarbrough formed The Order (also known as the Silent Brotherhood) in 1982, and was responsible for counterfeiting large amounts of currency, reportedly at the Aryan Nations headquarters. The Nations held gatherings of white supremacist groups, known as Aryan Nations Congresses, in 1984 and 1986. In 1985 a leading associate of the group, the Rev. Robert Miles (see Mountain Church), hosted a Christian Patriots Conference in Michigan with the participation of similar groups.

The 1986 Congress, held under FBI surveillance and with armed guards provided by supporters, was attended by 150 delegates from the US and Canada, including leaders of Ku Klux Klan factions, John Ross Taylor of Canada and revisionist historian Michael Hoffmann. The Congress included a cross-burning ceremony, held in private because of a 1982 state law backed by a local anti-fascist campaign.

Four Aryan Nations associates—Elliott Pires, David Dorr and Edward and Olive Hawley—were arrested after bombings in Coeur d'Alene, a town near Hayden Lake, in late 1986. The Hawleys already faced charges of counterfeiting for the benefit of the *Brüder Schweigend* Strike Force II, a splinter group of the Nations. Arms, explosives and other material were seized at the time of the arrests. In early 1987 several members of the Aryan Nations were being sought by the FBI in connection with bank robberies in Illinois and Indiana in 1986.

Policies. The group advocates the establishment of a "territorial sanctuary" and eventually of a White Sovereign National State of America in the north-west of what is now the USA. The group also opposes the existing US constitution and the federal administration, which it terms the "de facto" government or "Zionist Occupation Government" (ZOG), alleging that it is controlled by Jews. Some Nations supporters practise polygamy. In 1986 it was reported that the group was making a particular effort to recruit poor farmers, notably in Iowa.

Membership. The group refuses to disclose membership figures. Police estimate that its sympathisers number several thousands.

Associated organizations. See Church of Jesus Christ Christian, Christian Identity Movement and League of Pace Amendment Advocates. The Aryan Nations group is close to several Ku Klux Klan factions and attended the 1986 Klan gathering in Georgia. See also White American Resistance and National States Rights Party. An Aryan Nations leader, Louis Beam, maintains a computer network, the Aryan Liberty Net, linking far-right groups and providing information on "race traitors" and other enemies of fascism.

International affiliations. The group has members in Canada (see separate entry) and claims to have affiliates in Britain, Australia, the Netherlands, Scandinavia and France.

Aryan People's Party—see Social Nationalist Aryan People's Party.

Assembly of Captive European Nations (ACEN)

Address. 150 Fifth Avenue, no. 832, New York, NY 10011

Telephone. (212)255 9549

Leadership. Feliks Gadomski (general secretary)

Orientation. Anti-communist

History. The Assembly has been in existence since the mid-1950s.

Policies. The Assembly seeks to co-ordinate the policies and activities of anti-communist pressure groups and "liberation movements" representing the émigré communities of Albania, Bulgaria, Czechoslovakia, Estonia, Hungary, Latvia, Lithuania, Poland and Romania.

Publications. ACEN News

Associated organizations. Groupings representing each Eastern European country are affiliated to the Assembly.

Association of Former Intelligence Officers (AFIO)

Address. 6723 Whittier Avenue, Suite 303A, McLean, Virginia 22101

Leadership. David Atlee Phillips (founder and leader); John K. Greaney (director)

Orientation. Anti-communist

History. This organization, formed in 1976 as the Association of Retired Intelligence Officers, consists of right-wing former agents of US civilian or military intelligence services. Its leader, as head of Western Hemisphere Operations for the Central Intelligence Agency (CIA), was in a position to have known about CIA dealings with fugitive nazi war criminals. He is now a contributor to *Eagle* and *Soldier of Fortune*, the leading right-wing mercenary magazines.

Policies. The AFIO is staunchly anti-communist and supports a US military build-up to meet what it regards as an imminent Soviet threat.

Associated organizations. The AFIO is affiliated to the American Council for Peace Through Strength.

Brave America

Address. Box 247, 2265 Westwood Boulevard, Suite B, Los Angeles, California 90064

Orientation. Ultra-right

History. Brave America was established in the early 1980s to provide an information service on white racist and fascist groups in the United States.

Brüder Schweigend Strike Force II

Orientation. White supremacist

History. This group, which takes its name from the Silent Brotherhood (also known as The Order—see below), was established in the mid-1980s as a splinter group of the Aryan Nations. Two of its associates, Olive and Edward Hawley, were arrested for counterfeiting in 1986. Police reportedly believed that the Strike Force planned to mount a campaign of robbery, counterfeiting and murder.

Policies. The Strike Force seeks to create the conditions for the overthrow of the US government and to assist in the establishment of an exclusively white-ruled state.

Captive Nations Committee Inc.

Address. PO Box 540, New York, NY 10028

Telephone. (212) 439 8044

Leadership. Dr Lev Dobriansky (chairman); Horst-Adolf Uhlich (president)

Orientation. Anti-communist

History. This organization was established in 1959 with the aim of co-ordinating the political activities of various New York-based East European émigré groups and US anti-communist organizations. It sponsors annual "Captive Nations Week" programmes of demonstrations and rallies, and organizes publicity activities, consumer boycotts and information programmes.

Policies. The Committee seeks to raise public awareness of what it sees as the totalitarian nature of the East European governments.

Membership. 20,000.

Publications. Globe Eagle.

Cardinal Mindszenty Foundation (CMF)

Address. PO Box 11321, Clayton Branch, St. Louis, Missouri 63105

Telephone. (314) 991 2939

Leadership. Eleanor Schlafly (director)

Orientation. Anti-communist

History. The CMF was founded in 1958 and was named after a Catholic prelate who had come into conflict with the Communist Party government in Hungary.

Policies. The CMF seeks to expose communist infiltration and subversion of the United States, and to educate the public as to the goals and practices of the communist movement.

Publications. Mindszenty Report, monthly internal bulletin; *The Red Line*, monthly organ.

Associated organizations. Similar groups active in the 1970s included the Cardinal Mindszenty Study Club (Van Nuys, California) and the Cardinal Mindszenty Study Group (Williston, North Dakota).

CAUSA USA

Address. 4301 Harewood Road NE, Washington, DC 20017

Telephone. (202) 529 7700

Leadership. Sun Myung Moon (founder); Joe Tully (director)

Orientation. Anti-communist

History. CAUSA was founded in 1983 (as the Causa USA Foundation) by the Korean-born leader of the Unification Church prior to his imprisonment for tax fraud. It engages in a variety of activities designed to further the struggle against communism; it organizes seminars and conferences and bestows annual awards on US and foreign politicians and writers.

Policies. CAUSA exists to combat "ever-expanding communism" across the world. Its current priorities include lobbying for increased US funding for the Nicaraguan contras. The group describes itself as "a God-centred humanitarian educational movement".

Membership. 25,000 (1985) including about 20 full-time staff.

Publications. CAUSA USA Report, monthly; *CAUSA Magazine*, quarterly; monographs, conference proceedings and other material.

Associated organizations. See Unification Church. CAUSA has a number of subsidiary organizations aimed at particular interest groups, such as the CAUSA Ministerial Alliance which directs its efforts at the clergy of many denominations.

International affiliations. The group is part of CAUSA-International (see South Korea), which has affiliates in several countries, including France and Ireland, and is itself an affiliate of the World Anti-Communist League (see South Korea). CAUSA USA runs Project Tropical Light, which, according to its sponsors, provides assistance to anti-communist refugees, mainly from Nicaragua.

Center for International Security (CIS)

Address. 905 16th Street NW, Washington, DC 20006

Orientation. Right-wing conservative

History. The CIS was founded in 1978.

Policies. It lobbies for a strong national defence policy, supported by a foreign policy which provides backing to the allies of the United States, particularly in the Third World, and which challenges the country's perceived enemies, notably Libya.

Associated organizations. See Committee on the Present Danger.

Center for the Survival of Western Democracies

Base. New York, NY

Orientation. Right-wing

History. This organization, founded in the 1970s, achieved some publicity in the 1980s by its sponsorship of a Committee for an Alternative to the *New York Times*, which sought to end an alleged liberal monopoly in the serious press.

Policies. The Center carries out research on foreign policy and defence issues in conjunction with right-wing exile and academic groupings, and concerns itself with domestic political and media matters relevant to the international positions and strategies of the United States.

Christian Anti-Communism Crusade

Address. Box 890, 227 East Sixth Street, Long Beach, California 90801

Telephone. (213) 437 0941

Leadership. Dr Fred C. Schwartz (president); Rev. James Colbert

Orientation. Anti-communist

History. The Crusade, founded in 1953, was especially active in the anti-communist movement in the 1950s and '60s. It remained in existence in the 1970s, with offices in Long Beach, in Waterloo (Iowa) and in Houston (Texas).

A delegation from the organization visited South Africa in April 1986. Colbert was reported as stating that the unrest there was due to Marxist elements; that Marxists exploited religion; that the South African Council of Churches did not represent the majority of South African Christians, and that most "government people" favoured the dismantling of apartheid.

Policies. The Crusade campaigns against communism, which it defines in rather broad terms, on the domestic and international fronts. It is particularly concerned with uncovering subversion in the media and the US establishment, and with exposing the communist movement's strategy for world domination.

Membership. The Crusade does not disclose membership data. It has about two dozen full-time staff.

Publications. Newsletter, approximately monthly; occasional books and pamphlets.

International affiliations. The Crusade claims to have affiliates in 21 countries, including Australia, Brazil, India, Kenya and the Philippines.

Christian Citizens' Crusade (CCC)

Address. PO Box 1866, Greenville, South Carolina 29602

Leadership. Sherman A. Patterson (executive director)

Orientation. Ultra-right

History. The CCC, which was formed in the early 1950s, has been active in a number of right-wing causes. In the mid-1970s, when it was based in Atlanta (Georgia), its publication was called *Militant Truth*.

Policies. The CCC defines itself as representing Christian conservative patriots. It is anti-communist and has opposed school desgregation.

Publications. Independent Voice.

Christian Defense League (CDL)

Address. Box 493, Baton Rouge, Louisiana 70821

Leadership. James K. Warner

Orientation. Neo-nazi

History. The CDL was set up in the early 1980s by Warner, a former leader of the American Nazi Party and the New Christian Crusade Church (NCCC), and its name parodies that of the terrorist Jewish Defense League (JDL), a group based in New York. Alternatively, it may be a successor to an earlier Louisiana group, the Christian Defense Fund, based in Alexandria in the mid-1970s, or to a Californian group, which published the *Christian Defense Bulletin* from Idyllwild in the early '70s.

Policies. The CDL claims that there is a need to defend Christian America from a Jewish onslaught aimed at eventual world domination.

Publications. Christian Vanguard, tabloid monthly, formerly (in the 1970s) the organ of the NCCC; *The Christian Defense League Report*, internal bulletin.

International affiliations. The League appears on mailing lists linked with the World Union of National Socialists, but it is not a full member of the WUNS. A now-defunct UK affiliate of the NCCC published *Impact* bulletin in the mid-1970s.

Christian Identity movement

Orientation. White supremacist, neo-nazi

History. This loose network of churches, sects and groups developed in the late 1970s and early '80s to co-ordinate the activities of those who followed a "Christian" white racist philosophy. The most important elements in the movement in the 1970s were William Potter Gale's Ministry of Christ Church (now the Church of Christ), based in Mariposa, California, and James Warner's New Christian Crusade Church (now superseded by the Christian Defense League). Gale, who had led the paramilitary California Rangers movement in the 1960s and had also been involved in the Posse Comitatus movement, was arrested on conspiracy charges in March 1987.

Policies. The movement maintains that white people are God's chosen race, and that Jews are born of Satan through Cain. That part of its ideology may be traced to the 19th-century British Israel movement (see United Kingdom). It also advocates the establishment of a white racist state in the Idaho-Washington-Oregon-Montana-Wyoming region, as a refuge from the supposedly Jewish-controlled US government. This region is advocated because of its very low black population, partly a consequence of 19th-century racist legislation. Some supporters of the movement advocate polygamy as a means of ensuring white numerical supremacy.

Membership. The Jewish anti-fascist *B'nai Brith* organization estimates that the organizations comprising the Identity movement have a combined total of about 6,000 adherents.

Associated organizations. See Aryan Nations, Church of Jesus Christ Christian and allied organizations.

Christian Knights of the Ku Klux Klan

Base. North Carolina

Leadership. Virgil Griffin (Imperial Wizard)

Orientation. White supremacist

History. This Klan grouping has members in several states. The national leader of the Christian Knights is known as the Imperial Wizard, while state leaders are called Grand Dragons. The current Imperial Wizard was present at the Greensboro massacre of 12 left-wingers by Klansmen and nazis in 1979. In 1985 the Grand Dragon in Virginia, Jordan Gollub, was forced to resign after press reports of his Jewish parentage. The Christian Knights, who staged 35 marches in 1985 and 54 in 1986, recruited a large proportion of the membership of the White Patriot Party following the latter group's decision in early 1987 to disband.

Policies. The Christian Knights have anti-semitic neo-nazi policies.

Christian Mission to the Communist World, International (CMCW)

Address. PO Box 2947, Torrance, California 90509

Telephone. (213) 533 5872

Orientation. Anti-communist

History. The CMCW, which is possibly stronger in the United Kingdom than in the USA, is one of a large number of groups which both publicize alleged repression of Christians in the Soviet Union and other communist-ruled countries, and attempt to provide support to unofficial religious groups in such countries. The CMCW is particularly identified with unofficial Baptist groups in the western Soviet Union.

In the 1970s and early '80s the US and foreign affiliates of the CMCW were divided by protracted lawsuits which arose partly from the financial and managerial practices of the Mission's founders, Michael and Richard Wurmbrand, who had been involved in 1960-67 in a Bible-smuggling operation called Underground Evangelism before founding Jesus to the Communist World, Inc., a precursor of the CMCW.

351

Policies. The CMCW has produced a wide range of publicity material on the situation of religion in communist countries and on the evils of communist ideology, including, for example, accounts of Bible-smuggling and a leaflet setting out the argument that Karl Marx was a Satanist.

Associated organizations. Recently active groups with similar concerns include Christ for the Nations (Dallas, Texas); Christ for the World (Orlando, Florida); the Mission to Europe's Millions (Glendale, California), and *Religion in Communist-Dominated Areas* (475 Riverside Drive, New York, NY 10027), a bulletin on religious persecution.

Christian Vikings of America

Address. Box 12182, Indianapolis, Indiana 46222

Orientation. Neo-nazi

History. This small grouping was part of the National Socialist Movement's White Confederacy alliance during the 1970s.

Policies. It espouses white supremacist ideas, and more specifically the inherent superiority of the Nordic, Teutonic and Anglo-Saxon peoples over all other human beings.

Christian Voice

Address. 214 Massachusetts Avenue NE, Suite 120, Washington, DC 20002

Telephone. (202) 544 5202

Leadership. Rev. Bob Allen (president)

Orientation. Protestant right-wing

History. Christian Voice was founded in 1978 under the aegis of the Heritage Foundation, the leading radical conservative lobby. It has developed into a large and influential organization specializing in media campaigns.

Policies. It campaigns from a Protestant perspective against abortion, pornography, gay rights, the Equal Rights Amendment and liberalism in general.

Membership. 50,000, including more than 60 Congressmen of both parties.

Church of Jesus Christ Christian

Address. Box 382, Hayden Lake, Idaho 83835

Leadership. Rev. Richard Girnt Butler

Orientation. White supremacist

History. Butler (born 1919; a former aeronautical engineer) founded the Church as part of the Christian Identity movement, a white supremacist and anti-semitic religious tendency. Churches are not taxable under US law. The Church, which is virtually identical in membership and policy with the Aryan Nations movement, has adopted as its symbol a swastika-like cross, before which worshippers swear allegiance at the end of services. The Church hosted the 1986 Aryan Nations Congress, designed to bring together a wide range of racist groupings.

Policies. The Church shares the aims and objectives of the Christian Identity movement.

Membership. According to a press report the Church's Sunday congregations rarely exceed 10.

Associated organizations. See Aryan Nations (the secular wing of the Church) and the Christian Identity movement (of which tendency the Church is a part). Butler's organization is probably the same as the Church of Jesus Christ (Christian) which was reportedly active in St. Petersburg, Florida, some years ago, and the Church of Christ (Christian) of Wilmington, Ohio.

Citizens' Councils of America (CCA)

Address. 5430 Executive Plaza, Jackson, Mississippi 39206

Telephone. (601) 981 2020

Leadership. Robert B. Patterson (secretary)

Orientation. White supremacist

History. The CCA organization was formed in 1954, and was very influential in the campaign against the black civil rights movement until the late 1960s. By the mid-1970s Citizens' Councils were active in Alabama, Arkansas, California (which had at least four Councils), Florida (two), Kentucky, Louisiana (two), Mississippi (nine), South Carolina (four), Tennessee (three), and Texas (three).

Policies. The organization calls for state sovereignty over racial policy as a means of reintroducing segregation of education and of public places and facilities. It also advocates the "maintenance of racial purity" and researches and publishes studies on eugenics.

Membership. The organization's headquarters staff claim, somewhat improbably, that there are 750,000 members in over 1,000 local branches.

Publications. The Citizen, monthly, formerly the organ of the Greenwood (Mississippi) Citizen's Council. The Council in Ruleville, in the same state, produced *The Spartan,* which appears to have ceased publication.

Associated organizations. The CCA has had an Educational Fund, based in Mississippi, whose functions seem to have been assumed by the head office in Jackson.

Citizens' Council of America for Segregation (CCAS)

Address. 2302 Lawndale Drive, Dallas, Texas 75211

Telephone. (214) 942 6601

Leadership. Dr Carey Daniel (president)

Orientation. White supremacist

History. The CCAS, which now appears to be independent of the larger CCA, has been active at least from the early 1960s. It was known briefly as the National Association for the Advancement of White People, but is unconnected with the existing pressure group using that name.

Policies. The CCAS is against race-mixing and for segregation, which it sees as the answer to racial violence. It finds a biblical justification for its positions. The group is also stridently anti-communist and has argued that multi-racialism is a communist ploy to undermine American society.

Membership. About 1,000.

Citizens for America (CFA)

Address. 214 Massachusetts Avenue NE, Suite 320, Washington, DC 20002

Telephone. (202) 544 7888

Leadership. Lewis E. Lehrman (chairman); Joseph Coors (member of executive)

Orientation. Anti-communist

History. This organization was established by Lehrman, a Republican millionaire, a year after he lost the New York mayoral election in 1982. It was active in the mid-1980s in attempting to raise public support in the USA for the Nicaraguan counter-revolutionary movement. In 1985 more than half of the group's 40 workers resigned and another seven were dismissed, reportedly as a result of financial mismanagement. Coors, a brewing magnate, was a close political associate of Ronald Reagan as a member of his "kitchen cabinet" of right-wing businesspeople, as was Jacqueline Hume, who reportedly suggested the foundation of the group.

Policies. The CFA advocates rapid economic growth and a strong defence policy.

Publications. Reality Report, monthly; other reviews and pamphlets.

Associated organizations. The CFA is administered by the Heritage Foundation and is reportedly close to the Reagan White House. Its publishing arm is the tax-exempt CFA Educational Foundation.

International affiliations. The CFA was responsible for the 1985 conference which resulted in the formation of the Democratic International, uniting various counter-revolutionary groups from the Third World.

Civilian Military Assistance (CMA)

Address. PO Box 3012, Decatur, Alabama 35602

Telephone. (205) 353 5769

Leadership. Thomas V. (Tom) Posey (national director); Walton Blanton

Orientation. Anti-communist

History. This pressure group and mercenary organization, whose name is often reported incorrectly as Civil Military Assistance, Civilian Military Assistance Group or Civilian Material Assistance, has been involved since its foundation by Posey and Blanton in 1983 in the supply of funds, support, equipment and training to the Nicaraguan contras and possibly to other Central American right-wing guerrilla movements and, on a smaller scale, to the Salvadorean armed forces. Posey, a vegetable salesman, is a former marine and an ex-member of the John Birch Society; Blanton is a Special Forces veteran.

Several foreign mercenaries arrested in Costa Rica in April 1984 claimed to have been recruited for the contras by CMA. Two CMA members were killed in a raid on Nicaragua on Sept. 1, 1984, leading to an inconclusive congressional debate as to whether CMA's operations, which had at least the political support of the Reagan administration, were in breach of the US Neutrality Act. CMA supplied the security guards for a World Anti-Communist League (see South Korea) conference in Texas in 1985.

In 1986 an armed and uniformed group of CMA supporters, seeking to demonstrate the vulnerability of the United States' frontiers, seized 16 Mexicans on the southern border and held them for some time before handing them over to the Border Patrol. A US citizen who claimed to be a member of the group was arrested for spying in Nicaragua in December 1986 (see Phoenix Battalion).

Policies. The group seeks to encourage, organize and channel support from private individuals for "freedom fighters" in anti-communist guerrilla movements.

Membership. In 1986 the group claimed 5,000 members. Most of its support appeared to be in Alabama, Tennessee and Mississippi, with smaller followings in Michigan and Florida.

Clean Up TV Campaign

Address. 5807 Charlotte Avenue, Nashvile, Tennessee 37209

Leadership. John Hurt (director)

Orientation. Christian conservative

History. The Campaign was founded in 1978 as an outgrowth of the Protestant fundamentalist move into politics, as typified by the Moral Majority movement.

Policies. The Campaign seeks the censorship of television to prevent the broadcast of what it regards as immoral or offensive images or topics. To that end it compiles blacklists and organizes consumer boycotts of companies whose advertising appears during objectionable programmes.

Coalition for Peace Through Strength (CPTS)

Address. c/o American Security Council, Box 8, Boston, Virginia 22713

Leadership. Gen. John K. Singlaub (chairman); John Fisher

Orientation. Militarist

History. This pressure group, also known as the American Council for Peace Through Strength (ACPTS), was established in 1979. Its chairman is a key figure on the American and international right. Fisher is a long-standing associate of Dr Roger Pearson (see Council for Social and Economic Studies).

Policies. The Coalition advocates the retention and expansion of the US nuclear arsenal to meet what it sees as an imminent threat from the Soviet bloc.

Publications. Peace Through Strength Report, monthly.

Associated organizations. The CPTS sometimes operates as the National "Peace Through Strength" Campaign. See US Council for World Freedom; the CPTS is also closely associated with the American Security Council and with Western Goals, and has numerous domestic affiliates including the Association of Former Intelligence Officers.

International affiliations. Affiliates of the Coalition include several US and East European émigré groups associated with the World Anti-Communist League (South Korea).

Committee for the Free World (CFW)

Address. 211 East 51st Street, New York, NY 10022

Telephone. (212) 759 7737

Leadership. Midge Decter (director)

Orientation. Anti-communist

History. The CFW was established in 1981.

Policies. It campaigns for the maintenance of the American way of life and for the free enterprisesystem, and against communism as a threat to individual liberty.

Publications. *Contentions*, monthly.

Committee for the Jewish Idea (CJI)

Base. New York, NY

Leadership. Meir Kahane (founder)

Orientation. Anti-Arab

History. The CJI was formed in the 1970s to support the campaign of Rabbi Kahane, currently a member of the Israeli parliament (see *Kach*, Israel), for the Jewish domination of the Holy Land. It is sometimes regarded as a front for the Jewish Defense League (JDL), a terrorist group.

Policies. The CJI supports *Kach*, encourages Jewish emigration to Israel, opposes contact between Jews and Arabs and advocates the expulsion of all Arabs from Israel.

Committee on the Present Danger (CPD)

Address. 905 16th Stret NW, Suite 207, Washington, DC 20006

Telephone. (202) 628 2409

Leadership. Charles Tyroler II (executive director)

Orientation. Militarist

History. The CPD was founded in 1976 by right-wing activists; in 1978 some of its members were involved in the formation of the Center for International Security, based at thesame address. The CPD organizes seminars, study committees and conferences, and provides speakers on national security issues.

Policies. The CPD seeks to build public support for a strong national defence policy, increased military expenditure, the deployment of new weaponry, and the reinforcement of US foreign policy to meet a Soviet challenge.

Committee on State Sovereignty

Base. Florida

Orientation. Ultra-right

History. The Committee was established in 1958 in response to the increasing use of federal legislative and judicial recourses in furtherance of the civil rights movement.

Policies. It seeks a greater devolution of power to the individual states of the Union. The Committee is anti-communist, anti-socialist, anti-trade union and in favour of private enterprise and law and order.

Membership. 5,000 (1987 estimate).

Committee to Stop Chemical Atrocities

Address. 214 Massachusets Avenue NE, Suite 580, Washington, DC 20002

Telephone. (202) 543 1286

Leadership. Amy Moritz

Orientation. Anti-communist

History. One of many pressure groups based at the Heritage Foundation headquarters, the Committee was established in 1982 to publicize the alleged use of chemical weapons by the Soviet Union and its allies, notably "Yellow Rain" in South-East Asia.

Policies. The Committee appears to have dropped the "Yellow Rain" issue and now concentrates on allegations that the Soviet Union and China employ slave labour.

Publications. National Policy Watch, monthly.

Associated organizations. The Committee is closely associated with a National Center for Public Policy Research, which supplies material (from the same address) on domestic and foreign policy issues and which operates a speakers' bureau on the subject of Afghanistan.

Concerned Women of America

Address. 122 C Street NW, Washington, DC 20001

Leadership. Beverley Lahaye (president)

Orientation. Ultra-conservative

History. This group was founded in 1979 by Lahaye and other Baptist conservatives, and has grown into a national network of over 1,000 branches.

In 1986 the group funded a Tennessee court case aimed at forcing the withdrawal of a range of school textbooks deemed to be too liberal. The case, which evoked memories of the 1925 John T. Scopes "monkey trial" case on evolution teaching, achieved widespread publicity for the views of Protestant fundamentalists opposed to the alleged promotion of "secular humanism", feminism, homosexuality, non-Christian religions, internationalism, abortion and occult practices by the federal educational system. (The plaintiff in the court case, Vicky Frost, had sought to remove her child from school because she objected to the textbooks.)

Earlier cases, notably in Arkansas and Texas in 1982-84, had also attempted to challenge evolution teaching, and in 1986-87 there were attempts under way in some states to have "secular humanism" declared a religion, and thus to prevent its promotion by the public schools. The litigation, and the related activities of the Concerned Women of America, were occurring in the context of a determined effort by the religious right to reverse the effects of Supreme Court rulings of 1962-63 which in practice removed religious instruction, prayer and other religious activities from public-funded schools to avoid infringing the constitutional separation of church and state.

Policies. The Women combat the decline of Christian moral standards in public life.

Membership. About 500,000 (late 1986).

Associated organizations. There are literally thousands of pressure groups at local, state and national levels which share some of the concerns of the Women, but most are less right-wing, much smaller and rather less influential. Funding and support for the plaintiff in the Tennessee court case has come in part from the Moral Majority and from the Freedom Council Foundation, a pressure group led by religious broadcaster Pat Robertson, and, on the opposing side, from the American Civil Liberties Union and from People for the American Way, a group which monitors the religious right. The activities of the Concerned Women and similar groups are influenced by the work of Mel and Norma Gabler (Educational Research Analysts, PO Box 7518, Longview, Texas 75601), who review school textbooks from the point of view of their compatibility with fundamentalist Christianity. In federal politics most proponents of school prayer and similar causes are Republicans (including President Reagan and Senators Howard Baker, Paul Laxalt and Jesse Helms), while the Democrats have generally opposed such causes.

Confederation of Klans

Leadership. Bob Scoggins

Orientation. White supremacist

History. This grouping of Ku Klux Klan followers was represented at the annual Klan rally at Stone Mountain, Georgia, in 1986.

Policies. The Confederation, in common with other Klan groups, has white supremacist ideas and tends towards fascist social and economic policies.

Conservative Alliance—see NC-PAC.

Conservative Caucus

Address. 450 Maple Avenue East, Vienna, Virginia 22180

Telephone. (703) 893 1550

Leadership. Howard Phillips (national director)

Orientation. Right-wing conservative

History. This Republican Party pressure group, founded in 1974 (and based until 1984) in Falls Church, Virginia, supported Ronald Reagan's 1980 and 1984 election campaigns and has gained some influence with the White House. In 1986 it placed newspaper advertisements in the name of a National Coalition for Americans Committed to Rescuing Africa from the Grip of Soviet Tyranny. The Caucus holds frequent congresses and meetings at state and local level throughout the United States in order to debate and refine conservative agendas for local, state and federal governments.

Policies. The Caucus aims to keep right-wing domestic and foreign policy goals in the forefront of national political debate. In common with many conservative groups it campaigns for a reduction in income and other taxes (partly through its sponsorship of the Committee for a 10% Flat Tax, which is run by the Tax Reform Immediately section of the John Birch Society).

Membership. 700,000.

Publications. Conservative Manifesto, monthly magazine; *Members' Report*, quarterly bulletin; other journals and pamphlets.

Associated organizations. Campaigns run by the Caucus include the Victory over Communism Project. Organizations sympathetic to its positions are many, and include the American Conservative Union (which has 400,000 members and publishes *Battle Line*) and the American Conservative Trust, both based in Washington DC. The tax-exempt publishing arm of the Caucus is the Conservative Caucus Research, Analysis and Educational Foundation. Although the Caucus is generally identified with the Republican right, it has exceptionally offered support to right-wing Democrats opposing liberal Republicans. The first instance of this was in May 1984, when Phillips, together with Richard Viguerie (publisher of the influential

Conservative Digest) and Terry Dolan (of NC-PAC) supported an Illinois Democratic candidate for the US Senate.

Constitution Parties of the United States

Address. Box 608, White Fish, Montana 59937

Leadership. Dr Clarence Martin (executive director)

Orientation. Anti-communist

History. This network of state-level parties was formed in 1952, and has members in at least 23 states. Martin, the leader of the North Dakota Constitution Party in the 1970s, became national leader in the early 1980s.

Policies. The Parties work for the enhancement of state power over federal power, for Christian government, against communism and against the United Nations Organization, which they view as a conspiracy for world government.

Council on American Affairs

Address. Suite 210, 1785 Massachusetts Avenue NW, Washington, DC 20036

Leadership. Dr Roger Pearson (president)

Orientation. Right-wing

History. The Council was founded in 1975 by Pearson, a veteran right-wing academic (see Council for Social and Economic Studies). After the American Council for World Freedom had withdrawn from the World Anti-Communist League (see South Korea) in 1975, in protest against the involvement of many fascist and anti-semitic organizations, Pearson's Council became the League's American section.

It hosted the 11th annual WACL conference in Washington in 1978 with the help of the anti-semitic Liberty Lobby. Pearson chaired the conference; one of his assistants and an employee of the Council was Earl Thomas, a former member of the National Socialist White People's Party.

In 1979 a non-fascist lobby within the League began to conspire against Pearson and other ultra-rightists; Pearson resigned as WACL chairman in 1980, and in the early 1980s he was forced out of the League with the American WACL "franchise" returning to the Council for World Freedom. He is now active in the Council for Social and Economic Studies, which may have superseded the Council on American Affairs.

Publications. The Council co-operates with the American Foreign Policy Institute (see American Security Council) to publish the *Journal of International Relations*, whose general editors have included Pearson. An associate editor of the journal in 1984 was James Angleton, a former head of the Central Intelligence Agency.

Council for the Defense of Freedom (CDF)

Address. 1275 K Street, Suite 1160, Washington, DC 20005

Telephone. (202) 789 4294

Leadership. M. Lewis (chairman)

Orientation. Anti-communist

History. The CDF was formed in the early 1950s, and operated for a time as the Council Against Communist Aggression (based until the late 1970s in Orlando,

Florida). It lobbies government, conducts direct-mail campaigns, presents awards and provides speakers for public events.

Policies. The Council seeks to combat communist aggression in the international arena and to expose domestic subversion.

Membership. Over 6,000 (1984).

Publications. Washington Inquirer, weekly; *Bulletin*, monthly; pamphlets and tracts.

Council for Inter-American Security (CIS)

Leadership. L. Francis Bouchey (chairman)

Orientation. Anti-communist

History. In December 1986 Bouchey participated in a pro-contra Conference for a Free Nicaragua in London (England), which was organized by people associated with the Federation of Conservative Students (see United Kingdom) and the Heritage Foundation.

Policies. The CIS supports pro-US regimes and movements throughout Latin America.

Associated organizations. Michael Waller, a leading employee of the CIS, is also national secretary of Young Americans for Freedom.

Council for Social and Economic Studies (CSES)

Address. Suite 502, 1629 K Street NW, Washington DC 20006, or 1133 13th Street NW, Suite Comm. 2, Washington, DC 20005

Telephone. (202) 789 0321

Leadership. Dr Roger Pearson (founder)

Orientation. Ultra-right

History. This organization, founded in 1980 by Pearson and others associated with the Council on American Affairs (which it may have replaced) publishes an academic-style journal promoting the views of ultra-right politicians. Its founder received a testimonial letter from President Reagan in April 1982, in which the Republican leader praised his "substantial contributions to promoting and upholding those ideals and principles that we value at home". The letter, on White House paper, was used in advertising Pearson's journal. Among those associated with the journal have been Russel Kirk and Ernest van den Haag.

Pearson was born in England in 1927. In the 1940s and '50s he worked in India, where he established a racist journal, *Northern World*, in 1956. In 1958 Pearson set up the Northern League as an international co-ordinating body for ultra-rightists. This group remains in existence among Western European fascists (see Netherlands). His journal, which achieved a substantial circulation among foreign fascist groups, became *Folk* in 1963 and *Western Destiny* in 1964, by which time it was published in the USA where Pearson had become involved in Willis Carto's operations (see Noontide Press; Liberty Lobby). Pearson left *Western Destiny* in 1966.

During the 1960s and 1970s Pearson, then working as an anthropologist, became involved with a number of ultra-conservative and neo-fascist groups, including the American Security Council, the Heritage Foundation, the Pioneer Fund, the World Anti-Communist League (of whose North American Region he became chairman), the Council on American Affairs and the American Foreign Policy Institute. In the early 1980s, as part of a purge of fascist elements, Pearson was forced out of his leading position in the WACL and was succeeded by Gen. Singlaub of the US Council for World Freedom.

Publications. The Journal of Social, Political and Economic Studies, quarterly. Pearson has written a number of tracts and books on race and eugenics, several of which are sold through US and foreign fascist groups.

Associated organizations. See *Mankind Quarterly* (United Kingdom).

The Covenant, the Sword and the Arm of the Lord (CSA)

Base. Three Brothers, Arkansas

Leadership. James Ellison (leader); Kerry Wayne Noble (deputy leader)

Orientation. Nazi

History. This organization, which may be defunct, was part of the paramilitary "survivalist" movement which has gained many adherents on the ultra-right. It carried out numerous attacks on Jewish and homosexual targets in 1983-84. Its camp on the Arkansas-Missouri border was raided by the FBI in 1985, resulting in the seizure of a vast quantity of weaponry and in the sentencing of Ellison to 20 years in prison for racketeering offences. Six other CSA members—including Noble, imprisoned for five years—received lesser sentences on conspiracy and arms charges.

Associated organizations. Several members of another fascist paramilitary group, The Order, were found at the headquarters of this group during the FBI raid.

Democratic International

Address. 214 Massachusetts Avenue NE, Suite 320, Washington, DC 20002

Leadership. Lewis Lehrman (main sponsor)

Orientation. Anti-communist

History. This group was launched in June 1985 at a meeting, in a UNITA-controlled area of Angola, organized by the Citizens for America pressure group. The meeting was attended by a group of South African students and heard a message of support from President Reagan.

Policies. The International seeks to co-ordinate the publicity and fund-raising efforts of various anti-communist rebel movements, to publicize their causes in the United States and elsewhere, and to foster co-operation between the groups.

Membership. The International includes UNITA (Angola), which was represented at the inaugural ceremony by its leader, Jonas Savimbi; the Afghan *mujaheddin*, represented by Dastagir Ghulam Wardak; the Ethnic Liberation Organization of Laos, represented by Pa Kao Her, and the *Fuerza Democrática Nicaragüense*, led by Adolfo Calero.

Destiny Research Foundation (DRF)

Address. Box 333, Salem, Ohio 44460

Telephone. (216) 332 0100

Leadership. Frank Fiebiger (president)

Orientation. Anti-communist

History. The DRF was established in 1977.

Policies. The main aims of the Foundation are "to monitor and expose subversive threats to the US Constitution, and to set right distortions of history by subversives". It also campaigns against income tax and defends America against a world-wide socialist conspiracy.

Publications. Defender and *Research Report*, monthly; leaflets and other material.

Associated organizations. The DRF formed a National Coalition of Patriotic Associations in 1980, possibly as a successor to the American Coalition of Patriotic Societies (see American Security Council).

Eagle

Leadership. Jim Morris (editor)

Orientation. Anti-communist

History. This magazine is directed at anti-communist mercenaries and those interested in their lifestyle. Its editor addressed the 1984 conference of the World Anti-Communist League (see South Korea).

Associated organizations. One of its contributing editors, David Atlee Phillips, is leader of the Association of Former Intelligence Officers and a contributor, like several other *Eagle* writers, to the better-known *Soldier of Fortune* mercenary magazine.

Eagle Forum

Address. Box 618, Alton, Illinois 62002

Leadership. Phyllis Schlafly (president)

Orientation. Ultra-conservative

History. The Forum was founded in the early 1970s as the Eagle Trust Fund. In the late 1970s it operated partly through an anti-feminist pressure group called Stop ERA (i.e. the Equal Rights Amendment campaign) by Schlafly, whose magazine had for several years been one of the leading anti-communist periodicals in the United States.

Policies. The Forum works for the preservation of the nuclear family, for the devolution of federal powers to the states, and for strong foreign and defence policies.

Publications. The Phyllis Schlafly Report, monthly.

Endowment for the Preservation of Liberty

Leadership. Carl (Spitz) Channell (director)

Orientation. Anti-communist

History. This lobbying organization came to public attention in December 1986 when it was reported that it had spent between four and seven million dollars on US television advertising designed to further the cause of the Nicaraguan contras. The Endowment received illegal assistance from Lt.-Col. Oliver North, a serving officer then in charge of organizing secret funding for the covert war against the Nicaraguan regime. The director of the Endowment was until 1982 associated with the National Conservative Political Action Committee, and has more recently held senior posts in the American Conservative Trust, the Anti-Terrorism America Committee and the Sentinel lobbying group. In April 1987, during the so-called "Irangate" hearings, Channell pleaded guilty to criminal conspiracy to avoid paying taxes on $2,000,000 which he had raised to buy arms for the contras.

Policies. The Endowment aims to publicize and win support for anti-communist causes.

Eugenics Special Interest Group

Address. Box 5181, Austin, Texas 78703

Orientation. White supremacist

History. This Group has been active since the mid-1980s.

Policies. It provides advice on "racial science" to activist groups, and promotes the idea of the controlled breeding of intelligent white people to create a European renaissance.

Publications. Eugenics Bulletin, quarterly.

Euro-American Quarterly

Address. Box 2-1776, Milwaukee, Wisconsin 53221

Leadership. Maj. Donald V. Clerkin

Orientation. Anti-semitic

History. This journal specializes in the revision of history from an anti-semitic, pro-fascist perspective.

Policies. The *Quarterly* regards communism and Judaism as essentially the same thing, and reviles those sections of the right (such as the John Birch Society, which it calls the Jacob Belchstein Society) which admit Jews as members.

Excalibur Society

Address. Box 70434, Charleston Heights, South Carolina 29405

Leadership. Harold Covington (head)

Orientation. Nazi

History. The Society was formed around 1982 by Covington, who had led the National Socialist Party of America for a year after he achieved national prominence by winning 56,000 votes (43 per cent) as a nazi candidate in a Republican Party primary election for state attorney-general in 1980.

Policies. The Society advances classic national socialist policies on racial, social and economic matters.

Publications. Excalibur.

Executive Intelligence Review (EIR)

Bases. Washington, DC and New York, NY; *European offices*: Wiesbaden, West Germany, and London, England

Leadership. Lyndon LaRouche (founder)

Orientation. Conspiracy theorist, LaRoucheist

History. The EIR is a magazine set up by LaRouche, who is better known as leader of the National Democratic Policy Committee. The magazine purports to supply high-grade political and economic intelligence to important people in return for large sums of money. There have been reports that "agents" of the EIR have undergone paramilitary training and have disrupted left-wing rallies and meetings. The EIR is also said to have access to sophisticated computer technology and to top-level government contacts in several Western countries.

In October 1985 the EIR, which was previously published only from Washington, commenced operations in Europe. The launch meeting in London was said by *Searchlight*, a British anti-fascist magazine, to have been attended by Latin American and Middle Eastern diplomats, by East European émigrés and by leading British right-wingers.

Policies. The EIR advances the notions that Soviet and nazi forces are conspiring to take over the world, using the IMF, the drugs trade and the AIDS epidemic. It supports President Reagan's "Star Wars" plan for space-based military systems as a sensible and affordable strategy to meet that threat. In common with other LaRouche operations, the political stance of EIR is not presented as explicitly right-wing or left-wing.

Publications. Executive Intelligence Review, $400 per year; *Investigative Leads*, $80 per issue; other reports and monographs.

Fact Finder

Address. Box 10555, Phoenix, Arizona 85064

Leadership. Harry T. Everingham (editor)

Orientation. Anti-communist

History. This organization was active in the early 1980s. It has not been possible to establish whether it was connected with mid-1970s right-wing groups such as the Fact Finders Forum (Palm Beach, Florida) or, more plausibly, *Fact Finder* magazine (published by We, The People, a California-based group which had a chapter in Phoenix).

Publications. The American Patriot. (Not the same as the magazine of that name published from Carbondale, Pennsylvania, in the early 1970s.)

Fairness in Media (FIM)

Address. PO Box 25099, Raleigh, North Carolina 27611

Telephone. (919) 781 4842

Orientation. Ultra-conservative

History. The FIM was established in 1985. To date it has concentrated on a direct-mail campaign urging conservatives to buy stock in the CBS broadcasting network in order to pressure the network into removing or altering the programmes to which the FIM takes exception.

Policies. Its objective is to prevent the use of the mass media for the propagation of liberal ideas.

Freedom League

Address. 2140 West Chapman Avenue, Suite 223, Orange, California 92668

Telephone. (714) 385 1776

Orientation. Libertarian

History. The League was formed in 1978 in Orange County, which has long been recognized as a source of radical and innovative thinking on the right wing of the major parties. The League is positioned somewhere between the conservative tax-cutting movement led by Howard Jarvis, which won the Proposition 14 referendum in California in the mid-1970s, and the quasi-fascist survivalist and Posse Comitatus movements, which also have a significant following in California.

Policies. The League devotes its energies to developing the argument that there is no legal or constitutional basis for the US taxation system.

Publications. Newsletter, irregular.

German-American National Political Action Committee (GANPAC)

Address. Box 1137, Santa Monica, California 90401

Leadership. Hans Schmidt (chairman)

Orientation. Neo-nazi

History. The GANPAC was founded in 1982.

Policies. It is extremely anti-semitic and anti-homosexual, advocating the establishment of "Jew-free, AIDS-free" white colonies.

Publications. *GANPAC Brief*, monthly.

Heritage Foundation

Address. 214 Massachusetts Avenue NE, Washington, DC 20002

Telephone. (202) 546 4400

Leadership. Edwin J. Feulner Jr (president); Burton Y. Pines (vice-president); Jeffrey B. Gaynor (international director); Stuart Butler (domestic director)

Orientation. Right-wing conservative

History. The Heritage Foundation, usually known as Heritage, was an obscure ultra-conservative pressure group and "think tank" founded in 1973 by Paul Weyrich with a $260,000 grant from brewing magnate Joseph Coors. It has achieved national prominence only since the coming to power of Ronald Reagan at the head of a right-wing Republican administration. The Reagan government has put into practice most of Heritage's domestic and foreign policy recommendations, as set out in a 1,000-page book, *Mandate for Leadership*, published just after the 1980 election, and in a shorter sequel issued in 1984. Many Heritage staff have received important government posts, and President Reagan has attended Heritage events.

Prominent members of the Foundation in the mid-1970s included Roger Pearson, now regarded as something of an embarrassment because of his racist associations. The current leadership of the Foundation includes former Treasury Secretary William E. Simon; Richard Allen, a former National Security Council head; Coors; Midge Decter, executive director of the Committee for the Free World; and Lewis E. Lehrman of Citizens for America. Heritage has provided premises, facilities and support for many smaller single-issue pressure groups and lobbying organizations. The 1986 budget of the tax-exempt Foundation was almost $10,000,000.

Policies. The Foundation originally sought to provide research, policy support and advice to conservative Congressmen, but it has now developed into a major lobbying organization dedicated to free enterprise, monetarism, small government, a strong defence policy and individual liberty. It opposes equal pay for women and supports aid for foreign anti-communist guerrillas. It has been highly critical of the United Nations and has supported US withdrawal from UN agencies.

Membership. Heritage is supported by about 130,000 regular donors, including some 100 of the country's 500 largest businesses.

Publications. *Policy Review*, quarterly; *Heritage Today*, six per year; *National Security Record*, monthly; *Backgrounder* and *News*, occasional press releases; frequent position papers.

Associated organizations. The Young Conservative Foundation (YCF) was formerly regarded as the activist wing of Heritage. In 1986, however, it changed its name to the World Youth Freedom League and became the youth wing of the World Anti-Communist League (see South Korea), which is represented in the USA by the US Council for World Freedom. Another conservative youth group linked to Heritage is Third Generation, founded in 1984 and based, as are many right-wing pressure groups, at the Foundation's $9,500,000 headquarters building. Many hundreds of smaller groups throughout the United States share at least some of the Foundation's policies.

Heritage is one of about 100 groups forming the Coalition for the SDI (i.e. the Strategic Defense Initiative, the Administration's preferred name for what is usually called the Star Wars strategy, for space-based weapons systems). The most important of the other members are the NC-PAC and industry-funded electoral pressure groups such as Gen. Daniel Graham's 13,000-member American Space Frontier Committee (Box 1984, Merrifield, Virginia 22116). A similar coalition is called High Frontier.

Major institutional donors to the Foundation include the John M. Nolin Fund and the Oklahoma-based Noble Foundation.

International affiliations. The Foundation maintains contact with about 200 foreign right-wing groups, such as the Federation of Conservative Students and the Adam Smith Institute (United Kingdom). Many British Conservative politicians have visited the Foundation or written for its publications.

Heritage Library

Base. Velma, Oklahoma

Leadership. Lawrence L. Humphreys (head)

Orientation. Anti-semitic

History. The Library was founded around 1980 by Humphreys. In 1985 it became involved in a campaign to prevent banks foreclosing on an indebted farmer in Cochran, Georgia.

Policies. The Library maintains that the banking system has no legal basis.

Associated organizations. The Library appears to be in sympathy with groups such as the Aryan Nations and the Covenant, the Sword and the Arm of the Lord, which have argued that foreclosures are being used to ensure Jewish control of the agricultural industry.

Initiators

Address. Box 1257, Alpine, Texas 79831

Telephone. (915) 837 2258

Leadership. Marie G. McAfee (chairwoman)

Orientation. Anti-communist

History. This group was founded in 1962.

Policies. It opposes communism and internationalism, and works for a strong nation and the defence of liberty.

Membership. 100,000 (1984 claim).

Institute for Historical Review (IHR)

Address. Box 1306, Torrance, California 90505

Telephone. (213) 533 5061

Leadership. Tom J. Marcellus (editor, *Journal*); Willis Carto (founder); Keith Stimely (associate editor); H. Keith Thompson

Orientation. Revisionist history group

History. This organization, established in the 1970s with support from Carto's Liberty Lobby, belongs to the international revisionist history movement, which attempts to persuade people inter alia that the Nazi Holocaust never took place. As a publicity gimmick it offered a $50,000 prize for anyone who could prove that Jews had been gassed by the Nazis; it refused to pay the money to an Auschwitz survivor, who sued the IHR in 1985 and won damages of $90,000. The IHR holds annual conferences and publishes a pseudo-academic journal. Several IHR supporters are prominent nazis.

The first director of the IHR was an Irishman called Dave McCalden (also known as Lewis Brandon), formerly active in the National Front and National Party (United Kingdom). He left the IHR in 1979 amid mutual recriminations and was embroiled in a legal dispute with Carto in the mid-1980s; he went on to establish the rival Truth Mission. McCalden's allegations against Carto and his supporters included fraudulent appeals for funds, the operation of a secret gay nazi group within the Institute, and the recruitment of IHR members by the Scientology cult. Counter-claims from Carto are backed up by a dossier of letters from several revisionists associated with the Institute.

US-based revisionists on the editorial advisory committee of the IHR *Journal* include Arthur K. Butz, author of one of the best-selling Holocaust denial pamphlets; Austin J. App, George Ashley, Reinhard K. Buchner, Percy L. Greaves Jr, James J. Martin, Revilo P. Oliver, Charles E. Weber and Andreas R. Wesserle. All but Greaves use the title Dr, and most are or were employed in otherwise-respectable US universities.

Membership. The IHR reportedly has a mailing list of 30,000 names.

Publications. Journal of Historical Review, quarterly; *Newsletter* and *IHR Special Report,* occasional.

Associated organizations. See Liberty Lobby, whose Dr Martin A. Larson is also on the committee, and *New Libertarian,* represented on the committee by its editor Samuel E. Konkin III and contributing editor James Martin.

International affiliations. Revisionist historians are also active in most other countries with sizeable fascist movements, although few of them are prepared to admit membership of fascist groups. The IHR has contact with many foreign revisionists, including Walter Beveraggi (Argentina), Robert Faurisson (France), Wilhelm Stäglich and Udo Walendy (West Germany), Dietlieb Felderer (Sweden) and John Bennett (Australia), all of whom are on the *Journal*'s advisory committee. See also Jim Keegstra and Ernst Zundel (Canada); David Irving, Richard Verrall, Centre for Historical Review and Historical Review Press (United Kingdom).

Institute for Regional and International Studies (IRIS)

Address. Box 693, Boulder, Colorado 80306

Leadership. Alexander McColl (president)

Orientation. Anti-communist

History. The IRIS was founded in 1983.

Policies. It seeks to conduct research into "Soviet-sponsored subversion" in Central America.

Institute for the Study of Man Inc.

Address. 1716 New Hampshire Avenue NW, Washington, DC 20009

Orientation. White supremacist

History. This organization produces journals on race and eugenics which are widely circulated among US fascists.

Invisible Empire Knights of the Ku Klux Klan

Address. Box 700, Five Points, Alabama 36855

Telephone. (205) 499 2297

Leadership. James Farrands (Imperial Wizard)

Orientation. White supremacist

History. This KKK faction, also referred to as the Invisible Empire of the KKK or as the KKK—Invisible Empire, was created in Denham Springs, Louisiana, in 1975 by a split in the Knights of the Ku Klux Klan. It revived the name of a Klan group, first incorporated in 1915, which had died out in the 1960s. It grew rapidly in the late 1970s, and is strongest in Alabama, Georgia and other southern states, but it has members, including its current leader, in the north-east of the country. It had ten regional offices by 1982.

Virgil L. Griffin, then the Grand Dragon of the Invisible Empire in North Carolina, was among the group of Klansmen and nazis involved in the 1979 Greensboro massacre. The Knights' original leader, Bill Wilkinson, was compromised in Klan circles and lost many followers after the revelation in 1982 that he had been an FBI informer. He retained some prestige in the organization by refusing, in contempt of a court ruling, to release membership data required by a judge in 1983. A former high-ranking member, naval employee John Walker, was convicted in 1985 of spying for the Soviet Union. Another prominent member, Bill Allen, has defected to the White Aryan Resistance group.

A convention of the Invisible Empire in 1986, held in Connecticut, elected Farrands as the new leader, succeeding James E. (Jim) Blair of Alabama. Five members of the group were arrested during the gathering for drunkenness and other offences.

Policies. In common with other Klan factions, the group advocates white rule, racial segregation, patriotism and a hierarchical authoritarian state. In addition it espouses economic protectionism and, unusually for a Klan group, it wishes to be regarded as a bona fide political party. It encourages its members to own and use firearms and has conducted paramilitary training, even (through the Klan Youth Corps—KYC) for the children of its members.

Membership. In 1983, when he was forced to file for the bankruptcy of the group, Wilkinson claimed that it had 1,800 members, which at that time would probably have given it from 15 to 20 per cent of the national Klan following.

Publications. *The Klansman*, monthly; *KYC News*, quarterly.

Associated organizations. The same name was used around 1980 by a Klan group using a Louisiana address (Box 188, Swartz, LA 71281), which was led by Robert M. Shelton, one of the few nationally known Klan leaders (now leader of the United Klans of America). The Shelton group had extensive foreign contacts, mainly in the nazi network. It has not been possible to establish whether the two groups were or are connected.

John Birch Society (JBS)

Address. 395 Concord Avenue, Belmont, Massachussets 02178

Telephone. (617) 489 0600

Leadership. Charles R. Armour (president); A. Clifford Barker (chairman); John Rees (editor); John F. McManus (director of public relations); Gary E. Benoit

Orientation. Ultra-conservative, anti-communist

History. The JBS was founded in 1958 by confectionery manufacturer Robert H.W. Welch Jr, who had published the pioneering ultra-conservative magazine *One Man's Opinion* since the early 1950s. The JBS was named after the first US soldier to die at the hands of a communist army in the post-war era (a spy, shot in China in 1945).

In 1961 the JBS was involved in a major controversy when Maj.-Gen. Edwin A. Walker, a commander of US forces in West Germany, distributed its propaganda to serving soldiers. He was forced to resign and became involved in segregationist activities in the southern USA, being charged with sedition in 1962. He was denied a pension until a review of his case under the Reagan administration in 1982. During the 1960s the JBS acquired 400 bookstores and about 100,000 members. It supported the efforts of Senator MacCarthy and others to identify alleged communists and "fellow-travellers" throughout US society, but it went further than the Senator in naming President Eisenhower and the former Secretary of State, John Foster Dulles, as "dedicated, conscious" communist agents. The Society declined in membership during the 1970s and is now a pressure group and publisher rather than a mass movement.

The chairman of the JBS from the late 1970s was the only urologist ever elected to federal office, the right-wing Georgian Democratic Congressman Lawrence Patton (Larry) McDonald. In 1977 it was reported that McDonald had over 200 guns in his home. He was involved in promoting the spurious cancer drug laetrile, and attempted to stop sales of stockpiled silver in order to support the investments of his friend and fellow-member of the JBS, Texan billionaire Nelson Bunker Hunt. A member of the board of the Christian Voice new right pressure group, McDonald founded the Western Goals lobby shortly before his death in the 1983 KAL 7 airliner incident.

In 1982 the JBS organ, *American Opinion*, had a $400,000 libel award made against it, then a record amount. By 1986 the JBS was in serious financial trouble, with a deficit in the region of $9,000,000 as against assets of about $30,000. It was also divided ideologically, with the widow of Welch (who died in 1985, two years after retiring as president of the Society) opposing the anti-Reagan stance of the new leadership under Armour (elected as president at the June 1986 annual meeting).

Policies. The Society seeks to expose communist subversion and other threats to Western values and institutions, and espouses a strong US foreign policy backed by an enhanced military capability. It advocates free enterprise, low taxation, withdrawal from the United Nations and the cessation of all diplomatic and economic dealings with communist states.

Membership. Under 50,000.

Publications. The New American, weekly, founded 1985, circulation 30,000; *JBS Bulletin*, monthly. The JBS has produced many hundreds of books, booklets and periodicals in the anti-communist cause. Its best-known publications have been *American Opinion* (monthly), which was closed down in 1985, and *The Review of the News* (weekly).

Associated organizations. The tax reform department of the JBS uses the name and slogan Tax Reform Immediately. Truth About Civil Turmoil (TACT), run from California by C. Herbert Joiner, is a JBS-sponsored national network dedicated to exposing and countering the "subversive effects" of civil rights agitation and other urban activism.

Journal of Social, Political and Economic Studies—see Council for Social and Economic Studies.

Keep America Independent (KAI)

Address. 6609 Edenvale Road, Baltimore, Maryland 21209

Telephone. (301) 486 5909

Leadership. Alfred I. Aaronson (president)

Orientation. Anti-communist

History. The KAI was founded by Aaronson in 1981.

Policies. The KAI campaigns against what it sees as a socialist conspiracy for a "one-world" government.

Publications. KAI, monthly; the campaign also produces films and pamphlets, and grants awards to those in public life who have done most to further its aims.

Knights of the Ku Klux Klan (KKKK)

Address. Box 624, Metairie, Louisiana 70004; *or* c/o Patriot Press, 1214 Old Lee Highway, Tuscumbia, Alabama 35674

Leadership. Stephen Donald (Don) Black (Imperial Wizard, i.e. leader); Thomas Robb (national chaplain)

Orientation. Neo-nazi

History. This Klan group, founded in 1974, is one of many organizations claiming lineal descent from the original Ku Klux Klan (KKK), a white racist and anti-Catholic group founded in Tennessee and active in the Southern states from 1865 to about 1870. A feature of the first Klan movement which has been retained by later incarnations was the use of esoteric titles for officers of the organization, such as Exalted Cyclops, Grand Dragon, Imperial Wizard, Titan and Grand Chaplain. The KKK was reorganized by W.J. Simmons of Atlanta, Georgia, in 1915. The new Klan became extremely popular in the early 1920s, reaching a membership often estimated at about 4,000,000, mainly in the south and in Indiana, Oregon and Colorado.

It declined in influence in the late 1920s and the '30s, and was virtually destroyed by publicity given to its links with the nazi German-American Bund in 1939, and by a tax case in 1944. Attempts were made to reconstruct the Klan in the post-war era, notably by Dr Samuel Green of Atlanta, Georgia, but it never again achieved national significance.

By the mid-1960s there were estimated to be about 10,000 Klan members, mostly grouped in the following major factions: (i) the 5,000-member Knights of the KKK, based in Tuscaloosa, Alabama, and minor groups elsewhere affiliated to it through the United Klans of America Inc.; (ii) the 1,000-member Original Knights of the KKK, based in Louisiana; (iii) the clandestine 2,000-member White Knights of the KKK, based in Mississippi and having a reputation for violence; (iv) the 1,000-member North Florida Klan, based at Jacksonville, which regarded itself as a faction of the Knights of the KKK, and (v) the 500-member Association of South Carolina Klans. Members of many Klan groups were involved in violent confrontations with lblack civil rights campaigners in 1964-66.

Since the mid-1960s the rapid turnover of membership, FBI infiltration, and a confusing tendency to split, to change names and to readopt old names has made it somewhat difficult to chart the progress of the Klan movement. (The movement has, however, been closely monitored by the FBI and by groups such as Klanwatch—a project run by the Alabama-based Southern Poverty Law Center.) There have been instances of two or three rival groups using the same name, and most efforts to unite or merely co-ordinate the various groups have foundered. The Ku Klux Klan has since the early 1970s functioned mainly as a flag of convenience for the US national socialist movement, which has sought to acquire a history by identifying itself with the older tradition of southern racism still typified by the Klan-linked National States Rights Party.

In the mid-1970s, more than a dozen competing Klan groups were active: (i) a new organization called the Knights of the KKK, based in Louisiana but not directly descended from the 1960s Knights, and an identically-named group in Ohio; (ii) the Original Knights of the KKK, with at least four Louisiana sections; (iii) the White Knights of the KKK, with at least three Mississippi sections, publishing *Klan Ledger*; (iv) the United Klans of America, represented in Alabama, Indiana (two sections), Maryland, Michigan, North Carolina, Pennsylvania and South Carolina; (v) the Association of Georgia Klans; (vi) the Association of Arkansas Klans; (vii) the United Florida KKK; (viii) the National Knights of the KKK, based in Georgia (publishing *Imperial Nighthawk*), and strongly represented in Ohio; (ix) the Klan Youth Corps, Georgia; (x) the United Klans—Knights of the KKK, Georgia; (xi) the Mississippi Knights of the KKK; (xii) the Association of South Carolina Klans, which also operated as the Majority Citizens League of South Carolina; and (xiii) groups simply calling themselves the KKK, based in Georgia (three groups) and Florida.

In 1984 the Jewish pressure group *B'nai B'rith* estimated total Klan membership at 8,000 to 10,000, which it said represented a fall of about 35 per cent over the figure two years earlier. (Neo-nazi movements were said to have some 500 members.) The group surveyed activity from region to region, concluding that: (i) Klan activity was declining in Florida, Tennessee and Texas, but increasing in Georgia and North Carolina; (ii) there were only some 300 Klansmen in the north-east, with sustained activity only in Connecticut; (iii) in the Mid-West, there were three Klan factions in each of Ohio and Indiana, two each in Missouri and Kentucky and one in Illinois; (iv) in the West, there was little recorded Klan activity. Nationally, the movement continued to be fragmented and ineffective, although there were signs that small and more militant groups would emerge.

There have been scores of separate, and mainly short-lived, Klan groupings in the past decade, of which the Knights—organized in 1974 by a young nazi leader, David Duke, and apparently separate from the earlier Tuscaloosa group of the same name—have been one of the most successful. Several members broke away in 1975, forming the Invisible Empire Knights, and a former national organizer, Karl Hand, founded the National Socialist Liberation Front. Duke himself left the group in 1980 to found the National Association for the Advancement of White People.

The Knights were involved in a conspiracy in 1981 to invade the Caribbean island of Dominica. Black served a three-year prison sentence for his role in the affair. On his release in 1985 he announced plans to form a "Nathan Bedford Forest Brigade", named after the 19th-century founder of the Klan movement, with the aim of recruiting 120 Klansmen to help the Nicaraguan contras. Black was reported in early 1986 to be running for election to the Senate. The Knights were then reported to be strongest in the state of Alabama and their headquarters may now be in that state.

Policies. The Knights are more openly nazi in tone than some other white supremacist groups. Robb maintains that "the federal government controlled by the anti-Christ Jews" has as its goal "the destruction of our race, our faith and our people, and our goal is the destruction of them". The group was among the first Klan factions to organize women directly in its activities. It sees itself as defending white Christian America and Western civilization.

Membership. Reliable figures for the size of any Klan group are hard to come by, but Jewish and anti-racist groups have suggested that the Knights had about 2,000 male and 1,000 female members in 1983, making it one of the two or three largest Klan groups.

Publications. The White Patriot (formerly *The Crusader*).

Associated organizations. The youth wing of the movement is known as the Klan Youth Corps. Its publishing arms has used the names Empirical Publications and Patriot Press. In 1983 the Knights joined a loose Confederation of Klans also involving the National Knights of the KKK, the New Order Knights of the KKK, the White Knights and other groups. Black attended the 1985 Christian Patriots Conference, which involved the New Order, the American Nazi Party, the America First Committee and other racist groups. The Imperial Wizard and the national chaplain also attended the 1986 Aryan Nations Congress, and a meeting chaired by Robert Miles (see Mountain Church) and involving the White Patriot Party, the National Alliance and other groups. The KKKK has been associated with another Metairie-based organization, the New Christian Crusade Church (now effectively superseded by the Christian Defense League).

International affiliations. The KKKK is in contact with many foreign groups, including several member organizations of the World Union of National Socialists.

Ku Klux Klan (Ohio)

Leadership. Dale Reutsch

Orientation. White supremacist

History. The Ohio Klan is one of many small factions in the loose national network of Ku Klux Klan movements. It probably arose from within the National Knights of the KKK. Reutsch was arrested on arms charges in 1985.

Policies. Like other Klan groups, the Ohio faction preaches the genetic superiority of the white "race" and advocates white political supremacy.

Associated organizations. Reutsch was a speaker at the 1985 Christian Patriots Conference, which was attended by many KKK and nazi activists.

League of Pace Amendment Advocates

Base. Los Angeles, California

Leadership. Daniel Johnson

Orientation. White supremacist

History. This group is named after James O. Pace, whose ideas the group advances.

Policies. The League advocates the repeal of the 14th Amendment to the US Constitution, which extended the bill of rights to the states and guaranteed citizenship to all. It would follow the repeal by dispossessing and deporting non-white people.

Associated organizations. Johnson represented the League at the 1986 Aryan Nations Congress.

Liberty Bell—see *Der Schulungsbrief* (West Germany).

Liberty Federation—see Moral Majority.

Liberty Lobby

Address. 300 Independence Avenue SE, Washington, DC 20003

Telephone. (202) 546 5611

Leadership. Willis Allison Carto (leader); Vincent Ryan (managing editor, *The Spotlight*); Lois Petersen (secretary, Board of Policy); Trisha Kaston (assistant editor); Sara Bebko (executive secretary)

Orientation. White supremacist, anti-semitic

History. Carto, one of the leading figures on the American far right, is a follower of Francis Parker Yockey, an anti-semite and conspiracy theorist who died in prison in 1960. Carto founded Liberty Lobby in 1958, as a "Lobby for Patriotism" linked with the American Council of Christian Laymen, and has built it into a multi-million dollar propaganda operation and pressure group; he has used it to fund the election campaigns of ultra-right candidates of mainstream parties, and in the 1960s was involved in the presidential campaign of Senator Barry Goldwater and in the campaigns of Alabama politician George Wallace. In the 1970s there was a brief alliance with the John Birch Society, a larger but not anti-semitic group. In 1978 Liberty Lobby organized the Washington DC conference of the World Anti-Communist League (see South Korea) in conjunction with the Council on American Affairs.
In 1984 Carto established the Populist Party as his own political organ. He has also been involved in establishing a revisionist history institute and a publishing group with Klan and nazi links. Liberty Lobby was represented at a White Patriot Party rally in early 1986.

Policies. Liberty Lobby produces anti-semitic, anti-communist and anti-establishment propaganda. It aims to act as a point of contact between ultra-conservative and outright fascist organizations. It opposes the Equal Rights Amendment campaign, the United Nations, immigration, taxation, the federal government, gun laws, the welfare state and liberalism.

Membership. 30,000 (1986 claim).

Publications. *The Spotlight*, tabloid weekly, claimed circulation 150,000; other journals and books. In 1985 the paper was sued by William F. Buckley Jr, editor of the mainstream conservative *National Review*, after *The Spotlight* accused him of supporting paedophilia and the American nazi movement.

Associated organizations. See Institute for Historical Review; Noontide Press; Populist Party. Liberty Lobby also funds single-issue lobbying operations. Carto also established a Government Educational Foundation in the 1960s to manage property investments. The Lobby has worked through a front organization called Americans for National Security.

International affiliations. The Lobby has relations with the Crown Commonwealth League of Rights (see United Kingdom) and with the latter's affiliates in Britain, Canada, Australia and New Zealand. Its propaganda is widely circulated by other foreign ultra-right groups. *The Spotlight* has "international bureaus" or correspondents in Argentina, Australia, Canada, Central America, Taiwan, United Kingdom, Greece, India, Mexico, Portugal, Singapore, South Africa and Western Europe.

Mercenary Association

Orientation. Ultra-right

History. Members of this survivalist grouping ran paramilitary training camps in various areas in 1984 and 1985. In November 1985 one of their camps was raided by police; several members were arrested and charged with explosives offences.

Policies. The ideology and practices of the survivalist movement are described above; basically, it prepares members for a self-sufficient existence in the event of the collapse of social order.

Minutemen of Indiana

Address. Box 342, Danville, Indiana 46122

Orientation. Neo-fascist

History. This organization is almost certainly a remnant of the national Minutemen network of the 1960s.

The original Minutemen were militia volunteers who formed guerrilla bands during the War of Independence. In 1959 Robert Bolivar DePugh revived the name for a semi-clandestine organization which by 1961 claimed to have recruited about 25,000 members, in cells of five to 15 men, across 40 states. DePugh's organization was broken up in 1966-67, when he was imprisoned, with some of his followers, for firearms offences. The movement had allegedly tried to infiltrate the army reserve and planned to launch a campaign of political violence with racial overtones. DePugh maintained a small following in the 1970s (when his organization published *On Target*, from Box 68, Norborne, Missouri 64668), but his group appeared to have faded away by the early 1980s.

The Minutemen of Indiana, although reported as active around 1984, failed to respond to an enquiry and may also be defunct.

Policies. DePugh's Minutemen sought to resist communist subversion and propaganda, to support national defence and to uphold the right to own and bear firearms. The Indiana group appears to have white supremacist policies sympathetic to fascism.

Associated organizations. The Indiana Minutemen were affiliated in the 1970s to the White Confederacy, an alliance led by the National Socialist Movement. It is not known whether they were connected to the Minute Women of the USA (with addresses in Texas and West Virginia) or to the Minute Women of Virginia, which were small groups active until the late 1970s.

Monarchist Alliance

Orientation. Ultra-conservative

History. This organization was active in the early 1980s and may be defunct. (There are several other "monarchist" groupings in the United States, most of which are social or academic historical organizations whose members pursue their interest as a hobby; this appears to have been the only organization actually promoting monarchism as a political system for our time.)

Policies. The Alliance has sought to promote the monarchical system of government as the ideal arrangement for North America, and to promote monarchism in general and in particular foreign countries. It appears to be influenced by British Israel theory (see United Kingdom), which holds that the British and other European royal families rule by divine right and by traceable direct descent from early Biblical characters; it also appears to be associated with an authoritarian and fundamentalist version of the Catholic religion.

Moral Majority

Address. 305 Sixth Street, Lynchburg, Virginia 24504

Leadership. Rev. Jerry Falwell (president); Dr Ronald S. Godwin (vice-president); Charles E. Judd (executive director)

Orientation. Christian fundamentalist

History. Moral Majority, established in 1979, formally changed the name of its principal campaigning group to Liberty Federation as part of a reorganization in January 1986, with a small lobbying group being called Liberty Alliance and the name Moral Majority being retained for limited purposes; the change does not appear to have been widely accepted by the media, and the old name is used not just to describe all of Falwell's grouping but as a generic term for the Christian right.

This is perhaps the most successful of many pressure groups launched in the 1970s by Christian fundamentalists. The moving forces behind the initiative were Falwell, a religious broadcaster, and Howard Phillips of the Conservative Caucus. The group uses direct mail, rallies and paid advertising to favour election candidates of either major party who support conservative approaches to moral, social and political issues and who oppose abortion, gay rights and pornography.

In July 1984 Falwell launched a voter registration drive designed to enfranchise 2,000,000 conservative Christians, in an attempt to counter the registration of blacks and poor people by Rev. Jesse Jackson's Democratic supporters. In 1985 Falwell visited South Africa, where his description of Bishop Desmond Tutu as "a phoney" cost him some support in the United States.

The combined budgets of the three sections of Falwell's operation was about $12,000,000 in 1986. In early 1987 Falwell became involved in attempts to rescue the religious broadcasting operations of two rivals.

Policies. The group consists mainly of conservative Protestants anxious to preserve what they regard as Christian values from what they regard as an onslaught from secular and amoral forces. Particular concerns of its supporters include opposition to abortion, to homosexuality, and to feminism and feminist causes such as the Equal Rights Amendment campaign. Since the change of name in 1986 the Liberty Federation has expanded its campaigning activity to take in support for the Nicaraguan contras, for right-wing forces in the Philippines, South Korea, Taiwan and South Africa, and for space weapons systems, and has endorsed Vice-President George Bush as Republican candidate for the 1988 presidential election; the name of Moral Majority is now used solely for religious and "moral" campaigning.

Membership. Moral Majority may well be the largest conservative pressure group in the world, currently having 4,000,000 affiliates in 50 state groups. It claims to have had some 6,500,000 people join since 1979, most of whom are Baptists and other Protestants, with a sizeable proportion of Roman Catholics and a small number of Jews.

Publications. Liberty Report, monthly.

Associated organizations. Falwell also runs the Liberty University, founded in 1971 as the Liberty Baptist College, and a number of other educational and social projects. There are many hundreds of Christian fundamentalist groups with right-wing political viewpoints, many of which (such as the Christian Action Council and the Crusade for Decency) share the special concern of Moral Majority with the question of immorality and ungodliness in society. The most important of these on the national political scene is the movement led by the Rev. Pat Robertson—like Falwell, a television evangelist—who is expected to seek the Republican presidential nomination for 1988. Other Christian right groups include the American Coalition for Traditional Values and the Christian Voice Moral Government Fund.

Mountain Church

Address. Box 331, Cohoctah, Michigan 48816

Leadership. Rev. Robert E. Miles (pastor)

Orientation. White supremacist

History. This group, formed around 1972, is one of the leading components of the racist Christian Identity movement. It supported the 1980 and 1984 state congressional election campaigns of Michigan fascist Gerald Carlson, who won 18 per cent of the vote in 1980 and 40 per cent in 1984, having on both occasions won the Republican Party nomination against the party hierarchy's favoured candidate.

Miles, born in 1926, is a former Ku Klux Klan member. He received a six-year prison sentence for having bombed school buses in 1971 in protest at desegregation.

Policies. Miles has sought to foster co-operation among as wide a range as possible of white racist groups.

Publications. From the Mountain

Associated organizations. Among many groups with which Miles had contact in the early to mid-1980s were the Aryan Nations, the National Socialist White People's Party, the National States' Rights Party, the SS Action Group and the United Klans. He attended the 1986 Aryan Nations Congress. In the same year he was reported to have performed a marriage ceremony for the leader of the National Socialist Liberation Front, with as best man the leader of White Aryan Resistance, and to have been involved with the National Association for the Advancement of White People, the National States Rights Party and the Alabama Ku Klux Klan. He has hosted meetings of the National Alliance, the White Patriot Party and other racist groups.

Nation of Islam

Base. Chicago, Illinois

Leadership. Louis Farrakhan (leader)

Orientation. Black Muslim

History. This organization, while not avowedly ultra-rightist, has come to public attention largely because of apparently anti-semitic statements by Minister Farrakhan (as he styles himself), notably during Jesse Jackson's 1984 presidential election campaign when he described Jews as lying and deceitful, Judaism as "a gutter religion" and Hitler as "a great man". These pronouncements, and the Nation's advocacy of black separatism, have aroused the interest of white racist leaders, some of whom, such as Tom Metzger, Bob Hoy, Bob Miles and (in Britain) leaders of the National Front, have expressed support for Farrakhan.

Policies. In common with some white supremacist groups, the Nation of Islam calls for the creation of separate black and white states in North America. The publications of the group contain references to the machinations of "the Zionists" or "the Israeli lobby", which appear to mean Jews, and to "their Black and White political marionnettes".

Publications. The Final Call, editor Wali Abdul Muhammad.

International affiliations. Farrakhan staged a "world tour" in 1986 which included visits to Burkina Faso, China, Ghana, Iran, Japan, Libya (which has provided financial support for his operation), Pakistan, Saudi Arabia and the United Arab Emirates, although he was refused admission to Britain and to Bermuda, allegedly because of "the tentacles of the Israeli lobby".

National Agricultural Press Association (NAPA)

Leadership. Rick Elliott (leader)

Orientation. Nazi

History. The NAPA campaigned among poor farmers from the late 1970s, succeeding an earlier organization which had been active in the 1960s. Maintaining that farms loans made after 1974 were legally unenforceable it sponsored a large number of frivolous lawsuits in the early to mid-1980s. At least one NAPA member has staged an armed confrontation with police, resulting in his death (in Cairo, Nebraska, in March 1985); a Posse Comitatus and Aryan Nations member, who had killed two federal officers, had been killed in similar circumstances (in Arkansas, in early 1984), and two men on the fringes of the Posse movement had been arrested (in Rulo, Nebraska, in August 1985) for two murders.

In 1985 Elliott (born 1927) was charged with embezzling the Association's funds.

Policies. The NAPA has pursued extremely anti-semitic and pro-fascist policies, urging debt-ridden farmers in the Middle West to default on loans from "Zionist" banks. It has sought to expose Jewish control of the agricultural industry.

Membership. 3,000 in 30 states (1985 claim).

Publications. The Grass-Roots Courier, irregular (in succession to the *Primrose and Cattleman's Gazette*).

Associated organizations. The NAPA has been reported as being a front organization of the Aryan Nations; there would appear at least to be an overlap of membership. Similar groups campaigning among farmers in the mid-1980s included the Populist Party, the Posse Comitatus movement, the Committee to Restore the Constitution (Fort Collins, Colorado), which concentrates on land law issues, the Anti-Lawyer Party, the National Commodity and Barter Association (allegedly behind a multi-million dollar tax fraud) and numerous Ku Klux Klan groups.

National Alliance

Address. Box 3535, Washington, DC 20007

Leadership. William L. Pierce (secretary); Nick Camerota

Orientation. Neo-nazi

History. Founded in 1970 in Springfield, Massachusetts, as the National Youth Alliance, and originally controlled by Willis Carto's Liberty Lobby, the anti-semitic policies of this group attracted the attention of American Nazi Party activists who effectively took it over in the early 1970s. Pierce was then editing *National Socialist World*, the organ of the World Union of National Socialists (see below, and Denmark), and was responsible for party ideology in the US National Socialist White People's Party. He became the leader of the Alliance in 1972, succeeding Bill Gillespie and moving its operations to the capital, and changed its name to the present form in 1974.

Pierce is one of the senior figures of the American ultra-right, and has written (under the pseudonym Andrew Macdonald) a novel, *The Turner Diaries*, which has been described as the *Mein Kampf* of the 1980s; it describes a nazi guerrilla group, The Organization, and its takeover of California, the USA and eventually the world. The book is widely regarded as having served as the blueprint for the establishment of The Order, a defunct fascist paramilitary group, and it is sold by many fascist groups, including the British National Front.

Policies. The Alliance promotes belief in a Jewish conspiracy to destroy the white "race" through socialism, black power, the banking system and inter-racial sex. It is planning to create a white-ruled "New Community" in the Appalachian mountains, and advocates white unity to permit the building of a new order.

Publications. National Vanguard (formerly *Attack!*), normally monthly, edited by Pierce; *Bulletin*, internal monthly.

Associated organizations. The Alliance has held joint activities with groups including the National States Rights Party and the Southern White Knights.

International affiliations. The foreign links of the Alliance are particularly extensive. The *Vanguard* circulates among most nazi and neo-nazi groups. In 1979 John Tyndall, then leader of the British National Front, visited the Alliance leader. It was also in contact with other British groups including the National Party (since disbanded) and the League of St. George. See also Aurora Promotions (United Kingdom).

National Association for the Advancement of White People (NAAWP)

Address. Box 10625, New Orleans, Louisiana 70181

Telephone. (504) 831 6986

Leadership. David Duke (president)

Orientation. White supremacist

History. This organization, whose name parodies that of a civil rights group, the National Association for the Advancement of Colored People, was established in 1979 by Duke, a former leader of the Nazi Party and of a Klan faction. The intention was to build an elite organization of educated white racists, but the group has had little success.

It took part in a rally held early in 1986 by the White Patriot Party. Two to three hundred participants protested against the planned federal public holiday in honour of Martin Luther King. Other activities of the NAAWP include research and publishing on racial affairs, and initiating lawsuits against employers with affirmative action programmes (i.e. strategies designed to favour ethnic minority job applicants).

Policies. The NAAWP opposes the black civil rights movement, race-mixing, immigration, and bussing (the allocation of schoolchildren across districts to ensure the integration of each school); it maintains that the federal government and federal legislation discriminate against the interests of white people.

Membership. 2,800 in about 10 branches.

Publications. Action, monthly; *NAAWP News,* and various bulletins and leaflets.

Associated organizations. Duke was Imperial Wizard of the Knights of the Ku Klux Klan from its formation until 1979. (In 1978 he was expelled from Britain after addressing several meetings of Klan sympathisers.) This NAAWP is not connected with a Texan group which has used the same name (see Citizens' Councils for Segregation), nor with an identically named group which was active in Pittsburgh, Pennsylvaniain the early 1970s. In 1983 Duke's NAAWP set up a White Majority Lobby with the immediate aim of campaigning against an amnesty for illegal immigrants.

National Coalition for Americans Committed to Rescuing Africa from the Grip of Soviet Tyranny—see Conservative Caucus.

National Conservative Political Action Committee (NC-PAC or NCPAC)

Address. 1001 Prince Street, Alexandria, Virginia 22314

Telephone. (703) 684 1000

Leadership. John T. Dolan (chairman)

Orientation. Right-wing conservative

History. This fund was established in 1974 as part of the "new right" network composed mainly of Republican Party supporters including Richard Viguerie. Its principal method of operation is by paying for advertising in favour of the policies of right-wing candidates or against those of opponents, without going through the candidates' own campaign machinery, thereby circumventing restrictions on spending for electoral purposes. In 1980 it spent $2,100,000 on advertisements opposing President Carter and supporting Ronald Reagan, but in 1984 it cancelled pro-Reagan spending because, it said, the President had been too liberal in office. In the same year Dolan stated that there were probably "active Soviet agents" in the US media, which was "pro-Soviet".

The NC-PAC, as it is generally known, has almost always supported right-wing Republican candidates and occasionally right-wing Democrats; on one occasion, in the 1984 senate elections, it supported a liberal Democrat in Illinois, in order to depose a centrist Republican who was preventing the right-wing Republican Jesse Helms from chairing an important committee.

The NC-PAC has served as the model for the many hundreds of right-wing political action committees (PACs) which have sprung up in the last few years, most of which are ad hoc funds supporting or opposing a single politician or a single policy; there are also PACs representing trade unions, professions, business sectors, environmentalists and other domestic and foreign policy concerns.

Policies. The NC-PAC seeks to help hardline right-wing candidates for public office, mainly from the Republican Party.

Publications. The Conservative Report, monthly.

Associated organizations. The NC-PAC may succeed a National Conservative Council based in Richmond, Virginia, in the early 1970s. Groups which are based at the NC-PAC address, but which are organizationally independent of it, include the 137,000-member Conservative Alliance, the National Coalition for American Survival and Young Americans for Freedom.

Unconnected conservative and ultra-conservative pressure groups and lobbies which are currently active on many of the issues which concern the NC-PAC, and which are not listed elsewhere in this chapter, include the following: the American Council for Co-ordinated Action; the American Defense Federation (and Institute); the Black Silent Majority Committee of the USA; Christian Focus on Government; Christians for a Strong America; Citizens for Reagan; Citizens for the Republic; the Coalition for America; the Coalition for Freedom; the Committee for a Sound Economy; the Committee for Western Civilization; numerous independent Conservative Clubs; Conservative Majority for Citizens' Rights; the Conservative Opportunity Society; the New York-based Conservative Party, which operates as a pressure group within the Republican Party; the Conservative Youth Federation; Conservatives for a Constitutional Convention, and Educational Services International.

The Federation for Religious Action in the Social and Civil Order; the Free Congress PAC; the Fund for an American Renaissance; the Fund for a Conservative Majority; Independent Americans; the Institute on Religion and Democracy; The Jewish Right; the dozens of Liberty Amendment Committees; the National Congressional Club, comprising supporters of Sen. Helms; the National Forum Foundation; the National Pro-Family Coalition; the National Tax Limitation Committee; the National Traditionalist Caucus; the Order of the Cross Society; the Parents' Alliance to Protect our Children; the Public Service Research Council; the Religious Round Table (led by Ed McAteer); Students for America; United Parents Under God; the Voice of Liberty Association; We the People, and the Young Conservative Alliance (and Foundation).

National Council for Labor Reform (NCLR)

Address. 4065 Plymouth Court, Chicago, Illinois 60605

Orientation. Anti-union

History. The NCLR was formed in 1969. It engages in a range of activities including litigation, publishing, "educational" work, the provision of speakers for public events, and advising individual employers.

Policies. It opposes trade union power, and campaigns in particular against closed shops (union-only businesses) and minimum wage laws, and in favour of the right of non-union members to obtain employment. It supports efforts to decertify trade unions and to deunionize workforces.

Membership. 5,000.

Associated organizations. Apart from the vast number of employers' groups which are unsympathetic or hostile to trade unionism, there are a number of associations which, like the NCLR, actively campaign against unions. These include Americans Against Union Control of Government, the Center on National Labor Policy, Concerned Educators Against Forced Unionism and the National Right-to-Work Committee (and the NRW Legal Defenseand Educational Foundation). There are also commercial consultancies which assist employers to remove trade unions from their enterprises. Most, but not all, anti-union groups are motivated by ultra-conservative ideology.

National Democratic Policy Committee

Address. Box 17729, Washington, DC 20041; *headquarters based in* Leesburg, Virginia

Leadership. Lyndon H. LaRouche Jr (leader); Warren J. Hamerman (chairman); Elliot Greenspan, Paul Goldstein, Jeffrey Steinberg

Orientation. Conspiracy theorist, LaRoucheist

History. This organization is one of several run by the supporters of Lyndon LaRouche, a singular figure who maintains, among other things, that the Queen of England lives off the drugs trade. LaRouche, whose surname is also rendered as la Rouche and Larouche, was formerly known as Lyn Marcus and is thought to be a millionaire, although he claims to live from the charity of his followers. He established his organization in 1966, since when it has used a variety of names, becoming the NDPC in 1980.

The political background of LaRouche (born in 1923) is somewhat obscure, partly due to his own presentation of competing versions, but it would appear that he was attracted to Trotskyism in his youth and gravitated towards the extreme right in the 1970s. By his own account, LaRouche is "the leading economist of the 20th century to date" and has "some degree of importance in shaping current world history".

The NDPC has sought to achieve elective office by running its candidates under the flag of the Democratic Party, much to the latter's embarrassment. (It sometimes describes its candidates as "LaRouche Democrats"; in California it has also sought places on Republican Party slates.) LaRouche himself sought the Democratic presidential nomination in 1980 and 1984 (having run in 1976 as a US Labor Party candidate). In 1980 he received more than $526,000 in federal matching funds for his campaign, but he was at first denied federal funds in 1984 because of his failure to pay a fine and refund demanded because of fund-raising offences in 1980. In March 1986 the NDPC took advantage of the low turnout in primary elections to secure positions for two of its people high up on the Illinois Democratic Party's slate, causing the mainstream Democratic candidate for Governor, Adlai Stevenson III, to refuse to run alongside such "bizarre and dangerous extremists".

The LaRouche sect has been involved in several legal controversies. In 1982 Nancy Kissinger was acquitted of assaulting one of its members who had asked her husband Henry, in the course of an interview at Newark Airport, whether he slept with young boys at the Carlyle Hotel. In February 1985 LaRouche was ordered to pay damages of $202,000 to NBC News for attempting to sabotage a broadcast after he had been described as leader of a "political cult" which harassed its critics; in a separate case, LaRouche had failed to persuade a jury that the comments were libellous.

The organization has trained members in terrorism and guerrilla warfare, supposedly in order to protect LaRouche from what he has decribed as "specialized capabilities of an assassination-relevant sort". In 1983 it moved its offices from Manhattan to Leesburg, where it has acquired some $2,300,000 of property including a heavily fortified residence for its leader.

Police and legal moves in 1986-87 against LaRouche's organization, which the FBI suspects of a credit card fraud involving at least $1,000,000, included ten arrests in October 1986 and a further nine arrests in April 1987. The arrests have hampered the Committee's activities while providing it with further "evidence" for its bizarre theories which present the federal government as an anti-LaRouche conspiracy.

Policies. LaRouche, who describes himself as "an American Whig", espouses an extremely complicated conspiracy theory with a cast of thousands, including the Jews, the Russians, the Playboy Foundation, the CIA, Henry Kissinger (a "Soviet agent of influence"), the Trilateral Commission, the British secret service, Colombian drug pushers and Queen Elizabeth II. He also advocates compulsory AIDS tests and the quarantining of carriers, the hanging of George Shultz (Reagan's Secretary of State), the building of MX nuclear missiles at the rate of 1,000 per year, the expansion of the "Star Wars" space weaponry programme, and various populist causes related to farmers and blacks. LaRouche sometimes claims to be a left-winger, although his advocacy of conspiracy theory and his policies place him firmly in a right-wing tradition. The movement claims to be part of an international, enlightened "pro-growth" tendency, while its opponents are identified as supporters of a sinister "anti-growth" movement. LaRouche regards the US government as "criminal or insane" and his critics as "druggies or commies".

Membership. The organization claimed to have 47,000 members in the United States in 1984—a figure which was regarded by most of the media as an exaggeration, although there is agreement that the Committee has several thousand adherents. In 1986 it claimed to have 780 candidates currently seeking public office. By most accounts it has 200 to 300 staff in the United States, suggesting an annual turnover approaching $10,000,000.

Publications. *New Solidarity*, formerly the twice-weekly organ of the US Labor Party; published for the Latin American market as *Nueva Solidaridad*.

Associated organizations. The NDPC has no connection whatever with the Democratic Party, although it has on occasion claimed otherwise, notably when LaRouche contrived to obtain an audience in 1982 with the President of Mexico. The NDPC is the successor to LaRouche's US Labor Party, which also functioned as the National Caucus of Labor Committees, the International Workers' Party and the Revolutionary Youth Movement. LaRouche also runs a publishing operation, *Executive Intelligence Review*, and his group has several commercial offshoots. It also functions as the New Solidarity International Press Service.

International affiliations. The organization has affiliates in other countries, notably the European Labor Party (see France and Italy) and the Schiller Institute and Patriots for Germany group (West Germany). The co-ordinating body of these affiliates was known in the mid-1980s as the International Caucus of Labor Committees (ICLC).

National Determination Party

Address. Box 3646, Manchester, New Hampshire 03105

Leadership. Arnold Moltis (chairman)

Orientation. Fascist

History. This group was formed in 1975 as the American Majority Party, and adopted its present name in 1982.

Policies. It represents "white Protestant patriots" who seek to defend the American way of life; it favours an aggressive foreign policy and a strong military, and it opposes both communism and monopoly capitalism.

Publications. *Imperative News and Views*, monthly.

National Education Program (NEP)

Address. Route 1, Box 141, Enterprise Square USA, Oklahoma City, Oklahoma 73111

Telephone. (405) 478 5190

Leadership. Robert H. Rowland (president)

Orientation. Anti-communist

History. The NEP has been in existence for a little more than 50 years. It was based for much of its existence in Searcy, Arkansas.

Policies. It seeks to expose an international communist conspiracy and to promote free enterprise and the American way of life by means of syndicated radio programmes and press features.

National Endowment for Democracy (NED)

Address. 1156 15th Street NW, Suite 304, Washington, DC

Leadership. Carl Gershman (president)

Orientation. Anti-communist quasi-government agency

History. The NED was established by the Reagan administration in 1983 as a discreet and indirect means of channelling US government funds to foreign political parties and other organizations active in anti-communist causes. Its annual budget is about $18,000,000.

Policies. It seeks to promote democratic values worldwide and to increase the involvement of US individuals and groups in foreign affairs.

Associated organizations. Much of the NED funding was at first paid through the AFL-CIO trade union federation's international bureau, the Free Trade Union Institute. The proportion has now been reduced from about 77 per cent to less than 25 per cent.

International affiliations. Among causes funded by the NED in 1984-85 were, in France, the *Force Ouvrière* trade union ($830,000) and the UNI student group ($575,000); in the United Kingdom, the Labour Committee for Transatlantic Understanding ($49,000), the actors' union Equity ($10,000), and the pro-NTS emigré magazine *Soviet Labour Review* (see Soviet Union—$129,000); and a presidential candidature in Panama. Other money went to groups in Brazil, Chile, Nicaragua, Paraguay, the Philippines, Poland, Portugal and Suriname.

National Federation for Decency (NFD)

Address. PO Drawer 2440, Tupelo, Mississippi 38803

Leadership. Don Wildman (director)

Orientation. Christian conservative

History. The NFD was founded in 1977 as part of the conservative Protestant movement typified by Moral Majority.

Policies. It promotes Biblical ethics in broadcasting, and lobbies against indecency and immorality in the media.

National Knights of the Ku Klux Klan

Address. Box 111, Stone Mountain, Georgia 30083

Leadership. James Venable

Orientation. White supremacist

History. This organization, formed around 1960, was one of the smaller Klans until the mid-1970s, when it extended its organization into other parts of Georgia and into Ohio (where its leaders were F. Harvey, Parker Scott and William Smith). It hosted a unity rally at Stone Mountain in 1986. It had suffered a split in 1985-86 leading to the formation of the Southern White Knights faction.

Policies. Like other Klan groups, the National Knights regard blacks as genetically inferior and and support the political hegemony of the white "race".

Publications. Imperial Nighthawk (published in the 1970s, now possibly defunct).

Associated organizations. In 1983 the Knights formed a Confederation with other Klan groups including the Knights of the Ku Klux Klan, the New Order Knights and the White Knights.

National Review

Address. 150 East 35th St, New York, NY 10016

Telephone. (212) 679-7330

Leadership. William Rusher (publisher); William F. Buckley (editor)

Orientation. Right-wing conservative

History. This fortnightly publication, founded in 1955, has long been one of the most influential organs of the American non-fascist right. Rusher is widely regarded as the author of the strategy pursued from the late 1970s by the Republican Party in order to attract the support of traditionally-hostile manual workers.

Policies. The *Review* opposes government bureaucracy, restraints on private enterprise, the growth of the welfare state, and domestic and foreign threats to national security and individual liberty.

Circulation. 119,000

National Socialist League (NSL)

Base. Los Angeles, California

Orientation. Gay nazi

History. Although there has long been an element in the US homosexual sub-culture which has exhibited a fascination for items of nazi uniform, such as caps, badges and leather gear, usually in association with sado-masochistic sexual practices, the NSL, formed in 1975, is the only known nazi group which makes homosexuality the focus of its party activity. Some rival groups regard the NSL as a bogus organization designed to discredit nazi ideology, while others regard its occasional publications as representing humorous spoofs.

Policies. The NSL appears to function primarily as a social forum for gay fascists.

International affiliations. The NSL is in sympathy with the leadership of the Our Nation group (United Kingdom). It is probably not connected with NSL World Service, a merchandising operation based in San Diego, California, and dealing in nazi films and memorabilia. It is not clear whether the gay NSL is identical with the National Socialist League which issued anti-Jewish tracts in 1981 (from PO Box 26496, Los Angeles, California 90026).

National Socialist Liberation Front (NSLF)

Address. PO Box 1531, Metairie, Louisiana 70004; other offices in Chillicothe, Ohio, and Buffalo, New York

Telephone. (504) 835 5169

Leadership. Karl Hand, Jr (commander)

Orientation. Nazi

History. The NSLF was founded in Panorama City, California, in the early 1970s by Joseph Tomassi, who was killed in 1975 by a member of the rival National Socialist White People's Party. The current leader is a former national organizer of the Knights of the Ku Klux Klan. In 1983 the NSLF absorbed a smaller fascist group, the National Socialist White Power Movement. The name of the group, which is strongest in the southern states, was used in claiming responsibility for an attack on the home of the liberal television actor, Ed Asner, in 1985. The NSLF staged an SS-style wedding for its leader in early 1986. It has been reported that the NSLF functions as the paramilitary wing of the Oklahoma-based National Socialist Movement.

Policies. The NSLF advances unreconstructed national socialist policies based on anti-semitism, white supremacism, authoritarianism and admiration for the ideas and conduct of Adolf Hitler. It was reported in 1984 that the Front had stated that it had "repudiated mass tactics and... embraced armed struggle and political terrorism".

Publications. Siege!, edited by James Mason; *Defiance.*

Associated organizations. See National Socialist Movement (Oklahoma), whose White Confederacy alliance the NSLF joined in the mid-'70s. The merchandising arm of the NSLF trades as Valhalla Sales. In the mid-1970s the Front joined the National Socialist Movement, the National Socialist Party of America and foreign groups including the British Movement in a co-ordinating body known as the White Confederacy. The NSLF maintains contact with a number of like-minded US and foreign organizations. Groups represented at Hand's wedding included White American Resistance and Robert Miles' racist Mountain Church.

National Socialist Movement (NSM)

Address. Box 41503, Cincinnati, Ohio 45241

Orientation. Nazi

History. This small group was formed by hard-core nazi activists in the mid-1970s. Its members have been involved in many violent incidents. It has not been possible to establish whether this NSM is identical with the Oklahoma group of the same name.

Policies. The NSM advocates the revolutionary overthrow of the existing state and social order and the construction of a new white-ruled nation based on national socialist principles.

Publications. NS Reporter

National Socialist Movement (NSM)

Address. PO Box 388, Bartlesville, Oklahoma 74005

Telephone. (918) 336 2272

Leadership. Clifford D. Herrington (chairman)

Orientation. Nazi

History. The NSM was formed in 1975. It is unclear whether it is linked with the Ohio group of the same name. Some sources state that the Oklahoma NSM is the political wing of a movement whose paramilitary wing is the National Socialist Liberation Front.

Policies. The NSM is open to non-Jewish white people, and advocates standard national socialist policies on race, the economy, the social order and other matters.

Publications. Social Justice, every two weeks; *National Socialist Bulletin*, monthly; *NS Internationaler*, German-language bulletin, every two months.

Associated organizations. See NSM (Ohio) and NSLF. The NSM claims to have youth, student and prisoner groups, and to run a Sport Defense Guard along the lines of West German war sports groups. Membership of the NSM is open to members of other nazi and racist groups, including the NSPA, the American Nazi Party and Ku Klux Klan factions; it has sought to co-ordinate with such groups through the United Patriotic Front and the White Confederacy.

National Socialist Party of America (NSPA)

Address. Box 6414, Lincoln, Nebraska 68506

Leadership. Michael Allen (leader)

Orientation. Nazi

History. The NSPA is one of the two largest organizations to have emerged from the National Socialist White People's Party (NSWPP) of the 1960s, the other being the group now known as New Order (which also called itself the NSPA for a time). The NSPA was founded by Frank Collin, a partly-Jewish fascist expelled in 1970 from the NSWPP. His ancestry was the principal reason for attacks on him by rival groups. In the late 1970s the Party held rallies in the Jewish district of Skokie, near Chicago, achieving massive publicity. Collin's conviction for child sex abuse in 1980 led to his replacement by Harold Covington of North Carolina, who then won 56,000 votes in a state primary election for the Republican candidacy for attorney-general. He resigned in 1981 (to found the Excalibur Society) and was succeeded by Allen. In the same year members of the NSPA were charged with conspiring to plant bombs in Greensboro, North Carolina, and with involvement with Klansmen and others in a frustrated invasion of the Caribbean island of Dominica.

Policies. The NSPA preaches undiluted national socialist policies.

Publications. New Order, six per year.

Associated organizations. See National Socialist Movement (Oklahoma). The NSPA sponsors the work of the German nazi NSDAP-AO, led by Gerhard Lauck.

National Socialist White Workers' Party (NSWWP)

Address. PO Box 1981, San Francisco, California 94101

Telephone. (707) 528 8084

Leadership. James Mason (secretary); Erika Reich, Heinz Eichman, Allen Vincent

Orientation. Nazi

History. The NSWWP was formed in the early 1970s as a splinter group of the National Socialist White People's Party, then the leading US nazi group (and now known as the New Order). The NSWWP was originally based in New Berlin, Wisconsin. In 1983 the group came to public attention for organizing a Hitler birthday party in San Francisco.

Policies. The Party has classic nazi policies based on nordicism, white supremacy and anti-semitism. From within the German nazi tradition it draws particularly on the positions and ideas of Julius Streicher, editor of the fiercely anti-Jewish *Der Stürmer*.

Publications. The Stormer, edited by Mason; *White Power*

International affiliations. In 1981 the NSWWP was associated with the now-defunct British Movement.

National Sozialistische Deutsche Arbeiterpartei - Auslandsorganisation (NSDAP-AO)

National Socialist German Workers' Party - External Organization

Address. PO Box 6414, Lincoln, Nebraska 68506

Leadership. Gerhard Lauck (leader)

Orientation. Nazi

History. This group was formed in West Germany in 1973 by Lauck (also known as Gary Lock), but moved its operations to the USA following his expulsion by the German authorities in 1974. It claims to have many secret members in West Germany. In the early 1980s it was reported to be extending its activities to Scandinavia and Austria. In June 1982 an NSDAP-AO member, Helmut Oxner, killed three people in Nuremberg (West Germany) before committing suicide.

Policies. As the name suggests, the party regards itself as a successor to Hitler's nazi party, and its policies are in all important respects identical with those of its model.

Publications. The NSDAP-AO is supported by the NSPA publication, *New Order*, every two months. Its own organ is *NS Kampfruf* (Nazi Battlecry), a German-language quarterly; it also produces occasional leaflets, and many adhesive labels bearing nazi slogans.

Associated organizations. The Organization is thought to have received the financial backing of US nazi groups. It was originally based at the Virginia headquarters of the World Union of National Socialists, and is now assisted by the NSPA. It is unclear whether the NSDAP-AO is the same as an early 1980s group called the *NSDAP - Auslands- und Aufbauorganisation* (External and Development Organization), or as a mid-1970s NSDAP based in Silver Springs, Florida. That NSDAP, which was led by SS veteran Albert Brinkman, published *NS-Kurier* in German.

International affiliations. See Institute for Historical Research, *Österreichischer Beobachter, Nachrichten Austauschdienst, Deutsch-Österreichisches Institut für Zeitgeschichte, Arbeitkreis Internationale Zusammenarbeit* (Austria); *Nordland Förlag* (Denmark). According to press reports in 1984 the NSDAP-AO also had contacts in Sweden.

National States Rights Party (NSRP)

Address. PO Box 1211, Marietta, Georgia 30061

Telephone. (404) 427 0283; 422 1180

Leadership. Jesse B. Stoner (chairman); Dr Edward R. Fields (secretary)

Orientation. White supremacist

History. The NSRP was founded in 1958. J.B. Stoner (born in 1926), who had previously led a group called the Stoner Anti-Jewish Party, was an advocate of violent opposition to black civil rights, and he bombed a black church in his native Alabama in 1965 - a crime of which he was not convicted until 1980, when he received a 10-year sentence (confirmed on appeal in January 1985). Fields had a long record of activism in Georgian white supremacist groups. The NSRP has been one of the leading fascist parties since its foundation and has opposed both Republican and Democratic governments; it was reportedly implicated in a conspiracy to assassinate President Kennedy in the 1960s. In 1974 Stoner stood in a Georgia election, gaining 70,000 votes. In 1984 the organization underwent a crisis in which Ed Fields, who had become increasingly involved with the New Order Knights of the Ku Klux Klan, was challenged for the leadership, and for control of the party organ, by a faction led by W.E. Wilson. Fields, who apparently retained control of the paper but not of the party, was one of four fascists arrested in 1986 after an assault on an anti-fascist activist.

Policies. The NSRP regards federal power and the United Nations system as Jewish and seeks the return of effective power to state governments, partly in order to permit them to repeal civil rights legislation, gun controls and other "unpatriotic" measures. It advocates racial segregation and the eventual formation of a white-only nation, excluding Jews and communists.

Membership. About 1,500 (anti-fascists' estimate); 12,000 (NSRP estimate). There appear to be sections of the party in Georgia, Florida, North Carolina and Tennessee, with smaller groups in Ohio, Pennsylvania, Texas, Maryland and elsewhere.

Publications. *The Thunderbolt* (subtitled "The White Man's Viewpoint"), circulation about 15,000; the 1984 crisis left it uncertain whether the paper was Fields' personal organ or that of the party. There is also a monthly internal *Newsletter*.

Associated organizations. The NSRP has held joint activities with many other groups, including the Aryan Nations, the National Alliance, the White Patriot Party, the National Association for the Advancement of White People, Liberty Lobby, the Southern National Party and the Southern White Knights. A 1970s group called the American States Rights Party, which had addresses in Ohio and Georgia, was probably a splinter group of the NSRP. In early 1987, following his early release from prison, Stoner formed a Crusade against Corruption to oppose civil rights movements.

International affiliations. Both Stoner and Fields have cultivated foreign contacts, and on visits to Britain in 1975, '76 and '77 they dealt with the National Front, the League of St George and the British Movement; the then NF leader John Tyndall (now of the British National Party) visited the NSRP in 1979.

New America

Address. PO Box 1084, Mount Vernon, New York 10551

Orientation. Ultra-conservative

History. This organization was active in 1986.

New Christian Crusade Church (NCCC)

Address. PO Box 426, Metairie, Louisiana 70004

Orientation. Nazi

History. This Church was established in the early 1970s in Hollywood, California, but moved to Metairie in the mid-'70s. The NCCC appears to have been superseded by the Christian Defense League, run by the NCCC's founder, James K. Warner.

Policies. It preaches a version of Christianity which accommodates extreme anti-semitic and white supremacist views.

Publications. *Christian Vanguard*, monthly.

Associated organizations. Most members of the NCCC are also members of Ku Klux Klan factions and/or nazi parties.

New Libertarian

Address. PO Box 1748, Long Beach, California 90801-1748

Leadership. Samuel Edward Conkin III (founding editor)

Orientation. Libertarian

History. This magazine, which is one of the leading US libertarian journals, promotes economic and social deregulation and revisionist history theories including the Holocaust denial.

Policies. The magazine espouses an anti-state, quasi-anarchist philosophy which is very attractive to certain right-wing extremists.

Publications. *New Libertarian*, five per year.

Associated organizations. The paper is owned by the New Libertarian Company of Free Traders, which also trades as New Libertarian Enterprises, using the same address as the magazine. *New Libertarian* has been advertised by Truth Missions, a Holocaust denial group, and Konkin advised on the group's publications, but there may be no other connection between the two; Konkin and an assistant, James J. Martin, have long been associated with the rival Institute for Historical Review. Rival libertarian organizations identified with the right rather than with left-wing liberalism or anarchism include the Reason Foundation, the Ramparts Institute (California) and the Society for Individual Liberty (Pennsylvania).

International affiliations. Its UK and European editor in the early 1980s was Chris Tame, who runs a libertarian retail organization, the Alternative Bookshop, in London.

New Order

Address. PO Box 88, Arlington, Virginia 22210; has also used Box 5505, Arlington, VA 22205, and Box 50360, Cicero, Illinois 60650; headquarters at 2507 North Franklin Road, Arlington, VA 22201

Telephone. (703) 524 2175

Leadership. Matt Koehl (commander)

Orientation. Nazi

History. This group was founded in 1958 as the World Union of Free Enterprise National Socialists, soon became known as the American Nazi Party and in 1967 became the National Socialist White People's Party (NSWPP). It was founded by George Lincoln Rockwell, regarded as the father of the American neo-nazi movement, who was assassinated by a colleague in 1967. Some present-day American nazis regard Rockwell as a government informer and his successors as politically suspect. After Rockwell's death the 500 or so members split into various factions, with Koehl retaining the party name and headquarters and the largest following. The Party contested a number of local and state elections without winning posts, but occasionally rising to several thousand votes. In 1983 the Party, which has also been known as the National Socialist Party of America, adopted its present name as part of a general reorganization. The American Nazi Party title was formally adopted by one of the countless fascist groups formed by deserters from its ranks. Others include the

National Socialist Party of America, the National Alliance and the Christian Defence League.

Policies. The New Order espouses traditional white supremacist and anti-semitic nazi ideology. Much of its energy has been dissipated in attacks on the political legitimacy of rival nazi organizations. It opposes both communism and unrestrained capitalism and defines its outlook as "racial idealism".

Membership. About 200 full members and 400 active supporters. The New Order has about 40 local branches (in California, Colorado, Delaware, Indiana, Illinois, Michigan, Minnesota, New Hampshire, New Jersey, New York, North Carolina, Ohio, Oregon, Texas, Virginia, Washington state, West Virginia and Wisconsin).

Publications. *White Power*, monthly; the party also uses dial-a-nazi telephone advertising. It publishes *The National Socialist* on behalf of the World Union of National Socialists.

Associated organizations. The party has distinct youth and women's sections. It took part in the Christian Patriots Conference of 1985 (see Aryan Nations) along with the American Nazi Party, the America First Committee and other ultra-right groups. It corresponds with, collaborates with and sells the publications of many other groups including Liberty Lobby and the Mountain Church.

International affiliations. In 1962 the NSWPP re-established the World Union of National Socialists (WUNS), which had been founded by Colin Jordan of the National Socialist Movement (United Kingdom). Rockwell led the WUNS from 1962-67 and was succeeded by Koehl, but the European section of the WUNS, administered by the Danish nazi movement, has probably become more important than the section based in the USA. The US WUNS trades from the New Order headquarters, using the North Franklin Road address, and is still led by Koehl; it has contact with numerous foreign fascist groupings.

New Order Knights of the Ku Klux Klan

Address. PO Box 2345, Overland, Missouri 63114

Leadership. Rev. J.L. Betts (grand dragon)

Orientation. White supremacist

History. This Klan grouping attended the 1986 KKK rally at Stone Mountain, Georgia. It appears to be associated with a faction in the National States Rights Party.

Policies. The Knights, like other KKK factions, espouse quasi-fascist white racist policies.

The Noontide Press

Address. PO Box 1248, Torrance, California 90505

Leadership. Willis Carto (founder)

Orientation. Ultra-right

History. This publishing company was set up in the early 1960s with the support of Carto's Liberty Lobby in order to produce racist and anti-semitic books and journals. It was based in Los Angeles until the late 1970s.

Publications. The Press published Roger Pearson's racist journal, *Western Destiny*, in the 1960s (see Council for Social and Economic Studies). It now publishes a wide range of periodicals and other material.

Associated organizations. See Liberty Lobby. Noontide Press publications are also distributed through several Klan groups.

Nordic League

Address. PO Box 1057, Trenton, New Jersey

Leadership. Dwight Baldwin McMahon

Orientation. Fascist

History. From the available information it would appear that the League functions mainly as a merchandising operation specializing in nazi propaganda materials rather than as a membership organization.

Paladin Press

Base. Boulder, Colorado

Leadership. Peter Lund (owner)

Orientation. Right-wing

History. This publishing company specializes in books of interest to real and pretend mercenaries and others interested in survivalism, warfare, assassination and terrorism.

Associated organizations. It advertises in *Soldier of Fortune* magazine.

International affiliations. See The Paladin Press/Norway.

Patriot Press   see Knights of the Ku Klux Klan.

Patriotic Order of Sons of America

Address. PO Box 1847, Valley Forge, Pennsylvania 19481

Orientation. Ultra-nationalist

History. The Order was founded in 1847 as a fraternal society of veterans. Until the late 1970s it was based in Philadelphia, Pennsylvania.

Policies. The current preoccupations of the Sons include the monitoring and countering of leftist subversion, opposition to immigration and support for aggressive defence and foreign policies.

Associated organizations. Similar non-fascist ultra-patriotic organizations, not formally linked with the Order, include Americans United for God and Country, the Committee to Unite America (also known as For America), the Military Order of St Columbia's Shield and the National Committee for Responsible Patriotism. There are countless local groupings concerned with honouring the flag, promulgating the principles of the constitution, supporting the armed forces and the police, and generally furthering conservative nationalism.

Phoenix Battalion

Leadership. Sam Hall (only known member)

Orientation. Anti-communist

History. This self-styled intelligence agency, which apparently operates along similar lines to Lyndon LaRouche's *Executive Intelligence Review*, was reportedly founded in 1984. It came to public notice in December 1986 when Hall, the brother of a US Congressman, was arrested at a Nicaraguan military installation with maps hidden in his socks. He claimed at the time to be a member of Civilian Military Assistance, which disowned him. He was released in January 1987 by the Nicaraguan authorities, who appeared not to regard him as a threat to national security.

Policies. The aim of this group appears to be the gathering of intelligence data for sale to government agencies or private interests.

Pioneer Fund

Orientation. Right-wing

History. This foundation was established in the 1960s to provide financial support for academic research designed to support right-wing political viewpoints. Among its beneficiaries has been Dr Roger Pearson, a racist anthropologist (see Council for Social and Economic Studies), who has received grants of at least $36,000.

Populist Party

Address. Box 76367, Washington, DC 20013

Telephone. (202) 546 5530

Leadership. William Baker (chairman); Emmett Miller (secretary)

Orientation. Ultra-right populist

History. The party was founded early in 1984 by Willis Carto, a veteran right-wing activist associated mainly with the Liberty Lobby. Its founding members reportedly included people associated with the National States Rights Party, the Knights of the Ku Klux Klan and the Posse Comitatus movement. In its first year it received 66,000 votes in 14 states in the federal elections. Also in 1984, it recruited Victor Marchetti, who had achieved considerable publicity ten years earlier as a CIA "whistle-blower" when he published unauthorized memoirs of his time with the Agency.

The Party went through serious internal problems in 1985-86, when the chairmanship changed hands at least five times amid allegations of financial mismanagement.

Policies. The Party maintains that the US middle class is oppressed by the power of the rich and by the political influence and cost of maintaining the poor. It was reported in mid-1986 to be attempting to distance itself from Carto's anti-semitism and authoritarianism.

Publications. Carto's weekly paper, *The Spotlight*, is now complemented by a paper controlled directly by the party.

Posse Comitatus

Leadership. Rev. William Potter Gale; James Wickstrom

Orientation. Libertarian right

History. The Posse Comitatus movement (named from the Latin: county power) was founded in 1969 by Henry L. Beach (a veteran of the 1930s fascist Silver Shirts movement), developed in California in the 1970s and subsequently spread to at least 12 other states. After several of its supporters had been involved in violent incidents it was listed by the US Justice Department as a terrorist organization.

A leader of the movement, Gordon Kahl, was killed in the Ozark mountains in February 1983 after a three-month hunt in which two federal marshals and a sheriff were also shot dead. Four Arkansas right-wingers were later convicted of harbouring Kahl.

In late 1985 Michael Ryan and two other Nebraska men belonging to a survivalist group linked to the movement were charged with two murders, including the torturing and killing of a five-year-old boy. A police raid had captured weapons, ammunition and other military equipment. In May 1986 a couple subsequently identified as supporters of the Posse Comitatus movement held 150 Wyoming schoolchildren as hostages for 2 hours, demanding a multi-million dollar ransom to be used for the establishment of a white racist homeland (as advocated by the Christian Identity movement and other groups). The couple died of self-inflicted gunshot wounds after one of their bombs went off, injuring nine children.

The origins and early history of the Posse movement were extensively documented by the leading American anti-fascist researcher, Dixon Gayer, in his journal *The Dixon Line*, published in California in the 1970s.

Policies. The Posse Comitatus movement regards the federal and state governments as unlawful and maintains that there is no legitimate authority above the county level. On that reasoning it regards income tax and other federal taxes as unlawful; it advises its members, and tries to organize farmers, to refuse to pay taxes. It is heavily influenced by anti-semitic and white supremacist ideas.

Membership. Claims 2,000,000; press estimate 3,000.

Associated organizations. Within the organization there is an autonomous section, Veterans of the US Posse Comitatus, led by Bruce Goff and based in Maryland. See also Aryan Nations and Christian Identity movement. The Posse Comitatus movement has also been closely linked with some Klan factions, with the racist Ministry of Christ Church (which has since the early 1970s published *Identity*, from Box 423, Glendale, California 91209) and with the American Tax Freedom Movement.

The Public Interest

Base. New York

Leadership. Nathan Glazer, Irving Kristol (co-editors)

Orientation. New right

History. This journal has become one of the leading forums of "new right" or neo-conservative thought in the United States. Although more reflective and perhaps less radical than the Moral Majority-type movements, which some analysts regard as the true face of the new right, the positions adopted by this journal, its contributors and its competitors (such as *Commentary*) have been equally influential in moving the ideological focus of the Republican Party, and thus in effect moving American political debate, to the concerns of the authoritarian, nationalist right.

Policies. The journal publishes the work of many of the ideologists of the new Republican leadership, attacking the supposedly liberal media, immorality, "big government" and threats to private enterprise, the nuclear family and personal freedoms.

Publications. The Public Interest, quarterly.

Radio Free Europe/Radio Liberty—see West Germany.

Reason Foundation

Address. Box 40105, Santa Barbara, California 93103

Orientation. New right libertarian

History. This group was established in 1978 to publish a magazine and to promote and conduct research on economic, social and political issues of interest to libertarians. In 1984 it was involved in producing programmes setting out new right philosophy for the British Channel Four television station. Its budget in 1986 was about $1,500,000.

Policies. The Foundation is part of the libertarian new right, which advocates the rapid reduction of state involvement in the economy and the favouring of individual over collective rights.

Membership. 30,000.

Publications. Reason, monthly; many leaflets and monographs.

Republican Party

Address. Republican National Committee, 310 First Street SE, Washington, DC 20003

Telephone. (202) 863-8500

Leadership. Ronald Reagan (leader); Paul Laxalt (general chairman); Frank Fahrenkopf (national chairman); Jean Birch (secretary)

Orientation. Mainstream conservative

History. As one of the two parties dominating US politics, the Republican Party, founded in 1854 (and often known as the Grand Old Party, or GOP), has frequently been in government, including the two Reagan administrations from 1981. The rightwards shift during the Reagan era has made some positions which were previously regarded as belonging to an eccentric fringe now appear intellectually respectable to the main body of the party. We are concerned here not with the mainstream conservative Republican Party as such, but with its right-wing fringe.

The Republican right. In the 1960s and early 1970s the Republican right consisted of a small fringe, grouped around individuals such as Sens. Barry Goldwater (the party's candidate in the 1964 presidential election) and Jesse Helms and a few organizations such as the John Birch Society; this "old right", which remains in existence, was generally regarded in the 1970s as an eccentric and isolated element.

Many Republican personalities, including both veteran right-wingers and younger "new right" figures, have come to the fore in the past decade with radical policies, advocating privatization, the deregulation of industry, the dismantling of the health care and social security systems, an aggressively anti-communist foreign policy, massive rearmament, anti-labour legislation and other right-wing goals. Right-wing policies adopted by the present Republican leadership include the "new federalism" concept of removing from the federal government responsibility for a wide range of social expenditure, and thus in most cases reducing provision in the affected fields; a general verbal assault, with little actual effect, on the level of government spending in non-military areas; a foreign policy including heightened anti-Soviet rhetoric and the subvention of guerrilla wars against the governments of Afghanistan and Nicaragua;

deregulation of the economy, and a general reversal of secularizing and liberalizing trends in legislative, administrative and judicial spheres.

Right-wing "think tanks" and pressure groups which are influential with the current Republican leadership are the Heritage Foundation, the Hoover Foundation, the American Enterprise Institute, the Conservative Caucus, Moral Majority, the NC-PAC and others.

Prominent right-wing Republican individuals include President Reagan, who, apart from pursuing right-wing domestic and foreign policy goals, has been directly associated with right-wing projects and organizations, having, for example, sent messages of greetings to World Anti-Communist League meetings (see South Korea). Other leading Republicans associated with the fascist-infiltrated WACL have included Senators Jake Garn and James McClure, who attended its 1978 conference, and former Secretary of State Gen. Alexander Haig, who sent greetings to the 1980 conference. The more right wing of the Republican Congressmen during the Reagan era have included Representatives Mark Sijlander and Dan Burton and Senators Strom Thurmond, Orrin G. Hatch, John P. East and Jesse Helms (whose National Conservative Club has an annual budget of about $8,000,000). Right-wingers within the executive branch have included Patrick Buchanan, as special assistant to the President, and Richard Allen, a former National Security Council head. Caspar Weinberger, the Defence Secretary; Richard Perle, his Assistant Secretary (until 1987); William Bennett, the Secretary for Education, and Edwin Meese, Attorney General, have all been identified with the "new right".

Samizdat

Address. Box 11132-0132, Buffalo, New York 14211

Orientation. Anti-semitic

History. This publication, whose title derives from the Russian term (self-published) used to denote unauthorized opposition publications in the Soviet Union, was founded in Canada in the 1970s. Its grossly anti-semitic content brought it into conflict with the legal authorities and around 1983 its postal address was moved to New York state.

Policies. Samizdat promotes a Jewish conspiracy theory.

Senator Joseph R. McCarthy Foundation

Address. 212 West Wisconsin Avenue, Milwaukee, Wisconsin 53203

Telephone. (414) 276 0575

Leadership. Thomas Bergen (chairman)

Orientation. Anti-communist

History. The McCarthy Foundation was set up in 1962 to perpetuate the memory of its eponymous hero, a US Senator (1947-57) best known for his vigorous pursuit of communists, socialists and others whom he regarded as subversive, particularly through the medium of the congressional Committees on Un-American Activities.

The notion that left-wing ideas were incompatibile with "Americanism" was used by the Senator and his followers to legitimize a campaign, now abandoned and generally discredited, whereby purges and blacklists decimated the media and entertainment industries, as well as affecting other spheres of public life. The terms "McCarthyism" and "McCarthyite" have become established in the United States as pejoratives to denote an irrational and possibly paranoid approach to dissident individuals and movements.

The Foundation seeks to counter the received image of McCarthy as a populist "witch-hunter" by celebrating his achievements in other fields of political and public affairs, and also by maintaining that his anti-communist campaign was both necessary and effective in preserving the American way of life, and remains necessary in the present day.

Policies. The Foundation promotes patriotism and vigilance against Marxist-Leninist subversion, and honours the life and work of Joseph McCarthy.

Publications. Newsletter, monthly.

Sentinel

Leadership. Carl Channell (head)

Orientation. Anti-communist

History. This lobbying group paid for television advertising against liberal congressional candidates of both major parties whom it regarded as being "soft" on Central America. In particular it targeted Mike Barnes of Maryland, who lost his attempt to move from the House to the Senate after a campaign which likened him to Gaddafi, Khomeini and other hate-figures.

Policies. Sentinel exists to lobby for conservative causes and to oppose liberal or left-wing ideologies.

Associated organizations. Channell also directs the Endowment for the Preservation of Liberty.

'76 Press

Address. Box 2686, Seal Beach, California 90740

Orientation. Ultra-right

History. This publishing company, which specializes in Jewish conspiracy theory tracts, has been active at least since 1977, and has been in contact with many domestic and foreign national socialist organizations.

Siegrunen
Victory Runes

Address. Box 70, Mount Reuben Road, Glendale, Oregon 97442

Leadership. Richard Landwehr (pseudonym of editor)

Orientation. Nazi

History. This publication, produced since the early 1980s, extols the memory of the Waffen-SS, a section of the German Nazi armed forces.

Social Nationalist Aryan People's Party (SNAPP)

Address. Box 1474, Post Falls, Idaho 83854

Orientation. Nazi

History. The SNAPP, whose name suggests its derivation as a splinter group of the National Socialist White People's Party (see New Order), has been active since at least 1984, when a member was tried for killing two black men and a man whom he had mistaken for a Jewish professor. He said at his trial that he had intended to kill "as many blacks and Jews as I could... one thousand, one million, the more the better".

Policies. It holds traditional national socialist views.

Soldier of Fortune (SoF)

Leadership. Robert K. Brown (publisher); Dale Dye (executive editor); John Donovan, William Guthrie, Maj. Heine Aderholt

Orientation. Right-wing mercenary organization

History. This operation publishes a glossy monthly magazine aimed at mercenaries, survivalists and others interested in war and anti-communist rhetoric. It also assists in the recruitment of mercenaries for anti-communist revolutionary or counter-revolutionary causes, and was active in Central America in the 1980s, mainly in sending several training teams to El Salvador. SoF also supplies non-military equipment to the Nicaraguan contra forces and holds annual "mercenary conventions".

Brown, who served in the Vietnam war with the Special Operations Group, was approached in the 1960s by the fascist National States Rights Party to join a plot to assassinate President John F. Kennedy. He reportedly declined.

Associates of the Brown operation have included the late Mitch Werbell, a mercenary associated with Lyndon LaRouche and with the ex-King of Afghanistan; Hans Scharff, a high-ranking German nazi officer; Alan Ash, a British mercenary formerly active in the nazi British Movement and in the National Socialist Party of the UK; and Terry Cooper, a member of the National Socialist Movement in Britain in the 1960s who moved to Paris after a criminal conviction. Ash and Cooper were reported in 1985 to be attempting to recruit European mercenaries for Central America under Brown's direction.

Publications. *Soldier of Fortune*, monthly, claimed circulation 200,000.

Associated organizations. See Air Commando Association. Gen. Singlaub, of the World Anti-Communist League (see South Korea) and other anti-communist pressure groups, has attended Soldier of Fortune annual conferences.

International affiliations. Foreign right-wingers who have attended SoF gatherings include Afghan and Nicaraguan counter-revolutionary leaders Hassan Gailani and Edgar Chamorro.

Sons of Liberty

Address. Box 503, Brisbane, California 94005

Leadership. Joseph W. Kerska (president)

Orientation. Gun lobby

History. The Sons of Liberty group was founded in 1976 as one of the more explicitly conservative of the lobbying organizations opposed to legal controls on the ownership and carrying of firearms. It may be connected to an earlier Sons of Liberty, which was based in Los Angeles around 1973.

Associated organizations. Major gun lobby groups include the National Rifle Association, the American Firearm Association, the Citizens' Committee for the Right to Keep and Bear Arms (and the related Second Amendment Foundation), Gun Owners Inc. and the National Association to Keep and Bear Arms.

Southern National Party

Address. Box 18124, Memphis, Tennessee 38118

Orientation. White supremacist

History. This organization was represented at a rally held in 1986 by the White Patriot Party.

Policies. The Party seeks to restore white supremacist rule in the old Confederate states.

Southern White Knights

Base. Georgia

Leadership. Dave Holland

Orientation. White supremacist

History. This group, one of many Ku Klux Klan organizations, was formed after a split in the National Knights of the KKK in 1985-86. It attended the White Patriot Party conference and the annual Klan gathering at Stone Mountain, Georgia, in 1986. Holland was one of four fascists arrested in the same year for an assault on a member of the anti-fascist Center for Democratic Renewal.

Policies. The Knights share with other KKK groups a belief in white supremacy and authoritarian government.

Associated organizations. The Knights have held joint activities with groups including the National Alliance and the National States Rights Party.

SS Action Group

Orientation. Nazi

History. This organization was reportedly active in 1986 and was attempting to recruit skinheads in American cities.

Policies. The name of the group suggests a mainstream nazi (anti-semitic, white supremacist) ideology.

Steppingstones Publications

Address. Box 612, Silver Spring, Maryland 20901-0612

Leadership. Ernest Sevier Cox (publisher)

Orientation. Fascist

History. This anti-semitic and white supremacist book distribution operation was established in 1973 by Earl Thomas as White Legion, and adopted its present name in 1976. It is controlled by Cox, a former Ku Klux Klan leader who had helped to establish the Northern League, an international fascist co-ordinating body based in the Netherlands.

Policies. Steppingstones has a white supremacist and authoritarian philosophy.

Stop Forced Busing (S.T.O.P.)

Address. Box 133, South Boston, Massachusetts 02127

Leadership. Charlie Ross Jr (director)

Orientation. Ultra-conservative

History. This organization was founded in 1974, with the initial purpose of resisting the practice of bussing children to particular schools to ensure a racial balance throughout the public school system. It has since broadened its scope to take in other issues of particular importance to the right.

Policies. The organization campaigns for school prayer and traditional education, and against homosexuality, bussing, sex education, gun control, feminism and pornography.

Sword of Christ

Address. Box 88, London, Arkansas 72847

Orientation. Fascist

History. This Christian racist newsletter was published in the mid-1980s. It may have originated as *Sword of the Lord*, which was published from Murfreesboro, Tennessee, in the early 1970s; alternatively, the latter publication may have given rise to the group known as The Covenant, the Sword and the Arm of the Lord.

Policies. Although little information is available about *Sword of Christ*, a national socialist orientation may be inferred from its use of a post office box number, 88, which represents a code among modern-day nazis for the letters HH, standing for Heil Hitler. The term "88" is sometimes used as a closing salutation in nazi correspondence and appears in the addresses of other US nazi groups, for example the New Order and *Torch*, and in the names of groups such as Column 88 (United Kingdom), Column 88 Heil Hitler (France) or *Trinchera 88* (Chile).

Teutonia Film and Video

Address. 1961 Vista del Mar, Hollywood, California 90068

History. This company specializes in the supply of films and other materials on national socialism and Nazi Germany.

Associated organizations. Similar operations, not all of which may have a fascist orientation, include International Historic Films, Chicago, and Communications Archives Inc., New Jersey.

Teutonic Unity

Address. Box 148, Buffalo, New York 14225

Orientation. Nazi

History. This newsletter was produced around 1980 by supporters of Manfred Roeder, a German fascist activist (see *Deutsche Burgerinitiative*, West Germany). It may now be defunct.

Policies. The newsletter promoted the West German fascist movement and liaison between West German and US fascist groups.

Torch

Address. Box 88, Bass, Arkansas 72612

Orientation. Fascist

History. This tabloid publication was being published in the mid-1980s.

Policies. It espouses white supremacist and anti-semitic concepts.

Associated organizations. In the early 1970s a journal called *The Torch* was being published by the Christian Crusade, a Tulsa, Oklahoma, group better known for its periodicals *Christian Crusade* and *Weekly Crusader*. It has not been possible to establish whether the Arkansas *Torch* is connected with Christian Crusade.

Truth Missions

Address. Box 3849, Manhattan Beach, California 90266

Telephone. (213) 546 3689

Leadership. Dave McCalden (director)

Orientation. Revisionist history group

History. Truth Missions was set up in the early 1980s following McCalden's expulsion from the Institute for Historical Review after a dispute with the IHR's sponsor, Willis Carto. The new group was reported to have appropriated the IHR's mailing list and it may be assumed that there is an overlap in membership. The two bodies were involved in litigation in 1985-86.

Policies. As part of the international Holocaust denial movement, the Missions' publications claim that there were no nazi death camps for Jews and others.

Associated organizations. The group has advertised *New Libertarian*magazine, but states that there is no organizational connection.

International affiliations. Truth Missions has a British address at premises owned by the Hancock family (see Historical Review Press, United Kingdom).

Unification Church

Base. Manhattan, New York

Leadership. Sun Myung Moon (founder); Dr Mose Durst (president); Bo Hi Pak (chief administrator)

Orientation. Anti-communist religious cult

History. This sect, better known as the Moonie organization, was founded in the 1970s by a South Korean anti-communist, Sun Myung Moon (born in 1920), and gained a considerable following among US youth, using what were widely regarded at the time as brainwashing techniques. By the early 1980s there were signs that the sect had gained some measure of acceptance as a legitimate religion. Its annual budget in the United States 1984 was about $22,000,000.

In 1984 Moon received an 18-month prison sentence for a $150,000 tax fraud of which he had been convicted in 1982.

Policies. The religious element of the sect's philosophy might be described as a fundamentalist Protestantism. It is aggressively anti-communist and supports Western moral values.

Publications. The Moonie organization's New World Communications subsidiary has established three daily newspapers in the United States, the tabloid *The New York Tribune* and the Spanish-language *Noticias del Mundo*(News of the World), both in New York, and *The Washington Times* in the capital.

Membership. 45,000 in the United States (against a claimed world-wide figure of up to 3,000,000).

Associated organizations. See CAUSA and *The Washington Times.*

International affiliations. See CAUSA-International and Unification Church (South Korea), and national CAUSA organizations (France, Ireland etc.). The Moonie sect has followers in 120 countries.

United Klans of America (UKA)

Address. Box 2369, Tuscaloosa, Alabama 34501

Leadership. Robert (Bobby) Shelton (Imperial Wizard)

Orientation. White supremacist

History. This faction has since its formation in the early 1960s been one of the most important of the various Klan groupings. By the middle of the decade it had some 5,000 members, mainly in the southern states; at the time it also operated as the Knights of the Ku Klux Klan, which is now the name of an independent grouping. Three members of the UKA were imprisoned for 10 years for the murder in 1965 of a black civil rights worker. Under the joint leadership of Shelton and Robert Miles, the UKA adopted an extremely anti-semitic outlook in the 1970s.

The murder by two Klansmen (including the son of Bennie Jack Hays, "Titan" of the Alabama section) of a black youth in 1981 led to a series of court cases, culminating in February 1987 with the award of $7,000,000 damages against the UKA in favour of the family of the victim. The murderer, Hays, had been sentenced to death in 1984, but had not yet been executed. Shelton was obliged to resume his profession as a car salesman and the UKA headquarters, said to be worth $100,000, were expected to be sold. The UKA itself was thought likely to be bankrupted and dissolved.

Policies. It advocates white supremacy, racial segregation and authoritarian government.

Publications. The Fiery Cross

United Patriotic Front (UPF)

Address. Box 388, Bartlesville, Oklahoma 74005

Leadership. Martin Borman (secretary)

Orientation. Nazi

History. The UPF was established by the National Socialist Movement (based at the same address) in the early 1980s. It succeeds the White Confederacy alliance.

Policies. The UPF seeks to co-ordinate the activities of nazi and Klan groups.

US Campaign Academy—see World Youth Freedom League.

US Council for World Freedom (USCWF)

Address. 3003 West Northern Avenue, Suite 4, Phoenix, Arizona 85021

Telephone. (601) 864 9804

Telex. 165122UD

Leadership. Maj.-Gen. John K. Singlaub (chairman); Richard Coorsh, Marta Wintering

Orientation. Anti-communist

History. The USCWF was founded in 1978 as a direct successor to the American Council for World Freedom (ACWF), led by Lee Edwards and Stefan Possony, which was the US affiliate of the World Anti-Communist League (WACL) until 1975, when it withdrew in protest at fascist infiltration of the League. The Council on American Affairs, run by Roger Pearson, then affiliated to the League, with Pearson becoming chairman of North American Regional WACL (NARWACL).

In the early 1980s, after non-fascists had staged a "counter-coup" within the WACL, the USCWF came back as the US chapter under the leadership of former Army general John Singlaub, who had been in charge of the clandestine Special Operations Group in the Vietnam war. (The SOG was involved in the Phoenix Programme of mass murder of opponents of the US-backed South Vietnam government.) After being dismissed by President Carter in 1977 for insubordination, Singlaub had become openly involved in right-wing politics.

The USCWF has used its tax-free status to raise millions of dollars of private funding for the Nicaraguan counter-revolutionary guerrillas (the contras), much of which has been spent on military supplies. In April 1986 it received State Department approval for the gift to the contras of an army surplus helicopter, which it had bought with a donation from one supporter, Ellen Garwood of Austin, Texas. It has also supported other anti-communist rebels, notably in Kampuchea, Laos, Vietnam and Afghanistan; it maintains a permanent representative in Pakistan to channel funds to the *mujaheddin.*

Policies. The USCWF engages in lobbying, advertising, fund-raising and other activities in support of anti-communist causes.

Associated organizations. See American Council for Peace through Strength; American Security Council; *Soldier of Fortune*; Western Goals; World Youth Freedom League.

International affiliations. See WACL (South Korea). NARWACL, to which the USCWF is still affiliated, is currently led by John Gamble, a former Canadian Conservative member of parliament and head of the Canadian Freedom Foundation.

United States Defense Committee (USDC)

Address. 3238 Wynford Drive, Fairfax, Virginia 22031

Leadership. Henry Walther (president)

Orientation. Militarist

History. The USDC was founded in 1982 and has engaged mainly in direct-mail campaigning.

Policies. It seeks a more aggressively anti-communist foreign policy and increased defence spending. It is particularly concerned with the Central American situation, where it perceives Nicaragua as a threat to US national security.

Membership. The USDC claims 132,000 "correspondents".

Publications. Defense Watch, six per year.

The Washington Times

Address. 3600 New York Avenue, NE, Washington, DC 20002

Telephone. (202) 636-3000

Leadership. Col. Bo Hi Pak (chairman); Arnaud de Borchgrave (editor)

Orientation. Anti-communist

History. This conservative daily newspaper was founded with a $150,000,000 investment by Sun Myung Moon's Unification Church (the Moonies) in 1982 to counter an alleged liberal bias in the US media. James R. Whelan, the first publisher and editor of the *Times*, was dismissed in 1984, and claimed that the paper was completely controlled by the Moonie sect. He was succeeded by Smith Hempstone, who in turn was replaced in early 1985. The paper claims a circulation of about 101,000.

Policies. The aim of the *Times* is to provide a conservative alternative to the liberal-controlled serious press. Its coverage is sympathetic to right-wing causes around the world, notably in South Africa.

Western Goals

Address. 111 South Columbus Street, Alexandria, Virginia 22314

Telephone. (703) 549 6687

Leadership. Linda C. Guell (director); Lewis Walt (chairman); Gen. John Singlaub (member of advisory board)

Orientation. Anti-communist

History. This foundation was established in 1979 by ultra-right congressman Larry McDonald, who died in the KAL 7 airliner incident of 1984. One of its main activists is now Gen. Singlaub of the US Council for World Freedom and the World Anti-Communist League. There is an overlap in membership between the advisory committees of this group and those of other right-wing lobbying groups.

In 1983 the group began to assemble a computer database on left-wing Americans with the help of files stolen from the Los Angeles police. Two detectives were charged in connection with the thefts in February 1984.

Policies. Western Goals seeks to convince the public of the need for massive rearmament and preparation for all-out nuclear war with the Warsaw Pact. It also seeks to expose subversion and to oppose diplomatic and commercial dealings with communist nations. It is not aligned with any US political party.

Publications. The group carries out extensive (and expensive) press and television advertising campaigns in support of its policies.

Associated organizations. See American Security Council; American Council for Peace Through Strength; John Birch Society; US Council for World Freedom.

International affiliations. There is a similarly named sister organization in the United Kingdom, and a small support group in West Germany. See also WACL (South Korea).

Western Guard Party

Address. Box 1197, Buffalo, New York 14225

Orientation. Fascist

History. This Party was founded in Canada in the early 1970s, but opened a US branch around 1980 in order to facilitate the distribution of its propaganda, which mostly contravened Canadian legislation against incitement to racial hatred.

Policies. The Party has white supremacist, national revolutionary policies.

Publications. Aryan.

International affiliations. See Western Guard (Canada).

White American Political Association—see White Aryan Resistance.

White Aryan Resistance (WAR)

Address. Box 65, Fallbrook, California 92028

Telephone. (619) 728 6224

Leadership. Tom Metzger (leader)

Orientation. White supremacist

History. This group, founded in 1980 as the White American Political Association, is in effect a faction of the Ku Klux Klan. It has also been known as White American Resistance, but it adopted its present name in 1985. Metzger was formerly involved in both Klan and nazi party activities and had also been active in the Democratic Party. Together with the leader of the Aryan Nations, Richard Butler, he appeared in a Los Angeles court in 1986 in connection with a cross burning ceremony. Metzger was best man at the 1986 wedding of the leader of the National Socialist Liberation Front. In April of the same year the group was associated with a Hitler birthday party held in a Los Angeles restaurant.

The WAR's leading members include Bill Albers, formerly prominent in the Invisible Empire faction of the Klan.

Policies. The WAR promotes white supremacy and complete racial segregation. Metzger has advocated a tactical alliance between white nationalist groups and other minority separatist organizations, such as Louis Farrakhan's black Muslim movement.

Membership. 5,000, in about 20 chapters.

Publications. WAR, irregular (succeeds *WAPA Fact Ledger*). Metzger hosts a cable television show called *Race and Reason.*

Associated organizations. Metzger spoke at the 1985 Christian Patriots Conference (see Aryan Nations), which was attended by many leading nazi and KKK figures.

White Confederacy—see National Socialist Movement.

White Knights of Liberty

Leadership. Jerry Douglas Suits (Titan); Mary Vestal Suits (Queen Kleagle); Jerry Albert Henderson, Joe Grady

Base. North Carolina

Orientation. White supremacist

History. Four members of this Ku Klux Klan faction—which, through its affiliation to a United Racist Front, was implicated in the 1979 Greensboro massacre—pleaded guilty in December 1985 to a series of cross-burnings designed to intimidate inter-racial couples. A total of 12 members were arrested in early 1986 on conspiracy charges. Following their conviction later in the year it announced its decision to go underground.

Policies. The faction advocates the use of revolutionary violence to create a white-ruled nation in North America.

White Patriot Party (WPP)

Base. Angier, North Carolina

Leadership. Glenn Miller; Steve Miller (leaders)

Orientation. White supremacist

History. The WPP was founded in the 1970s as the Confederate (or Carolina) Knights of the Ku Klux Klan. The Knights were sued by the anti-Klan Southern Poverty Law Center after numerous incidents involving their paramilitary Special Forces; three members of the Knights were later charged with an arson attack on the Center. Their leader, Glenn Miller (born 1941), a former American Nazi Party activist and army sergeant, ran in a Democratic primary election for state governor in 1984, securing almost 1 per cent of the vote. In January 1985 the Knights were forced to agree not to harass blacks in North Carolina, as part of the settlement of a lawsuit brought by a black resident.

In early 1986 the WPP organized a rally against the new federal holiday marking Martin Luther King's birthday. During 1986 a North Carolina court convicted the Miller brothers of contempt of court arising from charges that the WPP ran a paramilitary organization, allegedly recruiting serving soldiers and buying some $50,000 worth of rocket launchers, grenades, mines and plastic explosives. A federal grand jury investigation was under way in late 1986. In the same year it was reported that Glenn Miller was running for election to the state Senate.

In the last weeks of 1986 a number of WRP activists were arrested and charged with conspiring to bomb a fast food outlet. A Party spokesman, Cecil Cox, was then quoted as announcing the impending dissolution of the WPP, but it appeared to be still in existence in early 1987 (although Cox had gone on to establish a Southern National Front, linked to the British NF). It was reported in February 1987 that the WPP had declared its policy of deporting blacks to Africa on "leaky ships... to help them leak, we would blow them up".

Policies. The WPP is concerned to expose the activities of "the international satanic Jew", who, it claims, has taken over the government of the United States. Reported policies of the Knights include the compulsory registration of communists, the flying of the Southern Cross (the Confederate flag) from public buildings, the establishment of armed patrols to protect white schoolchildren, the expulsion of immigrants and the introduction of education programmes to discourage "miscegenation".

Membership. The WPP claims 2,600 members but a monitoring group, Klanwatch, puts the figure at about 800; in 1985 the Confederate Knights were reported to have 600 members.

Associated organizations. The WPP was represented at the 1986 Ku Klux Klan gathering at Stone Mountain, Georgia. It has attended or held joint meetings with the National Alliance, the National States Rights Party, Liberty Lobby, the Southern National Party and the National Association for the Advancement of White People.

White Solidarity Movement (WSM)

Address. 2021 K Street NW, Room 305, Washington, DC 20006

Orientation. Nazi

History. The WSM was founded around 1978.

Policies. It promotes unity and co-operation among US and foreign white supremacist and fascist groups.

White Student Union

Base. Sacramento, California

Leadership. Greg Withrow

Orientation. White supremacist, neo-nazi

History. Withrow (born in 1961) attended the 1986 Aryan Nations Congress.

Policies. Withrow has been quoted as saying that "non-Aryan" people "shall be terminated or expelled" from America; "the next line of Aryan leadership shall be a generation of ruthless predators".

Associated organizations. See Aryan Nations.

Women for a Secure Future (WSF)

Orientation. Right-wing conservative

History. This lobbying organization was active in the mid-1980s.

Policies. It concentrates on military issues and is part of the lobby supporting the "Star Wars" space weaponry plans.

Membership. It includes a number of mainstream and more radical conservative women's groups, such as, respectively, the National Federation of Republican Women and the Daughters of the American Revolution (DAR).

World Union of National Socialists—see New Order (above) and see Denmark.

World Youth Crusade for Freedom (WYCF)

Address. 1735 De Sales Street NW, Suite 802, Washington, DC 20036

Leadership. J. Parker

Orientation. Anti-communist

History. The WYCF was founded in 1965.

Policies. It campaigns against what it sees as the liberal domination of the field of foreign policy teaching, and promotes exchange programmes and other initiatives to concrease conservative influence in that area.

Associated organizations. Among organizations sponsored by the WYCF are the Freedom Training School, the Student Committee for a Free China and the Center for the Study of American Foreign Policy.

World Youth Freedom League (WYFL)

Base. Washington DC

Leadership. David Finzer

Orientation. Anti-communist

History. This pro-Reagan youth group, founded as the Young Conservative Foundation (YCF), was closely associated with the Heritage Foundation. It started a "Save the Oppressed People" (STOP) campaign in 1985 aimed at persuading investors to withdraw from businesses trading with the "evil empire" of the USSR. In 1986 it adopted its present name on becoming the international youth wing of the World

Anti-Communist League (WACL), replacing the fascist-infiltrated Youth-WACL. It has announced plans to open a "US Campaign Academy" to teach young anti-communist activists from abroad how best to use the media and modern marketing techniques to "sell" their message.

Policies. The WYFL (the acronym is pronounced "wiffil") supports anti-communist causes throughout the world, including the Nicaraguan contras and other guerrilla organizations. It seeks to educate young people as to the dangers of communism and the need to protect individual liberties and Western moral values.

Associated organizations. See US Council for World Freedom and Heritage Foundation.

International affiliations. See WACL (South Korea). The WYFL reportedly receives funding from the South Korean WACL as well as from affiliated youth organizations. As the YCF, the group had extensive contacts with foreign right-wing youth groups, including the Federation of Conservative Students (United Kingdom).

WUN Enterprises

Address. PO Box 1445, Greensboro, North Carolina 27402

Orientation. Nazi

History. This book and merchandise distribution operation was active in the early 1980s.

Policies. It produces and sells nazi and white supremacist propaganda materials.

Young Americans for Freedom (YAF)

Address. PO Box 20090, 1001 Prince Street, Alexandria, Virginia 22320

Telephone. (203) 836 1960

Leadership. Terrel Cannon (chairman); Michael Waller (national secretary)

Orientation. Ultra-conservative

History. The YAF was founded in 1960. It has traditionally been strongest in California, Missouri, New York state, Ohio, Texas and Wisconsin, although it has had branches in most states.

Policies. It provides research and policy discussion activities for right-wing Republican and Democratic youth activists.

Membership. 90,000, in some 300 branches.

Publications. New Guard, quarterly.

Associated organizations. The YAF runs the United Students of America Federation, and is politically very close to the Heritage Foundation. It has run other right-wing groupings such as the Campaign Against East-West Trade.

International affiliations. Waller participated in the 1986 pro-contra conference held in London by members of the Federation of Conservative Students (United Kingdom).

Young Conservative Foundation (YCF)—see World Youth Freedom League.

Defunct organizations

American Birthright Committee: a ferociously anti-semitic grouping of the 1970s, it campaigned under the slogan "Communism is Jewish". It sought to get "the US out of the UN and the UN out of the US", and presented "race-mixing" and subversion as the results of Jewish conspiracies.

American Christian Party: this mid-1970s Party, which adopted the slogan "Christian American: Beware of Jewish Swine", promoted its version of Christianity in the context of a campaign against racial "miscegenation". It had an armed paramilitary section which called itself the American Legion, and used the Nordic sunwheel (or Celtic cross) as its symbol.

American Flag Committee: an anti-communist, anti-integration grouping formed in 1950, it published a monthly *Newsletter* at least until the late 1970s.

American Nazi Party: an inconsequential grouping of the 1930s, it was associated with the Berlin-funded German-American *Bund*, which organized almost exclusively among German immigrants and their descendants and was suppressed in 1940.

American Renaissance Party: this nazi organization was active from the 1950s, with H. Keith Thompson, now a supporter of Willis Carto's enterprises (see Liberty Lobby), as one of its leaders. The party was associated with the German Rights Party, a defunct West German fascist group, and may have been linked with the uniformed fascist National Renaissance Party, which was active in New York in the 1970s (led by H. Madole).

American Victory: a bulletin published in the 1970s by Bradley J. Smith of Salem, Wisconsin, it promoted McCarthyite anti-communism and US nationalism.

American White Nationalist Party: founded around 1972 by John W. Gerhardt, the AWNP and its organ *The White Nationalist* advanced straightforward national socialist concepts on racial questions; it also supported the strengthening of states' rights against those of the federal government, which it regarded as Jewish-controlled. Based in Columbus, Ohio, the AWNP joined the National Socialist Movement's White Confederacy alliance in the mid-'70s.

Americans for Western Unity: a Michigan-based group, it published *Western World* irregularly from 1973 to about 1977. It was primarily a white supremacist movement.

Anglo-Saxon Christian Crusade, Inc.: led by Russell R. Veh, this organization, which was particularly active in the mid-1970s, had a profoundly racist and anti-semitic platform. Its publication, the *Christian Advocate*, was subtitled "A real case against the Jews".

Anti-Communist League of America: active from the late 1960s to at least the mid-'70s, this group was based in Park Ridge, Illinois.

Apostoli Veritas: this magazine (Apostoles of Truth) was published in the 1970s by ultra-right Catholic traditionalists opposed to liberal interpretations of Christian doctrine.

Aryan Knights of the Ku Klux Klan: based in Waco, Texas, around 1960, this group was led by H.S. Miller.

Christian Educational Association: this group was founded in 1945 by J. McGinley to publish *Common Sense*, a journal which remained in existence until the 1970s, served as an open forum for the US fascist movement and was dedicated to exposing a supposed Jewish-communist conspiracy. The paper opposed the civil rights movement and sought white Christian supremacy. The Association was based in Union City, New Jersey.

Christian Heritage: an anti-communist pressure group established in the 1970s, and based until at least 1982 at Mount Kisco, New York, it may have been superseded by the American Society for the Defense of Tradition, Family and Property.

Christian Party: an early 1950s grouping led by J.B. Stoner prior to the formation of the National States' Rights Party.

Church of the Creator: a nazi, anti-Jewish and anti-Christian organization which sought in the 1970s to take advantage of the tax-free status of religious groups, the Church's leader (or Pontifex Maximus) was Ben Klassen. Its "Bible" was *Nature's Eternal Religion,* a book by Klassen which called for a white revolution. The Church was based in Florida, where Klassen had served as a state congressman.

The Columbians: a Klan-like white supremacist group active in the 1930s.

Committee to Impeach Earl Warren: a John Birch Society front of the late 1960s, it sought the dismissal of a Supreme Court justice of liberal views.

Confederate Knights of the Ku Klux Klan: see main entry for White Patriot Party.

Duck Club: this secretive anti-communist organization was active in the north-west of the United States in the early to mid-1980s, but was reportedly dying out in mid-1986. Its newsletters reportedly included articles to the effect that the United States was about to be invaded by tens of thousands of Chinese and Korean communists, who were supposedly massing on the Mexican border. On Dec. 24, 1985, one of its members, David Lewis Rice, murdered four members of a Seattle family in the belief that they were Jewish communists; he was in June 1986 sentenced to death.

Friends of Rhodesian Independence: a white supremacist front of the 1970s. Similar groups active at the same time included Americans for Independent Rhodesian Government, Connecticut Friends of Rhodesia, the New Hampshire Committee in Support of Rhodesian Independence, Friends of Rhodesia (California), the American Friends of Rhodesian Independence under Civil Authority (AFRICA—Mobile, Alabama), and two groups called American Friends of Rhodesia (one based in Berkeley, California, and the other a subcommittee of the segregationist Separate Schools Inc., Atlanta, Georgia).

German-American Bund: the main fascist grouping of the 1930s, it was also the principal channel of German funding for American fascism.

The Herald of Freedom: an anti-semitic, integrist and anti-communist fortnightly newsletter published from New Jersey by Frank A. Capell, it ceased publication in the late 1970s along with a sister publication, the *Confidential Intelligence Report.*

Institute of American Relations: this right-wing pressure group was active on foreign and defence policy issues in the late 1970s.

Legion of Decency: a Christian ultra-conservative pressure group led by Alfred E. Smith, it sponsored an anti-nudism bill passed in New York in 1935.

The Order: all 24 known members of this neo-nazi guerrilla group, also known as the Silent Brotherhood (or *Brüder Schweigend,* White American Revolutionary Army or Aryan Resistance Movement), were dead or imprisoned by mid-1986, and the group itself was thought to be defunct. It was founded by Robert J. Mathews, Gary Lee Yarbrough and seven others in 1983 as an offshoot of the Aryan Nations. Yarbrough had previously belonged to a loose-knit prisoners' group, the Aryan Brotherhood, while most of the others had been active in the Aryan Nations, the related Church of Jesus Christ Christan, and other nazi or Klan groups. The Order took its name, ideology and strategy from a 1978 novel, *The Turner Diaries* by William Pierce (see National Alliance), which describes a right-wing guerrilla war against the US government.

In 1983-84 members of The Order were accused of two murders, including that of a Denver radio presenter, and of arms offences, counterfeiting, bank and armoured car robberies totalling $4,000,000, and arson; one member was later convicted of murdering a Missouri policeman in that period. After the start of a federal grand jury investigation into the group, Mathews died in a confrontation with police in December 1984, and was succeeded as leader by Bruce Carroll Pierce, but the group began to disintegrate. Yarbrough, who had been arrested in November, was imprisoned in February 1985 on assault and arms charges, and Bruce Pierce was arrested in March. Four other members were arrested in April at an Arkansas camp belonging to Jim Ellison's group, The Covenant, the Sword and the Arm of the Lord, and others were held in various states, notably Alabama, California, Colorado, Idaho, Oregon and Washington.

Another leader of the group committed suicide, 11 pleaded guilty to less serious charges and were given short prison sentences, and in January 1986 10 other members (including Yarbrough and Bruce Pierce) were sentenced to up to 100 years in prison for racketeering—the first time that anti-racket legislation had been used in a political case. Evidence given in the 15-week trial indicated that hundreds of thousands of dollars stolen by The Order were given to other racist groups, including the Confederate Knights of the Ku Klux Klan, the White Aryan Resistance, the National Alliance and the Aryan Nations.

The Order's policies included armed resistance to what it termed the "Zionist Occupation Government" and advocacy of the establishment of a "White American Bastion" in the Pacific north-west states. The Order was honoured at the 1986 Congress of the Aryan Nations, which was attended by Mathews' widow and son and received a letter from one of the imprisoned activists, Richard E. Scutari, who had been "chief security officer" of The Order. His successor in that post, Elden Cutler, was convicted separately in 1986 of conspiring to murder the informer behind the mass trial.

The Plain Speaker: an anti-semitic journal published by George Knupffer in the early 1970s, it was an early supporter of the Holocaust denial movement.

Right: this anti-semitic magazine was published in San Francisco from the mid-1950s to the mid-'60s. It was circulated among many US and foreign fascist groups and its editor, Dr E.L. Anderson, became associate editor of *Western Destiny* (see Council for Social and Economic Research) when racist anthropologist Roger Pearson moved his operations to the United States in the early '60s. Another *Right* editor, Edward Vargas, became a contributing editor for *Western Destiny* along with Ernest Sevier Cox, a Klan revivalist (see *Steppingstones*), and other leading American and foreign right-wingers.

Sovereignty Commission: this Mississippi agency was created by the state government in 1956 with the brief of preserving and defending the practise of racial segregation, and studying "subversive, militant or revolutionary groups" in the state. The 12-man commission, which had an initial budget of $250,000, remained active until 1973 and in existence until 1977; it was particularly active in 1960-64 when, under the direction of Gov. Ross R. Barnett, it worked closely with private white supremacist groups including the White Citizens' Council. A similar Alabama Sovereignty Committee existed until the mid-1970s.

United White People's Party: a Cleveland (Ohio) organization of the mid-1970s, its slogan was "Race, Fatherland, God". It co-operated with the National Socialist Party of America.

The Voice of Liberty: a Georgia-based monthly publication of the 1970s, it promoted nationalism, fundamental Christianity and "constitutional government", i.e. the prevalence of states' rights over federal authority.

Other organizations

It would be difficult, if not impossible, to list in the present volume all the minor radical right-wing organizations which have been active in the United States in recent years. What follows is merely a selection of such groups, and groups on which insufficient information has been obtained. Most of those listed are known to have been active at some point during the past 10 to 15 years, but a large proportion are likely to have become defunct.

The Aaronic Order (Springville, Utah); *Action Bulletin* (Corte Madera) and *Action Magazine* (Glendale, both in California); the Action Group (Detriot, Michigan); the Action Patriots (Los Angeles, California), and the associated American Birthright Committee; the Adamic Knights of the Ku Klux Klan (Box 36, Ephraba, Pennsylvania 17622), a splinter group of the UKA; *AIM Report* (Washington DC), against "media distortions"; *Alert*, a newsletter of the 1970s (Virginia); the anti-communist Alert Americans Association (Los Angeles); the All-American Conference to Combat Communism (1028 Connecticut Avenue, Washington, DC 20006), which was active in the 1970s and may be defunct; the anti-communist émigré All-Slavic Publishing House (New York, NY); *The Alternative*; *Amer-Europa* bulletin (Panama City, Florida); at least two right-wing journals called *The American* (Somerset, Pennsylvania, and Odessa, Texas); the pro-Pinochet American Chilean Council; the American Conservative Party (Missouri); Carl Channell's American Conservative Trust (305 4th Street NE, Washington, DC 20002), active in the mid-1980s; the American Defense Preparedness Association (Washington DC); the *American Digest* (Box 1314, Mena, Arkansas); at least three bulletins called *The American Eagle*; the American Enterprise Institute (1150 17th Street NW, Washington, DC 20036), an industry-funded conservative economic "think tank"; the racist American Eugenics Party (Box 38068, Los Angeles, California 90038).

The American Guard and the American Mobilizers (both at Box 1084, Mount Vernon, New York 10551), led by Adam Link and publishing *The New America* monthly; *The American Patriot* (Box 277, Carbondale, Pennsylvania 18407), which may be the same as an identically-named journal (formerly called *Free Enterprise*) published in the late 1970s from Phoenix, Arizona; American Patriots for Freedom, active in the early 1970s; *American Survival*(Washington state) and *American Survival Papers* (New York, NY), both early 1970s precursors of the survivalist movement; the racist American Veterans' League (Box 7085, Hiland Station, Minneapolis, Minnesota 55411), which also functions as the National Society for the Preservation of the White Race; Americans in Action (118 South First Street, Lufkin, Texas 75901); Americans for Civil Harmony (Box 6061, San Jose, California 95150), which had fronts in the 1970s called Christian American Heritage and Americans for Independent Rhodesian Government; the anti-communist Americans to Free Captive Nations (c/o A. Korn, 1025 Gerard, Bronx, New York 10000); Americans for Law and Order; Americans for National Security (based in Washington DC, but with state chapters elsewhere, notably in Missouri); Americans for Patriotic Action (Los Angeles); Americans against Union Control of Government; America's Future; Anglo-Saxon Books, a Christian Identity publishing house (Box 1222, Los Angeles, California 90053) which has produced *Identity Directory* and which runs the Lost Tribes Tract Service; the Anglo-Saxon Federation of America (Merrimac, Minnesota 01680), publishing *Destiny* magazine; Angriff Press (PO Box 2726, Hollywood, California 90028); the Anti-Bolshevik Bloc of Nations, also trading as the American Friends of the ABN (526 Genessee Street, Buffalo, New York 14244).

The Anti-Communist Amateur Radio Network (Berkeley, California); the Louisiana-based Anti-Communist Christian Association; the Anti-Communist International, also known as the First Anti-Communist International (Box 1095, New York, NY 10017); Anti-Communist Liaison, publishing *Tactics* (Box 3541, Arlington, Virginia 22203); the Anti-Communist Seminar (64 Sigourney Street, Jamaica Plain, Minnesota 02130); the Arizona Patriots, a fascist guerrilla group which emerged in late 1986; the Aryan Publishing Company (Box 1972, Milwaukee, Wisconsin 53201); the Asatru Free Assembly (formerly the Viking Brotherhood), a Nordicist organization (1766 East Avenue, Turlock, California 95380) publishing *The Rune Stone*; the similar Asatruarfolk (2922 South Marvin Avenue, Tucson, Arizona 85730), led by Eirikur Thorarinsson; the Association of Southern Defenders (South Carolina); *Attack!* (Box 3535, Washington, DC 20007); the Austin Anti-Communist

League (Texas); *Awake America* (Burbank, California); the Black Silent Majority Committee (PO Box 7610, Washington, DC 20044); the Blue Shirts of Louisiana (Box 8351, New Orleans, Louisiana 70122); the Bob Jones University (Greenville, South Carolina 29601), a fundamentalist "degree mill" which advocates racial segregation and whose "graduates" include Ian Paisley (Northern Ireland); Books for Libertarians (Washington DC); *Breakthrough* (Detroit); *Calhoon Reports* (Placentia, California); California Citizens for Decent Literature, and other Citizens for Decent Literature groups in Ohio and elsewhere; the California Home Defenders (Los Angeles); the Cameron Employees' Anti-Communism Committee (Houston, Texas); *Capitol Voice* (Washington DC); the Catholic Freedom Foundation; Catholics for Race Preservation (184 Garfield Avenue, Mineola, New York 11501); Celestial Democracy (Box 158, Berkeley, California 94704), and the Center for Judicial Studies.

The pro-Wallace Christian American Heritage Guild (Box 15, Menlo Park, California 94025); the Christian American Party (3966 McGirts Boulevard, Jacksonville, Florida 32210), active in the early 1970s; Christian Americans, publishing *Facts and Revelation Newsletter* (Box 4405, Alexandria, Louisiana 71301); the libertarian Christian Anarchists League, publishing *American Spectator* (Chicago, Illinois); *Christian Beacon* (Box 218, Collingwood, New Jersey 08108); the Christian Coalition Party (North Dakota); the Christian Constitutional Education League; the Christian Crusade (or Christian Crusade Church), not thought to be connected to the New Christian Crusade Church; the Christian Constitutional Educational League, the Florida-based segregationist publisher of *White Sentinel* monthly; the probably defunct Christian Defense Fund (Louisiana); *Christian Israelite* (Oregon), an early-1970s precursor of the Christian Identity movement; the Christian Nation Association, run by the Carolina Christian Union; the Christian Nationalist Crusade (Box 27895, Los Angeles, California 90027), founded in 1941 by Gerald Smith, publishing *The Cross and the Flag* and *The News Letter* and including a Citizens' Congressional Committee; the Christian Patriotic League (Pittsburgh, Pennsylvania); the Illinois-based survivalist Christian Patriots Defense League, led by nazi activist John R. Harrell and independent of the Christian Defense League; the Missouri-based Christian Sons of Liberty, publishing *Alarming Cry*; Oren F. Potito's Christian Youth Corps (Box 1739, Ocala, Florida 32670), publishing *National Christian News* and probably related to the National Christian Church; and the Cinema Educational Guild, formed in the 1960s and probably defunct.

The Citizens' Anti-Communist Committee (805 Housatonic, Bridgeport, Connecticut 06604); the Citizens' Committee of California Inc., active from the 1960s; the Citizens' Committee to Keep America Free (Chatanooga, Tennessee); the Citizens' Defense Fund (Washington state); the *Citizens' Informer* (PO Box 2494, Overland, Missouri 63114), a journal serving Citizens' Councils in Illinois, Kentucky and Missouri; *Clarion Call* (California); G. Leuthold's anti-communist newsletters, *Closer Up* and *Don Bell Reports* (Marsh Inc., Box 2223, Palm Beach, Florida 33480); the Commandos "L", based in Florida and possibly connected with the CLNC, Alpha 66 or some other Cuban émigré group; the mid-1970s Committee to Improve Racial Relations (Pasadena, California), which put forward some unconventional ideas as to how that goal might be achieved; the Committee for the Investigation of the Department of State, an early-1970s group which sought to expose infiltration of the public service; the Committee for the Repeal of the Income Tax (Evanston, Illinois); the Committee to Restore our Constitutional Republic Under God; the Committee of the States, a segregationist anti-semitic group publishing *American Challenge*; the revisionist Committee for Truth in History; the Committee to Unite America (PO Box 556, Lennox Hill Station, New York, NY 10021); the Committee to Warn of the Arrival of Communist Merchandise on the Local Business Scene (Miami, Florida); the Committee for Western Civilization, whose leaders include Richard Allen, Edwin

J. Feulner of Heritage and Sen. Phil Gramm; Communications Inc. (formerly the Independent Citizens' Council of the United States); Community Crusades of Americanism (Box 15, Glendale, California 91209); Concerned Citizens of South Jersey Against Communism (New Jersey), and Concord Press (Seal Beach, California).

The Conservative Citizens' Council (Jacksonville, Florida); the Conservative Society of America; *Conspiracy Digest* (Box 766, Dearborn, Michigan 48121); Constitutional Revival (Enfield, Connecticut); Constructive Action, a late 1970s group (Whittier, California); the Co-operators for Constitutional Money (New York) and the related Social Credit Association (Washington state); the Cooperstown Anti-Communist Society (Cooperstown, North Dakota); the Council Against Communist Aggression; the Council on Un-American Activities (Venice, Florida); the anti-communist Crusade for a Christian Civilization (Box 1281, New Rochelle, New York 10802); the Crusade Against Moral Pollution (Washington DC); *Dan Smoot Reports* (Box 9538, Dallas, Texas 75214), an influential ultra-conservative newsletter; *Danica* (Chicago); the *Dartmouth Review*, a right-wing student paper (New Hampshire); the *David Stacey Letters* and *Grace and Race* (608 West Animas, Farmington, New Mexico 87401); Gen. DelValle's Defenders of the American Constitution (Box 1776, Annandale, Virginia 22003); Defenders of the Christian Faith (Kansas City, Missouri); Defenders of State Sovereignty and Individual Liberty (Box 153, Lynchburg, Virginia 24505); Defiance Press (Abington, Connecticut); the Destiny of America Foundation, active around 1974; *Double Eagle* (Box 281, Murray Hill Station, New York, NY 10016), a bulletin on alleged Soviet penetration of the US establishment; the Eastern Patriots' Association (Pennsylvania); *Eddas*, published in the 1970s in support of the Northern League (see Netherlands); the John Birch Society-linked Englewood Anti-Communist League (Englewood, New Jersey), publishing *Reveille to Wake Up America*, and Eye Opener Publications (Junction City, Oregon).

The Federation of Christian Laymen, possibly descended from the Committee of Christian Laymen (active in California in the 1970s); the Federation for the Restoration of the Republic; the "Fight Communism" Stickers campaign of the Veterans of Foreign Wars movement; Fighters for Democracy Inc. (Florida); The Finders, a small hippie cult led by Marion Pettie (and linked to a similar cult called The Seekers); the monthly *Flag of Truth* (Fort Worth, Texas); the Fluoridation Education Society (Washington DC) and other anti-fluoridation committees, many infuenced by libertarianism or by conspiracy theories (suggesting, for example, that Jews or communists were poisoning the water).

At least two For God and Country Study Groups; the Forum of Americans for Constitutional Taxation; the Missouri-based Foundation for Divine Meditation, publisher of the *National Christian Crusader*; the Franklin County Anti-Communist Study Group (Columbus, Ohio); Free Anti-Communist Literature (1831 West Main, Alhambra, California); a libertarian magazine, *Freedom* (5930 Franklin Avenue, Hollywood, California 90028); the Freedom Crusade (Portland, Oregon); the Freedom Fighter Network (Box 12434, Fort Worth, Texas 76116); the Freedom Foundation, established in the late 1960s; the Freedom Leadership Foundation (1365 Connecticut Avenue NW, Washington, DC 20036); *Freedom Today*, a libertarian monthly (Phoenix, Arizona); *The Freeman*, also a libertarian monthly (New York); Georgians Unwilling to Surrender, active in the 1970s; the Greater St. Louis School of Anti-Communism (Missouri); *Help Alert America* (Fullerton, California); *Hilaire du Berrier Reports*, a Monaco-based anti-communist newsletter operation with a US distribution network (PO Box 786, St George, Utah); the I am an American Committee; *The Independent-American*, an ultra-right newspaper; Indiana Patriotic Publications; Individuals for Freedom; *Instauration* (Box 76, Cape Canaveral, Florida 32920), a monthly on "the deterioration in Western culture"; the racist International

Association for the Advancement of Ethnology and Eugenics, Inc. (IAAEE—Box 3495, Grand Central Station, New York, NY 10017), which has published numerous tracts since the 1960s; the *Internal Security Report*; the *Internationale Freiheitsbewegung* (International Freedom Movement); the Irving Christian Anti-Communist Crusade (Irving, Texas); the "Jab a Liberal" publishing operation (California); and the Jamestown Foundation (1708 Hew Hampshire Avenue, Washington DC), led by William W. Geimer, which helps anti-communist refugees.

The Keep America Free Council (Canton, Ohio); the Labor Volunteers (New York); Laissez Faire Books, a libertarian shop in New York; the Laymen's Committee Against Communism (Box 1, Atlanta, Georgia 30301); the Legion for the Survival of Freedom Inc., publishing *American Mercury*; Let Freedom Ring (based in Sarasota, Florida); *Let's Fight Against Communism*, published by Dilys Publications (3607 South Union Avenue, Chicago, Illinois 60609); Libertarian Books (Chicago); the Libertarian Press (Illinois), which used to publish *First Principles*; the anti-semitic Christian Identity movement Liberty Bell Publications (Raybar Inc., c/o Georg P. Dietz, Box 21, Reedy, West Virginia 25270), which produces *The Liberty Bell*; several groups called Liberty League; H.L. Hunt's *Life Lines*; Loompanics Unlimited, a survivalist group (Mason, Michigan); the Loyalty to Christ Committee (San Francisco, California); the MacArthur Freedom Association (Michigan), publishing *Freedom's Voice* in the 1970s; the Majority Citizens' League (Box 63, West Columbia, South Carolina 29169), a Klan front ("majority" being adopted in the early 1970s as a code word for white); Militant Americans, also known as the Church of the Great Kali; the Military and Religious Order of St. George, "dedicated to the preservation of Western Christian civilization", organized in 1965 by ex-Marine Gen. P.A. delValle; the Monroe Doctrine National Party, a probably extinct New York grouping; the Moral Rearmament Crusade, which some would regard as centrist rather than right-wing; the Mothers' Crusade for Victory over Communism, with chapters in several states; Mothers Organized for Moral Stability (Moms), active from the late 1960s, and the Movement to Restore Moral Decency (Motorede), organized around 1970.

The National Alliance to Keep and Bear Arms (PO Box 71, Norborne, Missouri 64668); the National Americanism Commission, publishing *Firing Line*, for right-wing unity (700 North Pennsylvania Street, or Box 1055, Indianapolis, Indiana 46206); the National Americanism League (South Carolina); the National Anti-Communist League of America (516 Milton, San Gabriel, California 91775); the National Captive Nations Committee (1028 Connecticut Avenue NW, Suite 514, Washington, DC 20036; J.E. Scott's National Christian Church, and its subsidiary, the Knights of the White Camelia, active from the early 1960s; the fascistic National Christian Democratic Union, formed around 1980 by Gerald Carlson; the National Committee for Economic Freedom (New York); the Los Angeles-based National Congress of Parents and Teachers Against Bussing (or Busing); the early-1970s *National Defender* (Washington DC); NEWS (National Emancipation of our White Soul), led by Dewey H. Tucker, which publishes *Battle Axe News* (from Route 2, Box 184B, Danbridge, Tennessee 37725); the National Forum (Massachusetts); the fascist National Guard Party and its youth movement, the White Youth Alliance, both linked to the Canadian Western Guard, and publishing *Defiance* and *Battlefront* under the direction of J.D. Westra; the 1,700,000-member anti-union National Right-to-Work Committee (Fairfax, Virginia); the mid-1970s National Socialist Bookstore (Cleveland, Ohio), which may have been linked with the North American Alliance of White People, based in the same city around 1974 (and not to be confused with the other NAAWPs); the non-party *National Socialist Review*, founded in 1973; the National Socialist Student Alliance, a probably defunct section of the NSWPP (now the New Order); the National Socialist White Power Movement (NSWPM), which appears to have disbanded, and the National Strategy Information Center.

The Network of Patriotic Letter-Writers, a lobbying group (Box 2003D, Pasadena, California 91105); New America Publications; *New Patriot and Race* (Box 16079, Jackson, Mississippi 39209); New Right Coalition (Boston, Massachusetts); *Nuevo Orden* (New Order), a Spanish-language magazine published in the early 1970s from El Monte, California (and not connected to the present-day New Order); *Orbis* (Philadelphia, Pennsylvania); the Order of the Three Crusades (New England); Oregonians for Constitutional Government; the Organization to Fight Communism (Box 281, Cleveland, Ohio 44121); Our Western World (Box 6596, St Petersburg Beach, Florida 33736); the *Patriot's Primer* (Box 2333, Delray Beach, Florida33444); the Pasadena Anti-Communist League, publishing *Truth Forum*, and the rival Pasadena Committee for Exposing Subversive Activities (California); the Patriot Bookstore in Baton Rouge, Louisiana (run around 1980 by David Duke, now of the New Order); Patriotic Americans for Freedom (Washington state); People of the Rune, a Philadelphia-based Odinist group; the *Pink Sheet on the New Left*, published by Phillip Luce (8401 Connecticut Avenue, Washington, DC 20005); the *Pitysmont Post*; the Political Council of American Citizens of European Descent (publishing *Potomac*), a coalition of ultra-right East European émigrés; *Private Property—Free Enterprise* magazine, published in Illinois in the late 1970s; Project Alert (Pensacola, Florida); *Problems of Communism*; the mainly anti-abortion *Pro-Life Reporter* (Export, Pennsylvania); the mid-1970s Provisional National Government (PNG—New York); the Racial Purity Bible School, run in the 1970s by the Citizens' Council of America for Segregation; *Rally*; the Rally for God and Country (Dedham, Massachusetts), and the unrelated Rededication to God and Country (Miami, Florida); *Religion in Communist-Dominated Areas*, and the Remember the *Pueblo* Committee, formed around 1968, which commemorated a clash with communist forces off Korea.

The Remnant Church (California) and the *Remnant Review*, published by Gary North (PO Box 467, Lynden, Washington 98264); *Renaissance Records*; *Richard Cotten's Conservative Viewpoint*, a newsletter concentrating on "anti-white racism" (Box 17194, Dulles Airport, Washington DC 20041); *The Right Report*, a libertarian newsletter (7777 Leesburg Pike, Falls Church, Virginia 22043); Rights of White People; the Runic Society, an Odinist movement formed in 1974 by J. Minor (publisher of *Einherjar* quarterly) and closely linked to the Canadian publication, *The Odinist*; the *St. Croix Review*; the St. John's Study Group on Communism (North Carolina); the Save Christian America Foundation (Fletcher, Missouri 63030), publishing *Confederate Star*; *Siempre*; the anti-semitic *Social Justice* journal (Box 41503, Cincinnati, Ohio 45241); the Soldiers of Christ (Pennsylvania); the Sons of Liberty, formed in the mid-1970s (Box 214, Metairie, Louisiana 70004, or Box 1896, Los Angeles, California 90028); Stockholders for World Freedom (4623 San Feliciano Drive, Woodland Hills, California 91364); *Strategic Review*; Students Against Communism (San Leandro, California); many Support Your Local Police committees; Survival (Chicago, Illinois) and other survivalist organizations; the Susan and Tony Alamo Foundation, active in 1984, which advanced a conspiracy theory directed against the Catholic Church; *Tactics*, an anti-communist monthly published since the early 1970s by Edward Hunter (Box 3541, Arlington, Virginia 22203); the Tax Rebellion Committee (California); the Teens Against Communism Club (Houston, Texas); *Think America* (California); *Through to Victory* (Ridgecrest, California); *To the Point International* (Box 697, Hightstown, New Jersey 08520); *Triumph*; *Trud* (subtitled "Terror Removes Unwanted Democracy"), a fascist journal produced in the 1970s by John Sullivan; the *Truth Seeker*, a racist, anti-semitic and anti-Christian journal founded in 1873; *Twin Circle* and the Twin Circle Publishing Company (New York); the Ulster American Loyalist Party; United Patriotic People of the USA (Glendale, California); the United Racist Front; the United Republicans of California; the US March for Victory (Washington, DC); the United Taxpayers' Party (Brooklyn, New York); the United White Christian Majority (Box 3980, Dallas,

Texas 75208), active in the 1970s; the United White People's Party; the Universal Order, led by James Mason (Box 17, Chillicothe, Ohio 45601), with its monthly *Siege*; *Veritas Report;* the *Voice of Americanism* (Box 90, Glendale, California 91209); and the *Voice of Truth and Freedom* (Anaheim, California).

Wake Up America (Ontario, California); the *Wanderer*, a conservative Catholic weekly (128 East 10th Street, St Paul, Minnesota 55101); *Washington Intelligence Report* (8001 MacArthur Boulevard NW, Washington, DC 20034); The Way International, a Kansas-based cult; We Fight On (Phoenix, Arizona); the Western Foundation of Dualism (Box 1081, Reading, Pennsylvania 19603), and its white supremacist magazine *Dragonfire*; Dr Walter White Jr's quasi-fascist Western Front (Box 27854, Hollywood, California 90027); Western Islands publishing, a John Birch Society operation; the mid-1970s White Bookstore (Alexandria, Virginia), which may have been run by the defunct White Party of Virginia; the White Citizens' Councils; the White Equal Rights Party (Box 4322, Pittsburgh, Pennsylvania); White Legion Books (PO Box 612, Silver Spring, Maryland 20901); *White Lightning*, a probably defunct racist paper of the late 1970s; the White Majority Lobby; the White Party of America, based in Washington DC in the mid-1970s and publishing *White Letter* and *White World*; the anti-semitic "Aryan Christian" White People's Committee to Restore God's Law, led by T.A. Robb and publishing *The Torch*(formerly *The Message of Old Monthly*); the White Power Movement, possibly the same as the NSWPM; the White Youth Alliance; Widening Horizons; *The Woman Constitutionalist*; Women for Law and Order (Alton, Illinois); the Women's Patriotic Conference on National Defense; World Service; *World War III Battlecry* (Dallas, Texas); Youth Action (PO Box 3051, Alexandria, Virginia 22302); Youth Against Communism (New York); Youth for America; and Youth for Wallace, a probably defunct campaign backing George Wallace of Alabama.

Individuals

James and *William Demick:* two New Orleans nazis charged in 1984 with planning to blow up a local business.

Peter Grace: this Reaganite millionaire has been involved at various times in several right-wing causes. He has served on the Board of International Broadcasting, the government body responsible for the anti-communist Radio Liberty and Radio Free Europe (see West Germany); he headed a presidential commission on public spending cuts, in connection with which he expressed racist views about Puerto Ricans; he served on a Lay Commission on Catholic Teaching and the US Economy, a pro-capitalist Roman Catholic pressure group; he has long been associated with Lewis Lehrman of the Citizens for America group, and he has given a lengthy interview to the journal of the anti-semitic Liberty Lobby. Grace is involved in the Americares Foundation which has taken part in private sector assistance to Nicaraguan *contra* forces.

Michael Hoffmann: a "revisionist" historian, i.e. one of those who claim that the Nazi genocide of the Jews never took place; Hoffmann is close to the Aryan Nations movement and addressed its 1986 Congress.

Jerry Peters: this convicted bank robber and nazi activist from Baton Rouge, Louisiana, was arrested on arms and theft charges in 1984, but was freed when his brother accepted responsibility.

Dr William Shockley: this physicist has maintained that blacks are genetically inferior to whites; has advocated the sterilization of those scoring less than 100 on IQ tests; and has donated sperm to a project designed to breed super-intelligent children.

Frank Spisak: a former member of the NSWPP and of the American Nazi Party, he killed three black people at Cleveland University in 1982 in furtherance of a "race war", and was in 1983 sentenced to death.

Uruguay

capital: Montevideo   **population: 3,000,000**

Political system. The 1966 Constitution of the Eastern Republic of Uruguay provides for an executive President, a Vice-President, a 30-seat Senate and a 99-seat Chamber of Deputies, all directly elected for five-year terms.

Recent history. The dominant political parties since independence have been the conservative Blancos ("whites") and the liberal Colorados ("reds"), each currently having a number of competing tendencies. The Colorados were in power from 1880 to 1958. The late 1960s and early '70s saw the rise of a left-wing guerrilla movement, the Tupamaros, and an increasingly violent military response culminating in a virtual military takeover in 1973, followed by harsh and repressive rule. Democracy was not restored until 1985, when a Colorado regime under President Julio Sanguinetti assumed office.

The evolution of the far right. The period of military intervention in government from 1972 saw the banning of left-wing political parties, arbitrary arrests, imprisonment without trial, torture, illegal executions, censorship and other restrictions of civil liberties. This repression was supported by President Juan María Bordaberry Arocena of the Colorado Party, but he was ousted by the army in 1976 after repeatedly stating that he would not discuss a return to civilian rule.

The repression, however, did not cease until 1985. The last military government, headed by Gen. Gregorio Alvarez Armellino, sought to establish a pro-military political party to continue its right-wing policies after democratization, but it was unable to secure sufficient support and most of the democratic parties outlawed by the military were eventually reorganized and legalized.

Active organizations

British Schools' Old Boys' Society

Base. Montevideo

Orientation. Anti-communist

History. A delegation representing this group attended a right-wing youth congress in South Africa in 1985.

International affiliations. See Youth for Freedom (South Africa).

Centro de Estudios de América y de Europa (CEDADE)
Centre for Studies of America and Europe

Base. Montevideo

Orientation. Nazi

History. The formation of the Uruguayan section of the CEDADE was reported in November 1985. Its offices in Montevideo had reportedly been searched by police.

Policies. The CEDADE is a pan-Hispanist national socialist organization.

Publications. The Uruguayan CEDADE has reportedly published several pamphlets.

International affiliations. The main CEDADE organization is the Barcelona-based Spanish section (the *Círculo Español de Amigos de Europa*); other sections, variously

417

named but all using the acronym CEDADE, exist in France, Portugal, Ecuador, Argentina and elsewhere. For historical and geographic reasons it is likely that the Uruguayan section has particularly close relations with the Argentinian group.

Iglesia de Unificación
Unification Church

Orientation. Anti-communist

History. This political-religious sect, led internationally by Sun Myung Moon (see South Korea), has since 1978 had a presence in Uruguay, where, according to the *New York Times*, it invested some US$70,000,000 in the period 1981-83 (inclusive). Its activities have been opposed by leaders of the main political parties.

Policies. The Church promotes a personality cult around its leader and also espouses anti-communism and authoritartian precepts.

Membership. 20 in Uruguay (1984 estimate).

Publications. Ultimas Noticias, supposedly independent daily, circulation 19,000, edited by Julián Safi (formerly a spokesman for the military regime).

Associated organizations. The Church owns Editorial Polo, a Montevideo publishing house, and the Banco de Crédito, as well as having hotel, real estate and other commercial interests. Its political affiliate, Causa (see South Korea), also has a Uruguayan branch led by Safi (as president) and Segundo Flores (vice-president, and father-in-law of Gen. Alvarez); that branch has hosted international Causa congresses.

International affiliations. The Uruguayan section is in contact with other Latin American "Moonie" groups, which exist in Honduras, Chile, Bolivia, Paraguay (where its members include Juan Manuel Frutos, a leading government figure) and Brazil (where its 6,000-strong organization was largely destroyed by riots after unfavourable media coverage in 1982).

Defunct organizations

Comando de Caza de Tupamaros: the CCT (Commando for Hunting Tupamaros) was a right-wing death squad active in the early 1970s. Nelson Bardesio, a Uruguayan right-winger often named in connection with the CCT, emigrated to Mexico in 1974 and became a Methodist pastor, in which capacity he organized a tour of Mexico by US evangelist Billy Graham in 1976.

El Federal: this journal, published in the 1960s and '70s, adopted an extremely anti-semitic and anti-communist stance. Similar publications, which unlike *El Federal* ceased to publish under the military regime, included *El Degüello* and *Lucha.*

Other organizations

Other right-wing formations include two small allied parties, namely the *Unión Patriótica* (Patriotic Union), formed in September 1982 by the late Col. Néstor Bolentini (Interior Minister in 1973-74), and the *Partido Laborista* (Labour Party), formed in 1984. A magazine called *Azul y Blanco* (Blue and White), founded in Montevideo in 1965, appears to have ceased publication; it pursued anti-semitic, "national revolutionary" and anti-masonic policies.

Venezuela

capital: Caracas   **population: 17,200,000**

Political system. The federal Republic of Venezuela has an executive President, assisted by a Council of Ministers; the Congress consists of a Senate with 44 elected members (and all constitutional ex-Presidents as life members), and a 199-seat Chamber of Deputies. The President and most members of Congress are elected by universal adult suffrage for five-year terms.

Recent history. Venezuela's first democratic government, elected in 1947, was overthrown by a military coup, but the centre-left Democratic Action (AD) regained power in 1958, was returned in elections in 1963 and thereafter alternated with the Social Christian Party (COPEI), which won elections in 1968 and 1978, while the AD won those of 1973 and 1983. A left-wing insurgency started in 1962 but was effectively defeated by 1975.

The evolution of the far right. The 1952 coup instituted a dictatorship under Gen. Marcos Pérez Jiménez, which was overthrown by a popular revolt in 1958. Pérez remained active in national politics until the late 1970s, but failed to regain power; his supporters attempted a coup in 1966.

Active organizations

Tradición, Familia y Propiedad (TFP)
Tradition, Family and Property

Orientation. Anti-communist

History. This group was established in Venezuela around 1980 by the Brazilians Fernando Tele and Paulo Campos. It was banned in December 1984, one of its members having been arrested in September on suspicion of planning an attempt on the life of Pope John Paul II (who was to visit the country in January 1985). Two official commissions had by December begun to investigate its activities, with particular regard to its influence in the armed forces and its alleged "brainwashing" of young followers.

Policies. The TFP, in Venezuela as elsewhere, has sought to oppose communist and socialist influence in society, and modernism in general; it advocates a return to an authoritarian and fundamentalist Roman Catholic system. Although many of its members are in sympathy with the rebel "integrist" movement in the Church (see Lefebvrist movement, Switzerland), there is no evidence that the TFP as such sought to kill the Pope.

International affiliations. This group is an offshoot of the original TFP, established in Brazil in 1960 (by Plínio Corrêa de Oliveira). Other TFP groups exist in France, the United Kingdom, Chile (where it has been linked with the fascist *Patria y Libertad* group), Canada and many Latin American countries.

Other organizations

Other right-wing organizations include the *Movimiento de Integración Nacional* (MIN—National Integration Movement), led by Gonzalo Pérez Hernández; *Nueva Generación* (New Generation), founded in 1979 and led by Gen. Arnaldo Castro Hurtado; and *Rescate Nacional* (National Rescue), led by former Defence Minister Gen.

419

Luis Enrique Rangel Bourgoin. All three groupings contested the 1983 elections but only the MIN won a seat in Congress.

Vietnam

capital: Hanoi   **population: 61,000,000**

Political system. The Socialist Republic of Vietnam (or Viet-Nam) is governed by a National Assembly, elected by adult suffrage, which in turn elects a Council of Ministers, including a Prime Minister, and a Council of State, which functions as a collective presidency.

Recent history. Vietnam was divided in 1954 after the defeat of French colonial forces, with communists controlling the north and an anti-communist regime in the south. The southern regime, backed militarily from 1961 by the United States, faced a widespread insurgency backed by the north.

Following the communist victory of 1975, north and south were reunited. The Soviet-backed government's principal foreign policy concerns have been the flight of several hundred thousand refugees (including former government and military officials, but mainly comprising ethnic Chinese economic refugees), and the situation in neighbouring Kampuchea, where the current regime is maintained by Vietnamese military forces.

The evolution of the far right. In early 1945 Japan, which had occupied Vietnam in 1940 with French collaboration, seized complete control, which it maintained for the few months until the end of the Second World War. Despite a declaration of independence, French forces then regained control of southern Vietnam and began a war with the nationalists, who were mainly communist and mainly from the north. Despite the defeat and withdrawal of the French in 1954 a right-wing regime was established in the south, which became the Republic of Vietnam, under President Ngo Dinh Diem.

Diem's authoritarian government was overthrown in 1963, and he was eventually succeeded by Gen. Nguyen Van Thieu; a war with the northern Democratic Republic of Vietnam resulted in the defeat of Thieu's regime in 1975.

Most far-right groups currently active were formed after the communist victory, and are based in the émigré communities in the USA, France and Australia; some are led by prominent ex-members of the South Vietnamese government. According to informed sources there were in 1985 at least 72 Vietnamese anti-communist groups in the United States, most based in Orange County, California. Some Vietnamese refugees have become involved in the activities of the fascist organizations of the host countries, as, for example, in the French FANE.

According to some reports, there is also a large Vietnamese organized crime syndicate, possibly known as "the Association", in the United States; the former Prime Minister and Vice-President of South Vietnam, Nguyen Cao Ky, denied evidence given in 1984 to a US presidential commission to the effect that he was the leader of "the Association". Evidence to the commission stated that the syndicate operates under the guise of an anti-communist resistance movement supposedly raising funds for revolutionary activities. On the other hand, some experts in the field maintain that crime among the refugee community is rare and unco-ordinated.

Relations between Vietnam and countries where émigré organizations are based have been affected by the organizations' activities; informal protests were made to the United States in late 1984, and to the Australian authorities (after several attacks, including the firing of shots at the Vietnamese embassy) in mid-1985.

Active organizations

National United Front for the Liberation of Vietnam (NUFRONLIV)

Address. Box 7826, San José, California 95150, United States

Leadership. Nguyen Dong Son (leader); Hoang Co Minh (ex-leader); Pham Van Lieu (organizer); Tran Minh Cong (spokesman)

Orientation. Anti-communist

History. The NUFRONLIV was formed in 1980 or 1982 by US-based émigrés including Minh, a former admiral in the South Vietnamese Navy. The group claims to have a small guerrilla base operating on the Thailand-Vietnam border.

Policies. It seeks the overthrow of the Vietnamese communist regime and the creation of a free and independent republic aligned with the West. It also seeks to expose "Soviet expansionism", particularly in South East Asia.

Membership. The Front claims to have upwards of 100 branches in the United States, where there are about 450,000 Vietnamese. It has also claimed to have 10,000 guerrillas under arms in Thailand, but another émigré group put the figure at 60.

Publications. Kang Chien, monthly.

Associated organizations. The Front runs the National Resistance Council, composed of leaders of various anti-communist émigré groupings.

International affiliations. The Front has affiliates in Australia, Japan and Europe.

Vietnamese Organization to Exterminate Communists and Restore the Nation

Base. California, United States

Orientation. Anti-communist

History. This clandestine ultra-right death squad (whose name has also been translated as Vietnamese Party for the Annihilation of Communism and for the National Restoration) has been responsible for several murders in the United States, including that in 1981 of a pro-Hanoi journalist, in August 1982 of a Vietnamese publisher, and in 1983 of a refugee restaurateur and another US-based writer. A US professor with Vietnamese links was killed in unclear circumstances, possibly by a right-winger, in October 1984.

Policies. The apparent aim of the Organization is to intimidate émigrés not supporting the right wing.

Defunct organizations

Hmong army: an organization created by the US Central Intelligence Agency among the Hmong tribesmen of the Laos-Vietnam border region, it participated in a guerrilla campaign against the Vietnamese communist forces. It collapsed after 1975 although its leader, Gen. Van Pao, was reported in 1983 to have met the former US president, Richard Nixon, to discuss the possibility of US aid for the "resistance" movements. Also present at the meeting, which was reportedly unproductive, was Nguyen Ngoc Huy, who had led the opposition *Cap Tien* Party in South Vietnam and was in 1984 leader of a "resistance" group based on that party.

National Salvation Front: an allegedly Chinese-backed counter-revolutionary organization established in 1975 and disbanded, with several members being put on trial, in 1979.

Popular and Military Front for National Salvation: in March 1980 several members of this internal anti-communist group received sentences ranging from death to eight years' imprisonment.

Other organizations

Other Vietnamese right wing groups reported as active in the 1980s include the *Greater Overseas Alliance for the National Restoration of Vietnam*; the Chinese-backed *National Front for the Liberation of the Central Highlands*, formed in Thailand in 1981 as a successor to the United Front for the Struggle of the Oppressed Races (FULRO, active in the 1970s); the *National Restoration Movement*, which may have been a generic term for internal anti-communist movements around 1980, and the *United Organization of Free Vietnamese in Europe*, a Paris-based coalition of 16 right wing groups.

Religious dissidence, principally involving a section of the Buddhist establishment, falls outside our scope, as does dissidence arising from within the communist movement, as in the case of Truang Nhu Tang's Paris-based National Salvation Committee.

In addition to the Vietnamese organizations mentioned above, there exist in the United States several non-Vietnamese groups which are concerned with Vietnamese affairs, including war veterans' societies and pressure groups concerned with locating and repatriating, dead or alive, US soldiers listed as missing in action. Many of these groups have a right-wing, ultra-patriotic and anti-communist orientation, and one or two have sought, unsuccessfully, to rescue prisoners allegedly held in secret camps inside Vietnam or to secure evidence of the existence of such prisoners and camps.

Yugoslavia

capital: Belgrade   **population: 23,200,000**

Political system. Yugoslavia is a Socialist Federal Republic with a collective state presidency and a bicameral indirectly elected Assembly. There is only one legal political party, the League of Communists of Yugoslavia.

Recent history. Yugoslavia, which came into being in 1919 and assumed its present name in 1929, was under nazi occupation for part of the Second World War but the communist-led resistance movement under Josip Broz Tito formed the government after elections in 1945. Tito remained in power until his death in 1980, and his policies of non-alignment, decentralization and federalism continue under the current (1987) leadership.

The evolution of the far right. Yugoslavia had a royal and military dictatorship from 1929 to 1931. A fascist movement, the *Ustasha*, arose in 1932. The Prince Regent, Paul, pursued a pro-fascist foreign policy from the inception of his government in 1934 to his overthrow in 1941, after he had brought Yugoslavia into the Axis pact. The then Minister of War, Gen. Zhivkovitch, became a patron of the fascist movement in 1935, but was dropped from the cabinet in March 1936.

German, Hungarian and Italian forces then invaded and Ante Pavelic led a puppet government in Croatia under the *Ustasha*, which assisted in the deportation and mass murder of Jews, gypsies and non-Roman Catholic Serbs. The extent to which the Catholic Church, and specifically Archbishop Alojzie Stepanic of Zagreb (who was sentenced to 16 years' imprisonment after the war), collaborated with the *Ustasha*, is still a matter of some controversy in Yugoslavia. In Serbia, a right-wing royalist *Chetnik* movement collaborated enthusiastically with the Nazis after becoming involved in a civil war with Tito's Partisan movement. There were frequent atrocities in both Croatia and Serbia and war crimes trials have taken place from time to time since 1946; the latest, started in 1986, involved Andrija Artukovic, Interior Minister in the Croatian puppet government (who was extradited from the United States).

The *Chetniks* and the *Ustasha* both lost heavily in the fighting and no organized anti-communist group survived the establishment of the Socialist Republic in 1946, although there have been occasional outbreaks of nationalist activity in Croatia, among ethnic Albanians in the Kosovo region, and in other regions. (The secessionist movement in Kosovo—in Albanian, Kosova—not having a specifically anti-communist orientation, is excluded from this study, as are exiled socialist and Christian democratic, and internal socialist and communist, opposition groups.) The main Croatian nationalist organization is still the *Ustasha*, which now exists almost exclusively in exile. An anti-communist "government in exile" established after the war is no longer in existence.

Right-wing Croatian exiles, mainly associated with remnants of the *Ustasha*, have carried out numerous and often fatal attacks on Yugoslav diplomats and premises abroad. There have been a few trials of dissident intellectuals and some two dozen bombings of public buildings in Croatia and Kosovo (an ethnic-Albanian region) since 1946, the majority occurring since the death of Tito in 1980. There have been relatively few instances of internal or external Serbian nationalist activity. In January 1987 it was reported that a group of 19 students, including four Communist Party members, had staged what appeared to be a nazi rally in an apartment in Belgrade. It was not clear whether the meeting was a genuinely fascist event nor whether there were any arrests.

Active organizations

Chetnik movement

Orientation. Serbian nationalist

History. The *Chetnik* monarchist movement, led during the war by Gen. Draja Mihailovic, was virtually wiped out by the civil war with ended with the communist victory of 1945. There have been few reported cases of Serbian nationalist activity thereafter, although several alleged collaborators with exiled *Chetniks* (in Western Europe) were sentenced in Yugoslavia in 1972-76.

Four Serbian nationalists, including a leader of the pro-*Chetnik Ravnagora* movement and an editor of the anti-communist *Vascrc Spoije* newspaper, were killed in Brussels (Belgium) in 1975-76. In March 1976 a Yugoslav vice-consul in France was murdered by a Serbian group.

Policies. The movement seeks the creation of a separate and independent Serbian state with a monarchical form of government.

Croatian National Congress (CNC)

Base. New Jersey, United States

Telephone. (201) 825 0379

Leadership. Dr Matthew Mestrovic (president)

Orientation. Anti-communist

History. The CNC was founded in 1974.

Policies. It opposes the Yugoslavian communist government and works for the creation of a free and independent Croatian national state.

Publications. CNC Report, eight per year; *Vjesnik*, six per year.

HOP
Croatian Liberation Front

Base. United States

Orientation. Fascist

History. The HOP is the main descendant of the Croatian nationalist and fascist movement which, under German tutelage, proclaimed an "independent" Croatian state in 1941. The movement was generally known asthe *Ustasha* (also spelt *Hustasa*, *Ustase* or *Ustasa*) and its leader, Ante Pavelic, fled to Argentina after the war and re-established the movement there as the HOP. He was fatally wounded, probably by a Yugoslav agent, and died in Spain in 1959, being succeeded by Stjepan Hefer, who remained leader until his death in 1975. (The HOP leader in Spain, Gen. Luvuric, who became involved with local fascist groups, was also assassinated.)

The HOP, which has become increasingly associated with the Croatian communities of Australia and the United States, is thought to be the main guerrilla organization opposing the Yugoslavian government, and to have been responsible for many of the attacks on Yugoslavian diplomats, including the assassination of the ambassador to Sweden.

Policies. The HOP seeks the overthrow of the communist regime and the creation of a separate Croatian state under fascist rule.

International affiliations. The HOP is in contact with many foreign fascist groups, particularly in North America and Western Europe.

Hrvatsko Borboneg Zajednitsvo
Croatian Fighting Unit

Leadership. Stjepan Deglin (leader)

Orientation. Anti-communist

History. The Unit (the name of which has also been translated as Croatian Combat Unity) was reportedly founded by Deglin in West Germany and organized in north-west Yugoslavia around 1981. It was held responsible for eight minor bombing incidents in five Croatian towns over the following three years, but no further activities have been reported since 24 alleged members, including Deglin, were charged in three separate cases in Osijek, Zagreb and Varazdin in early 1985.

Ibo Turbanovic was sentenced in April 1985 to 14 years imprisonment for his part in the bombings; a co-defendant had committed suicide before the trial. The second trial had 11 defendants, who were in May sentenced to between seven months and 15 years in prison; the defendants in the third trial included Deglin, who was imprisoned in October for 20 years (with nine of his co-defendants being sentenced for terms ranging from nine moinths to seven years).

Policies. According to Deglin, who described himself as a social democrat, the aim of the Unit was not to kill but to force the regime to open a dialogue with the nationalist movement, with the hope of achieving a pluralist and democratic state in which Croatia would have greater autonomy if not independence.

International affiliations. The Unit was reportedly associated with *Ustasha* groupings in West Germany.

Spremnost

Base. Australia

Orientation. Fascist

History. This monthly journal has been published in Australia for many years. It is published in Croatian and circulates mainly among the Croatian community there, which numbers several thousand, mostly post-war refugees.

Policies. The journal supports the *Ustasha* and the political-military struggle against the Yugoslavian regime.

Ustasha

Orientation. Croat fascist

History. Many attacks and conspiracies involving the post-war Croatian nationalist movement have been attributed by the Yugoslavian authorities to, or claimed by participants as the work of, the *Ustasha*, even though no single organization of *ustashi* exists. It is best regarded as a generic term but in many instances it has been impossible to attribute such activities more precisely.

Among incidents attributed simply to the *Ustasha* have been the following: the bombing of a cinema in Belgrade in 1970, in which one person was killed; the seizure of hostages at the Yugoslav consulate in Gothenburg (Sweden) in February 1971, and the murder of the Yugoslav ambassador to Sweden in April; two bombings of Yugoslav property in Australia, and the hijacking of a Swedish airliner, in September

1972; agitation in Bosnia in 1973; the killing of a policeman near Rijeka in October 1974, and the bombing of a Zagreb post office in November; the bombings of a Yugoslav cultural centre in Munich in March 1982, of a bookshop in Stuttgart (West Germany) in May and of a tourist office and a shop in Stuttgart in December; four other bombings in and around Stuttgart in 1981-82; an assault on the Yugoslavian ambassador to Australia in early December 1985; and an alleged terrorist conspiracy, directed from West Germany, for which two students were imprisoned in Zagreb in September 1986 (possibly in connection with the Croatian Fighting Unit—see above).

In January 1984 a number of Croats were arrested in West Germany and arms, ammunition and other material seized.

Other Croatian nationalist activities not specifically attributed to organizations include the incident in Split in January 1985, when 14 young people were arrested for singing nationalist songs and "insulting the memory of President Tito". Several writers, students and others had been imprisoned for miscellaneous nationalist activities in the early 1970s.

Defunct organizations

Brotherhood of the Cross: a 200-member Croatian guerrilla group banned in West Germany in March 1963, some four months after mounting an attack on a Yugoslavian trade mission. Some of its members went on to found the HNO.

Croatian Liberation Army: an attempt to form an internal *ustashi* revolutionary group of this name was apparently foiled by arrests which resulted in the imprisonment in 1974 of 15 Croatians.

Croatian Liberation Fighters: a US-based *ustashi* terrorist organization, it has carried out attacks including the bombing of a Yugoslav bank in March 1980 and of a diplomat's home in June.

Croatian Liberation Movement: this internal group, founded in 1963 by Branimar Peterner, was dissolved by the authorities and its members imprisoned in 1966. (A similarly named group exists in the exile community.)

Croatian Revolutionary Brotherhood: the HRB, founded in the late 1950s, was an *ustashi* terrorist organization which was particularly active in Western Europe and Australia in the 1960s and '70s, as was the separate Croatian Revolutionary Organization. The HRB, which was banned in West Germany in 1968, was responsible for infiltration of 19 guerrillas (mainly from Australia) into Yugoslavia in June 1972 (of whom 18 were killed and one imprisoned).

Drina: a Croatian group banned in West Germany in 1976.

Hrvatski Narodni Odbor: the HNO (Croatian People's Resistance), founded in 1965 by Stjepan Bilandzic (who had bombed a Yugoslav trade mission in 1962 as a member of the Brotherhood of the Cross), was banned by the West German authorities in 1976; Bilandzic was arrested on new terrorist charges in 1978.

Matica Hrvatska: founded in the 1840s as a Croatian cultural group, the "Mother Croatia" organization was accused in 1971 of functioning as a cover for *Ustasha* and other nationalist activities. Several leading members of the group were subsequently sentenced for espionage, separatist pagitation and other offences.

Pre-1945 Ustasha: the original *Ustasha* movement, founded by Ante Pavelic in 1932, was held responsible for the assassination of King Alexander, who was killed in France (together with the French foreign minister) in October 1934. Pavelic was sentenced to death *in absentia* (while in prison in Italy, in February 1936), along with two other *ustashi*, while three were sentenced to life imprisonment. Pavelic remained in Italy until the Axis invasion of Yugoslavia in 1941, when he returned to head a collaborationist government of Croatia. That regime was responsible for many atrocities, particularly against the Orthodox Christian Serbian minority, thousands of whom were slaughtered in a campaign ostensibly aimed at forcing their conversion to Catholicism.

Yugoslav Army of the Fatherland: this group, led by Gen. Draza Mihailovic and known as the *Chetniks*, supported the royalist government-in-exile after the nazi invasion in 1941. Based in Serbia, the *Chetniks* obtained logistic support from the Allies, but then became involved in a struggle for power with the communist-led National Liberation Army, and sought the help of the occupation forces. The *Chetniks* lost the ensuing civil war and the entire leadership was executed or forced to flee the country; remnants of it have been active in exile.

Yugoslavian Party of Unity: this right-wing party was formed by the government in August 1935 by the fusion of Prime Minister Stoyadinovitch's Radical Party with the Slovene Clerical Party of Fr Koroshetz and the Bosnian Moslem Party of Dr Mehmed Spaho. The Party was strongly monarchist and in favour of a unitary state.

Other organizations

Other groups which have reportedly been active in Yugoslavia or, more usually, in the émigré communities, include the following: the *Croatian Association of Australia*; the *Croatian National Council (HNV)* and the *Croatian Democratic Committee* (also based in Australia); the international *Croatian Liberation Movement* (as distinct from the internal group of that name) and the *Croatian National Resistance*, both umbrella groups of revolutionary organizations; the exiled nationalist *Croatian Peasants' Party*; the *Croatian Youth* (or Croatian Youth Movement, as it is called in Australia), and the separate *World League of Croatian Youth*; the *Revolutionary Croatian Resistance*; the *United Croatians of West Germany* (which has had members outside Germany); the *Victorian Co-ordinating Committee of Croatian Organizations* (Australia), and *Voice of Croatia* magazine (Box 416, San Jose, California 95178, United States).

Zimbabwe

capital: Harare　　　　　　　　　　　　　　　**population: 7,800,000**

Political system. The Republic of Zimbabwe has, at the time of writing, a multi-party parliamentary system with a 100-seat directly elected House of Assembly and a 40-seat Senate nominated in various ways. A non-executive President, elected by Parliament, is advised by a Prime Minister and Cabinet. Twenty seats in the House are currently reserved for white, Asian and mixed-race voters (although there are proposals to abolish this distinction, and to introduce a one-party state).

Recent history. Zimbabwe, which was then known as Southern Rhodesia, became a British colony in 1923 and was partially merged with two other territories in 1953 as the Federation of Rhodesia and Nyasaland. The Federation was dissolved in 1963, a year after the Rhodesian Front (RF) had come to power on the basis of racially restricted elections. Ian Smith, who became RF leader and Prime Minister in 1964, reacted to British and black demands for an end to white minority rule by unilaterally declaring the colony's independence, as Rhodesia, in 1965.

A guerrilla struggle against the Smith regime, and limited international economic and diplomatic sanctions, forced negotiations which led eventually, after a failed "internal settlement" involving whites and conservative blacks, to the holding of British-supervised elections in 1980. Robert Mugabe's ZANU-PF party emerged as the largest bloc and led Zimbabwe to recognized independence in April 1980. It remains in power in 1987, following a broadly socialist and non-aligned policy.

The evolution of the far right. The hegemony of the white minority was never totally unchallenged, with black nationalist movements active from at least the 1930s and a liberal white government holding power for five years from 1953. There subsequently emerged a white reactionary movement aligned with the South African National Party. This movement, the RF, continues to exist as the Conservative Alliance of Zimbabwe (CAZ).

Active organizations

Conservative Alliance of Zimbabwe (CAZ)

Address. PO Box 242, Harare

Leadership. Ian Douglas Smith (leader); George Cluckow (chairman)

Orientation. Conservative, formerly white supremacist

History. This party was formed in 1962 as the Rhodesian Front (RF), a coalition of right-wing white groups opposed to any transition to majority rule. In December 1962 its founder, Winston Field, became Prime Minister after white-controlled elections, and in 1964 he was succeeded by his deputy, Ian Smith. The RF won all 50 white seats in the parliamentary election of 1965 and Smith declared independence without British agreement. With the support of the South African apartheid regime, and despite an active guerrilla opposition and a widely ignored international trade boycott, Smith led an RF government until 1978, when he entered into a power-sharing arrangement with right-wing blacks.

A new assembly elected in 1979 included 20 RF members holding all the white seats, and Smith remained in the Cabinet with reduced rank. Fresh elections in 1980 left the RF again with all 20 white seats, and established Robert Mugabe's black nationalist government which led the country to independence. The RF became the

Republican Front in 1981, and began to lose its monopoly of white representation; defections and elections reduced its support to seven seats by mid-1984, when it adopted its present name and for the first time announced that it would accept non-white members. In April 1987 Smith was suspended from Parliament for 12 months by a majority vote of the House of Assembly, in protest at a series of speeches abroad in which he had opposed sanctions against South Africa.

Policies. The CAZ now functions as a conservative opposition party, but it was regarded until recently as a white supremacist organization and remains the principal party of the white minority.

Zimbabwe African National Union—Sithole (ZANU-Sithole)

Address. PO Box UA525, Union Avenue, Harare

Leadership. Rev. Ndabaningi Sithole (president); Noel Mukono (general secretary)

Orientation. Anti-communist

History. Sithole was leader of a minority faction of the ZANU which withdrew in 1976 from the revolutionary African National Council, while Mugabe's faction remained a member; Sithole's ZANU took part in Smith's "transitional government" of 1978-79, and has since 1980 (when it lost its House of Assembly seats) formed part of the extra-parliamentary opposition to the Mugabe government. Sithole signed an agreement with the Mozambican rebel movement, the MNR, in the USA in August 1986, to the effect that they would co-operate in "fighting Marxism in Mozambique and Zimbabwe".

Policies. ZANU-Sithole opposes the Mugabe regime and supports a mixed economy and a democratic system of government.

International affiliations. See MNR (Mozambique).

Defunct organizations

Candour League of Rhodesia: an anti-semitic and white supremacist grouping related to the Candour League of Great Britain; it was active in the 1960s and 1970s, under the leadership of Ian G. Anderson, and published *Rhodesia and World Report* as its monthly bulletin.

Rhodesia Christian Group: a white anti-communist organization active in the 1970s.

Rhodesian Action Party: a white supremacist group active in the late 1970s.

Rhodesian National Socialist Party: a nazi party of the 1970s.

Rhodesian White People's Party: the RWPP, also known as the White People's Party of Rhodesia, was a nazi organization active in the 1970s. Its leader was Ken Roger of Bulawayo. The group, which corresponded with many foreign nazi organizations and affiliated to the World Union of National Socialists, maintained that there was a Jewish conspiracy to transfer power to the black majority. The RWPP was banned by the Smith regime in November 1976, and two US nazis were expelled from the country.

Save Rhodesia Campaign: one of the less successful white supremacist pressure groups of the 1970s.

Southern Africa Solidarity Congress: a group which sought in the 1970s to co-ordinate the activities of Rhodesian and South African white supremacist organizations.

SUBJECT INDEX

Page numbers for countries and for main entries are printed in **bold** figures. *Italics*
have been used for the vernacular names of organizations and for publications.

I